Cambridge in the eighteenth and nineteenth centuries was a place of sharp contrasts. At one extreme a gifted minority studied mathematics intensively for the tripos, the honours degree. At the other, most undergraduates faced meagre academic demands and might idle their time away. The dons, the fellows of the colleges that constituted the university, were chosen for their tripos performance and included scholars of international reputation such as Whewell and Sedgwick, but also men who treated their fellowships as sinecures.

A pillar of the Church of England that denied membership to non-Anglicans, the university functioned largely as a seminary, while teaching more mathematics than theology. This volume describes the complex institution of the university, and also the beginnings of its transformation after 1850 – under the pressure of public opinion and the state – into the university as it exists today: inclusive in its membership, diverse in its curricula, and staffed by committed scholars and teachers.

A HISTORY OF THE UNIVERSITY
OF CAMBRIDGE

GENERAL EDITOR
C. N. L. BROOKE

A HISTORY OF THE UNIVERSITY OF CAMBRIDGE

General Editor: CHRISTOPHER N. L. BROOKE

Dixie Professor Emeritus of Ecclesiastical History, University of Cambridge, and Fellow of Gonville and Caius College

This four-volume series will comprise the first substantial history of the university of modern times. Each of the volumes will carry extensive original research and a synthesis of modern scholarship, and will explore the institutions, studies, scholarship, society, sports and buildings of the colleges and university, without neglecting the schools and social context from which the students came. Although not planned on the massive scale of series such as the current *History of the University of Oxford* or the *Victoria History of the Counties of England*, the series will chart afresh and in detail a remarkable passage of history, bring current scholarship into the light of day, and inspire a new generation of students and scholars to fresh endeavour.

Volumes in the series:

1 The University to 1546
   DAMIAN RIEHL LEADER

2 1546–1750
   VICTOR MORGAN
   Forthcoming

3 1750–1870
   PETER SEARBY

4 1870–1990
   CHRISTOPHER N. L. BROOKE

A HISTORY OF
THE UNIVERSITY
OF CAMBRIDGE

VOLUME III
1750–1870

PETER SEARBY

CAMBRIDGE
UNIVERSITY PRESS

PUBLISHED BY THE PRESS SYNDICATE OF THE UNIVERSITY OF CAMBRIDGE
The Pitt Building, Trumpington Street, Cambridge CB2 1RP, United Kingdom

CAMBRIDGE UNIVERSITY PRESS
The Edinburgh Building, Cambridge, CB2 2RU, United Kingdom
40 West 20th Street, New York, NY 10011-4211, USA
10 Stamford Road, Oakleigh, Melbourne 3166, Australia

First published 1997

Printed in the United Kingdom at the University Press, Cambridge

Typeset in Bembo 12/13 pt.

A catalogue record for this book is available from the British Library

Library of Congress Cataloguing in Publication data

A History of the University of Cambridge
Bibliography
Includes index
Contents: v. 1. The university to 1546 / Damian Riehl Leader.
1. University of Cambridge – History. I. Brooke,
Christopher Nugent Lawrence.
LF109.H57 1988 378.426'59 87-25586

ISBN 0 521 32882 9 (v. 1)
ISBN 0 521 35060 3 hardback

VN

TO MY CHILDREN,
CATHERINE, SHELAGH, AND JOE
AND TO MY GRANDSON,
RUARIDH PETER GILL

CONTENTS

ix

ILLUSTRATIONS

Illustrations 1 and 2 are from Nichol's photographs of Cambridge, 1860–1880; these photographs, illustration 5, the painting by Robert Farren (illustration 11), and illustration 22 (from W. Farren, Theatrical Characters: ADC Actors, 1864–6) are in the Cambridgeshire County Library, Local Collection, Petty Cury, to which we are indebted. Illustrations 3, 6, and 9 are from Rudolph Ackermann, *A History of the University of Cambridge* (2 vols., London, 1815); illustrations 4, 7, 12, 13, 14, 15, 16, 18, 20, and 21 are from J. L. Roget, *A Cambridge Scrapbook* (1859); illustration 8 is from V. A. Huber, *The English Universities*, translated by Francis W. Newman (3 vols., 1843); illustration 19 is from J. J. Smith, *The Cambridge Portfolio* (2 vols., London, 1840); for all these we are indebted to the Syndics of the University Library. Illustration 10 is a photograph in the Wren Library, Trinity College; we are indebted to the Master and Fellows of Trinity College for permission to use it. Illustration 17 is a drawing by Elizabeth Thomson in the National Portrait Gallery, to which we are indebted.

List of illustrations

GENERAL EDITOR'S PREFACE

At the outset of his Introduction, Peter Searby imagines a walk across Cambridge in the middle of the eighteenth century – a rapid walk, taking only fifteen minutes from Peterhouse to Jesus, yet taking in by the way how sixteen colleges comprised a university of only 700 undergraduates and 400 fellows. But on this walk we would have passed a whole series of amazing monuments – the great castle tower of Queens', King's chapel on the scale of a cathedral, the monumental libraries of Trinity and St John's. A careful observer walking this ground today will note that the eighteenth and early nineteenth centuries have contributed much, very much, to the face of Cambridge as we know it. In the 1710s and 1720s Hawksmoor planned a complete court at King's, of which the Gibbs Building of the 1720s is a more modest successor. From the same period the Senate House, by Gibbs and Burrough, is a fragment of a great design. In the early nineteenth century the idea of a major rebuilding of the Old Schools and the old University Library was revived, and of this the Cockerell Library was the fruit, a worthy successor to Wren's Library at Trinity. Meanwhile Wilkins himself conceived the idea of making a Regent Street out of Trinity Street and King's Parade, and the preposterous Mr Bankes, in 1824, proposed a variant of this obliterating the front of Caius to make way for the Fitzwilliam Museum.[1] It was an age of vast ambitions only partly realised. But the work of Sir James Burrough in Peterhouse, Trinity Hall, and Caius, and of his pupil James Essex – who adapted the Tudor Gothic of Christ's and of the hall of Emmanuel to the eighteenth-century taste with daring

---

[1] Christopher N. L. Brooke, *A History of Gonville and Caius College* (Woodbridge, Boydell, 1985), p. 193.

imagination – have left their mark in many parts of Cambridge to this day. In the next generation, Wyatville was wholly to transform Sidney Sussex, and the young William Wilkins to plan Downing from scratch – and to go on to build the New Courts of Corpus and Trinity, and make a deep mark on King's. The tradition of great monuments was resumed in the later decades of the Searby era with the Fitzwilliam Museum and the Cockerell Library.

Observers may react most variously to notable buildings. 'Upon beholding the masses of buildings at Oxford, devoted to what they call "*learning*"', wrote William Cobbett in 1830, 'I could not help reflecting on the drones that they contain and the wasps they send forth.'[2] But most of these buildings reflect a love of dignity and architectural splendour, which was not the dream of an individual – like King's chapel – but the common mind of a group of ambitious fellows and the wide circle of benefactors they had to inspire if their projects were to bear fruit. These buildings show a part – a very significant part – of the image of the University of Cambridge in the eighteenth and early nineteenth centuries. The clatter of masons and carpenters must have been a constant interruption to the peaceful life of the 400 fellows.

The adventures of the masons and carpenters form a dramatic contrast to the stereotype of a decadent, shrivelled, somnolent seminary for Church of England clergymen on which many of us were brought up. The stereotype has a venerable origin: Henry Gunning, looking back from the 1850s to his student days in the 1780s, marked them as '(with the exception of six or seven years preceding) the very worst part of our history' – that is, the history of the university.[3] It has recently been much under revision, both in general studies like John Gascoigne's and in deeper reflection on the world from which Lord Kelvin and Charles Darwin were to spring. Peter Searby has lent depth and insight to our knowledge of Cambridge between 1750 and 1870. The resulting portrait is at once a great deal more sophisticated, complex, and interesting than the stereotype. It is ambivalent: Cambridge had plenty of drones and

[2] *Rural Rides* (1830), quoted in C. Brooke, R. Highfield, and W. Swaan, *Oxford and Cambridge* (Cambridge, 1988), p. 260.
[3] Henry Gunning, *Reminiscences of the University, Town and County of Cambridge, from the Year 1780* (2 vols., London and Cambridge, 1854), VOL. I, pp. xix–xx.

wasps as well as Oxford. But it also reflects – as it must, if it is to be convincing – something of the dedication and the ambitions which are reflected in a great age of college and university building.

Cambridge, June 1996 CHRISTOPHER N. L. BROOKE

ACKNOWLEDGEMENTS

This history has been made possible by the help of many people. Christopher Brooke, the General Editor of the series, has been constantly generous with his energy and support; he has read every chapter in draft and suggested ways in which our past might be approached and one's utterance improved. His counsel has been invaluable. My wife, Norma, has given a lay critic's judgement on every page, and typed much of the book onto the hard disk before I had mastered the word-processor. In this task I was taught a lot by Steve Hindle, who in a multitude of ways made composition easier, if not exactly easy; without his help the volume would have taken longer to produce than it did. To these three people I am very grateful.

Before writing began, one eminent Cambridge historian, since deceased, declared that the enterprise was impossible because the sources were too copious. He might very well have been proved right, but for the generosity of Cambridge University Press, and Gonville and Caius, St John's, and Trinity Colleges. They made it possible for me to engage help with research, in particular with the collection of the data on which the appendices and figures in the text are based. This work was carried out over many months by Richard Connors, Natasha Glaisyer, Anne Milovic, and Richard Whatmore, and to them I record my indebtedness, not least for the debates we enjoyed over the interpretation of the data, in which I learned a great deal. I am grateful too to Sarah Bendall, Jayne Ringrose, and Malcolm Underwood, the archivists respectively of Emmanuel, Pembroke and St John's Colleges, for making available the documents on which the appendices are based, and for guiding me and others through them.

Anyone writing Cambridge history is fortunate in the incomparable richness of the city's libraries. To the staffs of two in particular, the University Library and the Cambridgeshire Collection of the County Library, I acknowledge my gratitude for their eager acceptance of the many calls I made upon them. I am very grateful too to the librarians of Emmanuel, Fitzwilliam, St John's and Trinity Colleges, the London Library, and the National Library of Scotland.

Elisabeth Leedham-Green led me through the University Archives, and threw light on many dark corners in the university's history. Many friends drew my attention to unfamiliar sources and gave me advice from which my chapters have benefited at many points: for their help I am greatly indebted to Will Ashworth, Derek Beales, Betty Bury, Henry Button, Eamon Duffy, Boyd Hilton, Arnold Hunt, Bill Lubenow, David McKitterick, Mike Petty, John Pickles, Janet and John Shepherd, Carol Anelli Sheppard, Frank Stubbings, and John Topham. Harry Porter added to my understanding of the drama in Cambridge and commented on several of my chapters, as did Judith Oliver. I have also owed much to the encouragement of Paul Hirst, James Holt, Brian Jamset, Angela John, and Norman Pounds. The Master and Fellows of Fitzwilliam College, that most welcoming of Cambridge societies, have given me sympathetic support over many years. William Davies of Cambridge University Press waited patiently for this volume for a long time and was helpful throughout its progress. At the Press Jean Field meticulously combed the text and saved it from many infelicities of expression.

To many people, whose kindness has reminded me of the unselfishness of historical scholarship, I wish to register my thanks. They have helped to give this book what merits it possesses. For its faults, and its interpretation of the university's history, I alone am responsible.

A lasting debt is acknowledged in the dedication.

PETER SEARBY

ABBREVIATIONS

ADC	Amateur Dramatic Club
Cooper. *Annals*	C. H. Cooper, *Annals of Cambridge*, vol. IV (Cambridge, 1853); vol. V (Cambridge, 1908)
CUL	Cambridge University Library
DNB	*Dictionary of National Biography*
DSB	*Dictionary of Scientific Biography*
FA	Football Association
GCSE	General Certificate of Secondary Education
PP	Parliamentary papers
RCHM Cambridge	*Royal Commission on Historical Monuments for England, City of Cambridge*, 2 parts (London, 1959)
RFU	Rugby Football Union
RIBA	Royal Institute of British Architects
UFC	University Football Club
VCH Cambs.	*The Victoria History of the Counties of England, Cambridge*
Willis and Clark	Robert Willis and John Willis Clark, *Architectural History of the University of Cambridge*, 4 vols. (Cambridge University Press, 1886)

INTRODUCTION

In the middle of the eighteenth century one might walk across the University of Cambridge at its widest point – from Peterhouse to Jesus – in fifteen minutes. In less than half a square mile were placed the sixteen colleges that constituted the university, and in them lived their 700 undergraduates and the 400 fellows who were the university's teachers and administrators. This small world was part of the British, or more properly English, Establishment. Only members of the Church of England might be members of the university, or at all events might graduate from it and hold office within it. So far as we can tell the largest group of graduates became Anglican clergymen, while most bishops had been fellows of colleges in Cambridge or Oxford. The university had the functions of a seminary, and was to retain them until well after 1850: in this as in other respects the period 1750–1870 was one of very great continuity. But the intellectual character of the institution was quite unlike what one would expect a seminary to be. Cambridge was quite different, for example, from the theological colleges that the Victorians founded to improve the professional education of the clergy.

In 1700 the Cambridge arts curriculum was recognisably the Renaissance mixture that had been introduced 150 years earlier: an attempt to survey knowledge by teaching philosophy and divinity, mathematics and science, and the classical languages and literatures. Examinations were not written but oral, as they had been before the invention of paper many centuries previously: much about Cambridge might remind an observer of the Middle Ages – as some things do still. Between 1700 and 1740, however, the curriculum for the Bachelor of Arts degree was transformed, in the most important intellectual revolution which Cambridge has ever experienced, and which has left an enduring impression on the nature of the university.

The impetus for this transformation came from the genius of Isaac Newton. Newton explained the universe in mathematical terms; he showed its harmony and its consistency with a total persuasiveness that more recent physics has done no more than modify. He also appeared to give scientific validation for Christianity, or at least deism. Newton's natural philosophy (or as we would say, mathematics and physics) became the core of the BA curriculum, especially for the brightest undergraduates; and in an epoch when material circumstances are often held to be the source of fundamental change it is worth stressing that Cambridge's revolution was the result of intellectual discovery.

Newtonianism might be thought of as a sort of theology, but one cannot find evidence suggesting that it was taught or examined in that light in Cambridge. Its mathematical content, not its doctrinal purpose, was the subject of tutorial discourse. Other subjects remained in the BA examinations, but for the most talented they were greatly attenuated. Colleges continued to attach importance to them, especially to the classics, and classical learning survived in college teaching without making much impact on the instruction given to students, or at least the most gifted or ambitious students, for their degree examinations. In the 1740s a new kind of examination for the BA was introduced in the newly built Senate House. The Senate House Examination was a written test, the first example of the unseen examination that now dominates education worldwide. Its origin in Cambridge was perhaps provoked by the difficulty of testing knowledge of geometry or algebra orally. At all events a written examination made more feasible the task of differentiating between candidates, even those of like ability. The examination results were placed in a hierarchy. At its top were the minority who gained honours, while at their very top stood the Senior Wrangler, the most accomplished mathematician of his year and the victor in a fierce contest.

The tripos became more and more competitive, as candidates fought for places near the top of the ladder. The examinations became longer, and the mathematical content more sophisticated; anybody inclined to accept the old jibe that the student's life in

pre-1870 Cambridge was always a soft option should remember that
honours candidates in the Senate House Examination wrote for up
to eight hours a day for as long as eight days, in an unheated room in
January, when the ink sometimes froze in the wells overnight. One
might ask, Why did they bother? – to which one answer would be,
that from the beginning of the Senate House Examination it was
used as the main criterion in the election of college fellows:
'meritocracy' was a feature of Cambridge life from 1750 onwards. A
top position among the wranglers would gain the graduate a
fellowship, or in other words a secure middle-class income for life
provided that he did not marry (less formal links might well be
forgiven) and that in most cases he took holy orders. As in the
eighteenth and nineteenth centuries the rents of agricultural land
rose so did college incomes, and so the value of college fellowships
increased: the prizes became more worth fighting for because of the
Agricultural Revolution, which was for the university as integral a
part of its history as it was for Norfolk or for a great landed family.

'The Senior Wrangler is the winner of the Derby' was how one
don summed up in 1865 one theme in Cambridge life: the
competitive thrust for academic distinction, which was also an
instrument to secure material wealth. It sounds, for good and ill,
surprisingly like the 1990s – the very model of a modern university.
But some shading has to be given to the picture it may conjure up:
'Unreformed Cambridge' was less than the university has since
become, while also being in some respects rather more. Only a
minority of undergraduates had both the talent and the inclination
to spend over three years cramming mathematics for the Senate
House Examination. Students with high talents for other branches
of scholarship had no examination to turn to until the Classical
Tripos began in 1824, and until 1850 classics candidates had in any
case to take the mathematical examination first and get honours in
it, before they could proceed to the classics papers. Students who
did not aspire to honours had merely the slender intellectual
challenge of the ordinary or 'poll' degree, which left students with
much spare time to employ as they thought fit. Men who
deliberately opted for the poll degree included William Wordsworth and Charles Darwin, and their creative use of the Cambridge years brought benefits of transcendent value to poetry and

biological theory: opportunities given by the freedom of the old university have been lost in our totally examined world.

Still, most students taking the poll degree could consider no other choice. Colleges lacked any real test of merit for their entrants, and were therefore bound to include many who were not intelligent enough to contemplate honours in mathematics. Such men most often spent much of their time at Cambridge idling, and increasingly in the early nineteenth century there was a search in Cambridge for ways to give them a degree to aim for that was worthwhile but more accessible than the Mathematical Tripos. By the 1830s men like William Whewell believed that one possible source for such a degree was the subjects, such as the natural sciences and history, where there were professors and lectures but no examination of which people took much notice.

Mathematics was the star in the Cambridge firmament: the university gave, albeit to a small minority, the most intensive and searching mathematical training in Britain. But in the eighteenth century Cambridge mathematics became increasingly old-fashioned, staying too much in thrall to Newton's ways of reasoning, which were essentially geometrical, for far too long. Algebraic techniques developed in Europe in the eighteenth century were not adopted in Cambridge until well into the nineteenth, and even then Cambridge tended to lag behind Paris. Not until the end of the century was the university a world centre of mathematical thought.

But such facts were not appreciated by the general public in the 1840s. The cost of a Cambridge education was, and criticism of it went to the heart of the university's structure. College living was necessarily expensive for most; but this was not all. College fellows had few *necessary* duties. They were bound to the common meal in hall and the common worship of chapel; but many were lax in attendance, and some were wholly non-resident. In each college a few fellows were employed as tutors, and they provided teaching. But it was insufficient for undergraduates ambitious for high honours. So as the tripos became more demanding and competitive, candidates had perforce to pay for 'private' tuition, and the cost of this might add as much as a quarter to total costs.

In the 1830s and 1840s Cambridge, like Oxford, was assailed by public criticism for its costliness and the narrow range of subjects that might be taken for a degree, for closing its doors to non-Anglicans, for the freehold character of a fellow's tenure and the clerical orders obligatory for most and the celibacy required of all: in short an attack contrasting the university's great resources with their meagre or selfish exploitation. In all these respects Cambridge was compared with the four universities of Scotland – which were cheap, had no religious tests, taught a very wide range of subjects, and had no dons with life freeholds but few tasks. So much of the criticism of Oxford and Cambridge originated in Edinburgh that it might almost be called a campaign for Caledonianising the English universities: and this is ironic, since at the same time there was a struggle in Scotland to anglicise its universities by importing the specialised honours degrees that were the best feature of the southern institutions. One might sum up much history by saying that Cambridge was Caledonianised rather less than Edinburgh was anglicised.

But in Cambridge the struggle was long. In the 1840s the overwhelming majority of dons had been educated in Cambridge itself and were mostly mathematicians who were also Anglican clergymen. They were highly intelligent: their first degree results had been won by intellectual effort more exacting on average than today. But they were few in number, occupied a tiny area, and were used to frequent social intercourse without much intervention by outsiders; daily life reinforced the effects of similarity of background. Far too conscious that their university was the finest mathematical centre in the kingdom – or Europe, or the world – and believing that mathematics was the best education money could buy, they were reluctant to concede any lessening of its priority for Cambridge undergraduates. Most of them were very unwilling indeed to breach the Anglican monopoly and college structures and privileges in serious ways. It is significant that the very few dons who did want extensive change were mavericks who felt outsiders in Cambridge; they soon left it.

Nevertheless, steady pressure from the state and public opinion, and from dons gradually converted to new attitudes, meant considerable change between 1850 and 1870. New triposes were created, and some of them were flourishing by 1870, though it was a long time before mathematics lost its predominance. Religious tests were abolished for bachelor's degrees in 1856, and fifteen years later they were ended altogether except for teachers of divinity and the like. In the 1860s colleges were ending or mitigating the rule of celibacy, and beginning to link fellowships to specific tasks of teaching or administration; the road 'from clergyman to don' was long in Cambridge, but by 1870 some had travelled part of the distance along it and for everybody it was clearly the way ahead.

Such are some of the themes discussed in this book. But there are others. In Max Beerbohm's *Zuleika Dobson* the dons 'were conscious of an agreeable hush' when all the undergraduates drowned themselves for love of the heroine. Likewise, as Max also observes, 'generations of undergraduates had said that Oxford would be all very well but for the dons'. In Cambridge Wordsworth came close to saying just that in stanzas of *The Prelude*. The undergraduate lives described below reveal how much of the pleasure and happiness they derived from their sojourn in Cambridge – however intermeshed with the dons' – was created by their own exertions, and remind us that the success and reputation of a university depend on the vitality of its students, as much as on the learning of its senior members.

Chapter 1

TOWNSCAPE AND UNIVERSITY: TOPOGRAPHICAL CHANGE

THE SETTING

Beneath surface changes, the centre of Cambridge is still dominated by two roads which have been in use for at least 1,000 years, bringing traffic from London and Colchester respectively. These routes, Trumpington and Trinity Streets to the west and Regent and Sidney Streets to the east, rest on the terraces of gravel beds marking an ancient river valley; they were the driest ways to the river crossing below Castle Hill. The medieval settlement with its houses, churches, and monasteries grew along these streets and between the line of Trumpington Street and the river; here the wharves and warehouses of the inland port were constructed, along Milne Street and Salthythlane. This first Cambridge was transformed from the fourteenth century onwards. The commercial quarter was swept away to make room for university colleges, and when in the sixteenth century the monasteries were dissolved their sites too were taken over for new collegiate foundations, a process that concluded in 1596 with the planting of Sidney Sussex where the house of the Franciscan friars had stood.[1]

In the seventeenth and eighteenth centuries Cambridge expanded little outside its Elizabethan limits. Hamond's town plan (1592) shows development up to Mount Pleasant in the Huntingdon Road, and Custance's (1798) the same. In Trumpington Street building reached the present line of Fitzwilliam Street and the museum by 1600, and crept down by 1800 to Spital End, opposite the entrance to today's Engineering Department.[2] Within the

---

[1] J. A. Steers, ed, *The Cambridge Region* (London, British Association for the Advancement of Science, 1965), pp. 162–78. M. D. Lobel, ed., *An Atlas of Historic Towns*, vol. II (London, Scolar, 1975), pp. on Cambridge.

[2] See J. W. Clark and A. Gray, *Old Plans of Cambridge* (2 parts, Cambridge, Bowes and Bowes, 1921), part 2, plans 3 and 7.

1 Trumpington Street about 1860, looking south from the Pitt Building.

town, settlement became much denser in these two centuries.
Houses were constructed in gardens and yards, while there was
much replacement and renewal. Such is suggested today by the
small number of pre-1700 structures compared with eighteenth-
century ones – though sometimes an older remnant lies within a
modern case, as in 21 Trumpington Street. Despite the infilling, in

1800 much open space remained. To the north of Bird-bolt Lane (now Downing Street) the first University Botanic Garden stretched towards Bene't Street on the land that was in the Middle Ages the garden of the Austin Friars and is now covered by the Materials Science Building and the Corn Exchange. To the south of Bird-bolt Lane there was pasture land, St Thomas's Leys, which remained open till Downing College was built in 1807.[3] Further south still, towards Lensfield Road, Loggan's map records 'The Marsh', and in the 1780s that inveterate sportsman Henry Gunning could generally get 'five or six shots at snipes' nearby.[4]

Cambridge was hemmed in by its two sets of open fields. Loggan's panoramic views of the city in *Cantabrigia Illustrata* (1690) show sheep grazing on stubble to the east of Emmanuel and Jesus, and to the west of the river grain is being harvested on the site of the University Library. At the edges of Cambridge development could take place only by nibbling away at the strips; for example, as Maitland pointed out, Peterhouse 'stands on land that once lay in selions and was arable', and Mill Lane originally had the 'aratral twist', the flattened S-shape of ploughland.[5] The enclosure of the West Fields in 1805 and the East in 1811 made expansion of Cambridge possible. The opportunity was first taken in the east, where land stretching beyond Parker's Piece or Lensfield Road for a mile or so was opened up for housing.[6] Though there were some substantial villas, the greater number were modest dwellings for various layers within the middle class and the artisanate. Colleges were often the developers, as Trinity Hall was, for example, for the terraces near the Botanic Garden to which (predictably) the names Bateman and Norwich Streets were given; similarly Jesus exploited its land in the 'Kite' in the 1830s, building the spacious and carefully articulated New Square and letting properties on forty-year leases that protected the college freehold.[7] The bigger developments were the new University Botanic Garden in the 1830s, and the tracks and station of the Eastern

---

[3] Walking over the vestiges of it in the 1890s F. W. Maitland found traces of ridge and furrow. The new buildings on the 'Downing Site' soon obliterated them. F. W. Maitland, *Township and Borough* (Cambridge University Press, 1898), p. 115.   [4] Gunning, *Reminiscences* vol. 1, p. 40.

[5] *Township and Borough*, p. 111.

[6] See Cambridgeshire County Record Office, Enclosure award maps for parishes of St Giles (1804) and St Andrew the Less, Barnwell (1811).

[7] *RCHM Cambridge*, part 2, pp. 358–74. The first stages in the development of the East Fields may be seen in R. G. Baker's detailed plan of Cambridge, 1830.

2 Trumpington Street about 1860, looking north from the Pitt Building.

Counties Railway which reached Cambridge in 1845, linking it to London. The railway stimulated further growth in the east of the town, and by 1870 the brick terraces were advancing along Mill Road and between it and the Newmarket Road.

Today much of this post-enclosure construction has itself been redeveloped. The Kite and much of Newtown was renewed in the 1970s, mostly, it has to be said, to their betterment. 'Development' has had less happy results in the replacement of Lensfield House, one of William Wilkins's attractive additions to the Cambridge townscape, by the banal Chemistry Laboratory in 1955. The other classical mansion in the town was Clarendon House, built in the 1820s by Charles Humfrey, spectacular architect, property developer, and (eventually) bankrupt. We regret its demolition more than a century ago. Still, the Edwardian 'Queen Anne' buildings of Parkside Community College that occupy its site have themselves become regarded as part of our architectural heritage, while one of Humfrey's sycamore trees flourishes in the school grounds. Some links with the past are tenacious, while much change is in due time itself accepted as history to be guarded.

CLASSICAL CAMBRIDGE AND JAMES GIBBS

The university and its sixteen colleges were contained inside a rough quadrilateral with Magdalene, Peterhouse, Emmanuel, and Jesus at its angles: a small area, about two-thirds of a mile in length and breadth, containing in 1795 about 400 'dons' or teachers, and 736 undergraduates. St John's and Trinity, with 100 and 165 undergraduates respectively, were larger than the others (the smallest, King's, possessing only twelve students) and had greater wealth, pride, and academic success at the tripos examination. Colleges guarded their separate endowments, statutes, and traditions carefully and were sometimes jealous of each other. But in their way of life and philosophy dons tended to be of a pattern, and the colleges were far more like each other in ethos than they were like anything else, except perhaps Oxford colleges. Their squabbles and instinctive loyalties remind the chronicler of a large Victorian family – George Eliot's Dodsons perhaps: 'And it is remarkable that while no individual Dodson was satisfied with any other individual Dodson, each was satisfied, not only with him or herself, but with the Dodsons collectively.'[8]

---

[8] *The Mill on the Floss*, chapter 6.

In 1750 the university was smaller than it had been since before
1550. Over 400 had matriculated each year between 1615 and 1627,
its high point, and that number had almost been reached again after
the ups and downs of the Civil War and Commonwealth. A long
decline had started about 1670, and was to continue till 1763 when
only 100 matriculated.[9] There was steady growth thereafter (broken
by a dip in the 1790s), marked by much building from 1800 onwards
to house extra numbers. So in the eighteenth century there was no
need to build additional accommodation. But that did not mean
that there was no new construction; on the contrary, there were
some remarkable monumental buildings, while brick (which the
eighteenth century thought mean) was converted to the semblance
of stone by a meticulous process of embellishment that colleges
undertook.

The chapel of Peterhouse, consecrated in 1632, is one of the most
revealing historical documents in Cambridge. Its east window,
luckily clearly visible from Trumpington Street, is Perpendicular in
style and by the non-expert hard to distinguish from a building of
1500. Yet since 1560 Cambridge architects had been increasingly
expressing themselves in classical language, reflecting fidelity to the
values of the ancient world, and Peterhouse chapel was an
old-fashioned declaration. The classical pediment that crowns the
east end was added in 1665 by the one-time master, Cosin, who was
affected by the triumph of the classical in Restoration England.
Early in the next century the chapel colonnades were rebuilt and
made round-headed to give them an antique appearance.[10]

Classicism was not, however, a unified tradition. At one extreme
was the Baroque syntax of Vanbrugh and Hawksmoor, massive,
eclectic, and florid, to be seen in Blenheim and Castle Howard.
There is something of Baroque exuberance in James Gibbs's
Cambridge Senate House, and his Radcliffe Camera in Oxford.
Other artists stressed restraint and archaeological purity;[11] the most
important reflection of these qualities in Cambridge was William
Wilkins's Downing College (1805). Variations in classical utterance

---

[9] J. A. Venn, *Oxford and Cambridge Matriculations 1544–1906* (Cambridge, Heffer, 1908), graph.
[10] Nikolaus Pevsner, *Cambridgeshire* (2nd edn, Harmondsworth, Penguin, 1970), p. 132.
[11] Sir John Summerson, *Architecture in Britain 1530 to 1830* (4th edn, Harmondsworth, Penguin, 1963),
pp. 157–210, 245–321.

are less significant for our purposes, however, than the effect of the idiom itself on the Cambridge townscape. In eighteenth-century Cambridge there was distrust of the Gothic (though not of its supreme achievement, King's chapel) and a desire to disguise as masonry the brick that was the chief building material of the Gothic centuries in Cambridge. 'Ashlaring', covering brick with a skin of stone, was effected on parts of Peterhouse and Trinity Hall, and Caius, Christ's, Pembroke, and St John's colleges, while the First Court of Magdalene was stuccoed for the same reason.[12] Prominent in these practices were two local classical architects, James Essex the Younger, and James Burrough. Burrough as a young man helped to prepare the way for Gibbs's Senate House; in his maturity he refaced the main court of Peterhouse and added the Burrough Building; he refaced courts at Trinity Hall and Gonville and Caius; and he was the teacher and patron of James Essex the Younger. Essex was responsible for the Queens' building bearing his name, the Ramsden building in St Catharine's, and, perhaps the most notable proof of his classical preferences, the rebuilding of the west range of Emmanuel Front Court between 1769 and 1775, giving it the Ionic portico that is one of the landmarks of Regent Street.

The most important college construction of the eighteenth century was the Fellows' Building at King's, completed in 1731. Dynastic troubles and lack of funds had prevented completion of Henry VI's grand scheme for his college; the chapel was finished by Henry VIII, but it dwarfed the college's hall and chambers.[13] At last Dr John Adams, provost from 1712 to 1720, set about gathering a building fund. Plans drawn up by Nicholas Hawksmoor were not used; instead, the college turned to James Gibbs. The first British architect to receive professional training abroad (in Rome, under Carlo Fontana, the pupil of Bernini), Gibbs's creative fecundity led him to become by 1720 'the architect most in vogue'.[14] In that year he first became involved with two of his most sumptuous projects, the Radcliffe Camera at Oxford and St Martin-in-the-Fields.

[12] For these details see *RCHM Cambridge*, parts 1 and 2.
[13] The site is now occupied by the Library of Gonville and Caius and the West Court of the Old Schools.
[14] The words are Horace Walpole's, quoted in Terry Friedman, *James Gibbs* (New Haven, Conn. Yale University Press, 1984), p. 13. For what follows on Gibbs and King's, see Friedman, ibid., pp. 232–8.

Shortly afterwards he began to design new university buildings at Cambridge, on land immediately to the north of King's; Gibbs was therefore a natural choice as architect for the college. In 1724 he published designs for the three ranges to complete the court whose fourth side was the chapel. The great need was to make the new buildings 'answerable' to the chapel, which Gibbs regarded as 'one of the finest gothick Buildings that can be seen anywher', and the desire for harmony helped Gibbs to adopt a more chaste classical vocabulary than his baroque tastes led him to elsewhere. We are not able to judge fully the success of his grand scheme: as with other Cambridge plans in this epoch, funds were inadequate, in part because King's lost money in the South Sea speculation and fairly desperate ploys to raise more failed to reach the target. Thus only the Fellows' Building was completed, and Gibbs had to wait until 1742, eleven years afterwards, to get the balance of his fees.

Meanwhile, Gibbs had also designed his Senate House (with help from Burrough), one of the most imposing additions to its buildings that the university itself (as distinct from its colleges) has until the twentieth century enjoyed. Early in the eighteenth century the university's functions were meagre, confined to matriculating and examining undergraduates and a little teaching between those ceremonies; even so, its premises were inadequate. There was a building for the Professors of Anatomy and Chemistry in Queens' Lane, and another for the University Press next door. University lecture rooms and administrators' offices, such as they were, were crammed into what is now the East Court of the Old Schools; this also contained the Regent (or Senate) House – the present Combination Room – and the University Library. Its 16,000 books and manuscripts[15] lay in squalid confusion in two ill-tended rooms.

Between the Old Schools and Great St Mary's stood close-packed streets, High Street (that is, King's Parade) being much narrower than it now is. In the seventeenth century it was hoped to clear the area and build a new library and 'Commencement House', but little was done, though the problem helped to provoke Nicholas Hawksmoor into designing a baroque Cambridge. In-spired by the ruthless reconstruction of Rome effected by Pope

---

[15] About 1/250 of the current total. The two library rooms are now, after extensive rebuilding, the East and Council Rooms.

Sixtus V in the 1580s, Hawksmoor imagined much demolition and the erection of new university buildings, a Forum between Peas Hill and King's, a Circus between the Senate House and St John's, and a long vista from Christ's to King's chapel a quarter of a mile away, across the Forum. If achieved, the plan would have given Cambridge a centre as Roman as Rome, and altered profoundly the images that others had of the university and that it had of itself.[16]

Action on the Old Schools problem was forced by a magnificent gift. In 1715 the new sovereign, George I, bought the collection of the recently deceased Bishop of Ely, the bibliophile John Moore, and presented it to the University Library. Comprising 29,000 books and 1,800 manuscripts it trebled the library's stock; absorbing it took decades, given the library's torpid rhythms. Two additional rooms on the first floor of the Old Schools were taken for the library – the Regent House and the school of law (now the Syndicate Room); thus the library came to occupy interconnecting rooms round the East Court. This expansion was made possible by the building of the Senate House.[17]

In 1719 a syndicate was appointed to purchase and develop land to the east of the Old Schools, and building plans were submitted by at least four individuals.[18] One was James Burrough, aged thirty, a fellow of Gonville and Caius and a member of the building syndicate. His first substantial architectural essay was his design for the new Public Building, or perhaps Public Buildings since he suggested a three-sided court open towards Great St Mary's. In 1721, two years after development began, the syndics began discussions with Gibbs, who had been introduced to university circles by his patron Edward Harley of Wimpole Hall. Invited to comment on Burrough's proposal, he too submitted plans for a three-sided court. Gibbs's design was preferred, a decision Burrough accepted. Burrough continued to be involved in executing the scheme, and perhaps Sir John Summerson is right in contending that the Senate House as we see it owed much to him. The

---

[16] Kerry Downes, *Hawksmoor* (2nd edn, London, Zwemmer, 1979), pp. 117–21. David Roberts, *The Town of Cambridge as it Ought to be Reformed* (Cambridge University Press, 1955), reproduces Hawksmoor's plan, and includes 'before and after' drawings by Gordon Cullen.

[17] David McKitterick, *Cambridge University Library. A History: the Eighteenth and Nineteenth Centuries* (Cambridge University Press, 1986), pp. 147–66.

[18] For this section, Friedman, *James Gibbs*, pp. 225–32; Willis and Clark, III, pp. 43–54.

relationship between the designs of Burrough and Gibbs remains uncertain.[19]

The stem of Gibbs's three-sided court was to be attached to the east range of the Old Schools, and arms were to reach out towards Great St Mary's. In an heroic classical idiom befitting their significance for the university, Gibbs's blocks were each to have temple porticoes, and a Giant Order was to be repeated on all five fronts to the court. The north block was to be the Senate, the centre or west block the Royal Library, and the south the Register House. The design was several times modified, becoming larger and more stately, with temple porticoes added to the courtyard elevations of the north and south blocks, just as on the south face of the Senate House today.

From 1720 onwards land was acquired, houses pulled down, and construction of the Senate House begun, though it languished for lack of funds. Other parts of the scheme aroused one of those intricate controversies that mark Cambridge life and make outsiders wonder how anything at all gets accomplished. Gibbs's 'attaching' scheme, for a continuous three-sided court united to the Old Schools, would involve blocking the way to the Old Schools from Caius (the passage which of course remains open to this day). The 'detaching' scheme, to enlarge the east rooms of the Old Schools for library purposes and leave the Senate House standing separate, had its partisans; among them was Dr Gooch, Master of Caius, who paradoxically had as Vice-Chancellor been a keen supporter of the Public Building from 1717 to 1719. He now pressed his opposition to the 'attaching' scheme by a Chancery suit – which was sufficiently prolonged to bring Gibbs's grand scheme to a halt.

Cambridge would have possessed the most Palladian university ranges in the world. The Senate House, the only portion to be completed, was ready in 1730 (though the west end was not finished till 1766–8, by James Essex the Younger). There were few architectural precedents for its function, a single large room used for the conferring of degrees. Gibbs had to suggest solemnity without melancholy, grave but happy ceremony. He did so by adopting a Roman utterance, emphasised by using Portland stone, rare in

---

[19] Summerson, *Architecture in Britain*, p. 188.

3 Interior of the Senate House.

Cambridge at that time.[20] The form of the Senate House, a parallelogram suggesting a combination of temple and basilica, expresses dignity and religious ritual; significantly, it shares a common idiom with Gibbs's current design for St Martin-in-the-Fields. Balance comes from the decorative luxuriance of the plasterwork on the walls and the coffered ceiling, not at all ecclesiastical in spirit.

After the completion of the Senate House the Regent House was taken over by the library, and the adaptation for the library of the other rooms on the first floor of the East Court of the Old Schools proceeded, slowly. Not till 1753 did the university get round to reconsidering an essential part of the 'detaching' scheme. James Burrough, in middle age a respected don and architect, was naturally invited for the task; he proposed to rebuild the east front so as to give it a façade very like one published for the Royal Library by

---

[20] It was used by Wren for the west end of Pembroke chapel 1663–5, and by Gibbs himself for the Fellows' Building at King's.

17

Gibbs over twenty years before; the first-floor room, a main part of the book accommodation, was to be widened by two-thirds. But suddenly, in October 1753, the new Chancellor of the University, the meddlesome fusspot Duke of Newcastle, wrote to the Master of Peterhouse with plans cutting across Burrough's:

> I have directed Mr Wright, to prepare forthwith a Complete Design, for Building a wing to answer the Senate-House in front, and to the Regent-Walk; – And, also, of a new front to the Library ... I must beg, that you would give immediate attention upon an affair, in which the Ornament, and Conveniency, of the university, and my own Credit, are so much concerned.[21]

Stephen Wright had worked for the duke for some years. The university always found it best to follow his patron's wishes, which Newcastle supported with £500 for the building; Wright was given the commission for the library design. Burrough was one of the sixteen dons to vote against the grace authorising building. One source suggests that it was Newcastle himself who tried to smooth Burrough's annoyance by obtaining a knighthood for him. Wright's facade, quite unlike Burrough's and strongly influenced by the designs for the Horse Guards by William Kent, is the one we see now; despite its odd provenance and the somewhat dismissive comment of Sir John Summerson it is usually regarded as harmonising with the Senate House quite well. Wright's plan for the south wing, part of the idea of the Public Building since Gibbs, was not proceeded with; nor was it afterwards, apart from some preparing of the ground and of plans by architects that included Robert Adam and Sir John Soane.[22] New quarters for university administrators were not gained till King's Old Court was purchased in 1829.

THE GRAECOPHILS AND THE BUILDING OF DOWNING COLLEGE

'Wilkins to build the College after his Athenian model, he has been formally advised of this.'[23] In this way George Whittington

---

[21] McKitterick, *Cambridge University Library*, pp. 256–7. See the same volume for these paragraphs on Wright in general.
[22] Willis and Clark, III, pp. 72–4; James Lees-Milne, *The Age of Adam* (London, Batsford, 1947), pp. 137–40.
[23] George Downing Whittington to Lord George Gordon, fourth Earl of Aberdeen, 8 December

announced the decision to appoint William Wilkins to design Downing College, the first new college for two centuries. It was the first Cambridge commission for the young Wilkins, and began a busy and important local connection: in his work for Downing, Corpus, King's, and Trinity Wilkins stamped his mark on the university landscape as no other single architect had since the Middle Ages, save possibly James Gibbs.

Wilkins was born in 1778, the son of a self-taught Norwich architect who moved to Cambridge in 1780, later building for his own use one of the most notable Italianate villas in the city, Newnham Cottage in Queen's Road.[24] For the elder Wilkins an interest in medieval architecture led to acquaintanceship with East Anglian virtuosi, commissions to restore ancient structures, and membership of the Society of Antiquaries; in so many ways, his career seems to prefigure his son's. A pupil at Norwich Grammar School, William Wilkins then won a scholarship to Gonville and Caius; it was the college of James Burrough and thus became linked with the two most distinguished architects of local origin.[25] He was Sixth Wrangler in 1800, demonstrating by high honours in the intensely mathematical degree course of the day his intellectual drive and capacity for detail. His deeper energies were given to antiquity. Adding to the study of medieval architecture that his father's tastes made it easy for him to pursue, Wilkins became an enthusiast for the ancient world; and it is natural to see behind this predilection the effect of the classical components in the Cambridge course, subordinate to mathematics though they were, and the inspiring way they were taught at certain colleges. William Wilkins was thus one of the Cambridge Hellenists or 'Graecophils' in whom Greece and Rome were to be lifelong passions. Often men of independent means, they travelled in the Mediterranean, and published studies of the antiquities they surveyed and frequently collected. In Wilkins's Cambridge generation a most committed Graecophil was Edward Daniel Clarke, who returned from his tour

1805: BL Add. MSS 43229 fol. 117v., quoted in Cinzia Maria Sicca, *Committed to Classicism. The Building of Downing College, Cambridge* (Cambridge, Downing College, 1987), p. 47.

[24] *RCHM Cambridge*, part 2, pp. 375–6. Wilkins senior also collaborated with Humphry Repton the landscape designer, and at one time owned six theatres in East Anglia, which his son inherited: see below, chapter 19.

[25] R. W. Liscombe, *William Wilkins 1778–1839* (Cambridge University Press, 1980), pp. 1–21.

of Greece with a caryatid from the Inner Propylaea at Eleusis which stood for many years in the entrance to the University Library.[26] Other Hellenists were Robert Walpole, author of an influential work on Herculaneum, and Lord George Gordon, fourth Earl of Aberdeen. Members of a university small by today's standards the Graecophils were naturally drawn together by common pursuits. Their careers often intersected, Aberdeen for example collaborating with Wilkins in compiling *The Civil Architecture of Vitruvius* (1813 and later).[27]

In 1801 Wilkins was elected to a Worts Travelling Bachelorship, which in return for monthly letters (in Latin) to the Vice-Chancellor gave him £100 for his Mediterranean tour. His two years abroad deepened Wilkins's devotion to the classical world, which he gave expression to in his authoritative work *The Antiquities of Magna Graecia* (1807), written while he was sustained by a Caius fellowship. Wilkins was a leading architect in the so-called Greek Revival, a misleading term since the classical impulse had been active for over two centuries, but marking the new direction it took with the Cambridge Hellenists and others of their generation. Traditionally, classicism had been mediated through Renaissance ideas of the ancient world, and it could produce structures quite unlike anything ever built in Greece or Rome – for example, the three gates of Dr Caius at Wilkins's own college. In the eighteenth century, however, the need for faithfulness to ancient models themselves began sometimes to be emphasised, a landmark in this concern for authenticity being Robert Adam's *Ruins of the Palace of the Emperor Diocletian at Spalatro in Dalmatia* (1764) – though Adam was always eclectic in his use of classical inspiration.[28] In his zeal for exact representation of classical exemplars and his preference for Greece rather than Rome – for original chasteness and simplicity rather than elaboration – Wilkins was an archaeological purist, or as his critics have said, a classical

---

[26] It is now in the Fitzwilliam Museum. Clarke became Professor of Mineralogy and University Librarian. He was 'Stone' Clarke, to distinguish him from 'Bone' Clark the anatomist and 'Tone' Clarke the Professor of Music.

[27] On the Hellenists see David J. Watkin, *Thomas Hope 1769–1821 and the Neo-Classical Ideal* (London, John Murray, 1968), pp. 64–92, and J. Mordaunt Crook, *The Greek Revival. Neo-Classical Attitudes in British Architecture 1760–1870* (London, John Murray, 1972), pp. 29–62.

[28] Lees-Milne, *The Age of Adam*, pp. 67–9.

pedant. But Greek was not the only grammar he could command. His first antiquarian interests were medieval, his first published essay (*Archaeologia*, 1801) concerned Prior Crauden's chapel in Ely, and his Cambridge work shows Wilkins's adroitness in the Gothic idiom. His sense of the separateness and integrity of past epochs encouraged movement from one style to another.

The invitation to design Downing came in 1805, when Wilkins was writing *Magna Graecia*, eighty-eight years after the possibility of a new foundation was first hinted at. In his will of 1717 Sir George Downing left instructions for the endowment of a college, should a series of named kin die without direct male heirs. There was in fact no such issue, but the Downing estates were claimed – and the intention to found a college contested – by Sir George's kinswoman Lady Margaret Downing and her descendants, though if the original will were valid their contentions were without value. Here was material for a dispute as interminable as *Jarndyce* v. *Jarndyce*. First begun in the Court of Chancery in 1764, the case, indeed cases, were not settled till 1800. Though legal costs and the family had between them bled the Downing estate white, a royal charter for the new foundation was sealed, college statutes published and a building fund set up controlled by Chancery.[29]

When plans for the college were still very inchoate and a site not yet purchased, James Essex was chosen as architect, a commission that if effected would have crowned the career of this local man. After his death in 1784 his successor in the still as yet notional post was James Wyatt, well known for his design for the Pantheon, assembly rooms in Oxford Street modelled on the church of Saint Sophia in Constantinople. Soon after 1800 Wyatt produced plans for the college in Roman Doric style, and when St Thomas's Leys[30] were acquired as a site in 1804 there was hope that they would soon be carried out. At that moment, however, the Master of Downing, Francis Annesley, invited comments on Wyatt's design from Thomas Hope, a virtuoso from Scots merchant stock, and an enthusiast for ancient Greece. Hope criticised Wyatt's Roman theme; it was to be wished that 'instead of the degraded architecture of the Romans, the purest style of the Greeks had been exclusively

[29] Stanley French, *The History of Downing College* (Cambridge, Downing College Association, 1978).
[30] Also known as Pembroke Leys, lying to the south of Bird-bolt Lane, the modern Downing Street.

adhibited'.[31] He hinted that Wilkins, newly returned from Greece and versed in the appropriate aesthetic vocabulary, would be a more suitable architect. Though the details of their plot are unclear, Hope's letter no doubt in some way reflected the desires of the Cambridge Graecophils; and perhaps a prime mover in the affair was one at the heart of the Downing fellowship – Sir Busick Harwood, Professor of Medicine, whose varied pursuits and foibles are retailed in some of the liveliest pages of Gunning's *Reminiscences*. Harwood knew Wilkins, and in 1800 was one of his sponsors for membership of the Society of Antiquaries.

Hope's letter did not settle the matter, but it did lead the Master in Chancery (still powerful in plans for Downing) to reopen it. Designs were submitted by George Byfield, whose name seems to have been pushed by a prominent Downing man, Edward Christian, Professor of the Laws of England;[32] by Francis Sandys, in part responsible for the neo-classical extravaganza at Ickworth; by Lewis Wyatt, nephew of the original college appointee; and by William Porden and of course William Wilkins. Porden, a successful designer of Gothic country houses, submitted plausible Gothic Revival plans for the college – an early essay in the style that became as characteristic of academe as the neo-classical. Sandys's ideas are lost, but were most probably classical in nature, as were in their various ways those of the other three men. By a process that cannot in detail be traced but probably involved the conflict of personal and aesthetic factions, the candidates were whittled down to Wilkins and Lewis Wyatt, the latter being backed by pro-college members of the Downing family and therefore hard to dislodge. It fell to the Master in Chancery to decide the question, and his request to three architects to assess the two contestants' merits set a precedent for future architectural competitions. They judged that 'the general decorations of Mr Wilkins's design adopted from Grecian models possess more grandeur simplicity and classical effect than those of Mr L. Wyatt'. The choice of Wilkins was a clear victory for Graecophil sentiment.[33]

We can scarcely grasp the strength of Wilkins's collegiate idea

[31] Quoted in Watkin, *Thomas Hope*, p. 62.
[32] Brother of the *Bounty* mutineer, Fletcher Christian.
[33] Sicca, *Committed to Classicism*, pp. 20–48.

from the imperfect realisation we see today. The buildings were to be surrounded by thick belts of trees screening them from the town and the commercial market-place. The college was to be inward-looking and detached, its architecture expressing serenity, harmony, and the permanent values of disinterested scholarship. Buildings were to face each other across a quadrangle. This was to be unlike the usual Cambridge court because of its much greater size and the openness created by the discontinuity of its ranges. Though prefigured by Gibbs's unexecuted ideas for King's, Wilkins's plans were an early statement of what later was called a 'campus'; they were drawn up more than a decade before what is commonly thought to be its prototype, Jefferson's design for the University of Virginia, though there is no evidence that Jefferson learnt from the example of Downing or even knew of it.[34]

The court was to be grassed; in contrast with the plantations shielding the college from the outside world it was to have few trees, so that there was to be no visual disruption of the sense of inner unity. The entrance gateway on the north side was to be modelled on the Propylaea, the monumental entrance to the Parthenon, and to offer on the outer and inner porticoes Doric columns like its fifth century BC original. On the other side of the court was to stand a block containing hall, library, and chapel, and inspired by the Erechtheum, a temple of the cult of Athena adjacent to the Acropolis. Its Ionic columns were to be translated to the Downing south range; there were to be Ionic porticoes on its north and south sides and its east and west ends, and they were to be made more salient by the astylar austerity of the east and west ranges. The historically authentic use of both the Doric and Ionic orders was also aesthetically apt, hinting at asymmetry and so lessening a threat of excessive regularity.[35]

Wilkins's design for Downing has been severely judged by some, C. R. Cockerell calling its separated pavilions 'a string of sausages'. Perhaps its buildings are too low for the breadth of the court, Wilkins showing here the creative stiffness that was to mar his work on the National Gallery to a much greater degree. Also, his faithful

[34] Bryan Little, 'Cambridge and the Campus. An English Antecedent for the Lawn of the University of Virginia', *Virginia Magazine of History and Biography*, 79 (1971), pp. 190–201.
[35] Sicca, *Committed to Classicism*, pp. 52–7.

reproduction of classical detail has been described as doctrinaire, but the comment fails to register the nobility of Wilkins's conception or the integral place in it of authoritative classicality.[36] On entering the court, the visitor was to be surprised by 'the distant view of classical temples, unexpectedly rising from the ground, almost as if he had been transported to some remote plain in Greece, or to the Valley of the Temples in Sicily'.[37] Wilkins's Downing was to be a declaration in stone of the reverence for classical culture and its permanent worth that Whewell was to evince, thirty years later, in *On the Principles of English University Education*.

The Downing building fund proved too small for the design, whose cost Wilkins had himself underestimated. Only the east and west ranges could be afforded; for the north and south ranges Wilkins attempted vainly to design cheaper variants of his Propylaea and Erechtheum with their splendid porticoes. After Wilkins's death the college commendably stayed loyal to his ideas, and buildings were sensitively extended by Edward Barry in 1873. Twentieth-century additions have been less happy. Sir Herbert Baker's northern ranges of *c.* 1930 are notably inferior to the original vision, Baker abandoning 'Wilkins's design just enough to irritate'.[38] The Regent Street frontage of the 1980s marks an even more lamentable aesthetic decline. So the monumentality Wilkins planned for his north and south ranges can only be imagined; what we see is a shadow of his collegiate idea.

THE UNIVERSITY LIBRARY AND C. R. COCKERELL

'Very good indeed, especially the part about the Library', was the comment of the Registrary on the speech of the Senior Proctor, John Lodge, at the election of the Vice-Chancellor in November 1833.[39] Lodge (who crucially happened to be University Librarian too) criticised the gross congestion that made proper organisation of the library stock impossible. Accessions had increased greatly since the Copyright Act of 1814 had given the library the right to claim a

---

[36] Liscombe, *William Wilkins*, pp. 54–5; Summerson, *Architecture in Britain*, pp. 303–7.
[37] Sicca, *Committed to Classicism*, p. 57.
[38] Pevsner, *Cambridgeshire*, p. 68; Sicca, *Committed to Classicism*, pp. 67–79; Liscombe, *William Wilkins*, pp. 50–5.
[39] J. P. T. Bury, ed., *Romilly's Cambridge Diary 1832–42*, (Cambridge University Press, 1967), p. 41.

copy of every British publication. Print threatened to fill every corner.[40] Elsewhere in the university accommodation was needed for roomless professors and scientific collections. Adam Sedgwick, Professor of Geology, found that the growing pile of rock specimens was overflowing into his own apartments in Trinity, while a set of wax models bought for anatomy demonstration were decomposing in a cupboard. Without additional premises, William Whewell warned in 1828, Cambridge, facing international competition, would 'have the mortification to see herself left behind in the cultivation of such studies as are above-mentioned'.[41] As Whewell wrote, however, the university was hoping to buy and redevelop the Old Court of King's (the West Court of the Old Schools fills the site today) which the college would vacate when Wilkins's south range was completed for it. The Old Court abutted the University Library at its south-western corner, and free and easy Etonian Kingsmen made a row that readers had to suffer, while the arches supporting the library's Dome Room actually rested on King's land. The university bought the court for £12,000 in 1829, after four years of wrangling over the price.[42]

The redevelopment of the site, raising issues of finance and aesthetics, was certain to provoke controversy, especially since, whatever committees might recommend, the final say rested with a Senate vote.[43] The university undoubtedly mishandled the issue, which is an object-lesson in how not to run an architectural competition. Squabbling filled the 1830s; feelings were hurt, and Cambridge's reputation damaged. Nevertheless, a striking and attractive building did result. A syndicate appointed in 1829 decided, in view of the dilapidated state of much of the Old Court structure and the appeal of an entirely fresh start, to demolish the King's ranges and the Schools too and to construct new offices and museums with a library above on the first floor. They also resolved to invite five architects to compete for the design, but foolishly gave them no advice on style or cost. Of the five men, Wilkins and the partners Rickman and Hutchinson were responsible for much new

---

[40] McKitterick, *Cambridge University Library*, p. 414.
[41] Willis and Clark, III, pp. 98–101.
[42] Willis and Clark, I, pp. 321–33; McKitterick, *Cambridge University Library*, pp. 465–71.
[43] For what follows, see Willis and Clark, III, pp. 101–21, and McKitterick, *Cambridge University Library*, pp. 473–89.

college building in Cambridge, while Decimus Burton, born in 1800, had designed the Ionic screen at Hyde Park Corner in 1824; a brilliant career lay ahead for him (though not in Cambridge). The fifth man, Charles Robert Cockerell, aged forty-two in 1830, was an accomplished architect whose pronounced classical tastes owed much to his long sojourn in Mediterranean lands; his Grecian addiction is perhaps best shown by his Scottish National Monument on Calton Hill, modelled on the Parthenon in the 1820s. Cockerell's aloof and fastidious disposition may be sensed from the likeness sculpted by John Philip on the podium of the Albert Memorial.[44]

All five men submitted designs. Rickman and Hutchinson produced two, one classical in the Ionic order and the other a richly detailed exercise in Decorated Gothic which threatened dissonance with both the Senate House and King's College chapel. Decimus Burton also supplied classical and Gothic designs, while from Cockerell came two plans which naturally, given his tastes, were both Greek.[45] The syndicate recommended one of Cockerell's but another syndicate appointed to consider the cost of the project judged that it was too expensive. A cost-limit of £25,000 was set for a first phase of construction, and entries were invited for a fresh competition for which the Grecian style was specified. Though Burton took no further part, the other competitors resubmitted. Wilkins's drawing resembled his recent design for University College, London, its Corinthian portico harmonising with the Senate House nearby.[46] Strangely, it had no partisans in the university, apart from Wilkins himself.

The serious contest was between Rickman and Hutchinson and Cockerell, whose contributions were assessed by yet another syndicate (confusingly called 'the second') appointed in June 1830. Cockerell's was of sumptuous splendour. The east front was Corinthian, with an imposing prostyle portico and classical statuary

[44] David J. Watkin, *The Life and Work of C. R. Cockerell* (London, Zwemmer, 1974) esp. pp. xix–xxiii and plate 2.
[45] Rickman's designs are illustrated in David J. Watkin, *The Triumph of the Classical. Cambridge Architecture 1804–1834* (Cambridge University Press, 1977), plates 7 and 8; see also David J. Watkin, 'Newly discovered drawings by C. R. Cockerell for Cambridge University Library', *Architectural History*, 26 (1983), pp. 87–91.
[46] See Watkin, *The Triumph of the Classical*, pp. 33–4 and plate 4, whose caption has been transposed with plate 9.

on pediment and roof, while a watercolour of the interior by Cockerell himself suggests the luxuriance of its antique and Renaissance motifs. It would have been one of the most distinguished university buildings in the world, and both more attractive and serviceable than the design, by Rickman and Hutchinson, that the syndicate incomprehensibly preferred.[47] A partisan of Cockerell, George Peacock the Trinity mathematician, said of Rickman's design, 'There is a total want both of simplicity and of symmetry in the internal arrangements',[48] while William Whewell, also from Trinity, supported Rickman. Other dons intervened, and a vigorous pamphlet war ranged over questions of aesthetics, function, and finance, and there was general dissatisfaction with the plan to deduct contributions towards the cost from the library book-fund.

Several syndicates later, it was in 1835 decided for the time being to erect a more modest building on the site of King's Old Court – leaving the Schools intact – and to meet its cost by subscription. By the end of the year over £20,000 were raised. Participants in the earlier competitions were frugally compensated (Cockerell proudly refusing the offer) and yet a third competition was mounted in 1836. Cockerell was at last given reason to feel pleased (though Rickman the reverse) by winning the Senate vote on his new plans in May. Cockerell contemplated the eventual construction of a new library court that would at least in part replace the Schools building, and we are given a tantalising glimpse of its grandly colonnaded east front in Le Keux's *Memorials of Cambridge* (1841–2).[49] The need for economy forced the truncation even of the first phase planned in 1835, and all that was built, between 1837 and 1840, was the north range, on the site of the original hall and kitchens of King's College. Even the reduced structure cost £35,000, £12,000 more than had been subscribed, and paying for it strained university resources. Cockerell's vision was never realised, and he asked his friend Thomas

[47] Watkin, *C. R. Cockerell*, pp. 189–90 and plates 83 to 86.
[48] Quoted in McKitterick, *Cambridge University Library*, p. 480.
[49] Reproduced in McKitterick, *Cambridge University Library*, p. 487. Designs for Cockerell's 1835–6 court are reproduced in Watkin, *C.R. Cockerell*, plates 88–91, and its possible extent is hinted at in Willis and Clark, IV, plan 27, fig. 1, though one cannot reconcile their suggestion with the engraving in J. Le Keux, *Memorials of Cambridge: A Series of Views of the Colleges, Halls, and Public Buildings* (2 vols., London, 1841–2).

Acland to 'have mercy on my library – consider it a fragment of a great Quadrangle'.[50] Judgement has in fact been mixed. Pevsner is no more than merciful, adverting to its 'severely functional exterior', and the 'earnest, weighty and impressive' interior.[51] Cockerell's biographer points to the subtle and imaginative deployment of motifs from the classical world and Renaissance masters and the 'austerity and magnitude' of the Senate House Passage facade.[52] Unfortunately, the constricted site of the Cockerell Building prevents one from seeing it properly without straining one's neck. The building at first contained a lecture theatre and scientific museums on the ground floor with a library above linked to the existing library in the Schools east court.[53] In the rest of the century, book accessions led to expansion of the library into the ground floor of the Cockerell Building and the east court of the Old Schools, and into the new ranges that G. G. Scott and J. L. Pearson constructed at the south end of the King's Old Court site.[54] But the University Library scarcely ever caught up with its need for extra accommodation (similar problems face it today, with vastly more space than Cockerell dreamed of at his most expansive) and its plight was dire indeed until the new library was built on a greenfield site between 1931 and 1934, half its cost being met by the Rockefeller Trustees. Fortunately, while the book is being prepared for publication in 1996, the original majestic interior of the Cockerell Building is becoming visible as twentieth-century bookstacks are removed.

THE CONFLICT OF STYLES IN CAMBRIDGE: THE TRIUMPH OF THE CLASSICAL, AND THE FITZWILLIAM MUSEUM

The classical and Gothic styles were in conflict for much of the nineteenth century. As we shall see, Gothic was chosen by colleges, a trend reinforced by the increase in Gothic sentiment in Cambridge from the late 1830s onwards. But it was rarely thought appropriate for university buildings, an exception being the Pitt

---

[50] Quoted in Watkin, *C. R. Cockerell*, p. 196.
[51] *Cambridgeshire*, pp. 203–4.   [52] Watkin, *C. R. Cockerell*, pp. 192–5.
[53] The linking staircase may be seen through a glass screen at the entrance to the Regent House Combination Room, the one-time Catalogue Room of the University Library. At the time of writing (1996) the Cockerell Building is being refurbished to house the library of Gonville and Caius.   [54] McKitterick, *Cambridge University Library*, pp. 599–608, 741.

Building, designed by Edward Blore, a friend of Sir Walter Scott and adept at varied Gothic utterance. It was erected between 1831 and 1833 to commemorate the statesman and house the University Press.[55] For university buildings the classical style was usually preferred. For the observatory, built on a site near the Madingley Road thought to be distant enough from Cambridge smoke to guarantee clear vision,[56] the *ad hoc* syndicate chose, from thirteen entries submitted, a design by John Clement Mead, that he described as copied 'from the Temple of Minerva at Athens'.[57] This preference for classicality, also evinced over the University Library, was shown in the contest for the greatest university monument of the epoch, the Fitzwilliam Museum.

What the Vice-Chancellor called, when laying the foundation stone of the Fitzwilliam Museum in 1837, 'many choice and excellent productions of the Sculptor's and Painter's skill',[58] were bequeathed in 1816 by the seventh Earl Fitzwilliam, a graduate of Trinity Hall, together with funds to assist their housing. The university certainly showed no unseemly haste in building a permanent home for the lavish gift. But there were problems of site and finance, and the commissioning of the architect was tactfully undertaken, lessons being learned from the library fiasco. From 1816 to 1842 the collection was housed in the hall of the old grammar school building in Free School Lane, which was altered for the purpose by William Wilkins.[59] In the 1820s no fewer than eight sites were considered and rejected, stimulating fantasies of how different the cityscape would be if the Fitzwilliam had been erected at the south side of Senate House Yard, or where the Arts Theatre now stands. The eventual site was bought from Peterhouse in 1823. Though little cluttered by buildings it was by leases, and work could not be contemplated till the mid-1830s. A competition for designs was announced in 1834, and twenty-seven architects submitted thirty-six. Most have disappeared. Those that remain in the Fitzwilliam itself and the Royal Institute of British Architects show

---

[55] Willis and Clark, III, pp. 136–44.
[56] Another desire was to have sight of the tower of Grantchester church for a meridian-mark.
[57] Willis and Clark, III, pp. 190–8.
[58] Willis and Clark, III, p. 212; and pp. 198–224 for what follows.
[59] The school hall, encased in other structures like a fly in amber, now houses the Whipple Museum of Science.

that the museum idea was very variously interpreted (the university having given no stylistic guidance). A vision completely different from the one we see in Trumpington Street came from the partners Thomas Rickman and Richard Hussey. Victorians usually chose Gothic for college buildings because it evoked notions of a medieval community. In 1835 it was also chosen for the new Houses of Parliament, because it was felt that their Englishness 'was best expressed and upheld in an essentially English style'.[60] So Rickman and Hussey had some grounds for expecting that 'associationism' might favour a Gothic museum, as indeed it was to do in Oxford in 1855; one of their Fitzwilliam designs is a romantic Gothic folly recalling Fonthill Abbey, whose insubstantial tower collapsed in 1825 shortly after completion.[61] But in the 1830s a museum, very much a recent concept invented to house antiquities gathered from the Mediterranean, was naturally envisaged as necessarily Classical; Smirke's British Museum of 1823 was a model hard for Fitzwilliam competitors to avoid. In fact, along with their Gothic entry Rickman and Hussey also joined those submitting variations on Greek or Roman themes, offering to dominate Trumpington Street with an Ickworth-like rotunda massively squatting on Ionic porticoes.

Entries were exhibited at the Pitt Building for six months, and then the Senate balloted twice, each member casting four votes on the first occasion and one on the second. This unusual way to effect an artistic choice worked brilliantly, the Senate demonstrating its high degree of cultivation in selecting by clear margins the designs of George Basevi, aged forty-one, an ex-pupil of Sir John Soane. Like others chasing success amidst the eclectic tastes of early Victorian England, Basevi designed Gothic churches and Tudor almshouses when asked, but three years' travel in Greece and Rome had deepened an attachment to the Classical style. In this style he designed many houses in Belgravia and Kensington, but his greatest achievement is without doubt the Fitzwilliam Museum, with its 'opulent display of Graeco-Roman detailing'.[62] Building started in 1837, and by 1845 Basevi was about to complete the interior. In October, however, he

---

[60] Watkin, *The Triumph of the Classical*, p. 12, and pp. 11–15 and 41–58, and plates 12–24.

[61] Reproduced ibid., plate 19, and *VCH Cambs.*, III, p. 388.

[62] H. M. Colvin, *A Biographical Dictionary of British Architects 1600–1840* (London, John Murray, 1978), pp. 93–4. Basevi was a first cousin of Benjamin Disraeli.

was killed in Ely Cathedral, falling through a hole in the west tower floor.[63] The Fitzwilliam Syndicate then entrusted the completion of the museum to C. R. Cockerell, whose forbearance and professional skill during the library imbroglio had been noted. Cockerell's classicism also made him profoundly sympathetic to Basevi's intentions, which indeed Cockerell carried out with fidelity while here and there giving greater richness of effect. Money, which had been giving cause for concern for some years, ran out in 1847 when the museum had already cost £91,000. For quarter of a century the brickwork of the entrance hall was left bare and undecorated – a dispiriting introduction to the museum's treasures for mid-Victorian visitors.

The entrance hall was part of the large design problem that sprang from Basevi's vision that his building had to be prominent, separated from its neighbours on either side and standing above the street:

> the effect of the Portico of the Pantheon at Rome is injured by its present low position and the vicinity of the other buildings – and on the contrary how finely the detached and elevated situation of the Greek temples accords with their symmetry – in some places crowning an Acropolis – in others occupying a rising ground, and always standing on a high platform.[64]

The magnificent portico of the museum, with its densely foliated Corinthian columns, was therefore placed above steps rising from Trumpington Street. But owing to the comparative shallowness of the site,[65] the visitor, after climbing the steps, has almost immediately to descend to reach the street-level galleries: Basevi's plan risked giving entrants a psychological blow. Since nearby there had also to be a staircase ascending to first-floor galleries the space posed puzzles of great complexity. Basevi suggested in turn three solutions. None was effected before his death, and Cockerell's was not

---

[63] It is said that Basevi was walking on scaffolding with his hands in pockets, carelessness later cited as a warning to architects in training: Arthur T. Bolton, *Architectural Education a Century Ago* (London, Sir John Soane Museum [1930]), p. 10. Basevi is buried in the cathedral, where there is a memorial brass.

[64] Watkin, *The Triumph of the Classical*, p. 13, quoting Basevi's notes on his site plan for the Fitzwilliam design.

[65] This lack of depth also meant that Basevi could not place the building back from Trumpington Street as the example of the Parthenon would surely have suggested. The portico steps are uncomfortably close to the perimeter railing, and a good view of the entire frontage is only really possible from the east side of Trumpington Street.

fully completed before the money ran out. Matthew Digby Wyatt, the architect of Addenbrooke's Hospital, who was consulted on the question, called it 'by far the most difficult problem I have ever met with in my professional life'; his imaginative solution was not however accepted by the syndicate. Eventually E. M. Barry, relatively unknown son of a famous father (the architect of the Houses of Parliament) solved the 'descent' conundrum by hiding the staircases; at the same time he enlarged the sense of space in the entrance hall, while adding to Basevi's exuberance 'a rich cascade of sumptuous marbles'.[66]

With the rebuilding of Corpus, King's, and the Old Schools area, and the addition of the Fitzwilliam Museum, the heart of the university acquired some of its most famous modern features. An equally important change was the transformation of the land between the Old Schools and Great St Mary's. Remnants of ancient properties, houses ('hovels' indeed) at the west end of Great St Mary's and others in front of the Old Schools, were cleared away; Trumpington Street was dramatically widened; and the square between the street and the university buildings was turfed and paved. These improvements were not completed till 1833.[67] The present grand vista, the tourist attraction *par excellence*, is less than two centuries old: antique enough, but less so than it is sometimes assumed to be. Two or three hundred years ago the area was congested and miserable. Its present grandeur, like much 'heritage', we owe to ruthless rebuilders who would now be blocked by conservationists. We trust modern architects less than Burrough or Gibbs, but also less than the nameless builders of cruck cottages. Central Cambridge provokes reflections on our lack of aesthetic self-confidence.

WILKINS, RICKMAN, AND THE TRIUMPH OF THE GOTHIC

In 1746 a couplet in the *Gentleman's Magazine* referred to a place

> where the rude plans absurdity confess,
> In Gothic ornaments, and barbarous dress.[68]

[66] Watkin, *The Triumph of the Classical*, pp. 14, 41, 56–7.
[67] Willis and Clark, I, pp. 544 (plan) and 548, III, pp. 71–3.
[68] Quoted in James Macaulay, *The Gothic Revival 1745–1845* (Glasgow, Blackie, 1975), p. 89.

After the middle of the century such a dismissal of Gothic architecture became less and less likely. The cult of naturalness and spontaneity, albeit in tamed and unthreatening forms, which expressed itself in the gardens at Stourhead and the pseudo-epic 'Ossian' poems of James Macpherson, had its architectural counterpart in a renewal of interest in the Gothic, with its connotations of 'wildness' and irregularity, as opposed to classical restraint. One of its first enthusiasts was Horace Walpole, Kingsman and friend of Thomas Gray, and begetter of the Gothic Strawberry Hill (1753 onwards). Cambridgeshire possesses one of the first Gothic Revival structures in Britain, the folly (*c.*1750) in the grounds of Wimpole Hall, the work of Sanderson Miller and his patron Philip Yorke, first Earl of Hardwicke and High Steward of the university. A few years later, another local grandee, John Cotton of Madingley, re-erected at his stables, with Gothicised detail, the gateway (1470) removed from the Old Schools to make way for Wright's frontage.[69]

After the Napoleonic Wars a college building boom began because of the need for additional accommodation. Scott's novels, and his house, Abbotsford, added to the appeal of medievalism and the Gothic style; it competed powerfully with the Classical. William Wilkins, despite his adulation of Athenian utterance, was himself an accomplished practitioner in the Gothic. For example, when the fourth Earl of Rosebery wished to replace his wave-washed medieval castle on the banks of the Forth, Wilkins submitted two designs, for a Corinthian temple and a Tudor manor house, alternatives that neatly illustrate his willingness to cater for different tastes. The manor house was accepted. Modelled on East Anglian originals he had long known, Dalmeny, the house Wilkins built, offered greater practicality, privacy, and comfort (it was warm in winter) than other Neo-Gothic edifices.[70] In Cambridge Wilkins made major additions in Gothic at Trinity, Corpus, and King's. Trinity New Court was the first of these commissions, the master, Christopher Wordsworth, inviting in March 1821 designs for new accommodation; the college wanted rooms for the recent increase in matriculants that had so far to be lodged in the town, at expense

[69] Pevsner, *Cambridgeshire*, pp. 435, 492.
[70] Macaulay, *The Gothic Revival*, pp. 318–21; Liscombe, *William Wilkins*, pp. 83–6; Colin McWilliam, *Lothian* (Harmondsworth, Penguin, Buildings of Scotland series, 1978), pp. 170–2.

to college and damage to discipline. Wilkins was approached because of the reputation gained by his 'Athenian' colleges, Haileybury and Downing. A straightforward classical prescription was easier on these greenfield sites than at Trinity, where it was necessary to take account of ancient ranges as well as Wren's uniquely sophisticated library. Mindful of varying demands Wilkins prepared Gothic and classical designs. The latter, Greek Revival in its upper storeys but Baroque on the ground floor to attempt harmony with the Wren Library, underlines the aesthetic problem.[71] The college chose Gothic, believing that it was appropriate for a community whose buildings were mostly pre-Classical. The decision set a crucial precedent for other colleges. A detail is that the idiom of New Court is Tudor, the gateway for example owing much to the vestibule of Henry VII's Chapel at Westminster – a fitting influence, since his son founded Trinity.[72]

Corpus Christi quickly followed Trinity, in 1822 inviting Wilkins to submit plans for extra accommodation which the college had desired for two centuries. As a result, houses and ancient college buildings fronting Trumpington Street were replaced by the 'Tudor' New Court.[73] Though the gateway and the hall suggest that Wilkins had observed detail at Trinity and Christchurch, it is hard to disagree with Pevsner that the overall effect is 'institutional, not collegiate'. Wilkins's work at King's was happier, though it surmounted a greater challenge. The contract, which much to their disgust he won against the competition of Charles Barry, Decimus Burton, and others, entailed fitting a hall and additional accommodation into a constricted site, since the college failed to get others to agree to move King's Lane to the south. Wilkins had also to harmonise with the chapel's overpowering statement and with the Gibbs building. His solution for the latter problem indicates the limits of his sensibility. Regarding Gibbs's debt to the European Baroque as pseudo-classicality, he proposed to clothe his building in Gothic garb. John Nash and Jeffry Wyatt, consulted, acclaimed the idea; fortunately for us, in the event the college could not afford it.

[71] Watkin, *The Triumph of the Classical*, plate 9. Its caption has been transposed with plate 4.
[72] Willis and Clark, II, pp. 651–60; Watkin, *The Triumph of the Classical*, pp. 6–7; Liscombe, *William Wilkins*, pp. 128–31.
[73] Wilkins also constructed a Gothic chapel at Corpus Christi.

As to Wilkins's constructions at King's, that stern critic of his rivals' schemes, C. R. Cockerell, denounced them as 'conceived in a servile spirit of imitation'; but more apposite is Pevsner's verdict that 'the scale is right, the heights are right, the execution is substantial'. In particular, the King's Parade gateway and screen blend so well with the chapel that they are now often taken to be of the same date, the highest compliment to a Gothicist.[74]

Like other colleges, St John's needed new accommodation greatly in the 1820s, annual admissions having risen from forty to ninety since the 1790s. New Court, extending St John's to the west side of the Cam, was the largest college building erected in Cambridge up to that time. The college instructed architects 'to follow as nearly as may be the style of the present Second Court [*c.*1600], with such Improvements as the Architect may suggest'.[75] Three architects were invited to submit designs – Wilkins, Arthur Browne of Lincoln, and Thomas Rickman. Wilkins did not enter the competition, and Browne's scheme did not properly exploit the site. Nor did the unsolicited design of John Mead, architect of the Cambridge Observatory. The winner was Thomas Rickman, aged fifty, whose unusual and productive career has mystifyingly failed to attract a biographer.[76] Unhappy as a clerk to a Liverpool insurance broker, he turned in his thirties to making meticulous drawings of churches as a solace for his many misfortunes. Bringing exactness and scientific method into a field till then dominated by the amateur artist, he showed the sequence of detail in church development, and invented the typology still used today – Norman, Early English, and so on. Utterly lacking the professional education common for men like Wilkins and Cockerell, he was self-taught as an architect, yet soon after he opened his office in Liverpool in 1817 his energy and competence made him one of the busiest practitioners in Britain, specialising in Gothic churches for the Church Building Commissioners. Designed in conjunction with his partner Hutchinson, the New Court of St John's was the firm's most ambitious assignment.

[74] Willis and Clark, i, pp. 297–304, 564–6; Liscombe, *William Wilkins*, pp. 123–33; Pevsner, *Cambridgeshire*, pp. 64, 96.

[75] Willis and Clark, ii, p. 278, and pp. 277–9 for what follows. See also Alec C. Crook, *From the Foundation to Gilbert Scott. A History of the Buildings of St John's College, Cambridge* (Cambridge, St John's College, 1980), pp. 73–86, which draws on archive material not used by Willis and Clark.

[76] Colvin, *A Biographical Dictionary*, pp. 688–93.

Its detailing is Perpendicular, but its composition and symmetry give it an unmistakable Classical feel, and as Pevsner remarks a temple portico would not seem out of place.[77] Clearly Gothic Revival, it is quite unlike its intended model, the Second Court, especially in being faced with stone.

In the 1820s and 1830s accommodation in Gothic style was also built for Peterhouse, Christ's, Jesus, and Trinity Hall, and the popularity of the idiom was most spectacularly shown at Sidney Sussex by Jeffrey Wyatt's conversion of serviceable Elizabethan into patently mock Gothic, in the process creating an extra floor of chambers. In the 1860s Tudor was the style adopted at Trinity for new courts which gave an additional ninety-five sets on the east side of the college. The master, Whewell, turned for their design to Anthony Salvin, who had for decades been employing Tudor and Jacobean styles to construct or restore country houses. Salvin also built a Tudor hall and library block for Gonville and Caius.[78]

THE CAMBRIDGE CAMDEN SOCIETY: GEORGE BODLEY AND GEORGE GILBERT SCOTT

As the passions aroused by the Old Schools schemes suggest, many university men were interested in architectural matters. One such was William Whewell, the Trinity don (and from 1841 master) distinguished in so many intellectual endeavours. Keenly noting constructional detail while travelling widely in Europe (once in the company of Thomas Rickman) he wrote a learned work on the German Gothic, designed two 'Gothic' shops in Trinity Street (nos. 4 and 6), and published in *Fraser's Magazine* (1850) one of the most perceptive reviews of Ruskin's *Seven Lamps of Architecture*, pointing out the inconsistencies while praising the eloquence of that rallying-cry for the Gothic. A man of similar breadth to Whewell

---

[77] One of New Court's most famous features, the 'Bridge of Sighs' linking it with the older parts of St John's, was designed by Hutchinson to be sealed at the sides and top, so that 'the nocturnal inclosure of the students within the walls is preserved without interfering with free communication between the courts': Willis and Clark, II, p. 279.

[78] J. Stair Douglas, *The Life and Selections from the Correspondence of William Whewell D.D.* (London, Kegan Paul, 1881), pp. 251, 516–18; Jill Allibone, *Anthony Salvin. Pioneer of Gothic Revival Architecture, 1799–1881* (Columbia, Miss.: University of Missouri Press, 1987), pp. 20–94, 134–7, 177; Peter Salt, 'Wyatville's Remodelling and Refurbishment of Sidney Sussex College, 1820–1837', *Proceedings of the Cambridge Antiquarian Society*, 81 (1993), pp. 115–55.

was Robert Willis, fellow of Caius and from 1837 Professor of Natural and Experimental Philosophy (in effect, Engineering); he is chiefly known today for the monumental *Architectural History* which his nephew completed. His first book concerned medieval architecture in Italy and is clearly indebted to Whewell's penetrating comments on the nature of Gothic; like Whewell's, Willis's book was an important milestone in architectural history. He went on to write extensively on the English cathedrals. Ruskin read both men attentively and met them in 1851, staying with Whewell in the master's lodge and travelling with Willis and him to Ely. Willis designed the Perpendicular west window in the tower of St Botolph's, Trumpington Street, and an Early English chapel in Wisbech, now sadly demolished.[79]

The choice of Gothic for the new Houses of Parliament in 1835 both reflected and enhanced a growing preference for the style; and despite the support for Classical designs in the library and Fitzwilliam competitions Cambridge preferences seem to have been moving in the same direction. Medievalism was much discussed in university circles, a focus being the Cambridge Camden Society, named after the sixteenth-century antiquary William Camden. It was founded in 1839 by a group of undergraduates attracted by the Tractarian movement of Newman and others in Oxford, with its loving celebration of the Catholic tradition in Anglicanism. Prominent in the new society was John Mason Neale of Trinity (now chiefly famous as a hymnographer) who described himself as 'a great upholder and setterforth of Puseyism'.[80] Another young member was A. J. Beresford Hope, an undergraduate of Trinity and the son of the virtuoso and collector Thomas Hope.[81] The Cambridge Camden Society soon recruited over 650 university men of all ages, Robert Willis being among the several score of dons joining, and

[79] Nikolaus Pevsner, *Some Architectural Writers of the Nineteenth Century* (Oxford, Clarendon Press, 1972), chapters on Ruskin, Whewell, and Willis; David J. Watkin, Introduction to reprint of Robert Willis and John Willis Clark, *Architectural History of the University of Cambridge* (Cambridge University Press, 3 vols., 1988) vol. I, pp. vii–xx.

[80] James F. White, *The Cambridge Movement. The Ecclesiologists and the Gothic Revival* (Cambridge University Press, 1962), p. 27 and generally; Pevsner, *Some Architectural Writers*, chapter XIV. For a longer account of the Cambridge Camden Society, see Chapter 10, below.

[81] In later years Beresford Hope was MP for the university, a Conservative of uncompromising views, opposed to parliamentary reform and supporting Gothic architecture and the rights of the Established Church. He also wrote a successful novel, *Strictly Tied Up*.

over 100 from outside academic circles. Concerned like the Oxford Tractarians to encourage true piety, the society tended to stress not the doctrinal matters absorbing the Newman circle but ritual and architecture. Enthusiasm for Gothic was plainly widespread in Cambridge, and among the young men round Neale who effectively controlled the society's publications and pronouncements it became fanaticism – sometimes to the unease of their elders.

The young ecclesiologists (to use the name they gave themselves) regarded architecture as ineluctably the expression of society's spiritual health; since the period 1260–1360 was the age of the most profound faith, Decorated (or as Neale and company preferred to call it, Middle Pointed) was the only approved style.[82] Their journal, the *Ecclesiologist*, attacked other styles relentlessly, asserting that C. R. Cockerell's imposing Classical library was 'that monstrous shop-front library with which he has disfigured this University'. Taking a hand in the 'restoration' (reconstruction would be a better word) that affected, and often violated, so many parish churches in that epoch, the Cambridge Camden Society preferred to return to the church's original structure, discarding later accretions. Though caution or sheer ignorance of earliest intentions prevented wholesale destruction everywhere, many structures were ruthlessly altered. One of the most notorious examples was the Church of the Holy Sepulchre, Cambridge, the Round Church of the twelfth century. Under the society's auspices Anthony Salvin removed features clearly visible in the elder Pugin's engravings of 1815:[83] mostly Perpendicular, they included a chancel, an aisle, a vestry, and a bell tower. The changes, extending to the Norman fabric itself, made it very largely a Victorian building. Even in the 1840s, inclined recklessly to remove the past, a few voices protested at this loss. Far more fuss was made, however, about the stone altar and a credence table that were added at the restoration. The incumbent protested at these signs of Popery, and brought an action in the Court of Arches whose complex course is best summarised by saying that he won it. At the church's reopening in August 1845 the

[82] The distant parallel between these views and Ruskin's is worth noting. For Ruskin the right organisation of labour was the touchstone, and he was very suspicious of anything that smacked of Popery.

[83] James Ackermann, *A History of the University of Cambridge, Its Colleges, Halls, and Public Buildings* (2 vols., London, 1815), vol. II, plates 57 and 58.

Master of Christ's, John Graham, warned 'lest in reproducing the graces of medieval architecture, we should lay ourselves open to the suspicion of reviving medieval superstition'.[84] The Holy Sepulchre imbroglio brought to a head long-festering anxiety about the doctrinal destination that the young leaders seemed to be taking the Camden Society to, despite their denials of 'Romanism'. Bishops resigned as patrons. Dons such as Samuel Lee and Adam Sedgwick protested. At length, in 1845, 121 members including perhaps a score of dons resigned from the society, which itself moved to London, changing its name to the Ecclesiological Society and losing much of the vehemence that marked it when undergraduates had set the tone. Whatever their limitations, the Cambridge Camden and Ecclesiological Societies had great influence on church architecture. They were largely responsible for restoring the chancel (an emblem of priestly separation from the laity) to its medieval importance, and for introducing the Victorian stained glass and fittings that so many churches now possess.

Seceders from the Camden Society turned to the Cambridge Architectural Society, founded in 1846, to pursue an unsectarian and broad enthusiasm for Gothic. Robert Willis was a member, and his nephew J. W. Clark. So was another Trinity don, W. J. Beamont, whose extensive travels took him to the Crimea and the chaplaincy of the Sebastopol camp hospital; at length returning to Cambridge, he founded the Cambridge School of Art and brought Holman Hunt to the city to decorate St Michael's church.[85] Another member was Beresford Hope, whose book *The English Cathedral of the Nineteenth Century* (1861) was of seminal importance in diffusing admiration for Gothic architecture. The many dons and citizens in the Architectural Society were part of a British (or at all events English) movement for what was increasingly seen as the 'national style', the selection of Gothic for the Houses of Parliament and the Law Courts, for example, associating medievalism with imperial greatness. Thus in the memorial it offered to the Cambridge controversy on the new Guildhall in 1860, the Architectural Society urged 'the propriety of adopting pointed architecture in

[84] James F. White, *The Cambridge Movement*, p. 138.
[85] On his death he was given a fittingly medieval memorial, a full-length brass in Trinity College chapel.

preference to a necessarily debased and incongruous style [i.e. the classical], for a civic building destined to adorn a town which is already so largely indebted to the national style'.[86] But the competition arbiter, T. L. Donaldson, chose a Classical design instead, incidentally getting revenge for the insults heaped on his own Classicism by the *Ecclesiologist*. The society saw its principles given practical effect in 1859 in the construction of the royal Albert Almshouses at the corner of Brooklands Avenue and Hills Road, early Cambridge examples of the polychromatic Gothic that Ruskin praised in *The Stones of Venice*. (It was sometimes called the 'streaky-bacon' style.)

This rage for the Gothic left permanent marks on the Cambridge skyline, most visibly at the corner of Hills and Lensfield Roads where the Church of Our Lady and the English Martyrs was built in the 1880s, and in a host of college ranges and chapels. At Jesus College several fellows were keen ecclesiologists, notably John Sutton, who after helping to found the Camden Society was one of the very few members who became Catholic converts. An enthusiast for church organs, he designed the first one in Jesus. A friend of the most famous apostle of the Gothic, Augustus Welby Pugin, Sutton was in part responsible for bringing him to work on the chapel from 1846 onwards. After reinforcing the tottery tower (a task that reminds us that not all restoration was purposeless vandalism) Pugin with the assistance of the Cambridge carver James Rattee repaired the east end of the chapel, leaving much original work but also reconstructing much of the fabric. The lancet windows were filled with glass that carefully followed medieval models: Pugin travelled to Chartres for exemplars.

In 1860 Jesus College supplied land in Jesus Lane as a new site for All Saints Church, whose existing structure in St John's Street was cramped and inconvenient. An architect was sought, and a natural choice was the youthful George Bodley; he was restoring the chapel at Queens' at the initiative of a fellow of the college, William Campion, another active member of the Architectural Society.[87] Bodley had been a pupil of Sir Gilbert Scott. His professional

---

[86] See Duncan Robinson and Stephen Wildman, *Morris and Company in Cambridge* (Cambridge University Press, 1980), p. 23, and pp. 1–3, 20–44, for these paragraphs.
[87] Bodley constructed a new chapel for Queens' in the 1890s.

philosophy was transformed by reading Ruskin's *Seven Lamps of Architecture* and *The Stones of Venice*. Bodley followed Ruskin in seeing architecture as rightly founded on the excellence of the past, and as the expression of noble feelings in the form that can best reflect and perpetuate them. As he designed he would mutter 'I wonder what Ruskin would make of that.'[88] In working on All Saints Bodley was constrained by shortage of money and by the committee's insistence on a spire rather than the tower that Bodley regarded as a more effective emphasis on the verticality he was eager for. But not all dons were inhibiting. Two enthusiastic ecclesiologists from Jesus, George Corrie, the master, and John Gibson, a fellow, gave sympathetic encouragement to Bodley's ideas and deserve some credit for the result, the most impressive and beautiful achievement of the High Victorian Gothic in Cambridge – if we may judge by the assessment of experts:

> Without mimesis, but in idiom, Bodley's church possesses the character of an early-fourteenth-century Gothic parish church, while enjoying the fruits of modern craftsmanship, building techniques and decorative skill. All Saints' stands out in the history of English architecture, marking the point at which the Gothic Revival demonstrated the ability to learn from past styles and to build from their principles, rather than to plunder them for individual features and precedents.[89]

The many visitors to the church are also attracted to its interior decoration. Bodley followed the medieval practice of covering walls and roof with painting, employing the Cambridge craftsman F. R. Leach to realise his designs. Perhaps some of these were prepared by William Morris, since Bodley had known the Pre-Raphaelite group since 1858 and had already worked with them. In 1863 he engaged their firm, 'Morris and Company', to design windows in All Saints, and glass by Burne-Jones and Philip Webb is a glory of the church. The firm was involved to a greater extent in the restoration of Jesus College chapel, whose structural deterioration, despite Pugin's recent efforts, called for Bodley's intervention in 1864; the college was wise not to invite Salvin or Scott, whose

[88] David Verey, 'George Frederick Bodley: Climax of the Gothic Revival' in Jane Fawcett, ed., *Seven Victorian Architects* (London, Thames and Hudson, 1976), pp. 84, 95.
[89] Robinson and Wildman, *Morris and Company in Cambridge*, p. 30.

savage amputations may be imagined. Bodley wrote, 'I think the Conservative principle of retaining all the old historical features of the building which are not incongruous & unecclesiastical is in all cases the right principle of restoration.'[90] But in Jesus much had to be renewed, and Morris, Burne-Jones, and Webb added ceiling panels (a rebus playing on the name of Bishop Alcock) and a lot of very fine glazing.[91] Visitors to Jesus are as much attracted to it as to the medieval structures in the college, but their attitude was not Morris's; in the 1870s he came to regret his own part in Victorian restoration, and refused any longer to add new glass to old buildings. His comment in 1877 to the Dean of Jesus, E. H. Morgan, was: 'Your chapel is you see glazed but just in time.' In the same year Morris founded the Society for the Protection of Ancient Buildings ('Anti-Scrape'), the first conservationist body.

He did so in rage at Sir George Gilbert Scott's restorations of English churches, the plans for Tewkesbury Abbey being the immediate trigger. Scott's new chapel for St John's, built in the 1860s, touches on many issues that exercise architectural historians and conservationists.[92] As with Jesus College chapel, there was a need for some fresh construction; it was not mere vandalism. St John's old chapel, inherited from the medieval hospital of St John, was too small to accommodate all members of the college. For decades debated, action for a new building was stimulated by a rousing sermon from William Selwyn, Lady Margaret Professor of Divinity. Land was bought, a street closed, and a building fund collected, and it was decided to erect a new master's lodge at the same time. The old chapel seems to have been built in the Early English and Decorated styles with many later alterations, chiefly sixteenth century. Scott seized upon the existence of Decorated stonework as a justification for constructing the new chapel entirely in that idiom, his favourite. His building is archaeologically faithful to the Decorated. On the other hand the old chapel and hospital

[90] Robinson and Wildman, *Morris and Company in Cambridge*, p. 36.
[91] A. C. Sewter, *The Stained Glass of William Morris and his Circle* (2 vols., New Haven, Conn.: Yale University Press, 1974–5), vol. I, many references, and vol. II, pp. 42–4. Morris and Company also worked with Bodley in restoring Queens' hall in the 1860s and 1870s, supplying much-admired fireplace tiles and roof decoration. The firm's tiles and glass in Peterhouse Combination Room may also be mentioned.
[92] Alec C. Crook, *From the Foundation to Gilbert Scott*, pp. 90–114; Willis and Clark, II, pp. 324–44.

buildings were destroyed, as were not a few inns and unpretentious houses that the present generation would prefer to have, though contemporaries seem not to have regretted their passing. Questions were asked about the dominating scale of the chapel – only to receive from Scott assurances that today merely confirm the judgement that he was insensitive. The chapel overwhelms its side of the college, and is as salient at one end of the historic town as Our Lady and the English Martyrs is at the other.

PAST AND PRESENT IN THE CAMBRIDGE TOWNSCAPE

1870 is more than a convenient milestone for the landscape historian, since innovations then abruptly became more varied, and stressed the disappearance of the past. If Girton's buildings stayed within the collegiate Gothic tradition, Newnham's Queen Anne ranges definitely did not. Trinity Street was transformed by Alfred Waterhouse's construction, for Caius, of the largest French château north of the Loire, while the red-brick Louis XII range he erected for Pembroke on Trumpington Street glared its contrast both with its neighbours and the Caius addition. A gloomy apprehension that the pace of change was accelerating and a legacy of beauty being recklessly squandered may be discerned in the commentary composed about 1880 by Robert Farren, a Cambridge topographer and engraver, as he took his readers by the hand and led them down Castle Hill into the heart of the city, to look at the non-university buildings of the ordinary citizens' Cambridge that was his immediate concern. A Ruskinian, revering the Middle Ages and abhorring the recent past, he mingled praise of the few ancient structures he discovered with regrets that so many had been destroyed:

> Nestled in the very heart of the town are the two old Tudor Inns, the Falcon and the Wrestlers, and although they are battered and patched, & surrounded by modern ugliness of every degree there is enough left to make really good subjects for the needle, but alas! their days are numbered, and the next generation of our town will have lost another link with the past.[93]

[93] Robert Farren, *Cambridge and its Neighbourhood* (Cambridge, Macmillan, 1881), plate V.

Eight engravings were enough to record the non–university buildings Farren thought of aesthetic value in the city centre, which he abandoned to register his impressions of Stourbridge Common.

Farren uses language with which the late twentieth century can easily sympathise, and sometimes we find what he says plausible; few would deny that the new Petty Cury is less attractive than the old – whatever the decrepitude of the old or the commercial pressures that led to its demolition. But the passage of time leads to gain as well as loss, and the aesthetic account is often hard to draw up. The innovations of the last epoch cease to intrude, and in time may themselves be fully accepted as part of a much–admired urban patchwork. Such has happened, indeed, to the 'ugly brick boxes of the 19th century' that Farren hated, and even to Waterhouse's addition to Caius – though it is doubtful whether the Materials Science building will have the same fortune. It has to be added that Cambridge has been luckier than most cities in its physical changes during the last two or three centuries, and this is particularly true of the backbone, a mile from end to end, that runs from Magdalene Street along Trinity and Trumpington Streets. Near this route lie most of the buildings described in this chapter, and perhaps most observers would agree that with some striking exceptions (St John's College chapel above all) they are more beautiful than the structures that preceded them. They also together form a unity. Yet the street was not 'planned' like one of Haussmann's boulevards, and indeed individually they were apparently the result of academic politicking and caprice. Perhaps the townscape suggests something intelligible about the nature of the university itself: that the arguments of its dons, however unedifying and unseemly at any one time, are likely to lead to transcendent results because an underlying unity of attitude is far more productive than may be guessed from the superficial wrangles that mask it.

Chapter 2

THE UNIVERSITY: ITS CONSTITUTION, PERSONNEL, AND TASKS

THE UNIVERSITY

CHANCELLORS, VICE-CHANCELLORS, AND UNIVERSITY JURISDICTIONS

I come now to the town, and university of Cambridge; I say the town and university, for tho' they are blended together in the situation, and the colleges, halls, and houses for literature are promiscuously scatter'd up and down among the other parts, and some even among the meanest of the other buildings; as Magdalen College over the bridge, is in particular; yet they are all encorporated together, by the name of the university, and are govern'd apart, and distinct from the town, which they are so intermix'd with.[1]

It was hard to see where college buildings ended and citizens' houses began, and it was harder still to distinguish the colleges from the university. University employees, as distinct from college members wearing university hats for a period, were few in number. In the centre of the city the university had imposing buildings, the Old Schools, reserved for its use, and the new Senate House (built between 1722 and 1730) was one of the noblest structures in Cambridge. But college courts dwarfed these university premises, and visitors might be forgiven for assuming that the 'university' was merely a very weak federation, with a feeble central government. Yet only the university could carry out certain essential tasks, like matriculating freshmen and, three or four years later, examining them and awarding the bachelor's degree. These functions were carried out by men spending most of their lives doing rather different things for their colleges. Loyalties sometimes conflicted,

[1] Daniel Defoe, *A Tour Through England and Wales* (2 vols., London, Dent Everyman, 1928), vol. I, pp. 85–6.

while at every turn dons were hampered by a cumbrous constitution two centuries old, obsolete yet exceedingly prescriptive, that it was impossible to change.

This 'constitution' consisted of the Elizabethan statutes of 1570, and some letters patent of James I and Charles I. It laid down detailed programmes of studies for bachelor's and later degrees, and made their alteration possible only by further royal intervention. It reduced the powers possessed in medieval times by the Senate (the assembly of MAs) and the important officers, the Proctors, it elected, while increasing those of the Vice-Chancellor, and the 'Caput' (a committee of senior dons) and making the heads of houses a separate estate in the government of the university. The very substantial curricular changes of the seventeenth and eighteenth centuries were made possible by evading the statutes or interpreting them in tortured ways, and the Elizabethan constitution remained intact until the 1850s, placing real control in the hands of a few with a strong interest in keeping it.[2] Its shadow lies across these pages. In 1856 an Act of Parliament greatly revised it. While the oligarchy of the heads of houses retained a strong presence, democratic and representative elements were strengthened in a remodelled Senate and the newly created Council of the Senate. This pattern remains largely intact in the 1990s. The need to reconcile democracy with executive efficiency, however, is likely in the future to pose a threat to it.

From Elizabeth's time onwards it became usual to choose as Chancellor a statesman likely to bring fortune and favour to the university and jobs for its members. Chancellors varied in their usefulness in these respects, but good or bad they could not reside or exercise day-to-day power – though absence did not stop the Duke of Newcastle from constantly interfering. The Vice-Chancellor was therefore the busiest officer, and perhaps the most powerful one. His range of duties included correspondence, managing finance and estates, presiding at meetings, deciding on prizes, judging in matters of discipline, and granting licences.[3] He had authority in Cambridge city government. Among his many functions, at any rate till the 1830s, was opening Stourbridge Fair each September, a prelude to

---

[2] George Peacock, *Observations on the Statutes of the University of Cambridge* (London, 1841), pp. 1–72.
[3] Peacock, *Observations on the Statutes*, pp. 135–6.

the academical year. Consuming sherry wine and cake in the Senate House mid-morning, he and others went by carriage to the Newmarket Road to proclaim the fair; they ate several barrels of oysters, and rounded off the day with herrings, pork, beef, a goose, plum and pease pudding, and 'a huge apple-pie' – the day being typical of many in its gastric burden on the Vice-Chancellor.[4] Administration was a burden for him too. Assistance with his correspondence and accounts (indeed all his tasks) was meagre, and for much of the eighteenth century entirely lacking. Emoluments were tiny. Like other university officers the Vice-Chancellor was largely dependent on graduation fees that had not risen since the time of Elizabeth, giving him a mere 4d for every BA.[5] Office accommodation was unnecessary since the Vice-Chancellor used his master's lodge for university purposes. A room was provided for his Consistory Court at the south end of the east side of the Old Schools, on the ground floor.[6] Despite the drawbacks of the office few wished to decline election as Vice-Chancellor, habit, duty, and ambition for honour and status combining to influence the constituency, the heads of houses, from whom the Vice-Chancellor was chosen.

Collectively the heads of houses were more powerful than the Vice-Chancellor. They nominated two candidates for the office of Vice-Chancellor, and the Senate chose one. Although in theory any MAs were eligible, from Elizabethan times onwards the heads nominated only from within their own ranks, and this custom was by 1750 considered as binding as the statutes themselves – a good example of the way in which conservative instincts aggravated the authoritarianism of the written constitution; the few attempts there were to nominate humble college fellows were defeated. Nominations were made by rotation, seniority of degree weighing heavily in the priority. Despite the obvious difficulty an incumbent had in learning how to be Vice-Chancellor, heads of houses hated the idea of his serving for a second year; in those twelve months the obvious successor might lose his claim because somebody with a superior degree was appointed to a college mastership. The brevity of his

[4] Gunning, *Reminiscences*, vol. 1, p. 165.
[5] Robert Plumptre, *Hints Respecting some of the University Officers, its Jurisdiction, its Revenues, & etc.* (Cambridge, 1782), pp. 3–13   [6] Willis and Clark, III, pp. 22, 68.

tenure effectively limited the Vice-Chancellor's power. By custom, though not statute, the heads of houses acted as his advisers, regularly meeting him in the vestry of Great St Mary's after the Sunday service. He was not obliged to follow their advice, but since they included his predecessors in office and knew what they were talking about he would have been foolish not to.[7]

Apart from two occasions when Newcastle got his supporters' terms extended, only one Vice-Chancellor served for a second year between 1750 and 1800, and as we might expect the circumstances were highly unusual. In 1782 the next Vice-Chancellor, according to the rota, was John Torkington, Master of Clare, but his lack of intellect and scholarship were derided in Cambridge, and it was said that he owed his mastership to his aristocratic kin, from whom favours were expected. So he was passed over in the election, Richard Beadon, Master of Jesus, serving a second term instead. One year later the heads did not humiliate Torkington by passing him over again, and the verdict is that he was in fact competent enough. Really inefficient Vice-Chancellors seem in fact to have been few. One who stands out is Barton Wallop, Master of Magdalene – chosen for that office by the owner of Audley End, as was then the rule. Wallop has been described as 'a hard living, hard drinking, sporting country gentleman, totally without scholarship or intellectual tastes'. His mastership disgraced the university, though fortunately he did not reside. Against the wishes of the other heads of houses he pressed his claim to become Vice-Chancellor. The heads nominated him in 1774, while perhaps hoping that the Senate would elect the other nominee, Dr Thomas, Master of Christ's. But Thomas, an aged valetudinarian, begged not to be elected, and the Senate took him at his word. As to Wallop, Richard Watson, the Regius Professor of Divinity, took care 'to instruct him in his office and to make him read his speeches with a proper accent and quantity', and he left Cambridge for good after his year was over.[8]

The Chancellor, and in his absence the Vice-Chancellor, had by

---

[7] D. A. Winstanley, *Unreformed Cambridge. A Study of Certain Aspects of the University in the Eighteenth Century* (Cambridge University Press, 1935), p. 18.

[8] Winstanley, *Unreformed Cambridge*, pp. 9–21. Wallop's mastership of Magdalene is described by Eamon Duffy in Peter Cunich, David Hoyle, Eamon Duffy, and Ronald Hyam, *A History of Magdalene College Cambridge 1428–1988* (Cambridge, Magdalene College, 1994), pp. 180–4.

an Elizabethan charter jurisdiction within Cambridge and one mile around, in all civil proceedings and criminal ones except 'treason, felony and mayhem', provided that a member of the university was involved. Presiding over the court was one of the major stresses on any Vice-Chancellor, even though he was counselled on occasion by the heads of houses and by a lawyer called the Assessor.[9] There was a right of appeal for senior members, to the Court of Delegates,[10] and this sometimes lengthened proceedings, as in the case of William Frend in 1793.[11] Whether appeal could be made in disciplinary cases involving senior members was contended, and so matters were sometimes even further confused.

Much of the time of the Vice-Chancellor's Court was taken up with undergraduates' disciplinary offences, of which the following example was typical. One evening early in December 1819 two undergraduates, Thomas Hewett Key of Trinity and Edmund Meadowcroft of St John's, smashed a shop's windows when drunk in a Cambridge street. The shopkeeper, Bridges, chased and caught them, holding Key by his gown and demanding their names. The students refused and blows were exchanged; in court there was inevitably an argument over who struck first. Row, a porter of King's who came up to help Bridges, was also struck, and a general scuffle developed, watched by a crowd of bystanders. After ten minutes or so Key managed to slip out of his gown and escape, shortly before the Proctor appeared. The students' names were inevitably discovered. Tried in the Vice-Chancellor's Court, they were sentenced to declaim on the folly of drunkenness in the Law Schools at 2.30 pm the following Wednesday, to be publicly admonished, and to pay Row and Bridges compensation of £2 each.[12] Some notion of more serious (though rarer) offences may be gained from the words of Isaac Milner, Vice-Chancellor in 1809–10:

---

[9] This intermittently onerous post was usually held by the Commissary, himself not overworked.

[10] The complex mode of election for this court may be summarised by saying that it was chosen by the Proctors and the Caput.

[11] See pp. 418–19.

[12] CUL: University Archives: VCV 41, Diary of William Frere, Master of Downing and Vice-Chancellor, 1819, fols. 27–8. Key put the escapade behind him. Nineteenth Wrangler in 1821, he became Professor of Latin at the University of London, Headmaster of University College School, and President of the Philological Society. He became FRS in 1860. Meadowcroft cannot be traced.

Breaking of lamps and windows, shouting and roaring, blowing of horns, galloping up and down the streets on horseback or in carriages, fighting and mobbing in the town and neighbouring villages; in the day-time breaking down fences and riding over corn-fields, then eating, drinking, and becoming intoxicated at taverns or ale-houses, and lastly in the night frequenting houses of ill-fame, resisting the lawful authorities, and often putting the peaceable inhabitants of the town into great alarm.[13]

Perhaps several of these offences amounted to the 'riotous behaviour in the streets, at midnight' for which Milner fined four students from Trinity and St John's £50 each.[14]

The university jurisdiction was one of many sources of dispute between town and gown.[15] Citizens, irritated that the town was charged to land tax at £2,700 a year, the university £100 and the colleges nothing, were angered that the Vice-Chancellor had power to punish tradesmen for lending more than £1 to undergraduates without tutorial permission. While shopkeepers might well think the risk of bad debts was worthwhile if customers were captured, the university was anxious to prevent undergraduates being insupportably burdened. Thus in July 1752, for example, Mrs Arbuthnot, a local vintner, was fined £5 for having given credit of £5 6s 9d (presumably by way of drink) to an undergraduate without the consent of his tutor. This offence also sometimes led to a tradesman's being 'discommuned' by the Vice-Chancellor's Court – members of the university, that is to say, being ordered not to deal with him. The university's parental role, disciplining minors *in statu pupillari*, also lay behind the right of the Proctors to search the town for prostitutes and arrest them for adjudication by the Vice-Chancellor, punishments available including imprisonment[16] or

---

[13] Mary Milner; *The Life of Isaac Milner, D.D., Comprising a Portion of his Correspondence . . . hitherto Unpublished* (London, 1842), p. 399.

[14] Milner, *Isaac Milner*, p. 393. The students were also rusticated or suspended for periods of six months or a year.

[15] For what follows, see *Cambridge University Calendar for the year 1802*, pp. vii–viii; PP 1852–3, HC xliv [1559]: *Report of Commissioners Appointed to Inquire into the State, Discipline, Studies, and Revenues of the University and Colleges of Cambridge: Together with the Evidence, and an Appendix (Graham Commission Report and Evidence): Evidence*, pp. 35–46; Winstanley, *Unreformed Cambridge*, pp. 27–33, 346–7; D. A. Winstanley, *Early Victorian Cambridge* (Cambridge University Press, 1940), pp. 122–32.

[16] In the university prison or Spinning House, situated in Regent Street on the site of what is now the city's Housing Department and was until recently the headquarters of the Cambridge City Police.

banishment. Concern for morality was also said to justify the Vice-Chancellor's exclusive right to grant alehouse licences, but it was an endless irritant in the town. So was the claim of other university officials, the Taxors, to regulate weights and measures, even though they rarely exercised it, the Vice-Chancellor's power to forbid plays and concerts in the city, and the revival by the university in 1817 of the Magna Congregatio, a local assembly created by Henry III for peace-keeping purposes but long since disused. It involved the mayor and others in attendance at Great St Mary's, for no good reason.

The unreformed corporation could do little, but its replacement in 1835 by a properly elected body with specified duties meant that a fresh sense of civic confidence and efficiency began to challenge the university, which was just as determined to hold onto its privileges. Using their powers under sundry Acts of Parliament, the borough police and magistrates began to punish undergraduates for assaults and prostitutes for importuning. The magistrates started to issue alehouse licences, 200 innkeepers claiming them on the first day, and in 1838 they forced the Vice-Chancellor to defend his right to issue licences by bringing a Queen's Bench action.[17] On their side, in 1844 the heads of houses tightened the screw on Cambridge tradesmen by threatening discommuning for anyone attempting legal action to recover debt without first informing tutors.

Rival arguments on the privileged jurisdiction were fought out before the university commissioners in 1852. The tide of public opinion was moving against the university on the issue; it knew it, and inched towards compromise, agreeing to arbitration in 1855. This granted much of what the two sides desired, and was embodied in an Act of Parliament.[18] The university lost its powers over fairs and markets, weights and measures, and the licensing of alehouses; and though it could still regulate tradesmen's dealings with students and discommune those infringing them, it could no longer inhibit their legal capacity to recover debts. University and college property was to be assessed for rates.[19]

[17] Cooper, *Annals*, IV, pp. 603, 615–16.
[18] P.G. 19 & 20 Vict. c. 88: *An Act to make further Provision for the good Government and Extension of the University of Cambridge.*
[19] Winstanley, *Early Victorian Cambridge*, pp. 131–8.

One major privilege that remained, the power to arrest and punish alleged prostitutes, was however tenaciously insisted on by academic opinion as a necessary part of the tutorial function. Civic opinion was that the borough could carry out any policing necessary, and it was sometimes plausibly asserted that the young women were innocent. A series of cases made the university look clumsy and ridiculous and turned the public decisively against it. One case involved the Proctors' intercepting at Parker's Piece an omnibus that had been hired to take some young women for an evening party, followed by breakfast, at the De Freville Arms, Great Shelford; the women were taken to the Spinning House, one of them receiving a sentence of fourteen days. They claimed to be virtuous dressmakers, wrongfully arrested.[20] Two later cases involved a chase after Jane Elsden down Petty Cury, her capture, escape, and rearrest in Dullingham, blunders and lack of common sense on the part of the university authorities, accusations in the press and questions in the House. The dispute ended with the surrender of these proctorial powers by an Act of Parliament in 1894.[21] The extraordinarily privileged position that the university had been given by the Elizabethan constitution was recognised as an unsustainable anachronism.[22]

THE SENATE AND THE CAPUT

The university's legislature was the Senate. All MAs and doctors of the university were eligible to sit in the Senate provided that they kept their names on college books (for an annual fee of £4 or £5, a substantial amount) or were resident in Cambridge and registered with the university as *commorantes in villa*. Its decisions or orders were known as graces, or supplicats if they concerned the award of degrees, and were binding within the university. Certain meetings of the Senate, called Statutable Congregations, were fixed in advance for the usual routine of university business such as conferring degrees and electing officers. Extraordinary Congrega-

---

[20] Winstanley, *Early Victorian Cambridge*, pp. 380–1.
[21] L. & P. 57 & 58 Vict. c. lx: *Cambridge University and Corporation Act*.
[22] D. A. Winstanley, *Later Victorian Cambridge* (Cambridge University Press, 1947), pp. 91–143 – a highly detailed account, surprisingly sympathetic to the university's stance.

tions[23] were called by the Vice-Chancellor by a printed notice, displayed in college halls three days in advance. On the day of Congregation the bell of Great St Mary's was rung for one hour to summon members, twenty-six of whom formed a quorum. The Senate was divided into two houses for most purposes. The Regent House contained MAs of less than five years' standing,[24] and also the university officers and doctors of less than two years' standing. The Non-Regent House consisted of more senior MAs and doctors, though the latter group had the option of sitting in the Regent House, as did the Orator – a possibility that made votes on contentious matters hard to predict. The Senate's power was limited by the Elizabethan statutes, which had increased the powers of the Caput Senatus, the 'Head of the Senate', for that purpose.

The Caput included the Vice-Chancellor, a doctor in each of the Faculties of Divinity, Civil Law, and Physic, and two MAs, one from each house. Every October the Vice-Chancellor and both Proctors each nominated five men in these categories, and the Vice-Chancellor, heads of houses, doctors, and Scrutators[25] elected five from the fifteen; by the eighteenth century even the slight counterbalance to oligarchy provided by the Proctors' role was removed by the custom of choosing only the Vice-Chancellor's list. The Caput had to approve unanimously all graces before they were put to the Senate; so the constitution gave the Caput very strong negative power. The standard defence of it was that the Caput saw itself as a sort of steering committee whose job was to frame graces in a workmanlike way, and that vetoes were unusual. No doubt uncontentious administrative matters, of which there were many, were settled amicably. But in the pages that follow there are too many examples of vetoes, and therefore of discussion being blocked, for the defence to be entertained.[26] It is scarcely to the point that many graces, if put to the Senate, would have been voted down; in effect, the Caput inhibited debate and so contributed to

---

[23] A meeting of the Senate out of term was called a Convocation.

[24] This period was for MAs the time of their 'Regency', when in theory they could be called upon to preside at public disputations in the Schools; by the eighteenth century the practice had long been defunct. The Regent House was also known as the Upper or White-Hood House, and the Non-Regents as the Lower or Black-Hood House.

[25] The tellers in the Non-Regent House.

[26] Examples were the three successive vetoes of Jebb's examination proposal in 1773; see Winstanley, *Unreformed Cambridge*, pp. 320–1.

the complacency and mental rigidity that the university displayed when faced with calls for change in the 1830s and 1840s. As many complained, the cumbrous process that followed after graces were approved by the Caput made it hard to effect movement. The grace was introduced into each house, and after an interval of several days to allow issues to be discussed in colleges, it was read again in the Non-Regent House and voted upon if opposed. If agreed by the Non-Regents, it was read again in the Regent House, and if passed there, became valid.[27]

UNIVERSITY OFFICERS

The Proctors survived from the medieval university, in which they had important administrative duties. They were nominally elected by the Regents but in practice were chosen by colleges according to a complex cycle.[28] They took part in Senate House ceremonies and were responsible for the proper conduct of some of the exercises for degrees, but their ancient role had shrunk and their chief tasks were disciplinary. As they were to be till 1971, Proctors were often visible in the streets of the town with their assistants, the 'Bulldogs', checking the behaviour of undergraduates outside college premises (tutors being responsible inside colleges).

As Bagehot observed about the British constitution, parts of the university were more decorative than useful. The High Steward's office was thought to confer great honour on its holder, and certainly county magnates sometimes fought bitterly to be elected by the Senate to it. But his duties were insubstantial, and scarcely justified even the £4 that by the Elizabethan Statutes was his stipend. The Commissary also had a vestigial role, his jurisdiction having been overtaken by the Vice-Chancellor's court.[29] The Orator was the Senate's spokesman on public occasions, and presented 'persons of rank to honorary degrees with an appropriate speech'. The Esquire Bedells, besides sundry tasks in Congrega-

---

[27] *Cambridge University Calendar for ... 1802* (Cambridge, 1802), pp. ii–v; *Cambridge University Calendar for ... 1850* (Cambridge, 1850), pp. 1–2; PP 1852–3, HC xliv [1559]: *Graham Commission Report*, pp. 13–14; Winstanley, *Unreformed Cambridge*, pp. 24–7.

[28] The Taxors, possessing powers (largely disused) to inspect local weights and measures, were elected in the same way.

[29] The Commissary was appointed by the Vice-Chancellor.

54

tions, accompanied the Vice-Chancellor on solemn occasions, often carrying their silver maces before him as he processed through the town streets.[30]

The functions of some officers were the atrophied remnants of tasks once far more purposeful, and in this they were like so many offices in eighteenth-century Windsor, Westminster, and White-hall. Others were indispensable, and had plenty to do even if they were not worked off their feet. Among them was the Registrary. He was the university's record keeper for Congregations and the university court, part of his job being to translate graces into Latin. He took the subscriptions (affirmations and promises) of undergraduates on matriculation and of candidates for degrees, transcribed them into permanent books, and was responsible for getting the government stamp impressed on them in the Stamp Office. In an institution where accuracy of record was essential, it was fitting that the Registrary was the most highly remunerated university officer, receiving £400 a year in the 1840s, largely from fees paid by matriculants and graduates.[31] The Registrary's room (the university archives were stored there, too) was at the north-west corner of the Schools Quadrangle, on the ground floor and next to the Divinity Schools (where the Lauterpacht Room is today). Since the room was by 1831 too damp for the records the Registry was moved to the Old Court of King's College, and when that was demolished in 1836 to the Pitt Building, where it stayed for a century, till the construction of the present University Library made return to the Old Schools possible.[32]

Registraries in office from 1700 onwards were conscientious and competent, with the exception of Robert Grove in the early eighteenth century.[33] The most impressive was Joseph Romilly, who filled the post from 1832, when he was forty-one, till his death in 1864. Romilly came from prosperous Huguenot stock. Samuel

[30] The Orator, Esquire Bedells, Librarian, and Registrary were elected by the Senate, which chose between two candidates nominated by the heads of houses. The process gave considerable power to the heads.

[31] *Cambridge University Calendar for ... 1802*, pp. v–vii; *Cambridge University Calendar for ... 1850*, pp. 3–4; PP 1852–3. HC xliv [1559]: *Graham Commission Report*, pp. 9–12, and *Evidence*, pp. 36, 42, 63–5; Winstanley, *Unreformed Cambridge*, pp. 22–4, 33–7.

[32] Willis and Clark, III, pp. 22–3, 78, 142. Winstanley, *Early Victorian Cambridge* pp. 383–4.

[33] Dorothy M. Owen and Elisabeth Leedham-Green, 'Who deue wilbe a register ...': Catalogue of an Exhibition of University Archives (Cambridge University Library, 1984), pp. 1–6.

Romilly the legal reformer was his uncle.[34] He matriculated at Trinity in 1809, graduated as Fourth Wrangler in 1813, and became a fellow in 1815. A very genial man, fond of company, cigars, whist, and musical concerts (he was very widely read too) Romilly was also a devout Anglican, a clergyman indeed, like the great majority of dons – though he rarely preached and did not reside in the Glamorgan parish whose rector he was for seven years. Possessing forceful opinions, an enthusiastic Whig and university reformer, Romilly made astringent comments on the tedium and banality that varied the convivial Cambridge round. Yet one of his closest friends, John Lodge the University Librarian, was a convinced Tory. Romilly was very popular, and it was perhaps this fact that explains his election as Registrary, rather than any apparent great fitness or his determined canvass for it.[35]

The survival of Romilly's voluminous diary enables us to assess the nature of his job, and how it meshed with his Trinity fellowship and the life of a cultivated Victorian gentleman.[36] In 1836 he completed his fourth year as Registrary. Well into his stride, he was perhaps blasé, being absent from Cambridge from 8 July to 8 October, and spending three weeks with his sisters in Dulwich during the Michaelmas Term. Returning to Dulwich for Christmas on 17 December, he came up again on 7 January 1837, spending five and a half hours in the 'Star' coach. Soon after he was visited by the Vice-Chancellor 'who told me as a friend that it was remarked I was too much absent from Cambridge'. We hear of no more complaints thereafter. But though Romilly seems not to have been absent for an entire summer again, he still felt able to take frequent breaks from Cambridge. From 9 to 20 January was a busy period, Romilly being in his office every morning (and some evenings) to take fees from over 200 graduand bachelors, and their subscriptions to the Anglican Articles. He also by invitation attended two meetings of

---

[34] Henry Wagner, 'Some Romilly Notes', *Proceedings of the Huguenot Society of London*, 8 (1905–8), pp. 340–7.

[35] J. P. T. Bury, ed., *Romilly's Cambridge Diary 1832–42* (Cambridge University Press, 1967), pp. vii–xiv, 3–12. I have had many very helpful conversations about Joseph Romilly with Mrs M. E. Bury, and I express my warm thanks to her. Mrs Bury and Dr J. D. Pickles have edited a second volume of selections from Romilly's diary (1842–7, published 1994), and are editing a third volume.

[36] In what follows, J. P. T. Bury's edition, which includes only some of Romilly's entries on his professional tasks, is supplemented with the manuscript diary for 1837 (CUL Add. MS 6819).

the Caput concerned with supplicats for degrees, spent an evening arranging them, was present at the Bachelors' Commencement on 21 January, and then registered the details – a record we still rely on. From February to July he took on Registry business on between seven and fifteen days each month, sometimes between 10 am and 2 pm, sometimes for longer hours and evenings too: attending Congregations and meetings of the Vice-Chancellor's Court where delinquent undergraduates were tried, assisting the Vice-Chancellor with the licensing of Cambridge alehouses, and exceptional tasks, such as the twelve-hour stint on Saturday 8 April drawing up an affidavit for the Vice-Chancellor,[37] in the action over the licensing of alehouses brought by the Cambridge magistrates, and another entire day later in the month preparing documents for counsel. Romilly was able to leave Cambridge for a total of seven weeks in these months, and from 22 July to 12 September there was apparently no Registry business to speak of (and Romilly was away for August), the academical year's serious tasks starting for him with the opening of Stourbridge Fair on 23 September. The routine we have seen in earlier months was soon re-established, a busy time being the matriculation of 385 freshmen in early November. Romilly did not leave the Senate House till 3 pm on Monday 13 November. His year as Registrary finished with three or four mornings in the middle of December spent copying a manuscript in the University Library for the lawyer Grimaldi.[38]

Romilly was not a slave to the machine. Unlike a modern administrator, he was not a member of any university committees; indeed there may have been only three – the Caput, and the Library and Press Syndicates. He had a clerk, paid £30 a year, but perhaps this meagre stipend was for part-time services; Romilly himself undertook menial tasks that nowadays would be given to a school-leaver; in April 1837 for example he spent two days pasting into a manuscript book documents to do with G. W. Wood's parliamentary bill of 1834 to admit Dissenters to Oxford and Cambridge. Romilly also had work to do as a fellow of Trinity, marking Latin papers for fellowships and scholarships, and there were occasional meetings of the Seniority, the college's ruling

[37] See p. 51.
[38] Grimaldi was collecting material on the royal forests and the library's MS concerned Wychwood.

body; the last obligation of 1837 was a college meeting to choose a librarian, on Boxing Day. But it was an unusual day that did not allow a brisk afternoon walk to Trumpington and an evening in company or with one of Scott's novels. Still, he was a more assiduous Registrary than he needed to be and than his predecessors, themselves conscientious enough; he laboriously listed the contents of the volumes they had compiled, an achievement of great value to us.[39] It is not fruitful to compare his work rhythms with those of a modern administrator – carrying more insistent and complex burdens and assuming a 9 am to 5 pm working core to the day – and then to deduce some special torpor in the 'Unreformed' university. Romilly's irregular pattern was like that of many Victorian public servants of gentlemanly status, for example Matthew Arnold, HMI, whose school inspections left him free to spend many afternoons writing in the Athenaeum.

FINANCE

The university was run on a shoestring, but a tangled one, and the Vice-Chancellor managed its finances without help from 'any permanent officer in the capacity of Bursar'.[40] In each of the seven years that ended at Michaelmas 1851 the university's income was on average £18,200; the Vice-Chancellor received it and was responsible for it. Of this, £2,300 came from land, houses, and tithe-rents (in the parish of Burwell) that the university owned; nearly £900 from profits of Cambridge University Press; nearly £700 from annuities and dividends; £3,850 from fees and fines (chiefly for matriculation and degrees); and £221 from Cambridge wine-licences.[41] This total, nearly £8,000, was for 'general purposes'. The remaining income, about £10,200, was 'appropriated to specific objects', and came from a host of sources and special funds. The two largest amounts were £2,621, 'interest of money bequeathed by Viscount Fitzwilliam for the support of the Fitzwilliam Museum (deducting Income Tax)', and nearly £2,000 in subscriptions for

---

[39] Owen and Leedham-Green, 'Who deue wilbe a register', p. 6.
[40] For what follows, see PP 1852–3, HC xliv [1559]: *Graham Commission Report*, pp. 138–42, and *Evidence*, pp. 14–17.
[41] In addition, £2,774 from fees on matriculation and degrees went directly to university officers, for example the Proctors and the Registrary, as remuneration for their services.

the University Library, at 6s from 'every Member except Sizars'. Over £1,000, 'voted annually by Parliament', came from the Paymaster-General for the salaries of Regius professors, while in addition over £100 came from 'the Commissioners of Her Majesty's Woods and Forests' for sundry purposes – a good example of the complexity of the university's finances. The smallest amount recorded was just over £5 from 'interest of Government Stock, for the Ramsden Sermon, preached annually, on the subject of Colonial Church extension (deducting Income Tax)'.

The Vice-Chancellor was also responsible for disbursing money, though needing the consent of the Senate 'for every item of expenditure beyond the ordinary routine of business'. The library received over £3,800, much the largest item, and enjoyed its copyright privilege as well; so compared with the rest of the university it did not do badly. The observatory, botanic garden, and museums and lecture rooms got over £1,700, and the Spinning House (the prostitutes' prison) over £170. A substantial amount, £770, went to support the vicar and church of Burwell (whence the tithe rent-charge came), and nearly £200 to Great St Mary's for repairs and salaries. University 'stipends and salaries' totalled £1,100. Rates and taxes took £363, and £283 went to the Cambridge Improvement Commissioners for paving, lighting, and cleansing: the colleges paid seven times this amount. Paper and printing cost £530, a large amount in a total expenditure of £17,000. Receipts amounted to about £1,000 more, and so despite its meagre resources the university had been able since 1820 to contribute from its treasury ('the Chest') towards the capital cost of the library, the botanic garden, and museums. But any major developments, such as the university teachers recommended by the Graham Commissioners in 1852, could only be paid for from new sources. In practice that meant from the colleges, collectively richer than the university itself.

TERMS AND RESIDENCE

The Cambridge year was divided into three terms, as it still is; the names are the same too, though not the dates.[42] The Elizabethan

[42] For what follows, see Winstanley, *Unreformed Cambridge*, pp. 42–3.

statutes prescribed that the Michaelmas Term should extend from 10 October to 16 December, the Lent Term from 13 January to the tenth day before Easter, and the Easter Term from the eleventh day after Easter to the Friday after the first Tuesday in July. Twelve terms of residence were prescribed for the BA degree. But the heads of houses were adept at interpreting the statutes, and by the eighteenth century the number of terms was whittled down to ten. Thus for the majority of matriculants who came into residence at the start of the university year in October, January three years and a few months later was the earliest time that their degree might be taken: hence the apparent oddity of setting the Senate House Examination, when candidates had to sit at desks for four hours at a stretch, in an unheated chamber at the coldest time of the year.

January remained the month of graduation for all BAs until the change of university ordinances in 1859.[43] A period of nine terms was then laid down as the minimum for the ordinary BA, whose cycle was therefore separated for the first time from the honours cycle. The ordinary examinations were now held three times a year, and the period of residence required for this degree was reduced to nine terms.[44] A person who entered in October, it was pointed out, had the shortest course, 'owing to the fact that the Long Vacation [entered] only twice, and not three times, into his course' as it did for January or April matriculants. But the course for honours was still ten terms, and since the examinations were held only once a year, in January, entry in October was in effect entailed. This pattern lasted until the changes to the university timetable that took effect in 1882, when three-year triposes examined in the Easter Term became the norm.

STUDENTS

NUMBERS AND TRENDS

Introducing in 1843 an account of the English universities that he had translated from the German, Francis W. Newman wrote:[45]

---

[43] *Cambridge University Calendar for ... 1859*, p. 10.
[44] These matters are explained in J. R. Seeley, ed., *The Student's Guide to the University of Cambridge* (Cambridge, 1862), pp. 2–4, whence come the following quotations.
[45] V. A. Huber, *The English Universities*, an abridged translation by F. W. Newman (3 vols., London, 1843), vol. I, p. xxxv.

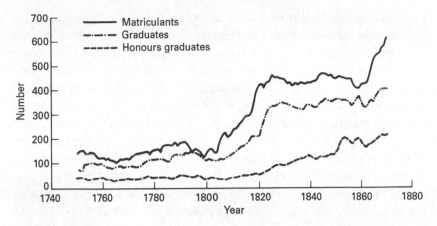

Graph Matriculants, graduates, and honours graduates, 1750–1870: three-year moving average.
Sources: Matriculants: J. R. Tanner, ed., *Historical Register ... to the year 1910*, pp. 987–90; graduates: CUL: UA, Degr. 9, Joseph Romilly, Graduati Cantabrigienses (1864), and Degr. 10, Henry Luard, Graduati Cantabrigienses (1873). I am grateful to Natasha Glaisyer for help in compiling this graph.

> The admirable material structure of our noble Universities, the broad basis which unnumbered zealous benefactors have laid, the schools connected with them which spread over the whole kingdom, the sympathies and venerable remembrances with which their names are entwined, give them substance for a perpetual youth, co-enduring with the energies of the British nation, the prime talent of which they will long have the means of picking.

As the account made amply clear, the popularity of Oxford and Cambridge among parents and their sons had varied greatly over the centuries; and the graph (*above*) is an attempt to represent these fluctuations for the period 1740–1870.

It was pointed out in the 1970s that the rates of admission to the two ancient universities 'rose and fell together in an extraordinary harmony' over a long period, and that the same causes were behind the fluctuations in both institutions.[46] The eighteenth century was a bad time for university recruitment. Student numbers fell while the

---

[46] Lawrence Stone, 'The Size and Composition of the Oxford Student Body 1580–1910', in L. Stone, ed., *The University in Society* (2 vols., Princeton, N.J., Princeton University Press, 1975), vol. 1, pp. 5–6, and for Graph 1 which shows the remarkable correspondence; pp. 37–57 for what follows.

population and living standards were rising quite dramatically; a Cambridge education was not desired, or could not be afforded. The poor students so prominent in the period 1550–1650 were squeezed out by lack of church livings as stipends rose and became attractive to the better off. As university numbers fell the proportion of wealthy matriculants rose. At Cambridge the percentage of fellow commoners rose from 10 in the first half of the eighteenth century to 18 by the end,[47] while in an epoch when the peerage remained static in size the numbers of peers and their sons who attended Cambridge rose too, from 30 in the years 1700 to 1719 to 61 in the years 1780 to 1799.[48] The wealthy, increasingly salient in the university, were in the 1780s blamed for 'the enormous, and enormously increasing, Expence in the education of young Men in this University'; they imported their expensive tastes, which others imitated, for extravagant dinners, stag-hunting, and hiring horses for rides on the Gog Magog Hills or trips to the Newmarket Races. 'Hunting, Racing, and Profligacy of every Sort, is and has long been, the Staple Commodity of this once flourishing University.'[49]

Obviously feeling that everything was going wrong everywhere, the anonymous writer blamed the college authorities for also permitting Methodism to grow and students to absent themselves from divine service, and for supplanting the classical learning for which the university was once renowned 'by a Study as useless for Clergymen and Lawyers, as it would be useful to a Carpenter, or Joiner. Not that I totally condemn the Study of Mathematical Science... But I would not have it made the Standard of Merit in every young Man, not the only Introduction to a Fellowship.'[50] In reprobating the emphasis placed on mathematics after 1750 for those wanting an honours degree the writer put his finger on the feature peculiar to Cambridge which was most probably responsible in some measure for the steep decline in admissions that occurred between 1750 and 1765. It was probably no mere coincidence that

[47] N. Hans, *New Trends in Education in the Eighteenth Century* (London, Routledge, 1951), p. 44.
[48] John Cannon, *Aristocratic Century. The Peerage of Eighteenth-Century England* (Cambridge University Press, 1984), pp. 14–15, 44–59. Cannon's argument runs counter to Lawrence Stone's (in *The University in Society*) to the effect that a smaller proportion of the 'social élite' was attending Oxford; and Cannon gives convincing reasons for doubting Stone's contention.
[49] *Remarks on the Enormous Expence of the Education of Young Men in the University of Cambridge* (London, 1788), pp. 1, 40.
[50] *Remarks on the Enormous Expence*, pp. 13–14, 15–21.

A Wine

4 A Wine.

the gap in enrolments between Oxford and Cambridge was widest between 1750 and 1800: Newtonian geometry is likely to have discouraged more people than it drew; Horace Walpole's remarks about triangles, quoted below, spoke for many.

The number of Cambridge admissions started to rise dramatically soon after 1800, threefold in twenty years from an annual total of about 150; there was then a plateau that lasted until after 1860. Trends were similar at Oxford though annual admissions were larger. Reasons for the initial spurt in growth are not hard to find, at least in outline, and as Stone writes, 'there can be no doubt that the pool of potential students was greatly increased by the demographic growth and the expansion of the middle classes profiting from the industrial and commercial revolutions'.[51] One result was the accommodation crisis and the spectacular expansion of collegiate buildings to meet it, notably in the biggest colleges, Trinity and St John's; the growth of lodgings under licence was a parallel expedient designed to retain tutorial control of students without going to the expense of

[51] 'The Size and Composition of the Oxford Student Body', p. 59.

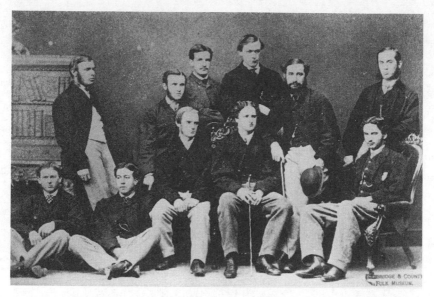

5 St John's Undergraduates 1864.

constructing bedrooms for them inside the college gates.

The plateau is harder to explain, since the growth in the middle class continued unchecked, and the development of many new boarding and day schools for its sons is proof that there was an eagerness to spend increased purchasing power on education. But whatever educational benefits for their sons parents hoped for, they were being told in the period 1825–60 that Oxford and Cambridge would disappoint them:[52] there was an unprecedented barrage of criticism for the ancient universities, scarcely a journalist having a good word to say for them. Their curricula were confined to two disciplines and they refused seriously to embrace science, from which forward-looking men and women expected so much. The exclusion of non-Anglicans gave deep offence, even though the exclusion could be evaded (at least in Cambridge), while the overwhelmingly clerical nature of college fellowships seemed an anachronism in an epoch when the secular character of scholarship itself was being argued by some. Tutors did not teach adequately, forcing men wishing to reach high honours to pay for private

[52] This criticism is described in chapter 11.

tuition: nothing caused more anger than the inflation of university costs that resulted.

So widely criticised were the ancient universities in the middle of the nineteenth century, and so out of harmony with the desires of the professional classes did their practices seem, that one highly perceptive observer wondered if they might decline from their pre-eminence in British society. Parents might well turn elsewhere: 'provincial University-towns are not likely to have all the advantages that professional students desire. The London University will have greater inducements to offer than its elder sisters.'[53] These vaticinations proved too gloomy. The steep rise in admissions from the late 1850s onwards coincided with, and no doubt was stimulated by, the beginning of change: the new triposes, greater emphasis on college teaching, the acceptance of religious diversity and the secular don: in short the coming of the modern university, whose development however had scarcely started at the date this volume ends, 1870.

MATRICULANTS, DROP-OUTS, AND GRADUATES

The Reverend C. A. Swainson, tutor of Christ's College, declared in 1851 that 'young men are frequently sent to the University, of whom from the first there is not the slightest hope of their passing the Final Ordeal. The parents are difficult to convince of this; after three years expense and delay they discover it, and the consequences of the discovery are at times fearful.'[54] At the same time the Reverend J. J. Smith of Gonville and Caius put his finger on a different problem: the existence of 'a multitude of students' who were enabled 'to spend their time ... in idleness and extravagance' by the 'facility of obtaining a degree'.[55] The requirements for the ordinary degree had to be kept low because at almost all colleges there was no matriculation test apart from a certificate of competence from an MA of Oxford or Cambridge. It was no doubt frequently written by the parochial clergyman and as insubstantial as

[53] John Conington, 'The English Universities', *North British Review*, 14 (November 1850), pp. 193–201.
[54] PP 1852–3: *Graham Commission Evidence*, p. 195. What follows is based on pp. 142–217.
[55] P. 189.

65

open testimonials usually are. Only Trinity had an examination, instituted in 1836, and 'of a very elementary character to which students are subjected on their first entrance upon residence'.[56] Yet support for a matriculation examination was confined to a minority of dons, because the university was the obvious agency to administer it and colleges were fearful for their autonomy; they also were afraid that its immediate result would be to reduce the number of entrants, even if in the long run 'it would serve as a stimulus to idle lads, and induce schoolmasters to give more attention to their less promising pupils' – as Henry Latham of Trinity Hall believed.[57]

The lack of any real intellectual test meant that the university comprised young men of very different mental endowments. But their inclinations varied even more widely, and given that colleges were unwilling to be vigorous enough in weeding out the unstudious, it was hard to see, stated Frere of Trinity, how university examiners looking at test papers could know anything 'of the Candidates beyond what appeared from the result of the Examination', and above all 'whether the applicant be of quiet and studious habits'.[58] An examination, feared W. H. Thompson of Trinity, might 'operate as an encouragement to extra-academical "cramming" by hireling tutors. The *general* cultivation of candidates for admission would be sacrificed to the *special* preparation required for this particular examination.' Any written test of competence would have admitted H. J. C. Blake, an undergraduate from 1810 to 1814, since he had been an Eton colleger, but his autobiography is innocent of any account of his studies before he took the poll degree.[59] He kept a black Newfoundland dog and greyhounds in his rooms at King's and spent as much time as possible defying gamekeepers on estates near Cambridge, and riding tandem to balls in Huntingdon and to races in Newmarket. His remembrance of things past at Cambridge concerned sport (and lacked apostrophes):

> Is there any one of my College readers, or others also, who in the cold autumnal or winter months, has not relished after a hard days shooting perhaps in the Fens, (his lower extremities pretty well

---

[56] P. 149.   [57] P. 172.   [58] P. 161, and p. 199 for the next quotation.
[59] See Henry John Crickitt Blake, *The Cantab, or, A Few Adventures and Misadventures in After Life* (Chichester, 1845), pp. 25–67, and p. 39 for the quotation. Blake was ordained priest in 1823, and served in several curacies until 1865 at least; he disappeared from Crockford in 1868.

saturated with liquid mud,) his dinner at six, and then his bottle of port accompanied by the fascinating walnuts, and his friend of the gun, with no little *gusto*? Those cold squashy feet, now comfortably cased, the game bags contents rather ostentatiously displayed in the *outer room*, to impress visitors with the success of the days sport.

Men of his predilections rarely wrote autobiographies, and they tend to be passed over in accounts of the university that naturally enough stress its academic nature. So it is hard to get a sense of their numbers and their outlook on life. In the 1840s dons like Whewell assumed that the follies of the eighteenth century had long been cast aside and that Cambridge was essentially a scholarly institution for all its members. J. D. Lewis's essay on 'The Fast Cantab' convincingly suggests the contrary, even if we have to peer beneath its facetious gloss.[60] 'The fast man usually rises at a late hour', with 'a strong sensation of rum-punch in his mouth'. He and three or four friends sit round the fire most of the afternoon, drinking pale ale and smoking meerschaums, until they go for a ride, tormenting Cambridgeshire farmers 'in galloping violently over wheat and seeds'. 'The fast man hurries off to chapel with curses both loud and deep'; he comes in late 'with his surplice unbuttoned, and holds his prayer book upside down'. In the evening 'there are his billiards, his whist, his *soirées* at the "Emperor's Head", with ostlers, and horse-dealers and blacklegs'. Hating solitude, he cannot study, and 'he hates the University, as a matter of course, longing for the time, as he tells you, when he is to get out into the world'. The fast man is often clever enough to pass the Previous Examination, a not very demanding test in any case.

Yet, it cannot be denied that of the number who annually fail at this examination, a large proportion belong to the class whom we are attempting to describe. It is curious to witness the effect which the approach of that epoch in his life produces on the habits of the fast man. For a whole term he repairs to a 'coach', from whom he expects to gain a thorough knowledge of Paley. He secludes himself from the haunts of men. After vain attempts to comprehend the first chapter he learns it off by rote, and in the senate house answers every question wrong. It is not uncommon to hear from a young

[60] 'John Smith (of Smith Hall)' [John Delaware Lewis], *Sketches of Cantabs* (London, 1849), pp. 10–22, from which the quotations are taken.

gentleman, who confesses that he cannot understand one word of Paley's Evidences, that he is going to the bar, and that he hopes to succeed there too! 'Do you really suppose there's any law-book harder than *that*' he cries 'blow it, I don't believe you'.

However exaggerated, these words betray the existence of men who were not sufficiently clever or diligent or bookish to profit from the university's academic offerings. Graph 1 reflects this reality. Some matriculants did not intend to take a degree, or were plucked by their college, and left before the normal ten terms had elapsed: hence the gap between matriculations and graduations. The second gap was between poll men and honours graduates. These gaps were always considerable. In 1777, 142 men matriculated, and in 1781, 113 men graduated; 104 graduated BA, 47 with honours. In 1837, 430 men matriculated, yet in 1841 only 314 men graduated; of the 300 who graduated BA only 118 gained honours in the Senate House Examination.[61] Between 1820 and 1860 the Senate House Examination became tougher and more competitive, as more candidates scrambled for the wranglerships that led to fellowships that were fixed in number – and so harder to get. Dons were apt to point to this increased rigour as a sign of the university's concern for self-reform, yet the proportion of matriculants unwilling or unable to enter for an honours degree was perhaps rising, while their numbers were larger than ever before. The ordinary degree was not a test that the university could regard as satisfactory, but many did not even aspire to that. The intellectual calibre of the university's entry was its Achilles heel.

PENSIONERS AND OTHERS

One writes of matriculants and undergraduates, or scholars and other students without their intellectual distinction. But undergraduates were separated into quite different categories related to social status: noblemen, fellow commoners, pensioners, and sizars. They paid different fees, enjoyed different rights and privileges, and sometimes wore different academic dress. The most select group

---

[61] I have taken the numbers of matriculants and honours graduates from J. R. Tanner, *The Historical Register of the University of Cambridge . . . to the year 1910* (Cambridge University Press, 1917), pp. 460 and 500 and 989–90, and of total graduates from Joseph Romilly, Graduati Cantabrigienses, 1760–1846 (Cambridge, 1846), pp. 429 and 435.

were noblemen, comprising peers proper and their sons, baronets and knights, 'persons related to the King's Majesty by consanguinity or affinity; provided that they be also honorable', and also their eldest sons.[62] This miscellaneous band paid £10 a quarter for tuition at the beginning of the nineteenth century, ate on high table, might wear hats instead of the academic cap, and were given an MA degree after two years residence only, and without any formal exercises – thus bypassing the BA degree.

Fellow commoners were a much larger group, enjoying privileges of table and apparel and scarcely distinguishable in standing from noblemen. They paid somewhat lower fees (£5 a quarter for tuition), but their families were necessarily wealthy, and some were from noble or landed stock. If entitled by birth they might take their MA in two years, though they had to take the Senate House Examination if they wished to have an honours degree (so did noblemen for that matter). Fellow commoners were often excused from attending college lectures and performing their exercises for the plain BA. James Scarlett, later Lord Abinger, came up to Trinity as a fellow commoner in 1785 and took advantage in his first year of the 'acknowledged licence of a fellow-commoner to abstain from all lectures', being 'kept in countenance by the noblemen and members of my own order, not one of whom, though the class was numerous, had ever shown himself at the lecture of the college Tutor'. The memoirs of John Trusler, a sizar at Emmanuel in the 1750s, throw light on the behaviour of fellow commoners in that college, which had many of them:[63]

> As to the fellow-commoners, they were always at Cambridge called 'empty-bottles' from the following circumstance that occurred at Emmanuel. Wine-merchants send their porters occasionally round the Colleges to collect the bottles; one of these men, during the hour of lecture, knocked at the lecture-room door by mistake, and called out 'empty bottles!' The tutor, then out of humour at being attended by only one fellow-commoner, when there were twenty in college, cried out, 'Call again another time; I have now but one'.

[62] See for example *Cambridge Calendar for . . . 1816*, pp. 145–6, and see for what follows Winstanley, *Unreformed Cambridge*, pp. 80–2, 197–202, and p. 199 for the quotations from James Scarlett.

[63] Quoted by Christopher Brooke in Sarah Bendall, Christopher Brooke, and Patrick Collinson, *A History of Emmanuel College* (forthcoming), chapter 11.

Fellow commoners have had a bad press over the centuries, but it is worth remembering the case of Philip Yorke, the nephew and heir of Lord Hardwicke, who in the 1770s was kept to a rigorous course of study by his martinet of an uncle, however complaisant the college might have been prepared to be towards him.[64]

Most undergraduates were scholars or pensioners. Scholars had considerable financial help from their college, and pensioners paid their fees and for their subsistence. It should be said that in practice the boundaries between the two categories were blurred; scholars found that their scholarships did not pay for everything, while pensioners themselves very often became scholars, or had sundry grants of money, because of their academic success. Pensioners and scholars paid £2 10s a quarter for tuition. Most men in both groups, or at least those for whom we have evidence, seem to have come from gentle and professional but not notably wealthy families, and very frequently they grew up in the rectories to whose like they returned after taking their degree, or enjoying the fellowship that their talents had gained them. 'Most of them were very ordinary young men with no very pronounced characteristics', wrote Winstanley in the 1930s; but since they included Charles Darwin and the future Lord Kelvin his remark is not particularly perceptive.

Sizars paid only 15s a quarter for tuition, a mere fraction of what a fellow commoner paid.[65] They lived more cheaply in Cambridge than other undergraduates, as the prodigious economies practised by men like William Bowyer early in the eighteenth century at St John's testify. In return they acted as servants in college. In Caius in the sixteenth century some, called 'public sizars', did the work of butler or steward; most, the 'private' or 'proper' sizars, were assigned to the fellows and fellow commoners, as waiters in hall and as valets; they dined on leftovers from high table. In the eighteenth century sizars were still acting as servants. For example, at St John's in 1765 nine were chosen to wait at the President's table, and when Isaac Milner came to Queens' in 1770 he had as sizar to ring the chapel bell and help to serve the fellows at dinner. But by this time attitudes towards the sizars' role were changing. In medieval and

---

[64] See chapter 14.
[65] On sizars, see J. Venn, *Early Collegiate Life* (Cambridge, Heffer, 1913), pp. 131–4, Christopher Brooke, *Gonville and Caius College*, pp. 117–18, and Winstanley, *Unreformed Cambridge*, pp. 201–3.

Tudor times it had not been thought degrading to act as a servant in this way, however irksome the duties might be. It was acceptable for a poor boy, often a poor member of a gentle family, to work his way through college; a sizar's tasks have also been compared to fagging in English boarding schools. But in the eighteenth century it came gradually to be felt demeaning for undergraduates to act as servants. In 1767, for example, the sizars at Caius seem to have struck against acting as waiters; the college agreed to provide two servants to replace the sizars at high table. Such changes were common at other colleges, while sizars were given 'commons' to eat at their own table instead of discarded fragments at the fellows'. Students, and college servants, became mutually exclusive categories; a sizarship provided education without strings. Usually, however, sizars still wore gowns that were different from the pensioners', and as late as 1840 they dined at Trinity after other undergraduates had finished, which suggests inferior status and perhaps inferior food.

In 1851 it was reported that 'the menial duties are in all cases abolished', and sizarships continued as a species of scholarship. In St John's and Trinity, the two colleges with much the largest numbers of sizarships, there were 54 and 32 respectively, while another 57 were distributed through another 10 colleges.[66] 'The benefits arising from these Sizarships are considerable', reported the Graham Commission, instancing the case of 'a Gentleman of St John's College, who was afterwards the Senior Wrangler of his year'. He wrote 'I consider mine to be no exceptional case. It was my duty to my friends to abridge my expenses, but I do not consider that I deprived myself of any advantages in pursuing my studies for the sake of economy.' The net cost of his ten terms at St John's was only £19, since in addition to his sizarship he was awarded 'allowances and exhibitions' totalling £135 to set against college bills of £154. Ominously, however, he added that 'private tuition cost me besides £111' – putting his finger on the item which raised costs for many in mid-nineteenth-century Cambridge, and drew more criticism from a concerned public than almost any other feature of the university.

[66] PP 1852–3, HC xliv [1559]: *Report of the Graham Commission*, pp. 195–6.

(a)

(b)

(c)

(d)

6 (a) Master of Arts of the Lower House; (b) Bachelor of Arts; (c) Fellow
commoner; (d) Pensioner.

73

ORIGINS AND DESTINATIONS: BACKGROUNDS OF
CAMBRIDGE STUDENTS AND THE OCCUPATIONS OF
ALUMNI

In 1952 two American scholars attempted to survey the origins and
vocations of a large sample of matriculants in the published listings of
the ancient universities over the period between 1752 and 1886; in
the case of Cambridge, they necessarily relied on Venn, *Alumni
Cantabrigienses.*[67] They suggested for fathers' occupations the figures
given in table 1. The table is open to the objection that there is no
differentiation across time: the century and a third in question was
after all a substantial epoch in which elsewhere in society very great
changes took place. Yet such evidence as the compilers are able to
present suggests that the social composition of Cambridge's intake
remained largely unchanged across the period. The table is also far less
helpful than it may seem in other respects. Venn was as detailed and as
· accurate as his sources allowed, but they were neither complete nor
infallible. His volumes contain many 'don't knows' concerning the
occupations of fathers and the graduates themselves. But the table
fails to reflect this very significant gap, and as a result probably
registers too high a percentage for a father's calling that is fully
recorded – clergyman. So all the table's categories are unprovable;
that is, they may be right, but there is no certainty that they are.

There is also the vagueness of boundary and definition in some of
the headings. In the age in question many clergymen were also
schoolmasters, perhaps keeping a small private school as a sideline,
as the Reverend Jeffrey Wortle did in his rectory at Bowick in
Trollope's novel *Dr Wortle's School* (1881). But he and others like
him were primarily clergymen, even though (it is likely) many of
them are included in the grouping 'academic'. The most problematic classification is however the 'plebeians', which 'ranged from
business employees, government employees (outside the topmost
ranks . . .), through yeomanry, husbandmen, writers and artists, and
miscellaneous occupations'. The authors conclude that 'at Cambridge plebeian representation never exceeded 2 percent until 1830,
after which it varied between 5 and 3 percent'. When one abstracts

---

[67] C. Arnold Anderson and Miriam Schnaper, *School and Society in England. Social Backgrounds of
Oxford and Cambridge Students*, Annals of American Research (Washington, D.C.: Public Affairs
Press, 1952), pp. 5–8 for what follows. The sampling technique is described on pp. 29–33.

Table 1

Occupation	Percentage
Nobility	7.2
Gentry	25.5
Clergy	32.6
Military	6.0
Law	5.3
Medicine	6.0
Government	1.5
Business	9.4
Academic	3.3
Plebeian	3.2
Total	100.00

Source: Figures from Anderson and Schnaper, *School and Society in England.*

from these 'plebeians' the sons of artists and tradesmen and the like, the inference is that the number of entrants from backgrounds of poverty must have been minuscule. But the very poor were the matriculants whose origins were least likely to be recorded. Nevertheless, it would be wrong to move from this lack of demonstrability to the conclusion that there were many poor men at Cambridge 'hidden from history'. This outcome would not be suggested by anything we know about the costs of a Cambridge education (which are treated below), or by our reflections on the difficulty of maintaining a son in a grammar school (even if it was nominally free) during six or seven years when his brothers would be working, in search of a career that lay over the horizon of the poor's customary expectations from life. 'The talk of the "continuous stream of poor boys" who are alleged to have entered the older universities before the twentieth century is humbug, if "poor" is taken to mean working class', is the robust summary of two college historians, though one should add that it is not clear that the allegation in question has ever been made.[68]

[68] Arthur Gray and Frederick Brittain, *A History of Jesus College, Cambridge* (London, Heinemann, 1960), p. 175.

There remains the general impression one derives from the table and it cannot be disregarded, even though its flimsy basis as a piece of social science has to be remembered. Most probably the university was the resort of the landed class and the professions, the church, the law, and medicine, the clergy being the largest single group.

The authors also list the social and occupational groups recorded for Cambridge alumni in the same period (1752–1886) and their findings are given in table 2. Once again the crucial importance of the 'don't knows' who do not appear in the table has to be borne in mind, and it would be very unwise to draw from a comparison of the two lists the inference that fewer alumni took to medicine or business than came from those backgrounds when they matriculated, since the margin for adjustment is so great. Still, one cannot discount the numbers known to have entered the church. The existence of Crockford's *Clerical Directory* means that we know about every graduate who became an Anglican clergyman, and the *apparent* percentage might have to be lowered if the fate of the 'don't knows' were discovered. But it would remain high, an assurance strengthened by our knowledge of the very large numbers of fellows who pursued careers in the church (Appendix VIII). In the few pieces of evidence of change across time that Anderson and Schnaper provide it is reported that 'at Cambridge ecclesiastical alumni dropped sharply after 1830, having receded from 76 percent in 1752–69 and reaching a low of 38 percent in 1870–86'. Nevertheless, the great attraction of the church was scarcely less striking at the end of the period than earlier. In other words, during the 120 years considered in this volume Cambridge was an Anglican seminary. The university's purpose was churchly and ecclesiastical. Paradoxically, however, the route to academic success for undergraduates was largely mathematical: there was a contradiction between the course they studied for an honours degree and the profession that most of them pursued afterwards.

COSTS

In his discussion of the costs of a Cambridge education Henry Latham, the tutor of Trinity Hall, wrote in 1862 that

Table 2

Occupation	Percentage
Nobility	4.7
Gentry	5.8
Clergy	54.3
Military	4.5
Law	11.2
Medicine	3.5
Government	1.6
Business	3.9
Academic	9.1
Plebeian	1.4
Total	100.00

Source: Figures from Anderson and Schnaper, *School and Society in England.*

only a small part . . . arises from fees or payments that are alike for whole classes of Students. College arrangements are so framed as to admit of the Undergraduates living together, all something in the same way, and dining at a common table, but so as to allow a considerable discretion to each in fixing his own scale of expenditure and style of living.[69]

These circumstances made it impossible to predict precise costs to future matriculants, and Latham's lengthy account could do no more than suggest some broad bands of choice. The historian's knowledge of expenditures is limited similarly, and sometimes the detail is missing altogether, particularly for the eighteenth century.

We know, however, that costs went up, and some of the evidence for the eighteenth century has been quoted. 'The cost of an Oxford education . . . appears to have increased five or sixfold from the early 17th to the mid-19th century, although the general cost-of-living index had risen by only two and a half times, and wages had barely kept abreast of the index.'[70] By 1715 the annual

[69] Seeley, *Student's Guide to the University of Cambridge*, p. 49.
[70] Stone, 'Size and Composition', p. 43.

costs of a commoner at Oxford (the equivalent of a pensioner at Cambridge) were thought to amount to £60, and a gentleman commoner's (the equivalent of a fellow commoner) might be about twice as much.[71] By 1750 a commoner might get by on £80 or £100, but by 1800 costs had more than doubled. As at Cambridge, the determinedly economical could manage on much less; in 1760 it was thought that a frugal servitor (sizar) could live 'pretty well' on £21 a year. Some corroboration from Cambridge of these trends comes from William Whiston, who wrote in the 1740s about his years as a sizar at Clare in the 1680s:[72]

> My Father being now dead, we were all of us under the Care of our Mother the Widow, whose comparative small Means for her seven Children, made it difficult for her to support me there. And had the Expences of a Collegiate life been as extravagant then as they are now come to be, or had I not lived as frugally as possible, she would not have been able to have given me my Degrees.

In 1795 it was said that £300 a year was too little for a fellow commoner who lived in Cambridge 'a great part of the year'.[73] The writer was William Burdon, a fellow of Emmanuel and private tutor to George Beresford, son of the Archbishop of Tuam. George, he wrote, 'has lived since he came here in a manner equally moderate and respectable, with a proper attention to his studies and a limited indulgence in pleasure'. Nevertheless, Burdon reckoned that college and personal expenses, including those 'which with young men are usually called pocket money, such as cards, music, balls, etc.', came to £360 a year. The archbishop was persuaded that a fellow commoner needed more money in Cambridge than some clergy supported families on in Tuam, and he increased his son's allowance. But as with other student budgets we have to question how far we can generalise from the Beresford story, since by 1796 he was in difficulties again and Burdon was telling him that gaming and Newmarket were his undoing.

More details of expenditures at Cambridge are lacking for the eighteenth and early nineteenth century, but we have abundant

---

[71] V. H. H. Green in Sutherland and Mitchell, eds., *The Eighteenth Century*, pp. 328–9.
[72] *Memoirs of the Life and Writings of Mr William Whiston* (1st edn, London, 1749), p. 23.
[73] The following details are taken from chapter 11, by Christopher Brooke, in Bendall, Brooke, and Collinson, *A History of Emmanuel College* (forthcoming).

evidence from the middle of the nineteenth century suggesting the range of costs, the possibility of a highly economical régime for the spartan undergraduate and the reality of an expensive stay at Cambridge for those of average predilections. In December 1844 H. W. Cookson, the tutor of Peterhouse, wrote a lengthy and considered account of a sizar's expenses:[74]

> At this college the annual expenditure for rooms, attendance, tuition & keeping the name on the college boards amounts to £14 9s 3d. There is no charge for dinner in the college hall.
>
> The expences of one of our own sizars, who does not appear to be extremely economical, but who is tolerably prudent, amounted in his first year (including furniture, matriculation fees, grocer's, shoemaker's bookseller's bills &c) to £72 11s 7d and in his third year to £58 2s 8d.

He also received money for prizes, scholarships and a chapel clerkship, amounting to £40 in his first year and £55 in his third; so

> if this gentleman had reduced his expenditure as low as some of the sizars do, his receipts in the two years ought to have abundantly covered his expences. The college bills of a sizar here frequently amount to less than £30 though they include almost every necessary article – I must add however that sometimes they exceed this considerably . . .
>
> It is generally considered imprudent to venture to college unless the friends of the student can hope to provide him with an allowance of nearly £100 per annum. Even this would not allow much for private tuition; though under favourable circumstances it ought to allow almost as much as would be required. – I must say however that if a youth be determined to deny himself luxuries he may live as a sizar for much less than £100 a year & pay his private tutor besides.

A detailed breakdown of the costs of the 'strictly necessary' costs of residence put them at around £69 a year for pensioners in 1863;[75] £18 was for college tuition (sizars paid much less, and fellow commoners much more), £10 for rooms, £6 5s for 'attendance' (or servants), £3 10s for coal (a high charge reminding us that

---

[74] CUL MS Add. 7342, C. 135: H.W. Cookson to James Thomson, 19 December 1844. Thomson was Professor of Mathematics at Glasgow and had enquired about chances for one of his students. His son William was already an undergraduate at Peterhouse: see chapter 17.

[75] For what follows, see H. Latham, 'University Expences', in *The Student's Guide* (1862), pp. 50–66. Notice that the costs of college tuition had risen since the beginning of the century.

Cambridge was a long way from a coalmine), £5 7s 4d for sundry college payments, £5 8s for the services of a laundress, and £20 12s 6d for food for 25 weeks' residence. But the food mentioned was basic.[76] It included no large meal after dinner in the afternoon, while dinner itself consisted very largely of meat as late as the 1860s – up to 2lbs of it. So payment for extras 'and all dishes furnished to an Undergraduate in his rooms' frequently 'much augments the College bill'. Thus college bills varied between £70 and £120 a year according to taste. The cost of grocers' and booksellers' bills, travelling expenses, pocket money and 'tradesmen's bills for personal expenses and entertainments' raised the annual totals to £125 for the economical and £250 for the indulgent.

The full details we have of the cost of William Thomson's stay at Peterhouse, from 1841 to 1844, show that he was a high spender, whatever he protested to his father.[77] William Thomson was a pensioner, living at a comparatively inexpensive college. In the three years he spent almost exactly £900. Excluding the cost of his private tuition, he spent about £250 a year on the ordinary items of residence, or in other words what a tutor at Trinity regarded as a 'high average' at his college, an expensive one with many well-to-do students.[78] Of Thomson's expenditure, £774 came from his father and £122 from the college in prizes and scholarship – evidence of how able and committed students might reduce costs significantly and of how hard generalisations about net expenditures are.

Thomson's case also provides strong evidence of the extra cost of a very good degree: £144 of Thomson's total expenditure, or nearly one-sixth, was for private tuition. As the Mathematical Tripos grew more demanding and more competitive, and as the rewards for success in it became larger, private tuition became a desideratum for a man hoping to become a wrangler, and a cause of the frequent accusation that Cambridge was too costly. The cost of Thomson's private tuition, it should be added, was not excessive for a man of his ambitions. A student reading 'for the highest honours, either in classics or mathematics' would usually pay £51 a year for

---

[76] It was often called 'Commons', while extras were 'sizings'.
[77] More is said about the cost of William Thomson's education in chapter 17.
[78] PP 1852–3, HC xliv [1559]: *Graham Commission Evidence*, p. 198.

private tuition in addition to an average cost of residence of £86, said the Reverend H. Arlett of Pembroke: or in other words private tuition would amount to nearly two-fifths of his costs, while another authoritative estimate, from J. J. Smith of Caius, put the highest cost of private tuition at £100 a year and a more usual amount at £72.[79]

To provide help with these costs there were in about 1850, as appendix X reveals, 401 open scholarships and 317 others restricted to certain schools or localities, and in addition 155 exhibitions in the gift of specific schools; often exhibitions could be held jointly with other awards. Appendix X may give a misleading impression of clarity for what was a confused and complicated matter about which exact accuracy is not easily recoverable from the sources; one suspects that some bursars had to think hard before they could be sure what their college had to offer. But at least we can be certain that in the eighteenth century there were more bursaries available than the total of scholars and pensioners combined – an intriguing fact – and that in 1850, after considerable growth, there were still fewer than two undergraduates for every bursary. One concludes that for most of the period 1750–1870 a student was certain to get help of some sort if he were averagely competent, and sometimes even if he were not. On the other hand no award equalled Latham's estimate for the lowest annual cost, £125, which also omits anything for private tuition. In other words, only the most ruthlessly self-disciplined of sizars could have covered all or nearly all the expense of their Cambridge years, and even they would have to find extra for private tuition. Perhaps William Thomson's experience in receiving £122 from his college towards total costs of £900 was quite typical, while we have to remember that Thomson was an exceptionally talented student whom Peterhouse was keen to help. These suggestions are the core of the argument, sketched earlier, that Cambridge could not have contained more than a handful of men from working-class backgrounds.

<hr>

[79] PP 1852–3, HC xliv [1559]: *Graham Commission Evidence*, pp. 143–4, 188.

Chapter 3

COLLEGES: BUILDINGS, MASTERS, AND FELLOWS

COLLEGES

COLLEGES: RESIDENTIAL COMMUNITIES

Among these narrow, ugly and dirty streets, are tumbled in, as it were at random (for the whole place looks as if it had been dancing to Amphion's music, and he had left off in the middle of a very complicated figure) some of the most beautiful academical buildings in the world. However their style of architecture may vary, according to the period at which they were built or rebuilt, they agree in one essential feature: all the colleges are constructed in quadrangles or *courts*; and, as in course of years the population of every college except one [Downing], has outgrown the original quadrangle, new courts have been added, so that the larger foundations have three, and one (St. John's) has four courts. Sometimes the 'old court', or primitive part of the building presents a handsome front to the largest street near it; but frequently, as if to show its independence of, and contempt for, the town, it retires from the street altogether, showing the passer by only its ugliest wall, and smallest, shabbiest gate.[1]

In thus introducing his account of his undergraduate life in the 1840s Charles Astor Bristed touches on what has always been most significant about Cambridge colleges: their faithfulness to an essentially medieval architectural idiom, many centuries after the Middle Ages ceased. In their style and quadrangular plan the first colleges remind us of late medieval mansions, Haddon Hall or the first buildings at Knole being examples, where impressive gate-

---

[1] Charles Astor Bristed, *Five Years in an English University* 1st edn (2 vols., New York, 1852), vol. 1, pp. 1, 14.

houses led into courts ranged round with dwellings, and fortification was ceasing to matter. Towers were added to colleges as embellishments rather than defensive features.[2] The most important rooms in a college were the chapel and the hall, where God was worshipped and the life of the community was celebrated in dinners that were as much ceremony as refreshment.

From the sixteenth century onwards the designers of country houses moved away from the courtyard plan in favour of the compact block, while within it the great hall was replaced by a series of smaller rooms that made possible the privacy of the owner's family and their separation from servants; Upstairs/Downstairs took the place of the unity of the household. But in colleges there were no resident servants, as distinct from the poorer students who acted as such. When they ceased to do so in the eighteenth century the servants who were employed in their stead did not reside.[3] Colleges were not country houses, and have remained attached to the great hall and the conventional courtyard plan for their own reasons; the nature of their sites has been a constraint, as has in recent centuries the idea of what a college ought to look like. Though the Gibbs Building at King's is very like a Palladian house, more typical of college construction in the last four centuries are the Wilkins courts in King's and Trinity – and, one might add, the courts of mid-twentieth-century Churchill and Fitzwilliam. There has been continuity in internal arrangements too. From about 1300 to the middle of the seventeenth century the courts in Oxford and Cambridge colleges very largely comprised 'chambers', small rooms each accommodating several fellows or undergraduates, while partitioned side-rooms gave privacy for study and sleep. This practice, 'chumming', decayed in the late seventeenth century as a result of falling numbers and of rising living standards; single occupancy became the rule.[4]

At the end of the twentieth century new college construction still very largely consists of small rooms for student accommodation, and often it is organised round staircases (rather than corridors) as it was

---

[2] Willis and Clark, III, pp. 266–73; Mark Girouard, *Life in the English Country House. A Social and Architectural History* (New Haven, Yale University Press, 1978), pp 66–71.

[3] Servants are discussed in chapter 4, pp. 142–6.

[4] Willis and Clark, III, pp. 297–327.

7 The Screens: where college notices are posted.

in the Middle Ages; thus the New Court of Fitzwilliam College (1986) interprets the staircase theme so as to heed both the tradition and modern safety regulations.[5] For centuries colleges have also erected small rooms for convivial gatherings.[6] At Emmanuel in the latter half of the eighteenth century, for example, the fellows' parlour was 'a favourite evening resort to all who loved cheerful talk

---

[5] Nicholas Ray, *Cambridge Architecture. A Concise Guide* (Cambridge University Press, 1994), p. 120.
[6] Willis and Clark, III, pp. 376–86.

and a glass of wine, especially on a Sunday evening', and these words may touch the memories of modern fellows.[7] Above all the large hall has survived as an essential feature of a college; it dominates Wilkins's King's College from the 1820s and Lasdun's Fitzwilliam built in the 1960s, thus showing in the most tangible way how college life, despite many changes, remains pervaded by the spirit of community and its expression through the habit of dining together.

COLLEGE CONSTITUTIONS

In seeking to instruct his fellow-countrymen about Cambridge, Charles Bristed took pains over what most puzzles people still, the constitutions of colleges and their relationship to the university:

> The first thing that the American reader has to impress on his mind is, that the several Colleges are distinct and independent corporations. They are on different foundations, that is to say, the funds that support them are derived from different sources; their officers are distinct, their lecture-room subjects different, though with a general resemblance; their very gowns vary. The confederation of these independent corporations constitutes the University, which may, in its relation to the colleges composing it, be compared to our Federal Government in its relation to the separate States – with this important historical difference, however, that the Colleges sprang into existence *subsequent* to the founding of the University.[8]

Like the university itself, colleges derived from royal charters their authority to carry out their academic functions, to govern themselves, and to hold property, and the charters gave sanction to the statutes that prescribed the day-to-day collegiate life.[9] Usually they went into considerable detail about worship in chapels and courses of study, and the rights and duties of members of the foundation – master, fellows and scholars – including the stipends they were to enjoy. By 1750 the most recent college, Sidney Sussex, was 150 years old, and statutes were, to say the least, out of date; stipends of

[7] E. S. Shuckburgh, *Richard Farmer, D.D., (Master of Emmanuel 1775–1797)* (Cambridge, 1884), p. 37
[8] Bristed, *Five Years in an English University*, vol. I, p. 13.
[9] For what follows, PP 1852–3, HC xliv [1559]: *Graham Commission Report*, pp. 150–3.

£3 or £4 had been made valueless by inflation, and nobody bothered any longer with Aristotelian philosophy. Statutes could be altered, but the process was lengthy and cumbrous, and there was the risk of tripping over the Elizabethan statutes of the university itself. It was thought better to ignore college statutes where it seemed necessary, and to bypass them by new expedients. In the early eighteenth century tutors, who had been in existence for several centuries and were responsible for undergraduate instruction, came to be more formally recognised and better remunerated.[10] But the office of tutor was not recognised in college statutes, while the lecturers that were by statute charged with the duties he performed had nothing to do and tiny stipends for doing it. Paradoxically, institutions that lived by the letter of the law on some occasions disregarded it on others.

The formative years for Cambridge colleges occurred long before this history begins, and by 1750 the colleges' structure was set. They were sixteen in number.[11] About fifteen we may with confidence generalise; differences, though sometimes made much of by college chroniclers, and occasionally indeed being of real importance, should not be allowed to undermine our sense of a common pattern. Each college had a principal, called 'master' except at Queens', where he was 'president'. There was also a body of undergraduates and a smaller group of senior members, the fellows. The fellows of a college, and among its students the scholars, were often referred to as being 'on the foundation', since they were supported by the endowments that over the centuries benefactors had made. Some of these had prescribed links with particular schools or areas – for example, the connection between Norfolk and Gonville and Caius – which gave an idiosyncratic local colouring to the society. But at all except one of the sixteen colleges the bond was not exclusive; members came from a wide range of schools, counties and regions. Very different was the sixteenth college, King's, which had a constitution quite distinct from the others.

'The peculiar circumstances' of its foundation had created 'great difficulties' for the Graham Commissioners when they came to write about it in 1852:

[10] Tutors are discussed in chapter 4, pp. 118–29.
[11] The only college to be founded in our period, Downing, received its charter in 1800.

The unusual constitution of the Society, its anomalous position in relation to the University, its intimate connexion with the Royal Foundation of Eton, the solemn prohibition imposed upon its members, against seeking or even accepting the smallest change in its laws, the magnificence of its collegiate buildings, the affluence of its resources contrasted with the paucity of its Undergraduate Students – all these, as well as other circumstances, involve difficulties and embarrassments of no ordinary weight.[12]

By its constitution of 1446 King's was intended by King Henry VI to be closely and exclusively linked to his other foundation, Eton; and so it remained, three and more centuries later. The heart of Eton College, the seventy scholars of the foundation, were chosen each summer, at the age of twelve or thirteen, by examiners that included the Provost and two fellows of King's; and on their ranking in the examination depended the place they would be given years later in the queue for King's scholarships.[13] None but Eton collegers were eligible for them, and there were very few undergraduates apart from scholars; in 1802, for example, King's had nine scholars, a fellow commoner, and two 'ten-year men'.[14] A scholar was certain, on graduating, to be given a life fellowship. An additional peculiarity of the college was that its members graduated without taking the university examinations: a privilege that arose in the sixteenth and seventeenth centuries and was justified by a false interpretation of an agreement of 1456 between the college and the university.[15] Thus a scholarship won when childhood had not ended might lead without further intellectual tests to an income lasting for seventy years – a strange amalgam of meritocracy and privilege. What this meant may be seen in the fortunes of Oscar Browning, elected Eton colleger in 1850 and afterwards scholar and fellow of King's. In a career of achievement, pathos, and not a little scandal he taught at Eton and King's, wrote many now forgotten books, helped to found the Faculty of History and the Department

---

[12] For this quotation and what follows, see PP 1852–3: *Graham Commission Report*, pp. 173–7; Winstanley, *Unreformed Cambridge*, pp. 189–92; Christopher Morris, *King's College. A Short History* (Cambridge, King's College, 1989), pp. 1–7.

[13] Unlucky candidates at the back of the queue were 'superannuated', crowded out by later elections.

[14] For 'ten-year men', see chapter 7, pp. 263–4.

[15] The agreement, the 'Composition' as it was called, merely exempted the college from the Chancellor's jurisdiction over legal cases arising in the college.

of Education, and died in 1923 – still enjoying the dividend from his King's fellowship.[16]

COLLEGE MASTERS

'All communications to the Master are to be addressed through the College Tutor', a Master of Trinity is reported to have said to an undergraduate who had ventured to remark that the day was wet when sheltering from the rain under the same arch as his head of house.[17] Heads of house were the most powerful group in the university. They were often consulted by the Vice-Chancellor and held weekly meetings to determine their collective view; they served as Vice-Chancellor in turn.[18] They were the only senior members of the university enjoying full college rights and privileges who were allowed to marry, though in the case of some colleges this permission was by custom only, not by statute.[19] This small number of dignitaries and their wives composed in the early nineteenth century Cambridge's upper-class society of mixed dinner parties and morning calls, more formal and more constrained by protocol than were bachelor fellows in college hall and combination room; the wives of heads of house were said to call only on other heads' wives – which is doubtless an exaggeration.[20] In their lodge heads were somewhat set apart from the fellows of their college, but statutes gave heads great power to initiate and to obstruct, and colleges languished, or prospered, largely as a result of their heads' energies.

In eleven colleges the master[21] was elected by the fellows, much as before the Dissolution monks elected their abbot. In the other six the choice lay elsewhere. In Trinity, a royal foundation, the

---

[16] Ian Anstruther, *Oscar Browning. A Biography* (London, John Murray, 1983); Peter Searby, *The Training of Teachers in Cambridge University: The First Sixty Years 1879–1939* (Cambridge, Department of Education, 1982), pp. 5–8, 25–7.

[17] A. E. Shipley, *'J.' A Memoir of John Willis Clark* (London, 1913), p. 17.

[18] Winstanley, *Unreformed Cambridge*, esp. p. 277.

[19] Strictly speaking heads of house were not 'fellows'. By university statute fellows were not allowed to marry, and men elected to professorships had to resign their fellowships if they wished to marry – a point not always made clear in modern works. In Cambridge there was a fringe university society of married MAs; one such was William Hopkins, on whom see chapter 16, pp. 633–5.

[20] Shipley, *'J.' A Memoir of John Willis Clark*, pp. 17–18 and 46–50.

[21] For what follows, see PP 1852–3: *Graham Commission Report*, pp. 152–3.

master was appointed by the sovereign or those acting on his behalf. The Master of Jesus was by its early sixteenth-century statutes nominated by the Bishop of Ely;[22] he also had a role at Peterhouse, choosing between two nominees of the fellows – one from the north of England and one from the south, an example of the regional prescriptions also found in fellowships. At Magdalene the process was unusual. The college was refounded by Henry VIII in 1542 after the Dissolution, and the royal letters patent gave to Thomas Audley, the king's agent in the matter, and to his heirs as proprietors of Audley End, the right in perpetuity to nominate the master.[23] In Downing, in 1800 the first college to be founded for two centuries, the master was chosen by the Archbishops of Canterbury and York and the Masters of St John's and Clare, a dispensation reflecting the wishes expressed in the will of Sir George Downing in 1717.[24]

The results of the various ways of choice may be seen in appendix II, which shows that, as with the fellowships whence they were promoted, the academic qualifications of heads of house steadily improved over the period. Before 1781 only one wrangler was elected. After 1831 firsts greatly outnumbered others. Nominators generally considered academic quality as much as fellows did. At Trinity the crown nominated four wranglers (two of them Senior Wranglers, including Whewell, the most distinguished Cambridge scholar of his generation), in addition to two junior optimes. The Trinity list resembles that for St John's, with its six elected masters: one Senior Wrangler and three other wranglers, one junior optime, and one poll man – William Samuel Powell, whose achievement as master might not have been predicted from his modest degree. The fellows of Queens' elected four wranglers, two of them being Senior Wranglers, and three out of the four elected Masters of St Catharine's were wranglers too (though the fact that one of them was the unfortunate Robinson shows that academic success need

[22] Gray and Brittain, *A History of Jesus College Cambridge*, p. 32.
[23] Cunich, Hoyle, Duffy, and Hyam, *A History of Magdalene College Cambridge*, pp. 31–41. By the statutes of 1926 the right of nomination was transferred from the owners of Audley End to the barony of Braybrooke.
[24] Stanley French, *Aspects of Downing History*, vol. II (Cambridge, Downing Association, 1989), pp. I, II.

not lead to happiness);[25] one of the three – Philpott, elected in 1845 – had been Senior Wrangler in 1829.[26] At Jesus the Bishops of Ely chose five wranglers and a poll man, and at Peterhouse too they acted well, except in the 1787 contest when the bishop mishandled matters dreadfully, nominating a man, Barnes, who did not want the job but clung onto it for forty-five years; despite being a prizeman Barnes was very unsuccessful in the post, another reminder that academic eminence was no guarantee of managerial ability.[27] At Magdalene the Portsmouth and Braybrooke families nominated kinsmen and others of varying quality. Daniel Waterland (master from 1713 to 1740) was a very distinguished theologian, but it was a long time before any successor was as eminent. Thomas Chapman (1746–60) is described by a college historian as 'even by the easy-going standards of the eighteenth century ... a shameless jobber, with all the delicacy of feeling of a hog',[28] while Barton Wallop (1774–81) deserved D. A. Winstanley's comment that he was a 'hard living, hard drinking, sporting country gentleman, totally without scholarship or intellectual tastes'.[29] Fortunately he rarely resided. His successors were at least gentlemanly, but masters of Georgian and Victorian Magdalene contributed little to such scholarly achievements as the college had to its credit.

The master of a college had oversight of all its affairs. He administered its property, saw to the learning and good conduct of its members, protected it against external attack through legal action or other means, and presided over meetings of the fellows, their majority assent being necessary for major decisions. He acted with others, usually for example leaving many financial concerns to the bursars. But he had an initiating and commanding role; for instance

---

[25] After his success in the magisterial election at St Catharine's in 1861 Robinson was accused of double-dealing in voting for himself instead of for his rival, Jameson, as he was said to have promised. As a result he was ostracised by Cambridge society. In his detailed discussion of the affair Winstanley, *Later Victorian Cambridge*, pp. 1–19, concluded that probably misunderstanding rather than turpitude explained Robinson's vote, and that his colleagues' harsh treatment of him reflected a judgement based on gossip.

[26] The fourth man was Lowther Yates, elected 1779; his degree was 'Ad Baptistam'.

[27] Winstanley, *Unreformed Cambridge*, p. 294; pp. 284–94 contain an extensive account of this dispute.

[28] Eamon Duffy, in Cunich, Hoyle, Duffy, and Hyam, *Magdalene College*, p. 171, and pp. 159–219 for this passage generally.

[29] Winstanley, *Unreformed Cambridge*, p. 19; E. K. Purnell, *Magdalene College*, College Histories Series (London, Robinson, 1904), pp. 162–99.

he appointed the tutor in whose hands lay the college's teaching.[30] In almost all cases a master's income reflected his status, being much greater than a fellow's.[31] In the middle of the nineteenth century, when for the first time we have figures for a majority of colleges, incomes ranged from £608 at Queens' to £1,518 at Trinity, in all cases a lodge and its maintenance costs being provided too.[32] As with other college officers remuneration often comprised several items, a large one tending to be a dividend from the profits of the college estates. At King's the master's dividend was three times a senior fellow's, and at Emmanuel over four times. Dividends had been rising, on a long view, for over a century because of agricultural prosperity, and of course masters' incomes had been rising with them. At St John's, for example, the master's component rose from £120 in 1755 to £480 in 1852 (the master's dividend being three times a junior fellow's); his total income in the middle of the century was £1,160.[33]

Masters did not always succeed in getting what they wanted or in creating happiness for themselves or their society. Perhaps the most instructive example of failure is Christopher Wordsworth, appointed Master of Trinity by Liverpool's government in 1820. The younger brother of the poet, he had graduated in 1796 as Tenth Wrangler from Trinity, where a fellowship followed. It was probably as an undergraduate that Wordsworth was private tutor to Charles Manners-Sutton; through him he became known to his father, the Bishop of Norwich and in due course Archbishop of Canterbury. Both father and son became his patrons, appointing him to a succession of church livings; they enabled Wordsworth to employ and reveal his considerable gifts. In 1805 he became chaplain to Archbishop Manners-Sutton, and so gained access to Lambeth Palace Library, and the opportunity to compose the six volumes of *Ecclesiastical Biography*; this scholarly work on the English church appeared in 1810 and was republished three times by the

---

[30] PP 1852–3: *Graham Commission Evidence*, pp. 306–429.
[31] The exception was Trinity Hall, where the master had a fellow's dividend plus commons; in 1850 the dividend was £150.
[32] Information is lacking on five colleges who did not reply to the Graham Commissioners' enquiry on this matter.
[33] PP 1852–3, *Graham Commission Report*, pp. 153–6, and *Evidence*, pp. 351, 427; H F Howard, *An Account of the Finances of The College of St. John the Evangelist in the University of Cambridge 1511–1926* (Cambridge University Press, 1926), pp. 137–8.

middle of the century. His appointment to Trinity at the age of forty-six was a recognition of his talents; he brought intelligence, vigour, and earnest religious principle to Cambridge.

As Vice-Chancellor he showed a capacity to work with others and to modify his own plans for the benefit of a more popular design; he contributed greatly to a notable reform, the setting up of the Classical Tripos. In Trinity he argued the need for more undergraduate accommodation soon after his arrival, and the New Court, completed in 1825, was the result of his energy and determination in the face of opposition. But overall as master he achieved little, perhaps precisely because he felt that his essential nature as master was challenged by disagreement. He became master after sixteen years away from Cambridge. His friends were elsewhere, and he gained few in the College. That was not because he was a Tory ruling Liberal dons; Cambridge friendships often transcended party differences. He lived in seclusion in the lodge; a widower and lacking a daughter who might preside over his household, he did not take the trouble to entertain fellows; there was little social intercourse to smooth the asperities created by his conduct of public business. He made the fatal error of interpreting the college statutes as though their tyrannical sixteenth-century utterance might be taken seriously in the nineteenth, and he failed to see that the college was (in the words of one fellow), 'like the soi-distant English constitution, a monarchical republic'. He accused the good-humoured and equable Joseph Romilly of 'an act of rebellion' because he had petitioned for the hour of dinner to be changed to 4.0 pm; and when at a college feast a fellow proposed the health of a college man who was a Whig politician, he rose to his feet and choking with rage protested that he was not being treated with proper respect as toasts ought to be proposed from the chair. He was excessively angry, too, when Connop Thirlwall, an assistant tutor, attacked the exclusion of Dissenters from the university and compulsory attendance at chapel. Wordsworth felt that the essential character of Trinity as an Anglican community was under threat. He forced Thirlwall to resign his tutorship, and wished his colleagues to deprive Thirlwall of his fellowship, which much as some of them disapproved of Thirlwall's pamphlet they refused to do. Whewell, as tutor, with difficulty persuaded some impetuous colleagues from appealing to the Visitor against the master – a threat raising the spectre of the dissensions of Dr Bentley's day. The Thirlwall matter, in 1834, left its lasting mark, and helped to persuade Wordsworth to resign in 1841 – a very unusual action for a Cambridge head of house.[34]

His contemporary, James Wood, Master of St John's from 1815 to 1839, was an even greater Tory than Wordsworth, wishing to preserve the university he had known in his youth. As Vice-Chancellor in 1817 he reconvened, with great obstinacy, the Magna Congregatio when only finicky legalism was on his side and the inhabitants of Cambridge were against him. His reactionary stance led to great bitterness in the town.[35] As Vice-Chancellor he also closed down the Union Society, regarding free-ranging undergraduate discussion, which sometimes even led to criticism of government policy, as an evil to be permanently suppressed.[36] He refused to permit further debate even when the society offered to exclude political topics. Wordsworth, when Vice-Chancellor a few years later, sensibly (if not *too* liberally) lifted the ban provided that political issues less then twenty years old were eschewed.[37] Yet, unlike Wordsworth's, Wood's years as master were thought by his colleagues to be highly successful. Like Wordsworth, Wood was responsible for increasing college accommodation (Rickman's New Court), but there the significant resemblances ended.

As Vice-Chancellor, Wood revealed the darker, though lesser, side of his character. St John's, where he lived for almost all his life from the age of eighteen onwards, gained his deepest loyalties and powers of self-effacement. The slight, stooped, and retiring figure in Dighton's engraving suggests his lack of a commanding presence; his voice was feeble and his conversation lacking in sparkle. 'His merit was of a kind which could not be duly estimated except after intimate acquaintance with him, and by intelligent people.'[38] Wood was the

---

[34] Winstanley, *Early Victorian Cambridge*, pp. 58–82, a very detailed account.
[35] See chapter 13, pp. 499–500.
[36] In the chair when the Proctors entered the debating chamber with the Vice-Chancellor's order was William Whewell, a young graduate and, eventually, Wordsworth's successor as Master of Trinity.
[37] Winstanley, *Early Victorian Cambridge*, pp. 26–7, 122–4.
[38] Wood's colleague Edward Bushby, quoted in Thomas Baker, *History of the College of St. John the Evangelist, Cambridge*, edited by J. E. B. Mayor (Cambridge, 1869), part 2, p. 1096. What follows is taken from this source, pp. 1094–104. See also A. F. Torry, *Founders and Benefactors of St. John's College, Cambridge, with Notes, chiefly Biographical* (Cambridge, 1888), appendix, pp. 568–9.

son of handloom weavers, and born in Bury, Lancashire. His father, self-educated, taught his son algebra; a local cotton manufacturer paid the fees for him at Bury Grammar School, whence he went up to St John's as sizar in 1778. Exhibitions and a scholarship followed. Wood lived in a garret in college. Too poor to buy candle and fire, he studied on the staircase near a rushlight, and with his feet wrapped in straw. He was Senior Wrangler in 1782. He soon became fellow and assistant tutor, and in due course tutor.[39] Wood, blessed with patient and economical energy, was a meticulous and thorough man of business; testimony to this is a detailed notebook on the college estates compiled on a rapid and productive tour in 1816.[40] His powers of organisation are shown in his textbooks on algebra, mechanics, and optics, elucidations of Newtonian natural philosophy that were in the hands of every undergraduate early in the century – though it is also typical of Wood's lack of intellectual creativity that he played no part in the mathematical thinking that superseded the old scheme. In college discussions Wood was flexible and accommodating. Kindly and lacking in egotism, he was on cordial terms with all his colleagues; he may indeed be criticised for lack of ruthlessness as master, since he permitted the long tenure as senior bursar of Charles Blick, whose incompetence had to be in part repaired by Wood's own donation of £12,000.[41] His weakness over Blick raises the question of what exactly 'success' as a master meant, and part of the answer is that colleges tended to value clubbability and to reject men of stiff or abrasive style; these preferences were natural enough since colleges were communities of residents, working and living together all the year round, their harmony and peace of mind dependent on the renunciation of egotism.

FELLOWS

FELLOWS: THEIR CONDITIONS OF TENURE

To the outsider all colleges seemed the same, and to consist of very similar men leading identical lives. To fellows, the heart of a college,

---

[39] For Wood's work as tutor, see pp. 125–6 below.
[40] Howard, *Finances of St. John's College*, pp. 156–8.
[41] Howard, *Finances of St. John's College*, p. 170. Wood also bequeathed £20,000 to St John's, from which fund the new chapel at length benefited.

their own institution seemed unique, its idiosyncrasies distinguishing it from others, and to be carefully nurtured or at times just as carefully resented. At the level of particularity colleges varied so greatly as to tax the powers of those (like the Graham Commissioners) who had to explain and categorise them; and of course lawyers having to adjudicate on niceties were enriched. Fellowships varied in the benefits they gave, as to the period of tenure, vocation and stipend prescribed; and in the persons qualified to hold them, as to their place of birth, schooling or even kin.[42] They varied too, occasionally, by virtue of those able to confer them. At Jesus the Bishop of Ely chose between two college nominees for all fellowships, while however invariably choosing the first man nominated and so leaving the effective decision to the college. At St John's the bishop had the full choice of one fellow, at Sidney the Fishmongers' Company chose another, while the two Dixie fellowships at Emmanuel were nominated by the founder's heir. Two Parke fellows at Peterhouse were chosen by the heir of Archbishop Sandys, and the master at the same college chose the two Ramsey fellows. The Master of Magdalene nominated to the Drury fellowship, which gave considerable funds for travel. But the great majority of Cambridge fellowship elections were made by the master and existing fellows (or the seniors among them) by the venerable principle of co-optation.

What was a fellowship *for* ? We naturally ask the question: the eighteenth century would have been puzzled or dismayed by it. Whatever expectations of scholarly endeavour those who centuries before had endowed fellowships had entertained of their holders, in law they were a species of property, like real estate, canal shares or annuities. They conveyed dividends, or shares in the profits from the college's estates, rather than salaries, and when Lord John Russell used the word 'salary' about them during a Commons debate on university reform in 1854 Charles Neate of Oriel College, Oxford, rushed into print to put him right: 'Does Lord John Russell know that I can mortgage my Fellowship, that I can make over to a creditor or an assignee the right to receive during my life my share of the revenues of my College? Salary indeed! I have no more a salary than Lord John Russell himself and I work less hard

[42] For what follows, see PP 1852–3: *Graham Commission Report*, pp. 156–72; *Cambridge University Calendar for ... 1802*, pp. 61–130, *Cambridge University Calendar for ... 1850*, pp. 198–347.

for it.'[43] This view, widespread in both universities, meant that reformers eager to turn dons into beavers had to remove or circumvent their indefeasible property right. When in 1810 Adam Sedgwick gained a Trinity fellowship through the mathematical grind his friend Samuel Duckworth congratulated him on escaping 'from the clutches of x and y ... no longer impelled to move in diagonal by the joint action of ambition and lucre on the one hand, and of indolence on the other, you may commit yourself entirely to the influence of the latter'.[44] Sedgwick did no such thing, but naturally valued his right to employ his time as he thought fit. Another fellow of Trinity, the radical reformer Benjamin Walsh, in the 1830s floated ideas for turning college fellows into public lecturers for the university as a whole. He suggested that they should be paid with lecture fees from clients – in effect, he thought of systematising private tutorships – but realising that fellows enjoyed indefeasible rights he was careful to add that 'those Fellows of Colleges, who chose to devote their days to port wine and whist, might continue to do so, just as at present'.[45]

The growing value of dividends made fellowships more coveted, and the surge in matriculants after 1815 made contest for them fiercer still. At the same time, the increasing complexity and sophistication of the tripos and the opportunity it offered to make discriminations on the tiniest of differences, made it a ready means of choosing fellows, as well as wranglers, in an objective way. It also magnified the aura of competitiveness attending the annual winter combat in the Senate House. 'People sometimes ask', wrote Leslie Stephen,

> What is the good of horse-racing? The respectable and ostensible reply is that it improves the breed of horses. Our educational system is supposed to improve the breed of undergraduates, and in very much the same way ... The examination is to the undergraduate what the racecourse is to the inferior animal ... The senior wrangler is the winner of the Derby.[46]

---

[43] Quoted in A. J. Engel, *From Clergyman to Don. The Rise of the Academic Profession in Nineteenth-Century Oxford* (Oxford, Clarendon, 1983), p. 65.

[44] Quoted in John Willis Clark and Thomas McKenny Hughes, *The Life and Letters of the Reverend Adam Sedgwick* (2 vols., Cambridge University Press, 1890), vol. I, p. 100.

[45] Benjamin Dann Walsh, *A Historical Account of the University of Cambridge, and its Colleges; in a Letter to the Earl of Radnor* (London, 1837), pp. 130–1.

[46] Leslie Stephen, *Sketches from Cambridge by a Don* (London, 1865), p. 35.

Stephen added that in both sorts of enterprise the real object was money, and he estimated the value of a fellowship to be £2,500. Stephen was made uneasy by the competition for fellowships and the intellectual narrowness it sprang from and sustained. But it was just as natural for his close friend Henry Fawcett to revere the integrity of the Cambridge process. From a modest background and lacking great aptitude for mathematics, after three years of courageous application and eight days of ferocious contest, meticulously assessed, Fawcett became Seventh Wrangler in 1856; a fellowship at Trinity Hall followed, carrying a dividend that maintained him after the sudden onset of blindness, and enabled him to study political economy – in which in 1863 he became the first professor. Fawcett defended fellowships as embodying intellectual meritocracy; they were entirely consistent with his dislike of privilege and veneration of free competition – or at least they would be when open to Dissenters:

> The race is a manly and a noble contest – manly, because no feelings of jealousy tarnish the keen competition; noble, because the contest is purely intellectual. What other coveted distinction is there which wealth and rank has no influence in securing? Cheap books and the extension of good schools have placed the rudiments, at least, of a good mathematical education within the reach of humble life . . . If, therefore, the religious disability upon fellowships was removed [as happened in 1871], they might be regarded as great rewards which our universities bestow upon the most intellectual of the nation. [47]

At the end of the eighteenth century there were about 381 fellows in Cambridge colleges.[48] In addition to 57 fellows at King's, whose peculiarities distanced it from other colleges, 272 fellows were on college 'foundations', and thereby entitled to many privileges and emoluments; 52 others were 'bye', or subordinate

---

[47] Henry Fawcett, 'On the Exclusion of Those who are not Members of the Established Church from Fellowships and Other Privileges of the English Universities', *Macmillan's Magazine*, 3 (1860–1), p. 414; Leslie Stephen, *The Life of Henry Fawcett* (London, 1885), esp. pp. 31–2, 90–2; Lawrence Goldman, ed., *The Blind Victorian. Henry Fawcett and British Liberalism* (Cambridge University Press, 1989), esp. pp. 6–7.

[48] The figure varied slightly from year to year because of unfilled vacancies. The total of 381 is based on details in the *Cambridge University Calendar* for 1802. Christopher Wordsworth, *Social Life in the English Universities in the Eighteenth Century* (Cambridge, 1874), pp. 641–2, suggests 392 for 1796, to which figure the five fellows of Downing, founded in 1800, would have to be added for any later total.

and less-advantaged fellowships. At most colleges at least some of the foundation fellowships were subject to geographical restriction. The exceptions were Trinity Hall and Trinity College, whose fellowships were open, in theory, to men from any nation provided that they met the requirements as to fitness, vocation, and a Cambridge background. Trinity College's sixty foundation fellowships were the largest number at any college and were competed for openly by Trinity's scholars; at the other large college, St John's, the fellowship was restricted to men born in England and Wales, as was Christ's, while at St Catharine's and Emmanuel only native English could be elected. One common limitation was regional. At Peterhouse the entire foundation (fourteen fellowships) had to be split equally between the north and south of England, the river Trent being the dividing line; Wales was split, too. The foundations of Clare, Christ's, and Jesus were subject to similar divisions. At eight colleges[49] there was a county restriction, it not being possible to have more than one or two fellows from the same shire at the same time. The purpose of these complicated rules had been to prevent the growth of the regional and clan disputes that had marred the university in the Middle Ages.[50] By the eighteenth century they served no useful purpose, and might be a nuisance, as the example of Henry Gunning shows. He was the grandson, son, and nephew of fellows of St John's, and would normally have been admitted to that college in the hope of continuing the family link. His county was Cambridgeshire. In 1782 (two years before he went up to university) the Cambridgeshire place at St John's was filled when James Hitch was elected fellow, while Zachary Brooke, also from Cambridgeshire and the son of a fellow, had already been admitted as an undergraduate and was therefore in the queue for the county place. Henry Gunning's father saw better prospects at Christ's. The Cambridgeshire slot there was filled, but by a man of advanced years (Adam Wall) who might be expected to die in time for young Henry to succeed him; Henry was therefore entered at Christ's.[51]

Some colleges had fellowships tightly reserved for graduates from

---

[49] Clare, Christ's, Emmanuel, Pembroke, Peterhouse, Queens', St Catharine's, and St John's.
[50] For a Victorian reformer's comment, see Peacock, *Observations on the Statutes*, p. xx.
[51] Gunning, *Reminiscences*, vol. 1, pp. 5–6. In the event, Wall lived till 1798 and Gunning did not become a fellow of Christ's.

named shires, schools or families. At Pembroke one foundation place was held for men born in Cumberland or Westmorland and preferably educated at St Bees Grammar School, which had been founded by Archbishop Grindal, a native of St Bees and Master of Pembroke before he became a bishop. Of the twenty foundation fellows at Caius, three had to come from Norfolk and three from the diocese of Norwich – reservations partly due to that cantankerous benefactor Dr Caius, whose mandate was felt to be a sore constraint by Caius fellows three centuries after he had made it. At Corpus, too, six fellowships (out of twelve) were kept for men from Norfolk or Norwich, while at Queens' two were appropriated to the county of Yorkshire, at Magdalene one to Shrewsbury School, and at Sidney Sussex two to Blundell's School, Tiverton. The largest number of reservations was at St John's, where twenty-one foundation fellowships, out of fifty-three, were specially appropriated.[52]

Almost all these fellowship restrictions dated from the sixteenth century or earlier. In the first half of the nineteenth century they were increasingly felt to be anachronisms, an impediment to common sense and straightforward fairness and to the spirit that regarded fellowships as prizes for wranglers. In the 1820s, 1830s and 1840s the regional or county quotas were abrogated through revision of statutes in Peterhouse, Clare, Queens', Jesus, St John's, and Emmanuel. St John's was, as we have seen, especially constrained by narrow limitations of kin or locality. Here the college's desire to free itself was supported by a legal decision in 1808. A member of St John's qualified by birth for the Rokeby fellowship, but when denied it, he appealed to the Visitor, the Bishop of Ely, Thomas Dampier. In his hearing the bishop had the assistance of his brother Henry, a baron of the exchequer and a well-known ecclesiastical lawyer. It was judged that in electing to the fellowship the college was right to insist on ability. 'The Foundress Dame Rokeby, must be supposed to have intended to confer a benefit on the town of Beverley, by encouraging its inhabitants to bring up their sons to useful learning, otherwise she might have granted an annuity, instead of founding a Fellowship.'[53] The college's power to

[52] 39 of the 75 Cambridge bye-fellowships were subject to geographical or kindred restrictions.
[53] PP 1852–3: *Graham Commission Report*, pp. 161–2.

disregard such restrictions was spelled out in revised statutes of 1848. Nevertheless, in the middle of the century appropriations were still powerful elsewhere, notably at Corpus and Caius, where in 1829 reforming fellows had failed to break the Norfolk stranglehold over certain fellowships. As provided by the college statutes, they appealed for an interpretation from the Vice-Chancellor and two senior doctors of divinity, who determined that the holders of the fellowships concerned had to be born in Norfolk.[54]

In eighteenth-century Cambridge 87 per cent of fellowships imposed on their holders the obligation to take holy orders within a certain time of their election.[55] At some colleges the rule applied to all fellows, like the 12 at Corpus and the 17 at Magdalene, while at St John's it applied to all save 4 of the 53 foundation fellows and all except 2 from Trinity's 60. Elsewhere a larger proportion of places was open to laymen (or, more precisely, to men not obliged to take orders by some specified time): for example, at Peterhouse about three-quarters and at Pembroke more than half. Some fellowships were expressly reserved for practitioners in law or medicine – the two lay professions that since medieval times universities had educated men for. At Caius 2 or 3 fellowships were kept for physicians, while another 18 were open to laymen generally – though as previously noted many of the total of 29 foundation and bye-fellowships were hedged about with restrictions nourished by the particularist loyalties of benefactors.[56] The most striking example of lay reservation was Trinity Hall. The founder in 1350, Bishop Bateman, wished to educate lawyers for church and state, and the college had a bias towards ecclesiastical and civil law from its early days, and kept it for five centuries.[57] Bateman's lawyers were

---

[54] PP 1852–3: *Graham Commission Report*, pp. 159–67; *Evidence*, pp. 311, 387. Edward Miller, *Portrait of a College. A History of the College of Saint John the Evangelist Cambridge* (Cambridge University Press, 1961), pp. 75–6; John Peile, *Christ's College*, College Histories Series (London, 1900), p. 279; John Twigg, *A History of Queens' College, Cambridge, 1448–1986* (Woodbridge, Boydell, 1987), p. 2224. Gray and Brittain, *Jesus College Cambridge*, p. 155.

[55] A sign of the complexity which makes generalising about Cambridge so difficult is that the requirements on ordination varied from college to college: for example, at Corpus fellows had to take orders within three years of election, and at St John's and Trinity within six and seven years respectively after taking their MA, which would be a year or two after election.

[56] PP 1852–3: *Graham Commission Evidence*, pp. 306–44; *Cambridge University Calendar for . . . 1802*, pp. 99–112.

[57] Damian Riehl Leader, *A History of the University of Cambridge: Volume I, The University to 1546* (Cambridge University Press, 1988), pp. 73–4, 85–6. For what follows, see G. D. Squibb, *Doctors'*

all clerics. Many gravitated towards Doctors' Commons, a sort of club for clerical lawyers founded in the fifteenth century; after the Reformation it became the equivalent of an Inn of Court for judges and advocates in the ecclesiastical and admiralty courts. The laicisation of Doctors' Commons began before Henry VIII abolished appeals to Rome but accelerated afterwards. By the eighteenth century only laymen might be admitted, and so the fellows of Trinity Hall had to be laymen too; more members of Doctors' Commons came from Trinity Hall than any other Oxford or Cambridge college. In the eighteenth century ten fellowships were usually given to graduates in law, and nine of the ten fellows listed in the *University Calendar* for 1802 were LL D or LL B.[58] The lay fellows were often non-resident, leaving college teaching and administration to the clerical fellows and returning to the hall for ten days of festivity at Christmas, 'boar's head, and game pie, and oysters, and certain tins of baked apples ripening before a generous fire'.[59]

The fellows of Trinity Hall were forbidden by college statutes to be absent for more than a month, apart from vacations; so a mere brief residence at Christmas was, in Cambridge parlance, 'unstatutable'. Other colleges had similar rules. But unless they were the minority who were tutors or other college officers, fellows had few tasks to perform: they were left to their own devices for a lifetime. So in the eighteenth century the residence rules came to be overlooked, it being of advantage to all fellows to be able to disregard them when they wished to play a role away from the tiny fenland stage.[60] We may trace the growth of non-residence in the eighteenth century at Caius, which is probably a typical example. In 1721 Dr Branthwaite, an advocate in the Court of Arches, was reminded that there was an 'order, of above twenty years' date, that

---

Commons. A History of the College of Advocates and Doctors of Law (Oxford Clarendon, 1977), pp. 25–9, 40–2. Trinity Hall still has a legal emphasis, though it is now less marked than two centuries ago.

[58] The tenth was John Robinson, fellow from 1750 to 1805, for whom no degree or other achievement is recorded. He was presumably elected because he was the brother of Matthew Robinson, fellow from 1734 to 1800 (the longest tenure of any Trinity Hall fellow), FRS, and MP for Canterbury.

[59] Stephen, *Life of Henry Fawcett*, p. 78; C. W. Crawley, *Trinity Hall. The History of a Cambridge College 1450–1975* (Cambridge, Trinity Hall, 1976), esp. pp. 1–12, 70–89.

[60] PP 1852–3: *Graham Commission Report*, pp. 171–2 and *Evidence*, pp. 347–8.

every Fellow is required to reside one quarter of every year'. In 1734 a further order warned junior fellows that they should 'reside for three months in each year, or be precluded from all prospect of further preferment'. These admonitions were obviously ineffective, since in 1751 junior fellows were again ordered to reside, this time for the lesser minimum of one month in each half-year. In 1809 the struggle was at last abandoned, it being agreed 'not to require for the present any residence in College from the junior Fellows'. The records of Queens' also suggest largely ineffective injunctions against non-residence, fellows merely returning to the college in January for the audit and election of new fellows. Perhaps the career of Henry Venn, the Evangelical cleric who was elected fellow of Queens' in 1749, was typical; he remained in residence for two years, but was granted leave of absence each year from 1751 to 1757, when he married and resigned his fellowship.[61]

Another prohibition, against marriage, applied to all fellows whether clerical or lay. It was difficult to evade and was rigidly enforced; fellowships were forfeited on marriage. In 1765 there was a campaign to end the restriction. Edward Betham, fellow of King's wrote:

> In the University we have all of late been in a most violent flame, labouring under the same disorder, that carried off poor Dr. M. some years agone. Young & old have formed a resolution of Marrying: the first desirous of loosing no time: the others, of making the speediest amends possible of what was already lost... The restraint from Marrying they look upon as a Remnant of Popery: a Doctrine fit only to be taught & maintained in the court of the Whore of Babylon.[62]

Some dons refused to take the idea seriously, while others were very irritated, prophesying the ruin of the university. The supporters quarrelled, and the plan fizzled out. Thirty years later a similar proposal was a damp squib, too. As Dr Plumptre pointed out in 1765, allowing absentee fellows to marry would have meant a deserted university; non-residence and marriage were in a sense

---

[61] John Venn, *Caius College*, College Histories Series (London, Robinson, 1901), pp. 196–7; Twigg, *Queens' College*, p. 186.

[62] Cooper, *Annals*, IV, pp. 340–1. Betham was writing to William Cole the antiquarian, 31 January 1766.

mutually exclusive options, as dons were aware.[63] Young dons
vacated their fellowships specifically to marry, and those retaining
them had varying reasons for accommodating themselves to
bachelorhood. Oscar Browning, and others with his predilections,
were not tempted to abandon it. For others celibacy did not
necessarily mean continence, as we are reminded by the most
perceptive critic of early Victorian Cambridge, the American
Charles Astor Bristed; he thought that the standard of sexual
morality in Cambridge was often low for undergraduates and
sometimes for dons too, and he was indignant over the conduct of
one fellow of King's and the mild punishment meted out by his
college.[64] Perhaps the most extraordinary non-celibate fellow was
George Green, the Nottingham miller and mathematical genius,
elected to a fellowship in Gonville and Caius in 1839 despite having
seven children by a woman he declined to marry. It seems too that
Robert D. Willis, fellow of Caius from 1790 to 1821, was not
married to the woman who bore him two children; the son of one
of them, J. W. Clark, wrote the *DNB* biography of the other, his
uncle and great architectural historian Robert Willis, but astonish-
ingly does not mention Willis's mother.[65]

THE ELECTION OF FELLOWS: THE RISE OF MERITOCRACY

> I once supposed (before I had seen so much of men's motives in the
> election of fellows), that merit might be the sole or the principal
> reason which guided the elector's mind, but it is impossible that I
> should offend any one by asserting a general truth which nobody
> who knows anything of the history of colleges will deny, viz., that
> the thing is by no means always so.[66]

So wrote Isaac Milner in 1803. Unfortunately, we lack much direct
evidence that would enable us to check his statement. Colleges
recorded the results of fellowship elections in conclusion books, and
the discussions that preceded decisions are hidden from us. It is
therefore difficult to know, for example, how effective were the
Duke of Newcastle's attempts to favour his candidates for fellow-

---

[63] Cooper, *Annals*, IV, p. 462; Winstanley, *Unreformed Cambridge*, pp. 299–301.
[64] Bristed, *Five Years in an English University*, vol. II, pp. 40–54.
[65] Christopher Brooke, *Gonville and Caius College*, pp. 195–6, 203–5.
[66] Milner, *Isaac Milner*, p. 270.

ships in the middle of the eighteenth century: in any case, as is argued in another chapter,[67] Newcastle was mindful of merit in his recommendations, and the fact that the men he favoured were sometimes chosen is no proof that such elections were grossly corrupt, however much outside interference offends twentieth-century ideas. Certainly the details of the one fellowship election cited by the historian most critical of Newcastle do not show that his candidate – in the event successful – was unworthy of a fellowship.[68] Also, such meddling by outside authority no doubt diminished significantly after Newcastle's death in 1768. But we can take for granted that in small communities where men lived cheek by jowl for years, there were strong personal feelings for and against candidates, and occasionally the sources reveal their effects.

In Corpus in 1782 a candidate with some claim on the college, William Masters (he had been a student at Corpus and his father had written its history) was rejected because of his 'obstinate, sour and ungovernable disposition'. In an unusual move, non-resident fellows came to Cambridge expressly to exclude William Masters from the fellowship.[69] Only Trinity held fellowship examinations,[70] for much of the eighteenth century candidates being interviewed by the master and the eight Seniors. The process was at least a step towards unbiased treatment, but it varied greatly in rigour, from the stringent testing of mathematical and classical attainments that Richard Cumberland was subjected to in 1752 to the superficial questioning of Stephen Whisson in 1741.[71] Perfunctory procedures in 1786 led, it seemed, to the choice of an inferior candidate while two wranglers were turned down. After much protest from fellows, and a hearing before the Lord Chancellor, Trinity's examinations were reformed; within a few years formal written papers were instituted, a guarantee of impartiality.[72]

---

[67] See chapter 11, pp. 397–402.
[68] D. A. Winstanley, *The University of Cambridge in the Eighteenth Century* (Cambridge University Press, 1922), pp. 14–16, describing a Trinity contest in 1762.
[69] Winstanley, *Unreformed Cambridge*, pp. 236–7.
[70] Rooke, Master of Christ's 1745–54, seems to have established a fellowship examination there, but it did not continue: Peile, *Christ's College*, p. 239.
[71] Richard Cumberland, *Memoirs*, edited by Henry Flanders (1856), pp. 76–8; Edward Thomas Vaughan, *Some Account of the Rev. Thomas Robinson* (London, 1815), p. 33.
[72] Winstanley, *Unreformed Cambridge*, pp. 240–55, a very full account of the Cumming scandal; G.M. Trevelyan, *Trinity College. An Historical Sketch* (Cambridge University Press, 1943), pp. 75–7.

The election of fellows: the rise of meritocracy

Trinity progressed towards accepting academic excellence as the overriding criterion for election to fellowships, and appendix III shows that between 1751 and 1870 the same was true of the foundationers with unrestricted fellowships (that is, not confined to men in narrow categories) in St John's, Pembroke, and Emmanuel Colleges, and we may take them to be representative of the university as a whole. In the largest group, St John's, the increasing tendency to choose excellence is most marked: from the 1770s the great majority of fellows possess wranglerships or other marks of outstanding achievement, while there are many fewer with seconds or ordinary degrees. In the case of Pembroke the trend is marked from the 1780s, while at Emmanuel its onset is not clear until much later, in the 1830s. The leadership of St John's in the march towards meritocracy was perhaps the work of its reforming master, W. S. Powell. It is tempting to criticise others, such as Emmanuel, for their seeming slowness to elect prizemen and wranglers as a matter of course, and no doubt conservatism had something to do with it. An indication of how colleges may have been unresponsive to wider inclinations is their overwhelming propensity to choose fellows from among their own graduates, as appendix IV attests. These tables reinforce the picture we derive from elsewhere – for example, their evidence to the Graham Commissioners – of colleges as inward-looking and particularist, marked by intense family loyalty. But there was no large pool of unrewarded wranglers, passed over for fellowships in favour of less distinguished graduates. For example, in 1763 seven out of the ten wranglers obtained fellowships, in 1773 nine out of the eleven, and in 1783 twelve out of fifteen.[73] Since some allowance has to be made for those graduates who did not wish to become fellows we may assume that it would not have been possible for all colleges to choose only wranglers and prizemen for fellowships; the supply was inadequate. In these circumstances it was easier for a very large college like St John's to be meritocratic since it had its own supply of wranglers at hand – though of course it might also be said that it had a lot of fellowships to fill. A precondition for the improvement in the intellectual quality of fellows after about 1830

[73] These figures have been calculated from the lists in J. R. Tanner, ed., *The Historical Register of the University of Cambridge ... to the year 1910* (Cambridge University Press, 1917).

was the increase in the number of firsts from about 1820, itself in part the result of university expansion.

We get a less certain impression of advance towards meritocracy when we contemplate reserved and appropriated fellowships. Much the largest number of these were at St John's.[74] Appendix V shows the quality of degree for those elected in two categories of fellowships – those 'restricted' yet available for wider candidature should men with the desired qualifications be lacking; and the 'fully restricted', for which there was no eligibility outside the specifically qualified. It is hard to discern any difference between these two groups; indeed, paradoxically, the fully restricted fellowships seem to have been filled earlier with highly qualified candidates. When considered together both groups suggest that electors were swayed by potentially incompatible impulses – to respect benefactors' prescriptions and to choose the most gifted candidates. The latter seems to have become stronger about 1820, and the effect of the college's victory in the Rokeby case[75] of 1808 may be detected here, in encouraging the college to elect men lacking the specified qualifications when those with them were inadequately talented. For many decades after 1750 there is a noticeable disparity between these restricted groups and the foundation fellows, the former including higher proportions of men with degrees in the second or lower classes. After 1850, however, the several categories are indistinguishable. The movement for collegiate reform is reflected in this trend, as it was in the new St John's statutes of 1860 that swept away all ancient particularisms marking fellowships.[76]

HOW LONG DID MEN RETAIN THEIR FELLOWSHIPS?

Appendix VII throws some light on this question, though it is not easy to interpret the figures. Quite apart from the problems caused by 'unknowns', it must be remembered that fellowships were vacated by death as well as resignation; and no doubt it thinned numbers at younger ages as well as older ones. Still, appendix VIIa suggests clearly enough that most St John's fellows enjoyed their

---

[74] PP 1852–3, HC xliv [1559]: *Graham Commission Report*, pp. 157–67.
[75] See pp. 99–100 above.
[76] Miller, *Portrait of a College*, pp. 85–6.

prize for more than a couple of years but less than eleven; and that the great majority vacated them through resignation. Thus, of the 21 foundation fellows elected at St John's in the 1750s only a couple resigned within five years, but 12 had gone within another six. Of the 35 elected in the 1830s 8 went within five years but 15 in six more. Most St John's fellows, that is to say, retained their prizes in their twenties but relinquished them by their early thirties. And though the incomplete nature of the evidence in college records and in Venn makes it hard to be sure, it seems right to assume that marriage (a certain disqualification for a fellowship) was the trigger for resignation.[77] Cambridge fellowships very largely comprised bachelors in their twenties, with a mixture of older dons, many of whom were the professional academics – tutors, bursars, and masters – who kept the permanent university machinery working. To choose at random from a multitude of examples, the St John's combination room contained in the late 1830s John Palmer, who had been a fellow since 1794 and had served as bursar and president of the college and as Professor of Arabic. Among younger men were William Hey, elected in 1836 at the age of twenty-five, and Samuel Laing, elected 1834 at the age of twenty-two. Palmer died in his college rooms in 1840 and was buried in the antechapel; Hey resigned his fellowship in the same year, becoming a clergyman in Yorkshire and the headmaster of St Peter's, York; Laing resigned in 1841 and achieved uniqueness among ex-fellows of St John's by becoming part-owner of the Crystal Palace, MP for Orkney, and managing director of the London, Brighton, and South Coast Railway. Relationships in the combination room among fellows of very different ages and predilections would repay investigation.

Fellows' length of tenure must in some way have been linked to the attractiveness of their fellowships and also to their ability to find alternative sources of income after resignation; whatever the dynamics of this complex relationship, such evidence as we have suggests that they changed in the period 1600–1750. At Queens' the average length of tenure of fellowships was six or seven years

---

[77] The St John's statutes of 1860 permitted married fellows to retain their fellowships only if they were professors or 'public lecturers' or had one of three specified university offices. Such slight modification of the college statutes was typical of the work of the Statutory Commissioners of 1856. Marriage was permitted to all fellows of St John's by the statutes of 1882.

between 1500 and 1640, and rose to nearly twelve years between 1660 and 1778; at Clare the average age of fellows rose from twenty-seven in 1600 to thirty-two in 1750.[78] Appendix VII shows that the length of tenure of the foundation fellows of St John's rose from over eleven years for men elected between 1751 and 1760 to nearly seventeen years for those elected between 1801 and 1810, and after falling to below ten years for those elected in the 1820s rose, fell and rose again with dramatic suddenness for following decades to reach over fourteen years for the generation elected in the 1860s. These peripeties may be most plausibly connected to the heyday of private tutorships in the mid-Victorian years and the growth in opportunities for academic careers for married fellows towards the end of the nineteenth century. But more continuous influences were the rise in college dividends that took place between 1750 and 1870, and also in the stock of livings that a college possessed for fellows to move to, since (as appendix VIII shows) fellows were more likely to proceed to a clerical career than any other.

At St John's considerable sums were spent on purchasing advowsons, from the Brackenbury and Robins funds set up for this purpose in 1692 and 1719 respectively, and later combined into the Livings Fund. In 1817, for example, the advowson at Holt (Norfolk) was bought for £3,000, and the fund was left in debt. Ten years later, however, the advowson of Murston (Kent) was purchased for £8,000; interest only was paid for eight years, when the college had just £2,000 in the Livings Fund and borrowed £6,000 for the balance from two fellows, one of whom, Tatham, became master. The debt to Tatham was not repaid till 1850. The sharp fall in the length of tenure of the 1801–30 generations of fellows suggests that St John's significantly improved its ratio of parishes to fellows.[79] We know that these matters were a serious concern at both universities, and that because of the purchase of advowsons for fellows the total of livings owned by Cambridge colleges seems to have risen from about 250 early in the eighteenth century to about 300 at its end. At that time the overall ratio of

---

[78] Twigg, *Queens' College*, p. 185; J. Gascoigne, *Cambridge in the Age of the Enlightenment. Science, Religion and Politics from the Restoration to the French Revolution* (Cambridge University Press, 1989), p. 15. [79] Howard, *Finances of St John's College*, pp. 81–2, 138–140.

college livings to fellowships was 3 : 4, and that at only two colleges (Catharine Hall and Magdalene) was it less than 1 : 2. The Mortmain Act of 1736 (which limited the number of livings that could be bought) is usually thought to have been an effective constraint, though if the St John's evidence is typical then shortage of money is likely to have been more important. But our knowledge of the colleges' skill in managing their superannuation resources is as insubstantial as our knowledge of their finances generally, and investigations of their record as large corporate property owners would yield some very fruitful results.[80]

IN SEARCH OF 'TYPICAL' FELLOWS

Is it possible to fit names to these numbers, and discover fellows who were 'typical' at each stage of their careers? One element of typicality not so far mentioned is that fellows appear to have come from humbler origins than most Cambridge undergraduates – for that is suggested by the very high proportions of fellows who had been admitted to their colleges as sizars, as appendix VI shows. Typical fellows proved themselves as high achievers and gained good degrees (and in the second half of the period probably outstanding ones); they resigned their fellowships by their early thirties, and turned to parochial duties as Anglican clergymen. Of the 320 men who were elected to foundation fellowships at St John's between 1751 and 1870, 46 met all these terms, persevering in the Clapham omnibus through every stage in its journey. The sparse biographical details we possess imply lives of exemplary ordinariness, typical of many being William Grieve Wilson, the son of a clergyman (like so many fellows and indeed graduates generally). An uncle, two brothers, and two cousins also graduated from St John's, the Wilsons being one of the Cambridge clans that may be traced through the columns of Venn. A sizar in 1838, Sixteenth Wrangler and Eighth Classic, he became a fellow in 1844, and in 1847 was appointed Rector of Forncett, a college living in

---

[80] I. G. Doolittle, 'College Administration', p. 236, in L. S. Sutherland and L. G. Mitchell, (eds.), *The History of the University of Oxford, vol. V, The Eighteenth Century* (Oxford: Clarendon, 1986); Twigg, *Queens' College*, pp. 166–7; Christopher Brooke, *Gonville and Caius College*, pp. 160–1; Gascoigne, *Cambridge in the Age of the Enlightenment*, p. 16.

Norfolk that he retained till his death in 1896, though he resigned his fellowship in 1849, marrying soon afterwards. Like many clergymen in the eighteenth and nineteenth centuries, some of the forty-six fellows became masters in grammar or public schools, and eight became heads, one of them succeeding another at Tonbridge where the college had links.

So many details suggest conventional lives, sustaining the existing fabric of the world. Perhaps we should not expect anything else from what was still essentially a clerical seminary. For a minority there were marked alterations in career or direction that imply collaboration with changes occurring in society. Joseph Woolley, Third Wrangler in 1840 and a fellow for six years, became a clergyman in Norfolk on his marriage in 1846. His mathematical attainments led to an interest in questions of ship design, and in 1848 he resigned his living to become the principal of the School of Naval Construction in Portsmouth Dockyard. Eventually he relinquished holy orders by means of the Clerical Disabilities Relief Act of 1870 that gave an escape route to those who had lost their faith. The most irregular person in the group of forty-six was John William Colenso, whose career reminds us that colleges contained, and encouraged, men with the strength to follow conscience even when it led to conflict with the orthodoxy surrounding them.

Colenso came from a Cornish family in straitened circumstances, and only great talent and the energy that his piety stimulated enabled him to reach St John's. At college his poverty was alleviated through the kindness of his tutor, John Hymers. Colenso became Second Wrangler in 1836. A fellow from 1837 till his marriage in 1846, he then served seven years in a college living in Norfolk. His reputation was bright,[81] and in 1853 he became Bishop of Natal. From youth attracted to the challenge of the mission field, he proved an evangelist of genius; he mastered the Zulu tongue, publishing a grammar and a dictionary and translations of the scriptures, and (what was very rare among white men) he took the Zulus' part in their growing quarrel with the colonisers. His great conflict with orthodox authority was caused by the five volumes,

---

[81] In part owing to the school mathematics textbooks (still found on dusty bookshelves) that he composed using his tripos expertise. In 1853 Colenso sold his copyrights for £2,400, equal to at least £100,000 in 1990s money.

and 3,500 pages, of *The Pentateuch and the Book of Joshua Critically Examined* (1862–79). Colenso was part of the Broad Church movement that attempted to reconcile Christian doctrine with modern scientific truth and method; another famous landmark in the movement was *Essays and Reviews* (1860). A detailed study has described Colenso's achievement as 'the most remarkable ... by a British scholar in the field of Old Testament criticism in the nineteenth century'.[82] He 'took account of German criticism in a manner that had not been done before' and that was to be without equal in Britain until the 1880s. Colenso disproved the assumed unitary character and literal truth of the ancient texts, showing that they came from several hands and were inaccurate; he used his arithmetic skills to show the impossibility of many treasured totals, for example the number of Israelites alleged to be in the wilderness after the Exodus. The length at which he elaborated his arguments itself now seems absurd, but has to be understood as necessary to demolish contentions very stubbornly held. It took great courage to persevere, not least when the Archbishop of Capetown tried to depose him from his see,[83] and many clergy refused to recognise his authority. To these moves Colenso replied: 'it seems to me to be my duty to proclaim the truth, as I see it, though all the clergy and laity of England and Natal were banded against me'.[84] Colenso was unusual among Cambridge fellows, yet there are enough examples like him to show that the university could foster steadfast independence of spirit.

WHAT DID FELLOWS WRITE?

It has been possible to assess the literary productivity of a sample of fellows, the group, as before, being the 320 foundation fellows of St John's College elected between 1751 and 1870. The results of this investigation are given in appendix IX, its basis being the fellows'

[82] John Rogerson, *Old Testament Criticism in the Nineteenth Century. England and Germany* (London, 1984), p. 232 and pp. 220–37 for this paragraph generally; it also draws on Josef L. Altholz, 'The Warfare of Conscience with Theology', in *The Mind and Art of Victorian England* (Minneapolis, Minn., University of Minnesota Press, 1976), pp. 58–77, and George W. Cox, *The Life of John William Colenso, D.D., Bishop of Natal* (2 vols., London, 1888).
[83] Considering only the question of ecclesiastical jurisdiction, the Judicial Committee of the Privy Council declared the deposition null and void.
[84] Cox, *The Life of John William Colenso*, vol. 1, p. 248.

published works as recorded in the catalogues of the college and university libraries and in the Advocates' Library in Edinburgh, which has an especially good deposit of eighteenth-century Cambridge authors. The accuracy and reliability of a careful bibliography is not claimed for it, however. Papers in journals are not systematically recorded, and the omission must have reduced the totals credited to some fellows, especially in the nineteenth-century heyday of the quarterly; some men known to be affected are mentioned below. On the other hand it seems likely that few fellows are seriously disparaged since the abundance of sermons, pamphlets and offprints in the catalogue listings concerned reveals that the libraries cast their nets widely. Also, no attempt is made in the appendix to discriminate between works of very different length, and so, for example, the publications separately recorded for Colenso include many sermons and in addition, again as one item, the five volumes of *The Pentateuch and Book of Joshua Critically Examined*. Still, it seems that rough justice is done to *relative* quantities, and rather more than that to the direction of a fellow's intellectual life.

What does this appendix tell us about how fellows spent their time? This question, plainly akin to the enquiries into dons' productivity carried out today by the Funding Councils, is less revealing and straightforward than might be hoped. More useful is a second question, Does appendix IX tell us anything about Cambridge's permanent legacy to the culture of its fellows?

Perhaps it should again be stressed that until the reforms of the 1870s Cambridge fellows did not have an obligation to perform tasks in return for their guaranteed stipend; the burdens of scholarship and tuition were voluntary, and were assumed by men like Adam Sedgwick and James Wood because they were naturally industrious. However, appendix IXa shows an increase in literary productivity that paralleled, though not with close congruence or consistency, the rise in fellows' degree results. Eighteenth-century fellows wrote, or at all events published, very little. During the tenure of their fellowships the cohorts of the 1750s and 1760s produced only one and two authors respectively, and those of the next two cohorts none. If we broaden the investigation to include lifetime productivity the totals rise, but not by very much. The

Wooden Spoon is held by the cohort of the 1780s, only one of whose fellows appears to have published anything. This person was William Lambe, Fourth Wrangler in 1786 and a fellow from 1788 to 1794. Graduating MB in 1789 Lambe acquired a medical practice in 1790, and in the course of a long career as a medical practitioner became an enthusiast for a régime of vegetarian food and filtered water, and it is for this prescription, and writings related to it, that he is chiefly known.[85] One necessary comment is that whatever the clinical value of his medicine, the Senate House Examination was a wholly inappropriate preliminary to it.

In the nineteenth century fellows became more productive, though not so as to astound us by their industry. The cohort of the 1830s was the most productive, 23 out of its 35 members publishing something. Appendix IXb shows, however, the immense variation between individual performances, J. W. Colenso's forty-three works being balanced by six colleagues who seem to have produced only one each. And it is important to stress that it is *lifetime* utterance that is being compared here. Only 9 of the 23 fellows published during the period of their fellowships; and brevity of tenure cannot explain the silence of the other 15. But the productivity criterion, so taken for granted today, would have seemed alien to a fellow in the 1840s, and at best very limited to the most professionally minded successor in the 1940s.

The most striking example of a non-publishing don in this cohort was W. H. Bateson, elected a fellow in 1837 at the age of twenty-five, and in office continuously until his death in 1881 aged sixty-nine. Bateson, whose oeuvre apparently consists of two modest pamphlets on university matters, expended himself as bursar and Master of St John's, Vice-Chancellor, secretary or member of royal commissions on university matters, and as secretary of the Council of the Senate and in a host of now forgotten syndicates where his presence seemed indispensable. 'He was distinguished by an acute judgment and a remarkably sweet and tender character', wrote Oscar Browning in the *DNB*; 'his patience and industry made him an excellent man of business'. On the other hand, G. F. Reyner, fellow from 1840 to 1876, is also credited with only two

[85] H. Saxe Wyndham, *William Lambe, M.D. A Pioneer of Reformed Diet* (London, The Vegetarian Society, 1940).

short works and leaves us wondering how he did spend his time after discharging his duties as a college lecturer in mathematics. Charles Merivale may be compared with both men. Graduating senior optime and Fourth Classic, he became a fellow in 1833. Greatly attached to his classical studies, and having 'a desperate horror of the battle of a professional life' such as his father had had as a barrister,[86] Merivale hoped to occupy his time as a fellow and tutor 'with congenial associates and studies while waiting for the college living which was in due time' to set him 'at liberty' and give him the 'literary leisure' he longed for. Merivale certainly taught and studied conscientiously during his fellowship years and laid the foundations for his major publications on classics and ancient history. But they appeared *after* he became Rector of Lawford (Essex) in 1848. 'My parish', he wrote before moving to it, 'will not be so large or full of work as to occupy my time to the exclusion of my immortal interests', and so it proved. Merivale is a good example of the Cambridge scholar for whom a church living was a means of continuing college pursuits with the added advantage of allowing marriage, which he had been forced to abjure many years before by his desire for a fellowship.

It was thought legitimate to employ a fellowship and its guaranteed income to prepare for a career not directly served by Cambridge's academic specialisms, and such labour gave little time for authorship even if one had the inclination. W. Martin, Twenty-sixth Wrangler and Fourth Classic in 1829, read for the bar at Lincoln's Inn in his seven years as a fellow from 1831 to 1838; from 1841 to 1857 he was Chief Justice of New Zealand. In 1860 and later he published two studies of New Zealand politics and *Inquiries concerning the structure of the Semitic languages* – a result, it seems safe to guess, of his classical studies of many years before. The careers of Percival Pickering and Lancelot Shadwell were very similar, fellowships of eight years or so being used to prepare for the law, with authorship being taken up years later.

Professional clerics were a large group in Cambridge fellowships and there were 18 in the 23 'publishing' fellows in the 1830s cohort,

---

[86] Judith Anne Merivale, ed., *Autobiography of Dean Merivale with Selections from his Correspondence* (London, 1899), pp. 78, 90–1 and 176 for the quotations that follow, and pp. 52–93 for Merivale's Cambridge years generally.

mostly working as parish priests or grammar-school headmasters, but occasionally advancing to prominence, as did H. Cotterill who was Bishop of Edinburgh from 1872 to 1886, or even notoriety as in the case of Colenso. Representative of a humbler position was John Doudney Lane, curate of St Andrew-the-Less, Barnwell from 1839 to 1844, where his ministry is touched on in one of the most widely read volumes of Evangelical exhortation.[87] The effective role of the university as a clerical seminary explains the weight of religious works in the fellows' published oeuvre, just as the variety in Joseph Woolley's work is explained by his disavowal of clerical status and his new calling as naval architect.[88] A scholarly interest of the Victorian clergy is reflected in W. Hey's special study of the beetles of Yorkshire when he was Archdeacon of Cleveland.

W. Nathaniel Griffin, Senior Wrangler, and fellow from 1837 to 1848, published three mathematical treatises while at Cambridge, and four school mathematical texts from his Kent vicarage. Another ex-fellow whose published works bore the impress of his wrangler-ship was Charles Pritchard, for many years the highly successful headmaster of Clapham Grammar School. Possessing a small observatory in Clapham, he distinguished himself as an astronomer; at the age of sixty-two he became Savilian Professor of Astronomy at Oxford, and in the twenty years before his death contributed fifty papers to learned societies;[89] 'nothing could be more admirable than the vigour and originality' with which he discharged his Oxford duties, wrote Agnes Mary Clerke in the *DNB*. Another lifelong mathematician was Colenso, while among the non-clerics Percival Frost[90] was a professional mathematician; he supported his family as a private tutor – like William Hopkins he lived in Fitzwilliam Street – after vacating his fellowship on marriage, and he published many more papers than the five recorded in appendix IX. These four examples, though distinguished in quality, seem remarkably few from a total of twenty-three of the university's outstanding mathematical graduates. Their scant number reinforces one's impression that the Senate House Examination was an initiation rite

---

[87] 'Old Jonathan' [J. A. Doudney], *Try and Try Again* (London, 1863). J. A. Doudney was J. D. Lane's uncle.   [88] See p. 381.

[89] Pritchard is one member of the sample whose published work is certainly under-recorded in appendix IX.   [90] Frost was ordained deacon but did not proceed to priest's orders.

that many ambitious young men steeled themselves to excel in, for the sake of the glittering prizes it led to, and that as soon as possible thereafter they bade farewell to Newton's world.

Imaginative literature is even more meagrely represented. There are only two examples: Percival André Pickering, the lawyer, published a very feeble *Essay on Friendship* (1875), and Samuel Laing jr. (b. 1812), a two-volume novel, *The Sporting Quixote* (1886); the University Library's many fiction-readers have not bothered to cut their copy's pages and peruse the sporting and romantic adventures of the Honourable Augustus Fitzmuddle. Serious literary talent and the willingness or ability to cram for the Senate House Examination may have been mutually exclusive. William Wordsworth did not bother with honours, despite his early interest in Newton's thought; his brother did, but then Christopher was not much of a poet.

Yet one is tempted to linger over Laing's publications because of the diversity and unusualness they share with his life: it is hard to fit him, and some of his writings, into traditional categories. A fellow of St John's for seven years during which he read for the bar, Laing resigned in 1841 and afterwards was very successful as a civil servant at the Board of Trade, financial minister in India, and managing director of the London, Brighton, and South Coast Railway. A Peelite Conservative as a young man, he moved to the left and was a Liberal Imperialist in old age; he was for long periods Radical MP for Wick, and Orkney and Shetland. Publishing works on railway taxation and politics in his thirties, and the *Prehistoric Remains of Caithness* (1866) in his fifties, Laing showed his vigour and the extent of his informed reading in seven works published after the age of seventy. *Human Origins* (1892), which appeared when Laing was eighty-one, is a conspectus of ancient civilisations and prehistoric cultures that shows what he described as his 'faculty for lucid condensation'. In surveys of the science of Darwin, Huxley, and Herbert Spencer he argued its incompatibility with revealed religion while expressing the hope, with a long quotation from *In Memoriam*, 'that somehow good will be the final goal of ill'. Though as attached to its period as his other works, *Problems of the Future* (1889) impresses still with the breadth of its knowledgeable reference, from Malthus to Lord Kelvin, and its blend of foreboding and optimism that reminds us of the scientific romances that H. G. Wells was to write a few years later; though classed as 'biological science' in appendix IX, it might just as well be termed 'prophecy'. But we are now a long way from Laing's undergraduate experiences sixty years earlier, and as so often when we assess the achievements of a graduate's maturity it is impossible to know what the university may be given credit or blame for; however greatly fellows' careers bore the mark of their Cambridge years, fortunately native talent or disposition was responsible for much, too.

Chapter 4

COLLEGES: TUTORS, BURSARS, AND MONEY

TUTORS

JOHN WRIGHT AT TRINITY

In the month of October, eighteen hundred and fifteen, I, and lots more, first saw the light as sons of Alma... Furnished by a friend with a letter to the tutor, the present worthy and learned rector of Kendal,[1] in Westmoreland, I made my way with all speed to that spot of all spots – Trinity College.[2]

With his momentous climb up the stairs to Hudson's room John Wright, from King's Lynn Grammar School and the Lincolnshire village of Frampton, begins the account of his chequered years at Cambridge: fittingly so, since the Trinity tutor (or as we would say, Senior Tutor) gave him advice that stimulated one side, the scholarly side, of Wright's dual personality, and started him on the road that led to some academic success; and if Hudson and his colleague, Brown, who became personally responsible for Wright, did not prevent the misadventures that befell their pupils it was not for want of effort. On that initiation day in October 1815 Hudson enquired into Wright's knowledge of mathematics and the classical authors, and was unimpressed by a recital of mere reading:

Then know, Sir (was the fag-end of the examination), that at this place, all things – prizes, scholarships, and fellowships, are bestowed, not on the greatest readers, but on those who, without any assistance, can produce most knowledge on paper... You must *'write out'* all you read, and read and write some six or eight hours a

---

[1] John Hudson, Senior Wrangler 1797 and fellow of Trinity 1798.
[2] A Trinity Man [John Martin Frederick Wright], *Alma Mater; or, Seven Years at the University of Cambridge* (2 vols., London, 1827), vol. II, p. 4. Wright in fact matriculated in 1814 and made a late entry to his studies the following year.

day; and then you will have no reason to repent of your labour. Don't be alarmed at your scanty progress in the mathematics. When I first entered college, Sir, I knew less of them than you do.[3]

Hudson gave Wright a list of books to cram for his first-year courses, and he proceeded to borrow them from Trinity library and a circulating library. At Trinity first-year men were taught in classes by separate tutors for mathematics and classics, but despite the numbers involved there was a good deal of personal attention. For example, Brown, who taught mathematics, checked attendance and took the men carefully over the steps to the Pons Asinorum. Wright answered well Brown's question about axioms.

> Very good, Sir, though not precisely in the language of Euclid. But what is the first axiom of Euclid, or of Geometry, as I may say, the terms being synonymous?

> Things which are equal to the same, are equal to one another. Very good, Sir . . .[4]

> Mr Brown gave us daily a number of neat questions for solution the day following, and shewed great ingenuity in his ineffectual endeavours to bring Jemmy Wood and the numerous family of the Thickheads, to a better understanding. In the doctrine of proportions, a subject extremely embarrassing to these gentlemen, Mr B. gave very numerous illustrations in order to show that the things compared must be homogenous [*sic*] or of the same kind. One of these was, 'Do I make myself perfectly understood, Mr. D.?' – 'Not quite, Sir' – 'I'll go over it again. You cannot state the terms of a proportion thus, "Ten pounds of sugar, are to twenty pounds of beef, as ten gallons of rum, to twenty gallons of ox-tail soup" . . . Do you now comprehend me, Mr. D.?' – 'I think I do, Sir.'[5]

In Wright's detailed account Brown comes across as a conscientious and highly competent teacher. When in their third year Wright and other talented students were tackling Newton's *Principia*, Brown helped them invaluably by lending MSS that were essential for students wanting to excel in the tripos, 'inasmuch as they contained the aggregate of the results of the labours at Cambridge, to clear up the obscurities of Newton, ever since he had been read there'. Observing that Wright was better off working in

---

[3] Wright, *Alma Mater*, vol. I, p. 6.   [4] Wright, vol. I, pp. 120–5.   [5] Wright, vol. I, p. 170.

his own rooms than with him, 'who must wait even for the slowest capacities', Brown allowed him to cut lectures and study privately.[6] Like others hoping for high honours Wright took the services of a private tutor; and the need for intensive tuition shows the inadequacies of official college teaching, even a man like Brown being hampered by the mixed-ability character of the class.[7] Still, when Wright's academic prospects collapsed Brown 'consoled me in every way he could think of, strenuously advising me against the determination I had now formed' to cut the written papers.[8] Taking an ordinary degree, Wright went on a pleasure jaunt in London, fell on hard times (the details are skated over in *Alma Mater*) and was helped through the winter by a personal loan of £50 from Brown. Brown was a generous man whose efforts on behalf of his pupil were vindicated in the love of mathematics that Wright evinced after his follies at Trinity.[9] Brown's selflessness was typical of many tutors, though not of all; it is very difficult to generalise about the competence and assiduity of tutors in the eighteenth and nineteenth centuries.

THE RISE OF THE TUTORS AND THEIR FUNCTIONS

Who were they, these college officers responsible for so much of the university's real work? By the sixteenth century they already

[6] Wright vol. II, pp. 24–5. The manuscript papers were usually in the hands of private tutors, and explain why ambitious undergraduates had to resort to them: a theme for the sociologist of knowledge.

[7] Wright, *Alma Mater*, vol. I, pp. 171–3.

[8] Wright, *Alma Mater*, vol. II, p. 60. Wright (vol. II, pp. 46–97) alleges that he was gored by a bull in Petty Cury, and so missed an important exercise in the Schools. As a result given an inferior preliminary grade, he quarrelled with the examiner, Peacock, and decided to withdraw from the tripos. Wright was 'gulphed', given an Aegrotat degree, awarded to those 'who but for sickness, or some other sufficient cause, might have obtained an Honour'. He got off lightly.

[9] Wright, *Alma Mater*, vol. II, pp. 105–11. Wright certainly upheld his claim to be an accomplished mathematician. Between 1825 and 1832 he was the author of works – such as commentaries on examination questions and on Newton's *Principia* – designed for use within the Cambridge world of intensive private tuition for the Senate House Examination; for a time he was a private tutor himself. In 1827 *Alma Mater* was published; it was unfavourably reviewed in the *Atlas*, and Wright lost a libel action complaining of the excessively personal remarks in the review. The report of the action shows that John Wright was indeed the author of *Alma Mater*: see *The Times*, 11 July 1827, for which reference I am grateful to Arnold Hunt. Then Wright made a career change that was startling after his youthful divagations. Taking holy orders in 1828, he became a successful clergyman in Malvern and elsewhere, and chaplain to the Duke of Cambridge. He died in 1893 in his hundredth year. See *Notes and Queries*, 22 January 1949 and the introductions to Wright's works in Trinity College and Cambridge University libraries.

formed the core of the teaching system, being given responsibility for the education and welfare of pupils; they supplemented the instruction given by the official college lecturers. Until the eighteenth century each tutor had charge of just a few undergraduates; the office might be held by many fellows in turn and for a brief time by any one of them. The change to a post with longer tenure, held by a small number of fellows carrying almost all the college work, was occasioned (it seems very probable, though the connection has not earlier been made) by the rise of Newtonian mathematics as the dominating theme in the university curriculum, and the need for experts to teach it. It is significant that whereas in 1725 there were twelve tutors at Trinity and eight in 1745, in 1755 the college entry was split into just two 'sides', each the responsibility of a tutor. Meanwhile the official college lecturers, whose functions had been laid down centuries before, became unimportant throughout the university in the eighteenth century. They were not competent to teach the new mathematical learning and in any case their stipends, fixed by ancient statutes, had been made laughable by inflation.[10]

In the second half of the eighteenth century each college seems to have had one or two tutors, or at most three. Though at Trinity or St John's their workload was heavy, usually tutors looked after a handful of undergraduates. As Gunning wrote about the early 1780s: 'The number of admissions at Christ's in my year was only three; two of the men professed not to read, and I was ignorant of the first Proposition in Euclid.'[11] The tutor at Christ's, Thomas Parkinson, lacked professional commitment. He was an accomplished mathematician who had supported himself as an undergraduate by calculating tables of parallax and reflection for the Board of Longitude;[12] he was Senior Wrangler in 1769. Gunning thought him 'one of the most kind-hearted and benevolent men breathing ... much interested for all his pupils'.[13] But at the point of contact his handful of pupils were an irritation, since on three mornings a week Parkinson wanted to ride eighteen miles into Suffolk to visit his fiancée, and his anxieties were increased by his poor prospects

---

[10] Winstanley, *Unreformed Cambridge*, pp. 267–70; W. W. Rouse Ball, *Cambridge Notes: Chiefly concerning Trinity College and the University* (2nd edn, Cambridge 1923), pp. 34–7.

[11] Gunning, *Reminiscences*, vol. I, p. 6.

[12] Parkinson's work thus helped marine navigators.

[13] Gunning, *Reminiscences*, vol. I, pp. 6–10 for the following quotations.

(he had failed to be elected Master of Christ's)[14] and debts to the college cook. 'We were lectured immediately after chapel, and generally in a very hasty manner, as Parkinson not unfrequently was equipped in boots and spurs, which his gown but ill concealed.' Lectures were in any case hurried, since they were commonly compressed into the second division of term, a month or so. Unable to keep pace with Parkinson and taking his difficulties to him, Gunning was told that 'I cannot make it any plainer, Sir; it requires only common sense to understand it.'

Disheartened, and resolved 'to give up reading altogether', Gunning was rescued from idleness by a sudden access of concern in Parkinson; talking to Gunning over breakfast, he urged him not to waste 'opportunities never to be recovered'. Gunning was reinvigorated, but to be taught he turned not to Parkinson but to a second-year undergraduate,[15] a skilful mathematician who tutored Gunning patiently in the first five weeks of the Lent Term before lectures started at the end of February, when they were the only two undergraduates in college. Taking him through his difficulties, Hartley lent Gunning a manuscript that filled the gaps in Maclaurin's algebra textbook; from Hartley Gunning 'derived all the advantage I could have received from a private tutor'. Hartley continued to teach Gunning during his second year, while for all this time his ostensible tutor was content to offer reading lists and a weekly examination. In 1786–7, Gunning's third year, when he was preparing for his acts and opponencies, Hartley was busy with his own tripos and later with family matters, and Parkinson taught Gunning for two hours a week in the Michaelmas and Easter Terms for an hour each alternate day, taking him through Newton's *Principia*, particularly the tricky ninth and eleventh sections;[16] 'by his

---

[14] A post that would have permitted him to marry while remaining in Cambridge. As a fellow he was of course celibate, needing a well-paid church living to marry on. In the end Parkinson's fiancée married someone else.

[15] Richard Hartley, Sixth Wrangler in 1787. For these lines and quotations, see Gunning, *Reminiscences*, vol. I, pp. 10–17, 49, 79–87.

[16] The first eight sections of *Principia* consider the motion of bodies in fixed elliptical orbits, and the ninth section considers for the first time the situation where an elliptical orbit rotates about one of its foci. Section XI introduces a further complication. Until then Newton has been concerned with attractions due to gravity of bodies towards a fixed centre, such as the sun. But in practice the sun is no more fixed than the earth is, and Section XI introduces the study of the mutual gravitational attractions of collections of bodies, regarded now as revolving about one another rather than about a fixed centre.

illustrations he rendered it highly interesting'. The following Michaelmas Gunning was reading hard for his tripos in January 1788, and was placed in the preliminary first class, for candidates who might expect to become wranglers. 'Hartley was with me the next morning before I had risen, bringing under his arm the *Meditationes Algebraicae* of Waring, six of whose forms he said it was absolutely necessary I should make myself acquainted with, as some of them would be sure to be set amongst the Evening Problems.'[17]

Thus in his ten terms of mathematical instruction Gunning owed at least as much to a fellow student as he did to his tutor. In contrast to this pattern was the sustained professionalism of J. B. Seale, the junior tutor – Seventh Wrangler in 1774 – who lectured on classics, moral philosophy, and logic, taking several years together so that he had classes of a dozen or more; the small-scale patterns of eighteenth-century Cambridge sometimes made specialised instruction as remote a possibility as in the country grammar schools many undergraduates hailed from. Nevertheless, Gunning never missed Seale's lectures,[18]

> as they were to me very interesting, except when he lectured on the *Metre* of the Greek Choruses, of which I knew nothing, but on which he had (unfortunately for me) published a book. He was a man of very strong prejudices, and accustomed himself, when he wanted to illustrate his subject by an example, to introduce the name of some man who was obnoxious to him. He particularly disliked the Master of his own college; and when speaking of the force of habit, he cautioned us against acquiring bad habits, and generally added, – 'for want of observing this rule, our *Warden* indulges himself in the most filthy and disgusting of all habits, that of chewing tobacco, which renders him unfit for decent society' ... Nothing could be pleasanter than the hour passed at Seale's lectures, – such was his kindness to all, particularly to those who wished to profit by them. When any ludicrous blunder occurred (which was not unfrequently the case), he joined in the laugh as heartily as any of us.

A sense of tasks undertaken by a highly conscientious classical tutor is given by the teaching notes prepared by Seale's contemporary William Bennet of Emmanuel, fellow from 1769 and tutor from

[17] The additional tests given to prospective wranglers.
[18] Gunning, *Reminiscences*, vol. I, pp. 17–19.

1779 or 1780 until 1790.[19] Bennet was fascinated by Roman roads, and travelled widely in search of them with his friend Thomas Leman, another fellow of Emmanuel; the two men compiled a volume of notes on the roads. Bennet's teaching notes on six classical texts survive; they are very thorough, and testify to the care that the most conscientious Cambridge tutors took with their pupils. Two of the sets of notes are in Bennet's own hand, commentaries on Cicero, *De Oratore* Book I and Sophocles, *Electra*. They deal intensively with usage and content and are three or four times longer than the texts with which they are interleaved; they were compiled for meticulous line-by-line scrutiny.[20] There is evidence, however, that Bennet read the texts with private pupils in what we might term supervisions, but delivered formal lectures to his college pupils: so it may be that some of his undergraduates got especially helpful instruction – which is a hint of the differences certainly common in the 1840s.[21] Four other of his sets of notes survive in another hand, and seem to have been copied for use by his successor as tutor, Robert Cory, which is a strong suggestion that not all tutors were as conscientious as Bennet. Bennet's pupil John Fane, tenth Earl of Westmorland, appreciated his former tutor's labours enough to take him to Ireland as his chaplain when appointed Lieutenant-Governor in 1790.[22]

Tutors were in a paradoxical position. Their office was not usually mentioned in ancient college statutes, as the college lecturers were. On the other hand they enjoyed power unequalled by any other statutable college officer with the exception of the master – and in some respects more than he. Once he was appointed by the master (a right incidentally that gave the master considerable influence on the future direction of the college) the tutor had sole control of large amounts of money. Among them were the tutorial

---

[19] For what follows on William Bennet I am indebted to Christopher Brooke's long account in 'The Society in the Eighteenth Century', a chapter in Bendall, Brooke, and Collinson, *A History of Emmanuel College*; I am also very grateful to Frank Stubbings for his comments on Bennet and his manuscripts.

[20] Emmanuel MSS 2.2.16 and 2.3.19 (141 and 163 in Montagu Rhodes James, *The Western Manuscripts in the Library of Emmanuel College* (Cambridge University Press, 1904)).

[21] A classical supervision of the 1840s is described in chapter 16, pp. 607–8.

[22] Frank Stubbings, *Forty-Nine Lives, an Anthology of Portraits of Emmanuel men* (Cambridge, Emmanuel College, 1983), #25. Bennet also became Bishop of Cork and Ross, and was translated to Cloyne.

fees, paid by each man *in statu pupillari* to his college tutor. Before 1721 such sums were small, and the caution monies were insufficient to protect the tutors. So in that year forty-two tutors (perhaps the university total) petitioned the Vice-Chancellor and heads of houses, and as a result quarterly fees were agreed for all colleges, ranging from 15s for a sizar to £3 10s for a fellow commoner; their cautions were to be £10 and £25 respectively. Thus all colleges charged the same for undergraduate instruction while additional costs for residence varied greatly from one to another. Amounts were increased for most students in 1767 and again in 1802 after a decade of high inflation. The sizar's fee was then, as always, 15s a quarter, a pensioner's £2 10s and a nobleman's £10. This scale of fees was not reduced when the cost of living fell after 1820; so the real expense of college tuition rose for much of the nineteenth century.[23]

So therefore did the real income of college tutors. They received the fees, paying them into their own bank accounts and paying stipends to their assistant tutors, who had 'nothing whatever to do with the discipline and pecuniary affairs of their pupils', but were 'merely officers paid by the Tutor . . . for their services in lecturing his "side" or "class"'.[24] Other college bills were also submitted to the tutor, who passed them to undergraduates or their parents, received and banked their payments, and settled with the creditors. Sometimes there was a gap between transactions that allowed a useful amount of interest to mount up for the tutor. On the other hand the tutor was responsible if debtors defaulted. Tutors' bills reminded pupils that they could not remain in college if they were one quarter in arrears,[25] and debtors were also ineligible to enter examinations. Trouble was possible when undergraduates were permitted to run up arrears and did not wish to take a degree anyway, and very occasionally the tutor had to bear the loss himself.[26]

One such case plagued James Wood, tutor of St John's, who left copious evidence of his scrupulous and conscientious character. In

[23] Cooper, *Annals*, IV, pp. 167–8. 350; PP 1852–3: *Graham Commission Report*, p. 82.
[24] Walsh, *Historical Account of the University of Cambridge*, pp. 36–7.
[25] See for example the bill that Brown sent to Wright on Lady Day 1820, reproduced in *Alma Mater*, vol. II, p. 112.
[26] Malcolm G. Underwood, 'A Tutor's Lot', *Eagle*, 69 (1984), especially the letter quoted on p. 3.

1790 the college matriculated William Whelpdale, an illegitimate protégé of the Earl of Lonsdale. Lonsdale was described by Alexander Carlyle as 'truly a madman, though too rich to be confined': 'more detested than any man alive, as a shameless political sharper, a domestic bashaw, and an intolerable tyrant over his tenants and dependents'.[27] Whelpdale went down after three terms, leaving a debt of £274 9s 3d – 'a sum [Wood wrote to Lonsdale] of very great importance to me, and which I trust your lordship will now order to be remitted'.[28] That was in April 1792. Wood wrote to the earl five times in the next eight years, without result. Lonsdale dying in May 1802, Wood applied to Lord Lowther in June, and was told that the amount would be considered with other demands against the estate; he was still trying in May 1804, when corroboration was proving difficult because of the death of the Lancaster solicitor who had secured Whelpdale's admission fourteen years before: 'the Master of St. John's, Dr Craven, however, recollects the transaction, and I have Mr. Saul's letters which I will, if your Lordship's steward wishes it, transmit to him'.[29] Nothing was heard, and Wood seems finally to have dropped the matter. Lonsdale's default was exceptional, it should be noted; Wood's letter book records only four other (and lesser) cases of bad debt over fifteen years.

Among Whelpdale's debts there were, no doubt, sums owed to Cambridge shopkeepers.[30] In most colleges tutors accepted bills from Cambridge tradesmen for 'necessities', such as 'grocers, tailors, hosiers, shoemakers, hatters, booksellers, and licensed lodging-house keepers', and gave accounts their sanction so that parents were more likely to settle them promptly, through the tutor, who would in due course pay the tradesmen. In this way tutors could watch for signs of overcharging by shopkeepers as well as of student extravagance. Apart from the power they had to suggest the names of approved tradesmen, tutors could get those guilty of bad dealing 'discommuned', though this severe punishment was rarely inflicted.

The threat of discommuning reflected the grip the university had

[27] Alexander Carlyle, *Autobiography* (3rd edn, Edinburgh, 1861), pp. 418–19.
[28] St John's College Archives, TU.1.1.2, letter book of James Wood, 1792–1807.
[29] St John's College Archives, TU.1.1.2, Wood to Lord Lowther, 25 May 1804.
[30] For what follows, see PP 1852–3: *Graham Commission Evidence*, pp. 140–217.

long had over townspeople. As we have seen, in Victorian times they had a new self-confidence, and they increasingly resented their subordination.[31] In 1844 some shopkeepers brought actions against students for the recovery of debt without previously informing their tutors. Tutors were quick to retaliate, pushing the heads of houses into threatening discommuning for shopkeepers who took such action. This warning was not lightly meant; in February 1848 a local hairdresser was discommuned for a month for suing, without giving previous notice to his tutor, a BA of Trinity who had gone down and was living in Yorkshire. The debts had been incurred while he was *in statu pupillari*, which for the university was the crucial point.[32] Tutors were touchy over the growing public criticism of their alleged neglect of duty; the royal commission was seen by many as a threat. Pride brought tutors and shopkeepers into conflict. In 1847 the tutors induced the heads of houses to order local tradesmen (under pain of discommuning) to send to tutors each quarter the names of pupils owing more than £5. In the settlement of disputes between town and gown in 1856 the university sacrificed the 1844 rule, but the 1847 one remained as part of the range of powers over pupils that tutors retained for many decades – but very few of which they still possess.[33]

Victorian tutors were confident that their powers sufficed to control the compliant majority. They were unhappy about the tiny minority, estimated by Henry Latham of Trinity Hall to be 1 per cent, who were extravagant and reckless, and who were eagerly abetted in their folly by confectioners, wine merchants, and horse-dealers. Students who cocked a snook at the Cambridge rules might run up debts all over town but keep each one below £5, or borrow cash from shopkeepers under the fiction of buying goods, or deal with London tradesmen, who were quite outside the tutors' authority.[34] James Cove Jones, matriculating at St John's in 1807, managed very soon to outwit his family and his tutor, James Wood. In October 1808 Jones's guardian told Wood 'that the extravagance of J. C. Jones makes it necessary to adopt strict measures of

---

[31] See above, pp. 51–2.   [32] Cooper, *Annals*, IV, pp. 667–8.
[33] Winstanley, *Early Victorian Cambridge*, pp. 137–8; Cooper, *Annals*, IV, p. 195; P.G. 19 & 20 Vict. c. 88: *An Act to make further Provision for the good Government and Extension of the University of Cambridge*.
[34] PP 1852–3: *Graham Commission Evidence*, pp. 140–217.

restraint'. Wood was to allow £50 a quarter for Jones's bills, an ample amount for keep and tuition, with a modest £5 for pocket money. Wood was to order any books Jones needed. 'I am also to acquaint the tradesmen that any extravagant bills will not in future be paid.'[35] Early in 1809, however, the 'tradesmen pretended particularly the taylor, not to have received or to have forgotten the order'[36] and so were able to indulge Jones with goods he bought on credit all over the city; the extent of his bills became apparent only after Jones left Cambridge in the summer to read medicine at Edinburgh. Wood thought that 'tradesmen who are so ready to furnish young men with every article of luxury and extravagance deserve punishment. I will send for some of them in a day or two & consider what steps are to be taken . . . I will take all the blame of the non-payment of the bills upon myself.'[37] A week later Wood reported: 'Have seen Pratt, Curtis, Beales and Rutledge [Cambridge shopkeepers] who could give no satisfactory reason for having trusted J. C. Jones. Hope all may be delayed till they feel impropriety of conduct.'[38] As to stopping credit for pupils really determined to get it, Joseph Blakesley, tutor of Trinity, wearily commented: 'A college tutor is . . . quite as helpless . . . as the colonel of the regiment of Life Guards is with regard to the subaltern officers.'[39]

One of the tutor's chief tasks was to guard the welfare of his pupils, the great majority of whom were legally minors; towards them the tutor was *in loco parentis*, to use a phrase often uttered in Cambridge. Pupils needed their authority to leave Cambridge during the term and to live outside college – even though many had to in the great expansion of undergraduate numbers that followed the French wars; for example, in 1822 (before Wilkins's New Court was built) only 100 out of the 350 members of Trinity were able to live in the college itself. Alleged undergraduate orgies, their quantities of drink and numbers of prostitutes probably much exaggerated in the telling at tutors' gatherings, seemed to be corroborated by the death from exposure, one night in February 1818, of a drunken undergraduate who had fallen into a ditch on

[35] St John's College Archives, M.I.3, Abstract letter book of James Wood, 1808–36, 1 October 1808.
[36] Ibid, 7 February 1809.   [37] Ibid., 2 January 1810.   [38] Ibid 9 January 1810.
[39] PP 1852–3: *Graham Commission Evidence*, p. 147.

his way home from a lodging house in Bridge Street. A committee of tutors thereupon suggested regulations which the heads of houses approved and which demonstrate the tutors' determination to keep a tight control over their pupils' morals. Lodging-house keepers were in future licensed by the Vice-Chancellor and Proctors, on condition they pledged to inform an undergraduate's tutor if he returned after 10 pm, and even to refuse to supply supper without tutorial sanctions. Tutors inspected their college's lodging houses, of which in the 1820s there were over 200 in Cambridge. Probably it was the difficulty tutors faced in inspecting widely dispersed lodgings that caused the decision, in 1826, not to license any more houses outside a half-mile radius from Great St Mary's.[40]

As at Christ's in Gunning's description, in the second half of the eighteenth century in most colleges two tutors seem to have divided the tuition between them. Such a pattern may be discerned at the beginning of the following century, when there were 31 tutors for the 16 established colleges, and in addition 12 or 15 assistant tutors or lecturers, sharing teaching but not the pastoral and financial responsibilities of the tutors proper. St John's had 3 tutors with 3 assistants, and Trinity 2 with 4. At the other extreme, King's had merely one tutor, whose duties must have been varied. By 1830 the total of assistants had doubled, the number of tutors remaining the same. St John's now had 8 teachers altogether, and Trinity 9, while smaller colleges possessed 2 or 3, and King's, still just one. By the middle of the century there were 34 tutors, but over 40 assistants, 10 of them at Trinity. At the same time there were 356 fellows, between one-quarter and one-fifth of whom were therefore engaged in official college teaching.[41] This increased establishment made possible specialised teaching, at all events in the larger colleges. At Trinity junior sophisters were divided into two sets, by mathematical proficiency, and seniors into three, while a small college like Corpus had separate sessions for 'high and low honourmen'.

[40] Winstanley, *Early Victorian Cambridge*, pp. 58–60; PP 1852–3: *Graham Commission Evidence*, pp. 156–7; Cooper, *Annals*, IV, pp. 520, 553.
[41] *Cambridge University Calendar for ... 1802*, pp. 61–130; *Cambridge University Calendar for ... 1830*, pp. 228–371; *Cambridge University Calendar for ... 1850*, pp. 198–347.

PRIVATE TUTORS

This official teaching was not the only sort, since as tutors grew in number so did 'private tutors', instructors paid by students themselves, as a result of the Senate House Examination and the competitive spirit it helped to engender. Richard Watson supplemented his meagre resources by becoming a private tutor in 1756 (just a few years after the examination began) when he was merely a junior sophister, a second-year undergraduate;[42] and by the 1760s it seems to have been believed that private tutors were advisable for men desiring high honours.[43] Private tuition led to accusations that examiners showed favouritism towards their private pupils; Richard Watson, Second Wrangler in 1759, thought he lost the senior position to a lesser mathematician, Massey of St John's, who was a private pupil of another Johnian who also happened to be a senior moderator.[44] Anxiety was general enough for the Senate to agree in 1781 to a grace excluding from honours those who had employed a private tutor within two years of the Senate House Examination. But private tutors (themselves members of the Senate) disliked the rule, and in 1807, 1815, and 1824 it was successively reduced to six months. In fact, the legislation seems never to have been taken seriously anyway,[45] while by the nineteenth century the existence of the partiality so feared earlier was explicitly disavowed.[46] The growth in the number of candidates and examiners, to cite an obvious material circumstance, would have made favouritism at least very difficult.

In 1800 private tutors were still uncommon, college lectures being regarded as sufficient by many students.[47] The dramatic rise in the number of private tutors came about 1830, with the increasing demands of the Senate House Examination, for which official college teaching was inadequate. Colleges, like modern comprehensive schools in accommodating an immensely wide spectrum of talent, did not create groups of sufficiently equal competence in the

---

[42] Richard Watson, ed., *Anecdotes of the Life of Richard Watson, Bishop of Llandaff* (London, 1817), pp. 10–11.
[43] Edward Thomas Vaughan, *Some Account of the Rev. Thomas Robinson*, p. 29.
[44] Watson, (ed.), *Anecdotes*, p. 18.   [45] Winstanley, *Unreformed Cambridge*, pp. 332–3.
[46] Gunning, *Reminiscences*, vol. I, p. xx.
[47] George Pryme, *Autobiographic Recollections* (Cambridge, 1870), p. 48.

simple 'streaming' they managed in their official teaching, especially since in mathematics differences in intellect have an immediate and acute effect on performance; in addition, many freshmen came up to Cambridge very ill prepared. Private tuition (usually one-to-one, though the tutors most in demand taught in classes) was therefore regarded as essential in the middle of the century. Three undergraduates in four had recourse to one for at least part of their ten terms, paying £14 a term for an hour's tuition every weekday, or £7 for alternate days; a long-vacation tutor cost £30, and help at Christmas or Easter, £10. Even at Trinity, priding itself on the efficacy of its college teaching, it was usual for honours men to have help from a 'half-tutor' for three terms, while the 7 or 8 per cent of its undergraduates who were hoping for the highest wranglerships turned to one of the top men for six terms and two long vacations. 'In a small College [averred the Revd C. A. Swainson of Christ's in 1851] the funds provided for maintaining the staff of Tutors and Lecturers are not sufficient for such a multiplication of Lecturers as would render private Tuition unnecessary.'[48]

Private coaches were useful for many candidates for ordinary degrees, 'persons of idle habits or inferior abilities', whose crammers 'were rarely men of any superior attainment'[49] and lacked honours degrees themselves. All the honours coaches had come up the Cambridge ladder, and indeed there was nowhere else they could acquire the special expertise necessary. Some half-dozen or so were full-time professionals. One such man was Richard Shilleto, the leading classical coach for thirty years, who ministered to the needs resulting from the institution of the Classical Tripos in 1824. He graduated Second Classic in 1832 (while showing his comparative incompetence at mathematics by being 'Wooden Spoon').[50] An early marriage removed the chance of a Trinity fellowship, and he stayed outside the dons' innermost circle until elected a fellow of Peterhouse in 1867.[51] Shilleto supported his large family by teaching

---

[48] PP 1852–3: *Graham Commission Evidence*, pp. 193 and 140–217 for this section generally. The relationship of one undergraduate, William Thomson, with his private tutor William Hopkins, is described in chapter 17.

[49] *Graham Commission Evidence*, pp. 165 and 198.

[50] The Wooden Spoon was the last junior optime, scraping into the honours list, and so (in Shilleto's day) barely qualifying to attempt the Classical Tripos. Below him were the great mass of poll men, with ordinary degrees.

[51] He was the first man to be elected under a new college statute permitting married fellows.

(at all events during full term) from 9.0 am till 8.0 pm. He stimulated his energies by a constant supply of tea or beer, his pint mug of the latter being refilled through a hatch near his chair; and he punctuated his teaching with frequent pinches of snuff from a packet on the table before him, while the floor was littered with discarded handkerchiefs and books. But, said a pupil about his learning, 'he spoke with authority, and the outpouring of references (by chapter section or line), without opening a book, simply took your breath away. If you turned them out afterwards, lo they were correct. Truly an astounding feat of memory.'[52] Though one of the greatest Greek scholars of his generation in Cambridge, Shilleto's publications were few; he was a *teacher*, rather than a *writer* as a modern don is assumed to be.

Most private tutors were young (and of course unmarried) fellows, teaching the arcane learning they had recently acquired – and naturally adding noticeably to their dividends by doing so; a private tutor taking two pupils for three terms and three vacations earned £184 for daily tuition. The term 'private tutor' was therefore somewhat misleading, since such a person was for all practical purposes an inseparable part of the university system; only his contract of payment was 'private'. It would have improved matters to 'either double or treble the public tuition (as a matter of ultimate economy), and then by means of this source of income employ the whole body of resident Fellows as a staff, distributing the different subjects in such a manner as to secure competent lecturers or teachers in each department'.[53] But dons were much slower to recommend this remedy than its obvious merits might suggest to us, and their readiness to stick to an arrangement that was both irrational and financially advantageous to individuals helps to explain why tidy-minded reformers were so suspicious of them. There were naturally strong doubts about the real educational value of private tuition. It was cramming for examinations, thus 'preventing that salutary intellectual discipline which arises from the student having to overcome difficulties for himself'.

A 'market' defence of private tuition could be advanced: it enabled pupils to buy exactly what help they needed. The strongest

---

[52] W. E. Heitland, *After Many Years* (Cambridge University Press, 1926), pp. 129–30.
[53] PP 1852–3: *Graham Commission Evidence*, p. 202, and p. 204 for the following quotation.

indictment of the system, however, was that private tuition led to a neglect of the official instruction that colleges existed to provide. 'The public lecturer', reported the Senior Fellow of Pembroke, the Reverend H. Arlett, 'has no inducement to exert himself when he finds his best pupils pre-occupied by their private tutors'; his lecture, in consequence, 'usually takes the form of a short daily examination'.[54] W. E. Heitland's judgement on his 'deeply learned' tutors in the late 1860s at St John's (by general consent offering with Trinity the best college instruction) was that

> somehow we did not seem to profit much by their instruction . . . they did not study their pupils personally so as to diagnose individual cases. Even the set lectures to full classrooms were apt to be a blend of what men either knew already or did not want to know at all. Graves was an exception . . . and Mathematical men spoke well of Horne, if he were out of bed in time for an 8 o'clock lecture. Those Classical lecturers who took the small Composition classes were generally content with exposing grammatical blunders and giving you a 'fair copy'.[55]

At Caius in the 1850s, 'we all alike had to attend the same lecture', despite their great variety of attainments:

> the destined high wrangler, who had read his conic sections as a schoolboy, and the youth to whom Euclid and his mysterious pictures were a daily puzzle . . . Under the circumstances of our lecture system you will understand that it was quite natural to say, as one came out of the room, 'Now I can begin my work'; and that no sarcasm was intended when we agreed that one great advantage of the Long Vacation was that we were then entirely unhindered by lectures.[56]

WEALTH AND ITS MANAGEMENT

LAND, LEASES, AND DIVIDENDS

At college feasts thanks were given to the benefactors whose generosity had made possible the subsistence and comfort of master,

---

[54] PP 1852–3: *Graham Commission Evidence*, pp. 143–4. D'Arcy Wentworth Thompson, at Pembroke from 1849 to 1852, felt at his first classical lecture that he was back as a junior at Christ's Hospital, while the mathematical tutor 'muttered in an indistinct voice some puerilities regarding mathematical trifles that had been familiar to me for years': *Wayside Thoughts* (Edinburgh, 1868), pp. 95–9.   [55] Heitland, *After Many Years*, p. 128.   [56] Venn, *Early Collegiate Life*, pp. 258–9.

fellows, and scholars. A typical gift was made in 1515 to Catharine Hall by 'John Mylbourn and Joan his wife',[57] and consisted of £124 to buy land of the clear annual value of ten marks, which was to maintain as a fellow 'an honest priest of good name, fame and conversation, and a Master of Arts and student in Divinity'. By virtue of such benefactions, St Catharine's, like other colleges, came to possess widely scattered estates. In the detailed inventory of 1872,[58] the college owned fifty parcels of land in Cambridgeshire, Essex, Lincolnshire, and Yorkshire, ranging in size from a holding of 329 acres in Fockerby (Yorkshire) to a plot of 5 perches in Linton-on-Ouse; since colleges were precluded by Elizabethan legislation from alienating land the 1872 survey gives a helpful impression of the distribution of their holdings a century or two earlier (though of course colleges also bought land with surplus cash). In addition, St Catharine's possessed fifteen cottages in Queens' Lane, Silver Street, and Trumpington Street, Cambridge – occupied in 1872 mostly by college servants. Other colleges were similarly endowed; Cambridge was a sort of 'company town', and no county in England lacked its scattering of college lands.

Colleges had other sorts of property too.[59] Rectorial tithes might be donated or purchased on lands that a college did not own; often the tithes were leased to the vicar, as St John's for three centuries did with the tithes of Holme on Spalding Moor (Yorkshire) that it bought with a bequest in 1638; but sometimes it was worthwhile to collect the tithes in kind, and in 1822 St John's built an expensive barn in Cherry Marham (Norfolk) to contain the tithes that Sir Ralph Hare had given the college the right to in 1623. Advowsons were bought by colleges too – useful properties for societies wishing to find livings for fellows displaced on marriage. A minor source of

---

[57] W. H. S. Jones, *A History of St. Catharine's College once Catharine Hall Cambridge* (Cambridge University Press, 1936), p. 209.

[58] PP 1873, HC xxxvii (iii) [C.856–II]: *Report of the Commissioners appointed to Inquire into the Property and Income of the Universities of Oxford and Cambridge and of the Colleges and Halls therein [Cleveland Commission]* vol. III, *Returns from the University of Cambridge, and from the Colleges therein*, pp. 250–9.

[59] What follows is drawn from Howard, *Finances of St. John's College*; the chapter by J.P. Dunbabin, 'College Estates and Wealth 1660–1815', in L. S. Sutherland and L. G. Mitchell, eds., *The History of the University of Oxford, vol. V, The Eighteenth Century* (Oxford, Clarendon, 1986), pp. 269–301; E. J. Gross, *Chronicle of the College Estates* (Part 2 of John Venn, E. S. Roberts and E. J. Gross, *Biographical History of Gonville and Caius College*, vol. IV, Cambridge University Press, 1912), pp. i–x; and Twigg, *A History of Queens' College, Cambridge*, pp. 110–20, 300–5.

income was 'profits of courts' – the right to take manorial dues from its tenants; colleges might also have to pay them, in respect of lands it had by copyhold where the manorial rights were owned by somebody else. In 1857 St John's spent a substantial sum enfranchising its Kentish Town copyholds. Colleges also had some stocks and shares, perhaps starting with investment in the South Sea scheme and going on later in the eighteenth century to Consols and canal and turnpike ventures. But these were essentially outlets for surplus balances. As they had since their foundation (and as for that matter did the cathedral chapters, almshouses, and hospitals that in wealth they may be compared with) colleges drew most of their income from land. Rarely farming it directly, they leased it.

Until 1858 colleges were controlled in their leasing policy by several Elizabethan statutes. They could not sell it, or lease land for more than twenty-one years or three lives, forty years being however the limit for houses. Lastly, at least one-third of rent was to be index-linked to the market-price of wheat. Thus while inflation made colleges' fixed statutory stipends valueless, corn-rents were a way of keeping ahead of it. Like churches and other corporate owners of property, colleges let their freehold land on 'beneficial' leases; a low unchanging customary rent was complemented by a large entry fine for renewal. Entry fines, like corn-rents, gave colleges a means of profiting from inflation. They were usually paid after 7 years of the lease had elapsed (or 14 years in the case of urban property); following the fine the lease would be extended for a further 20 or 40 years, so the fine-payer was in effect buying the renewal of the original lease 13 or 25 years ahead. The way beneficial leases worked may be illustrated from the example from Muggington, in Derbyshire, where St John's bought an estate of 88 acres in 1590, with a bequest. In 1783 it was leased to Lord Scarsdale for 20 years at a customary rent of £26 and a fine of £299. In 1800 the lease was renewed for 9 times the net annual value, or £470. Further renewals followed in 1807 for £161, in 1826 for £815, and in 1833, 1840, and 1847 for £230 on each occasion. Lord Scarsdale bought the land outright in 1866 for £6,860, the Universities and Colleges Estates Act of 1858 having made land sales possible.

Beneficial leases were often taken out by middlemen who sub-let land to the actual cultivator. They could be profitable to the leaseholder, and there was competition for them. The leaseholder was in a strong position; if he declined to renew mid-term the lessor would have to wait till the lease expired to get his entry fine. On the other hand at a time when rents were static or falling, as in the early eighteenth century, rack-rent leases might be no advantage to the landowners. The great benefit of long leases to absentee owners such as colleges was that they did not constantly have to discover how profitable their soil was: a task that would have been considered burdensome before the new professional land agents became common and roads improved at the end of the eighteenth century; in 1788 Henry Gunning had to travel very hard for three days to get from Cambridge to Herefordshire.[60]

By the time of the Civil War it was an established practice to pay fellows dividends made up of entry fines, corn-rents, and all kinds of other minor dues. By the eighteenth century dividends formed the most important item in fellows' income, dwarfing the old fixed statutory fees and reflecting agricultural prosperity.[61] In St John's the dividend for junior fellows, the great majority, was £20 in 1736, and rose to £40 in 1755, £50 in 1775, £70 in 1795, £100 in 1801, £150 in 1818, and £160 in 1821.[62] Similar rises occurred elsewhere. At Emmanuel dividends were increased on five occasions between 1807 and 1861, when fellows received between £268 and £318 according to their status.[63] In 1850 fellows' emoluments varied between £140 (for junior fellows) at St John's and £330 at Magdalene, plus free food and (usually) free rooms. A fellow's income depended on the wealth of his college, and on the number of fellows it was shared among; St John's, though corporately one of the richest, gave a low amount to each fellow because it had so many.[64]

With some fluctuations, the years 1750 to 1815 were a boom time for the colleges. They watched the progress of agriculture closely,

---

[60] Christopher Clay, 'Landlords and Estate Management in England', in Joan Thirsk, ed., *The Agrarian History of England and Wales, vol. V, 1640–1750, part 2, Agrarian Change* (Cambridge University Press, 1985) esp. pp. 201–2; Gunning, *Reminiscences*, vol. I, pp. 96–8.

[61] On the many minor sources of fellows' income, see pp. 139–40 below.

[62] The eight most senior fellows of St John's received dividends one and a half times greater than a junior's.

[63] E. S. Shuckburgh, *Emmanuel College*, College Histories Series (London, 1904), pp. 170–1.

[64] PP 1852–3: *Graham Commission Report*, p. 167. Downing, a new and impoverished college, gave its fellows £100.

investing large sums in constructing new farmhouses and enclosing open fields. Between 1770 and 1813 enclosure cost St John's over £8,000, or more than one year's income. The boom finished with the French wars, and the depression that followed lasted till the late 1830s caused belt-tightening in colleges. In St John's, where the slump was aggravated by the incompetence of Charles Blick (bursar 1816–46), the dividend, £160 in 1821, was reduced to £100 in 1830 and fluctuated till 1847 when it was raised to £140. At Queens' in the 1820s feasts were twice reduced in number, fellow commoners' fees were raised, and debtors actively pursued. Rents began to pick up again in the 1830s, and from the 1840s to the mid-1870s there was an agricultural boom – the mid-Victorian Golden Age – from which colleges profited greatly.[65] Dividends rose. The St John's dividend was £300 in the early 1870s, and other colleges raised stipends similarly.[66]

From about 1830 colleges increasingly replaced beneficial leases with rack-rents (annual renewable tenancies), sharing the dislike of long leases generally that landlords and tenants alike felt in the early nineteenth century. Such leases made it hard for owners to benefit from rising prices (as in the French wars) but also forced them to grant abatements during depressions. Tenants often feared that they might never recoup their investment in the farm that a lease made them responsible for.[67] Of the twelve colleges that gave details of their finances to the Graham Commission eight reported that they were ending their beneficial leases, while three more had never had many.[68] Rack-renting exploited college estates more efficiently. The mid-Victorian urban housing boom was another opportunity for the many colleges with land strategically placed. Letting land on lease and then drawing ground rents was the obvious expedient, but colleges were hampered by Elizabethan legislation that forbade leases of more than forty years, a limit that discouraged property developers; until 1858 colleges had to circumvent it with legal

[65] Some enjoyed large windfalls from coprolites mined on their estates. In the 1860s St John's coprolite receipts totalled £12,595, almost half one year's gross income. See also Peile, *Christ's College*, p. 284.
[66] See Shuckburgh, *Emmanuel College*, pp. 170–1, and Peile, *Christ's College*, pp. 257–84.
[67] J. V. Beckett, 'Landownership and Estate Management', in G. E. Mingay (ed.), *The Agrarian History of England and Wales, vol. VI, 1750–1850* (Cambridge University Press, 1989), pp. 612–15.
[68] PP 1852–3: *Graham Commission Report*, pp. 197–8. See also J. R. Wardale, *Clare College*, College Histories Series (London, 1899), pp. 204–5; and Peile, *Christ's College*, p. 284.

ingenuity. The Universities and Colleges Estates Act, 1858,[69] allowed colleges to create building leases of up to ninety-nine years' duration, and assisted the more profitable use of urban land. Building leases provided an increasing share of colleges' income, and helped to tide them over the Great Depression that had such dire effects on agricultural rents (and on colleges abnormally dependent on them). Colleges' gross income from land declined from £135,200 in 1871 to £119,800 in 1913, while from houses it rose from £22,600 to £62,500 in the same period.[70] College enterprise in the housing market may be best seen, naturally enough, in Cambridge itself; the enclosure of the parish of Barnwell (St Andrew the Less) in 1807 was followed by the leasing of much college land for building purposes, distinguished college members being commemorated in street names such as Glisson and Harvey in the Caius estate to the east of Hills Road that was developed after 1870. These two roads reveal, in their architectural contrast, a policy of targeting different layers of tenantry within the middle class, while the terraced houses that Caius developed off Mill Road in the 1880s and later (and named after Caians such as Willis, Guest, and Mackenzie) were aimed at artisans. A similar variety of customers was in mind for the Trinity Hall Newtown estate, with artisan property in Norwich Street and middle-class villas in Bateman Street. Such adroit grasping of opportunity suggests how prudently collegiate wealth was husbanded at the end of the nineteenth century.[71]

BURSARS AND ACCOUNTS

Colleges spent their income on maintaining their master, fellows, and scholars and the army of servants this task made necessary. They repaired and extended college buildings (sometimes doing so almost bankrupted a college, as for example the construction of the New

---

[69] P.G. 21 & 22 Vict., c. 44.

[70] J. P. Dunbabin, 'Oxford and Cambridge College Finances, 1871–1913', *Economic History Review*, 2nd series, 28, 4 (November 1973), p. 638. A few colleges whose different sources of income are hard to separate are omitted from the calculation by Dunbabin.

[71] Christopher Brooke, *Gonville and Caius College*, p. 252. College land in this area, from Trumpington Road to the river, is shown on the enclosure award map for the parish of St Andrew the Less (1807): Cambridgeshire County Record Office.

Court of St John's in the 1820s), and kept their agricultural estates in trim by draining and enclosing land and building farmhouses. Items such as taxes, fire insurance, and donations to charities were also costly. College accounts were necessarily complicated, and were often made more so by book-keeping techniques that obscured balances and by the traditional practice of tying items of expenditure to specific receipts. 'Between the 16th and 19th centuries, as in the cathedral chapters, every office, every fellowship and scholarship was a kind of benefice, separately funded, separately endowed.'[72] In St John's, for example, the bequest of William Platt in 1684, consisting of estates in London and Kentish Town, was kept separate from the main college accounts till 1858, while the nine exhibitions founded by James Wood, Master of St John's 1815–39, were linked to the receipts from land at Chawridge, Berkshire. Complexity also attended the remuneration of college fellows and officers, largely because the stipends set down in ancient statutes had by the eighteenth century been made derisory by inflation, and it was easier to add other payments from various sources than it was to change the statutes.[73] Once instituted these separate payments were not consolidated. The most important was the dividend that had become common by 1640. There were many smaller ones too. The statutory stipend of the Master of St John's was £14 12s, but he received in 1770 an extra total of £173 13s 4d under eight different heads including dividends of £120, £2 allowed for pigeon corn and £12 as a substitute payment for 120 lb of brawn, and half the college admission fees.[74] At Emmanuel, likewise, the fellows added to their dividends and their stipend of £5 buttery profits amounting to £10 each, and shared each month a levy of 4s on every 240 loaves the college bought (the butler getting another 1s); the lecturer's meagre stipend was supplemented by levies of 1d a quarter on every undergraduate.[75]

It was sometimes hard to persuade one of the fellows to become

[72] Christopher Brooke, *Gonville and Caius College*, p. 102.
[73] It was for this reason that when tutors became fully responsible for college teaching they were given receipt of the tutorial fees and so built up financial systems separate from their colleges.
[74] Howard, *Finances of St. John's College*, pp. 132–7.
[75] Emmanuel College Archives: MSS 3.2.21, William Bennet's Register, vol. 1 (1773), p. 89; MSS STE 1.6, Steward's Accounts 1759–72, p. 1, 'Directions for making up the accounts'. See also Shuckburgh, *Emmanuel College*, pp. 146–50.

bursar and administer this jungle of anomalies and perquisites. Colleges might in desperation force fellows to take on the job in rotation,[76] but that might mean a succession of novices never in the job long enough to learn it properly. A bursar happy to stay in post would probably not be disturbed, and so would be able to exploit the jungle to his own advantage. In the first half of the eighteenth century the senior bursar of St John's was able to bank in his own name the surpluses that were accruing and take the interest on them (thus imitating the tutor) without having to submit to regular audit. Because of this latitude William Wood,[77] senior bursar from 1795 to 1797, was able to speculate with college money which was then lost in a banking crisis, leaving a deficiency of between £4,000 and £5,000 that caused a reduction in dividend and was recovered by the college with difficulty. Bursars were also able to buy goods at one price and sell to the college at a higher one, and to take commission from suppliers too. At St John's a college order of 1769 laid down that

> the Junior Bursar for the future shall make no charge to the College for any additional price of charcoal beyond what he pays, or for boiling brawn; nor shall receive any present from the charcoal merchant; nor shall claim any old iron or copper out of the kitchen which shall always be sold for the benefit of the College, and that in lieu of the above perquisites he shall charge the College in his own accounts the sum of £22 yearly.[78]

This order was part of the financial reforms devised by William Samuel Powell, Master of St John's from 1765 to 1775 and diehard Tory – as opposed to removing the disabilities of Dissenters as he was enthusiastic about improving the administration of his college.[79] He began the semi-annual examinations of St John's undergraduates, and introduced a clearer and more logical system of accounts that made it easier for contemporaries (and historians) to assess the college's financial condition. Powell began a process of financial rationalisation that continued after his death. In particular,

[76] See, for example, Thomas Alfred Walker, *Peterhouse* (Cambridge, Heffer, 1935), p. 77, and Twigg, *A History of Queens' College*, p. 303.

[77] His brother James had been senior bursar before him; neither is to be confused with James Wood, tutor from 1789 to 1814 and master from 1815 to 1839.

[78] Howard, *Finances of St. John's College*, p. 136.   [79] Miller, *Portrait of a College*, pp. 64–8.

fellows' perquisites in kind were steadily commuted for cash allowances that were easily monitored. For example, in 1779 the bursar was allowed five guineas a year in lieu of his perquisites of wine, and in 1787 one guinea for his loss of brawn and capons. Many of the most glaring perquisites had been ended by 1828. The follies of William Wood in the 1790s showed that stricter control of college funds was necessary, and this was realised in 1802. An order enforced deposit of monies in a college bank, though interest on it was to be shared among the officers – an indication of how prevalent still was the notion of remuneration by fees. Still, the tutor's transactions – dealing with the heart of the college's educational function – remained outside the college accounts, while the career of Charles Blick, senior bursar of St John's from 1816 to 1846, shows how greatly the college administration needed to be reformed in the early nineteenth century. Blick was left by his colleagues to get on with the job, but mismanaged the financing of the construction of New Court, meeting little of the cost through revenues and so incurring excessive loans and interest. As Howard wrote in the 1930s, 'It is difficult to condone the application to College finance of methods following the lines of the hire purchase system.'[80] When Blick was dismissed by the fellowship in 1846 (he was presented to a college living as compensation) St John's was left with unclear accounts and a burden of debt costing £3,000 a year to service.

Balances were created and accounting procedures transformed by William Henry Bateson, senior bursar from 1846 to 1857. He was secretary to the Graham Commission of 1852, played a large part in amending the statutes of St John's in 1848 and 1857–60, and as master of the college from 1857 to 1881 presided over it in years of crucial change; Bateson stood at the centre of university reform. The Graham Commission had remarkably little to say about college finances, but the demand for change, expressed in commission, country, and colleges themselves, could not have been met without rational and efficient administration. The revised statutes of St John's of 1860 recognised the need; building on Bateson's work as bursar, 'they mark a complete departure from the earlier codes.

[80] Howard, *Finances of St. John's College*, p. 172.

They omitted all reference to obsolete offices, emoluments and practices ... and they provided for the developments of the future by giving the College power to create new offices and to assign suitable stipends to the holders thereof.'[81] As a result of the new statutes and of regulations based upon them, the Platt foundation was merged with the college's main estates and a fixed stipend for the master replaced the medley of ancient payments. Similar rationalisation occurred with the fellows' dividend; ancient offices were abolished and the duties of others more fittingly defined; detailed provision was made for the audit of accounts, and the governing body was to have control of the tuition fees, even though they were to continue to be paid to the tutors. Many of the mid-Victorian reforms were administrative in nature. The process of change, known to us in detail in the case of St John's, may be traced in other colleges, though earlier generations of college historians tended to ignore so mundane a matter as perquisites and audit.[82]

SERVANTS

Colleges were households, the master and fellows (and in term the undergraduates) taking the place of the noble or gentle family whose comfort, health, and worldly contentment it was the function of a host of servants to serve. This provision was a prerequisite for a college's higher activities, yet it is singularly ignored in most college histories that dilate on the triumphs of the boat club, and is scarcely mentioned in the 900 pages of the eighteenth-century volume on the history of the University of Oxford. Many people are in this fashion hidden from history. Two conflicting tendencies affected servant numbers. One, economy, reduced them, while another – a lesser force, however – was pushing them up. Until the second half of the eighteenth century such waiting at table as was undertaken was the responsibility of sizars, and sometimes scholars. Sizars were relieved of these menial tasks between 1760 and 1790: at Caius in 1767, at Queens' in 1773,

---

[81] Howard, *Finances of St. John's College*, p. 192.
[82] Wardale, *Clare College*, p. 207; Shuckburgh, *Emmanuel College*, pp. 170–1; Christopher Brooke, *Gonville and Caius College*, pp. 251–2; Twigg, *A History of Queens' College*, pp. 306–7.

and at St John's (where scholars gave up waiting in 1765) in 1786.[83] Women bedmakers were employed instead to wait at table.

Early in the nineteenth century, if we judge from incomplete yet complementary sources, St John's College had about 140 servants (100 being bedmakers or laundresses) and in 1870 after several economy drives it had about 110.[84] In the same period its total of undergraduates rose from 125 in 1800 to 361 in 1870, while its fellows totalled about 55 throughout the period. The ratio of servants to gentlemen resident at St John's was therefore about 3 : 4 in 1800 and 1 : 4 in 1870. The application of these ratios to university totals suggests that there may have been about 750 college servants in 1800 and the same number seventy years later. But there are many imponderables in this estimate, not the least being that many servants may not have been in full-time employment and may therefore have figured on the books of several colleges.

Like dons, college servants were traditionally paid in part by fees and perquisites. It was easy to use them to supplement established stipends that were laughably small, and no doubt this explains the levies of a few pennies a term that in the eighteenth century undergraduates at Emmanuel paid to the gardener, cooks, janitor, and the library-keeper.[85] At St John's early in the nineteenth century undergraduates paid fees to servants when they first dined in hall, when they changed their status and their table, and when they took degrees, while the chapel-clerk took fees from newly elected fellows and scholars. Much more substantial amounts were accumulated by cooks and butlers, at the top of the college hierarchy; they ran kitchens partly as personal ventures, taking large profits from a clientele that was captive or complaisant, charging over the odds for incidental meals in individuals' rooms, and exploiting their perquisites of 'waste' food and drink – still today an

---

[83] John Venn, *Caius College*, College Histories Series (London, Robinson, 1901), pp. 191–4; Twigg, *A History of Queens' College*, p. 193; Malcolm Underwood, 'Restructuring a Household. Service and its Nineteenth Century Critics in St. John's', *Eagle*, 72 (1990), p. 10. These paragraphs are greatly indebted to Malcolm Underwood's pioneering article.

[84] St John's College Archives: JB 3.1, First Junior Bursar's Account, 1807–29; TUI.3.2, Payments to bedmakers and laundresses, 1839–53; C5.4, Conclusion book 1846–72, order concerning appointment and dismissal of college servants, 17 March 1860; D33.10.21, Lists of college suppers for servants, 1864–9.

[85] Emmanuel College Archives MSS STE.1.6, Steward's Accounts 1759–72, p. 1, 'Directions for making up the accounts'.

area that catering managers find it hard to fix bounds to. In St John's in the 1760s the money needed to provide 'commons' was 'left entirely to the management of the butler, who, finding that his computation of this article was never examined, has for many years constantly inserted in it charges which could not have been allowed had they been known; besides almost every week he has made errors in his arithmetic to his own advantage'.[86]

Looking back in the 1920s on his experience of Cambridge in the late 1860s, W. E. Heitland averred that

> College Kitchens were a standing provocation to extravagance. They were I think all leased to speculators, who made their profit out of undergraduate luxury. Thus they compensated themselves for having to provide dinner in Hall at a low contract price. Their position was a strong one, and it was not easy for College authorities to check the growth of an Undergraduate's Kitchen bill, or indeed to exercise any pressure on the College Cook... In such an economic atmosphere as this no wonder College servants were tempted to plunder their masters.[87]

On his first evening in St John's Heitland arrived too late for hall, and took up his gyp's offer to fetch a cold fowl from the kitchen, 'having in prospect several meals at no great cost'. Heitland ate about a quarter of the bird. The following morning he hoped to add some chicken to his allotment of 'commons', bread and butter, but found that his fowl had disappeared.

> On the gyp's return, I asked what had become of it. He replied with easy assurance that the Gentlemen always left the remainders of dishes to their gyps. I thanked him for his care of my social proprieties, adding that I would consult my Tutor on the matter. He at once deprecated troubling a busy official with so trivial an issue, and generously offered to waive his own rights in the future for my benefit. So I held my ground; but he ate that fowl, and the Cook charged it to me at the peculiar College price.[88]

In the mid-1850s the net income of the butler of St John's was £299 a year (about £50 more than a senior fellow's);[89] over £200 came

---

[86] Underwood, 'Restructuring a Household', p. 11, quoting William Samuel Powell.

[87] Heitland, *After Many Years*, pp. 103–4, for the quotations in this paragraph. See also Gray and Brittain, *A History of Jesus College*, p. 174, on private contractors in the kitchen.

[88] At Trinity fifty years earlier, servants took clothes, crockery, and linen as perquisites when students went down for the last time: [J. M. F. Wright], *Alma Mater*, vol. II, p. 260.

from profits on the sale of butter and ale, and the rest from a miscellany of fees, allowances, and services such as carrying letters for undergraduates. The junior butler's net income was £179. Both St John's butlers, like butlers and cooks in other colleges, recruited and paid their assistants, and given the slack in the system and the number of relatives they wished to oblige it is not surprising that colleges were overstaffed, a fault that their archaic patterns of establishment aggravated; St John's had a separate scholars' cook, supported by his own staff of foreman, accountant and house-keeper. There were different people to wash dishes and plates, while the presence of so many shoes with lazy owners enabled the college shoeblacks to employ deputies on journeymen's wages.

Perquisites in Cambridge colleges remind us of practices in the royal dockyards, where the ancient right to carry off 'chips' for firewood had by the eighteenth century been so exploited that workmen were cutting up ship timber in work-time to create 'scraps' that could be sold for 1s each outside the yard. Other parallels with Cambridge were that management was implicated in practices equally dubious, and that 'chips' were defended as customary rights compensating for inadequate wages. Such ex-actions were common in industry.[90] Still, the spirit of the age was against them; after decades of ineffective prohibitions dockyard 'chips' were replaced by cash payments in 1805, and these were discontinued in 1830. In Cambridge reform began in the eighteenth century, William Samuel Powell of St John's being notably active; under his direction the college took its first steps towards replacing fees and perquisites with stipends, a task resumed in the 1830s. But until the middle of the century changes were piecemeal (and less substantial than parallel reforms in the way fellows were remuner-ated). Enough traditional customs remained to attract the powerful criticism of the Graham Commission. Their particular concern was the way in which the costs of undergraduate residence were higher than they needed to be, and they therefore judged that

> we think it desirable that College servants should be paid by fixed stipends, and not by perquisites, and in particular that the system of

[89] PP 1852–3: *Graham Commission Evidence*, p. 397.
[90] See John Rule, *The Experience of Labour in Eighteenth-Century Industry* (London, Croom Helm, 1981), pp. 124–9.

profits on the sale of commodities, wherever it prevails, should, as far as practicable, be discontinued. Care should also be taken, that the prices of all articles supplied for the use of Students, should be frequently revised and made known in the College, and provision made for the frequent information of the Student, as to the amount, and the several particulars, of the liabilities he has incurred.[91]

Two years after these criticisms St John's appointed a committee on service that began in earnest the reduction of sinecures, the direct employment of college servants, and the replacement of fees and perquisites by fixed salaries. The same changes may be traced at other colleges.[92] They took some time to complete, and as Heitland's experience shows 1870 was not a decisive turning-point in the process but a stage in a lengthy transition. Some words in a letter of 1890 from the Dean of St John's to the bursar suggest how attitudes had changed in the century and yet what still had to be accomplished. He was

> astonished to learn that there is a system of heavy perquisiting in connexion with the communion wine. The chapel clerk asked whether three bottles would be required or two. I thought he meant for the term, but the senior dean tells me that he meant for the day... It is part of the wretched old plan which made all these men drunkards in the past. Perquisites in drink belong to an order of things which can no longer stand the daylight.[93]

[91] PP 1852–3: *Graham Commission Report*, p. 149.
[92] See for example Wardale, *Clare College*, p. 207.
[93] Underwood, 'Reconstructing a Household', p. 17.

Chapter 5

MATHEMATICS, LAW, AND MEDICINE

THE ORIGINS OF THE MATHEMATICAL TRIPOS

ISAAC NEWTON AND NEWTONIANISM

When Isaac Newton, a yeoman's son, entered Trinity College in June 1661 he brought from his grammar school in Grantham proficiency in Latin (an excellent preparation for his correspondence with foreign savants), some Greek, and skill in constructing working models of windmills and other contrivances.[1] At Trinity he was put through the arts course prescribed by the Elizabethan statutes of the university, in which Aristotelian logic and natural philosophy, inherited from the medieval curriculum, had a prominent place. Such was the fate of other undergraduates in seventeenth-century Cambridge (and Oxford), a fact that has led scholars like Christopher Hill to criticise the universities as sterile, and hostile to the new science of Copernicus and Galileo. Such comments underestimate the value of Aristotelianism, not merely as mental gymnastics but as a persuasive cosmology that even practitioners of the new science like Bacon and William Harvey still in large measure accepted.

Aristotelianism was in fact a flexible system that accommodated discoveries, and in retaining it the universities did not exclude scientific advance. Many dons were interested in the new science, and knowledge of it percolated down to students through the unofficial curriculum, mediated by tutors, that complemented the official one. One of Newton's notebooks reveals that he read the

---

[1] For the details of Newton's biography that follow, see R. S. Westfall, *Never at Rest. A Biography of Isaac Newton* (Cambridge University Press, 1980), pp. 55–237; John Fauvel, Raymond Flood, Michael Shortland, and Robin Wilson, eds., *Let Newton Be!* (Oxford University Press, 1988), pp. 1–99.

work of the new scientists, Kepler, Galileo, Gassendi, and Descartes; and we know that much of Newton's impetus came from a desire to counter what he saw as Descartes's faulty reasoning. It is perverse for some of Newton's biographers to ignore the most probable influence of those around him, including his tutors, in leading him to these thinkers; and to argue that he was therefore a solitary and self-taught scientist. The scientific culture of Cambridge stimulated Newton. But of course it does not account for his transcendent genius.[2]

Newton graduated early in 1665. From 1664 onwards, in Cambridge and while exiled in Lincolnshire by the plague epidemic, he advanced at phenomenal speed to make discoveries in mathematics, optics, and celestial dynamics that were the foundation for his revolutionary achievement. Returning to the university he became a fellow of Trinity and at the age of twenty-six, in 1669, Barrow's successor as Lucasian Professor, a chair he retained till 1701. Newton made what has been described as the most important mathematical innovation since the ancient Greeks – the infinitesimal calculus (which he called 'fluxions'); it solved the immemorial problem of how to measure areas under curves and the volumes of solid figures, and it has proved a versatile instrument in the natural and social sciences. His invention of the binomial theorem or formula was a gain in mathematical economy, enabling complex and tedious multiplications to be dispensed with; while his work on optics was a considerable advance in explanation of the nature of light and how it behaves. Any one of these additions to our understanding would have brought him lasting fame. His greatest achievement was to perceive the dynamic harmony of the universe that he elucidated in *Principia Mathematica* (1687). Terrestrial and celestial motion alike were to be explained by gravity: a single force exerted between heavenly bodies and indeed between any two pieces of matter in the universe, a force that causes objects to fall to

[2] W. T. Costello, *The Scholastic Curriculum at Early Seventeenth-Century Cambridge* (Cambridge, Mass., Harvard University Press, 1958); Mark Curtis, *Oxford and Cambridge in Transition 1558–1642* (Oxford, Clarendon Press, 1959), esp. pp. 241–50; Mordechai Feingold, *The Mathematicians' Apprenticeship. Science, Universities and Society in England, 1560–1640* (Cambridge University Press, 1984); Mordechai Feingold, ed., *Before Newton. The Life and Times of Isaac Barrow* (Cambridge University Press, 1990), esp. chapters by Feingold and John Gascoigne; John Gascoigne, 'The Universities and the Scientific Revolution: The Case of Newton and Restoration Cambridge', *History of Science*, 23 (1985), pp. 391–434.

earth and at the same time keeps the moon revolving round it and the planets in motion round the sun.

When Newton died in 1727 he lay in state in Westminster Abbey for a week. At the funeral his pall was borne by two dukes, three earls, and the Lord Chancellor, causing Voltaire to remark that 'He was buried like a king who had done well by his subjects', while Alexander Pope conveyed something of what his contemporaries found in him in his famous couplet:

> Nature, and Nature's Laws lay hid in Night.
> God said, *Let Newton Be!* and All was *Light.*
> *Epitaph XV*

Newtonianism affected thinkers somewhat remote from mathematics and natural science: the theory of vibrations, which underlay Hartley's associationist psychology, was prompted by Newton's concepts of motion and the ether, while de Buffon, in his *Histoire Naturelle*, tried to argue that the laws of chemical affinity were the same as the law linking the celestial bodies. One of the strongest proofs of Newtonianism's pervasiveness is its popularisation in works such as *The Newtonian System of Philosophy Adapted to the Capacities of Young Gentlemen and Ladies...* by Tom Telescope, A.M. Alternative scientific explanations did criticise Newtonianism, or parts of it, but they were not generally persuasive, even though they often contributed insights to later scientific endeavours undreamed of in the eighteenth century.[3] Thus in his *History of the Inductive Sciences* Whewell wrote that Newton was 'altogether without a rival or neighbour' and that his work on universal gravitation was 'indisputably and incomparably the greatest scientific discovery ever made'.[4]

Intellectual pre-eminence goes a long way to explain why Newtonianism came to dominate Cambridge. Still, it was not nearly such a paramount force at Oxford, and rival ideologies seem to have played a part in causing the two universities to diverge. So although in the late seventeenth and early eighteenth centuries there was a group of Newtonians in Edinburgh and

[3] Fauvel, Flood, Shortland, and Wilson, eds., *Let Newton be!*, pp. 23–41, 203–39.
[4] W. Whewell, *History of the Inductive Sciences* (3rd edn, 3 vols., London, 1857), vol. II, pp. 136–7.

Oxford who were Tories and High Anglicans,[5] Newtonianism was more consistently supported by the Low Church or Latitudinarian section of the Church of England.[6] Eager to emphasise the role of reason in the apprehension of religious truth, and the importance of natural religion – truth as displayed in the physical world – Low Churchmen saw that the Newtonian cosmology, and particularly the universal law of gravitation, gave proof of design by a Divine Artificer, and perhaps also of his immanence in the world. High Churchmen, on the other hand, stressed the superiority of Revelation to frail human reason where the two were in conflict; they tended to be wary of an explanation that conflicted with the scriptural account and relegated God to the status of a craftsman. In the early eighteenth century Tory High Churchmen were powerful in Oxford, and Whig Latitudinarians in Cambridge.

The spread of Newtonianism in Cambridge owed much to such men, or so it seems, though it is necessary to remember that even the most committed Latitudinarians were not mere propagandists but scholars persuaded of Newtonianism's truth by the majestic rationality of its argument. Chief among these enthusiasts for the new mathematical cosmology was Richard Bentley, brilliant classicist and Master of Trinity (1700–42), in whose career intense dedication to learning and disputatious egotism were promiscuously mingled.[7] Bentley read the *Principia* soon after it was published in 1687. In 1692 he gave the first of the Boyle lectures, endowed by the scientist Robert Boyle to uphold the truth of Christianity; they became a platform for the latitudinarian argument. Bentley used the *Principia* to provide evidence for God's providential design of the universe.[8] At Trinity Bentley was a patron of Roger Cotes, the first

---

[5] Anita Guerrini, 'The Tory Newtonians: Gregory, Pitcairne, and Their Circle', *Journal of British Studies*, 25 (1986), pp. 288–311.

[6] For what follows, see Gascoigne, *Cambridge in the Age of the Enlightenment*, pp. 142–84; John Gascoigne, 'Politics, patronage and Newtonianism: The Cambridge Example', *Historical Journal*, 27, 1 (1984), pp. 1–24.

[7] Bentley is the only head of house ever to be deprived (in 1719) of all his degrees by the Senate, outraged at his behaviour; they were restored in 1724, after lengthy litigation. See John Henry Monk, *The Life of Richard Bentley, D.D.* (2 vols., London, 1833) for details of his extraordinary career.

[8] Margaret C. Jacob, *The Newtonians and the English Revolution 1689–1702* (Sussex, Harvester, 1976), pp. 32–2, 145–7.

Plumian Professor of Astronomy and the editor of the second edition of the *Principia* (1709) which clarified Newton's argument. Bentley also assisted William Whiston, Newton's successor as Lucasian professor and a champion of the apologetic value of his work: 'Mechanical philosophy, which relies chiefly on the Power of Gravity, is, if rightly understood, so far from leading to Atheism, that it solely depends on, supposes and demonstrates the Being and Providence of God; and its Study by consequence is the most serviceable to Religion of all other.'[9] Other Newtonians, to varying degrees known to Bentley and to each other, and to varying degrees, also, Latitudinarian in sympathy, included Robert Smith, Bentley's successor as Master of Trinity and author of a Newtonian textbook much used in the university, Nicholas Saunderson, the blind Lucasian professor (1711–39), and Richard Laughton, a tutor of Clare.

An early indication of the way in which the Cambridge curriculum came to include Newton's work is given in the diary of William Stukeley, who came up to Corpus in 1704 and took an MB in 1708.[10] Stukeley's tutor was Thomas Fawcett, and he was also taught by Robert Danny, a fellow of Corpus and a friend of Roger Cotes. Danny taught Stukeley 'Arithmetic, Algebra, Geometry, Philosophy, Astronomy, Trigonometry' using 'all Newton's and Boyle's works' (which must be an exaggeration) together with textbooks such as 'Tacquets Geometry by Whiston' and 'Rohaults Physics by Clark'.[11] A few years later, in 1710, Richard Laughton promoted Newton's ideas when acting as Proctor. Claiming his ancient right to preside in person at the disputations in the Schools, he persuaded William Browne of Peterhouse to choose mathematical themes for his disputations by promising him an honorary

9 Quoted in Gascoigne, *Cambridge in the Age of the Enlightenment*, p. 145. For Whiston, see James E. Force, *William Whiston: Honest Newtonian* (Cambridge University Press, 1985).

10 W. C. Lukis, ed., *The Family Memoirs of the Reverend William Stukeley, M.D. and the Antiquarian and other Correspondence of William Stukeley, Roger & Samuel Gale, etc.* (Surtees Society Publications, vols. 73, 76, 80, (1882–7), vol. 73 (1882), pp. 20–1, 143. Stukeley (1687–1765) became a clergyman after practising medicine, and wrote extensively on antiquarian matters – most notably, Stonehenge. See Stuart Piggott, *William Stukeley, an Eighteenth-Century Antiquary* (Oxford University Press, 1950).

11 Samuel Clarke published a Latin translation of Rohault's *Traité de physique* (a Cartesian textbook) in 1697; in a later edition in 1702 Newtonian elements were added, and these were strengthened in a third version in 1710. Clarke, a Latitudinarian, was involved in notable theological controversy.

proctor's optime degree.[12] Twenty years later Newtonian topics were commonplace, if we may judge from Thomas Johnson, *Quaestiones philosophicae* (1735), a guide for students preparing disputation topics. Those defending the proposition 'Whether the cause of gravity may be explained by mechanical principles' were urged to read works by Descartes and others, while opponents were told to consult the *Principia* and *Opticks*. Advice was also given on how to prepare for other topics where knowledge of Newton's ideas was essential, for example 'Whether Newton's three laws of nature are true', 'Whether light is a body', and 'Whether electrical phenomena can be explained by mechanical principles'. Such disputations came at the end of the BA course, and detailed guidance on how to organise four years of study in mathematics (as well as in classical and theological matters) was given in a booklet by Daniel Waterland, the Master of Magdalene: *Advice to a Young Student. With a Method of Study for the First Four Years*, which he published in 1730;[13] a revised version came out in 1740. The reader is advised to study elementary arithmetic and geometry texts in his first year, proceed to Newtonian popularisations by Clarke, Keill, and Whiston, and open Newton's *Opticks*, a difficult work, only in his fourth year.[14]

Waterland's guide also shows that the scholastic philosophy had disappeared from the Cambridge curriculum by the early eighteenth century. Nor is Aristotle included in another list of philosophers recommended for student reading about 1730, though Hobbes, Descartes, Leibnitz, Butler, Berkeley, and Locke are. From among this group Waterland singles out for study Locke, *Essay on the Human Understanding*, in the Lent Term of the second year.[15] Locke's rejection of the notion of innate ideas and emphasis on the importance of experience and reason were congenial to many (though not by any means all) of the Latitudinarians who

---

[12] The Proctors had the right, as did the Vice-Chancellor and the Senior Regent, to insert one candidate at any position in the degree list they chose. The right was not exercised after 1797, and abolished in 1827; it was never regarded as more than an honorary distinction, akin to the statesman's Litt. D today.

[13] It had been composed about 1706, and published in a pirated edition in 1729.

[14] Details of Waterland's booklet are given in Christopher Wordsworth, *Scholae Academicae. Some Account of Studies at the English Universities in the Eighteenth Century* (Cambridge, 1877), pp. 330–7.

[15] Christopher Wordsworth, *Scholae Academicae*, pp. 120–34, 333. For what follows, see Gascoigne, *Cambridge in the Age of the Enlightenment*, pp. 171–4.

promoted Newton, and they were at the same time antipathetic to the high churchmen unenthusiastic about him. In 1696 it was remarked about Locke's view that the idea of God was not innate, that 'now we find Mr Bentley very large upon it, in his sermons at Mr Boyle's lectures . . . And Mr Whiston, in his new theory of the earth.' On the other hand, Robert Jenkin, a nonjuror who became Master of St John's, said of Locke's work that it 'offered violence to Scripture and every thing else that opposes it'.

In compiling his student guide Waterland seems to have had in mind the majority of undergraduates who were intending to be clergymen, and for them he advised the concurrent study of three branches of knowledge – religion, classics, and philosophy (which included mathematics and much else). In March and April of an undergraduate's fourth year, for example, he recommended study of Newton's *Opticks*, J. Clarke's Boyle lectures on the origin of evil, *De Veritate Religionis Christianae* by Grotius, and Thucydides' *Peloponnesian War* (the Greek text, of course). The modern reader would not guess that this fare was recommended for the penultimate term before the final disputations, for the BA degree, which concentrated on natural and moral philosophy and included no questions on Greek. Waterland was propounding the tutorial, collegiate curriculum, not a 'university' scheme focused on the degree exercises. For three centuries (until the mid-nineteenth) the collegiate curriculum, devised by tutors like Waterland, included a wider range of studies than was required for the degree.[16] In particular, while tutors taught much classical literature to their pupils, knowledge of it was tested in the degree exercises merely in the indirect sense (albeit a considerable one) that Latin was the language in which they were conducted. Disputations had been devised in the Middle Ages for contentious and debatable topics; classical literature, added to courses in the sixteenth century, did not lend itself to the adversarial format.

Over the centuries the great change in the university curriculum was that Aristotle became replaced by Newton and Locke, and we now turn to the way these two masters were examined.

---

[16] See Curtis, *Oxford and Cambridge in Transition*, pp. 83–125.

DISPUTATIONS AND THE SENATE HOUSE EXAMINATION

'My heart was in my cause, and proudly measuring its importance by the crowd it had collected, armed, as I believed myself to be, in the full understanding of my questions, and a perfect readiness in the language, in which our disputations were to be carried on, I waited his attack amidst the hum and murmur of the assembly.'[17] Richard Cumberland, after weeks of intensive preparation, was in the Philosophical Schools in the Lent Term 1750, ready to take part in his first Latin disputation for the BA degree. These exercises had occurred since the Middle Ages, and in an unchanging form, but in 1750 they were being overtaken in importance by the new Senate House Examination, though they continued, in dwindling fashion, till 1839.

Preparing for the exercises, the two moderators in charge received from college tutors lists of their third-year pupils, with comments such as 'reading', 'hard-reading', or 'non-reading' man.[18] Using these judgements, the moderators then chose likely men to open disputations as respondents, and sent by hand slips of paper commanding them to appear in two or three weeks, for example: 'Respondeat Gunning, Coll.Christ 5ᵗᵒ die Februarii 1787. T.Jones, Modr.' Giving 6d to the servant bringing the note, a respondent replied to the moderator with a list of three topics on which he proposed to argue, perhaps choosing them from a manual of stock subjects like Thomas Johnson's *Quaestiones* (Cambridge, 1735), a book that also very handily suggested possible lines of argument. Respondents selected propositions from Newton's *Principia* and other mathematical authorities such as Halley and Maclaurin. Philosophy questions reflected Locke and Berkeley and asked if matter could think, or whether touch and sight yielded similar information. The respondent sent his list of three topics to the moderators, who generally allowed them, though propositions taken from Euclid were usually disallowed because it was hard to refute them. Heretical theses were frowned on too, such as William

---

[17] Richard Cumberland, *Memoirs* (2 vols., London, 1807), vol. 1, pp. 100–1. Cumberland, the grandson of Richard Bentley, became well known as a dramatist.

[18] This account of the exercises is taken from Christopher Wordsworth, *Scholae Academicae*, pp. 33–43, and W. W. Rouse Ball, *A History of the Study of Mathematics at Cambridge* (Cambridge, 1889), pp. 164–86.

Paley's proposal in 1762 to deny the eternity of hell's torments; Paley compromised by affirming his question instead. The moderators chose three opponents for each respondent, taking care to match men of equal weight, and sent them notice of the questions, and the time of meeting.

Henry Gunning was horrified in January 1787 that he was 'to open the schools' on 5 February, a very stressful task performed before an audience of other members of the university. Getting a 'dormiat' from the dean of Christ's (which excused him from early morning chapel) Gunning read till late at night in his selected pages.[19] As was usual, Gunning had his opponents to tea.[20] Opponents entertained their respondent in turn, the custom being for him to leave early on the last occasion to enable the opponents to co-ordinate their arguments to the thesis he had chosen to advance. Gunning and his three opponents met in the schools before 2.0 pm on 5 February; the Elizabethan statutes laid down that exercises should last from the 'first to the third hour', but it was considered that the rubric was obeyed if debate began before 2.0 pm and lasted till after 3.0 pm. Disputations therefore usually lasted for seventy minutes.[21]

'Ascendat Dominus Respondens': obeying this command from the moderator the respondent mounted his rostrum on the other side of the room, carrying a Latin thesis (one that survives covers eight and a half closely written pages of a quarto notebook) on the topic he preferred. Usually this was philosophical in nature: mathematical theses demanded less Latin, but handling complex algebraic proofs orally was also difficult. The thesis would usually take about ten minutes to read. The first opponent then climbed into a box near the moderator, and argued against the thesis in syllogisms, according to the strict rules of formal logic, thus: major premise, if A is B, then C is D; minor premise, A is B, and therefore C is D; conclusion, therefore C is D. The respondent attacked any weak links in this chain, perhaps admitting that A was B, but alleging that it did not follow that C was D. The argument swung

---

[19] Gunning, *Reminiscences*, vol. 1, pp. 80–4.
[20] Wine is said to have been usual until 1782, when James Wood, the future Senior Wrangler and Master of St John's, suffered badly from its ill-effects.
[21] Gunning, *Reminiscences*, vol. 1, pp. 82, 144.

back and forth until the second and third opponents were given their briefer opportunities. At last, the respondent was examined by the moderator on his mathematical knowledge, and dismissed with a conventional Latin phrase suggesting the class to which he might aspire in the tripos. A man praised with 'summo ingenii acumine disputasti' would hope to be numbered among the highest wranglers. 'Optime disputasti' rewarded more modest attainments, and it is from this phrase that the second class in the Mathematical Tripos gets its name. Very occasionally utter incompetence brought the dismissal 'Descendas', whose shame was keenly felt. Moderators marked performances with a spread of literal grades, recording them in a book before them. Performances that were better than expected were noted. In 1752 sixteen names of putative poll men were moved up, after doing well in the schools, into the provisional junior optimes; and after the Senate House Examination this was the class awarded to them. In other words the exercises were used as a preliminary filter for the Senate House Examination as it became more significant in the grading and classification process. The filter became more refined and discriminating from 1763 onwards, as is explained later.

The most accomplished disputants appeared eight times in the exercises, twice as respondents and six times as opponents, in the Lent and Easter Terms of their third year and the Michaelmas of their fourth. Traditionally fellow commoners were excused all attendance, while by the end of the eighteenth century the non-reading men, likely to end in the *hoi polloi*, were invited to take part on only a few occasions – their painful maladroitness being no help to the undergraduates in the audience. But omitting the exercises meant infringing the strict terms of the Elizabethan statutes. So by ingenuity common in the university when rules had to be accommodated to the facts of life, weaker candidates 'huddled' the disputes they needed to complete their statutable number. A respondent said 'Recte statuit Newtonus', and the opponent countered with 'Recte non statuit Newtonus'. This counted as a disputation, and the game was played as many times as were necessary, men changing places to argue the contrary of their earlier assertion and polishing off many acts and opponencies in a few minutes.

The moderator in 1819, William Whewell, commented: 'As we are no longer here in the way either of talking Latin habitually or of reading logic, neither the one nor the other is very scientifically exhibited. The syllogisms are such as would make Aristotle stare, and the Latin would make every classical hair in your head stand on end.'[22] Sometimes the moderator himself spoke dog-Latin. William Farish of Magdalene, vicar of St Giles and Professor of Chemistry but no classicist, reproved a poll man running into the Schools without full academical dress: 'Domine opponentium tertie, non habes quod debes. Ubi sunt tui . . . eh! eh! Anglice "bands"?' The opponent replied, 'Domine moderator, sunt in meo . . . Anglice "pocket".'[23] The proposal made by the reformer John Jebb and others that the exercises should be held in English was not taken up. They therefore became ever more anachronistic, especially when in the 1820s advanced algebra was included in the tripos; it was of course exceedingly difficult to demonstrate it orally.[24] So from 1830 onwards the exercises ceased to be any real test, as candidates rehearsed their arguments elaborately in advance, perhaps even memorising much of the Latin, and staged a mock performance in the schools. So the moderators of 1839 abolished the ancient system on their own responsibility, apparently arousing no dissent. Nevertheless, until their last years acts and opponencies had considerable value. Those stern critics Jebb and Whewell regarded them as good tests of knowledge, while Gunning averred that they usually discerned the ability later revealed by the Senate House Examination: 'for many years no man was ever a Wrangler who was not placed in the first or second class [i.e. in the exercises]; and it generally (though not invariably) happened that a first-class man was placed higher on the Tripos than a man in the second class'.[25] Augustus De Morgan, who proved his talent by becoming Fourth Wrangler in 1827, wrote of the act he kept in 1826:

> I was badgered for two hours with arguments given and answered in Latin, – or what we called Latin – against Newton's first section,

[22] Isaac Todhunter, *William Whewell, D.D. Master of Trinity College Cambridge: An Account of his Writings with Selections from his Literary and Scientific Correspondence* (2 vols., London, 1876), vol. II, p. 35.
[23] Christopher Wordsworth, *Scholae Academicae*, pp. 40–1. A poll man (pronounced like 'polly') was a member of the *hoi polloi*, the lowest stratum.
[24] See p. 171.   [25] Gunning, *Reminiscences*, vol. I, p. 82.

Lagrange's derived functions, and Locke on innate principles ... I never had such a strain of thought in my life. For the inferior opponents were made as sharp as their betters by their tutors, who kept lists of queer objections drawn from all quarters.[26]

At the other end of the spectrum, the disputations did not test the talents of the *hoi polloi* who 'huddled' their tasks. But the fault lay not in the nature of the exercises themselves, but in the university's failure to devise a curriculum, or a pattern of teaching, truly appropriate for profoundly unacademic students.

The Senate House Examination of the eighteenth century became the Mathematical Tripos in the nineteenth, and is the prototype, therefore, of all today's honours examinations. But the original examination itself was not invented: it evolved slowly from a much older test, mentioned as 'accustomed' in the Elizabethan statutes.[27] Undergraduates having completed their disputations and been given the rank of 'questionists', were tested in the Schools. By the end of the seventeenth century these tests lasted for three days in the middle of January, and any MA could pose questions; the examination was naturally in Latin. At this stage it was less important than the acts and opponencies, on whose results was compiled, most probably, the Ordo Senioritatis, the degree list. This indicated a simple 'pass' for many men, though ranking others at the head of the list in an order of merit. In 1710–11, however, this merit group was split into two, the 1st and 2nd Tripos,[28] a development perhaps reflecting the increasing importance now being given to the post-exercises examination. Forty years later, after a process regrettably shadowy, the examination (held in the Senate House after its completion in 1730) was beginning to be taken more seriously than the disputations, a development no doubt linked to the printing of the examination results in 1747–8;[29] while the division in 1753 of the merit or honours group into three classes

---

[26] A. De Morgan, *A Budget of Paradoxes* (London, 1872), p. 305.

[27] As is convincingly argued by Winstanley, *Unreformed Cambridge*. The account that follows is based on Winstanley, *Unreformed Cambridge*, pp. 47–57, 350–2, Ball, *A History of the Study of Mathematics at Cambridge*, pp. 187–211, and Christopher Wordsworth, *Scholae Academicae*, pp. 44–58.

[28] The examination was held in January, 1710 Old Style, 1711 New Style. From 1714 onwards the two divisions in the merit group were known as '*In Comitiis prioribus*' and '*In Comitiis posterioribus*'.

[29] For this reason 1748 is usually regarded as the first year of the Mathematical Tripos: J. R. Tanner, ed., *The Historical Register of the University of Cambridge ... to the year 1910* (Cambridge, 1917), p. 351.

instead of two – the wranglers, and the senior and junior optimes – is a sign of the growing weight being given to the assessment of the most talented candidates.

From about the middle of the century onwards the examination was conducted in English. Knowing that it is the ancestor of all our modern written examinations we might assume that from the earliest days it had the form that is today customary – of printed papers being given to candidates as they enter the examination chamber, and answers being composed on paper provided. The transition from an oral test was in fact slow. At first men were questioned viva voce by the moderators, and also by any MA who chose to exercise his right to intervene in the examination. It soon became usual for candidates for the highest honours to be given additional questions, called 'problems', which were tackled on paper.[30] Problems were however *dictated* to candidates, a practice that saved examiners the trouble of composing them long in advance but must have led to confusion over complex mathematical terms. After about 1772 it began to be customary to dictate questions to the generality of candidates and of course to require written answers. The printing of papers did not start till the 1790s, and even then only for problems; dictation remained for other questions till 1827, printed papers coming in the following year as one of many changes in the examination.

By the 1740s, at the latest, the examination was largely mathematical in content,[31] and it was certainly an ordeal for questionists desiring honours. After his success in the Schools Richard Cumberland was in 1751 grilled in the Senate House, a trial made worse by his rheumatic fever. He wrote, 'It was hardly ever my lot during that examination to enjoy any respite. I seemed an object singled out as every man's mark, and was kept perpetually at the table under the process of question and answer. My constitution just held me up to the expiration of the scrutiny.'[32] He collapsed soon after and was ill

[30] They are mentioned in the lengthy description of the examination given by John Jebb: see John Disney, ed., *The Works of John Jebb . . . with Memoirs of the Life of the Author* (3 vols., London, 1787) vol. II, pp. 284–300.
[31] See the quotation from Bodleian Library, MS Gough gen. top. 39, f.311v, cited in John Gascoigne, 'Mathematics and Meritocracy: The Emergence of the Cambridge Mathematical Tripos', *Social Studies of Science*, 14 (1984), p. 553.
[32] Richard Cumberland, *Memoirs* (2 vols., London, 1807), vol. I, p. 105.

for six months, comforted by gaining sixth place in the examination. Dimmer men, known from their record and their performance in the schools to be destined for the poll, were however rarely bothered in the Senate House. Hanging about for three days, they played push-pin on the benches.[33]

Originally, all the questionists from a given college were examined together, without regard to their different attainments. This procedure led to accusations of bias on the part of examiners eager to benefit their own college. So when he was moderator in 1763 Richard Watson began to classify men according to their performances in the disputations; at first eight in number, after a few years there were six such classes, separately examined. 'By this arrangement', Watson claimed, 'persons of nearly equal merit are examined in the presence of each other, and flagrant acts of partiality cannot take place'.[34] If accusations of bias did not entirely cease (as the case of William Gooch shows, cited below), the change certainly had far-reaching effects. The mathematical character of the examination encouraged belief in the preciseness and certitude with which candidates' talents were assessed; now, after Watson's changes, very fine discriminations between candidates were made possible, by the use of what one observer termed the 'abstruse labyrinths' of mathematics. Thus in the latter part of the century the examination became steadily more competitive, candidates vying for numbered rungs on the ladder of distinction. The screw was given a further twist in 1779 with the introduction of 'brackets', groupings of candidates of equal merit effected in the course of the examination as stimuli to struggle between them.[35] In 1779, too, the number of moderators was increased from two to four, and a day added to the three given over to the examination.[36] Perhaps as a result of the increasing demands of the examination fewer MAs after 1779 exercised their right to question candidates, and after 1785 it apparently ceased to be claimed though formally continuing.

Apart from differences of detail the test remained very much the same from the 1780s to 1827. It was held in January, the worst month in the year to sit in the Senate House, since, as Whewell

---

[33] *Memoirs of the Life of Dr Trusler* (Bath, 1806), p. 15.
[34] Richard Watson, *Anecdotes*, p. 19.
[35] Gascoigne, 'Mathematics and Meritocracy', p. 568.   [36] In 1805 a fifth day was added.

sardonically remarked, no stove was allowed to disfigure its classical purity. Once, it is said, the ink froze in the wells. About 1800 candidates attended on Monday and Tuesday from 8 am to 5 pm, with three hours of intervals. Candidates sat at three tables according to the classes they had been provisionally placed in following their performance in the disputations. The examiners moved about the room, dictating questions. Speed of working and writing was at a premium, as it is today in all written tests for which the Mathematical Tripos was the prototype.

> It requires every person to use the utmost dispatch; for as soon as ever the Examiners perceive anyone to have finished his paper, and subscribed his name to it, another Question is immediately given. A smattering demonstration will weigh little in the scale of merit; every thing must be fully, clearly, and scientifically brought to a true conclusion.[37]

Questions varied in difficulty according to which class of questionists they were given to. Talents differed enormously, the least numerate getting pass degrees on elementary arithmetic, quadratic equations, and the simplest ideas in Euclidean geometry – mathematics now handled by bright pupils of fourteen. At the other extreme the most talented were tested on their understanding of Newton's *Principia*. As we have seen, they were given additional 'problems', both in the Senate House during the day and on Monday and Tuesday evenings in the moderators' college rooms, where questionists were given fruit and wine.[38] Wednesday was devoted to logic, moral philosophy, and religion. Little weight was given to these topics and many candidates were, like Gunning, examined for one hour only. They spent much of the day playing 'teetotum' below stairs in the Senate House. Working hard, the examiners produced for 8 am on Thursday the 'brackets', each grouping together candidates of equal marks. In 1802 there were fifteen brackets. Throughout Thursday questionists were examined in mathematics, their positions in the rank order being adjusted every few hours. Dissatisfied candidates could challenge men in the bracket above to a play-off, and then the moderators might call on the Proctors and

---

[37] *Cambridge University Calendar*, 1802, p. xx, a detailed account of the examination.
[38] Gunning, *Reminiscences*, vol. 1, p. 89.

other MAs for help in adjudicating. This task was tricky. The examination procedures themselves aggravated stress. So did the favours sometimes shown by examiners and private tutors to men from their own colleges. But examiners from other colleges were watchful. There was also a desire for a fair result. Thus an arbitrator like the redoubtable Isaac Milner, President of Queens', was of great help. 'Being a man of strong nerves, and caring very little about the opinions of others, he got into frequent disputes with the Praelectors of colleges who ventured to remonstrate with him on the positions in which their men were placed in the Tripos.'[39]

Tensions in the Senate House are captured in William Gooch's letters to his parents in Brockdish (Norfolk).[40] From the first day of the examination onwards Gooch (Caius) was fighting to be Senior Wrangler with Daniel Peacock of Trinity. William Lax, also of Trinity,[41] was moderator, and tried to favour Peacock, though perhaps of most significance is that Gooch accepted that the result was fair.

> *Monday 1/4 aft. 12.*
>
> From 1 till 7 I did more than Peacock; But who did most at Moderator's Rooms this Evening from 7 till 9, I don't know yet; – but I did above three times as much as the Senr Wrangler last year, yet I'm afraid not so much as Peacock.
>
> Between One & three o'Clock I wrote up 9 sheets of Scribbling Paper so you may suppose I was pretty fully employ'd.

> *Tuesday Night.*
>
> I've been shamefully us'd by Lax to-day; – Tho' his anxiety for Peacock must (of course) be very great, I never suspected that his Partially [*sic*] wd get the better of his Justice. I had entertain'd too high an opinion of him to suppose it. – he gave Peacock a long private Examination & then came to me (I hop'd) on the same subject, but 'twas only to *Bully* me as much as he could, – whatever I said (tho' right) he tried to convert into Nonsense by seeming to misunderstand me. However I don't entirely dispair of being first, tho' you see Lax seems determin'd that I shall not...

---

[39] Gunning, *Reminiscences*, vol. I, pp. 91–2, 258.
[40] Printed in Christopher Wordsworth, *Scholae Academicae*, pp. 319–29.
[41] Daniel Peacock, later vicar of Sedbergh, was a member of a prolific Cambridge clan. Lax was Senior Wrangler in 1785, Lowndean Professor 1795–1836, and vicar of St Ippolyts, Herts., where he built an observatory.

Wednesday evening.

Peacock and I are still in perfect Equilibrio & the Examiners themselves can give no guess yet who is likely to be first; – a New Examiner (Wood[42] of St John's, who is reckon'd the first Mathematician in the University . . .) was call'd solely to examine Peacock & me only. – but by this new Plan nothing is yet determin'd. – So Wood is to examine us again tomorrow morning.

Thursday evening.

Peacock is declar'd first & I second . . . I'm perfectly *satisfied* that the Senior Wranglership is Peacock's due, but *certainly* not so very indisputably as Lax pleases to represent it – I understand that *he* asserts 'twas 5 to 4 in Peacock's favor. Now Peacock & I have explain'd to each other how we went on, & can *prove indisputably* that it wasn't 20 to 19 in his favor; – I *cannot* therefore be displeas'd for being plac'd second, tho' I'm provov'd [*sic*] with Lax for his false report (so much beneath the Character of a Gentleman.)

A few months later Gooch sailed as an astronomer on Vancouver's voyage to the Pacific; he was murdered by natives on the island of Oahu.[43]

In the last third of the eighteenth century, on average 114 men took bachelor's degrees, of whom 45 were awarded honours.[44] The lists were in rank order. The Senior Wrangler was of course the hero of the week, while the last junior optime was awarded the Wooden Spoon. Funnily enough, the man immediately below him, the Captain of the Poll, was regarded as having distinguished himself. At the tail came the men who had just scraped their degrees. They were given nicknames that depended on the size of their group – the Twelve Apostles, the Seven Wise Men, or the Three Graces.

JOHN JEBB'S PROPOSED REFORMS, 1772

The first proposal for change in university examinations came in 1772.[45] Though in the event it was defeated, it raises in a pregnant

---

[42] James Wood, later Master of St John's: see pp. 93–4.

[43] See Greg Dening, *History's Anthropology: The Death of William Gooch*, Association for Social Anthropology in Oceania, Special Publications no. 2 (Lanham: Md., University Press of America, 1988).

[44] For BAs, see Ball, *Study of Mathematics*, p. 249. Figures for honours are calculated from Tanner, *Historical Register*, pp. 453–69.

and succinct way some issues that continued to be important: the crucial effect of personality in university struggles, the difficulty of manoeuvring reforms through the university's archaic constitution, and the prickliness of colleges when their interests seemed to be menaced by the university – even though collectively they composed it.

The proposals were put forward to the Vice-Chancellor by the impetuous but resolute John Jebb in 1772. Perhaps influenced by the frequent examinations held at his own first university, Trinity College, Dublin, he suggested annual ones at Cambridge, to spur students before their final trial in the Senate House; they would be tested in classics, history, international law, and philosophy as well as mathematics. He also wished noblemen and fellow commoners to be subject to the same examinations as others. Consulting the heads of house, the Vice-Chancellor found little support and took no action. Jebb tried again, this time proposing to the Caput, the powerful committee that steered the Senate, four graces in succession, each being negatived in the Caput by a pretext. A fifth grace passed by the Caput and both houses of the Senate led to the question being considered by a syndicate. Composed of heads of houses, Regius Professors and tutors and reflecting academic conservatism, it duly rejected Jebb's plans.

The Caput knew that annual university examinations would control the college curricula far more continuously than the Senate House Examination; they would undermine the accepted convention that 'the business of education, both of government and instruction, is conducted with more success, as it has been conducted for some ages, under the domestic discipline of each college than it could be under the direction of the Senate'.[46] Tutors might often have to revise their lectures, or might have the frailty of their knowledge exposed by bad examination results. The threat to collegiate autonomy was uppermost with William Samuel Powell, the autocratic and weighty Master of St John's, even though he had begun semi-annual examinations there, of course under college control. 'At Emmanuel', wrote Robert Plumptre, the President of

---

[45] For what follows, see Winstanley, *Unreformed Cambridge*, pp. 318–30.

[46] William S. Powell, *An Observation on the Design of Establishing Annual Examinations at Cambridge* (Cambridge, 1774), quoted in Winstanley, *Unreformed Cambridge*, p. 318.

Queens', 'it was said that the public examinations proposed would be the ruin of the University. The explanation of which, as I understand, is that such noblemen and fellow-commoners, as were not distinguished in the examinations, would conceive a disgust against the University and be its enemies for ever after.'[47] Jebb was disliked and distrusted personally, too, because of his involvement with the subscription issue and parliamentary reform.[48] On the other hand the university Chancellor, the Duke of Grafton, favoured giving idle fellow commoners some hard work, while some dons might look forward to being examiners at £10 a year. Opinion in the university as a whole was balanced. Jebb believed that the Vice-Chancellor had arranged a vote in the syndicate at a time when most members could not be present.

Jebb tried again, and with a new Vice-Chancellor, Lynford Caryl of Jesus, and a new Caput that did not include Powell, he succeeded in getting, in March 1774, a more balanced syndicate than its predecessor. It recommended examinations for pensioners and sizars in their second year, and for noblemen and fellow commoners in their first and second. Put to the Senate, a series of graces containing these ideas was lost by narrow majorities in the Non-Regent House (that is, consisting of the more senior and more conservative dons).[49] Hopeful that an attempt to accommodate college opinion might succeed, Jebb put forward a scheme to link examinations 'with the settled lectures of the Tutors'; approved by the Caput and presented in the Non-Regent House, the crucial grace was lost by 39 votes to 38 in October 1774.[50] Jebb wanted to try again, but damaged his chances by at last resigning his Anglican livings and openly avowing the unitarian beliefs that his lectures on the New Testament had since 1770 been making Cambridge suspect; 'I am easy in the thoughts of being delivered from what I esteem worse than Egyptian bondage', he wrote.[51] In February 1776 Philip Yorke, an undergraduate at Queens', wrote that 'Mr Jebb is to propose his graces for the public examinations tomorrow for the last time, but I believe without any hope of success, for he is

[47] BL Add. MS 35628, fol. 191, quoted in Winstanley, *Unreformed Cambridge*, p. 325.
[48] See pp. 406–11.
[49] By 47 to 43, 48 to 41, and 49 to 38: Cooper, *Annals*, IV, p. 371.
[50] Cooper, *Annals*, IV, p. 374.
[51] Quoted in Winstanley, *Unreformed Cambridge*, p. 328.

so obnoxious a person himself that every plan or proposal, however good in itself, provided it comes from him, is sure to be rejected.'[52] The graces were lost by thirteen and fourteen votes. When examination reform was next seriously mooted in the 1820s, Jebb's plans were brought in evidence by both sides in the dispute.

REFORMING THE SENATE HOUSE EXAMINATION

THE PREVIOUS EXAMINATION AND THE CLASSICAL TRIPOS, 1822

Classics and theology were anomalous studies at Cambridge.[53] Many dons were interested in them. There were endowed professorships to foster them, and prizes of various sorts for undergraduates excelling at them – perhaps the most highly esteemed rewards being the Chancellor's gold medals for classical learning.[54] They were also taught and examined in colleges. But neither classics nor theology was examined in the tripos. The exclusion of classics was unfair to undergraduates keen on literary pursuits,[55] and it seemed absurd to omit divinity when most undergraduates became clergymen. Change seemed logical, but as so often it was not easy to effect it. Some feared any encroachment on the sovereignty of mathematics. This issue was entangled with that of college teaching and the sovereignty of tutors; some colleges might not be able to teach for new examinations and so teaching might fall into the hands of the university.[56] Graces proposed between 1818 and 1820 to extend the range of examinable subjects were vetoed in the Caput, and so never reached the Senate. At length the Senate was brought in 1822 to agree to two examinations, a compulsory one in the fifth term, the Previous Examination, and a voluntary Classical Tripos to be held shortly after the mathematical examination in the eleventh term.

Both examinations were compromises; both had enemies. The Previous tested knowledge of the classical tongues and Paley's

---

[52] BL Add MS. 35377, fol. 271, quoted in Winstanley, *Unreformed Cambridge*, p. 329. Jebb left Cambridge to live in London in September 1776.
[53] For what follows, see Winstanley, *Early Victorian Cambridge*, pp. 65–71, a very detailed account.
[54] Instituted by the Duke of Newcastle in 1751.
[55] This matter is treated on pp. 184–6.
[56] Which in large measure is what in the twentieth century has occurred, for the reason expected.

Evidences of Christianity. It was to prove a very real hurdle for generations of dim pass men who never ceased to lament it. 'For a whole term he repairs to a "coach" from whom he expects to gain a thorough knowledge of Paley. He secludes himself from the haunts of men. After vain attempts to comprehend the first chapter he learns it off by rote, and in the senate house answers every question wrong.'[57] The low standard of the examination was criticised by purists like Christopher Wordsworth, but given the unfiltered university entry any compulsory test could be no more than elementary. The Classical Tripos was voluntary,[58] but candidates had to have achieved honours in the Mathematical Tripos; the supremacy of mathematics remained, and the double load of revision was hard for classicists, as the memoirs of Charles Astor Bristed testify.[59] To have included theology in the new tripos, as Wordsworth wished, would have nominally improved the preparation of future ordinands but at great cost in extra burdens while mathematics was such an obstacle. It was not lowered till a Senate vote, in October 1849,[60] opened the Classical Tripos to men who had qualified for an ordinary degree by taking the first part of the Mathematical Tripos. Though contested by the mathematical lobby,[61] the change was probably inevitable since ordinary graduands were allowed to enter for the new Moral and Natural Sciences Triposes set up the year before. The requirement for classicists was lightened again in 1854, when it was agreed that they merely had to pass the Previous Examination. But this was itself made more severe, by the inclusion for honours candidates (in all triposes) of additional mathematical topics. A suggestion that poll men should also have to face them was turned down – an indication of contradictory attitudes in Cambridge: mathematics was essential for everybody, and all intelligent undergraduates had to study as much of it as was feasible, while the threshold had to be kept very low for poll men.

---

[57] 'John Smith', *Sketches of Cantabs*, p. 18.
[58] Wordsworth failed in 1821 to persuade the Senate to agree to a Classical Tripos obligatory for all save the first ten wranglers. Typical of Wordsworth's lack of common sense, that scheme would have proved a disaster.   [59] See p. 609–10.
[60] For what follows, see Winstanley, *Early Victorian Cambridge*, pp. 216–18, 279–82.
[61] The votes were 43 to 31 in the Non-Regent House and 38 to 26 in the Regent House.

THE RECEPTION OF ANALYSIS IN CAMBRIDGE

An inspiration to progress at the beginning of the century, Newton's legacy was a constraint in Cambridge at the end: dons tended to rest on the laurels that he had won.[62] In one respect they retreated from his achievement, ceasing for the most part to use it for apologetic purposes, as a buttress for the argument from design, that in 1700 men like Bentley had seen as one of its great benefits. Confining themselves to Newtonian mathematics, they created the efficient and systematic Senate House Examination; but after 1750 (apart perhaps from Francis Maseres and Edward Waring)[63] they failed to add to mathematical understanding, and for a long time they ignored the way in which Newtonian mathematics was being overtaken by continental discoveries.[64] Newton was inclined to geometrical reasoning and used in his calculus a notation (his 'fluxions') that was akin to it. Leibnitz, who invented the calculus at very much the same time, used a different notation derived from algebra and was given in general to advanced algebraic (or analytical) reasoning. Especially when developed and refined by late-eighteenth century savants such as d'Alembert, Euler, Lagrange, and Laplace, analytical methods became greatly superior to Newton's; they were more economical, and facilitated mathematical progress. But at the turn of the century it was rare for Cambridge undergraduates to be introduced to the new techniques. The most popular textbooks of the era for the Senate House Examination were six produced by Samuel Vince and James Wood[65] in the 1790s; they were almost entirely geometrical in reasoning.

English mathematicians were usually suspicious of analysis. There was more enthusiasm for it in Scotland. John Playfair, Professor of Mathematics at Edinburgh from 1785 to 1819, was a notable supporter. A close friend of Henry Brougham, and a member of the liberal group centred on the *Edinburgh Review*, he

---

[62] For what follows, see Gascoigne, *Cambridge in the Age of the Enlightenment*, pp. 180–2, 270–99.

[63] Maseres was a fellow of Clare from 1756 to 1769, and was later a barrister and judge. Waring, a fellow of Magdalene, and Lucasian Professor of Mathematics from 1760 to 1798, became famous as the author of 'one of the most abstruse books written on the abstrusest parts of Algebra'.

[64] It is however true that Newtonianism stimulated other sciences in Cambridge, for example David Hartley's associationist psychology.   [65] Of St John's: see pp. 93–4, 125–8.

published his views on analysis in its columns. By contrast, the Tory *Quarterly Review*, founded in 1809 to oppose the *Edinburgh*, praised the Newtonian legacy while the *Eclectic Review* was anxious about the fate of the young if they were expected to read works by French mathematicians who were atheists. This debate took place during the French wars, and mathematics became entangled with patriotism and morality, so delaying the reception of French analysis in Cambridge.[66]

Cambridge had an early enthusiast for analytical mathematics in Robert Woodhouse, Senior Wrangler in 1795 and a fellow of Caius from 1798 to 1823. At the age of thirty, in 1803, he produced *Principles of Analytical Calculation*, a work whose cogency was much increased by its judicious correction of some continental methods. Woodhouse was aiming to convert his fellow teachers. He was unsuccessful, at least in the short term, and the book's compressed and difficult style was in part responsible. He also had to contend with established loyalty to Newton and the defence (specious though it often was) of geometry's superiority. Also strong, though scarcely ever admitted, was tutors' investment in lecture notes. Woodhouse's next work, *Elements of Trigonometry* (1809), was directed towards undergraduates, and Woodhouse's influence in helping to bring about the new mathematics was mediated through them, and therefore slow to take effect.[67]

Such influence may perhaps be detected in the shadowy career of John Toplis, who graduated Eleventh Wrangler from Queens' in 1801. Headmaster of Nottingham High School from 1806 to 1819, he was a partisan of the analytical approach, translating Laplace, *Mécanique céleste*, and inspiring the mathematical discoveries of George Green, the Nottingham miller whose genius, in large measure self-taught, led him to publish in 1828 one of the first attempts to apply mathematical theory to electrical phenomena; it has been described as 'the beginning of mathematical physics in England'.[68]

[66] Philip Charles Enros, 'The Analytical Society: Mathematics at Cambridge University in the Early Nineteenth Century', (PhD thesis, University of Toronto, 1979), pp. 49–79.

[67] Ball, *A History of Mathematics at Cambridge*, pp. 118–20.

[68] *An Essay on the Application of Mathematical Analysis to the Theories of Electricity and Magnetism*. Green published nine further investigations. In 1833 he matriculated at Gonville and Caius; Fourth Wrangler in 1837, he was elected a fellow of Caius. He died in 1841, aged forty-seven. Green's

Woodhouse's utterance also affected Charles Babbage, the genius described as 'the pioneer of the computer'.[69] In his home in Devon Babbage, 'being passionately fond of algebra', had learned of the new notation as a schoolboy through the works of Woodhouse and others; he spent seven guineas on the great book on the calculus by Lacroix before coming up to Trinity in 1810.

> I had ... met with many difficulties, and looked forward with intense delight to the certainty of having them all removed on my arrival at Cambridge... After a few days, I went to my public tutor Hudson, to ask the explanation of one of my mathematical difficulties. He listened to my question, said it would not be asked in the Senate House, and was of no sort of consequence, and advised me to get up the earlier subjects of the university studies.

Babbage suffered two further unsuccessful attempts to gain enlightenment from other dons. 'I thus acquired a distaste for the routine of the studies of the place, and devoured the papers of Euler and other mathematicians, scattered through innumerable volumes of the academies of Petersburgh, Berlin, and Paris, which the libraries I had recourse to contained.'

Joining with other undergraduates angry with the superannuated character of Cambridge mathematics, in May 1812 Babbage formed the Analytical Society, dedicated to furthering the new methods.[70] Other leading lights were John Herschel (the son of a famous astronomer and himself destined to be another) and Alexander D'Arblay (whose mother was Fanny D'Arblay, better known perhaps as Fanny Burney, the novelist). Before coming to Cambridge all three had learned of analysis, D'Arblay in France. There were no more than twenty members altogether, almost all of them undergraduates. 'Of course we were much ridiculed by the Dons; and, not being put down, it was darkly hinted that we were young

name was after his death rescued from obscurity by William Thomson, Lord Kelvin, who recognised the originality of his genius. In this century Green's techniques have been of great value in quantum physics. See D. M. Cannell, *George Green, Mathematician and Physicist, 1793–1841: The Background to his Life and Work* (London, Athlone, 1993).

[69] For what follows, see Charles Babbage, *Passages from the Life of a Philosopher* (London, 1864), pp. 26–7. See also Anthony Hyman, *Charles Babbage. Pioneer of the Computer* (Oxford University Press, 1982).

[70] What follows is greatly indebted to Enros, 'Analytical Society', pp. 103–66; see also Hyman, *Charles Babbage*, pp. 25–8.

infidels, and that no good would come of us.'[71] Babbage and Herschel dominated its proceedings and wrote all the papers (which were austerely mathematical) in the *Memoirs of the Analytical Society* (1813). They attracted little attention outside Cambridge and not much more in it. Babbage and Herschel graduated in 1813, and when deprived of their energy the society soon collapsed. Continued life for the Analytical was in any case made unlikely by the ascetically scholarly nature of its activities, which lacked any hint of youthful levity. Nevertheless, its chronicler P. C. Enros is too severe in his judgement that the society was a comparative failure, since it played a large part in assisting the introduction of analysis to Cambridge by fostering it in members later powerful. Three, George Peacock, Richard Gwatkin, and John William Whittaker, became private tutors after their wranglerships, and Peacock became an assistant public tutor at Trinity in 1815. The three men were therefore able to act as missionaries for analysis among their pupils, and Peacock's influence on undergraduates is suggested by J. M. F. Wright's purchase in 1816 and 1817 of Woodhouse's *Elements of Trigonometry* (1809, a key work in the new mathematics) and *Traité élémentaire de calcul différentiel* by Lacroix, which Wright perhaps obtained in the translation of 1816 by Babbage, Herschel and Peacock; but Wright also had to cram many pages in Wood's pre-analytical textbooks.[72]

Peacock was able to exert more leverage when in 1817 he became moderator in the Senate House Examination.[73] His fellow-moderator, John White of Caius, and the two examiners (in charge of proceedings) would not heed his call for change, and he was able to introduce analysis only into his own papers. Whewell's comment was that Peacock had turned it 'naked' among the dons: 'Of course all the prudery of the university is up and shocked at the indecency of the spectacle.'[74] Still, most of the younger members of the university were converted to the analytical cause, and when in 1819 Peacock was moderator again his colleague Gwatkin joined him in adopting it. The following year William Whewell was moderator, and he

[71] Babbage, *Passages from the Life of a Philosopher*, p. 29.
[72] Wright, *Alma Mater*, vol. I, pp. 184, 206–7. Wright came up in 1815.
[73] For what follows, see Enros, 'Analytical Society', pp. 213–55, and Ball, *Study of Mathematics at Cambridge*, pp. 120–3.
[74] Todhunter, *William Whewell, D.D. Writings*, vol. II, p. 16.

adopted it too.[75] Whewell, younger than Babbage and Peacock, had not been a member of the Analytical Society, and had studied analysis only after graduating in 1816. While never fanatical about analysis he saw its power as a mathematical tool, and worked to add it to established geometrical approaches in the Cambridge curriculum. By the early 1820s it was firmly established in Cambridge, its position being consolidated by a new generation of textbooks, superseding the geometrical standbys. In 1832 Herschel wrote: 'at this moment we believe that there exists not throughout Europe a centre from which a richer and purer light of mathematical instruction emanates through a community, than one, at least, of our universities'.[76] From 1832 to 1847 the weight given to analysis in the tripos steadily increased; 'pure geometrical reasoning was altogether abandoned, and the attention of the Students, by the questions proposed, was unduly fixed upon the dexterous use of symbols'.[77]

There was a reaction, and in it William Whewell was very significant.[78] Regretting the enthusiasm he had as a young graduate felt for analysis Whewell came to believe in the 1830s that it should be subordinated to geometrical reasoning in the university curriculum. Geometry forced the student to reason by stern and exacting logic, step by step towards the truth. Analysis, on the other hand, allowed him to exchange facts for symbols whose manipulation made reasoning easier.[79]

> In the one case, that of geometrical reasoning, we tread the ground ourselves, at every step feeling ourselves firm, and directing our steps to the end aimed at. In the other case, that of analytical calculation, we are carried along as in a rail-road carriage, entering it at one station, and coming out of it at another, without having any choice in our progress in the intermediate space.

The greater celerity, economy, and neatness of analysis in mathematical calculation were admitted. Future professional mathema-

---

[75] What follows on Whewell is based on Enros, 'Analytical Society', pp. 236–52, an account exploiting new manuscript sources.   [76] Quoted in Enros, 'Analytical Society', p. 242.

[77] PP 1852–3, HC xliv [1559]: *Graham Commission Evidence*, p. 229.

[78] What follows is greatly indebted to Harvey W. Becher, 'William Whewell and Cambridge Mathematics', *Historical Studies in the Physical Sciences* 11 (1980), pp. 1–48.

[79] For what follows see William Whewell, *Of a Liberal Education in General; and with Particular Reference to the Leading Studies of the University of Cambridge* (2nd edn, London, 1850), pp. 38–77; the three quotations are taken from pp. 41, 77, and 43 respectively.

ticians would certainly need to study it. But 'the use of mathematical study, with which we have to do, is not to produce a school of eminent mathematicians, but to contribute to a Liberal Education of the highest kind': that is, for men of a wide range of professions. In any case, analysis itself could only be fully understood by those who had learned to reason through the superior agency of geometry. 'And the habit thus advancing, with clear conviction and active thought, from step to step of certain truth, is an intellectual habit of the greatest value; which a good education ought to form and render familiar; and which nothing but geometrical study can impart.'

Whewell was prominent in the campaign to 'regeometrise' the Cambridge curriculum, serving on the syndicate that considered the faults in existing procedures. Weaker candidates lacked the time or the talent to be competent at everything, and they gambled by cramming portions of higher mathematics, analysis included; they went to much trouble 'not to overcome the real difficulties of the subject, but to seize some such portion of it, or to put it in some such form, as may fall in with the turn that the Examination may take' (in other words, question-spotting).[80] To discourage them, Whewell made in 1845 a proposal to divide the tripos into two parts, and to make success in the first a requirement for entry to the second. The first was to consist very largely of the geometrical and non-analytical usage whose essential nature as a 'permanent' study in a liberal education Whewell wished to stress, and the second to contain the advanced and 'progressive' elements necessary for future professional mathematicians. The Senate acted upon the proposal, and with effect from 1848 the tripos was split into two parts, separated by a gap of eight days – a change that was an important feature of the 'internal reform' that the university undertook in the 1840s. All candidates took the first part of the examination. Only those candidates acquitting themselves well in the first part might proceed to the honours papers in the second; others might be held to have qualified for the mathematical section of the ordinary degree.

Whewell wished the university to create a Board of Mathematical Studies, composed of the professors and others and reflecting

---

[80] Whewell, *Of a Liberal Education*, 2nd edn, Part 1, p 197.

established opinion. Though in 1843 the Senate rejected the idea by nine votes, five years later it agreed. In 1849 and 1850 the new board suggested, and the Senate agreed, that certain topics recently added to the tripos should be eliminated from it. Very important amongst them were theories of magnetism, electricity and heat; excluding them meant restricting mechanics in the tripos to explanations derived from the *Principia,* 'which had been made into a mathematically consistent and stable system in the eighteenth and nineteenth centuries. The experimental and hypothetical frontiers of physics were excluded.'[81] The scope of the 'reNewtonisation' of the tripos may be seen in the questions asked in 1854. Analysis was less important than it had been ten years earlier. Problems calling for geometric solutions outnumbered those demanding algebraic solutions; there was a renewed emphasis on the Newtonian tradition rather than continental mathematics, and on applied or mixed rather than pure mathematics, embracing mechanics, hydrodynamics, astronomy and planetary theory, and physical and geometrical optics.

In 1866 James Clerk Maxwell introduced some tripos questions dealing with current concerns in physics – heat, electricity and magnetism – and in 1873 the subject matter excluded in the middle of the century was restored. Still, Cambridge mathematics retained its distinctive character after that, and there was good and bad in it. Though it was highly competitive and physically and intellectually demanding for those seeking the highest honours, it remained behind the continent in the quality of its 'pure' higher analysis. Thus Isaac Todhunter, Senior Wrangler in 1848, claimed in a textbook published in 1871 that there had not been 'any real improvements' in the 'methods of explaining and developing the principles' of the calculus for twenty years; yet he manifested his ignorance of recent advances in his own references to the calculus.[82] Arthur Cayley, the Sadleirian Professor of Mathematics from 1863 to 1895, was a lone enthusiast for pure mathematics, and failed to attract many undergraduates to his lectures.[83] One of his students, Andrew Forseyth, Senior Wrangler in 1881, tried to update Cambridge analysis but

[81] Becher, 'Whewell and Cambridge mathematics,' p. 44.
[82] Becher, 'Whewell and Cambridge mathematics,' p. 42.
[83] J. J. Thomson, *Recollections and Reflections* (London, 1936), p. 47.

used obsolete methods. He was judged not 'very good at delta and epsilon', he looked 'backward to Lagrange' in his research on differential equations, and he wrote a textbook on the theory of functions, sections of which 'read as though they had been written by Euler'.[84] 'As an undergraduate', wrote Bertrand Russell, Seventh Wrangler in 1893,

> I was persuaded that the Dons were a wholly unnecessary part of the university. I derived no benefits from lectures... My mathematical tutors had never shown me any reason to suppose the Calculus anything but a tissue of fallacies... The mathematical question had already in the main been solved on the Continent, though in England the continental work was little known. It was only after I left Cambridge and began to live abroad that I discovered what I ought to have been taught during my three years as an undergraduate.[85]

On the other hand Cambridge mathematics was a leading route to the profession of physicist, and different from the *experimental* route that was constructed after the start of the Natural Sciences Tripos in 1851. Thus in the second half of the century wranglers filled nearly half the chairs in physics in British universities.[86] The emphases of the Mathematical Tripos tempted the handful of very talented students inclined to research to investigate the mathematical bases of the physical world rather than the theoretical bases of pure mathematics in the continental way;[87] and their researches were shaped by the concern of the tripos, inherited from Newton, with the mathematical explication of the dynamics of the universe. Different though their interests and findings were, Cambridge physicists with a background in the Mathematical Tripos were united in stressing the special status of mechanics, the science of

[84] Becher, 'Whewell and Cambridge mathematics', pp. 42–3, quoting Roth, 'Old Cambridge Days,' *American Mathematical Monthly*, 78 (1971), pp. 229–31.

[85] Bertrand Russell, *The Autobiography of Bertrand Russell* (3 vols., London. Allen & Unwin, 1967–9), vol. 1, pp. 67–8.

[86] P. Forman, J. L. Heilbron and S. Weart, 'Physics *circa* 1900: Personnel, Funding and Productivity of the Academic Establishments', *Historical Studies in the Physical Sciences*, 5 (1975), p. 32. For Cambridge physics, see chapter 6, pp. 226–31.

[87] For these lines see P. M. Harman, ed., *Wranglers and Physicists: Studies on Cambridge Physics in the Nineteenth Century* (Manchester University Press, 1985), esp. the chapters by Harman and D. B. Wilson, pp. 1–48; also D. B. Wilson, 'Experimentalists among the Mathematicians: Physics in the Cambridge Natural Sciences Tripos, 1851–1900', *Historical Studies in the Physical Sciences*, 12 (1982), pp. 325–71.

matter in motion, as the zenith of physics and a paradigm of physical theory. Within a mathematical framework of interpretation, they emphasised 'a commitment to the mechanical view of nature, which supposed that matter in motion was the basis of all physical phenomena and that mechanical explanation was the programme of physical theory'.[88] Many leading late-Victorian physicists, among whom one may mention George Stokes, William Thomson (Lord Kelvin), and Joseph Larmor, came from this tradition, were immersed in its deductive, mathematical, and dynamical spirit, and were inclined to relegate experimental findings to a subordinate place in the scheme of things, however much they were themselves willing to embrace experimentalism.

Against this pervasive culture experimentalism at first found it hard to contend. But Clerk Maxwell, though himself Second Wrangler in 1854, urged the need for an alternative approach in the 1860s; his appointment in 1871 as the first Cavendish Professor of Experimental Physics was a landmark, as were the opening of the Cavendish Laboratory in 1874 and the start there of courses in experimental physics in 1876–7. If the weakness of those educated through the Mathematical Tripos was a tendency to neglect experimental methods, in the early years NST physics students were inadequately prepared in mathematics. The remedying of this anomaly by J. J. Thomson helped to lead to the growth in success, reputation, and self-confidence in the Cavendish in the 1890s: in short, it moved out of the shadow of the Mathematical Tripos.

THE NATURE OF THE MATHEMATICAL EXAMINATION, 1824–1870

THE EXAMINATION BECOMES EXCLUSIVELY MATHEMATICAL

After the setting up of the Classical Tripos in 1824 the Senate House Examination remained as the inescapable route to the bachelor of arts degree; only graduates with honours in it could enter for the new tripos, and that remained true till 1850. For many years the Senate House Examination was nominally for honours men and *hoi*

---

[88] Harman, *Wranglers and Physicists*, p. 2.

polloi too, though from 1828 onwards the tripos and poll examinations were taken at different times and had different question papers.[89] As their intellectual content diverged, this fiction of a common test with two sections became increasingly transparent, and in 1858 the poll examination was separated from the Mathematical Tripos.[90]

Proposals for change in the 1770s and 1810s had aroused contention because they threatened college autonomy or the supremacy of mathematics. In contrast, changes within the Mathcmatical Tripos (as we should now call it) that were developed from the 1820s to 1870s through dialogue between mathematicians, menaced no vested interest and caused no serious dispute, though certainly the syndicates overseeing the evolution talked for many sessions. A departure from tradition was the practice, from 1827 onwards, of giving candidates printed papers for all questions, and not merely the 'problems'. A link with the Middle Ages, the disputations that preceded the written examination, became less and less important in the 1820s. They would have done so inevitably, and the coming of algebraic notation[91] speeded the change up: 'the nature of the new kind of mathematics, addressing itself, as analysis does, to the eye, and difficult to express in an oral form, made the disputations in the Schools much less intelligible and interesting, and gave an increased importance to the paper Examinations'.[92] The preliminary classes (originally eight, then six) were based on the disputation results, and became less coherent as these did. The classes had always been separately examined[93] by the moderators, whose questions naturally differed. Difficulties thus arose:

> The Examiners, in giving different questions to different Classes, endeavoured to proportion the difficulty of the questions to the attainments of the Class; and again, to proportion the credit to the difficulty, in judging the answer... If the questions proposed to the lower Classes were proportionably too easy, the members of those Classes obtained more marks than those who, being in the higher

[89] For what follows, see Ball, *History of Mathematics at Cambridge*, pp. 211–16, and Whewell, *Of a Liberal Education in General*, 2nd edn, Part 1, pp. 186–97. For the ordinary degree examinations, see p. xxx.   [90] See p. 183.   [91] See p. 172.
[92] Whewell, *Of a Liberal Education*, 2nd edn, Part 1, p. 186.
[93] For this purpose the classes were grouped in twos.

Classes, had probably read higher parts of mathematics than they had... An examination such as that which was finally established, in which the same questions were proposed to all the candidates, has, in that respect a very great advantage, as a means of forming a just list of merit.[94]

The classes were reduced from six to four in 1827 (examined in two groups of two). They were abolished altogether in 1838, and the ending of the disputations followed naturally the next year.

Between 1827 and 1848 (when the examination was given the form it had till 1873) the number of days within the tripos given over to mathematics was in several stages increased from three to eight. In the same process the day traditionally given over to 'brackets' was scrapped, as was the religion and philosophy day, dropped about 1840; so perished the last vestige of the Aristotelian bias that university studies had possessed in the Middle Ages.[95] The tripos became exclusively mathematical. The total of hours grew from twenty-three in 1827 to forty-four and a half in 1848, far more than today, when in addition triposes are split into at least two parts (in different years) each rarely exceeding eighteen hours. Evening sessions disappeared in 1832, so at least an examination day was less hectic than it had been for Gunning's generation. Examiners were also given some leeway; at the beginning of the century they were said sometimes to have to mark all night, but the division of the tripos into two parts from 1848 onwards[96] meant that in the middle there was a gap of eight days in which examiners could mark the Part 1 papers.[97] In the middle of the century twenty-one days elapsed between the beginning of the tripos and the day the results were published.[98]

We get a striking picture of the examination as it was about 1860 from William Everett, a member of a patrician New England family whose father had been ambassador to the United Kingdom in the 1840s.[99] William Everett, after a period at Harvard, was a pensioner

---

[94] Whewell, *Of a Liberal Education*, 2nd edn, Part 1, pp. 192–3.
[95] 'Religion' was reintroduced in 1846 in the form of papers on the New Testament, Paley, and ecclesiastical history. They were usually neglected by candidates since no account was taken of their marks in drawing up the final list. In 1855 they were deleted, and not restored again to the Mathematical Tripos.   [96] See p. 173.   [97] By 1860 the gap had grown to ten days.
[98] PP 1852–3, HC xliv [1559]: *Graham Commission Evidence*, p. 259.
[99] William Everett's Cambridge years are treated at length in chapter 16.

and then a scholar at Trinity. He was at the head of the second class in the Classical Tripos in 1863. One year later he conveyed the charm and oddity of Cambridge life to a Boston audience in lectures he gave in the Lowell Institute.[100] We are in the Senate House on a Tuesday morning early in January, Everett writes:

> As the hands of the great University clock on the church outside are seen to approach nine, an examiner, or some University official, takes his station at the head of each of eight lines of tables, with a pile of the printed examination papers, damp from the press. The instant the first stroke is heard, a rapid race down the tables begins, a paper being dropped at every man... They contain, on this first day, questions on the elements of mathematics, the divine Euclid, and other easy geometrical subjects, – all such as can be found in approved treatises, or easily deducible therefrom...
>
> Over this paper of questions the candidates are allowed three hours, but may go out as much sooner as they wish, – not of course to come in again; – for it is a maxim running through the whole of Cambridge instruction, that a man is not to be put to do more than he wants to. If his declining to work on a paper subjects him to failure and loss, that is his lookout. At twelve, then, they must stop. At one, another three hours' paper. The next day, the same, and the next. Then a pause of ten days, while the work of the previous three, all on the easier departments of mathematics, is looked over. All those who have passed the minimum asked by the examiners, are now announced as 'having acquitted themselves so as to deserve mathematical honours'. The rest, O dreadful word, and thrice dreadful fate, have their names published no more, and are 'plucked'. The degree of Bachelor of Arts is not for them as far as mathematics goes. With these three days, the ambition of most stops...[101] On the tenth day after they end, begins the five days' examination, on real tough mathematics, *beginning* with the differential calculus, and going up to the highest calculation of astronomy and optics. 'Few are the stragglers, following far', who stay in after the prescribed half hour in the last

---

[100] William Everett, *On the Cam. Lectures on the University of Cambridge in England* (London, 1866), pp. 53–6 for what follows.

[101] Candidates for the Classical Tripos (one being Everett himself) met their mathematical requirements by success in the first three days. After 1854 candidates for classical honours who passed the Previous Examination at an honours level might then drop mathematics altogether. Presumably Everett's results in the Previous had not been outstanding and so he took the first three days of tripos papers.

8 Presentation of the Senior Wrangler in the Senate House by the praelector of Trinity, January 1842. The Vice-Chancellor is George Archdall, Master of Emmanuel. The Proctors are on his left. The Senior Wrangler is Arthur Cayley; he became a fellow of Trinity and in 1863 Sadleirian Professor of Mathematics. The informality of this scene is remarkable, compared with the ceremony of similar occasions today.

few papers of these dreadful five days, three hours morning and afternoon...

After the five days, everybody takes a rest. On the last Friday in January, or thereabouts, the result of their examination is announced. Again the candidates assemble in the Senate-House a few minutes before nine, or rather their friends, for the candidates themselves don't like to go much. A proctor appears in the gallery with a list. Five hundred upturned faces below listen eagerly for his first words. The clock strikes nine. 'Senior Wrangler, – Romer of Trinity Hall.' A tumultuous, furious, insane shout bursts forth, caps fly up into the air, the dust rises immeasurable, and it takes many minutes to restore the order that greets the announcement of the greatest honour that the University can bestow for that year. 'Second Wrangler, – Leeke of Trinity.'[102] Another burst of cheering that would be called terrific, had the other not preceded it. 'Third', and so on down through the Wranglers, or first class. Now look out. The proctors in the gallery, each armed with his file of printed lists, proceed to scatter them to the multitude below. Talk of Italian beggars, beasts at a menagerie; why, the rush, the scuffle, the trampling, the crushing of caps and cap-bearers in a shapeless mass, the tearing of gowns, coats, and the very papers that come slowly floating down, beats any tumult I ever saw.

THE MATHEMATICAL TRIPOS: ITS DEFENCE AND ITS LIMITATIONS

'A Senior Wrangler, as he would urge, might be absolutely ignorant of law; but three years after his degree he would be a far better lawyer than the man who had been crammed with legal knowledge in place of being trained in the use of his logical faculties.'[103] By the middle of the nineteenth century the Mathematical Tripos had been so developed and refined as to be a subtle and sophisticated competition, discriminating exactly between fine shades of talent and accomplishment; the Reverend T. Gaskin (moderator in the tripos in 1842) reported that less than one and a half per cent in the total number of marks had been known to mark a difference of

---

[102] Romer and Leeke achieved these honours (and also tied equal for the Smith's Prize) in 1863, the year that Everett himself took the first three days' papers, and shortly afterwards the Classical Tripos.

[103] Leslie Stephen, *Life of Henry Fawcett* p. 91, and 90–2 for what follows.

three places among the wranglers.[104] The examination exploited and assessed a narrow range of gifts, and its content scarcely ever proved useful in the graduate's vocation; but it was praised as an excellent 'mental gymnastic' and a scrupulously just test of intelligence, and therefore a perfect meritocratic instrument, when administered with the utmost fairness as it was by the university examiners. Such was the robust defence offered by dons like Henry Fawcett (Seventh Wrangler in 1856 – a result that disappointed him); Fawcett proved his own intellectual tenacity by becoming a successful scholar and politician, Postmaster-General in Gladstone's government of 1880–5, after being afflicted by blindness.[105] Fawcett's friend and biographer Leslie Stephen exposed the frailty of these arguments in the amusing sketches he wrote with tongue in cheek for the *Pall Mall Gazette*.[106] Success in the tripos was not attempted by undergraduates for the sake of mental cultivation. 'I remember a rash youth who stated to his friends that he was studying mathematics with a view to improving his mind. It became a standard joke against him ever afterwards.' Undergraduates pursued wranglerships for fellowships, assessed by Stephen as worth £2,500 each, and for the glory, which since it helped to bring success in the church or at the bar came 'to very much the same thing'. And though the minds of a gifted minority might be developed by the rigorous training, that was certainly not true of most:

> nothing can be more absurd than to make five hundred young men ... give up three years to reading classics or mathematics for their own sake. Perhaps fifty of them may be improved by such a discipline ... The 'gymnastic theory', as applied to those below the first-class, is a mere farce ... If any one doubts this, he may ask himself whether he would recommend a stupid lad of eighteen living in London, who was to enter a profession in three years' time, to pass the intervening years in attending third-rate lectures on Greek and Latin.

The tripos also-rans were of two sorts, which overlapped: the highly intelligent whose predilection was for literary pursuits, not

---

[104] PP 1852–3, HC xliv [1559]: *Graham Commission Evidence*, p. 230.
[105] On Fawcett see Goldman, *The Blind Victorian*, and Leslie Stephen, *Life of Henry Fawcett*, one of the most elegant of Victorian biographies.
[106] Reprinted as *Sketches from Cambridge*, by 'A Don' (London, 1865), pp. 31–43 for what follows.

mathematical ones, and the dullards, very common in the university when entry was much less competitive than the degree examination. The range within the spectrum of honours candidates (about one-third of the total taking BA degrees) was itself great, but we need also to take into account the poll men. In 1843 the bottom junior optime gained one-twentieth of the marks of the Senior Wrangler: perhaps 4 per cent as against 80 per cent. The number of men allowed honours was itself artificially inflated at that time because of the requirement that those wishing to proceed to the Classical Tripos had to gain mathematical honours first, and by the fact that those failing honours could not use their marks to qualify for the mathematical section of the ordinary degree. Ten years later new regulations had removed these restrictions, and within the honours category marks now varied by a factor of no more than four or five, very similar to the modern disparity.[107] But of course in the meantime the tail of poll men had just been lengthened, whereas today the number of ordinary graduands is tiny.

As to these poll men, we are not surprised to learn that they failed to profit from mathematical instruction. J. M. F. Wright was despite his talents relegated in 1819[108] to the eighth (the lowest) category of questionists, the future *hoi polloi*: 'a man from the opposite side of the table, having for the last ten minutes been leaning his head upon his hand, excogitating most intensely, exclaimed, "I shall be plucked to a certainty, and if so, I may as well hang myself, my father having again and again threatened to disinherit me if I am plucked – do help me over this difficulty, Sir".'[109] 'Bearing in mind', said Gaskin thirty years later, 'the difficulties which abstruse subjects present to many men whom we should be most sorry to exclude from an academical degree, I think that it is impossible to make the standard anything but very low.' Candidates for the ordinary degree had to attempt just three papers: on arithmetic and simple algebra, the first three books of Euclid and six propositions of Book VI, and some elementary propositions in mechanics and hydrostatics with simple examples – at a generous estimate, no more than would have been known by a bright pupil of fourteen when in the 1960s

---

[107] PP 1852–3, HC xliv [1559]: *Graham Commission Evidence*, pp. 227, 250, 267a. I owe the modern comparison to Michael Potter of Fitzwilliam College.
[108] See p. 120.   [109] Wright, *Alma Mater*, vol. II, pp. 67–8.

Euclidean geometry was last taught in British schools. Poll men were more able to memorise propositions than to understand principles. On the arithmetic paper, it was said, the examiners were 'obliged to be satisfied with less than one-third of the paper'; otherwise they would have been 'reduced to the necessity of refusing degrees to a large proportion of the Candidates'.[110] The least talented of these candidates was the 'fast man', too stupid to benefit at all from his studies or to enjoy any intellectual interests. 'He hates the University, as a matter of course, longing for the time, as he tells you, when he is to get out into the world.' His conversation was vapid, and his pleasures drink, betting, and racing.[111] Such men were unable to study anything, but nothing was less likely than mathematics to engage their attention.

William Whewell built his educational philosophy on the necessary combination of mathematics and the classical tongues,[112] but the predominance of mathematics in the Cambridge curriculum meant that those with literary preferences were disadvantaged. Horace Walpole (whose letters are incidentally testimony to the early predominance of mathematics at Cambridge) revealed his literary tastes and talents at Eton and continued to do so after coming up to King's as a fellow commoner in 1735, for example writing a Latin poem that the university published on the occasion of the Prince of Wales's marriage in 1736. Walpole attempted to learn mathematics with Saunderson, the blind professor, but was told after a fortnight that it was robbing him to take his money since he could never learn it. Walpole wept with humiliation and engaged a private tutor, but soon had to admit that Saunderson had been right. Commiserating with his friend at Christ Church, Richard West, at their 'two barbarous towns o'errun with rusticity and mathematics',[113] he complained that:

> Great mathematicians have been of great use: but the generality of them are quite unconversible ... by living amongst them, I write of nothing else; my letters are all parallelograms, two sides equal to two

110 *Graham Commission Evidence*, pp. 226, 236.
111 'John Smith', *Sketches of Cantabs*, pp. 15–20.
112 Whewell, *Of a Liberal Education*, 2nd edn, Part 1, pp. 106–8.
113 Wilmarth Sheldon Lewis, ed., *The Correspondence of Horace Walpole* (48 vols., New Haven, Conn.: Yale University Press, 1937–83), vol. XIII, pp. 93–4, Walpole to Richard West, 9 November 1735.

sides; and every paragraph an axiom, that tells you nothing but what every mortal almost knows.[114]

Walpole expressed no affection for Cambridge until many years later.[115]

Eighty years afterwards T. B. Macaulay, aged twelve, wrote from his school in Little Shelford: 'The books which I am at present employed in reading to myself are, in English Plutarch's lives and Milner's Ecclesiastical History, in French Fenelon's dialogues of the Dead.'[116] The letters of the youthful prodigy are peppered with references to his omnivorous reading, from Boccaccio to Byron, and no Cambridge undergraduate of the century (he went up to Trinity in October 1817) was more suited to literary studies. In August 1820 he was 'deep in Plato, Aristotle and Theocritus', and a year later his 'admiration of Homer increases with every perusal'.[117] Wishing to achieve honours in the tripos he kept on resolving to work hard at mathematics, and in the Trinity freshmen's examination he did well enough to get into the first class. Even so, Macaulay had already revealed his feelings a few months earlier: 'I can scarcely bear to write on mathematics or mathematicians. Oh for words to express my abomination of that science ... this miserable study! Discipline of the mind! Say rather that it is starvation, confinement, torture, annihilation of the mind. But it must be ... Farewell then Homer and Sophocles and Cicero.'[118] We are not surprised to learn, however, that in his tripos in January 1822 he withdrew after two days knowing that he would not achieve honours; he had not been able, wrote his father, 'to sacrifice his more miscellaneous reading to Mathematics'.[119] Macaulay was 'gulphed', given a pass degree but not made to suffer the mortification of seeing his name in the list of poll men.

The Classical Tripos, instituted two years later, was meant to give an opportunity to men of literary talent, but would not have helped

[114] W. S. Lewis, *Correspondence*, vol. XIII, pp. 107–8, Walpole to West, 17 August 1736.
[115] R. W. Ketton-Cremer, *Horace Walpole* (3rd edn, London, Methuen, 1964), pp. 32–40.
[116] Thomas Pinney, ed., *The Letters of Thomas Babington Macaulay* (7 vols., Cambridge University Press, 1974–), vol. I, p. 28, TBM to Selina Mills Macaulay, 20 April 1813. For what follows, pp. 1–169, and John Clive, *Thomas Babington Macaulay. The Shaping of the Historian* (London, Secker & Warburg, 1973), pp. 21–60.   [117] Pinney, *The Letters*, vol. I, pp. 145, 163.
[118] Pinney, *The letters*, vol. I, pp. 122–3, TBM to Selina Mills Macaulay, 24 February 1819.
[119] Quoted in Pinney, *The Letters*, p. 169.

Macaulay since candidates had to gain honours in the Mathematical Tripos first. In the 1840s Charles Astor Bristed, the Yale graduate extending his education at Trinity, complained that this rule was far more onerous than the classics hurdle in the Previous Examination was for mathematicians. Hating the spherical trigonometry he was revising in the last intensive months – 'the feeling was exactly like that of eating sawdust'[120] – Bristed tried to quench the burning temptation to read Homer by keeping it in a separate room – only in the end succumbing. Bristed would have liked the jokey ignominy of the 'Wooden Spoon' but instead was two places above it; three weeks later he took the second place in the second class of the Classical Tripos. His considered judgement – surely correct – was that it was fruitless to try to force a specialism on a mind disliking it, while 'Mathematical annoyances' occasioned 'petulance and irritability' among enthusiastic classicists that were 'matter of notoriety' among students in general.

LAW AND MEDICINE

Arts were not the only field in which one might acquire a bachelor's degree. There were also bachelors in divinity, law, and medicine, though in the eighteenth century none of them attracted the prestige or the numbers of the arts degree.[121]

LAW

There were three legal traditions in England, all originating in the Middle Ages: canon law, civil law, and common law.[122] Canon law was the law of the church, and civil law consisted of the texts composed by jurists in the Roman Empire, and later interpretations of them; often it was called Roman law. The chief text was the *Corpus juris civilis* – hence the term 'civil law'; it is not to be confused with civil actions as we know them today. Common law was created by lawyers in the king's courts, case by case; it was also

---

[120] C. A. Bristed, *Five Years in an English University*, vol. 1, pp. 298, 292 for the later quotation, and 279–305 for these sentences in general.
[121] For degrees in divinity, see chapter 7, pp. 262–5.
[122] For what follows, see J. H. Baker, *An Introduction to English Legal History* (London, Butterworths, 1971), esp. pp. 29–77.

modified and created by statute. In the Middle Ages canon and civil lawyers were trained in the universities, and common lawyers in the Inns of Court or more likely through self-help. At the Reformation the study of canon law was ended at Oxford and Cambridge, while civil law remained.

There was hostility between the jurisprudential systems. Roman lawyers regarded theirs as intellectually superior, since it was based on coherent principles; common lawyers feared encroachment by 'civilians' on their courts of King's Bench and Common Pleas.[123] The struggle ended, particularly after the Revolution of 1688, with the victory of the common lawyers; they confined the actions of civil law to a few courts – the most important being the Court of Admiralty and the ecclesiastical courts responsible for matters of divorce and probate, the chief of these being the Court of the Arches.[124] There were only between twenty and thirty advocates working in this court at any one time, and only one or two were admitted each year; so opportunities for civil law graduates were limited, though they might turn to other careers, like diplomacy, where knowledge of civil law was useful because most European legal systems were based on it – as international law was.

Civil law languished at Cambridge. The statutes required residence for six years for the bachelor's degree.[125] Only one exercise was required to graduate, but it was supposed to be kept against the professor or a doctor of law, and so was potentially tougher than the exercises arts candidates faced, against other undergraduates. Practice lagged behind. In 1684 the heads of house decided that three years' residence would suffice – a typical example of the way departures from statutes were allowed when they suited the university. After three years' absence candidates returned to take their act, but meanwhile they were not required to study law; the exercise became perfunctory and the degree a soft option. Few people took it – a handful each year in the first half of the eighteenth century and less than twenty, it seems, in the second half. In 1766 the President of Queens', Dr Plumptre, denounced it as 'the refuge

---

[123] For what follows, see J. L. Barton, 'Legal Studies', in Sutherland and Mitchell, *Oxford: The Eighteenth Century*, pp. 594–6.
[124] So called because it sat under the arches of the church of St Mary-le-Bow. It was usually called the Court of Arches.   [125] Winstanley, *Unreformed Cambridge*, pp. 57–9.

of idleness and ignorance' that gave an advantage over candidates for the BA.[126] In 1768 a grace laid down that nobody except a bachelor of arts could graduate in civil law unless he got a certificate to prove attendance at the professor's lectures for three terms. This was a first tentative step towards a proper examination.

One Cambridge college, Trinity Hall, was very much 'a nursery for civilians'.[127] It was bound by its statutes of 1350 to the study and practice of civil and canon law, and the link with civil law remained after the Reformation, when canon law was proscribed in the universities. Between 1512 and 1856 (when advocates in the civil courts ceased to be a separate category) 85 of the 462 men admitted as advocates, or nearly 20 per cent, were from Trinity Hall; the only college that came near to rivalling it was All Souls, Oxford. Of the 16 Masters of Trinity Hall between 1552 and 1803, 15 had been advocates, while between 1666 and 1873 all 12 Regius Professors of Civil Law were Trinity Hall men by origin or adoption. The advocates had a formal society, the College of Doctors and Advocates of the Court of the Arches, familiarly called Doctors' Commons, and from 1567 to 1768 Trinity Hall was its landlord; it leased from the Dean and Chapter of St Paul's Cathedral the premises that in turn Doctors' Commons rented from the college.

Unlike some others the Professors of Civil Law did lecture, which was fortunate since colleges did not as a rule provide teaching.[128] One reason for their diligence was their power to charge fees, a supplement to their meagre stipend of £40, fixed in 1540 and not enlarged afterwards. The university was not 'the theatre of the Professor's most engrossing labours'. Some were also clergymen; Henry Maine, professor from 1847 to 1854, was a barrister.[129] Samuel Hallifax, better known as a churchman and for his controversy with his cousin John Jebb, was professor from 1770 to 1782, and in 1774 published *An Analysis of the Roman Civil Law*, which also offered a comparison with English law. Based on Hallifax's lectures, it went through four editions in twenty years, and was republished in 1836. As late as 1850 the Bachelor of Law

---

[126] Quoted in Winstanley, *Unreformed Cambridge*, p. 59.
[127] Crawley, *Trinity Hall*, esp. pp. 70–89.
[128] For what follows, see Winstanley, *Unreformed Cambridge*, pp. 123–7, and PP 1852–3, HC xliv [1559]: *Graham Commission Evidence*, pp. 77–9; p. 79 for the first quotation.
[129] Later the writer of *Ancient Law* and many other works, and Master of Trinity Hall.

(LL B) course followed Hallifax's scheme, which indicates considerable intellectual competence on his part, and some inertia perhaps on the part of his successors. The only comment we have on Hallifax's lectures, however, is that they were 'too fast' for note-taking. His successor Joseph Jowett of Trinity Hall, professor until 1813, was one of the university's leading Evangelicals; his law lectures, and his comparison of Roman and English law, were commended.

When Jowett died he was succeeded as Regius Professor by James Geldart, a graduate in law from Trinity Hall.[130] His literary endeavour was confined to a new edition of Hallifax's book, but in 1816 he initiated annual examinations for men in his civil law classes, to add to the academic status of the LL B degree. In the first two years the degree was divided into two classes, and from 1818 onwards three. In 1816 there were fourteen candidates, and in 1857, the last year of this examination, twenty-four; so numbers were always modest. One-third of all the candidates, and one year in two the top man, came from Trinity Hall;[131] in 1850 it was said that Trinity Hall supplied most of the LL B candidates who intended to be lawyers. The rest, without legal ambitions, wanted the degree as a substitute for the Bachelor of Arts degree, and luckily the bishops accepted it on this basis for ordination. The period of residence was shorter than for the BA by one term. Henry Maine, who succeeded Geldart in the Regius chair in 1847 when he was twenty-five, gave evidence as professor to the Graham Commission, and was unhappy about the status of law in the university (while in addition the meagre stipend of the Regius chair was a lasting grievance). Though residence for the LL B was three years, graduands had to wait three more years to get the degree, and five after that to obtain a vote in the Senate. He perceived 'a belief that the tests in Law' were 'more easily satisfied than those in Arts', which 'tended to cover the whole Faculty with a discredit which is most assuredly undeserved, but which it is beyond the power of a Professor to remove by his single-handed exertions'.[132] Maine was right in arguing that the LL B was tougher than the poll degree. But it was certainly easier

---

[130] For what follows, see PP 1852–3, HC xliv [1559]: *Graham Commission Evidence*, pp. 77–9.
[131] Crawley, *Trinity Hall*, pp. 88–9; Tanner, *Historical Register*, pp. 844–53.
[132] *Graham Commission Evidence*, pp. 78–9.

than the Mathematics Tripos, which made the LL B the refuge of many weak students who could not face grinding at geometry for ten terms. The law faculty suffered from their presence: on the other hand, the law syllabus was at least as satisfactory for them as the course for the ordinary BA. Maine's opinions, like those of so many others in the middle of the century, rotated round the question, What do we do about our less talented undergraduates? In 1857, when the civil law examinations ceased, Cambridge had had a second chair of law for over seventy years. In 1788 the university had appointed Edward Christian as Professor of the Laws of England, in other words the common law. Two sets of circumstances lay behind this decision. It had long been said by many that the universities should add English law to their curricula,[133] and in 1758 Oxford appointed William Blackstone as the first such professor, under the bequest of Charles Viner.[134] The encouragement of legal studies in Cambridge was an aim of Francis Annesley, nominated as Master of Downing College in 1778 or 1779 (the date is not certain) by the heirs-at-law of Sir George Downing the original benefactor.[135] Annesley, a wealthy bibliophile and connoisseur of the arts, was a member of Gray's Inn, and from 1770 MP for Reading. When appointed master he had some reason to expect that he would soon be able to put his educational plans into effect, but the interminable Downing legal disputes kept him in the wings until 1800, when the charter for the new college for 'law, physic and the other useful arts and learning' was sealed.

Edward Christian, professor since 1788, became the first Downing Professor of the Laws of England, to which a fellowship at the college was attached. Christian, the elder brother of the *Bounty* mutineer Fletcher Christian, came from a Cumberland family and was Third Wrangler in St John's in 1779. He never fulfilled his early promise and was said to be much derided in Cambridge; he 'was frequently seen in the public walks, where his society was avoided by every one whose time was of any value. He died in 1823, in the full vigour of his *incapacity*'.[136] His successor, Thomas Starkie, was

---

[133] For example, Thomas Wood, *Study of the Laws of England in the Two Universities* (Oxford, 1708).
[134] L. G. Mitchell and L. S. Sutherland, eds., *Oxford: The Eighteenth Century*, pp. 600–5.
[135] Stanley French, *Downing College*, pp. 68–82.
[136] Gunning, *Reminiscences*, vol. I, pp. 210–20, and p. 220 for the quotation.

Senior Wrangler at St John's in 1803. He was later called to the bar at Lincoln's Inn and practised on the Northern Circuit. His high competence as a lawyer is shown by his many legal publications. Like the incumbents of the Regius chair, Starkie did not regard his professorship as a full-time job. His stipend was meagre, but on the other hand he had little to do.[137] On appointment in 1823 he gave twenty lectures on 'civil contracts, the law of real property, and the criminal law'. As to students:

> I think I had the first year somewhere about 10 or 12; the next year not so many; the fact is, that Downing College, where the lectures are given, is at some distance from the general colleges, St. John's and Trinity, and at those lectures it would be vain to expect an attendance except in the morning, and the hour in the morning which was appointed interfered with the college lectures which a young man was obliged to attend to; it would be no excuse his attending law lectures, and therefore they found it so inconvenient that there was a very slight attendance.

After a few years attendance ceased altogether, and Starkie gave up his lectures about 1826. The fact that his course did not lead to any qualification was a great disincentive for students. Even those intending to be lawyers preferred to give all their energies to the Senate House Examination, because if they gained a fellowship they could then spend years in uninterrupted legal study. Starkie appeared to have hardly any contact with his colleague the Regius Professor, though like him he resented the low status of law in the university.

The concerns of the two law professors overlapped with views widely expressed in Cambridge at the time. Many students found the two existing and narrowly specialised triposes, in mathematics and classics, uninteresting or too difficult.[138] Dons felt a need to provide both fresh goals for them to aim at for a degree, and industrious students to fill the empty chairs at professors' lectures. The Moral and Natural Sciences Triposes (1851 onwards) were the result. At first they had an *ad hoc* quality; they looked, and in fact

---

[137] For what follows, see PP 1846, HC x (686): *Report of the Select Committee on Legal Education in England and Ireland*, pp. v–vi, 1–4, including the quotations. This Parliamentary Paper has been misdescribed in indexes from 1846 onwards as relating solely to Ireland.

[138] The foundation of the Moral Sciences Tripos is dealt with at greater length in chapter 6.

were, cobbled together from existing resources. 'The list of sciences included in this Examination was selected rather as comprising subjects already recognized in the University by the existence of Professorships tending to promote their cultivation, than with a view of offering a complete scheme of Moral Sciences.'[139] Five subjects were joined together for the new degree: moral philosophy, modern history, political economy, jurisprudence, and the laws of England; all subjects had to be attempted by candidates. The two law professors came together for academic purposes for the first time, examining the degree with the professors of the other subjects. In the first year, 1851, an extra examiner was appointed, and the six men outnumbered the four candidates, all of whom got Firsts. One was Fenton Hort, who reported his reaction to the law papers in a letter to a friend: 'Tuesday, 9–12, Maine, General Jurisprudence, – a capital paper, of which I did about half; 1–4, a detestable mass of bad poetry, puns, and anecdotic gossip, with a screed or two of absurd law, called Laws of England.'[140] 'I did all the Moral Philosophy very fully, about half the History, and two or three scraps of the other things.' In the next nine examinations there was a yearly average of five candidates. In 1860, there were none.

In the 1850s two concerns in Cambridge affected the future of law in the university. One was the crowded nature of the Moral Sciences Tripos, which forced rapid cramming of too many subjects in a brief time, and resulted in a low academic standard. So in 1860 the subjects were placed in two groups, of which candidates were expected to take one. Jurisprudence was placed with political economy, with history and political philosophy also forming part of the same group. The 'laws of England' were omitted from the tripos altogether.[141] There was also much anxiety in the middle of the century about the defective state of legal education in the Inns of Court and the universities. Barristers and solicitors were trained largely through practice. This state of affairs, reported a select committee of the House of Commons in 1846, and a royal

---

[139] Whewell, *Of a Liberal Education in General*, 2nd edn, Part 2, p. 44.
[140] Anthony Fenton Hort, *Life and Letters of Fenton John Anthony Hort* (2 vols., London, 1896), vol. 1, pp. 180–1.
[141] Peter Slee, *Learning and a Liberal Education. The Study of Modern History in the Universities of Oxford, Cambridge and Manchester, 1800–1914* (Manchester University Press, 1986), p. 33. More is said about these matters in chapter 6.

commission eight years later, was unacceptable in a developed and civilised country.[142]

The Law Tripos, which replaced the classes in civil law in 1858, was Cambridge's response to these worries, and to some extent it was modelled on the academic structure suggested by the royal commission in 1854. But placing more emphasis on Roman (that is, civil) law, the new tripos reflected its higher status in Cambridge, where it had a long tradition as compared with English law. Especially influential on the tripos, too, were the ideas of Henry Maine, expressed in 1856 in his essay 'Roman Law and Legal Education' in the volume entitled *Cambridge Essays*. Regarding English common and statute law as deficient in theory, and believing that a proper legal education had to have a theoretical structure,[143] the whole essay is a plea for the acceptance of

> Roman law as the grammar of all advanced legal systems. It was not so much a knowledge of its particular rules but rather an understanding of its concepts and its ways of thinking that was essential for the new generation of educated lawyers, who, he hoped, would drag English law into the modern world.

The two professors (still in the 1860s the only two teachers of law in the university) co-operated in the new degree,[144] but neither of the two men who served as Downing Professor in the 1860s acted as examiners for the degree that they taught for. Roman Law still dominated the tripos in the 1880s. As with so many academic disciplines, in 1870 legal studies in Cambridge had scarcely begun to develop the sophisticated structure characteristic of a modern university.[145]

MEDICINE

In 1750 Cambridge educated men for three great vocations – the church, law and medicine. The church was much the most

[142] A. H. Manchester, *A Modern Legal History of England and Wales 1750–1950* (London, Butterworths, 1980), pp. 54–8.
[143] Peter Stein, 'Maine and Legal Education', in Alan Diamond, ed., *The Victorian Achievement of Sir Henry Maine. A Centennial Reappraisal* (Cambridge University Press, 1991), p. 204, and pp. 195–208 generally.
[144] See J. R. Seeley, ed., *The Student's Guide to the University of Cambridge* (Cambridge, 1862), p. 173.
[145] Christopher Brooke, *A History of the University of Cambridge, vol. IV, 1870–1990* (Cambridge University Press, 1993), pp. 216–18.

important for the university: almost all Anglican clergymen were graduates of Oxford or Cambridge, and the largest single group of graduates became clergymen. Law and medicine were different. In both professions most practitioners were not graduates, and the two faculties were much smaller than the Faculty of Arts. Between 1660 and 1760, 678 men received 'all or a substantial part of their medical education in Cambridge', an average of 7 a year.[146] Many medical practitioners received licences through the Royal College of Physicians, while other practitioners were surgeons or apothecaries, who qualified by apprenticeship, or the 'empirics' at the bottom of the profession with little formal education. The professional training represented by these qualifications might be much or little, though it should be borne in mind that a practitioner who seemed ignorant would be unlikely to prosper.

A careful calculation has established that of the 475 medical graduates in England listed in various sources for the year 1780 Oxford and Cambridge provided only 60 graduates each, as against 259 from Scottish universities. In 1850 the total from Cambridge had risen to 84 and from Oxford to 73, but these were lower percentages of the grand total, 1,717, of which no fewer than 1,279 came from Scottish universities.[147] These figures indicate dramatically the slight importance of Cambridge as a centre of medical education, though it is true that some doctors originating from there did not receive degrees. Some men who studied medicine briefly acquired enough knowledge to practise, which until 1727 the university might recognise with its Licence to Practise Medicine; such licentiates were often graduates in arts who were unwilling to spend the time needed for the Bachelor of Medicine degree.[148] According to the statutes a candidate for the MB had to reside and attend lectures for six years, and conduct two disputations against the opposition of other undergraduates. But several evasions of statute that were initiated by the heads of houses meant that by the beginning of the eighteenth century all that was required of

[146] Arthur Rook, 'Medicine at Cambridge, 1660–1760', *Medical History*, 13 (1969), pp. 110–11.
[147] A. H. T. Robb-Smith, 'Medical Education at Oxford and Cambridge Prior to 1850', in F. N. L. Poynter, ed., *The Evolution of Medical Education in Britain* (London, Pitman, 1966), pp. 50–1. At both dates much the largest number of practitioners were apothecaries or surgeons – 4,870 in 1780 and 12,899 in 1850.
[148] For what follows, see Winstanley, *Unreformed Cambridge*, pp. 60–1, and p. 77 for the quotation.

candidates was to keep their names on college books for five years, to reside for nine terms, to witness two dissections and to conduct one disputation. Thus while the BA was made tougher by the Senate House Examination the MB was made easier, and this consideration lies behind the bad press that the medical faculty of the Unreformed University has usually received, notably from its twentieth-century historian, D. A. Winstanley. Music, he remarks, was the Cinderella among the faculties, but medicine 'probably deserved to be'. These pages argue that while the medical faculty by no means approached the quality achieved by Edinburgh or Leyden, or by mathematics in Cambridge itself, it was not as bad as has usually been asserted. This is not an accolade to take much pride in, however.

Medicine had been taught in Cambridge in the Middle Ages, when as at other universities the course was literary, comprising the intensive study of ancient texts to which canonical value was ascribed.[149] In the sixteenth and seventeenth centuries medicine was transformed by new habits of empirical observation, in which Cambridge shared and was sometimes in the lead. One departure was the foundation of the Regius Professorship of Physic in 1540, and another the refoundation in 1557–8 by John Caius, the eccentric polymath, of the college that bears his name, and to which he gave a pronounced medical emphasis.[150] Among the medical scientists educated there was William Harvey, who discovered the circulation of the blood; his career however was not spent in Cambridge. Another Caian, John Glisson, became Regius Professor, one of many from his college. Among his copious medical writings perhaps the most important was his detailed account of rickets, based on very careful observation of its symptoms. It has to be said, however, that because of the very limited knowledge of therapeutics that pervaded the epoch he was unable to advance the treatment of the disease, and its causes could not be understood till the discovery of vitamins.[151] Similar reservations have to be borne in

---

[149] What follows is based on Johanna Geyer-Kordesch, Mark Weatherall, and Harmke Kaminga, *The History of Medicine in Cambridge: Education, Science and the Healing Arts* (Cambridge, School of Clinical Medicine, 1990), pp. 13–27.

[150] On the life of John Caius, see Christopher Brooke, *Gonville and Caius College*, pp. 55–60.

[151] Walter Langdon-Brown, *Some Chapers in Cambridge Medical History* (Cambridge University Press, 1946), pp. 34–9.

mind about other branches of medical science before recent times. There is also some doubt about how far Glisson may be described as a *Cambridge* scientist: much of his time as Regius was in fact spent in London. In other words, statements praising the character of Cambridge medicine have to be qualified in various ways.

One of the chief benefits to medicine of the new learning of the sixteenth century was a concern with anatomy and its corollary, the practice of dissection. In theory the university made provision for the teaching of anatomy in 1562, but seems largely to have neglected this task for many decades. Still, the pluralism of Cambridge meant that anatomy was intermittently taught at colleges, particularly Gonville and Caius, and by private tutors who gave instruction in return for fees, just as Isola was to teach Italian to Wordsworth in the 1780s.[152] One such anatomy tutor was James Keill, who flourished in the 1690s and published in 1698 a students' text, *The Anatomy of the Human Body Abridged*, which was widely used in the early eighteenth century. The professorship of anatomy, the first in England, was founded in 1707, and the Anatomy School was opened in Queens' Lane in 1716. The first professor, George Rolfe, was however deprived of his post in 1728 for persistent absence from his duties.

These sentences show the difficulty of generalising about Cambridge medicine in this era. The university was sometimes committed and active, but not continuously, as is attested by the fortunes of the botany chair, so important for its bearing upon materia medica.[153] But to some extent private and informal research and teaching served the purposes that the twentieth century turns to the university to meet, but which the eighteenth might obtain from a wider field. At all events that is strongly implied by the lives of Stephen Hales (1677–1761) and William Stukeley. They met at Corpus, where Hales was elected a fellow in 1703 and Stukeley began medical studies in 1704. His account of them suggests that self-education supplemented the instruction that Stukeley received. He and the small group of enthusiastic medical students round him went on botanical expeditions in the Cambridgeshire countryside; he visited London to attend a dissection (none being on offer in

---

[152] See chapter 15, pp. 571–6.   [153] See chapter 6, pp. 209–12.

Cambridge), and an apothecary's shop to gain knowledge of drugs. At Stukeley's instance Hales and he undertook an enormous number of experiments in anatomy and physiology in their rooms in college; they assembled skeletons, including human ones, and devised a model of the bronchial tree.[154]

John Francis Vigani, an Italian, taught in Cambridge from 1683 to 1708, offering an annual course of twenty-five lectures on the medical applications of chemistry, and also a separate course directly concerned with materia medica; the title of Professor of Chemistry (though there was no stipend) was conferred on him by the Senate in 1703. Vigani's successors as Professors of Chemistry, notably John Mickleburgh who served from 1718 to 1756, also lectured on materia medica.[155] In Catharine Hall, John Addenbrooke taught materia medica for some years from 1705 onwards, when as a young MA he was himself studying for the MD. He used in his teaching the extensive collection of drugs that he had assembled, including many of plant or animal origin and also chemicals such as arsenic and bismuth; the collection suggests the wide range of treatments available to practitioners three centuries ago, and the importance attached to making them known to doctors through courses on materia medica.[156]

Over the centuries many quite useless remedies had crept into the pharmacopoeia, and purging them from the lists was a task that 'the most important figure in eighteenth-century Cambridge medicine' set himself.[157] This was William Heberden, a graduate of St John's who lectured on materia medica from 1734 to 1748, when he moved to London, where Samuel Johnson was one of his many patients. His perceptive *Commentaries*, assembled from his case notes at the age of seventy-one, display a habit of meticulous and sceptical observation that set him apart from most practitioners of his day. It is the judgement of an historian who spent many years researching eighteenth-century medicine in Cambridge that 'it was ... largely

---

[154] See Piggott, *William Stukeley*, pp. 22–6, and A. E. Clark-Kennedy, *Stephen Hales, D.D., F.R.S., an Eighteenth-Century Biography* (Cambridge University Press, 1929), pp. 14–21.

[155] For these lines, see Rook, 'Medicine at Cambridge', pp. 117–18, and also Arthur Rook, Margaret Carlton, and Graham W. Cannon, *The History of Addenbrooke's Hospital, Cambridge* (Cambridge University Press, 1991), pp. 15–16. More is said about Vigani and chemistry in chapter 6, pp. 217–26.   [156] His drug cabinet is now in the possession of St Catharine's.

[157] On Heberden, see Langdon-Brown, *Some Chapters*, pp. 53–60.

due to Heberden's pupils that the medical school did not die completely even at the worst period'.[158] For example, one such pupil was Robert Glynn, a fellow of King's and for many years a practitioner in the city and district; in 1751 and 1752 he lectured on medicine in the Anatomy School.[159]

The three Regius Professors of Physic in the period 1700–1817 seem to have taught very little.[160] On the other hand, Charles Collignon, Professor of Anatomy from 1753 to 1785, a highly competent doctor who was highly esteemed by his contemporaries, lectured regularly during his long tenure of his chair and illustrated his lectures with dissections when corpses were available; they were perhaps in short supply.[161] The most famous anatomist in eighteenth-century Cambridge was Sir Busick Harwood, who was professor from 1785 to 1814, and simultaneously Downing Professor of Medicine from 1800 to 1814.[162] He like Collignon has recently benefited from a careful study that rehabilitates his reputation. In Harwood's case the damage was first done by Gunning. His malicious and implausible account has been disproved in detail, though the story of Harwood's serving turbot from yesterday's dissection table will no doubt be told for many years yet. Harwood lectured regularly in both of his professorial capacities, and the schedules that he published, and the students' notes that survive, show that he ranged widely over the medical field; his lectures ostensibly on anatomy also included much physiology and pathology, with incursions into materia medica and forensic medicine too. In his lectures he referred to the latest discoveries by scientists, and he illustrated his sessions with specimens which were injected with contrasting colours to achieve clarity. He carried out experiments, particularly on techniques of blood transfusion, and

[158] Rook, 'Medicine at Cambridge', p. 121.
[159] Arthur Rook, 'Robert Glynn (1719–1800), Physician at Cambridge', *Medical History*, 13 (1969), pp. 251–9.
[160] Arthur Rook, 'Medical Education 1600–1800', in Arthur Rook, ed., *Cambridge and its Contribution to Medicine* (London, Wellcome Institute for the History of Medicine, 1971), p. 60.
[161] Arthur Rook, 'Charles Collignon (1725–1785): Cambridge Physician, Anatomist and Moralist', *Medical History*, 23 (1979), pp. 339–45. The paper seeks to redress Winstanley's unsubstantiated attack on Collignon's competence.
[162] What follows is based on Raymond Williamson, 'Sir Busick Harwood: "A Reappraisal"', *Medical History*, 27 (1983), pp. 423–33. See also Bernard Towers, 'Anatomy and Physiology in Cambridge before 1850', in Rook, *Cambridge and its Contribution to Medicine*, pp. 72–7.

the one volume that was published of his intended survey of physiology dealt with the olfactory organs with erudition and perceptiveness; it came from 'a man with a very active mind'.[163] Harwood's period, so far from being the nadir of Cambridge medicine that it has often been considered, stands out in comparison with much that had preceded it.

Still, no one would argue that even at its best eighteenth-century Cambridge medicine was the equal of Edinburgh. At a low point, in 1759, Richard Davies, a fellow of Queens' College, attacked the lack of equipment, facilities, and clinical practice, and concluded, 'In short if we consider the difficulties and discouragements that attend the study of physic in both Universities it must be a matter of surprise that physicians have arrived at that respect and dignity of character which they have long maintained in the world'.[164] With the exception of the period when Harwood was professor a medical student could not gain from *university teaching* anything like adequate knowledge. There were other sources for it in Cambridge, but however widely one locates this medical endeavour it remained patchy and sporadic. It is not surprising that many Cambridge men visited medical schools elsewhere; for example between 1630 and 1730 between 12 per cent and 35 per cent of men with some experience of medical study at Cambridge travelled to Leyden, albeit sometimes for short periods. By the end of the century Edinburgh appears to have taken Leyden's place as a supplement to what Cambridge offered.[165] Perhaps one way or another Cambridge-educated doctors managed to achieve professional competence, but the university could not take much credit for that fact.

A new departure occurred when John Haviland was appointed Regius Professor of Medicine in 1817.[166] Like so many practitioners the son of a doctor, Haviland graduated Twelfth Wrangler at St John's in 1807; he studied medicine at Edinburgh for two years and

---

[163] Williamson, 'Sir Busick Harwood', p. 430.

[164] From Richard Davies, *The General State of Education in the Universities with a Particular View to the Philosophical and Medical Education* (1759), quoted by A. H. T. Robb-Smith, 'Medical Education Prior to 1850', pp. 42–3.

[165] Arthur Rook, 'Cambridge Medical Students at Leyden', *Medical History*, 17 (1973), pp. 256–65.

[166] For what follows see PP 1852–3: *Graham Commission Evidence*, pp. 80–2, and Winstanley, *Early Victorian Cambridge*, pp. 160–6.

at St Bartholomew's Hospital for three more. His small university stipend made private practice necessary; if we may judge by the frequency with which he is mentioned in Romilly's diary it was large, and testimony to his competence. But unlike his predecessors he did not use his private practice as an excuse to neglect his official tasks. From 1819 onwards he lectured on the principles of medicine, being the first Regius to lecture since the seventeenth century. His efforts were complemented by those of the scientific professors, among whom may be especially mentioned William Clark ('bone Clark') the Professor of Anatomy from 1817 to 1866; so for the first time there was in Cambridge a group of medical teachers working to some extent as a team, though the university did not yet possess an integrated medical course. Soon after he was appointed Haviland initiated examinations for the MB degree, in effect to replace the undemanding 'acts'. The examinations were strengthened in 1827, when the Senate agreed that medical students should attend the lectures of the Downing Professor and the Professors of Anatomy, Botany and Chemistry,[167] and that these men should assist the Regius in the examinations. Papers were to be taken each term on a wide range of medical topics. Unlike the medical schools in the Scottish universities and the London teaching hospitals the course lacked clinical experience, and this gap Haviland resolved to fill. He had the means at hand in the Cambridge licence to practise medicine, a qualification separate from the MB degree, and given two years after graduation – or in other words four years after the obligatory three years of residence. Through a series of Senate decisions Haviland ensured that those four years, or a substantial part of them, were employed in clinical practice whose efficacy was tested before licensing. Some time in the 1830s such practice began to take place in Addenbrooke's Hospital, and clinical teaching by the hospital staff was associated with it. At first private and informal, this teaching became public and systematic lectures in 1842, in which year clinical examinations began – the first to be given in the United Kingdom. In this work of steady improvement Haviland was assisted by George Paget and Frederic Thackeray, physician and surgeon respectively at the hospital.[168]

---

[167] These sciences are discussed in chapter 6, pp. 205–26.
[168] See Rook, Carlton, and Cannon, *Addenbrooke's Hospital*, esp. pp. 235–7, and Arthur Rook, 'The

Despite these advances Haviland reported to the Graham Commission that medical studies were 'at a very low ebb' in Cambridge.[169] There was an '*entire want* here of teachers in some very important and necessary branches of Medicine, as Forensic Medicine, Hygiene, Comparative Anatomy, &c', while the teaching year was too short, however much it suited 'Students of Classical Literature and Mathematical Science'. Unfortunately Cambridge was geared to their needs. In short, the reform of medicine was not fast enough to stop medical schools in London and elsewhere from overtaking Cambridge: the number of its students was declining.

The university did endeavour to improve matters. On the recommendation, in May 1854, of the Studies Syndicate that was set up to consider the findings of the Graham Commission a Board of Medical Studies was created to give direction to change.[170] In the next few years the regulations for medical degrees were overhauled, a move made the more desirable by the creation by an Act of Parliament in 1858 of a structure to guarantee high standards within the medical profession and the agencies educating doctors. By the early 1860s Cambridge possessed a pattern for medical education quite like the one that exists today: a total of five years of professional training devoted to the systematic accumulation of knowledge that was reflected in the splitting of the MB into parts.[171] There survived, however, an insistence on the need for Cambridge to provide an education in at least the basics of classics and mathematics; all those intending to read medicine had to spend their first year reading for the Previous Examination with their college tutors before professional training began, and it was suggested in the *Student's Guide* (1862) that some might like also to take the Classical or Mathematical Tripos. Such men would spend at least eight years at university. Ancient assumptions were very tenacious, and the university was slow to meet the needs that followed from the new medical structure. Lecture-rooms and other

Thackerays and Medicine', *Medical History*, 15 (1971), pp. 12–22. Frederic Thackeray's father was the great-uncle of the novelist William M. Thackeray.

[169] PP 1852–3: *Graham Commission Evidence*, p. 81.

[170] Cooper, *Annals*, v, pp. 166–70. For what follows, see Geyer-Kordesch, Weatherall, and Kaminga, *Medicine in Cambridge*, pp. 38–43, and G.M. Humphry, 'Medical Education', in Seeley, *Student's Guide to the University of Cambridge*, pp. 196–214.

[171] The university also began a Bachelor of Surgery degree overlapping greatly with the MB.

facilities were poor, as the university admitted in 1854, yet it could not afford to spend more than a fraction of the £23,000 required, while the colleges failed to respond to an appeal for funds.[172] There remained too the need for more teachers that Haviland had adverted to: and not merely more *university* appointments, but also college tutorships, which were overwhelmingly in classics and mathematics. Unfortunately, *The Lancet* remarked in 1875, 'no inducements are offered for a sufficient number of young men to remain and engage in the work of medical teaching',[173] while there was also a shortage of dedicated scholarships for medical undergraduates; only Gonville and Caius enjoyed such provision. Medicine shared all these difficulties with the natural sciences, and like them real change did not come until after 1870.[174] In many ways, 1870 was a turning point in the university's history.

[172] Winstanley, *Early Victorian Cambridge*, p. 274.
[173] Quoted in Geyer-Fordesch, Weatherall, and Kaminga, *Medicine in Cambridge*, p. 43.
[174] For the fortunes of the Natural Sciences Tripos at this time, see chapter 6, pp. 231–3.

Chapter 6

SCIENCE AND OTHER STUDIES

PRELUDE: THE NEW TRIPOSES, 1850

Geology seems to have been tolerably done by all, brilliantly by none. If the paper had been a quarter of the length, it would have been more satisfactory to all parties. Fuller says Sedgwick boasted of having made it a 'very complete' paper, and got *all* geology into it, to be written out in four hours! We all (i.e. all the first class) did very well in the general paper. I was glad to find that Fuller thinks two subjects as much as anyone can manage.[1]

So wrote one candidate, Fenton J. A. Hort, for the first examination, in Lent 1851, for the Natural Sciences Tripos. Another tripos, in moral sciences, also began at the same time, and Hort was a candidate for that too.[2]

The triposes were set up following considerable pressure from within the university and outside it. For a long time there had been a sense of unease at the contrast between the distinguished scholarship and reputation of the university's professors and their detachment from Cambridge's chief intellectual purpose, the gift of a liberal education based upon mathematics and classics to undergraduates, as measured by the Senate House Examination and the Classical Tripos. These two subjects were taught by *colleges* almost entirely; professors were little concerned with them. Other subjects were not examined; nor were they taught except by the professors. So Whewell's writings on the nature of a university, which expressed the views of so many at Cambridge, were a defence of the dominant position of mathematics and classics within Cambridge, together with an ingenious plan for assured though subordinate

---

[1] Fenton J. A. Hort to his mother, 8 March 1851, in Hort, *Life and Letters of Fenton John Anthony Hort*, vol. I, p. 191. [2] See chapter 14, p. 513 for details of the legislative origins of the tripos.

places for the natural sciences and the humanities (the 'moral sciences') within the examination hierarchy. The new triposes would be taught and examined by their professors, whose role within Cambridge would therefore become more recognised and certain, while a Natural Sciences Tripos, Whewell asserted, would be a means 'of removing the alleged neglect of the Inductive Sciences in the University, without any great disturbance of our existing system'; that is, without challenging the preponderance of mathematics and classics. A Moral Sciences Tripos would have a very similar function.[3]

When the new courses started, the professors' rooms were soon crowded with candidates for the ordinary degree who were to qualify for it, in part, by attending the lectures. But the *triposes* attracted few candidates at first. Entry was only possible for men already qualified for the BA; they had only one year to prepare for their examinations, and in each tripos they had to take papers in five subjects; more specialised degrees seem to have been ruled out of consideration because except in one or two cases each professor was the only teacher of his subject in Cambridge, and the burdens of instruction and examining therefore needed to be shared as widely as possible. In due course logic was to lead to some specialisation, and from it sprang modern Cambridge with its host of single-subject honours degrees each cutting very deeply and rather narrowly, and each taught by scores of experts.

The new departures of 1850 looked forward to a different kind of university from Unreformed Cambridge, but began because of an odd and particular characteristic – professors who had little apparent function and needed to be found one. Their lives display the intellectual diversity of Old Cambridge, and some of its strengths and weaknesses. To some of these men we now turn, choosing because of the importance of their pursuits the Professors of Botany, Chemistry, Geology, and Physics among the natural sciences, while history is taken as an example in the humanities because we have abundant knowledge of its professors and their teaching.

---

[3] Whewell, *Of a Liberal Education*, 2nd edn, pp. 225–8.

THE NATURAL SCIENCES

THE SCIENTIFIC PROFESSORS

In the late eighteenth century there were eight scientific professor-ships. The Regius Professorship of Physic (that is, medicine) was founded by Henry VIII in 1540, and the others after 1700: chemistry in 1702, the Plumian Professorship of Astronomy and Experimental Philosophy in 1704, anatomy in 1707, botany in 1724,[4] the Woodwardian Professorship of Geology in 1728, the Lowndean Professorship of Astronomy and Geometry in 1749, and the Jacksonian Professorship of Natural Experimental Philosophy in 1783. Their stipends ranged from £99 to £300,[5] modest sums even in 1830, and at best less than half the lowest stipend for a head of house.[6]

The concern for self-reform which was apparent in Cambridge after the Napoleonic Wars may be discerned in the university's natural sciences. But since mathematics dominated the university all men who might be recruited as scientific professors took the Senate House Examination. The modern world is used to specialisation at the undergraduate stage, and looks askance at Cambridge mathematicians converting themselves to something else. Yet the task was easier then than it would be now, and it was usually undertaken conscientiously after 1820. Some characteristics of the transition may be illustrated by the example of mineralogy. In 1807 Edward Daniel Clarke began 'his spectacularly successful annual courses of lectures',[7] and in 1808 the university founded the chair of mineralogy which he occupied. Clarke was a gifted populariser, and 'his historical position is difficult to assess in that the importance of his influence so far outweighs that of his scientific achievement'. His immediate successor, John Stevens Henslow, attended lectures in chemistry and mineralogy as an undergraduate, and had a 'reputation in the University as a talented young natural historian with

---

[4] A Regius chair of botany was founded in 1793, and in 1825 the original chair was suppressed. In 1857 botany ceased to be a Regius chair.

[5] Winstanley, *Unreformed Cambridge*, pp. 95–182. In addition, the Lucasian Professorship of Mathematics (1663) should be mentioned.

[6] With the exception of Trinity Hall and (perhaps) St Catharine's, from the twelve detailed in PP 1852–3, HC xliv [1559]: *Graham Commission Report*, pp. 154–5.

[7] Duncan McKie in the *Dictionary of Scientific Biography*, from which the following quotations are taken.

skills in geology, chemistry, mineralogy and mathematics'.[8] Any further development as a mineralogist was prevented by his becoming Professor of Botany in 1825; he gave his energy to his new position though he retained the chair of mineralogy for three more years. Henslow's successor, Whewell, prepared for the professorship of mineralogy from 1821 onwards, studying in the 'best Mineralogical Schools in Germany', and presenting papers which were said by the President of the Royal Society 'to be an admirable application of mathematical to physical science'.[9] Whewell was professor for four years and did a great deal to restate mineralogy in geometrical language. His successor, William Miller, was professor from 1832 to 1880 and a mathematical mineralogist of substantial achievement, with scientific knowledge of 'exceptional breadth'.[10]

ACCOMMODATING THE SCIENCES

The university's record in supporting the professors with what are now termed 'physical resources' was intermittent and variable. The Botanic Garden was the largest resource. The first garden, five acres to the north of what is now Pembroke Street, was given to the university by Dr Richard Walker, the Vice-Master of Trinity College, in 1762. Its purpose was to allow 'trials and experiments' to be 'regularly made and repeated' to discover the 'virtues' of plants, 'for the benefit of mankind' – a reference to their value as materia medica, one of the main justifications then for the study of botany. In the garden the university erected modest lecture rooms costing £1,800 for the Professors of Botany and Experimental Philosophy.[11] By 1830 advances in botany meant that far more plants needed to be grown than the original gardens could accommodate, while jackdaws regularly stole the wooden species labels for their nests in the buildings that hemmed the gardens in. To gain a new

---

[8] Harvey W. Becher, 'Voluntary Science in Nineteenth Century Cambridge University to the 1850s', *British Journal for the History of Science*, 19 (1986), p. 61.

[9] Becher, 'Voluntary Science', pp. 61–3, for these lines.

[10] Duncan McKie in the *Dictionary of Scientific Biography*.

[11] Willis and Clark, III, pp. 145–54; S. M. Walters, *The Shaping of Cambridge Botany* (Cambridge University Press, 1981), pp. 40–4. The jumbled stone and concrete of the New Museums Site now occupies the original Botanic Gardens.

9 The old Botanic Garden.

garden in 1831 the university agreed to a transfer of land with Trinity Hall; the college exchanged thirty-eight acres near the Trumpington Road for seven acres in Newtown plus £2,200. After delay because of the need to allow expiry of a lease the thirty-eight acres became the present Botanic Garden, much the largest area developed by the university in the nineteenth century.[12]

The observatory built on the Madingley Road in 1822–4 was a special example of university commitment to the sciences; it apparently cost the chest over £12,000, more than twice its liability as originally estimated. The Plumian Professor, George Airy, stated to the Senate in 1828 that 'all the Astronomers who have seen it, English and Foreign, agree in declaring it to be better adapted to its purpose than any similar building in Europe'.[13] On the other hand most of the other scientific disciplines had quite inadequate lecture rooms and museums for many years. Anatomy, medicine, and modern history were cramped into a house next to the Pitt Building in Trumpington Street. There was no provision whatever for

[12] Willis and Clark, III, pp. 157–8; Walters, *The Shaping of Cambridge Botany*, pp. 55–62, 72–82.
[13] Willis and Clark, III, pp. 190–8. See also above, chapter 1, pp. 28–9.

mineralogy, which by its nature required a display room, while for over a century from 1735 geology occupied a room in the Old Schools described by Adam Sedgwick as 'small, damp, and ill-lighted, and utterly unfit for a residence or a lecture-room'.[14]

The university felt guilty about its failure to provide proper premises, and between 1818 and 1824 three syndicates reported on the need to do something. In 1828 Whewell drafted a document detailing all deficiencies graphically and calling firmly for remedies:

> The continual progress of such sciences cannot be understood, except the Museums be capable of admitting the objects which illustrate this progress. It is beyond a doubt, also, that if the University were possessed of space for the reception and exhibition of such collections, the regard of its members towards it, their zeal for science, and numberless opportunities perpetually occurring, would augment and complete its stores.[15]

Detailing the way in which Oxford and Paris were actively meeting similar needs, Whewell remarked that Cambridge might 'have the mortification to see herself left behind in the cultivation of such studies' at a time when professors were 'zealous' and students were 'daily growing in activity and intelligence'. Whewell's ambitious plans were accepted, and combined in a complex scheme for the expansion of the University Library, itself very short of space. Unfortunately, however, the hopes of the scientific professors were not fulfilled, and even the library extension (Cockerell's Building) was not begun until 1837 and ready for use until 1844. The merits of rival architectural plans led to a bitter and protracted dispute, the chief combatants being George Peacock and Whewell, and this was one cause of delay. But it seems that in any case the university could never have afforded the original scheme in full without stringent economies elsewhere, for example in the library's book fund. Of the scientific interests originally under consideration, only geology and mineralogy were accommodated in Cockerell's Building, on the ground floor.[16] Premises for anatomy and chemistry were pro-

---

[14] Willis and Clark, III, pp. 154–5.   [15] Willis and Clark, III, pp. 97–100.
[16] Willis and Clark, III, pp. 101–21; 155. McKitterick, *Cambridge University Library*, pp. 473–86; Becher, 'Voluntary Science', pp. 76–7. The construction of Cockerell's Building is dealt with above, chapter 1.

vided in 1832–3 by extending the buildings within the old Botanic Garden,[17] and after the garden was vacated in 1852, the use of its space for new university accommodation was debated, an urgent matter since the Natural Sciences Tripos had begun in 1851. There were endless frictions over aesthetics, amenity, and money, but between 1864 and 1866 museums were ready for zoology and comparative anatomy;[18] they formed the first stage in the development of the New Museums Site that has gone on continuously ever since, and has marked Cambridge with one of the ugliest and most ill-assorted architectural jumbles in any British university precinct.

BOTANY

Because of his background John Henslow was less suited to mineralogy, his first chair, than to botany. He was one of the 'galaxy of congenial spirits' who were swept by enthusiasm for natural history in the early nineteenth century – a movement that helps to explain the growth of science in Cambridge, since undergraduates came prepared to turn to it.[19] Henslow, the son of a solicitor, began collecting butterflies as a schoolboy. He naturally took the mathematical course at St John's (1814–18) and became Sixteenth Wrangler, and in 1822 was elected Professor of Mineralogy. But there is probably much truth in the statement of his first biographer, Leonard Jenyns, that 'the Professorship of Botany was the one to which he had been looking for some years, and for which he had been preparing himself at a time when he never anticipated that the chair of Mineralogy would be open to his acceptance first'.[20] He was certainly a more distinguished botanist than his predecessor, Thomas Martyn. Professor from 1762 to 1825, Martyn was a descriptive botanist, a competent classifier on Linnaean principles – the dominant approach in the science in the eighteenth century – but in his last thirty years Martyn was an absentee. Henslow held the chair until his death in 1861, but from 1839 onwards he lived in Hitcham, the Suffolk parish whose rectory he was glad to accept

[17] Willis and Clark, III, pp. 156–7.   [18] Willis and Clark, III, pp. 157–81.
[19] See Lynn Barber, *The Heyday of Natural History 1820–1870* (London, Jonathan Cape, 1980), p. 14.
[20] Quoted in Walters, *The Shaping of Cambridge Botany*, p. 49, and pp. 36–47 for what follows.

from the Crown, with its stipend of £1,000 that dwarfed his professor's pay. He gave his energies to Hitcham,[21] and though his contribution to Cambridge botany was by no means negligible after 1839, his most productive years as professor were from 1825 to 1839.

By the greatest good fortune for world science they included the years that Charles Darwin was an undergraduate at Christ's (1828–31), a circumstance that has added to Henslow's fame. From his childhood onwards Darwin was as enthusiastic over natural history as the young Henslow. Dismayed by his years spent studying classics at Shrewsbury School and in the anatomy lecture room during his abortive two years of medical training at Edinburgh, he came to Christ's College intending to be ordained after his degree. Working for a poll degree he found most of its academic requirements uncongenial but managed to graduate. 'But no pursuit at Cambridge was followed with nearly so much eagerness or gave me so much pleasure as collecting beetles.'[22]

Henslow saw that 'many persons, both within and without the Universities, suppose its [i.e. botany's] objects limited to fixing names to a vast number of plants, and to describing and classifying them under this or that particular system'.[23] Henslow replaced this vestige of the science's origins as an adjunct to medicine with 'a very active, vital botany based on appreciating plants as living organisms',[24] botany as an observational science. Henslow 'neglected nothing in his power to make his lectures attractive and popular', wrote one student, Leonard Jenyns of Bottisham Hall.[25] 'Large-scale diagrams strengthened students' understanding, as did "demonstrations" ... from living specimens ... of some of the more common plants, such as the primrose ... which the pupils, following their teacher during his explanation of their several parts, pulled to pieces for themselves.' Another of Henslow's innovations was botanical field trips into the Cambridgeshire countryside, two

---

[21] Jean Russell-Gebbert, *Henslow of Hitcham. Botanist, Educationalist and Clergyman* (Lavenham, Suffolk, Terence Dalton, 1977) is largely concerned with his Suffolk years.

[22] Charles Darwin and T. H. Huxley, *Autobiographies*, ed. Gavin de Beer (Oxford University Press, 1974), p. 34. See Janet Browne, *Darwin*, vol. 1, Voyaging (London, Jonathan Cape, 1995), pp. 1–116 for these lines on Darwin.

[23] Quoted in Walters, *The Shaping of Cambridge Botany*, p. 57.

[24] Browne, *Darwin*, p. 122. [25] Quoted in Walters, *The Shaping of Cambridge Botany*, p. 51.

or three times in each session. 'He used to pause every now and then and lecture on some plant or other object; and something he could tell us on every insect, shell, or fossil collected... After our day's work we used to dine at some inn or house, and most jovial we then were.'[26]

Darwin said that his friendship with Henslow 'influenced my whole career more than any other',[27] because of his exceptionally lively teaching, and also because of his gift of affectionate understanding and sympathetic support for unshaped talent. Darwin's

> early life was characterised by a constant need for this kind of quasi-parental support... Darwin's greatest gift at this time was not so much the ability to understand nature's secrets, if he had it to any degree as an undergraduate, but a capacity to identify the people capable of giving and inspiring in him the loyal affection he desired. On such affections his ultimate success as a naturalist depended.[28]

Soon well acquainted with Henslow, Darwin 'took long walks with him on most days' during 'the latter half' of his time at Cambridge, so that he 'was called by some of the dons "the man who walks with Henslow"'.[29] Other men's biographies, were equal details known to us, might show more fruitful contact between dons and undergraduates than would be guessed from the gloomy lines of *The Prelude*. It was at Henslow's Friday soirées, 'where all undergraduates and several older members of the University, who were attached to science, used to meet in the evening', that Darwin became acquainted with Whewell and Sedgwick. Darwin sometimes walked home with Whewell at night, conversing 'on grave subjects', while his friendship with Sedgwick led to Darwin's accompanying the geologist on a field-trip to North Wales soon after he gained his poll BA. During this excursion a letter arrived at the Darwin home in Shrewsbury inviting him to serve as a naturalist on Captain FitzRoy's surveying voyage in the *Beagle*. FitzRoy had asked Francis Beaufort, the Admiralty Hydrographer, to find him a gentleman companion with scientific interests; Beaufort had approached George Peacock, who wrote to Henslow. In this way

---

[26] Quoted in Walters, *The Shaping of Cambridge Botany*, pp. 50–1.
[27] *Autobiographies*, pp. 35–6.   [28] Browne, *Darwin*, p. 124.   [29] *Autobiographies*, p. 36.

Darwin was chosen for his great expedition, one of the most momentous enterprises in the century that added incalculably to our knowledge of nature. There is no stronger demonstration of the Cambridge network's importance.[30]

GEOLOGY

The early history of the professorship of geology, founded in 1728, provides the most glaring examples of sloth and incompetence in the eighteenth-century university.[31] The chair was founded with a bequest from John Woodward, an amateur natural historian who left a collection of fossils to the university, and gave the professor the task of looking after it; he was also to remain in residence for most of the year, could not marry, and had to give lectures. None of the first five appointees lectured significantly or advanced geology in other ways. The sixth professor, John Hailstone, elected in 1788 at the age of twenty-eight, was more conscientious; while knowing nothing of geology when appointed, he studied afterwards in Germany with Werner, one of the masters of a rapidly developing science, and on his return to Cambridge published *A plan of a course of lectures in Mineralogy*, in the hope of arousing interest in a science which had 'hitherto been suffered to languish in unmerited obscurity' in the university. Unfortunately, he could not deliver his lectures since he could not assemble a class. He took far greater care of the fossil collection than any of his predecessors, but his long tenure of the chair (he died in 1818) is eclipsed by his successor Adam Sedgwick, one of the greatest of nineteenth-century geologists and Cambridge dons, and the most striking example of the university's power of self-renewal.

The years 1780–1860 have been called the Heroic Age of British geology,[32] and the title might also be given to the science itself as a world phenomenon. The rational explanation of the universe that Galileo and Newton had composed in earlier centuries was not followed with a science of the earth itself until the end of the

---

[30] Browne, *Darwin*, pp. 144–61.
[31] The following details are taken from Winstanley, *Unreformed Cambridge*, pp. 167–71.
[32] Roy Porter, 'The Natural Sciences Tripos and the "Cambridge School of Geology", 1850–1914', *History of Universities*, 2 (1982), p. 193.

eighteenth century. British and continental savants liberated the rocks from the chronology of Genesis, and by 1830 interpretations looked towards two contrasting hypotheses to explain how the earth's crust had been shaped over many millennia. They were christened by Whewell the 'uniformitarian' and 'catastrophist' hypotheses. The leading uniformitarian was Charles Lyell,[33] whose *Principles of Geology* (1830–3) was very widely read; Darwin took it with him on the *Beagle*. Lyell, it has recently been written, 'seemed to ignore the evidence of greater movements in favour of the continuous action of small causes' in the earth's crust.[34] His version 'is true most of the time', but the disturbances that the catastrophists looked to

> have a role much greater than might be inferred from their rarity and what we have seen of them. Again, it is the use of our life span to measure rarity or regularity that is at fault, and the same holds true for the use of our size to measure the extent of geological disturbance. 'Such [great] catastrophes have not occurred since the existence of man, at least since the existence of written records.'[35]

In due course a consensus emerged that synthesised both hypotheses, and British geologists helped to create it. The Geological Society, founded in 1807, and the official Geological Survey, begun in 1835, were an impetus to activity and forums for debate, for the assortment of gentlemanly amateurs, university professors, and state employees that composed the geological Establishment.

Adam Sedgwick was renowned among British geologists and among Cambridge dons. The length of his career, the vigour of his physique and his intellect, the variety of his pursuits and the contradictions of his personality, drew attention to him constantly. His energy was matched by hypochondria, and his emotional temperament could result in deep friendships and intense loyalty to university and college, and also in touchy polemic; in the famous quarrel that ruptured his friendship with Roderick Murchison both men were at fault for taking differing interpretations of evidence

---

[33] Also a leading publicist of university reforms. See chapter 12, pp. 436–7.

[34] Mott T. Greene, *Geology in the Nineteenth Century. Changing Views of a Changing World* (Ithaca, N.Y., Cornell University Press, 1982), p. 165, and generally for these lines.

[35] This last sentence is a quotation from vol. 1 of *The Face of the Earth* (1904–9) by the Austrian geologist Eduard Suess.

10 Adam Sedgwick, a photograph taken about 1860, when he was aged seventy-five.

personally,[36] but Sedgwick more so – even though he paid the price of losing touch with one of his closest friends, Lady Murchison. Like many imperfectly integrated scholars Sedgwick found fulfil-

[36] The quarrel is fully chronicled in James A. Secord, *Controversy in Victorian Geology. The Cambrian-Silurian Dispute* (Princeton, N.J., Princeton University Press, 1986)

ment in teaching; 'he had a direct and informal manner that made him accessible to students', it is said in a recent assessment of his achievement.[37] But his written utterance was cumbrous and 'he found the formal composition of scientific papers irksome', so that their completion was delayed by ill-health and the abundance of other tasks. 'His published works . . . hardly reflect the full extent of his achievement.'

Whatever may be suggested about the way others prepared for chairs for which their degree studies had not familiarised them, Sedgwick's biographers aver that while he may have known something of mineralogy before he became Professor of Geology, 'there is no evidence that he had ever troubled his head with cosmical speculations' (that is, geology); Sedgwick's 'personal character' led to his election. A few years later 'he seemed a master of the subject'.[38] Like most British geologists of his epoch Sedgwick was by instinct a catastrophist, since the hypothesis was most easily reconciled with the Mosaic deluge, their 'favourite catastrophe'.[39] Though Lyell's criticisms led them to abandon their correlation of the Flood 'with the phenomena of geology', Sedgwick and others rightly remained unconvinced that Lyell's uniformitarianism was a wholly adequate explanation of geological change; Sedgwick was much influenced by the way the great French scientist Elie de Beaumont combined in his interpretations the regularity of slow causes with sudden and much faster paroxysms.[40]

All British geologists of Sedgwick's epoch saw the hand of God in the rocks: geology was proof of Design, and its apologetic function helps to explain the popularity of the science.[41] But for uniformitarians God was remote, the First Cause but not one that constantly intervened, which was the way catastrophists tended to see Him. After ceasing to believe in the Flood and attendant occurrences that furnished a providential explication, Sedgwick was left finally with one certain proof of divine intervention – the separateness and

[37] Martin Rudwick in the *Dictionary of Scientific Biography*.
[38] Clark and Hughes, *Adam Sedgwick*, vol. I, pp. 159, 161, 164.
[39] The phrase was coined by Charles Coulston Gillispie in his account of the controversy around the conflict between biblical and other chronologies and their connections with geology and religion: *Genesis and Geology* (Cambridge, Mass., Harvard University Press, 1951), p. 143.
[40] M. T. Greene, *Geology in the Nineteenth Century*, pp. 91, 95, 120.
[41] For what follows, see Gillispie, *Genesis and Geology*, pp. 216–28, and Martin Rudwick's essay in the *Dictionary of Scientific Biography*.

immutability of each living species and the uniqueness of human-kind. He was more influenced than he was inclined to admit by Paley's demonstration of the designful beauty of the kingdom of life. Such a view was challenged by a theory of the transmutation of species by natural means, and so he felt unable to accept the central argument of Darwin's *Origin of Species* (1859), which seemed to undermine Sedgwick's faith in the necessary concordance of science and religion.

Thus Sedgwick's 1859 class examination paper contained this question: 'Is there a shadow of proof from the ethnographical, and physical history of man that any one of his oldest varieties was derived from a quadrumanous progenitor [that is, a non-human primate]?'[42] But he aimed at open intellectual debate, not indoctrination, and to one paper appended this note: 'If in any instance you think you differ in opinion from the proposer of the above questions, you are requested to state your own opinions without hesitation and to give your reasons for them.' His question papers, writes Roy Porter, were 'concerned to elicit methodical patterns of thought. Candidates were asked to *evaluate* and to *test* theories alongside available evidence... There was a concern, very characteristic of Sedgwick and Whewell, with the principles of reasoning.'

The teaching that lay behind this endeavour was of legendary quality, attracting many voluntary students to his classes in the years before the institution of the Natural Sciences Tripos. Thus in November 1849 Richard Wilton, an undergraduate from St Catharine's, wrote:

> Coleridge used to attend Sir Humphrey Davy's lectures, he said, in order to increase his stock of metaphors; and anyone might with advantage attend Sedgwick's merely for the same purpose, tho' he were uninterested by the mysterious truths which he developes. His lectures are a rich mine of strong, rugged, and picturesque English; and I am confident that Tennyson has worked in it assiduously. I could quote many passages to prove that he has studied and imitated Sedgwick's grand, nervous style. I wish I could preserve for you a lecture in its integrity, but even then the vehemence of his voice and the energy of his manner

---

[42] Roy Porter, 'The Natural Sciences Tripos', pp. 201–7 for these lines and the quotations.

would be wanting. His appearance is captivating. While gazing on his time-worn, weather-beaten face,[43] you cannot help remembering that it is no idle spectator you are listening to, but a philosopher indeed, the friend of Cuvier and Humboldt and Buckland and other veterans of modern science; one who recounts facts from his own observations, who had himself groped in dark caves in search of wild beasts' bones, and dredged whole days, through shine and shade, in river beds... He is indeed a grand living example of the truth of Wordsworth's philosophy. He has been schooled by Nature into a 'divine old man'.[44]

Sedgwick was the most memorable character among Cambridge scientists, and perhaps the greatest lecturer within the university. But for almost all his career he was the only Cambridge geologist. Perhaps the support and influence of colleagues would have moderated his waywardness most notably in his quarrels with Murchison and the Geological Society. Certainly, 'by the end of his long life Sedgwick had in effect survived into a new period in the history of science: and although he was widely admired and even loved as a warmhearted and noble character, many of his scientific views seemed remote and antiquated'.[45]

After Sedgwick's epoch the number of geologists in Cambridge increased, separately funded by both the university and the colleges, in step with the demand for their services from larger cohorts of candidates. To this growth in faculty personnel, and the abundant resources that lay behind it, has been attributed the excellence of Cambridge geology in the years 1870–1920: a function of the division of labour, the diversity of intellect and outlook, and the competitive edge that numbers brought.[46] These qualities, it should be noted, were inherent in Cambridge science as a whole in these decades of development.

CHEMISTRY AND TECHNOLOGY

'Where have we any thing to do with Chimistry, which hath snatcht the keyes of Nature from the other sects of Philosophy, by

---

[43] Sedgwick was sixty-four when Wilton wrote.
[44] Roy Porter, 'The Natural Sciences Tripos', p. 201, quoting an original in the Sedgwick Museum.
[45] Martin Rudwick, in the *Dictionary of Scientific Biography*.
[46] Roy Porter, 'The Natural Sciences Tripos', pp. 201–10.

her multiplied experiences ?'[47] So asked in 1649 John Hall of St John's, in a pamphlet calling for 'the advancement of learning and reformation of the universities'. Cambridge gave a positive response to his question about 1682, when John Vigani, an Italian who had studied chemistry widely in Europe, was welcomed as a teacher in Cambridge. Treating chemistry largely in relation to its medical uses (an emphasis that remained for many years), he gave lectures in Queens' and had a laboratory in Trinity. In 1703 the Senate created a chair for him. Though it was at first non-stipendiary, the professorship was permanent, and in 1716 a university lecture room in the New Printing House in Queens' Lane was attached to the chairs of chemistry and anatomy.

Vigani died in 1713. We know little about the next two professors, but John Hadley of Queens', professor from 1756 to 1764 and a close friend of John Gray, the poet, published a *Plan of a Course of Chemical Lectures* that strongly suggests his competence. That also seems to have been a quality of the next professor, the famous Richard Watson, whose uneven career as Professor of Divinity and Bishop of Llandaff is discussed elsewhere.[48] Though ignorant of chemistry when elected to the chair in 1764 at the age of twenty-seven, Watson prepared for lecturing by fourteen months in the laboratory. He gave a course every Michaelmas Term, and published a paper of 'considerable merit' (in W. H. Mills's words) in the *Philosophical Transactions of the Royal Society* for 1770, on the changes in volume consequent upon the solution of salts in water. He also succeeded in getting a stipend for his chair, from the Crown, though the £100 scarcely satisfied Watson's financial ambitions. Watson's tenure of the chemistry professorship was abruptly ended by his election to the Regius Professorship of Divinity in 1771, but he continued to publish papers on chemistry; paradoxically, he was more distinguished as a chemist than as a bishop or Professor of Divinity.[49]

[47] Quoted by W. H. Mills, 'Schools of Chemistry in Great Britain and Ireland, 6: The University of Cambridge', *Journal of the Royal Institute of Chemistry*, 77 (1953), p. 423, and pp. 423–31 for the following paragraphs.
[48] See chapter 8, pp. 286–94.
[49] He was interested in industrial chemistry, and 'advocated the recovery of the volatile products discharged from coke ovens and the condensation of the fumes and sulphurous gases given off during the roasting of lead ores'. He also advised the government on the manufacture of a more explosive gunpowder: see Mills, 'Schools of Chemistry', p. 426.

Watson was succeeded in the chemistry chair by Isaac Pennington, who seems to have continued the stress on its medical orientation. During his tenure, in 1783, a new professorship, the Jacksonian, was endowed as a result of a bequest. Its holder was to have a wide choice of approaches – between chemistry and 'natural experimental philosophy'; either of them might be freely interpreted, but lectures were to be illustrated by experiments, and some attention was to be paid to the affliction of gout. There followed an exciting period in Cambridge chemistry, containing colourful personalities, and some solid achievements and fresh departures. The period is also confusing to the modern student, with men moving from one professorship to the other while chairs change character, too, and two chemists bore the same unusual surname, Wollaston.

The first Jacksonian Professor, Isaac Milner, gave early evidence of a lifelong interest in practical mechanics by designing a sundial at the age of eight, and after taking his BA he studied chemistry with Watson and taught it as Pennington's deputy. As professor he both gave lectures and conducted practicals, being the first occupant of the rooms constructed in the old Botanic Garden in 1786. The verdicts on him are mixed – a contrast that would suggest the difficulty of attempting wide expertise at a time when the sciences were rapidly developing. William Smyth, Professor of Modern History from 1807 to 1849, thought him a 'very capital lecturer. The chemical lectures were always well attended; and what with *him*, and what with his German assistant, Hoffman, the audience was always in a high state of interest and excitement.'[50] While reporting that the chemistry lectures were judged 'very excellent',[51] Henry Gunning felt that Milner 'did not treat the subjects under discussion' in his practical sessions 'very profoundly', though 'he contrived to amuse' the audience and get them 'laughing heartily' at mishaps:

> In order to prove that a guinea and a feather would descend *in vacuo* in the same time, he made use of a glass tube hermetically sealed, in which the guinea and the feather were enclosed; it so happened, that in several attempts the guinea *had the advantage*: he then managed to

---

[50] Milner, *Isaac Milner*, p. 32, and pp. 3, 14–15, 18, 37–8, 51, 70 for other references.
[51] Gunning, *Reminiscences*, vol. II, pp. 259–60 for what follows.

place the guinea above the feather. At the end he exclaimed, 'How beautifully this experiment has succeeded for if you observed attentively, you would perceive that the feather was down sooner than the guinea.'

Fortunately, Milner's reputation is as a divine.

This was a time of rapid development in chemistry in Cambridge and elsewhere. Milner was an ardent believer in 'phlogiston'[52] and was very reluctant to accept that its existence was disproved by Lavoisier. In his syllabus of lectures for 1783 Milner wrote in the old terms of 'dephlogisticated air', 'hydrogen air', and 'carbonic acid air'.[53] But when he resigned in 1792 Milner was succeeded as Jacksonian professor by F. J. H. Wollaston, a man abreast of recent advances in knowledge. Wollaston, the son of an astronomer clergyman and like his father a graduate of Sidney Sussex, was Senior Wrangler in 1783. In his syllabus for 1794 Wollaston wrote of 'oxygen air' and 'hydrogen air', and by 1805 was using the modern terms, 'oxygen', 'hydrogen', and so on. Wollaston showed 300 experiments in his course of lectures, and added to knowledge himself – perhaps most notably by measuring the height of Snowdon accurately.

His contemporary in the chemistry chair (he succeeded Pennington in 1794) was William Farish, son of a Carlisle clergyman, and successively sizar of Magdalene, Senior Wrangler 1778, and fellow of his college. Finding 'the province of reading Lectures on the principles of Chemistry already ably occupied by the *Jacksonian* professor', he chose 'the Application of Chemistry to the Arts and Manufactures of Britain'.[54] His activities as vicar of St Giles, Cambridge, reveal that displays of mechanical ingenuity were very congenial to him; he created over the pulpit 'a paraboloid sounding-board, which was likened to a tin coal-scuttle bonnet'.[55] His lecture syllabus shows that 'he had an extensive knowledge of

---

[52] Phlogiston – a name used in the eighteenth century for a supposed substance emitted during combustion. A modern chemist sees a gain or loss of oxygen, but earlier chemists an inverse loss or gain of phlogiston.

[53] Mills, 'Schools of Chemistry', pp. 428–9 for what follows.

[54] Quoted in Mills. 'Schools of Chemistry', p. 429.

[55] Christopher Wordsworth, *Scholae Academicae*, pp. 40–1. In his house in Queens' Road (now Merton House) he constructed a movable partition which might divide either a bedroom or the dining-room below. On occasion this caused embarrassment. Merton House still has 'a large door raised by pulleys' between two *ground-floor* rooms: see *RCHM Cambridge*, Part 2, p. 379b.

contemporary manufacturing processes . . . to illustrate his lectures he provided himself with a set of interchangeable cogwheels, shafts, clamps etc.', an early version of Meccano.[56]

The men and ventures so far described suggest more interest in the marvels of the natural world, and more ingenuity and freshness of approach in teaching them, than some accounts of eighteenth-century Cambridge have prepared us for, though rarely obvious in these men's careers are additions to knowledge or attempts at them – in our idiom, research. But two men with Cambridge connections – Smithson Tennant and William Hyde Wollaston – were among the most distinguished scientists of their day, and their achievements deserve to be recorded at some length. Tennant, the son of a fellow of St John's and the vicar of Selby,[57] was in 1781–2 a medical student in Edinburgh, where Joseph Black's chemistry lectures were important to him. Tennant studied medicine at Christ's and later Emmanuel from 1782 to 1788, but though he did graduate MB he was little attracted by his formal studies and learnt most from his attention to chemistry and botany. He made original investigations during these Cambridge years but did not publish them. So far, his career may give us an impression of desultoriness, but in his years of widespread travel (he had private means and did not practise medicine) Tennant built a formidable reputation on papers published by the Royal Society. He added greatly to the work of Lavoisier on the composition of the diamond, showing that it was chemically identical with charcoal. His most important achievement was the discovery of two new elements within platinum ore, in which research he added to the findings of scientists in France and Sweden.[58] Because of his contributions to knowledge Tennant was elected Professor of Chemistry in 1813, and he gave a course of lectures which attracted large audiences including Milner and Whewell. But what promised to be a distinguished tenure of the chemistry chair ended in his death when a drawbridge collapsed beneath him in Boulogne in February 1815.

W. H. Wollaston's brother, Francis, was Jacksonian professor

[56] Mills, 'Schools of Chemistry', p. 429.

[57] What follows is based on the detailed account in Mills, 'Schools of Chemistry', pp. 429–31, and the lengthy biographies in the *DSB* by D. C. Goodman.

[58] He called the new elements iridium (because of its colours) and osmium (because of its distinctive odour).

from 1792 to 1813.[59] William's scientific achievement was far greater. Another child of the vicarage, William Wollaston came up to Gonville and Caius on a Tancred studentship, an award to assist men reading medicine; this was a college specialism that was however more latent than apparent in the 1780s, when there were only two medical students in Caius. Tennant was reading medicine at the same time, and the two men formed a lasting friendship. On graduating in 1787 Wollaston was able, because of his college's emphasis, to move straight to a senior fellowship, which he kept until his death in 1828, though 'he was a rare visitor in Caius'.[60] Practising medicine in London and elsewhere, he gave it up in 1800 on inheriting a fortune. Thenceforth he devoted himself to chemistry, which Tennant had stimulated him to address while he was an undergraduate. The great variety of his successful scientific endeavours ranged from advocacy of the imperial gallon to adding to atomic theory; they brought him the Presidency of the Royal Society for a time. Chief among them was the invention in his private laboratory of a technique for refining platinum in malleable form, a task that had puzzled some eminent men. His researches paralleled Tennant's, and about 1800 the two men formed a partnership to produce platinum vessels for the concentration of sulphuric acid. These two men, especially the more diligent Wollaston, have a meaningful place in the annals of the Industrial Revolution, in which Cambridge is rarely credited with any share. The very freedom and leisure of students' time, and exceptional and seemingly unjustified endowments, made possible the pursuit of talents outside the academic cursus.

In his evidence to the Graham Commissioners Henry Bond, the Regius Professor of Physic, stressed the place of chemistry, and other natural sciences, in his plans to bring the Cambridge medical curriculum up to date. After the 'matured liberal education' provided by the BA course medical students should study chemistry, to acquire 'rather the means of ensuring a philosophical foundation for the subsequent *professional* acquirements of the Medical Student' than actually contributing much to them.[61] James

---

[59] On William Hyde Wollaston, see, in addition to the sources already cited, Christopher Brooke, *Gonville and Caius College*, pp. 186–7, 288.
[60] Christopher Brooke, *Gonville and Caius College*, p. 187.

Cumming, the Professor of Chemistry from 1815 to 1861, shared this sense of the subject's purpose while appreciating its agency in liberal education.[62]

Cumming, a graduate of Trinity, was Tenth Wrangler in 1801. In 1825 he published a detailed syllabus listing, in addition to the basics of the science and the latest developments in electro-chemistry, the chemistry of bodily fluids, the detection of poisons, and the analysis of mineral waters, all important matters to doctors. He lectured regularly but for much of the time failed to attract more than four or five medical students.[63] Cumming was disappointed in his research too, being anticipated in his work on heat and electricity in the 1820s, and he began to give more time to his other avocation, his rectory, that usual concomitant of a Cambridge professorship. Still, though he was seventy-four when the Natural Sciences Tripos began in 1851, he does seem to have kept his lectures on the principles of chemistry up to date in the next decade. The NST examination papers show that students 'were meant to obtain a broad, uncontroversial understanding of the basic principles of chemistry', and were expected 'to be able to "explain", "describe" or "prove"; they required basically the same skills as those cultivated for the Mathematical Tripos'. But candidates were not asked to 'solve original problems or to perform chemical operations'.[64]

Cumming's successor was George Downing Liveing. Born in 1827 when Hallifax and Jebb might be remembered in the university, he died in 1924, within the memory of men and women still vigorous in Cambridge in the 1990s. Eleventh Wrangler in 1850, Liveing was at the head of the six candidates in the first Natural Sciences Tripos the following year, with a distinction in chemistry and mineralogy.[65] After some months of study in Berlin and the Royal College of Chemistry in London,[66] he returned to Cambridge to teach practical chemistry to medical students, with

[61] PP 1852–3, HC xliv [1559]: *Graham Commission Evidence*, p. 83.
[62] For what follows see article in the *Dictionary of Scientific Biography* and Gerrylynn K. Roberts, 'The Liberally-Educated Chemist: Chemistry in the Cambridge Natural Sciences Tripos, 1851–1914', *Historical Studies in the Physical Sciences*, 11 (1980–1), pp. 160–1.
[63] PP 1852–3, HC xliv [1559]: *Graham Commission Evidence*, p. 102.
[64] Roberts, 'The Liberally-Educated Chemist', p. 161.
[65] On Liveing, see Roberts, 'The Liberally-Educated Chemist', pp. 161–4, and W. C. D. Dampier's essay in the *Dictionary of National Biography, 1922–30*, from which the next quotation is taken.
[66] It became Imperial College.

the support of the Professor of Physic, 'in a primitive laboratory fitted up in a cottage in Corn Exchange Street'. In 1853 his college, St John's, elected him a fellow, founded for him a lectureship in chemistry, and provided a laboratory too: early examples of college involvement in the new sciences. In Cumming's declining years Liveing in effect took on his professional duties.

He became professor in name (the pay remained a frugal £100) in the first year of the autonomous NST honours degree. He immediately threw his energies into updating the syllabus and pressing for better accommodation than the lecture room he had to share with two other professors. Chemistry benefited from the building the university undertook on the old Botanic Garden;[67] by 1867 'Liveing rejoiced in a university laboratory that had space for thirty-five to forty students and apparatus for half that many', ample space for the maximum of twenty chemistry students that might be expected about 1870.[68] In addition, at about this time two more college laboratories were opened: a development reflecting appreciation of the new degree. But it was not wholly satisfying to Liveing, who would have preferred central *university* provision (over which the professor would have had some control) to the fragmentation of resources between many colleges. Liveing's prescription has been followed in the twentieth century because of pressing necessity: even the richest college would now quail at the prospect of equipping a range of laboratories. In Liveing's epoch, however, Cambridge was feeling its way towards a new concept of the multi-faculty university staffed by professional teachers and researchers, and we receive confused signals from it. Liveing requested three additional chemistry professors, and Gerrylynn Roberts thinks that he may have wanted one of them 'with a view to counteracting the appeal of the college laboratories by offering college-style tuition in a University setting'. The university's response, the appointment of three assistants, was less than hoped but more than might have been expected, while the university did quintuple the professorial stipend to £500.

Transition is also revealed by the chemistry examination papers in the period 1862–75. Some questions kept 'abreast of new

[67] It is now known as the New Museums Site.
[68] Roberts, 'The Liberally-Educated Chemist', p. 162, and pp. 163–4 for the next quotation.

knowledge rather than discovering or debating it'; they were 'in the Cambridge tradition', since little chemistry research was being undertaken in the university, even by Liveing. Other questions stressed 'factual areas of descriptive chemistry rather than broad understanding'. Still, these defects may to some extent reflect the inexperience of many examiners, an understandable result of the novelty of the degree itself. The *teaching* seems to have been at a higher level. As with other sciences, there were new departures in chemistry from the 1870s onwards – more students and staff, and a greater range in teaching, output of research, and sophistication in examination questions;[69] and though there were also weaknesses Cambridge chemistry was becoming far more capable of responding to the variety of demands usual in a modern university.

One of the most distinguished Cambridge men of the century was Robert Willis, Jacksonian Professor and famous as the author of the architectural history of the university that his nephew J. W. Clark completed.[70] An illegitimate son of R. D. Willis, fellow of Caius and therefore necessarily unmarried, Robert Willis showed in childhood the mechanical aptitude that lent distinction to his Jacksonian lectures. Graduating Ninth Wrangler in 1826, he was elected a fellow of his college, Caius, resigning it in 1832 on his marriage.[71] In 1837 Willis was elected Jacksonian Professor, retaining his chair until his death in 1875.

Willis delivered fluent and captivating lectures without notes, improving and modernising Farish's mechanical apparatus consisting of machine parts which Willis assembled before his crowded audiences. Writing much on the science of machinery, his stature led to his advising the official world, notably as a member of the royal commission considering the application of iron to railway structures and as a juror in the Great Exhibition.[72] Willis was a pioneer of Cambridge engineering. He is famous for his outstanding talent for revealing the historic growth of ancient buildings, yet

[69] Roberts, 'The Liberally-Educated Chemist', pp. 163–75.
[70] This account is based on J. W. Clark's biography of his uncle in the *DNB*, one of the best Cambridge entries in it; on Bernard Roth's entry in the *DSB*; on Christopher Brooke, *Gonville and Caius College*, esp. pp. 203–5, 214–15; on Nikolaus Pevsner, *Some Architectural Writers of the Nineteenth Century*, pp. 52–61; and on T. J. N. Hilken, *Engineering at Cambridge University 1783–1965* (Cambridge University Press, 1969), pp. 50–7.
[71] His wife was the daughter of Charles Humfrey, the architect of Maid's Causeway and much else.
[72] Willis was also a vice-president at the Paris Exhibition of 1855.

he also perceived that their construction was an *engineering* process, and his elucidation of the Gothic remains authoritative.[73]

PHYSICS

'The word "physics" acquired its modern connotations, as the science of mechanics, electricity, optics and heat, and as employing a mathematical and experimental methodology, in the first half of the nineteenth century.'[74] But versions of the science existed before the word. In the eighteenth century it was 'natural philosophy' (as it is still termed in Scotland), and Newton described himself as a natural philosopher, *Principia* being an explanation of the physical universe in mathematical terms, and more specifically in geometrical ones. Questions on mechanics and optics, very much Newtonian interests, were common in the Senate House Examination, if we may trust the 1802 problem paper;[75] and one may quote as an especially striking example of the way Newton's reasoning was called upon the following question on an unlikely incident in the motion of the heavenly bodies: 'If half the earth were taken off by the impulse of a comet, what change would be produced in the moon's orbit?' The Newtonian and geometrical bias of Cambridge mathematics was partly corrected by the influence of the Analytical Society, and questions entailing analytical techniques and pure mathematics were common in Senate House Examination papers of the 1830s and 1840s,[76] but the underlying concern of many Cambridge men continued to be 'mixed mathematics', comprising mechanics, hydrodynamics, astronomy and planetary theory, and physical and geometrical optics. The continued appeal of this Newtonian approach is shown by an analysis of the research papers published by Cambridge mathematicians in the years 1815–40.[77] Notable among them was George Biddell Airy (1801–92), the son

[73] The lack of a full-scale biography of Willis is one of the great gaps in Cambridge historiography.
[74] Harman, *Wranglers and Physicists*, p. 2.
[75] It is detailed in Christopher Wordsworth, *Scholae Academicae*, pp. 50–2.
[76] For what follows, see Becher, 'Whewell and Cambridge Mathematics', pp. 1–48, and David B. Wilson, 'The Educational Matrix: Physics Education at Early-Victorian Cambridge, Edinburgh and Glasgow Universities', in Harman, *Wranglers and Physicists*, pp. 12–48.
[77] I. Grattan-Guiness, 'Mathematics and Mathematical Physics from Cambridge, 1815–40: A Survey of the Achievements and of the French Influences', in Harman, *Wranglers and Physicists*, pp. 84–111.

of an excise officer and educated at Colchester Grammar School; a sizar at Trinity, he graduated as Senior Wrangler and First Smith's Prizeman in 1823. He became Plumian Professor in 1828; his *Mathematical Tracts* (1826 and later) were standard texts for Cambridge 'mixed' mathematicians, and in them and elsewhere he published much on astronomy, dynamics, the theory of tides, and the undulatory theory of light – all attempts at scientific (i.e. physical) explanation through mathematical means. This approach was shared among others by his successor as Plumian Professor, James Challis,[78] and by the most famous and influential of the mathematical coaches, William Hopkins. The return of the examination to a more geometrical and 'mixed' approach at the expense of abstract analysis owed much to Whewell, but it also reflected predispositions widespread in the university.

The 'mixed' approach emphasised in the Senate House Examination in the 1840s and later provided a thorough education for physicists of a certain definite type. The rationale of this education was most trenchantly explained by John Herschel (1792–1871), the astronomer and the most eminent member of an illustrious family containing four other astronomers.[79] Senior Wrangler and First Smith's Prizeman in 1813 he was elected immediately to a fellowship in his college, St John's. Though he resigned his fellowship in 1829 his influence in Cambridge was very great, especially through his *Preliminary Discourse on the Study of Natural Philosophy*, published in 1830 as the opening volume in Lardner's Cabinet Cyclopaedia, a series of thoughtful popularisations. The key to progress in advanced areas of science, Herschel argued, was 'a degree of knowledge of mathematics and geometry altogether unattainable by the generality of mankind'.[80] Sometimes scientific proof required a mathematical chain of reasoning so long and complicated 'that no *mere* good common sense, no general tact or ordinary practical reasoning, would afford the slightest chance of threading their mazes'. Such cases 'are the triumph of theories. They show at once how large a part pure

[78] In 1836 Airy became Astronomer Royal.
[79] John's father, two sons, and his aunt, Caroline.
[80] Quoted in Wilson, 'Physics in the Natural Sciences Tripos', *Historical Studies in the Physical Sciences*, 12 (1981–2), pp. 328–9.

reason has to perform in our examination of nature.' Especially was this so in the case of dynamics, 'the science of force and motion'; it described nature's most widespread activity, manifested the closest alliance between mathematics and science, and 'is thus placed at the head of all the sciences'. Herschel, in short, thought experimentalism a lesser means to truth than mathematical deduction.

Herschel arranged the sciences in a spectrum with dynamics at one end and chemistry at the other. To be sure, quantification was entailed in chemistry, but the science was so undeveloped that Herschel scarcely considered it as part of natural philosophy. Of all the sciences, chemistry was perhaps 'the most completely an experimental one', and its theories were 'generally intelligible and readily applicable', demanding 'no intense concentration of thought', and leading 'to no profound mathematical researches'. The other sciences – astronomy, optics, heat, electricity, and magnetism – ranged between dynamics and chemistry in their mathematical content and the extent to which they had become dynamical in character, astronomy and optics being nearest to dynamics on these criteria. In this scheme of things hypothesis and theory were sometimes valuable, but depended so greatly on mathematical verification that it was wise to rely first on the agency of mathematics.

These ideas might be a list of instructions for much of the work of the leading Cambridge scientists of the next fifty years: G. G. Stokes's dynamical theory of diffraction, Kelvin's dynamical theory of heat, and Clerk Maxwell's dynamical theory of the electromagnetic field, and much of J. J. Thomson's research in the 1880s.[81] In 1888 Thomson, in *Applications of dynamics to physics and chemistry*, declared that the result of the previous half-century's advances 'has been to intensify the belief that all physical phenomena can be explained by dynamical principles and to stimulate the search for such explanations'.[82] The case of J. J. Thomson is particularly striking, since eventually he was to lead the new departure in Cambridge physics, the *experimental*. It shows how greatly Cambridge approaches in the 'Reformed' period after 1850 were

---

[81] See Wilson, 'Physics in the Natural Sciences Tripos', pp. 330–3.
[82] Wilson, 'Physics in the Natural Sciences Tripos', p. 332.

conditioned by an ideology constructed in the 'Unreformed' period before it. 'At least five convictions', writes David B. Wilson,

> pervaded the atmosphere surrounding mathematical and physical studies at Victorian Cambridge. (1) Mathematics was necessary for physical research, even for experimental work... (2) Advanced mathematics was conceptually difficult and could be mastered only by a few, many fewer than could do experimental work... (3) A man should study mathematics when young. One could successfully take up experimental research after mathematical studies, without extended training in experimental physics. As [J.J.] Thomson noted, 'there have been many great physicists who never attended any demonstrations in practical physics – Joule, Stokes, Kelvin, Rayleigh, Maxwell to take only English examples – and I am not sure that they lost much by the omission'.[83]

Testimony as to the creative power of this mathematical tradition came from Osborne Reynolds writing about J. P. Joule.[84] He argued that William Thomson (Kelvin) developed Joule's work,

> and carried it into a region where the language was such that Joule, with his scant mathematical education, was ill-qualified to follow, much less to lead the advance... He evinced an admiration which almost amounted to reverence for the mathematical powers displayed, himself looking on until demand was made for further experimental work on incidental points, when he again lent his unequalled powers to the mathematicians.

From 1851 onwards it was possible to study physics in both the Mathematical and the Natural Sciences Triposes, although the NST did not become an autonomous degree until 1861 and physics did not become a separate subject within it until 1873.[85] For the first twenty years of the Natural Sciences Tripos, therefore, physics had subordinate status. In the Mathematical Tripos, much the larger in the period 1850–70, the physics topics were essentially those within

[83] 'Physics in the Natural Sciences Tripos', pp. 334–5. Thomson's words occur in *Recollections and Reflections* (1936), p. 134. He should have written *British* examples, since Kelvin (William Thomson) and Clerk Maxwell were Scots. It should also be said that Joule was renowned for his experimental skills rather than his mathematics.

[84] Osborne Reynolds, 'Memoir of James Prescott Joule', *Memoirs and Proceedings of the Manchester Literary and Philosophical Society*, fourth series, 6 (1892), p. 137. Reynolds, a wrangler from Queens' College, was for many years Professor of Engineering at Owen's College, Manchester.

[85] For what follows, see Wilson, 'Physics in the Natural Sciences Tripos', pp. 335–65.

the Newtonian framework – statics, dynamics, hydrostatics, optics, and astronomy. Heat, magnetism, and electricity were excluded until the efforts of Stokes, Airy, and Clerk Maxwell led to their addition from 1866 onwards. They occurred in NST examinations, but on the other hand mechanics and optics, the province of the Mathematical Tripos, did not.

NST physics was not as yet experimental in nature. Yet owing to pressure from Clerk Maxwell and others and the recommendations of a Physical Sciences Syndicate a chair of experimental physics was established (Clerk Maxwell was the first incumbent, in 1871) and the Cavendish Laboratory was opened in 1874. The appointment by Trinity College in 1869 of Coutts Trotter as a lecturer in physics was another significant development; an experimentalist who had studied in Germany, he seems to have provided most of the teaching for NST physics in the 1870s – his lectures being open to students from other colleges on payment of a fee. Clerk Maxwell began courses in experimental physics in 1876–7. They required no more than elementary mathematics, and had experiments for illustration only, not to be performed by students. Student experimentation did not start until 1879.

In the 1880s, however, the Natural Sciences Tripos developed considerably, and on different lines from the Mathematical Tripos (MT). Both sets of students studied physics, and MT students did far more mathematics, but could not conduct experiments; there were many men 'who could solve the most complicated problems about lenses, yet when given a lens and asked to find the image of a candle flame, would not know on which side of the lens to look for the image'.[86] J. J. Thomson lamented that the Mathematical Tripos produced men who 'look on analytical processes as the modern equivalents of the Philosopher's Machine in the Grand Academy of Lagado, and [who] regard as the normal process of investigation in this subject the manipulation of a large number of symbols in the hope that every now and then some valuable result may drop out'. In contrast, NST students were not expert mathematicians, but had to conduct experiments and answer questions on experimental apparatus. Though it was possible to combine both triposes, or

---

[86] Wilson, 'Physics in the Natural Sciences Tripos', p. 355, and p. 356 for the next quotation.

elements from them, in fact few did so. It is true, however, that such 'combining' students formed a high proportion of those taking NST advanced physics, half of whom (17) had already taken the Mathematical Tripos in the years 1871–81, and two-thirds (30) in 1882 to 1889. The combination was cumbrous, involving duplication of effort. It seemed to J. J. Thomson, Cavendish Professor from 1884, that the remedy was to fill in the gaps in each tripos, and though an attempt to add experiments to the Mathematical Tripos was not successful, the addition of mathematics to the Natural Sciences Tripos was. It changed the character of the degree, and helped to cause the swing that occurred in the 1890s towards preparing for a career as a physicist solely through the NST. Of the 39 men and women who took NST advanced physics in the years 1890–1900, only 8 had previously taken the Mathematical Tripos; the other 31 took the NST alone.

THE DEVELOPMENT OF THE NATURAL SCIENCES TRIPOS, 1851–1870

In 1863 the President of the new Cambridge University Natural Science Society wrote in his report for the Easter Term that he hoped its members would

> go forth into the world, not only to pursue Science as a recreation whilst engaged in other duties of the Church, the Bar or the Medical professions; but to rank amongst our Professed Naturalists and such as devote themselves exclusively to the advancement of the various departments of science, the encouragement of which the Society sets before it as its object.[87]

The tentative yet hopeful quality of these words catches the ambivalent character of the tripos in its first twenty years, looking forward to Cambridge's becoming the great scientific centre that its stature implied, while reflecting the hesitation of the tripos's beginning.

Between the years 1851 and 1860 the greatest number of

[87] Roy Macleod and Russell Moseley, 'Breaking the Circle of the Sciences: The Natural Sciences Tripos and the "Examination Revolution"', in Roy Macleod (ed,), *Days of Judgement. Science, Examinations and the Organization of Knowledge in Late Victorian England* (Driffield, N. Humberside, Nafferton Books, 1982), p. 194.

candidates was six and the lowest three; meanwhile there were always six examiners.[88] Despite the excellence of much of the teaching, candidates might be forgiven for feeling that the cards were stacked against them. Required to possess bachelor's degrees in mathematics or classics, they had to take papers in six scientific subjects in the Lent Term in which all tripos examinations were held. After merely one year's study, complained an anonymous writer in *Fraser's Magazine* in 1852, 'young men are to be examined in half a dozen sciences at once, each of which may, or rather, if any progress is to be made therein, *must* be the study of a whole lifetime'.[89] There were complaints at the lack of college preferment for scientists, by way of scholarships and fellowships. It matched, and helped to explain, the indifference towards it of the schools that traditionally provided Cambridge matriculants. 'The wonder,' lamented a writer in the *Lancet* in 1867, 'is that the Tripos keeps on its legs at all . . . Those who seek reward as well as honour, and they constitute the mass of hard-working students, see that the path of Natural Science will lead to little or nothing, and turn in the better-paid ways of Classics and Mathematics.'[90]

Still, matters were changing. Writing in *Nature* in March 1870, T. G. Bonney of St John's remarked that the 'Coldness and even dislike with which the study of natural science was once regarded here is rapidly passing away . . . the University is fully alive to the wants of the age.' Four colleges (Trinity, St John's, Sidney Sussex, and Downing) had appointed six lecturers in the natural sciences and were providing at least ten scholarships and exhibitions for natural sciences between them. These were merely the beginnings of the large increase in both university and college appointments in science that took place steadily thereafter, and still continues more than a century later. The spur was the setting up of the independent Natural Sciences Tripos in 1861, for which no other tripos was a prerequisite, a change that began a virtuous circle of growth for Cambridge science. Its prestige grew as students were able to devote more time to it, and as larger numbers of specialist dons added to knowledge through their researches. Growth was most dramatic in

[88] Tanner, *Historical Register*, pp. 737–9.
[89] Quoted in Macleod and Russell, 'Breaking the Circle', p. 195.
[90] Quoted in MacLeod and Russell, 'Breaking the Circle', p. 193, and p. 195 for the next quotation.

numbers of candidates. A modest increase in the 1870s was followed by a surge after 1881, when the tripos was divided into two parts, Part 1 for men and women wanting a general education in a wide spread of sciences, and Part 2 for those wanting to follow it with a specialism in one science.[91] In 1880 there were 32 candidates, in 1890, 82 (Part 1) and in 1900, 145 (Part 1).

A MORAL SCIENCE: HISTORY

THE FIRST REGIUS PROFESSORS

In 1724 George I established in Oxford and Cambridge Professorships of Modern History and Modern Languages at a stipend of £400 a year.[92] 'Two persons of sober conversation and prudent conduct ... skilled in modern history and in the knowledge of modern languages', were to educate 'constant supplies of learned and able men to serve the publick both in church and state'. The two professors were to pay from their own stipends for at least two persons at each university 'well qualified to teach and instruct in writing and speaking the said languages', who were to instruct twenty king's scholars.

The purpose of this scheme was to educate men for the government diplomatic service and to act as travelling tutors for gentlemen. It originated with Edmund Gibson, Bishop of London and friend of the Hanoverian dynasty.[93] But neither he nor anybody else created any means of ensuring that the professor carried out his duties properly; in fact the Whig ministry seems to have regarded the chair merely as a useful piece of patronage. The first professor, Samuel Harris, a Whiggish fellow of Peterhouse, gave an inaugural lecture but no others, though he did appoint instructors in French and Italian and report twice on the twenty scholars' progress. He wrote a lengthy commentary on the fifty-third chapter of Isaiah and no history. By the time of his death in 1733 the government had ceased to nominate any scholars, and appointed as successor to Harris a man, Shallet Turner, with no qualifications whatever apart

---

[91] This essential division remains. Cambridge thus retains the wide scientific coverage that characterised the first Natural Sciences Tripos.

[92] Cooper, *Annals*, IV, pp. 182–3.

[93] For what follows, see Winstanley, *Unreformed Cambridge*, pp. 154–62.

from his being a fellow of Peterhouse. He allowed, wrote William Cole, 'some small pittance to the French and Italian teachers in the University',[94] but did nothing else. Laurence Brockett, a fellow of Trinity, is described by Winstanley as the 'third and most scandalous' Professor of History; he owed his place to a friend's intercession with Lord Bute when he was a power in the government, did nothing in his six years in the post (1762–8), and was killed by falling off his horse in a drunken stupor when riding to Cambridge from his vicarage at Over one evening in July 1768. The fourth professor was the most famous incumbent ever, the poet Thomas Gray, who began intending to lecture, in response to the hints that came from government and university. But sadly he died in 1771 without having lectured, though he read a great deal of history and assisted Horace Walpole by sending much 'information about the fifteenth and early sixteenth centuries, with copious extracts from English and French historians'.[95]

His successor, John Symonds, was far more conscientious, and with him systematic history teaching began in Cambridge. The son of a Suffolk clergyman, Symonds graduated BA in St John's in 1752 and was elected a fellow of Peterhouse in 1754; he was then twenty-four. He probably owed his election to the university's Chancellor, the Duke of Grafton.[96] Like Grafton, Symonds was an advanced Whig. In May 1776 he was 'highly pleased and satisfied' with a sermon Richard Watson gave in Great St Mary's on the dispute with the Thirteen Colonies, telling Philip Yorke its 'plain tho' not absolutely open allusions to the venality of the majorities in the House of Commons ... contained a genuine Whig doctrine, and fully answered his ideas of the principles of the Revolution'.[97] In 1778, at the height of the War of Independence, Symonds published a pamphlet denying Britain's right to tax the American colonies.[98]

---

[94] Quoted in Winstanley, *Unreformed Cambridge*, p. 156.
[95] See Arthur Lytton Lytton Sells, *Thomas Gray: His Life and Works* (London, Allen & Unwin, 1980), pp. 41, 74, 95.
[96] On this point, see Winstanley, *Unreformed Cambridge*, p. 368, note 179. For much of what follows, see pp. 158–62.
[97] BL Add. MS 35377, fols. 312–13, 316. Philip Yorke to the Earl of Hardwicke, 2 June and 9 June 1776.
[98] John Symonds, *Remarks upon an Essay, Intituled the History of the Colonisation of the Free States of Antiquity, Applied to the Present Contest between Great Britain and her American Colonies* (London, 1778).

Symonds was Recorder of Bury St Edmund's, and lived in a 'handsome house' in the Adam style on St Edmund's Hill. A 'tall man, of pleasing manners and intelligent conversation' and 'distinguished for his literary attainments' he had many friends in county society.[99] Among the closest was one of the most famous Suffolk men of the day, Arthur Young, the writer on agriculture.[100] Symonds spent five or six years studying agriculture in Italy and the way local circumstances affected it, and he contributed seven articles on Italy to Young's *Annals of Agriculture*, describing irrigation systems, soil, chief crops, and climate in considerable detail.[101]

Symonds valued his professorship and was assiduous in it, regularly travelling the thirty miles to the university to lecture. There seems to have been anxiety lest Symonds's lectures should draw undergraduates from their college tasks; at all events he had to agree with the heads of houses that not more than twenty-six might attend.[102] We have testimony about the lectures from Philip Yorke who attended them in 1774, 1775, and 1776; unfortunately, it is somewhat contradictory. A survey course from 'the four first empires' onwards, it was given by Symonds 'without book', with 'a few notes lying before him to refresh his memory'. Yorke regarded his delivery as too slow and his pronunciation as 'affected'; and so people disliked the lectures 'which is unjust, as they are very clever in themselves'. Yorke thought that students found Symonds's lectures too desultory to note down, but on the other hand 15 or 16 out of the 25 or 26 undergraduates on the list did attend regularly – a proportion that would convince a modern history lecturer in Cambridge that he was a riotous success, especially if his course was not examined. Yet, Yorke also thought Samuel Hallifax *too fast* to take notes from; and he constantly gives the impression of seeking excuses for the brevity of the notes he submitted to his egregious uncle.[103]

[99] Sir Egerton Brydges, *Autobiography, Times, Opinions and Contemporaries* (2 vols., London, 1834), vol. I, pp. 64–5; John Nichols, *Literary Anecdotes of the Eighteenth Century* (9 vols., London, 1812–16), vol. IV, pp. 382–3.

[100] John G. Gazeley, *The Life of Arthur Young 1741–1820* (Phildelphia, Pa., American Philosophical Society, 1973), esp. pp. 148, 158–9.

[101] Mauro Ambrosoli, *John Symonds. Agricoltura e Politica in Corsica e in Italia (1765–1770)* (Turin, Einaudi, 1974) is a detailed study.

[102] Winstanley, *Unreformed Cambridge*, p. 159. Winstanley was inconsistent on this point; see note 183 on p. 368.

[103] BL Add. MS 35377, fols. 131–2 and 267, Philip Yorke to the Earl of Hardwicke, 19 November 1774 and 18 February 1776. See also chapter 15, pp. 558–9 for Yorke's attitude to Symonds.

Symonds was helpful to Yorke, taking tea with him and answering queries about the lectures, though it might be remarked that somebody in his position was likely to try to please the heir of Cambridgeshire's leading nobleman.[104] Symonds lectured every year, changing the content frequently. 'The matter and number of the lectures have been altered almost every year, the Professor sometimes omitting two or three entirely in order to introduce new circumstances.'[105] Attendance at his sessions became thin by 1777, and the discouraged professor decided not to lecture at all in 1778–9, and beginning again the following year was disheartened once more by the presence of only nine students and withdrew till November in the hope of attracting sixteen or so. Fortunately he seems to have done so, and the lectures proceeded.[106] The hint of hypersensitivity is reinforced by the strange statement of his successor as professor, William Smyth, that Symonds destroyed his lectures and all his historical papers.[107] Perhaps the impression one derives from these blurred yet overlapping images is of a worrying and far more conscientious disposition than eighteenth-century professors are usually credited with, serving a competent but lacklustre lecturing style.

WILLIAM SMYTH

Far more is known about William Smyth, professor from 1807 to 1849, an animated, emotional, highly social man who had many Cambridge friends of both sexes;[108] reminiscences record the rapid pace of his tall figure, dressed in the 1830s in the style of 1770, 'flying from one side of the way to another, as this and that person to whom he had a word to say, crossed his path'.[109]

---

[104] BL Add. MS 35377, fols. 139 and 143, Philip Yorke to the Earl of Hardwicke, 4 December and 11 December 1774.

[105] Winstanley, *Unreformed Cambridge*, p. 160, quoting the *University Calendar* for 1802.

[106] Winstanley, *Unreformed Cambridge*, p. 161, and p. 369, note 191.

[107] K. T. B. Butler, 'A "Petty" Professor of Modern History: William Smyth (1765–1849)', *Cambridge Historical Journal*, 9 (1947–9), p. 220.

[108] What follows is based on the brief autobiography which is the prelude to William Smyth, *English Lyrics* (5th edn, London, 1850), pp. v–xiv, and on Butler, 'William Smyth', pp. 217–38, a very full account which leaves Smyth better documented than any other history professor before Sir James Stephen. There are family reminiscences of Smyth (mostly inaccurate) in the autobiography of his great-niece, Dame Ethel Smyth, *Impressions that Remained* (1919).

[109] Quoted from Mary Ann Kelty, *Reminiscences of Thought and Feeling* (London, 1852), p. 155. Kelty, the daughter of an Irish surgeon, was a prolific writer of religious works and novels, and one of Smyth's Cambridge friends.

Smyth was the son of a Liverpool merchant (and mayor of the city) from Anglo-Irish gentry stock. Like another son of Liverpool commerce, W. E. Gladstone, William went to Eton, where he formed 'a little coterie of half a dozen, devoted, like myself to the pleasures of poetry', the start of a lifetime pursuit.[110] After studying for a period with a mathematics tutor in Bury (Lancashire) he matriculated as a pensioner in Peterhouse, and forcing himself to mathematics for the sake of a fellowship became Eighth Wrangler in 1787 and a fellow of his college. He helped a few young men to understand the intricacies of Euclid; one, Stratford Canning, wrote that he 'explained the point of difficulty in popular terms so clearly that I went to work again with fresh zeal'.[111] But Smyth was far fonder of young people than of mathematics, and gives the impression of carefully constructing his own network detached from academic Cambridge. A member of the Liverpool literary circle round William Roscoe, the author of *Lorenzo de Medici*, a friend of R. B. Sheridan, Samuel Rogers, Sir James Mackintosh, Sir Samuel Romilly, Mrs Barbauld, Mrs Opie, Lucy Aikin, and many others, his interests were in literature, Whiggish notions of reform, and parliamentary debate (he was often in the Commons gallery). His poems, *English Lyrics*, were first published in Liverpool in 1797 and had three further editions during his lifetime. Perhaps forgotten now, they were mildly successful in their day, and were among the very few Cambridge products Byron felt able to praise in *English Bards and Scotch Reviewers* (1808):

> Oh! dark Asylum of a Vandal race!
> At once the boast of learning, and disgrace,
> So sunk in dulness and so lost to shame
> That Smythe and Hodgson scarce redeem thy Fame.[112]

Byron's poetic taste was very like Smyth's – who preferred eighteenth-century poets such as Pope and Gray to 'Wordsworth

---

[110] W. Smyth, *English Lyrics*, p. viii.
[111] Quoted in Butler, 'William Smyth', p. 224. Stratford Canning became a diplomatist and is most famous for his period as ambassador in Constantinople, from 1842 to 1858.
[112] These lines (981–4) occur in early editions of the poem. In later editions the second couplet drops the references to Smythe and Hodgson, while still berating Cambridge. Francis Hodgson (1781–1852), an Etonian elected to a scholarship at King's in 1799, was a fellow of King's from 1802 to 1814, an intimate friend of Byron, and the author of *Leaves of Laurel* (1812) and other verse. He became a clergyman and Provost of Eton.

and his School', who 'seem to tell the Youth of both Sexes ... that no Poetry is to be found save in their own Productions'.[113] As we might expect, Smyth found much in Cambridge antipathetic. Writing to Scott, who in 1806 proposed to visit him, he offered to show him 'our Monks, our Monasteries ... But what I must confess to you! I cannot show you a single person that ever wrote a single stanza in his life, or cares a farthing about such things ... For my part I never hear more of the Muses here than I should in Lapland.'[114] Like others, he found his greatest Cambridge pleasure in music, 'on which I have lived so many years', as he wrote in 1841.[115] We catch glimpses of him in the writings of his close friend Mary Ann Kelty. In her episodic work *Visiting My Relations*, part fictional vignettes, part Cambridge reminiscence, she describes Smyth ('the Professor') at one of his Peterhouse concerts, 'cheerful, social, and welcoming his coming guests with a genial pleasantry peculiarly his own, and which diffused a feeling of ease and enjoyment over all of them'.[116] As Smyth stood by the side of an 'enchanting singer', 'I saw the smile of rapture on his countenance – I heard the little burst of feeling "Ah charming! charming!" from his lips.'[117] Even the slightest interruption 'catches the Professor's notice in a moment. He frowns – he lifts his finger; – the more experienced visitants smile – the culprit looks a little perplexed; but he has learnt the lesson that all have to learn who visit that concert-room – that not the faintest sound of a word is permitted while the music is going on.'

[113] From a letter to William Roscoe (1822) quoted in Butler, 'William Smyth', p. 226. C. A. Bristed records a story alleging that Smyth, examining Tennyson's entry for the Chancellor's Medal for English Verse (1829), was astonished that Tennyson had broken away, with blank verse, from the convention of heroic couplets, and drew the other examiners' attention to it with a pencilled exclamation. Misinterpreting it and trusting Smyth's apparent judgement they wrongly awarded the prize to Tennyson. *Five Years*, vol. 1, pp. 154–5.

[114] Butler, 'William Smyth', p. 224, quoting *The Private Letter-Book of Sir Walter Scott*, ed. W. Partington (London, 1930). Romilly and Bristed strongly suggest that Cambridge's literary life was less benighted than Smyth asserted.

[115] Quoted in Butler, 'William Smyth', p. 237, from a letter to William Roscoe junior, dating from the late 1840s. The letter records Smyth's sadness at his loss of hearing. Perhaps this affliction had led to the ending of his Peterhouse concerts, which would explain William Thomson's failure to mention Smyth in his reminiscences of Peterhouse music, *c.* 1841–5.

[116] Mary Ann Kelty, *Visiting My Relations, and its Results; A Series of Small Episodes in the Life of a Recluse* (London, 1851), pp. 332–4.

[117] The 'charming singer' was perhaps Mrs Frere, the wife of the Master of Downing. The beauty of her voice was renowned in Cambridge. Smyth dedicated his *Lady Morley's Lecture* (Leeds, 1840) to Mrs Frere, 'to whom I have been indebted for many of the happiest hours of my life'.

In 1807, when he was forty-two, this sociable, cultivated and sentimental don was appointed Regius Professor of Modern History by Lord Henry Petty, Whig MP for the university and later the third Marquis of Lansdowne. Another Whig, Sir James Mackintosh, heard the news out in Bombay, and wrote to a friend: 'I was highly pleased, indeed, with the last act of Lord Henry Petty at Cambridge, in securing the comfort and rewarding the merits of our amiable and accomplished friend Smyth'.[118] Gillray caricatured 'A Petty Professor of Modern History', a slightly timid pigtailed figure in old-fashioned garb, facing from the lecturer's desk a gang of ferocious, screaming Yahoos, though such undergraduates would be unlikely to attend voluntary lectures.[119] A modern appointments committee would not consider Smyth for the professorship. So far he had not written any history, and had two extra disabilities: though the Regius Professor had responsibility for teaching foreign languages Smyth could not speak any (though he could read French) while throughout life he was liable to inflammation of the retina if he read for more than two or three hours a day or at any time after nightfall.[120] To get round his eye weakness Smyth had a reader in the evenings, and pondered his lectures during long solitary walks. He faced other difficulties too. The colleges feared the threat his lectures posed to sacrosanct mathematical studies; he was confined to the Michaelmas Term, and only third and fourth year men were allowed to attend.

Yet this beneficiary of Whig patronage, given an apparently hopeless assignment that he might have been expected to regard as a sinecure, was more successful as History Professor than any of his predecessors, and one or two of his successors also. From 1809 to about 1840 he gave a course on European history, with a strong emphasis on England, from the fall of Rome to the American War of Independence, and in 1826 and some later years he also gave a more detailed course on the French Revolution, whose events he graphically recalled and regarded as of great

---

[118] Quoted in Butler, 'William Smyth,' p. 226.
[119] The caricature is reproduced in K. T. B. Butler's article.
[120] *English Lyrics*, p. x.

importance to students only three or four decades distant from them.[121]

Though it is now hard to capture a sense of Smyth's inner character, he seems to have been a lateral thinker, with enough self-reliance to refrain from attempting too much and to turn his weaknesses into strengths. He took his audience into his confidence in the lecture that introduced his European history course in 1809, which he published towards the end of his career.[122] Disarmingly, he confessed that he did not as yet know enough to compose the supranational account of 'the great community of Europe' which would be ideal, and that lectures on special topics such as the Age of Louis XIV would be too much like monographs. Smyth settled on guiding his audience rather than giving them masses of historical detail:

> my hearers are not to resort to me to receive historical knowledge, but to receive hints that may be of use to them while they are endeavouring to acquire it for themselves. The great use, end, and triumph of all lectures is to excite and teach the hearer to become afterwards a lecturer to himself... A hearer is not to sit passive, and expect to see performed for him those tasks which he can only perform for himself.

So essential features of Smyth's teaching were his discussions of authorities in the body of his lectures, and his recommendations for further reading. After some years Smyth published *A List of Books Recommended and Referred to in the Lectures on Modern History*.[123] Smyth tried to make his lists as short as practicable, since it was 'in vain to recommend to the generality of readers books, which it might be the labour of years to peruse'.[124] On the other hand he advised against 'general histories' except as introductions to 'more

---

[121] In writing these lectures Smyth profited from the memories of John Mallet, the son of Mallet du Pan and an eye-witness of the Terror; from him he obtained for the University Library a complete set of the *Mercure de France*, which Mallet du Pan had edited. The lectures were first published in 1840: *Lectures on History. Second and Concluding Series on the French Revolution* (3 vols., London, 1840).

[122] *Lectures on Modern History, from the Irruption of the Northern Nations to the Close of the American Revolution* (2 vols., London, 1840). The 'Introductory Lecture, 1809' is in vol. I, pp. 1–24; the quotations that follow occur on pp. 1 and 16.

[123] Cambridge, 1815 (UL Cam.c.815.11). Later editions are also in the Cam Collection, one with manuscript notes.

[124] W. Smyth, *Lectures on Modern History*, vol. I, pp. 7 and 9 for these quotations.

minute and regular histories'. Always aware of the pressures of time, Smyth often suggested reading specified sections or chapters. There were later editions of the reading lists. Some titles were added in the edition of 1823, but no more thereafter. Nor, apparently, were the lectures revised. By 1840, when the lectures were published, their scholarship and the reading lists seemed distinctly old-fashioned, and like Smyth's apparel, essentially eighteenth century.

Each lecture in the European course (there are thirty-six in all) is about 8,000 words in length, which would take an hour or perhaps a few minutes extra to enunciate, rather more than a Cambridge lecturer plans to take today.[125] Smyth's style, if not lacking the periphrasis usual in lectures of the day, was at least more simple and direct than most, and often indeed reached a punchy clarity – for example in his pages on the American Revolution, perhaps because his party feelings were closely engaged. His delivery seems to have been somewhat tentative and subdued, as we might indeed expect from the handsome yet diffident figure in the engraving that prefaces *English Lyrics*. His friend Mary Kelty listened 'to his pleasant lectures, not indeed either eloquently or strikingly delivered; but with simplicity, good sense, and a sprinkling of serene, philosophical remark, most agreeably impressive'.[126] Rather higher praise was bestowed by the author of an article about Cambridge published in 1825.[127] The author, who claims to have been Senior Wrangler in Smyth's first years as professor, hardly has a good word to say about anything or anybody in Cambridge, but named Smyth as the 'second man in the university', the first being Herbert Marsh, the Lady Margaret Professor of Divinity, who though an 'intolerant bigot' supported 'his opinions like a man'.[128] Smyth's lectures were 'admirable alike for their eloquence, and various information and profound research'.

> The man who has an opportunity of attending these lectures has reason to congratulate himself on his good fortune; for my own part, I have only regretted since that I did not devote my days and nights

---

[125] He or she has to fit into a schedule that assumes that students will move from one lecture to another, on the hour. By comparison, Smyth was 'free-standing'.
[126] *Visiting My Relations*, p. 332.
[127] 'Struggles of a Poor Student Through Cambridge', *London Magazine and Review*, NS, 1 (1825), pp. 491–510.   [128] Pp. 503–4.

to the mastering thoroughly the rich stores of thought and knowledge which they would have developed. The publication of these lectures would be an invaluable treasure to the youth of this country.

Smyth was a Whiggish historian, for whom the human chronicle is a march towards liberty with many wrong turnings led by bigots. Christianity was good, but Mahomet was a force for evil because he did not advance 'the civil liberty of his followers'.[129] The central theme of English history from the Middle Ages onwards is the advance of parliament, while the Reformation gave an opening to 'criminal' tendencies – 'the inherent intolerance of the human heart ... Pagan or Christian, Protestant or Roman Catholic'. Smyth devoted three lectures to Charles I and the Civil War, far more than to any other forty years. In some ways a subtle account – for example showing how writers like Hume and Clarendon could find it possible to justify Charles – it is nevertheless one replete with moral judgements, and possessing no heroes since everybody turned his back on the cause of liberty; one cannot tell what Smyth would himself have *done* in any crisis in the years 1649–60. He failed to appreciate the circumstances that made men what they were, and he always seems to be pleading a cause, liberty, that was rarely being given voice at all at the time he was writing about. Still, his lectures were often lively, and we can see why he was praised as instructive. One reviewer asserted that 'the language has too much succulence and waste of fertility', but 'every fibre and vein of argument and illustration are fresh with life'.[130] Another, an American, took Smyth to task for his major fault, his failure to take account of recent works,[131] but rejoiced to find a British historian giving a pro-American interpretation of the War of Independence, and urged adoption of the lectures as a Harvard textbook to do good 'throughout our community'. An American edition for Harvard students was in fact published very soon, while the British publication records of Smyth's lectures suggest their popularity; there were five editions of *Lectures on Modern History* between 1840 and 1848, and two editions of the lectures on the French Revol-

---

[129] For these quotations see W. Smyth, *Lectures on Modern History*, vol. I, p. 71 and 247–8.
[130] 'Arnold and Smyth on Modern History', *Fraser's Magazine*, 26 (1842), p. 642.
[131] *Christian Examiner and General Review*, 29 (1840–1), pp. 367, 372–3. (Published in Boston, Mass.)

ution. Both sets were given a place in Bohn's Standard Library in the 1850s, by the side of Goethe, Guizot, and Adam Smith.

In 1840 Smyth was seventy-five years old, and suffering from frailties which included the deafness that so often seems to afflict the musical. Perhaps the publication of his lectures in that year stimulated him to retire from lecturing. Joseph Romilly still records meeting him in the street, 'with his stick & gouty shoe, & [we] were glad to find him much better than he was a year ago: he was very cheerful & conversible in spite of his deafness'. That was in September 1844. Eighteen months later Smyth had retired to Norwich, where Romilly found that though he was deaf 'he hears my shrill voice better than anybody's'. On 31 December 1847 Romilly 'was very sorry to hear today that dear Professor Smyth had had a stroke of apoplexy'.[132] He lingered until 1849. His death marked the end of an era. By 1851 history lectures had ceased to be entirely voluntary, and were a component in the new Moral Sciences Tripos. There was a new professor too, of a very different sort from Smyth – James Stephen, a retired civil servant.

JAMES STEPHEN

James Stephen was the third son of another James, a lawyer who was in due course appointed Master in Chancery as a reward for political services: hatred of slavery that followed a period in the West Indies brought the elder James Stephen close to Evangelicals, who were prominent abolitionists, and he became an Evangelical too.[133] His son inherited his father's faith and his hatred of slavery. The younger James Stephen matriculated at Trinity Hall in 1806, at the age of seventeen, and wrote later that the 'three or four years during which I lived on the banks of the Cam were passed in a very pleasant, though not a very cheap, hotel. But had they been passed at the Clarendon, in Bond Street, I do not think that the exchange would have deprived me of any aids for intellectual discipline.' He did not sit the Senate House Examination, but gained the LL B in 1812. A

---

[132] M. E. Bury and J. D. Pickles, eds., *Romilly's Cambridge Diary 1842–1847* (Cambridgeshire Record Society, 1994), pp. 134, 163, 241.

[133] What follows is based on Leslie Stephen's perceptive study of his father (James later Regius Professor) in *The Life of Sir James Fitzjames Stephen* (London, 1895), pp. 31–65. J. F. Stephen was Leslie Stephen's brother. The quotation that follows occurs on pp. 31–2.

lawyer in private practice, in 1813 he was drawn into work for the Colonial department by Lord Bathurst, an Evangelical, and in 1825 became a full-time Counsel there. Until 1847 he devoted his very considerable talent and energy to it, having more influence on British colonial policy than any other person, though as his son Leslie Stephen points out his reasoning was concealed behind the names of the politicians whom he advised. His power being guessed, Stephen was sometimes called 'Mr Mother Country' by his critics. His talents took him in 1836 to the post of Under-Secretary of State in the Colonial Department, the highest position for a civil servant.

Stephen was not popular in the office. Disposed to very hard work by his Evangelical discipline, he was a hard taskmaster to subordinates, while standing aloof behind a pompous formality. It masked an intensely shy, thin-skinned, and pessimistic nature: Stephen could not abide mirrors that reminded him of his own appearance, and he abhorred the celebration of his birthday. His work in the Colonial Department did not satisfy the spirit; and though he was confident of his talents his exercise of them was merely dutiful. Overwork was very stressful, and Stephen could hardly have laboured so long without the librating serenity of his wife, Jane Catherine Venn, daughter of the Evangelical clergyman, John Venn. The Stephens suffered greatly at the time of the sudden death of their eldest son in 1846. The following year Stephen resigned, aged fifty-eight, and received a knighthood.

But Stephen soon recovered some of his strength, while the habit of work was deeply ingrained. Government thought his pension inadequate and cast around for a new post. Several options were considered. Stephen himself is said to have been hoping to become the Downing Professor of the Laws of England,[134] but William Smyth's death in 1849 made the Regius Professorship of History available for the government's patronage. Stephen had some serious claim to consideration. As he later wrote, in a typically laborious locution: 'though there were many men much more conversant than I am with the events of former times, there was no candidate for the office who could in any degree claim equality with myself in

---

[134] See Slee, *Learning and a Liberal Education*, p. 24, where however no traceable authority is cited for the statement.

that kind of historical knowledge which is derived from a long and intimate connection with the actual government of mankind'.[135] Also, while labouring in the Colonial Department Stephen had published lengthy articles in the *Edinburgh Review*, composing them 'early in the morning or late at night, or in the intervals of his brief holidays'.[136] In these writings, republished as *Essays in Ecclesiastical Biography* (1849), Stephen wrote with enthusiasm about Hildebrand and Ignatius Loyola as well as Martin Luther and John Wesley; his wide-ranging study broadened his sympathies and softened his Evangelical rigour.[137] His son's judgement was that 'putting aside Macaulay's "Essays"', none of the writings republished from the *Edinburgh Review* 'indicate a natural gift for style equal to my father's ... my father, had he devoted his talents to literature, would have gained a far higher place than has been reached by any of his family'.[138]

At all events, Sir James Stephen was not lacking in the mental endowment needed in his new post. His experience in it, however, revealed the imperfections in the structure of the new triposes, which all subjects, and not merely history, suffered from. The schemes had been devised very largely to give employment to distinguished scholars in the professoriate, but linking them to the various demands of the BA degree gave some of them (certainly Stephen) greater burdens than they relished, since in almost all subjects the professor was the only teacher. Stephen's case also exposed the folly of the government – the very agency most eager for university reform – in regarding the Regius Professorship as a sort of supplementary pension.

There were five subjects in the new tripos, which had to be completed in one year – a tough assignment.[139] The Regius Professor, the only teacher of history, had only twenty lectures to

---

[135] Caroline Emelia Stephen, ed., *The Right Honourable Sir James Stephen. Letters with Biographical Notes* (private publication, 1906), p. 154, letter to Bishop Wilson of Calcutta, 18 April 1852.
[136] Leslie Stephen. *James Fitzjames Stephen*, p. 55, and pp. 56–8 for what follows.
[137] One result was his being denounced in 1849 as a Latitudinarian, and for doubting 'the eternity of future punishment' by the Reverend William Bonner Hopkins, fellow of St Catharine's – criticisms that Stephen accepted. See C. E. Stephen (ed.), *The Right Honourable Sir James Stephen*, pp. 134–9.
[138] Leslie Stephen, *James Fitzjames Stephen*, p. 55. The judgement at the end of the quotation is ludicrous, but Leslie Stephen was as adept at self-depreciation as his father.
[139] For what follows see Slee, *Learning and a Liberal Education*, pp. 25–8.

communicate his knowledge, which he thought unlikely to be supplemented by wide reading because of the pressure of time. Stephen rejected a superficial survey course of European history, and opted for a narrower theme. Whewell, thinking of the poll men who were likely to form the bulk of his audience, pressed for English history. Instead, Stephen chose French history, on the dubious grounds that for the 'last six centuries' the French had 'been the arbiters of peace and war', as well as the dominant European culture.[140] The real reason was that France was the only country whose history he knew much about. He got contrary advice on how to tackle it from his friend John Austin, who suggested stressing the French monarchy, and Macaulay, who opted for the Wars of Religion and also urged Stephen to prepare for at least two years before he lectured – unhelpful words since Whewell told him that he would be expected to teach 'without delay'. Stephen set about his task vigorously.

The family moved to Cambridge, and at first Stephen thought it 'the best place of residence we could have selected. The libraries are excellent.'[141] A constant succession of 'little collegiate circumstances' kept at bay 'the stagnation of an ordinary country town'. The countryside was 'a prodigy of ugliness', but Stephen could 'trudge pleasantly along these most unpleasant roads' because he was planning his lectures. He gave his first course in the May Term, twelve lectures on French history from 'The Decline and Fall of the Romano-Gallic Province' to 'The States-General of the Sixteenth Century'.

At first the lecture-room was filled; dons came, and 'gownswomen' sat in the gallery.[142] Stephen told the senior members that he 'had nothing to offer which invited, or which would reward, their attention'. He had prepared 'nothing which was not perfectly simple, familiar, and elementary'.[143] Not surprisingly, the dons soon stayed away. Leslie Stephen, explaining the ennui that his father

---

[140] Sir James Stephen, *Lectures on the History of France* (2nd edn, 2 vols., London, 1852), vol. I, pp. 7–8, and p. vi for what follows.

[141] In a letter to Henry Taylor, 15 January 1850, in C. E. Stephen, *The Right Honourable Sir James Stephen*, p. 141.

[142] C. E. Stephen, *The Right Honourable Sir James Stephen*, p. 145, letter to Henry Taylor, 4 May 1850. 'Gownswomen' were the wives of heads of houses and of resident members of the Senate such as private tutors. In a later letter Stephen calls them 'donnesses'.

[143] Sir James Stephen, *Lectures* (2nd edn, 1852), vol. I, p. xiii.

soon felt, remarked that the 'young gentlemen' he was left with consisted very largely of poll men seeking certificates, since few honours candidates felt they could spare time for history.[144] Stephen had 'to choose between speaking over the heads of his audience and giving milk and water to babes'.

Stephen published his lectures in 1851, and implied that the printed text was the one he had delivered.[145] In fact, each lecture contains more than 11,000 words, suggesting sessions lasting ninety minutes each, which seems unlikely. Still, even if the text was stretched for publication we may assume that it remained close to Stephen's speaking style. It is heavy and literary, quite lacking in the lightness of touch appropriate for lectures and which Smyth certainly managed at times; it comprises ponderous complex sentences, replete with unusual words that only well-educated students would understand. Everything we know about the weaker poll men – who would find difficult modern examinations for school students aged sixteen – tells us that they would not comprehend or enjoy hearing the following typical sentences, which begin and conclude a paragraph on Merovingian France:[146]

> Between the mercurial Gaul and his saturnine conqueror, amalga-mation, whether social or political, was therefore of very tardy growth... The Meroving thus reigned over a state in which the great mass of the people regarded his rule with aversion and his person with contempt, and derided the convenient dulness which gave such ample scope to their own encroaching subtlety.

Perhaps Stephen knew very well that he was above the heads of many in his audience, and this was why when his lecture course had scarcely begun he wrote to his friend Henry Taylor that he was already 'beginning to tire of the publicity and the excitement of this unwonted labour'.[147] At all events, within a few weeks Stephen suffered a breakdown, involving 'great depression of spirits and a considerable increase of his characteristic sensitiveness'. Recovery was slow until the family visited Paris in the autumn.[148] Stephen

---

[144] *James Fitzjames Stephen*, p. 90.   [145] P. xv (2nd edn).

[146] Lecture 2: 'On the Decline and Fall of the Merovingian Dynasty', p. 61.

[147] C. E. Stephen, *The Right Honourable Sir James Stephen*, p. 145, letter of 4 May 1850, and pp. 148–9 for the next quotation.

[148] C. E. Stephen, *The Right Honourable Sir James Stephen*, pp. 148–9.

gave his second round of lectures in the May Term 1851, and they formed the second volume of his published series.[149] Stephen continued to lecture till he died in 1859.

But he was disenchanted with his job.[150] 'I am extremely sceptical as to the real value of public oral teaching on such a subject as mine', he wrote in 1852, and he therefore thought of his published lectures as an undergraduate textbook, none being available in English. Stephen also felt (very rightly) that the Moral Sciences Tripos asked far too much of candidates in expecting competence in five subjects after one Cambridge year of study. For example, a student of English law in such circumstances would not know 'any thing, worth the knowing, of that boundless, and toilsome, and ever-shifting field of enquiry. Yet an adroit and dexterous man may, even under such circumstances, assume the deceptive semblance of such knowledge.' So Stephen had come to view examining 'as of very doubtful utility'. Still, 'my duty' was 'to obey the law as I found it': in other words, life as Regius Professor had become, as it had been during his long years in the Colonial Department, the performance of imposed obligation that his Evangelical upbringing had prepared him for.

Stephen and his family ceased to reside in Cambridge in 1850, and after some wanderings settled in Westbourne Terrace, near Paddington Station in west London. Stephen stayed in the University Arms Hotel during his Cambridge lecture stints, which were 'not very exhilarating times', wrote his daughter, since by 1851 the audience had become 'very small',[151] though it still seems to have included several score because of the need for attendance certificates.[152] 'Many boys coming to be certificated and examined', Stephen wearily wrote in December 1853.[153]

One gentleman has been with me now three times, and three times has failed to answer the question, 'Tell me anything you

[149] These twelve lectures examined the growth and power of the French monarchy from the sixteenth century to the beginning of the eighteenth. There were also three 'On the Power of the Pen in France', dealing with Rabelais, Montaigne, Descartes, and others, which are not well linked to the main theme and may have been included because Stephen knew a lot about them.

[150] For what follows, see *Lectures on the History of France* (2nd edn), vol. I, pp. ix–xii.

[151] C. E. Stephen, *The Right Honourable Sir James Stephen*, p. 149.

[152] Thus on 9 May 1854 Stephen wrote that a concert in King's College reduced his audience from 70 to 30: p. 200.

[153] In a letter to his wife, Jane Catherine Venn. Stephen was attending the Christmas festivities usual in his college, Trinity Hall: p. 175.

know?' or any other of my questions. 'What', I asked, 'is your plan of life?' 'I mean to take orders.' 'How long have you been here?' 'Four years, having lost one by missing my Little Go.' 'Then you must lose another by missing my certificate.' And to this dunce and idler the Church of England is to confide the training of immortal souls for a bliss or a woe which the same Church believes to be eternal.

Even High Table made him miserable. Attending 'a large College dinner party' in May 1854 he wrote that 'nothing, multiplied by a thousand, will still be nothing; and dullness is not the less dull because there is a larger quantity of it.'[154] In January 1855 Stephen became Professor of Modern History and Political Economics at the East India College near Hertford, for the last three years of the college's life; he easily combined the post with the Regius Professorship, and the Stephen family lived in their house at the college for most of the year.[155] Meanwhile he laboured to complete two further volumes of lectures on French history, but they did not appear.[156] Early in 1859 his health began to decline (he was seventy years old), and the lectures he gave that year were intended to be his last. He died in September.[157]

THE DEVELOPMENT OF THE MORAL SCIENCES TRIPOS: CHARLES KINGSLEY

In 1859, his last year as Regius Professor, James Stephen wrote: 'We have this year just three candidates to be examined, and I think five if not six examiners, which is absurd'.[158] Between 1851 and 1859 the annual average of candidates for the Moral Sciences Tripos was only seven, and though there were far more attending the lectures as candidates for the ordinary degree, the new tripos itself was clearly not a success. Critics agreed with James Stephen's oft-repeated judgement that the tripos demanded far too wide a spread of

---

[154] P. 201. Letter to Mrs Stephen, 25 May 1854.
[155] C. E. Stephen, *The Right Honourable Sir James Stephen*, p. 217. Stephen taught a course in Indian history at the college.
[156] P. 234, letter of November 1856 to Mrs Sarah Austin, wife of the jurist John Austin.
[157] Pp. 276 and 285.
[158] Slee, *Learning and a Liberal Education*, p. 32, and pp. 31–5 for what follows, including the quotations.

knowledge from candidates with so little time to prepare for it, and that concentration on one field would be greatly preferable. One of the chief agents of change was W. H. Drosier, a medical lecturer and fellow at Caius; against those who contended that the university should not abandon 'the antient landmarks that hitherto have guided her' (that is, reliance on mathematics and classics) he pressed the educational claims of new subjects, provided that each was given proper opportunity. These ideas lay behind the new prescription of February 1860 for the Moral Sciences and Natural Sciences Triposes. The mathematical or classical hurdle no longer stood in the way, and the demands of the new triposes were abridged. The 'Laws of England' were dropped from the repertory of subjects, and mental philosophy, logic, and political philosophy were added. Subjects were grouped: mental and moral philosophy and logic formed one section, while history and political philosophy, political economy and jurisprudence formed the other. Students had to take one section; in other words, they could seek to explain the individual mind and the roots of human action, or the development of society itself.

History was coupled with political philosophy, a deliberate move by the newly formed Board of Moral Sciences to remove the charges of spoonfeeding which had justly been levelled at history previously, notably by Stephen himself. He was however unhappy at the discussions that led to this new partnership, fearing a departure from the facts that were history's bedrock. The board announced with 'regret that they have not had the assistance of a Professor of Modern History in making these arrangements', and went ahead devising a course that was far more philosophical than historical. The history of constitutional growth was the process that philosophy sought to explain, and so the coupling seemed natural to some, but the course fulfilled Stephen's fears. The list of books prescribed for students suggested a concentration on the close study of texts, from Plato and Aristotle to less lasting modern writers, Hallam and Brougham. The examination papers were focused on political philosophy too, and were very remote from the concerns of Stephen's successor, Charles Kingsley, who was not consulted by the Board of Moral Sciences about the scope of the history course it envisaged, and who in turn did not trouble himself much about the

Moral Sciences Tripos.[159] The gap between the examinable history course and the one man who was there to teach it was just one reason for Kingsley's unhappiness in Cambridge. In 1867 history was expelled from the Moral Sciences Tripos altogether, on the grounds that it could not be organised for the purposes of mental training, as mathematics or classics could. Kingsley was not made any happier by this downgrading of his subject in the last few years of his professorship.

The Regius Professor was appointed by the Crown, which in practice meant the Prime Minister, and therefore in 1860 Lord Palmerston. From within the university the only name that

> was widely canvassed was Dr Woodham of Jesus College, an eccentric with a repute for vast learning, epicurean manners and hatred for heads of houses, who were unwilling to serve with him on committees. In one year he contributed more than a hundred articles to *The Times*, all in vile handwriting, and willingly took up any subject the editor wanted, from war in Paraguay to the American elections. W. H. Thompson, soon to be Master of Trinity, and famous not only for his judgement but for the barbs in his words, once wrote of Dr Woodham, in a sentence intended for the eyes of a prime minister, 'I would have called him "original", if I could point to anything of importance that he had originated.'[160]

Palmerston refused to consider him, and offered the chair to J. W. Blakesley, the Trinity don who was now vicar of Ware in Hertfordshire, and perhaps also to George Stovin Venables, a one-time fellow of Jesus College and a frequent contributor to *The Times*. Neither had any claim to be a modern historian, though they might well have been thought of as candidates to teach political thought.

Kingsley was born in 1819, and was well known in Cambridge – though not for ventures that could be described as historical – when he was appointed to the Regius chair in 1860. He was much disliked in the university for his criticisms of it in his novel *Alton Locke. Tailor and Poet* (1850), a product of Kingsley's brief sympathy with

[159] Slee, *Learning and a Liberal Education*, pp. 34–6.
[160] Owen Chadwick, 'Charles Kingsley at Cambridge', in *The Spirit of the Oxford Movement: Tractarian Essays* (Cambridge University Press, 1990), p. 107.

Chartism in the 1840s,[161] which was soon to give way to paternalist Toryism and vigorous English Protestant nationalism. The fluctuating moods that Kingsley's tempestuous energies led him into are a main theme in the perceptive biography which was produced by his widow – who although in his shadow, like so many Victorian wives, was herself a person of many talents.[162] To this Victorian classic at least five modern biographies in English have been added, often with new material, but offering little increment in interpretation.

The son of a clergyman, Kingsley grew up in an oppressive Evangelical rectory, and its effect on him may be discerned in his lifelong restlessness – he could not sit still even for the duration of a meal – and an incapacitating stutter that only the excitement of public speaking could diminish. A shy, sensitive, and unformed youth, he went up to Magdalene in 1838, and threw off his strict upbringing at the card-table, the college boat-club, and a Barnwell brothel.[163] A conversion to academic work in his last months gained him a first class in the Classical Tripos in 1842, and a return to religious faith led him to become an energetic parish clergyman. His prophetic sense of the challenge from the dispossessed in the turbulent 1840s led to his dabbling with Chartism, his ardent advocacy of social reform, particularly in public health and education, and his involvement with Christian Socialism – essentially a bridge between radicalism and the paternalist Toryism that Kingsley was more deeply attached to. All this activity brought him public attention, and perhaps as much came from his extensive

---

[161] Fit to be compared with *Sybil* and *Mary Barton* as a powerful 'social novel' of the 1840s, *Alton Locke* is concerned with Cambridge's disdainful treatment of a self-educated working man. Alton Locke himself is based on the Leicester Chartist, autodidact and poet Thomas Cooper, whom Kingsley befriended. Cambridge is described as 'the scene of frivolity and sin, pharisaism, formalism, hypocrisy, and idleness' (1st edn, 1850, vol. I, p. 200).

[162] Frances Eliza Kingsley, ed., *Charles Kingsley. His Letters and Memories of His Life* (2 vols., London, 1877). Later editions were abridged, but nevertheless contain additional material. These lines on Kingsley are based on this work, and on the most thoughtful and convincing modern study, Marc Reboul, *Charles Kingsley. La Formation d'une personnalité et son affirmation littéraire (1819–1850)*, Publications de l'université de Poitiers, Lettres et sciences humaines XIII (Paris, Presses Universitaires de France, 1973), esp. pp. 63–94. Leslie Stephen's essay in the *DNB* remains one of the best studies of Kingsley.

[163] An illuminating guide to Kingsley's undergraduate years and the inner compulsions that the rectory had taught him to think shameful is Susan Chitty, *The Beast and the Monk. A Life of Charles Kingsley* (London, Hodder & Stoughton, 1974), esp. pp. 51–86; Chitty quotes extensively from Kingsley's love letters to his fiancée and prints some of his extraordinary erotic drawings.

religious utterance – Kingsley thought of himself as an Anglican pastor above all things – and his writings on the natural world that showed a gentle and serene side to his character that was often suppressed.

However, it was Kingsley's erstwhile Chartist sympathies and his ignorance of history that were uppermost in the mind of James Cumming, the Professor of Chemistry, who 'fell in with' Joseph Romilly on Sunday 10 June 1860, and '(like [W.H.] Thompson etc. etc.)' was 'highly indignant at the appointment of Kingsley as Prof. of Modern History'.[164] A few days later Romilly met W. H. Thompson of Trinity in London. 'Thompson was very amusing. He says that Ld. Palmerston (on being reproached with the appointment of Kingsley to the Chair of Modern History, – of which he [i.e. Kingsley] knew nothing) exclaimed "Why! he wrote '2 years ago', & if that is not mod. hist. what is?".'[165]

These initial reservations over Kingsley's appointment were to be recalled in later years when it had come to seem a great mistake, but in 1860 there was no settled hostility. Whewell wrote a generous letter of welcome, and Kingsley in his reply 'dedicated all his energies to the work of historical writing'.[166]

In his first three years as Regius Professor Kingsley was happy in the university. He and Frances lived in St Peter's Terrace, Trumpington Street, while regarding the rectory in Eversley, his Hampshire parish, as their true home. He taught the Prince of Wales during his period at Trinity, meeting him and eleven other carefully selected undergraduates in St Peter's Terrace twice a week, and supervising him alone on Saturdays. This sort of intimate encounter brought out Kingsley's intuitive sympathy, and the prince became a friend.[167] During these happy transactions Kingsley wrote his most unforced and tranquil work, *The Water Babies*, and in 1862, from an impulse whose source is uncertain, he rewrote the two Cambridge chapters of *Alton Locke* so as to smooth away much

---

[164] CUL MS. Add. 6840: Diary of Joseph Romilly, 10 June 1860, and 18 June 1860 for the next quotation. I owe these references to Mrs M. E. Bury.

[165] *Two Years Ago* (Cambridge, 1857) concerns many topics like all Kingsley's novels: social class, religion, the Crimean War and a cholera epidemic.

[166] Chadwick, 'Charles Kingsley at Cambridge', p. 107.

[167] Margaret Farrand Thorp, *Charles Kingsley 1819–1875* (Princeton, N.J., Princeton University Press, 1937), p. 151.

of their savage criticism. There are hints that his move was seen as too ingratiating and that he should have left matters alone.[168]

Soon there was a disconcerting change of front. Departing from the views on slavery he had expressed in *Two Years Ago*, Kingsley took the Confederate side in the American Civil War, and reproved the North for wishing to abolish slavery, in lectures on America delivered in 1863 two years after the war had started. A Cambridge paper wrote 'the Rev. Charles Kingsley seems to be losing the popularity he once enjoyed amongst Liberal folk'.[169] Suffering from malarial infections in Cambridge's damp winter, he gave up the Cambridge house and travelled up from Eversley to give his lectures, very much as Stephen had done. T. G. Bonney the geologist met him as a north-east wind was blowing along King's Parade, 'his shoulders up to his ears, his attitude and face expressive of acute discomfort. As we met he ejaculated, "What a miserable day!"'[170]

Behind physical afflictions lay the beginning of the ninth nervous breakdown Kingsley had suffered since 1848,[171] as he oscillated between euphoria and melancholy and aggravated his illness by compulsive overwork. Perhaps only mental unbalance can explain his crazy dispute with J. H. Newman in 1864; Kingsley, an obsessive anti-Papist, recklessly impugned Newman's truthfulness when reviewing Froude's *History of England*. In the pamphlet war that followed Kingsley was crushed by a far cleverer opponent (who also produced a masterpiece out of the dispute, *Apologia Pro Vita Sua*). The episode did Kingsley harm in the university, and added to the unhappiness resulting from the reception of his lectures. Here lay a fundamental cause of Kingsley's illness.

KINGSLEY'S LECTURES

Kingsley's inaugural lecture was keenly awaited in the university. On Monday 12 November 1860, the day he was to speak, 'every

---

[168] F. E. Kingsley, *Charles Kingsley*, vol. II, p. 409, quoting a letter of John Howson.

[169] *Cambridge Independent Press*, 5 December 1863. The strong racist strain in Kingsley was shown again in 1865–6, in his approval of Governor Eyre's brutal suppression of black rioters in Jamaica: see, for example, Robert Bernard Martin, *The Dust of Combat. A Life of Charles Kingsley* (London, Faber, 1959), pp. 259–60.

[170] T. G. Bonney, *Memories of a Long Life* (Cambridge, Metcalfe, 1921), p. 105.

[171] F. E. Kingsley, *Charles Kingsley*, vol. II, pp. 191–2. Susan Chitty, *The Beast and the Monk*, p. 239, dates his illnesses.

available place' in the Senate House was occupied before 2.0 pm, with heads of houses and other seniors on the floor and undergraduates crowding the gallery.[172] 'Previous to the entrance of the Lecturer, the Undergraduates in the gallery, according to "ancient usage", amused themselves with cheering and groaning for the popular and the unpopular.' Garibaldi, Lord Derby, and F. D. Maurice were cheered, and so was the Pope though he got groans too. 'Three cheers had just been given for "muscular Christianity", when the new Professor of Modern History made his appearance, and, after a perfect storm of cheers, silence reigned throughout the delivery of the lecture.'

Romilly complained that the lecture, entitled 'The Limits of Exact Science as Applied to History', lasted more than one hour and three-quarters; he found it unexciting, and remembered very little applause.[173] Though others praised it in letters to Kingsley, the modern reader is likely to agree with Romilly.[174] Kingsley chose to cast himself as an intellectual dealing with complicated ideas, a role he was deeply unsuited to though one natural enough for a Regius Professor of History. He argued for the influence of individuals and against determinist philosophies of history and the usefulness of universal explanations that seemed to undervalue free will and the effects of particular circumstances. Thus his inaugural stands at the opposite pole from the views that another novelist, Tolstoy, was to scatter through *War and Peace* a few years later. Tolstoy is perverse, but he does give the impression of having considered the issues involved with great intelligence. Kingsley, on the other hand, seems not to understand, and to revel in misrepresenting, the contentions he wishes to discount. It is hardly proof that the law of gravity, while potentially 'immutable', actually 'can be conquered by other laws', to point out that a stone falling to the ground can be caught and held in the hand.[175] And anybody in the audience with a passing acquaintance with the work of Malthus must have seen how fatuous it was to declare that the immense amount of slaughter in

---

[172] *Cambridge Independent Press*, 17 November 1860.
[173] Chadwick, 'Charles Kingsley at Cambridge', p. 112.
[174] It is printed in Charles Kingsley, *The Roman and the Teuton* (new edn, London, 1875), pp. 307–43.
[175] P. 317, and p. 322 for the next quotation.

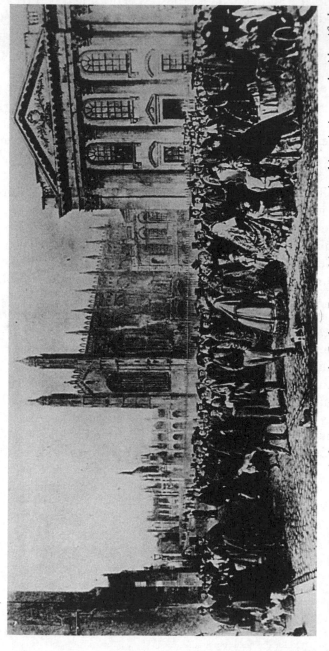

11 'Degree Day, January 1863', from a painting by Robert Farren. Many persons in this painting can be identified.

human history makes it impossible 'to arrive at any exact laws of the increase of population'.

Kingsley was highly conscientious. He lectured every year and on a greater range of topics, from early medieval Europe to the history of science, than Smyth or Stephen had attempted.[176] But his words were not well received by scholars. In 1864 he published as *The Roman and the Teuton* his lectures on the barbarian invasions of the Roman Empire. The commentators gave him reason to regret his action bitterly. A particularly savage review attacked the glibness and ignorance of this 'clever, impulsive, one-sided writer of popular literature ... so excitable, so apt to start off at a moment's notice, so incapable of seeing two sides to a question'.[177] The only other British review that I have traced remarked that 'his mind is essentially feminine' (a word that must have deeply wounded Kingsley, who was forever banging the noisy drum of his masculinity).[178] 'He cannot grasp the totality of a great historical event. He is lost in the parts and ... confused amidst effects, which he often mistakes for causes.' Lectures that Kingsley gave in the Royal Institution were published in 1867 and received equally critical notice, especially by *The Times*, and Kingsley's resignation from his professorship was his response to these sustained attacks.[179]

But a more measured assessment of his achievement was given by Friedrich Max Müller, the Oxford orientalist, in his preface to a new edition of *The Roman and the Teuton* in 1875, the year of Kingsley's death.[180] Müller admitted that the collection was not 'throughout what academic lectures ought to be', not being based on much 'original research' or a 'critical appreciation of the authorities', or 'well arranged, systematic or complete', or 'always written in a perfectly impartial and judicial spirit'. But they were above all things interesting to listen to. There were 'whole chapters full of excellence, telling passages, happy delineations, shrewd remarks, powerful outbreaks of real eloquence': in short, all the skills of a successful novelist – a varied and colourful style, the alternation of long and short sentences, and an often melodramatic

---

[176] Chadwick, 'Charles Kingsley at Cambridge,' pp. 122–3, lists his lecture courses.
[177] *Saturday Review* (9 April 1864), pp. 446–8.   [178] *Anthropological Review*, 4 (1866), pp. 22–33.
[179] *Three Lectures ... on the Ancien Régime as it Existed on the Continent before the French Revolution* (London, 1867). For the critical reviews, see Chadwick, 'Charles Kingsley at Cambridge,' pp. 137 8.   [180] Pp. v–xxix, and pp. xi–xiii for these quotations.

idiom. 'According to the unanimous testimony of those who had heard them delivered at Cambridge, they stirred up the interest of young men, and made them ask for books which Undergraduates had never asked for before at the University libraries.' Kingsley was 'an eloquent interpreter of the purposes of history before an audience of young men to whom history is but too often a mere succession of events to be learnt by heart, and to be ready against periodical examinations'.

Testimony also comes from a man who heard him as an undergraduate, and at the time of writing was 'a Rector in the North'.[181] As Kingsley lectured, 'We crowded him out of room after room, till he had to have the largest of all the schools, and we crowded that – crammed it.' They were attracted by his obvious sincerity, his sense of the comic, his open emotionalism, his

> warm, passionate admiration for fine deeds. His eye used to glisten, his voice in its remarkable sea-like modulations to swell like an organ as he recounted something great, till his audience listened – quiet, spell-bound, fixed, till the climax came, and then rushed into a cheer before they were well aware of it. He was so modest and humble he could not *bear* our cheers. He would beckon for quiet; and then in a broken voice and with dreadful stammering say, 'Gentlemen you must not do it. I cannot lecture to you if you do.' But it was no good ... we could not *help* it.

We should discount the gloss that the lapse of twenty years has caused the writer to apply to these words, but an impression of Kingsley's power over Victorian undergraduates remains – though it is certain that Kingsley's self-presentation would not appeal today.

It is necessary to remember that many in his audience – to be specific, a large number of the poll men – had a lesser mental endowment and academic ambition than modern undergraduates; in attainment and outlook they were schoolboys, and an exciting *teacher*, which Kingsley certainly was, had more to give to them than an unexciting scholar, however accurate. After the dryasdust monotony of Stephen, the semblance of scholarship without its substance, it is no wonder that he was such a success with them.

But he thought of himself not merely as a teacher, but as a scholar;

---

[181] See F. E. Kingsley, *Charles Kingsley* (abridged one-volume edition, 1883), pp. 239–41.

and that was what his Cambridge colleagues expected him to be, buoyed up as they were by a feeling of impending change for the better in Cambridge's attitude to learning and a hope that Kingsley would contribute to it. Missing from their assessment was any thought of what such a man might be able to offer the poll men. They were given only perfunctory attention, yet they were in the majority, because the university, or rather its constituent colleges, refused to have a test of admission that was as searching as their academic pretensions truly demanded. But if they had instituted such a test it would have been hard to find qualified matriculants rich enough to fill the colleges; intellectual advance had to wait for the expansion of secondary schools and bursaries. Here was a contradiction, or set of contradictions, at the heart of the Cambridge of the 1860s, and for that matter later decades too.

Kingsley's appointment was a mistake. But it was committed not by the university but by the government, responsible for naming Regius Professors. Here was another contradiction: that Palmerston, so eager that Cambridge should reform itself, should have appointed to the history chair someone who manifestly did not have the qualities expected in its incumbent. Some of the blame for the delay in university reform should be laid at the door of the state itself.

Chapter 7

RELIGION IN THE UNIVERSITY: ITS RITUALS AND SIGNIFICANCE

THE RELIGIOUS ESTABLISHMENT: COLLEGE CHAPELS

In the afternoon of Tuesday 29 July 1710 Zacharias Conrad von Uffenbach, a visitor from Germany, toured the buildings and courts of St John's College, and crossed the bridge over the Cam into the garden and bowling green.[1]

> We did not however stay long in the garden, but as we heard the bell ring for sermon, went to *King's* chapel, the finest here. It is certainly an incomparably elegant building of stone, especially as regards the quantity of carved work about it. But it is no such great miracle, as it is made out to be in the *Délices d'Angleterre*, Tom. I, that it is without pillars, for, though long and lofty, it is not at all broad. We heard the sermon, and admired exceedingly the goodness of the organ; for it is small, and yet of a deep and extremely pleasant tone.[2]

So even von Uffenbach, whose diary is described by his editor as 'full of girdings and sniffings at the people and things he sees', was impressed, like all visitors, by King's College chapel. Dwarfing the meagre secular buildings of King's College and the Old Schools nearby, the university's premises and the home of its library, the chapel was the most imposing structure in the city, and far larger than any parish church. It was much the most visible symbol of obligations embodied in university and college statutes, in the duties of college fellows and the observances laid upon undergraduates, and in the curricula of their studies. The university and its colleges were in the Middle Ages religious agencies, and so in very great measure they remained in the eighteenth century.

---

[1] New Court and later buildings now occupy this ground.
[2] J. E. B. Mayor (ed.), *Cambridge under Queen Anne* (Cambridge, 1911), p. 130.

There were two chairs of divinity, the Lady Margaret and the Regius,[3] no other area of intellectual concern having more than one. There was an official university church, Great St Mary's, where – to choose one example from many – the Regius Professor was required on 8 May each year to commemorate Henry VII.[4] Most fellows had to take holy orders within a given term of years (usually five) after election; many fellows became parish clergymen in the city or its vicinity, combining their curacy or living with their fellowship and high table, as Richard Farmer, a fellow of Emmanuel, did while curate of Swavesey – while finding time to be a keen member of London literary circles and to write an essay, still esteemed, on the *Learning of Shakespeare*.[5] Many other fellows took college livings on marriage, as Appendix VIII and memorial tablets in many parts of England and Wales testify. The most substantial group of undergraduates came from clerical backgrounds, and the church was the destination for the largest number. And of course all sixteen colleges had chapels, and though no other was as large as King's much care was lavished on them. The chapels of Clare and Sidney Sussex were built in the eighteenth century,[6] and the chapels of Trinity Hall and Gonville and Caius altered. Magdalene's was renewed between 1733 and 1755, and again in the 1840s, and Trinity's in 1832 and between 1867 and 1875.[7] The most spectacular events in this sequence concerned Jesus and St John's. The chapel at Jesus was transformed by Pugin and Morris and Company between 1846 and 1877 so as to become one of the most appealing Victorian statements in the university; while the medieval chapel at St John's was demolished in the 1860s, to be replaced by Gilbert Scott's massive structure. The aesthetic exchange effected by Scott was at best of very doubtful value, like some of the earlier transactions mentioned; but they collectively seem to bear witness to the strength of faith in the university. The underlying reality was however more complex.

---

[3] By the will of John Norris of Caius, a third chair was endowed in 1777.
[4] Great St Mary's remains the university church, special sermons being given there; its upkeep falls to some extent upon university funds. The circle within which university officers have to reside has its centre at Great St Mary's.
[5] Bendall, Brooke, and Collinson, *A History of Emmanual College* (forthcoming), chapter 14.
[6] Sidney Sussex's chapel was rebuilt again in 1912.
[7] These details are taken from *RCHM Cambridge*, and Pevsner, *Cambridgeshire*.

DEGREES IN DIVINITY

Within and without the universities, Oxford and Cambridge were widely regarded as seminaries for Anglican clergy, and most of their alumni were destined for holy orders. The chapels thus reflect the colleges' basic purpose. Their courses of instruction do not; surprisingly, Cambridge was very late in developing courses to prepare young men for the clerical careers so many were to enter. There was no first degree, in divinity, equivalent to the BA or to the bachelor's degrees in civil law and medicine.[8] The Bachelor of Divinity was a postgraduate qualification, taken by MAs. It was a survival of the medieval assumption, reflected in the Elizabethan statutes, that the bachelor's degree was merely a first step in a long ascent up the mountain of learning, via the MA, to a higher degree, or perhaps several higher degrees. The BD would therefore be taken fourteen years after matriculation. The Elizabethan statutes did not envisage the seven-year stint (after the MA) as a soft option, even if it was not expected to be continuously demanding. Resident masters choosing the divinity degree were to attend lectures, preach in Great St Mary's, and keep one divinity act and two opponencies. By the eighteenth century attendance at lectures had gone by the board (they were not always given, anyway) but the other obligations remained, and the divinity act was a tough assignment. The respondent had to propose two questions and to read a thesis on the first. The thesis was criticised by three opponents, and care was taken that at least the first of them was a powerful antagonist; also, the Regius Professor of Divinity acted as moderator and might criticise the thesis. When a candidate had a high reputation, his act drew a large audience: when Isaac Milner was respondent in 1786 the Divinity Schools were 'filled with auditors from the top to the bottom'.[9] Respondents prepared thoroughly. In April 1829 Adam Sedgwick remarked that as one of the tasks that were keeping him busy in Cambridge he was 'reading the Fathers and School Divines by way of preparation for my Divinity Act, which I must keep on

---

[8] For this paragraph, see Winstanley, *Unreformed Cambridge*, pp. 64–8. The LL B and MB degrees are described in chapter 5, pp. 186–202.
[9] Richard Watson, *Anecdotes*, p. 22. Milner's act is said to have been distinguished, but opinions differ on the quality of the debate: see Gunning, *Reminiscences*, vol. II, pp. 47–8.

the 30th of this month'.[10] Sedgwick's labours seem all the more serious to us when we reflect that as a geologist he had no intention of taking a divinity degree; but as a resident MA who had not declared for either law or medicine he was assumed to be reading divinity, and he was therefore called upon to keep his act. Ancient though the examination technique was, it seems that the exercises were a fitting test of candidates' capacities. At all events the Regius Professor of Divinity, J. A. Jeremie, replied to the Graham Commissioners' enquiry of 1850 about the exercises thus: 'I am inclined to think that, unless the period required for the degree of B.D. and D.D. be abridged, it is not desirable to change, to any considerable extent, the nature of Exercises which being in conformity with long established usage, appear to be well adapted to the age and position of the candidates.'[11] The Graham Commissioners accepted this admittedly less than effusive endorsement, remarking that the exercises were probably 'sufficient to deter and repel such persons as are conscious of deficiency in the command of the Latin language and in Theological knowledge'.[12] There was, however, another and less worthy route to the BD.[13] A medieval statute intended to permit monks and friars to bypass the MA requirement for the BD was adapted to the post-Reformation world by the Elizabethan code. The statute laid down that candidates over twenty-four years of age might proceed to the BD after the passage of ten years without taking an MA, provided that they devoted themselves entirely to study and that all the appropriate exercises were kept. As was pointed out by George Peacock, the Erskine May of the Victorian university, the Elizabethan statute enjoined, or at least assumed, ten years' continued residence.[14] But by the beginning of the seventeenth century residence was not required, so that the ten years might elapse without continuous study. A decree of the heads of houses in 1788 enforced residence for three terms in the last two years. Even so, a major anomaly remained. So far few people had been involved, being mainly clergymen of mature years who desired a degree. Between 1803 and

---

[10] Clark and Hughes, *Adam Sedgwick*, vol. 1, p. 339. Sedgwick was writing to R. I. Murchison.
[11] PP 1852–3, HC xliv [1559]: *Graham Commission Evidence*, p. 76.
[12] *Graham Commission Report*, p. 30.   [13] See Winstanley, *Unreformed Cambridge*, pp. 69–72.
[14] Peacock, *Observations on the Statutes*, appendix A, p. xlvii, note.

1825, however, the number of ten-year men enrolled rose from 33 to 230. Reformers in the university argued that the loophole should be closed. Candidates could buy ready-made theses and arguments for their exercises, and revealed in the schools great ignorance of theology and the classical tongues: 'surely we cannot be astonished that the divinity School is considered by freshmen and undergraduates as a temple of fun and frolic'.[15] In 1849 a syndicate recommended abolition of the ten-year privilege, and the Graham Commissioners agreed. It found no place in the revised statutes of 1858.

The summit of the academic Everest was the doctorate in divinity, for which according to the statutes BDs had to spend five more years in systematic study, attending lectures and performing exercises.[16] By a process already familiar to us, by the eighteenth century most of these requirements had lapsed. The need to keep an act remained, however, and it was usual to test the candidate severely against formidable scholars. As Conyers Middleton wrote:

> The principal and most celebrated exercises of this kind were usually those of doctors of divinity, as oft as any man of figure and learning appeared as candidates for that degree. For they were always opposed by the Professors in person who laboured to exert themselves on such occasions, and had by custom brought upon themselves a very difficult task which was commonly called the unravelling of the respondent's thesis, that is the answering it ex-tempore and offhand, though it is usually an hour long, and by the force of memory running over all its parts again, exposing its weakness and making the most probable objections to the matter as well as the form of it.

But there was another and a more usual route to the DD. By a strained interpretation of the statutes[17] it was possible to take the degree without performing the exercises. This bypassing of the Elizabethan code was convenient for dons chosen for offices where the DD was a necessary qualification, and it was often followed by those about to be elected heads of house. For example, when on 15

---

[15] An anonymous pamphleteer of 1825, quoted in Winstanley, *Unreformed Cambridge*, p. 71.
[16] See Winstanley, *Unreformed Cambridge*, pp. 72–5. The quotation from Conyers Middleton below occurs on p. 73.
[17] This very complex matter is explained in Peacock, *Observations on the Statutes*, appendix A, pp. xvii–xviii, note.

May 1798 Lort Mansel learned that he was to be appointed Master of Trinity, he immediately made arrangements to take his DD just one week later *per saltum*, that is without performing the exercises.

PREPARING STUDENTS FOR ORDINATION

The higher degrees in divinity were not taken by the great majority of MAs. They therefore did not provide a professional education for clerical careers. Also, the theological accomplishments of the minority who took the BD or the DD were not necessarily very great. But the biggest single group of graduates became parish clergymen, and, as we know, after a tripos course that was mathematical. Where did they get their theological instruction?

In 1841 George Peacock, the Dean of Ely, and one of the foremost reformers in the university,[18] published his *Observations on the Statutes of the University of Cambridge*, combining constitutional analysis of great perceptiveness with pleas for change.[19]

> At least one-half the students in the university are designed for the church, and no provision (the lectures of the Norrisian professor alone excepted) is made for their professional education; this is a deficiency in our academical system, which, in the present state of public opinion on this important subject, it will be impossible long to overlook. We believe that there are few members in the university who are not prepared for the adoption of the most prompt and decisive measures for the effectual remedy of so great an evil.

Peacock's assertions were quite justified, but for the sake of balance we should take note of the university's 'considerable provision for the small number who wished to study theology seriously on their own'.[20] The possibilities may be illustrated by the example of Harold Browne 'the one really distinguished' fellow elected at Emmanuel in the 1830s. Browne, the son of wealthy parents, whose four years at Eton were supplemented by a private tutor before his

[18] A decade later Peacock served on the Graham Commission.
[19] The following quotation occurs on p. 168.
[20] These words are quoted from Christopher Brooke's chapter on Victorian Emmanuel in the forthcoming history of the college. What follows on Browne, including the quotations, is taken from this source, which Christopher Brooke has kindly made available to me.

Cambridge career, in 1827 came up to Emmanuel, where (he later wrote) 'the idle habits of Eton came back to me' despite his talents. Wasting time in the college boat he was low down in the list of wranglers, and gained only a third in the Classical Tripos. But from 1833 to 1835 he was supported in theological study by two scholarships, the Crosse and the Tyrwhitt Hebrew; and he also won the Norrisian Prize. 'In these years he laid the foundation of the deep, if fairly conventional, learning in biblical and patristic studies which were to qualify him for the Hulsean Professorship twenty years later.'

Browne's experiences show what surprising good fortune might be plucked from the interstices of Old Cambridge, but by their very nature they could not be for more than a minority. Perhaps a chief purpose of university reform was to extend to the generality of students opportunities traditionally only available to a lucky minority. The bishops required Cambridge candidates for ordination to show, by means of a certificate, that they had attended the lectures of the Norrisian Professor of Divinity, whose chair was founded in 1777. That some did not however take this duty seriously is evident from the fate of James Fawcett, the Norrisian Professor from 1795 to 1815. Fawcett, of frail health since birth and disliking large gatherings of people, laboured under 'a certain thickness in his speech, an awkwardness of manner in a crowd, a want of energy, and an easiness of temper, little calculated to curb the sallies of a large assembly of young men, constrained to sit out a lecture of an hour in length'.[21] What may be surprising to us is not that a professor should have an unfortunate manner of speech, but that prospective ordinands should have caused a disturbance.

In 1822 Christopher Wordsworth attempted to get examinations in classics and theology added to the requirements for the BA, but the desire to retain the pre-eminence of mathematics was the stumbling-block; the Classical Tripos was set up, but as an optional addition to the Senate House Examination.[22] The Previous Examination, henceforth obligatory for all undergraduates in the Lent Term of the second year, could hardly be said to offer much by way

[21] T. S. Hughes, *Discourses by William Samuel Powell D.D. and James Fawcett B.D., with Some Account of Their Lives* (London, 1832), Fawcett, pp. viii–ix.
[22] For this section, see Winstanley, *Early Victorian Cambridge*, pp. 66–71, 169–74.

of professional education for intending clergymen; till 1920 all candidates had to pass in Paley's *Evidences of Christianity*, and one of the Gospels or the Acts of the Apostles in Greek. In 1837 theology was added to the subjects in the ordinary BA examination, candidates being tested on parts of the Acts of the Apostles and one or two of the Epistles.[23] Paradoxically, this move gave most to the students who were least talented and least likely to become bishops. The need to give professional education to the prospective clergymen with the greatest intelligence (that is, those taking the Mathematical Tripos) remained acute, and the university's failure to do so was thrown into sharp relief by its reply to the Dissenters' demand for admission – that Cambridge's great task was to prepare young men for the Anglican priesthood.

The church was anxious to improve the theological education of ordinands, and the diocesan colleges that were being founded in the 1830s[24] showed the way to Cambridge, yet were also a threat to it. So was Oxford's scheme for better theological instruction. In March 1841 the Bishop of London, Blomfield, wrote to Charles Perry of Trinity to urge 'that no time should be lost, for the work is actually in hand at Oxford, and Cambridge, if it does not move forthwith, will have only the second rate praise of reluctantly copying the example of her Sister University'. A scheme was promoted by John Graham, the Vice-Chancellor,[25] for a voluntary theological examination to be held in the fourth year of residence; it was damned by its suggestion that to make unnecessary any lengthening of an undergraduate's period at Cambridge the mathematical course for the Senate House Examination should be shortened by two terms.[26] But because of a widespread perception of the need for action the syndicate considering the question recommended a voluntary examination to be held in the Michaelmas Term for graduates. Surprisingly, the scheme was passed despite the vehement opposition of one of the men who might be expected to administer it – G. E. Corrie, the Norrisian Professor, whose writings are replete with Pooterish reflections on the evils of

---

[23] Ecclesiastical history was added later.
[24] F. W. B. Bullock, *A History of Training for the Ministry of the Church of England . . . 1800 to 1874* (St Leonards-on-Sea, Budd & Gillatt, 1969).
[25] Graham, the Master of Christ's, was to be Bishop of Chester and chairman of the royal commission that enquired into the university, 1850.
[26] Graham was in effect suggesting three-year degrees, which came to pass in the 1880s.

Popery and government interference with universities. Corrie, not noticeably overworked, wrote that: 'I told them that the lack of time and strength was a reason I could not change; that the duties of my office in College and of my Professorship were all I could get through, although I was out of bed eighteen hours out of every twenty-four.'[27] The new examination, which was first held in 1843, was therefore left in the hands of the Regius and Lady Margaret Professors. Fortunately, most of the bishops responded to a plea from the Vice-Chancellor, Whewell, to make it compulsory for candidates for ordination. J. J. Blunt, the Lady Margaret Professor of Divinity, reported to the Graham Commission: 'The Voluntary Theological Examination came into operation in 1843, in which year there were 14 candidates; in 1844 there were 36; in 1845, 83.'[28] Further increases followed, and in 1850 there were 205 candidates. 'The amount of knowledge displayed by the candidates of successive years, though naturally not increasing in the proportion of the numbers, has been increasing very perceptibly.' In 1850 it became a requirement that candidates for the examination should, by means of a certificate, show that they had 'attended the lectures delivered during one Term at least by two of the three Theological Professors. This regulation has the effect of swelling the amount of attendance, and ensuring, so far as it goes, an identity in the parties lectured and the parties examined.'

COMPULSORY CHAPEL

One stanza in a Cambridge parody of Gray's *Elegy* runs:

> Haply some friend may shake his hoary head,
> And say: 'Each morn, unchill'd by frosts, he ran,
> With hose ungarter'd, o'er yon turfy bed,
> To reach the chapel e'er the psalms began'.[29]

Chapel was in theory compulsory, but many slid out of it very often, or attended half-heartedly. Gilbert Wakefield wrote: 'The morning

---

[27] M. Holroyd, *Memorials of G. E. Corrie*, p. 182, quoting his diary for 14 February 1842.
[28] PP 1852–3, HC xliv [1559]: *Graham Commission Evidence*, p. 88.
[29] J. Duncombe, *An Evening Contemplation in a College* (1753), quoted in Charles Smyth, *Simeon and Church Order. A Study of the Origins of the Evangelical Revival in Cambridge in the Eighteenth Century* (Cambridge University Press, 1940), p. 117. The poem was printed in *The Cambridge Tart* (1823) and also in *The Oxford Sausage* (1821). Duncombe cannot be traced in Venn, *Alumni Cantabrigienses* or in Foster, *Alumni Oxonienses*.

and evening prayers (which are much too long) are *seldom* attended *at all* by the fellows: and with *no seriousness of devotion* by the undergraduates.'[30] Some colleges insisted on ten attendances a week, some on eight, and none on fewer than five; sometimes the number varied according to seniority.[31] Some colleges employed markers to prick off the names of worshippers with a pin. 'Winter and summer to matins we are summoned at seven in the morning, and unless we arrive in time for the Markers to get a glimpse at, and run their pins through us, we may as well be hugging the pillow', wrote that cynical observer J. M. F. Wright about the Trinity scene *c.* 1815.[32] The marker boy, he alleges, was often bribed with beer to prick the names of late sleepers; while those who neither worshipped nor bribed were punished by the dean:

> one week being 'put out of Sizings and Commons', another getting an '*Imposition*', in the shape of having to get by heart a satire of Juvenal, a book of Homer, [or] to give an analysis of Butler's Analogy... Times many, on surplice mornings, my duty to his deanship has been so somnolent that, having slumbered to the last tingle of the bell, sans inexpressibles, sans almost everything, I have whipped on the full-flowing surplice, and just saved my bacon.

In his memoir of his student days at Trinity (1851–6), J. W. Clark recalled that chapel attendance was not 'more irksome than ordinary duties' and that behaviour was usually proper. Still, he does not give an impression of as much seemly observance as might be expected in, say, a parish church: '"Iniquity Corner", as the space at the east end on each side of the altar was called, may occasionally have effectually sheltered card-playing; but when a young snob went so far as to light a cigar there he had the pleasure of finishing it in the country, for he was rusticated.'[33]

E. S. Appleyard, the author of *Letters from Cambridge* (1828), judged that obligatory chapel 'does produce a marked effect, and you may mark it through life, if you please. It produces listlessness and indifference, and it stifles true piety.'[34] Perhaps the absence of fellows and tutors from the services obligatory for their pupils had

---

[30] Gilbert Wakefield, *Memoirs* (2 vols., rev. edn, London, 1804), vol. I, p. 152.

[31] [E. S. Appleyard], *Letters from Cambridge* (1828), pp. 102–3.

[32] *Alma Mater* (1827), vol. I, p. 31, and p. 32 for the following quotation.

[33] Shipley, '*J.*' *A Memoir of John Willis Clark*, p. 38.

[34] P. 102. Appleyard, BA Trinity 1827, himself took holy orders in 1828, the year *Letters from Cambridge* was published.

12 Iniquity Corner.

the most corrosive effect on undergraduates. The serious-minded
William Wordsworth, coming to Cambridge with 'a clear sense of
what was noble, just, and true', was certainly more likely to attend
chapel than many undergraduates.[35] But he 'looked in vain' in St
John's chapel

> for the presence of many of those who ate the bread of the founders,
> and were supposed to administer the statutes, and had bound
> themselves by solemn engagements to observe the laws of the
> college, and to be examples to the younger members of the society,
> and especially to maintain that collegiate unity which cannot subsist
> without religious communion.
>
> He felt that there was something like hollow mockery and
> profane hypocrisy in this. He resented it as an affront to himself and
> to his fellow-students, as members of the academic body.

[35] Christopher Wordsworth, *Memoirs of William Wordsworth* (2 vols., London, 1851), vol. I, pp. 46–7.

Long before he voiced these sentiments to his nephew, Wordsworth had criticised compulsory chapel in *The Prelude*:

> Was ever known
> The witless shepherd who would drive his flock
> With serious repetition to a pool
> Of which 'tis plain to sight they never taste?
> A weight must surely hang on days begun
> And ended with worse mockery. Be wise
> Ye Presidents and Deans, and to your bells
> Give seasonable rest, for 'tis a sound
> Hollow as ever vexed the tranquil air,
> And your officious doings bring disgrace
> On the plain steeples of our English Church,
> Whose worship, 'mid remotest village trees,
> Suffers for this.[36]

Nearly fifty years after William Wordsworth was at St John's, Connop Thirlwall, a fellow of Trinity, criticised obligatory chapel for very similar reasons – that it was harmful to real religion: 'with an immense majority of our congregation it is not a religious service at all, and that to the remaining few it is the least impressive and edifying that can well be conceived'.[37] Five days after Thirlwall's pamphlet appeared the Master of Trinity, Christopher Wordsworth, invited him to resign his assistant tutorship, which he did. A few years later Wordsworth and the Trinity fellows ordered all undergraduates to attend chapel at least once each weekday, and twice on Sundays. The moving spirit was Carus, the senior dean, an ardent Evangelical (eventually Simeon's biographer), and needless to say hostile to Thirlwall's attitude. A deputation of undergraduates got no satisfaction from Carus, and there followed an incident worthy of a Gilbert libretto – the formation of a Society for the Prevention of Cruelty to Undergraduates. In February and March 1838 the society each week published sheets detailing the chapel attendances of the fellowship, with comments.

---

[36] 1805 Book Third, 11. 415–27. Wordsworth expressed the same opinion in his 1838–9 revision: see *The Prelude* 1850 Book Third, 11. 408–21. But in vol. II of his *Memoirs of William Wordsworth*, pp. 265–6, Christopher Wordsworth makes clear that his uncle wished in his late years to retain obligatory chapel.

[37] From a *Letter to Turton* (1834) quoted in C. H. Smyth, *Simeon and Church Order*, p. 125. What follows is based on pp. 123–8, and on W. W. Rouse Ball, *Cambridge Papers* (London, Macmillan, 1918), pp. 71–83.

The Society regret much that during the last week great laxity has prevailed among the Fellows in general with regard to their attendance in chapel . . . The Society, however, still hopes that in the ensuing week they will be able to make a more favourable report both of their attendance in chapel, as also of their good conduct when there. As was before stated, any Fellow who shall, owing to any wine-party, or other sufficient reason, be prevented from attending, will be excused on sending a note previously to the Secretary of the Society, and his absence will be counted as presence.[38]

In the last week the society published a class list: 'in arranging the different classes the Secretary has attached to each person's name his number of marks, in order to do away with any appearance of favour shewn more to one than another, as is too often the case in other Examinations'. Three fellows were placed in the first class, Carus gaining 72 marks, or 12 fewer than the possible maximum. Wordsworth and Whewell were in the second class. Two fellows, with no attendances, were unclassed. 'The Prize Medal for regular attendance at chapel and good conduct when there, has been awarded to Mr Perry, who has passed an examination highly creditable to himself and family.'[39]

There the matter rested. Undergraduates wearied of noting fellows' attendance, which of course kept somebody as busy as did worship itself. For its part, the college dropped the 1838 regulations, for when C. A. Bristed was an undergraduate in the 1840s, he found an 'indulgent standard', which was not 'rigidly enforced. I believe if a Pensioner keeps six chapels, or a Fellow-Commoner four, *and is quite regular in all other respects*, he will never be troubled by the Dean.'[40] In the next quarter-century college demands seem to have become less pressing. W. E. Heitland, an undergraduate at St John's in the late 1860s found that six chapels were required.[41] 'But you were free to keep them in the evening, if you thought morning Chapel at 7.0 am too early. Also, if you kept two Chapels on Sunday, you could get off with three in the rest of the week.' At his public school, Shrewsbury, religious observances had been rigidly disciplined. But they were 'henceforth on a new footing. Spiritual influences needed to be very

[38] Quoted in Ball, *Cambridge Papers*, p. 78. The following quotations are taken from pp. 80–1.
[39] The prize, a Bible bound in calf, is now in the Wren Library.
[40] Bristed, *Five Years in an English University*, vol. I, p. 22.
[41] Heitland, *After Many Years*, pp. 175–8.

13 Trinity Ante-chapel, after service on a Sunday Evening.

powerful if they were to retain their virtue in the tainted atmosphere of a tariff.' Heitland found that 'to get any spiritual nourishment out of the Chapel services, you had to take it in with you'. Nor did the dons help; some were doctrinally easy-going, some bigoted, some colourless. Sermons that gripped were few. One evening, 'two of the elders took to preaching at each other on issues of orthodoxy. One evening there was even a slight ironical applause from the benches.' Sermons had to be dropped altogether because the two dons were too antagonistic to each other. The episode places in a new perspective the building of a very large new chapel in St John's in Heitland's time, in theory because of pressing spiritual need. The abolition of religious tests by the act of 1871 removed any obligation from college members who were not Anglicans, and the struggle to make it compulsory for those that nominally were was a rearguard action ending in defeat this century – most probably, immediately after the First World War, when veterans with memories of the trenches seem to have been determined that chapel was one obligation of university life they would ignore.[42]

When chapel was compulsory, at some colleges Holy Communion was, too, although it was usual to celebrate it infrequently. The

[42] I owe this suggestion to Christopher Brooke, who has examined the attendance sheets at Gonville and Caius for the period in question. See also his *History of the University of Cambridge, vol. IV*, pp. 111–21.

enormity involved in making 'the most awful ceremony of the Christian church' a disciplinary matter for men quite unready for it was dilated on by E. S. Appleyard in 1828:

> Whenever celebration of it is enjoined, you must attend: no scruples of conscience are admissible; no sense of unworthiness can be pleaded. If you have just risen from a debauch, your senses steeped in wine, your better feelings unawakened to a sense of duty – well: – if, the bread touched, and the tremendous cup tasted, you return to the carousal you have quitted – no matter: – an imperious necessity commands, and you hope ... the shame, and the guiltiness of the deed, will rest on their heads who dragged you to it.[43]

Perhaps few undergraduates were as badly prepared as that. Yet there are pieces of evidence suggesting that ordinands, who naturally were firmly obliged to communicate, sometimes took their duty frivolously, as Walter Besant shows in a passage that also makes clear the assiduousness of others, and therefore underlines the difficulty of generalising about Cambridge behaviour. Besant was an undergraduate at Christ's from 1855 to 1859.

> Those of the undergraduates who were religiously disposed indulged in a sort of gluttonous banquet of services. One man, I remember, would take a Sunday school at eight a.m., go to chapel at half-past nine; to a morning service at eleven; to the university sermon at two; to King's College Chapel at three; to the college chapel at six; to evening service in some church of the town at seven, and end with a prayer meeting and hymn singing in somebody's rooms. But such men were rare. For my own part, though still proposing to take orders, I was so little moved by the responsibilities before me that though it was necessary, in order to obtain the proper college testimonials, to attend three celebrations of Holy Communion in the three years of residence, I forgot this requirement, and, on discovering the omission, attended all three in the last two terms. This was thought somewhat scandalous and I nearly lost my college certificate in consequence.[44]

William Everett, an American undergraduate at Trinity, was scandalised by a minority of Cambridge ordinands; their fitness

---

[43] *Letters from Cambridge*, pp. 104–5.
[44] Walter Besant, *Autobiography* (London, Hutchinson, 1902), pp. 90–1. Perhaps wisely, Besant rejected the thought of holy orders soon after graduating, and after a spell as mathematics teacher made a career as an author, becoming a well-known man of letters and philanthropist.

attested after a perfunctory college enquiry, they appear in chapel some time after graduating, 'to keep their sacraments', as a mere formality. 'I saw many things in England that pained me as to their estimation of sacred things, but never anything like this gross levity as to the communion.'[45]

On the other hand it was the requirement to attend communion, when he was an undergraduate at King's, that caused the conversion of Charles Simeon in 1779. In the three weeks of preparation, 'I made myself quite ill with reading, fasting, and prayer. From that day to this, blessed, for ever blessed, be my God, I have never ceased to regard the salvation of my soul as the one thing needful.'[46] The name of Simeon reminds us that some Evangelicals (though not all) stood out from their fellow-undergraduates because of the intensity of their piety. The irregularity in chapel duty so often ascribed to others was rarely alleged against them; and John Jerram's memory of his friendship with Thomas Thomason at Magdalene in the 1790s shows us how joyous attendance was held to be by one Evangelical group.[47]

> Many and happy were the seasons we spent together in reading the scriptures and in prayer, and now and then, when we could do it without the risk of drawing upon us invidious notice, we heightened our social pleasures by singing our favourite psalms and hymns . . . I can truly say . . . that these engagements were not only the happiest, but the most profitable of our college occupations. They greatly tended to relax the weariness of the same routine of reading; they counteracted the chilling effect of abstract studies, and the unchristian tendency of Pagan literature and profane mythology.

Another qualification should be made to the impression of lukewarm undergraduate worship coming from accounts of compulsory chapel. The university church, Great St Mary's, had large congregations, including undergraduates, if it had a good preacher.[48] Though Thomas Gray claimed that there were only three people, plus the heads of houses,[49] to hear Mr Sturgeon preach on 23 April 1757, the Reverend James Scott regularly drew crowds in the 1760s. His sermons were quite unlike the 'studiously abstruse'

[45] Everett, *On the Cam*, pp. 251–3.
[46] Quoted in C. H. Smyth, *Simeon and Church Order*, p. 120.
[47] J. Sargent, *The Life of the Rev. T. T. Thomason* (London, 1833), p. 38. Thomason was later Simeon's curate at Holy Trinity.
[48] For what follows, including quotations, see C. H. Smyth, *Simeon and Church Order*, pp. 130–43.
[49] Who were very much expected to attend.

ones that were usual; 'the subjects of his discourses attracted attention, the discussion of them awakened the feelings, and the elocution of the preacher delighted and fascinated the hoary sage, the ingenuous youth, and the unlettered Christian'. Adam Sedgwick, who was always eager to praise the quality of university worship, claimed in 1834 that a bystander in Great St Mary's 'may sometimes see six or seven hundred Undergraduates in the performance of a voluntary worship, and hanging with deep attention on the accents of the preacher'. But they could be very critical. Preachers who were disliked might be punished with 'scraping', or shuffling feet, and this was done to the Reverend Julius Hare on Advent Sunday, 30 November 1828, when he preached for eighty minutes on 'The Children of Light'. Greater disorder had occurred in 1773, when on 23 April the Reverend John Wilgress, a fellow of Pembroke, preached what John Jebb described 'as a most papistical sermon', during the subscription controversy.[50] 'He shewed that there was an absolute necessity for an uniform profession of faith; and talked of that faith being the true one, which had ubiquity, universality, antiquity on its side . . . He attacked the latitudinarians vehemently, and maintained that the liberty of private opinions rent the church of Christ.' Already annoyed with Wilgress's behaviour as Proctor, the undergraduates 'scraped' him. After the sermon the Vice-Chancellor called to the Proctors to take the names of undergraduates in one of the galleries. There was a 'general hiss' and many rushed out before the door could be fastened.

> At length, the bishop of Peterborough [the Master of Trinity, John Hinchliffe], the two proctors, and the vice-chancellor, arrived at the foot of the stair-case. The young men made a push, and broke the door off its hinges, and multitudes escaped. The names of the rest were taken, and a meeting of the heads followed; but, as all were guilty, all escaped unpunished. Such indecency was never seen, and they will have riots upon riots, unless some scheme is thought of to employ the active spirits of young men.

[50] Disney, *The Works of John Jebb*, vol. I, pp. 57–8. Disney is quoting a letter from Jebb.

Chapter 8

THE ORTHODOX AND LATITUDINARIAN TRADITIONS, 1700–1800

THE TWO TRADITIONS DEFINED AND COMPARED

His politics are Leviathan, and his religion is Latitudinarian, which is none; that is nothing that is *positive*, but against every thing, that is positive in other religions; whereby to reduce all religions to an uncertainty, and determinable only by the civil power... He is own'd by the Atheistical wits of all *England* as their true Primate and Apostle... He leads them not only the length of Socinianism... but to call in question all revelation, to turn *Genesis* & etc. into a mere romance.[1]

So wrote Charles Leslie in 1695 about John Tillotson, the recently deceased Archbishop of Canterbury. Leslie was one of that minority of Anglicans who felt that their faith was betrayed by those in power in the 1690s, and later. Refusing to take an oath of allegiance to William and Mary (hence the name 'Non-Jurors') Leslie and his colleagues remained loyal to the Stuart cause, despite the follies of James II which had so gravely tried their patience. They used the term 'Latitudinarian' to describe all they abominated in the Established Church, and the word continued to be employed abusively in the eighteenth century by the Non-Jurors' successors as upholders of firm High Church Anglicanism.

Since Latitudinarianism was especially associated with Cambridge, rather than Oxford, and continues to be associated with the university by historians now, we should pay attention to it. But it is hard to define with brevity because it was so inclusive and wide-ranging, as we might indeed expect of a word that began as criticism. Latitudinarians[2] stressed bonds of harmony within Protes-

---

[1] Thomas Birch, *The Life of Dr John Tillotson* (London, 1752), pp. 323–4.
[2] The discussion that follows is based on John Walsh, Colin Haydon, and Stephen Taylor, eds., *The*

tantism rather than the forces dividing it; they favoured at least the toleration of Dissent and sometimes attempts at 'comprehension', or some sort of institutional Protestant unity. There were many doctrinal similarities, and bonds of sympathy, between Latitudinarians and Old Dissent;[3] and they were alike too in greatly distrusting the Roman Catholic Church and its intellectual authoritarianism. Latitudinarians differed in their beliefs, sometimes very significantly; for example, Samuel Clarke of Caius went further than other Latitudinarians in doubting the Trinitarian nature of the deity. But Latitudinarians tended to agree in valuing simplicity and moderation in religious utterance and in accepting the Bible alone as a sufficient guide to doctrine; they believed that the biblical message was accessible to all men, and that truths not contained in it were matters of opinion. Naturally, they disliked the obligation to subscribe to the highly specific Thirty-nine Articles; as we shall see, the subscription issue reached crisis point in the 1770s, and split the Latitudinarian movement. Latitudinarians regarded Christianity as a faith based on the truths of natural religion, which revelation served to confirm. They also distrusted sacerdotalism, or as Bishop Burnet defined it, 'the raising of the power and authority of sacred functions beyond what is founded on clear warrant in scripture';[4] thus the Latitudinarian Bishop Hoadly caused great controversy within the Established Church by his depreciation of the priestly office.

Latitudinarians repudiated Jacobite claimants to the throne, fearing absolute monarchy and Roman Catholicism; they were ardent supporters of the Hanoverian dynasty. Politically, they were enthusiastic Whigs. As to the Established character of the Church of England, they were Erastians, stressing its subordination to the civil power rather than its separate and co-ordinate quality proclaimed by High Churchmen.

Latitudinarianism was in part a response to the changed fortunes of the Church of England at the end of the seventeenth century; the

> *Church of England c. 1689–c. 1833* (Cambridge University Press, 1993), and esp. the essays by John Walsh and Stephen Taylor, and Martin Fitzpatrick, pp. 35–41 and 209–13; Ernest Gordon Rupp, *Religion in England 1688–1791* (Oxford University Press, 1986), esp. pp. 28–39; John Gascoigne, *Cambridge in the Age of the Enlightenment*, esp. pp. 4–6, 40–1; Norman Sykes, *From Sheldon to Secker. Aspects of English Church History, 1660–1768* (Cambridge University Press, 1959), esp. pp. 145–52.
> [3] Sects of seventeenth-century origin – Baptists, Congregationalists, and Presbyterians – and distinguished from the groups created by the Evangelical Revival.
> [4] Quoted in Walsh, Haydon, and Taylor, *The Church of England*, p. 37.

reign of James II showed what tyranny would be brought about by anyone still believing in the Divine Right of Kings, and the legal toleration of Dissenters that followed the Glorious Revolution of 1688 made Anglicans conscious of the strength of other varieties of Protestantism. But in a more fundamental and long-term sense Latitudinarianism was but one result of the profound revolution, in the sixteenth and seventeenth centuries, in humankind's view of the universe: it ceased to be small, earth-centred, and human in scale, and became vast, its size beyond human comprehension, and exhibiting magnificent harmony in its structure and operation – the articulation of its myriad parts and the majesty of its motion. Newton's thought was the crown of this new cosmology. The universe itself proved design by a divine artificer, and was an argument for natural religion rather than revelation, and for the use in human affairs of the reason that had made the mysteries of the cosmos clear. And since the universe and its design were displayed to all humankind the effect, in the minds of some, was to lessen the importance of doctrinal divisions and sectarian disputes. The underlying forces that led to Latitudinarianism also led to the various forms of Christian Unitarianism, to deism and to atheism. But though different destinations on the same intellectual journey, these beliefs were often not in sympathy.

Latitudinarian ideas were powerful in Cambridge after the Glorious Revolution, and they go a long way to explain the Whiggism of the eighteenth-century university that so sharply differentiated it from Oxford. But it is important to register the variety of religious views within the university. Latitudinarianism was a set of linked attitudes rather than a totally consistent ideology; men in some ways alike might emphasise quite different aspects of religion, as we shall see in a detailed discussion of Richard Watson and William Paley. Moreover, there were dons whom it is impossible to fit plausibly into any Latitudinarian framework. In particular, there was a large representation within eighteenth-century Cambridge of the Anglican tradition exemplified by Edmund Gibson, Bishop of London from 1723 to 1748, whose career has been discussed in a definitive study.[5] Gibson was certainly

---

[5] See Norman Sykes, *Edmund Gibson. Bishop of London 1669–1748* (Oxford University Press, 1926).

a convinced Whig and partisan of the Hanoverian monarchy, but he was also jealous of the distinctive principles and theology of the Established Church, hostile to those stressing overmuch the place of natural religion or impugning the Trinitarian basis of Christianity or the special function of the priestly office, and unwilling to grant Dissent any more than the limited concession made by the Toleration Act of 1689. Such divines welcomed the new cosmology – after all many of them had a large draught of Newtonianism as undergraduates – and regarded it as complementing revelation rather than supplanting or conflicting with it.

Within this tradition was Daniel Waterland, Master of Magdalene, a powerful figure within the university and representative of a salient theological viewpoint within it.[6] J. M. Rigg, who wrote Waterland's biography in the *Dictionary of National Biography*, judged that he 'did more than any other divine of his generation to check the advance of Latitudinarian ideas within the church of England. His deep and accurate learning and his command of nervous and perspicuous English rendered him unusually formidable as an antagonist.'[7] Like so many Cambridge men the son of a clergyman, Waterland, after education at Lincoln Grammar School and Magdalene College became a fellow there in 1704 and Master in 1713, at the young age of thirty. The appointment was made by Henry Howard, Earl of Suffolk, who under the college's strange constitution had that power. Waterland had been tutor to his son, but there is independent testimony to his talents as a teacher. In any event Waterland's intellectual achievements vindicated the earl's decision. In 1714 Waterland performed his act for the degree of BD, his thesis prefiguring a later preoccupation with Arian subscription. 'This theological disputation', it is said,[8] 'excited an uncommon sensation, not confined to the University: ... Waterland being the respondent and Sherlock the

---

[6] What follows is based on William van Mildert, *A Review of the Author's Life and Writings*, in *The Works of the Rev. Daniel Waterland* (10 vols., Oxford, 1823), vol. I; and Robert T. Holtby, *Daniel Waterland 1683–1740. A Study in Eighteenth Century Orthodoxy* (Carlisle, Thurman, 1966).
[7] Vol. 20, p. 447.
[8] Edward Carpenter, *Thomas Sherlock 1678–1761* (London, SPCK, 1936), p. 7, quoting Hughes, *The Works of Bishop Sherlock*. Sherlock was the Master of St. Catharine's. Carpenter mistakenly believes that Sherlock was the candidate; he was already DD, and therefore a natural opponent for someone supplicating for the bachelor's degree.

opponent.[9] The unusual circumstances of a public debate between two heads of houses, the general interest of the topic, and
still more the learning, ingenuity and fluency of the combatants,
made a great and lasting impression.'

Little of the vast documentation pertaining to Waterland tells us
much about his personality, but we learn of an exemplary devotion to
study that is said to have shortened his life. His most famous work,
*Advice to a Young Student. With a Method of Study for the Four First
Years*,[10] is remarkable for its sternly moralising tone and its counsel to
students to spend all their waking hours in study or devotions; no
time is allotted to leisure, although by contrast even Philip Yorke,
inditing a rather implausible schedule of his studies for his ferociously
didactic uncle, admitted to a few hours of diversion.[11]

Serving as Vice-Chancellor from 1715 to 1717, years of crucial
importance for the new Hanoverian dynasty, Waterland acted with
his friend Richard Bentley to strengthen support for it and the
Whigs in Cambridge, where opinion was at first divided. He was
rewarded with sundry pieces of ecclesiastical preferment. Waterland's labours on behalf of traditional Anglican orthodoxy were at
least as significant. He is described by Eamon Duffy as 'without any
question the ablest and one of the best-read theologians in England
in the 150-year period between the seventeenth-century Revolution and the Oxford Movement';[12] his voluminous 'writings on
the Trinity represent the most sustained defence of Chalcedonian
[i.e. Trinitarian] orthodoxy ever constructed in English', remaining
'standard resources well into the nineteenth century'. Not the least
of the opponents against whom Waterland deployed his arguments
were in Cambridge, or at least spent many years in it. It is to the
chief of these, Samuel Clarke, and his controversy with Waterland,
that we now turn.

Clarke, a Norwich boy, went up to Gonville and Caius, then
essentially an East Anglian college, in 1690.[13] He was only fifteen

---

[9] Thomas Sherlock was the Master of St Catharine's, and was to become bishop in the sees of Bangor, Salisbury, and London.
[10] On this, see chapter 5, pp. 152–3. The *Advice* is detailed in Christopher Wordsworth, *Scholae Academicae*, pp. 330–42.   [11] See chapter 15, pp. 550–1.
[12] Cunich, Hoyle, Duffy, and Hyam, *A History of Magdalene College Cambridge*, pp. 161–3.
[13] What follows is drawn from J. P. Ferguson, *An Eighteenth Century Heretic. Dr. Samuel Clarke* (Kineton, War., Roundwood, 1976), pp. 1–46.

on his admission, perhaps a sign of his exceptional promise. He was twelfth in the *Ordo Senioritatis* for 1694–5,[14] out of a total of 134 graduates, a very respectable result; he was a fellow of Caius from 1696 to 1700. As a graduate he became friendly with William Whiston, Newton's successor as Lucasian Professor; through Whiston he met John Moore, the Bishop of Norwich, who became his patron and gave him ecclesiastical preferment. He attracted attention through his talented writings: a popularisation of Descartes, a translation of Newton's *Optics*,[15] and works of theology. In these he gave little sign of the heresy that eventually entangled him in his spectacular dispute with Waterland; rather, he established a reputation as an orthodox Latitudinarian, stressing the complementarity of reason and revelation, or natural religion and revealed religion, a distrust of enthusiasm, or emotional excess, and a preference for a reasonable faith enabling an individual to co-operate with his Creator in his own salvation instead of relying upon the gift of Grace, as Calvinists did. Well known as a Christian apologist by the early eighteenth century, Clarke was in 1704 accorded the honour of an invitation to deliver the Boyle lectures, a series devoted to the persuasion of infidels, in which Clarke had been preceded by some distinguished people. His lectures, directed at proving the existence of God to atheists, were so successful that he was most unusually invited to give a second series. These, aimed at deists, aroused some disagreement, but it was easy for theological utterance to do so in that epoch, and Clarke's Boyle lectures broke no bones. Winning much praise, they went into many editions. Waterland, later Clarke's doughty antagonist, recommended them to students in his *Advice*, along with a wide variety of others. Waterland was typical of Cambridge tutors in being eclectic in his teaching. But they did not tolerate heresy; in 1710 Whiston was expelled from the university for his Arianism, an offence close to the one Clarke was to be accused of. Clarke's theological bombshell was produced at the

[14] The *Ordo* was the list of those graduating BA. It exists from 1499 onwards. Originally reflecting both academic precedence and intellectual merit, it came to record merit only, probably in the first half of the eighteenth century; it thus became the Mathematical Tripos list, dating from 1748, which until 1909 was published in strict rank order of marks, that is with the Senior Wrangler at the top and the Wooden Spoon at the bottom.

[15] From the original English into Latin, to make the book accessible to a wider European audience.

heart of the ecclesiastical establishment, and naturally created all the more stir because of it.

In 1712 Clarke published *The Scripture-Doctrine of the Trinity*, examining the scriptural authority of the Athanasian Creed.[16] An essential part of Roman Catholic and Protestant doctrine, the creed stated that God comprised a Trinity of three co-equal and co-eternal persons. In early centuries it had been deployed against the Arian heresy – that Christ was the first of created beings, and therefore greater than man, but not of the divine substance – and in the seventeenth century Trinitarians were in dispute with the similar heresy of Socinianism. Arianism and Socinianism, quasi-Unitarian convictions, left their mark on Restoration England, though in several acrimonious disputes between scholars rather than in widespread acceptance of either belief. The Toleration Act of 1689 did not offer its benefits to anti-Trinitarians, and the Arianism of the eminent scholar William Whiston led to his expulsion from the university in 1710.

In a huge labour of scholarship Clarke examined 1,251 texts of the New Testament that touched upon the nature of the divinity, and concluded that 'from all these passages, it appears beyond contradiction that the words God and the Father, not God and the Three Persons, are always used in Scripture as synonymous terms'.[17] The Son and the Holy Spirit are not self-existent, but derive their being from the Father. Although Clarke contended that his arguments were consistent with Anglican doctrine, most of the copious commentary they attracted was highly critical; in particular, Clarke was condemned by the Lower House of Convocation, and it was made clear that he was not going to be promoted to the bishopric that his learning might have led him to expect.[18] Waterland entered the dispute in 1719.[19] There followed a wordy battle between the two camps that quickly became a duel between the two protagonists, lasting till Clarke's death in 1729. Comprising many titles and countless thousand words (some of the books ran to 500 pages) the struggle was over highly complex data and ideas that

---

[16] For what follows, see Ferguson, *Samuel Clarke*, pp. 47–58.
[17] Quoted in Ferguson, *Samuel Clarke*, p. 54.   [18] Ferguson, *Samuel Clarke*, pp. 59–123.
[19] *A Vindication of Christ's Divinity: Being a Defence of Some Queries, relating to Dr. Clarke's Scheme of the Holy Trinity, in Answer to A Clergyman in the Country* (1719).

were often ambiguous, not to say impalpable.[20] It demonstrates the seriousness of eighteenth-century religious controversy. Waterland, the most learned and intelligent of Clarke's opponents, pointed out that while Clarke might deny it his ideas were Arian and therefore in Anglican terms heretical. Modern biographers of the two men agree that Clarke may have got the better, by a narrow margin, of the technical dispute over what Scripture purported on the nature of the Trinity; but that Waterland also took into account, with skill and subtlety, explanations of the Trinity that had been developed by the early church and represented in the creeds, to reconcile monotheism with the divinity of Christ: in other words, Waterland defended orthodox Anglicanism that rested on revelation as well as reason.

Clarke had supporters in Cambridge or among its graduates, for example Joseph Wasse of Queens', John Balguy of St John's, and John Laurence of Clare. Waterland had his supporters too, notably Thomas Bennet and Dr John Edwards of St John's, and Edward Potter of Emmanuel.[21] It is necessary to register the existence of this 'orthodox', High Church group within Cambridge churchmen since in his wide and careful recent study John Gascoigne has suggested that by the middle of the century Latitudinarianism was the prevailing body of ideas in the university.[22] Yet when we examine the crucial subscription controversy of the 1770s, an issue likely to unite the various elements among Latitudinarians, we find that their arguments were defeated in every vote.[23] In other words, it is difficult to contend that Latitudinarians ever formed the *majority* of dons.

Eighteenth-century Cambridge contained a variety of religious views, and mutual toleration (within limits) was advised by the structure of the university itself. In the 1990s dons increasingly live as others do: in sharply separated chambers, at 'work' during the day and at 'home' in the evening perhaps fifteen miles away, often within a family whose existence and interests have few links with the university. In the 1790s their family was the other fellows of the college where they both resided and laboured. While propinquity

---

[20] For this discussion, see Ferguson, *Samuel Clarke*, pp. 123–49, and Holtby, *Daniel Waterland*, pp. 12–49.   [21] John Gascoigne, *Cambridge in the Age of the Enlightenment*, pp. 122–3.   [22] Pp. 126–7.   [23] See chapter 11, pp. 409–10.

might allow irritation to simmer, the need to foster quiet and comfort prevented it from boiling over often; and the need to co-operate in a myriad of intercollegiate concerns with the fellows of other colleges also held back eruptions. Disputes occurred, and they were sometimes spectacular, but there was a common interest in assuaging them. So Cambridge's story is not for the most part one of conflict, in all matters including religion, where the impulse to tranquillity mitigated theological bitterness.

Sometimes departures from orthodoxy were too great to be ignored; thus the Arianism of William Whiston led to his expulsion, as did the deism of William Woolston in 1721 and the atheism of Tinkler Ducket in 1739.[24] Yet the career of the Trinity don and cleric Conyers Middleton shows how with caution and craft it was possible to express heretical views but escape unscathed. Middleton, who richly deserves a biography, was friendly with Horace Walpole and the antiquarian William Cole; his house overlooking Senate House Yard[25] was said by the poet Thomas Gray to be 'the only easy Place one could find to converse in at Cambridge'.[26] Middleton had a lively wit and a penetrating intellect, yet also a restless and unreasoning ambition; he resented his lack of clerical preferment, and coveted the Regius Professorship of Modern History while already holding the chair of geology and a post at the University Library.[27] So his appetite for advancement made him present his heresies in a prudent fashion that reminds one of pre-glasnost Russia. Edward Gibbon's judgement was that 'his bold criticism ... approaches the precipice of infidelity'.[28] Replying to Daniel Waterland's arguments he attacked the reliability of miracle stories in detail. Middleton published his work[29] anonymously, but his authorship naturally became known in a community as small and leaky as Cambridge. The Public Orator Dr Williams declared that unless Middleton recanted he should be banished from the university. Middleton was not as forthright as Woolston or Ducket, and

[24] Gascoigne, *Cambridge in the Age of the Enlightenment*, pp. 135–7.

[25] It has since been demolished.

[26] Quoted in McKitterick, *Cambridge University Library*, p. 170. These paragraphs draw on the many references to Middleton in this volume, and on Leslie Stephen, *History of English Thought in the Eighteenth Century*, (3rd edn, 2 vols., London, 1902), vol. I, pp. 255–73.

[27] He was *protobibliothecarius*, a post specially created for him by his friends.

[28] *Autobiography*, World's Classics Edition (Oxford University Press, 1907), p. 46.

[29] *A Letter to Dr. Waterland, containing some Remarks on his 'Vindication of Scripture'*.

decided 'to make as reputable a retreat as I can manage into the quarters of Orthodoxy'.[30]

In 1748 Middleton published an extended criticism of miracle stories. David Hume said it 'eclipsed' his own essay, which by a strange coincidence appeared the same year. Middleton explained the tales as caused by the gullibility of the age they came from – a more intelligent and persuasive line than the usual one, fraud and imposture; he compared them to seventeenth-century witchcraft narratives. But he confined his attack to the Christian epochs after the first; so he seemed not to challenge the crucial earlier stories. This argument briefly served to convert Edward Gibbon to Roman Catholicism since he felt that the integrity of the first miracles outweighed the frailty of later ones. Middleton had coded his message too well to lay himself open to a conviction for heresy; but as Leslie Stephen remarked, 'he was far too able a man to be blind to the tendency of his arguments'.[31]

RICHARD WATSON

HIS CHARACTER AND CAREER

Writing in 1834 about society in the Lake District at the end of the previous century, Thomas De Quincey remarked that:

> At that time the leading person about the Lakes, as regarded rank and station, amongst those who had any connexion with literature, was Dr Watson, the well-known Bishop of Llandaff... Those who have read his autobiography, or are otherwise acquainted with the outline of his career, will be aware that he was the son of a Westmorland schoolmaster. Going to Cambridge, with no great store of classical knowledge, but with the more common accomplishment of Westmorland men, and one better suited to Cambridge, viz.,– a sufficient basis of mathematics, and a robust, though commonplace intellect, for improving his knowledge according to any direction which accident should prescribe, – he obtained the Professorship of Chemistry without one iota of chemical knowledge up to the hour when he gained it: and then setting eagerly to work, that he might not disgrace the choice which had thus distinguished him, long

---

[30] A letter to Lord Harley of 25 January 1732, quoted in Gascoigne, *Cambridge in the Age of the Enlightenment*, p. 139.   [31] In his essay on Middleton in the *Dictionary of National Biography*.

before the time arrived for commencing his prelections, he had made himself capable of writing those beautiful essays on that science, which, after a revolution, and a counter-revolution, so great as succeeding times have witnessed, still remain a cardinal book of introductory discipline to such studies ... With this experimental proof that a Chemical Chair might be won and honoured without previous knowledge even of the chemical alphabet, he resolved to play the same feat with the Royal Chair of Divinity; one far more important for local[32] honour, and for wealth. Here again he succeeded: and this time he extended his experiment; for whereas both Chairs had been won without *previous* knowledge, he resolved that in this case it should be maintained without *after* knowledge. He applied himself simply to the improvement of its income, which he raised from £300 to at least £1,000 per annum. All this he had accomplished before reaching the age of thirty-five.[33]

This passage concerns Richard Watson, perhaps the best-known Cambridge professor, Latitudinarian, and absentee bishop of the eighteenth century. It is accurate enough in most details, but singularly unjust in what it says about Watson's theology. In alleging ignorance De Quincey was however merely guided too much by Watson's autobiography.[34] As always when the subject's memoir is the most salient source, the task of Watson's biographer is complex, particularly in what is for our purpose most important, elucidating Watson's theological views. Upon close examination they prove to be much more sophisticated, thoughtful and orthodox than at first glance they appear, and very different from, say, John Jebb's; and as a result, Cambridge Latitudinarianism turns out to have been more subtle and various than it is often taken to have been.

Watson came from Westmorland 'statesman' (yeoman) stock. Like his fellow-countryman William Wordsworth, he came to Cambridge knowing that he could look forward to little family wealth. In his singular autobiography he remarks that after leaving his grammar school[35] for a sizarship at Trinity in 1754, 'I commenced my academic studies with great eagerness, from knowing

---

[32] De Quincey meant honour in Cambridge.

[33] Thomas De Quincey, *Recollections of the Lakes and the Lake Poets*, ed. David Wright (London, Penguin, 1986), p. 83. The essay, one of a long series in *Tait's Edinburgh Magazine*, was originally published in 1834.   [34] Richard Watson, *Anecdotes*.

[35] Heversham, where his father had been headmaster.

that any future fortune was to be wholly of my own fabricating.'[36] Hard work converted his sizarship into a scholarship, and made him Second Wrangler in 1759. He was elected a fellow of Trinity, and soon after gave a sign of the pride he was to display throughout life by refusing a curacy offered by the Vice-Chancellor: 'it would give me an opportunity of recommending myself to the Duke of Newcastle, then Chancellor of the University', with whose Whig views Watson emphatically agreed; 'but then and always prizing my independence above all prospects, I declined accepting the offer'.[37] Like so many Cambridge men he soon tired of mathematics, and within a few years he applied for the chair of chemistry. 'As there is no stipend annexed, I believe he will meet with no opposition', wrote a fellow of Clare to the Chancellor. 'He is a man of reputation, and purposes reading lectures.'[38] There followed the prodigious intellectual endeavours described by De Quincey that were the very attractive side of Watson's character. But he was above all things restlessly ambitious, and secured the Regius Professorship knowing little theology. His political friends the Dukes of Grafton and Rutland won for him some church livings (he did not of course reside) to augment the modest stipend of his chair; and in 1782 they gained for him the bishopric of Llandaff. Separated from Cambridge by more than 200 miles and some difficult roads, and offering only £500 a year, it was an unappealing prospect. Still, Watson hoped for the quick translation to a richer see that other Welsh bishops enjoyed.

He did not get it. Too proud to be a sycophant to exact favours, he nevertheless expected gratitude for services he thought he had rendered. When it was not shown him, he retired into self-pity. De Quincey,[39] who was puzzled by the personality he came to know in the Lake District, contrasted his pleasant and kind manners – 'his Lordship was a joyous, jovial, and cordial host' – with the 'querulous egotism' gnawing away underneath.

In 1786 Watson inherited an estate that he sold for £23,500.[40] He bought another estate, not in South Wales as might have been

---

[36] Richard Watson, *Anecdotes*, p. 7.   [37] Richard Watson, *Anecdotes*, p. 21.
[38] BL Add. MS 32963, fol. 409, William Talbot to the Duke of Newcastle, 15 November 1764, quoted in Norman Sykes, *Church and State in England in the Eighteenth Century* (Cambridge University Press, 1934), p. 334.   [39] *Recollections of the Lakes and of the Lake Poets*, pp. 84–6.
[40] Perhaps £1,000,000 in 1993 prices.

expected, but on the shores of Windermere, 250 miles from Cambridge, and nearly as far from his diocese; it could not have been less conveniently placed for Watson's duties. In a backward glance (written about 1810) at his life at Calgarth, Watson obviously had neither university nor bishopric in mind in his list of concerns:

> I pursued my intention of retiring, in a great measure, from public life, and laid, in the summer of 1789, the foundation of my house on the banks of the Winandermere. I have now spent above twenty years in this delightful country; but my time has not been spent in field-diversions, in idle visitings, in county bickerings, in indolence or intemperance: no, it has been spent, partly in supporting the religion and constitution of the country by seasonable publications; and principally in building farm-houses, blasting rocks, enclosing wastes, in making bad land good, in planting larches, and in planting in the hearts of my children principles of piety, of benevolence, and of self-government. By such occupations I have much recovered my health, entirely preserved my independence, set an example of a spirited husbandry to the county, and honourably provided for my family.[41]

Watson blamed his lack of promotion on his forthright Whig principles. His views were no doubt abominated by government, but he had no real complaint; his behaviour as a bishop was reason enough to sideline him. Norman Sykes has pointed out that he was more conscientious than his residence in the Lake District would lead us to expect; 'it would appear probable that Watson paid an annual visit to his see-city to ordain in his cathedral on Trinity Sunday', and made more extensive visits every three years.[42] Still, better arrangements could have been made. Since his total income was very large[43] there was no material reason why he could not have followed his duty as a churchman and lived in his diocese. As to his professorship, he did appoint a deputy[44] when he left for Calgarth, at two-thirds of its value, but there is no evidence that for the nearly thirty years remaining till his death he ever visited Cambridge; resignation would have been the more fitting course. George III's

---

[41] Richard Watson, *Anecdotes*, pp. 239–40.   [42] Sykes, *Church and State in England*, pp. 367–71.
[43] De Quincey states that it was £7,000 a year.
[44] His deputy from 1787 to 1802 was Thomas Kipling. His bad Latin was much criticised by Gunning: *Reminiscences*, vol. II, pp. 49–51.

comment on Watson was that 'eminent talents and discretion were not always allied and no stronger instance could be given than himself of the truth of that position';[45] that was true enough, though perhaps not exactly for the reasons the king had in mind. Watson's behaviour was not typical of eighteenth-century professors and bishops, though it is sometimes cited as though it were. But it did show what you could get away with in that century.

WATSON'S THEOLOGY AND POLITICAL VIEWS

Watson was a lifelong Whig, and in a minority in Cambridge in not changing his allegiance during the French Wars. Writing at the end of his life he remained sure that 'let the pensioners and place-men say what they will, *Whig* and *Tory* are as opposite to each other as Mr *Locke* and Sir *Robert Filmer*, as the soundest sense, and the profoundest nonsense'.[46] A convinced follower of John Locke, he believed that in the last resort authority sprang from the people. He supported the movement for parliamentary reform of Wyvill and others in the 1780s,[47] while however distrusting the call for manhood suffrage of his erstwhile colleague John Jebb. He disliked the 'mobs' that sometimes accompanied demands for reform, 'thinking senseless popularity beneath the notice of genuine Whiggism'.[48] As he made clear to Wyvill in 1784 when he was pressing Pitt to effect parliamentary reform, 'I am not one of those who stickle for the abstract right of every individual having a vote in the election, nor for the ancient practice of having a new parliament elected every year, provided the integrity of parliament could be obtained by other means.' Most important was 'the introduction of honest and independent members into the House', and Watson was searching for the expedient that would effect it.[49]

Like some other Whigs Watson was exhilarated by the liberal monarchy proposed for France by the constitution of 1791, an example without parallel in history, 'of a whole people ... divesting themselves of the prejudices of birth and education, in civil and

---

[45] Quoted in Sykes, *Church and State in England*, p. 342.
[46] Richard Watson, *Anecdotes*, p. 57. This section is indebted to this source, and to John Gascoigne, 'Anglican Latitudinarianism and Political Radicalism in the Late Eighteenth Century', *History*, 71 (1986), esp. pp. 34–6.
[47] See chapter 11, pp. 410–11.   [48] *Anecdotes*, p. 34.   [49] *Anecdotes*, pp. 134–5.

religious concerns, and adopting the principles of philosophy and good sense'.[50] With the courage that was one of his most attractive qualities Watson opposed the war with France, and two years after it began he supported a motion for peace in the House of Lords, being the only bishop to do so.[51] The French threat in due course made him as patriotic as anybody, as he attested in his very popular *An Address to the People of Great Britain* (1798), for which he was denounced as an apostate by his former radical friends Gilbert Wakefield and Benjamin Flower. Yet when they were prosecuted for sedition he remained staunch in defence of the freedom of the press, 'the palladium of the constitution'.[52] He remained a reformer to his death in 1816.

Watson's stance as a political radical was never very far from that of men such as Jebb and Lindsey who left the Church of England for Unitarianism in the 1780s. It has therefore been natural to regard him as perhaps almost a Unitarian too (he was after all friendly with the Duke of Grafton, who was of that persuasion) and certainly very far from Anglican orthodoxy in his reliance upon scriptural authority only. It is also true that Watson gave plausibility to such a judgement in his autobiography:

> I determined to study nothing but my Bible, being much uncon-
> cerned about the opinions of councils, fathers, churches, bishops,
> and other men, as little inspired as myself... I used to say... holding
> the New Testament in my hand... Here is the fountain of truth,
> why do you follow the streams derived from it by the sophistry, or
> polluted by the passions of man?[53]

Yet it was pointed out in 1991[54] that Watson's theology was far more subtle than that, and that Cambridge Latitudinarianism was therefore more varied than is sometimes averred: simply equating it with the views of Samuel Clarke and John Jebb is not persuasive. If we look behind the 'boastful, octogenarian ramblings about the events of forty-six years before' in Watson's *Anecdotes*, to the six volumes in his *Collection of Theological Tracts*, published in 1785,[55] we

---

[50] *Anecdotes*, p. 256.   [51] *Anecdotes*, p. 271.   [52] *Anecdotes*, pp. 305–6.   [53] *Anecdotes*, p. 39.

[54] A. M. C. Waterman, 'A Cambridge "Via Media" in Late Georgian Anglicanism', *Journal of Ecclesiastical History*, 42 (1991), pp. 419–36. Much of what follows on Watson is taken from this article, esp. pp. 425–7.

[55] And so, it is worth noting, before Watson had left Cambridge for the Lake District.

discover a far greater reliance on the authority of the church than on individual judgement. As Watson described them, the *Theological Tracts* were readings for ordinands from 'books of such acknowledged worth, that no Clergyman ought to be unacquainted with their contents'. Certainly, 'Their Bible is the only sure foundation upon which they ought to build every article of faith which they profess', but the 'decisions of councils, the confessions of churches, the prescripts of popes, or the expositions of private men' ought not

> to be fastidiously rejected as of no use, for although the Bible be the one infallible rule by which we must measure the truth or falsehood of every religious opinion, yet all men are not equally fitted to apply this rule, and the wisest men want on many occasions all the helps of human learning to enable them to understand its precise nature, and to define its certain extent. These helps are great and numerous; they have been supplied in every age, since the death of Christ.[56]

The *Tracts* include twenty-three excerpts from eighteenth-century theological writing, some of them being of book length; his annotations and suggestions for further reading leave no doubt that he had read very widely. Among the authorities he recommends is the *Summa Theologiae* of Thomas Aquinas,

> for notwithstanding the ridicule which usually, in these days, attends the mere mention of the *Angelic* Doctor, I will venture to affirm, That in that work there are, mixed indeed with many difficult subtleties and perverse interpretations of Scripture, not a few Theological questions of great moment stated with clearness and judgement.

Watson added that 'new books are not so much wanted ... as inclination in the younger clergy to explore the treasures of the old ones'.[57] In the light of these utterances, Watson's variety of Latitudinarianism seems close to orthodox and mainstream Anglicanism. As the most recent commentary on him avers, 'the Anglican biblicism he took for granted was sufficiently protected by

---

[56] Richard Watson, *Theological Tracts*, (6 vols., Cambridge, 1785), I, pp. v, xii, quoted in Waterman, 'A Cambridge "Via Media"', pp. 425–6.
[57] *Theological Tracts*, vol. I, pp. xxxii, vii, quoted in Waterman, 'A Cambridge "Via Media"', p. 426; the next quotation occurs on the same page.

theological learning against "enthusiasm", and clearly separated, by its rejection of "system", from the related errors both of popery and of Calvinism'.

Watson and his colleagues rejected both Rome and Geneva because of their 'blind attachment to system'. 'Established systems' impeded truth because they tried to derive more information from scripture than it could rightly yield. The countervailing error 'spurns with contempt the illusions of fanaticism and the tyranny of superstition . . . magnifying every little difficulty attending the proof of the truth of Christianity, into an irrefragable argument of its falsehood'; so those 'unlearned in Scripture knowledge' are prey to the infidelity of 'Bolingbroke, Voltaire, Helvetius, Hume'.[58]

The distinctive characteristic of Watson and his associates was an epistemological *via media*: 'the proper course is to affirm all that scripture clearly affirms, and where scripture is doubtful or ambiguous to go on using the actual words and phrases without insisting on any exclusive interpretation'. This 'becoming modesty about the possibility of theological knowledge which steers well clear of Hume's defeatist scepticism'[59] entailed of course toleration of the views of others and a willingness to engage in open-ended discourse, which would lead to a firmly grounded faith, not unbelief. As Watson himself put it in his reply to one of the age's most significant sceptical statements, 'free disquisition is the best means of illustrating the doctrine and establishing the truth of Christianity'.[60] On the other hand human reasoning had limited powers, and the more one exercised it the more one realised that there were some things about which the Christian could not be certain; about them, therefore, it was wise to be undogmatic:

> The most undecided men on doubtful points, are often those who have bestowed most time in the investigation of them . . . He who examines only one side of a question, and gives his judgment, gives it improperly, though he may be on the right side. But he who examines both sides, and after examination gives his assent to

[58] *Theological Tracts*, vol. I, pp. xiii, x, xii, quoted in Waterman, 'A Cambridge "Via Media"', pp. 426–7.   [59] Waterman, 'A Cambridge "Via Media"', p. 427.
[60] *An Apology for Christianity, in a Series of Letters Addressed to Edward Gibbon, Esquire* (Cambridge, 1776), quoted in Waterman, 'A Cambridge "Via Media"', p. 423.

neither, may surely be pardoned this suspension of judgment, for it is safer to continue in doubt than to decide amiss.[61]

This scrupulously rational approach to religion was a strong characteristic of Cambridge Latitudinarianism.

Watson was naturally much in favour of tolerating all varieties of Protestantism, following John Locke's arguments on the question. In 1787 he was one of only two bishops to vote for the abolition of the Test and Corporation Acts, and he clearly revealed by the public nature of his avowal the courage that was one of his most attractive qualities.[62] His tolerance extended to Unitarians, to whom many Anglicans denied even the name of Christian. Watson was a close friend of the Duke of Grafton, one of Britain's leading Unitarians:

> we had not always agreed either in our political or religious opinions; but we had both of us too much sense to suffer a diversity of sentiment to deaden the activity of personal attachment. I never attempted either to encourage or to discourage his profession of *Unitarian* principles, for I was happy to see a person of his rank, professing with intelligence and with sincerity Christian principles. If any one thinks that an Unitarian is not a Christian, I plainly say, without being myself an Unitarian, that I think otherwise.[63]

Like other Latitudinarians, Watson was less eirenic in his attitude towards Roman Catholics, conceding of course their right to free worship,[64] but wishing at first to deny them full political equality 'till it shall be clearly proved, that if they had the opportunity they would not use it to the oppression of the Protestants'.[65] Yet Watson was uneasy, caught on a classical liberal's dilemma; and during the French wars, when the need for imperial unity suggested the wisdom of conciliating Irish opinion, he eagerly pressed for political equality for Catholics and government help for their church in Ireland.[66]

Watson's ideas both overlapped and contrasted with those of William Paley, the most widely read and influential of the Cambridge Latitudinarians.

---

[61] Richard Watson, *Anecdotes*, vol. I, p. 59, quoted in Walsh, Haydon, and Taylor, *The Church of England*, p. 221.   [62] *Anecdotes*, p. 162.   [63] *Anecdotes*, pp. 46–7.
[64] John Gascoigne is mistaken in arguing that Watson was at first against extending toleration to Catholics: 'Anglican Latitudinarianism and Political Radicalism', p. 35.
[65] *Anecdotes*, p. 156.   [66] *Anecdotes*, pp. 309–11, 382–3.

WILLIAM PALEY

HIS LIFE

In his remarkable essay on William Paley in the *Dictionary of National Biography* Leslie Stephen wrote of his 'peculiar compromise between orthodoxy and rationalism'. Paley used the arguments of natural religion to prove the existence of the deity, and the tactics of common sense to show the truth of the miracle-stories on which so much Christian orthodoxy depended; the tone was quiet, reasonable, friendly, and enticing as though he were leading the reader by the arm – a far less portentous voice than was usual in Anglican apologetics; but the destination was far more orthodox than was implied, if not *totally* orthodox. In effect a skilful defender of theological conservatism, he was equally adroit in his defence of society's status quo, by replacing traditional theology with secular reasoning to justify social obligation. His message was very largely old; his idiom was very largely new, and therefore singularly persuasive. He was the most famous and the most influential of the Cambridge Latitudinarians.

Like Newton of yeoman stock, and like his Cambridge acquaintance Richard Watson the son of a northern grammar-school master, Paley was educated by his father at Giggleswick.[67] A good-natured and clumsy boy (he was always a poor horseman) he early displayed the curiosity and lively intelligence that marked his writing. On one occasion he sat up all night to watch soap being boiled, and after seeing a quack doctor performing an operation he was found trying to extract a girl's tooth. There were eight scholarships for Giggleswick boys at Christ's College, and he followed his father there after preparing for the Cambridge course with a mathematics tutor near Ripon. Paley matriculated in 1759, aged sixteen; at first a sizar, he soon became a scholar. 'The uncouthness of his dress and manners', it is said, 'caused not a little mirth amongst his fellow collegians, but as the superiority of his genius and his real worth were soon discovered,

---

[67] This account of Paley's life is based on George Wilson Meadley, *Memoirs of William Paley*, 1st edn (Sunderland, 1809); Edmund Paley, *Life of William Paley*, in *The Works of William Paley* (4 vols., London, 1838), vol. I, pp. xv–ccxvii; and M. L. Clarke, *Paley. Evidences for the Man* (London, SPCK, 1974), pp. 1–56.

these singularities did not deprive him of their esteem and admiration.'[68]

Paley was gregarious and very much liked. Later in life he claimed that in his first two years at Christ's he had lived entirely for convivial company, until a change was brought about by a friend's solemn warning over the proper use of talents; thereafter Paley rose at 5 am and worked solidly all day save for a frugal supper.[69] The operatic starkness of this tale is doubted by his biographers, but it does seem that Paley early in his student life took up a tough régime of hard work. With the aid of a private tutor in his third year (Paley is an early case of a student known to have been coached) he became Senior Wrangler in 1763. After a period as an usher in a bleak private school in Greenwich, he was ordained in February 1766 and became a curate in Greenwich. In June he was elected a fellow of Christ's. After coming into residence he quickly took up sundry university and college posts, including that of assistant tutor.

In 1772 he became joint tutor with John Law, who was to be a lifelong close friend.[70] Law taught mathematics and natural philosophy, and Paley metaphysics, ethics, and the Greek Testament. The material he compiled for his ethics classes he afterwards used in his *Moral and Political Philosophy*. Paley's methods of teaching were strikingly successful, and it is important to register the debt they owed to his informal, relaxed, and friendly personality. It also shone through his writing: he was a world away from the desiccated dons so gloomily reprobated by William Wordsworth. Dressed without thought of effect, his wig awry, working from a dog-eared copy of Locke that was scrawled over with notes, restless in his chair, he questioned his pupils in an animated yet comfortable manner: 'in the most familiar manner he discussed some subject in moral philosophy, pointing out the passages we were to read for the next lecture day and explaining everything in such a manner that the driest subjects were made interesting'.[71]

Paley took a full part in meetings of the Hyson Club, a society

---

[68] G. W. Meadley, *Memoirs of William Paley*, 2nd edition (Edinburgh, 1810), quoted in Clarke, *Paley*, p. 6.

[69] Edmund Paley says that his father supped off bread and cheese in Dockrel's coffee house in Trumpington Street.

[70] The son of Edmund Law, who was the Master of Peterhouse and from 1769 Bishop of Carlisle.

[71] *Universal Magazine*, 4 (1805), pp. 414–17, quoted in Clarke, *Paley*, p. 16.

founded in 1758 by Cambridge men with literary interests, for informal conversation over cups of china tea; Boswell's *Johnson* makes us familiar with this sort of genial gathering. Members included Isaac Milner, the Queens' Tory, the equally forthright John Gordon from Peterhouse, and John Jebb, the multi-purpose reformer from the same college who regularly beat Gordon in argument. Jebb asked Paley to support his anti-subscription case, to which Paley replied (despite his known support for reform) that he could not afford to keep a conscience – a remark that brought much condemnation, though it is highly probable that he was masking disapproval of Jebb's methods[72] with facetiousness.

In 1774 Paley published a pamphlet supporting the anti-subscribers though not perhaps the abolition of all tests, which any church might require. Paley wrote at greater length on subscription in *Moral and Political Philosophy*, published in 1785. He was much attacked by reformers like Gilbert Wakefield for 'shuffling', but Paley's approach seems a typical example of his philosophical style in giving a reasoned defence of a modified orthodoxy. Tests ought to be made as simple and undemanding as possible, since 'they check inquiry; they violate liberty; they ensnare the consciences of the clergy, by holding out temptations to prevarication'.[73] Meanwhile, he argued that many who could not accept all the Thirty-nine Articles might nevertheless subscribe to them with a clear conscience provided that they were not among the groups, such as Roman Catholics and Anabaptists, which it was their purpose to exclude when they were devised in 1571.

> They who contend, that nothing less can justify subscription to the Thirty-nine Articles, than the actual belief of each and every separate proposition contained in them, must suppose, that the legislature expected the consent of ten thousand men, and that in perpetual succession,[74] not to one controverted proposition, but to many hundreds. It is difficult to conceive how this could be expected by any, who observed the incurable diversity of human opinion upon all subjects short of demonstration.[75]

---

[72] Jebb's pushfulness and expectation of immediate results were disliked in Cambridge.
[73] *Works of William Paley* (1838) vol. III, *Moral and Political Philosophy*, p. 324 (Book 6, chapter 10).
[74] The clergy of the day and their successors.
[75] *Moral and Political Philosophy*, p. 102 (Book 3, Part 1, Chapter 23).

George Dyer, the Unitarian and friend to Jebb and reformers in general, commented that Paley's protest against subscription was not inconsistent with his guidance to subscribers:

> that being, in fact, the last effort of an ingenious mind to soften the rigour of a practice, which he could not seriously approve, but which he could not effectually alter; and is indeed a guide to people, not how they may believe before they subscribe; but how they may subscribe without a very hearty assent.[76]

Very typically for a Cambridge don, Paley moved to a church living after ten years as a fellow, in 1776, resigning his fellowship on marriage soon after. His new life was in the diocese of Carlisle, whither he was drawn by his friendship with Edmund Law, the bishop. Paley acquired a medley of benefices and ecclesiastical offices, holding them jointly in the custom of the age but carrying out his duties conscientiously and paying his curates, it is said, very liberally. Spare time was filled with conversation, whist and fishing, and also with much study and writing, which gave him his place in any discussion of Cambridge religion. This work continued after he moved in 1795 across the Pennines, to the rectory of Bishop Wearmouth, in Durham. It was there that he wrote *Natural Theology*, published in 1802, three years before his death.

PALEY'S THEOLOGY

The argument of natural theology is that the wonders of nature attest the existence of God, the Divine Creator.[77] As old as the ancient Greeks, it is common in Christian theology and science; Newton breathed new life into the ancient theme. Paley's *Natural Theology* (1802) is the most successful exposition of the epoch, because of the number and variety of the examples he cites and the adroitness and elegance with which they are described. The book was written towards the end of his life, but was the crown of a lifetime's fascination, from childhood onwards, with the natural world and mechanical processes. For his writing Paley drew upon copious

[76] George Dyer, *Privileges of the University of Cambridge; together with Additional Observations* (2 vols., London, 1824), vol. II, section 2, p. 108.

[77] This section is based on Leslie Stephen, *English Thought in the Eighteenth Century*, vol. I, pp. 405–20, D. L. Le Mahieu, *The Mind of William Paley. A Philosopher and his Age* (Lincoln, Nebr., University of Nebraska Press, 1976), pp. 29–90, and Clarke, *Paley*, pp. 89–99.

reading in texts like Maclaurin's popularisation of Newton, conversation with savants, and most strikingly his own observations. His son tells us that 'he used to take from his own table to his study the back-bone of a hare, or the pinion of a fowl, or some little bone in the head of a fish; and on coming home from a walk would pull out of his pocket a stone or a plant to illustrate what he had himself found, or seen advanced by others without sufficient minuteness'.[78]

The result of so much effort was a very long and densely detailed celebration of natural marvels and of the artificer to whose skill they bear witness.

> Were there no example in the world, of contrivance except that of the *eye*, it would be alone sufficient to support the conclusion which we draw from it, as to the necessity of an intelligent Creator ... Its coats and humours, constructed as the lenses of a telescope are constructed, for the refraction of rays of light to a point ... the farther provision for its defence, for its constant lubricity and moisture, which we see in its socket and its lids, in its gland for the secretion of the matter of tears ... these provisions compose altogether an apparatus ... [that bears down] all doubt that can be raised on the subject.[79]

Countless other marvels could only be the products of deliberate design; they could not, as proto-evolutionists such as Buffon were beginning to suggest, have arisen spontaneously from their environment, since their purposes and their host species were so narrowly specific. The pelican's pouch may have arisen from its storing of food over a long period of time, but 'the like conformation might be expected to take place in other birds, which fed upon fish. How comes it to pass, that the pelican alone was the inventress, and her descendants the only inheritors, of this curious resource?'[80]

Paley's God is beneficent: 'It is a happy world after all.' The 'sportive motions' of new-born flies, 'their wanton mazes, their gratuitous activity, their continual change of place without use or purpose, testify their joy, and the exultation which they feel in their lately discovered faculties'.[81] Paley was driven to argue that pain was merely an aberration, followed by periods of relief that were

---

[78] Edmund Paley, *Life of William Paley* (vol. 1 in *Works of William Paley*, 1838), p. cxcvi.
[79] *Works of William Paley* (4 vols., London, 1838), vol. 1, *Natural Theology*, pp. 37–8 (chapter 6).
[80] *Natural Theology*, p. 215 (chapter 23).   [81] *Natural Theology*, p. 224 (chapter 26).

positively pleasurable – writing this even when he was suffering from intestinal cancer. The existence of evil was one of the criticisms David Hume had advanced against the plausibility of the proof from Design for the existence of a benign deity, and Paley failed to grapple with it, as he did also with Hume's other objections – the anthropomorphism of the concept, and the difficulty of infinite regress that the notion of a Final Cause entails. But Paley was seeking not to convert the infidel by logic, but to reinforce the faith of the believer who was in doubt.

Paley's views on natural theology complemented his views on Revelation, and were logically prior to them.[82] One large strand in Enlightenment thought was suspicious of revealed religion, regarding it as confuted by the regularity and uniformity of the universe to which Newton was the most important witness. Reliance upon natural religion alone sustained Unitarian, or deist, ideas, and Paley might seem to us a deist were it not for his *View of the Evidences of Christianity* (1794) and related writings. A sequence of deist critics, and the atheist Hume, argued that the miraculous events recorded in the New Testament were fraudulent, and that the alleged witnesses to them were rogues or deluded fanatics; appeals to humankind's common experience suggested the implausibility of the tales they told. Butler's *Analogy of Religion*, preceding Paley's *Evidences* in defending the credibility of miracles, argued that they could be made 'to stand upon the same foot of historical evidence' as any other historical event.[83] Paley took the same line, and sustained his case with a great mass of evidence – the book's great strength (as it was for *Natural Theology*) and an explanation in part of its popularity. For Paley, the New Testament miracles were of crucial importance – proofs of the truth of Christianity and of the life hereafter, and proffered so as to convert observers – Paley assuming that the Apostles were to be persuaded by rational demonstration like Enlightenment philosophers. If the lessons of natural theology were accepted, then the authenticity of miracles might be accepted too, since they were the sort of happenings which we might presume God to cause, and since He devised the laws of nature in

[82] For this section, see Leslie Stephen, *English Thought in the Eighteenth Century*, esp. vol. I, pp. 405–20, Le Mahieu, *Paley*, pp. 91–114, and Clarke, *Paley*, pp. 100–13.
[83] Quoted in Le Mahieu, *Paley*, p. 93.

the first instance we might presume He had the power to suspend them for persuasive purposes. Here we see the interlocking character of *Natural Theology* and *Evidences*.

So far Paley goes no further than to predicate the essential plausibility of miracles. The heart of *Evidences* is a demonstration of their veracity, Paley drawing greatly on the *Credibility of the Gospels*, a work of seventeen volumes which Nathaniel Lardner, a congenitally deaf Nonconformist, had laboured for thirty-three years to produce earlier in the century. Paley sifted the abundant evidence bearing upon the dependability of the Gospels, refuting the contention that they were forgeries and sufficiently establishing that the fundamental accounts were composed by trustworthy witnesses and were substantially in harmony; Paley's skill is still thought to be worth heeding even though he of course lacked the techniques in biblical criticism that have been elaborated since his day. He faced Hume's assertion that witnesses to the miracles were not reliable because they were without the education and caution needed to separate fact from fantasy, and might indeed be suspected of a wish to deceive. This argument reflected Enlightenment prejudice against the ignorant and the unsophisticated, and was one of the weakest parts of Hume's case. Paley counters with the witnesses' courage and perseverance, as proofs of their integrity and conviction. In a passage showing the force and cogency of his utterance, Paley tests 'Mr Hume's theorem' on their testimony:

> If twelve men, whose probity and good sense I had long known, should seriously and circumstantially relate to me an account of a miracle wrought before their eyes, and in which it was impossible that they should be deceived; if the governor of the country, hearing a rumour of this account, should call these men into his presence, and offer them a short proposal, either to confess the imposture, or submit to be tied up to a gibbet; if they should refuse with one voice to acknowledge that there existed any falsehood or imposture in the case; if this threat were communicated to them separately, yet with no different effect; if it was at last executed . . . Now I undertake to say that there exists not a sceptic in the world who would not believe them, or who would defend such incredulity.[84]

[84] *Works of William Paley* (1838), vol. II, *Evidences of Christianity*, p. 6 (Preparatory Considerations).

It is worth noting that neither Hume nor Paley seriously contemplated the possibility of honest delusion. Still, within its limits Paley's reasoning reinforced the faith of the orthodox, who viewed matters within the same limits. The devout and orthodox Samuel Johnson traversed the same ground in a conversation on 21 July 1763, and Boswell's account suggests how Paley's detailed and evidential substantiation was welcomed by believers.[85]

Paley's *Evidences* draws us to the question of his own orthodoxy, or lack of it, his relationship to the Trinitarian theology of the Established Church: an issue that puzzled and disconcerted his contemporaries and intrigues historians still. Plainly he (and Watson too, it might be added) did not share the unitarian certitude of Jebb and his associates; Paley declined to push the Feathers Tavern petition or to leave the Established Church.[86] On the other hand he did not present a clear and consistent doctrinal stance either. In part it was a question of language: Paley offered different sorts of utterance according to his surroundings. In his three famous didactic books he turned to deductive, common-sense argument very largely free from liturgical reinforcement, and they were all the more persuasive because of it, in their effect on the sympathetic yet sceptical Christian. The evidence we have of his teaching at Christ's suggests a similar 'Latitudinarian' approach – even if our witness was most probably Frend, whose views were certainly those that he attributes to Paley:

> We had not, you may be sure, any rigmarole stories about the Trinity, or such stuff; the five points (of Calvinism) were left to repose in antiquated folios; the thirty-nine articles were never hinted at; the creed of Calvin ... was never thought of, and Paley seems to have taken for his model Locke on the Reasonableness of Christianity and his comments on the Epistles.[87]

But from the text of his published sermons, a very different impression is gained, and on the crucial question of the Trinity Paley appears to be nearer orthodox Anglicanism – although the task of explication is made difficult by Paley's ambiguity and by the many fine shades of difference between, and within, orthodox,

---

[85] James Boswell, *Life of Johnson* (Oxford University Press Standard Authors edition, 1953), pp. 314–15.   [86] On the Feathers Tavern petition, see chapter 11, pp. 407–8.
[87] *Universal Magazine* (November 1805), p. 416.

Arian, and Socinian (i.e. Unitarian) views.[88] These difficulties arose
for his contemporaries. While the Bishop of St Davids appealed to
Paley's sermons for Trinitarian support in attacks on unitarianism in
1813, others thought him a Unitarian too. A helpful comment on
the question came from a commentator in the *Quarterly Review*: 'On
the whole, this, we think, has been proved – that he was nothing
like a modern Socinian, that is he was, at least, something more than
an ancient Arian; but that the precise shade of his creed cannot be
determined by us, and perhaps had not been determined by
himself.'[89] Some words of Paley himself on the Trinity stress how
difficult it is to attain exact knowledge:

> We hear, nevertheless, of three divine persons – we speak of the
> Trinity. We read of the 'Father, Son and Holy Ghost'. . . . What is
> that union which subsists in the divine nature; of what kind is that
> relation by which the divine persons of the Trinity are connected,
> we know little – perhaps it is not possible that we should know
> more: but this we seem to know, first, that neither man nor angel
> bears the same relation to God the Father as that which is attributed
> to his only-begotten Son, our Lord Jesus Christ.[90]

Discussion was the way to elucidate those truths that might be
known, but contention over inevitable mysteries should be eschewed and other seekers after truth at least tolerated. So Paley
attended Methodist meetings and welcomed the sincere piety he
found there, and on an occasion that showed warmth towards the
other end of the confessional spectrum, sent a cart laden with
vegetables to a party of Roman Catholic priests, emigrés from
Revolutionary France, who were staying in Sunderland.[91] Scepticism over exactness of knowledge Paley shared with Watson,
and was a consistent theme in Cambridge Latitudinarianism –
the university's distinctive contribution to eighteenth-century
Anglicanism.

---

[88] For this paragraph, see G. A. Cole, 'Doctrine, Dissent and the Decline of Paley's Reputation, 1805–1825', *Enlightenment and Dissent*, 6 (1987), 19–30; also Waterman, 'A Cambridge "Via Media"'.
[89] Quoted in Cole, 'Decline of Paley's Reputation', p. 25.
[90] Quoted in Waterman, 'A Cambridge "Via Media"', p. 428.
[91] Meadley, *Memoirs of Paley*, 1st edition, p. 161; Ernest Barker, *Traditions of Civility* (Cambridge University Press, 1948) p. 227.

PALEY'S MORAL AND POLITICAL PHILOSOPHY

For Cambridge as for British society as a whole Paley's moral and political philosophy were at least as important as his religious ideas.[92] These two sets of views were profoundly linked, and in combining them Paley was following a long tradition. His immediate predecessors as thinkers – with the signal exception of David Hume – derived their sense of the good from some notion of universal harmony that we may call divine, or at least deist, and ethical behaviour was that which was most congruent with it. Even though some thinkers, notably Shaftesbury and Butler, located the human impulse to act well in an innate moral sense while Paley followed Locke in attributing all our thoughts to sense-experience, Paley's place in the tradition is very apparent in every chapter of his *Moral and Political Philosophy*.

His argument is this. We know that God designed the world, and since He is beneficent,

> God, when he created the human species, wished their happiness...
> The world abounds with contrivances: and all the contrivances which we are acquainted with, are directed to beneficial purposes... Teeth are contrived to eat, not to ache; their aching now and then, is incidental to the contrivance, perhaps inseparable from it: or even, if you will, let it be called a defect in the contrivance; but it is not the *object* of it.

It follows that to discover how religious principle assesses a given action we should 'inquire into the tendency of that action to promote or diminish the general happiness'.[93]

Christian revelation enhances the tendency towards rightful conduct by holding out both an inducement and a deterrent. 'Virtue is "the doing good to mankind, in obedience to the will of God, and for the sake of everlasting happiness".'[94]

---

[92] For this section, see Leslie Stephen, *English Thought in the Eighteenth Century*, vol. II, pp. 1–129; Clarke, *Paley*, pp. 57–88; Le Mahieu, *Paley*, pp. 115–52; Barker, *Traditions of Civility*, pp. 193–262 ('Paley and his Political Philosophy'); and Robert Hole, *Pulpits, Politics and Public Order in England 1760–1832* (Cambridge University Press, 1989), esp. pp. 73–82.

[93] *Moral and Political Philosophy*, pp. 33–4 (Book 2, chapter 5).

[94] Paley, *Moral and Political Philosophy*, p. 20 (Book 1, chapter 7). These words, which Paley italicises, are the epigraph to chapter 7, and a quotation from Edmund Law.

It seems most agreeable to our conceptions of justice, and is consonant enough to the language of Scripture,[95] to suppose that there are prepared for us rewards and punishments, of all possible degrees, from the most exalted happiness down to extreme misery; so that 'our labour is never in vain'; whatever advancement we make in virtue, we procure a proportionable accession of future happiness; as, on the other hand, every accumulation of vice is the 'treasuring up so much wrath against the day of wrath'.[96]

Thus Paley first demonstrates that the divine purpose of human life, and political society, is happiness, and then he crucially reinforces his argument by invoking the promise of heaven and the threat of hell. What might have been, and from other hands often was, a secular body of theory, becomes transformed into a Christian argument. In the words of Leslie Stephen, 'Bentham is Paley *minus* a belief in hell-fire'.[97]

In defining right conduct as that leading to happiness Paley was in the English Utilitarian tradition founded by John Locke. He denied that there were innate ideas. Beliefs were the result of experience, or sense-impressions, and moral principles reflect the basic human appetites, 'a desire of happiness and an aversion to misery'. 'Good or evil are nothing but pleasure and pain, or that which occasions pleasure and pain to us.'[98] Locke's most distinguished and penetrating eighteenth-century successors in this line of argument were David Hume and Jeremy Bentham. They were not Christians or deists, which made their task as Utilitarian philosophers easier. Other writers did attempt to reconcile empirically derived morality with the notion of divine ordinances; among them were Locke himself, Daniel Waterland and Edmund Law (whom Paley quotes), but none made an especial mark in this context. The most determined and lengthy attempt so far was *The Light of Nature Pursued* (1768–78) by Abraham Tucker, 'a rich country gentleman', delighting to follow philosophical theories 'through all the intrica-

---

[95] At this point Paley quotes in a footnote some texts of Scripture that support his argument: e.g., 'He which soweth sparingly, shall reap also sparingly; and he which soweth bountifully, shall reap also bountifully' (2 Cor. 9: 6).

[96] *Moral and Political Philosophy*, p. 24 (Book 1, chapter 8).

[97] *History of English Thought*, vol. II, p. 125.

[98] Quoted from the *Essay on the Human Understanding* in Leslie Stephen, *History of English Thought*, vol. II, p. 81.

cies of some speculative labyrinth', so that his writings were 'not seldom wearisome and immeasurably prolix'.[99] Paley's striking, persuasive and constantly readable text, published in 1785, stood out by contrast with these earlier writers, expertly demonstrating consistency between Christian doctrine and Locke's psychology. *Principles of Moral and Political Philosophy* appeared when Bentham's *Principles of Morals and Legislation* was in the press, though not yet published – one of the greatest coincidences in literature.

In uniting Utilitarian and traditional Christian modes of thought Paley performed a service for the Established Church that was to be of inestimable value until well into the nineteenth century; he updated the idiom of argument. In the eighteenth century the theories of social obligation that were proffered by Anglicans were couched in religious terms, often scriptural in origin and drawing on the sayings of St Paul. Thus in 1767 Robert Lowth, the Bishop of Oxford, stated in a sermon that:

> Government in general is the ordinance of God: the particular Form of Government is the ordinance of man ... The form of government therefore has not an absolute, but only a relative, goodness; ...
> It follows that it is the duty of every individual to acquiesce in that form of government, under which Providence hath placed him.[100]

Bentham transformed the debate about polity and governance, in the sense that he offered an exceedingly simple and plausible criterion for assessing the worth of a system of government, the utilitarian 'felicific calculus' about the 'greatest happiness of the greatest number'. His reasoning was secular – Bentham had no time for Paley's Christian Utilitarianism – and his arguments could not be ignored or dismissed by those wishing to offer a Christian political philosophy: they had in some way to be embraced, much as Keynesian economics had to be confronted in the 1940s and 1950s. This accommodation Paley achieved in the *Principles of Moral and Political Philosophy*, and at the same time he served the cause of conservatism. Bentham's ideas were taken up by radicals, among others; Paley advanced, as we shall see, a theory of social obligation

---

[99] Leslie Stephen, *History of English Thought*, vol. II, pp. 110–11.
[100] Quoted in Hole, *Pulpits, Politics and Public Order*, p. 15. This paragraph is indebted to this work, •
esp. pp. 1–31, 73–82.

little different in outcome, though not origin, from Bishop Lowth's. 'The political thought of a large number of Anglican clergy in the early nineteenth century was based on Paley's *Principles of Moral and Political Philosophy* which they had studied at university and which gave them this rational, secular and human view of political society.'[101]

In his own day Paley was sometimes regarded as a dangerous radical because of some of the things he said, whereas underneath he was as firm a conservative as Samuel Johnson or Burke. His well-known parable of the pigeons satirises the structure of society and its distribution of property, ninety-nine out of a hundred 'gathering all they got, into a heap' and keeping it for 'one, and that the weakest, perhaps worst pigeon of the flock'.[102] This passage earned him the nickname 'Pigeon Paley', and is said to have helped to persuade George III that he was 'Not orthodox, not orthodox' and so unfit for a bishopric.[103] Similar criticisms of the rich and powerful strike the reader in Paley's remarks on poverty. In 1802 the *Anti-Jacobin Review* 'hesitated not to affirm' that in the *Moral and Political Philosophy* 'the most determined Jacobin might find a justification of his principles, and a sanction for his conduct'.[104] Yet it has been pointed out that 'Paley went occasionally to the brink of radicalism and then drew back'.[105] After all, he fully justifies the unequal distribution of property: it 'flows from those rules concerning the acquisition and disposal of property, by which men are incited to industry, and by which the object of their industry is rendered secure and valuable'.[106] Meanwhile, the delights of riches are balanced by the gratifications of common life – the routine of toil that brings health, the pleasures of simple food and rest after labour, and freedom from the ambition that unsettles the rich.

When he turns to look at political organisation Paley makes clear his essential conservatism. He rejects the idea of a social contract, or compact, that was especially linked with the name of John Locke, as a dangerous fiction. 'In private contracts, the violation and non-performance of the conditions, by one of the parties, vacates the

---

[101] Hole, *Pulpits, Politics and Public Order*, p. 82.
[102] *Moral and Political Philosophy*, pp. 50–1 (Book 3, Part 1, chapter 7).
[103] Clarke, *Paley*, p. 43.   [104] Quoted in Waterhouse, 'A Cambridge "Via Media"', p. 423.
[105] Hole, *Pulpits, Politics and Public Order*, p. 75.
[106] *Moral and Political Philosophy*, p. 53 (Book 3, Part 1, chapter 3).

obligation of the other.'[107] So any government would find itself threatened by rebellion every time it seemed to be overstepping the mark: 'the position that every such transgression amounts to a forfeiture of the government, and consequently authorizes the people to withdraw their obedience, and provide for themselves by a new settlement, would endanger the stability of every political fabric in the world, and has in fact always supplied the disaffected with a topic of seditious declamation'. After stating in two propositions that God wills human happiness and that civil society exists to promote it, Paley proceeds: 'Civil societies cannot be upholden, unless, in each, the interest of the whole society be binding upon every part and member of it.' This is the third step, and conducts us to the conclusion, namely, 'that so long as the interest of the whole society requires it, that is, so long as the established government cannot be resisted or changed without public inconveniency, it is the will of God (which *will* universally determines our duty) that the established government be obeyed', – and no longer. Thus the right of rebellion is apparently conceded, but when Paley examines the specific case of the American War of Independence, concluded just three years before *Principles* was published, he shows how constrained he conceives this right to be.

> Had I been an American, I should not have thought it enough to have had it even demonstrated, that a separation from the parent-state would produce effects beneficial to America; my relation to that state imposed upon me a farther inquiry, namely ... whether what Great Britain would lose by the separation, was likely to be compensated to the joint stock of happiness, by the advantages which America would receive from it.

Though a few lines later Paley seemingly envisages a justified separation when the Thirteen Colonies were mightier than the United Kingdom (so that the balance of the greater happiness to be consulted had moved across the Atlantic) it is clear that this was thought of as being far in the future. In Paley's scheme of things the colonies would have stayed in the British Empire till well into the nineteenth century.

Like the eighteenth-century commentators Montesquieu and

---

[107] The quotations here are taken from *Moral and Political Philosophy*, pp. 237–42 (Book 6, chapter 3).

Blackstone, Paley praises the British constitution for the quality of balance between monarchical, aristocratic, and democratic elements, preventing any one interest from dominating others. Admitting defects, but warning that changes apparently justified might have unintended results, he berates 'that distempered sensibility, which is alive only to perceptions of inconveniency, and is too impatient to be delivered from the uneasiness which it feels, to compute either the peril or expense of the remedy'.[108] On a great debating-point of the age, parliamentary reform, Paley admits that there were rotten boroughs and so forth and that only a minority of men had votes. But denying the so-called 'natural right' to the franchise, he asserts that 'if men the most likely by their qualifications to know and to promote the public interest, be actually returned to parliament, it signifies little who returns them. If the properest persons be elected, what matters it by whom they are elected?' Thus Paley advocates the sort of highly cautious conservatism associated with his contemporary Edmund Burke.

PALEY'S IDEAS IN CAMBRIDGE

Paley's three works explained and justified the universe in a coherent, logical, and elegantly articulated way.[109] They proved the existence of God, and the rightness of Christian orthodoxy and the organisation of society. Densely empirical and packed with examples from everyday life, they were an excellent complement to Newton's deductive demonstration of the harmony of the universe. It was natural for his own university, where half the clergymen in the Established Church were educated, to adopt his texts – especially since much of the material in them had been honed for presentation to undergraduates by Paley in his teaching at Christ's. The first to be adopted was *Principles of Moral and Political Philosophy*, published in 1785 and introduced for the degree exercises in the following year by Thomas Jones, the moderator in the Senate House Examination.[110] Thereafter the other works were adopted for college reading lists or university examinations, the widespread

[108] *Moral and Political Philosophy*, p. 263 (Book 6, chapter 7).
[109] This section draws on Le Mahieu, *Paley*, pp. 153–83.
[110] Meadley, *Memoirs of William Paley*, 1st edn, p. 93.

use of *Evidences*, for example, being followed by its becoming a set text for the Previous Examination at its outset in 1822. In contrast, Paley was much less widely listed at Oxford. His books also provided an occupation for Cambridge's Grub Street, that curious twilit world where commentaries and cribs on examination texts were written. In 1836 Thomas Coward[111] published his *Analysis of Paley's Evidences of Christianity, with Examination Questions to Each Chapter*. 'How does Paley establish the position that the pleasures of ambition and superiority are common to all conditions? What are adventitious rights? How are they created?'; these are samples of the questions Coward cited. The guide was often reprinted, and similar volumes appeared at regular intervals, until as late as 1910.

Generations of undergraduates found Paley's direct technique attractive. Thomas De Quincey, at Worcester College Oxford early in the nineteenth century, disliked what Paley said but found the way he said it beguiling. 'Homely, racy, vernacular English, the rustic vigour of a style which intentionally forgoes the graces of polish on the one hand, and of scholarly precision on the other – that quality of merit has never been attained in a degree so eminent.'[112] Charles Darwin, at Christ's College a quarter-century after De Quincey's sojourn at university, found the Cambridge mathematical and classics curricula tedious. But, he added,

> In order to pass the B.A. examination it was, also, necessary to get up Paley's Evidences of Christianity and his Moral Philosophy. This was done in a thorough manner, and I am convinced that I could have written out the whole of the Evidences with perfect correctness, but not of course in the clear language of Paley. The logic of this book, and as I may add of his Natural Theology gave me as much delight as did Euclid. The careful study of these works, without attempting to learn any part by rote, was the only part of the Academical Course which as I then felt and as I still believe, was of the least use to me in the education of my mind. I did not at that time trouble myself about Paley's premises; and taking these on trust I was charmed and convinced by the long line of argumentation.[113]

---

[111] He cannot be traced and presumably was not a Cambridge student.

[112] David Masson (ed.), *Collected Writings of Thomas de Quincey* (Edinburgh, 1889–90), vol. II, *Autobiography and Literary Reminiscences*, p. 62.

[113] Darwin and Huxley, *Autobiographies*, pp. 32–3.

In his preface to his new edition of Paley's *Moral Philosophy* in 1859, Archbishop Whately declared that

> having long been an established Text-book at a great and flourishing University, it has laid the foundation of the Moral Principles of many hundreds – probably thousands – of Youths while under a course of training designed to qualify them for being afterwards the Moral instructors of Millions. Such a work therefore cannot fail to exercise a very considerable and extensive influence on the Minds of successive generations.[114]

By the middle of the century, however, *Principles of Moral and Political Philosophy* had lost its central place in discourse. Its utilitarian ethics – the calculating expediency that it was plausible to impute to them – were distrusted by several schools of thought; Evangelicals believed the source of right conduct was a God-given moral sense, rather than sense–impressions. The Evangelical attack on him began a few years after *Principles* appeared, with the publication in 1789 of *Principles of Moral Philosophy* by Thomas Gisborne.[115] In his much reprinted attack on Paley Gisborne warned that 'General expediency is an instrument not to be wielded by a mortal hand'.[116] Expediency had no biblical warrant, and it led to the evasion of moral responsibilities. Gisborne, wrote Wilberforce, had 'fully established his charge against Paley, and [had] shown with great effect how little such a principle as general expediency is fit for man'.

The strongest denunciation of Paley came from Calvinist Evangelicals such as John Overton, a Yorkshire clergyman educated at Magdalene, a leading Evangelical college of the epoch. His *The True Churchman Ascertained: or his Apology for those of the Regular Clergy of the Establishment who are Sometimes Called Evangelical Ministers* (1801) contended that 'Paley and his School' asserted, 'with almost one voice, like the Papists, the doctrine of *freewill*; our Reformers say, that the Papistical doctrine of freewill is *abominable* in the sight of God, and to *be abhorred* by all Christian men'.[117] Evangelicals such as

---

[114] Richard Whately (ed.), *Paley's Moral Philosophy* (London, 1859), p. iii.
[115] Gisborne, from a Derby family whose members were often educated at St John's, was Sixth Wrangler in 1780, and afterwards a country squire and clergyman; he was an intimate friend of Wilberforce, whom he met as an undergraduate, and prominent in Evangelical circles.
[116] Quoted in Le Mahieu, *Paley*, p. 156. These pages draw on this book, pp. 153–83.
[117] Quoted in Waterman, 'A Cambridge "Via Media"', p. 433.

Charles Simeon were more moderate than this. Nor of course did everybody approve of Evangelicals anyway. But some of their sternest critics disliked Paley too, as Edward Pearson showed in his *Remarks on the Theory of Morals* (1800). A graduate of Sidney Sussex, Pearson became master in 1808. An energetic controversialist, he was often in debate with the leading Cambridge Evangelical Charles Simeon. Meanwhile, the most famous Canta-brigian to attack Paley was Samuel Taylor Coleridge, in several writings between 1809 and 1818. Coleridge, having by now abandoned his early Unitarianism for Anglicanism, regarded Paley's prudential basis for virtue as akin to Enlightenment rationalism, in the encouragement it gave to selfish individualism; Paley taught '*obey* God, *Benefit* your neighbour; but love YOURSELVES above all'. Christian virtue was founded on self-denial and self-restraint.[118]

Amid this chorus of criticism from voices not otherwise in harmony, notes of approval were comparatively few, the chief being *Vindication of Dr. Paley's Theory of Morals* (1830) by Latham Wainewright, a graduate of Emmanuel (BA 1802) and rector of Great Brickhill. *Principles* ceased to be an accepted authority in Cambridge in the 1830s (though it continued as a set text for some time), its fall being announced by Adam Sedgwick's attack on it in 1833. Concerned for student morals, Sedgwick, after praising Paley's 'homely strength and clearness of style, and his unrivalled skill in stating and following out his argument', reproves him for 'denying the sanction and authority of the moral sense'.

> Amidst all the ruin that is within us, there are still the elements of what is good; and were there left in the natural heart, no kindly affections and moral sentiments, man would be no longer responsible for his sins; and every instance of persuasion against the impulse of bad passion, and of conversion from evil unto good, would be nothing less than a moral miracle. On such a view of human nature, the Apostles of our religion might as well have wasted their breath on the stones of the wilderness as on the hearts of their fellow-men in the cities of the heathen.[119]

---

[118] Hole, *Pulpits, Politics and Public order*, pp. 180–1.
[119] Adam Sedgwick, *A Discourse on the Studies of the University*, 1st edn (Cambridge University Press, 1833), pp. 49–51.

By contrast, there was continued vitality in Paley's theological writings. Though his detail might seem obsolete, his underlying theme, that reason and revelation were reconcilable, satisfied generations of churchmen and dons, and there were many acknowledgements of his name in the *Bridgewater Treatises* (1825) in which eight authors, including William Whewell, attempted to demonstrate 'the Power, Wisdom, and Goodness of God as manifested in Creation'. And, while criticising *Principles of Moral and Political Philosophy* in 1833, Adam Sedgwick at the same time praised *Natural Theology*. Referring to the 'very important and elaborate treatises' that had recently appeared 'enforcing different parts of the great argument to be drawn from final causes', Sedgwick believed that it was 'impossible that any one of them, or all of them together, should supersede the work of Paley'.[120] However, Darwin's convincing evolutionist case, the *Origin of Species* (1859) finally made *Natural Theology* seem obsolete as a statement about how God affected the universe. 'Whereas Paley's argument assumed a fundamentally static universe whose creation had been the single act of an enormously wise and powerful Creator, Darwin substituted an ongoing process which accounted for the various functions of natural phenomena by the specific exigencies of a particular place and time.'[121] By the middle of the century, too, *Evidences* seemed fatally damaged as a help for Christians anxious to reinforce faith. Its survival seemed to depend on admitting the need for a less literal, more metaphorical interpretation of scripture, and dispensing with the idea of miracles altogether; such was the theme of *Essays and Reviews* (1860). Nevertheless, *Evidences* continued to be set for the Previous Examination till 1920, while very old-fashioned dons like J. P. Taylor commended its 'practical wisdom' and 'admirable good sense' and tried to defend it from the accusation, prevalent in Cambridge, that it was terribly out of date.[122] The fact that *Evidences*, written at the end of the eighteenth century, was crammed for examination by men and women still living at the end of the twentieth, is proof of just how set in their ways academics can sometimes be.

---

[120] *A Discourse*, p. 88.   [121] Le Mahieu, *Paley*, p. 179.
[122] *A Consideration of Some Recent Strictures on Paley's Evidences of Christianity* (Cambridge, 1898).

Chapter 9

CAMBRIDGE RELIGION
1780–1840: EVANGELICALISM

THE EVANGELICAL AWAKENING

In 1744 a British soldier, Sampson Staniforth, had a religious experience while on guard duty during a military campaign in Flanders:

> As soon as I was alone, I kneeled down, and determined not to rise, but to continue crying and wrestling with God, till He had mercy on me. How long I was in that agony I cannot tell; but as I looked up to heaven I saw the clouds open exceedingly bright, and I saw Jesus hanging on the cross. At the same moment these words were applied to my heart, 'Thy sins are forgiven thee'. My chains fell off; my heart was free. All guilt was gone, and my soul was filled with unutterable peace. I loved God and all mankind, and the fear of death and hell was vanished away. I was filled with wonder and astonishment.[1]

Staniforth's words describe two chief features of Evangelicalism, a movement that swept through Protestantism in the eighteenth century: the sense of being justified, in other words that one's sins had been forgiven through the atoning death of Christ, and secondly that one's human nature had been renewed at the time of conversion, through a 'new birth'. Evangelicals, reaffirming traditional Protestant trust in the Bible, believed that all spiritual truth was to be found in its pages; and they felt an urgent sense of mission to spread this truth to those lacking it. Their religion was active and vital.

[1] Quoted in Mark A. Noll, David W. Bebbington, and George A Rawlyk, eds., *Evangelicalism. Comparative Studies of Popular Protestantism in North America, the British Isles, and Beyond, 1700–1990* (Oxford University Press, 1994), p. 4. What follows draws on chapter 1 of this work: John Walsh, '"Methodism" and the Origins of English-Speaking Evangelicalism', pp. 19–37; and also on D. W. Bebbington, *Evangelicalism in Modern Britain. A History from the 1730s to the 1980s* (London, Unwin Hyman, 1989), pp. 1–74.

The Evangelical awakening

Though our focus is on the University of Cambridge, it is helpful to remember that Evangelicalism affected far more than this tiny fragment of Christendom. Beginning in Central and Eastern Europe amid Protestants oppressed by resurgent Catholicism,[2] it spread westwards to the Atlantic and beyond it, to the British territories in North America. In a movement so widespread, where generic and local causes were intertwined in highly complex patterns, its dynamic remains in some respects mysterious, despite great scholarly effort to explain it: why, for example, did separate though nearly simultaneous awakenings occur in Wales and Massachusetts in 1734–5? Yet however inexplicable their effect in particular circumstances, the importance of some forces seems clear enough. Among them in Britain were the refugee Moravian Brethren who in the 1730s so greatly influenced the most famous Evangelical of all, John Wesley. The Moravians traced their descent from the Hussites of the fifteenth century, and British Evangelicalism had roots in seventeenth-century Protestant forms, notably Puritanism. But it seems also to have been a reaction against the spiritual depletion of much contemporary religion: the rationalism of the deists and Latitudinarians seemed arid compared to the Evangelicals' emotional certitude and sense of joy.[3] In part, Evangelicalism was in revolt against much in Cambridge.

The movement affected all Protestant churches and dominated some. John Wesley and his immediate associates in 1738–9 were High Church Anglicans, and the Methodism that he founded began within the Established Church and overflowed its boundaries, eventually separating from it. By the end of the century the Dissenting churches were Evangelical in outlook, and there were Evangelicals within the Anglican church itself, like the famous pastors Henry Venn at Yelling (Huntingdonshire) and John Berridge at Everton (Bedfordshire);[4] they had close links with the Evangelical group, all of them necessarily Anglican, in the nearby university. There were also many in the Church of England, such as Bishop Porteus, who sympathised with Evangelical moral ideas, for example on slavery, without agreeing with their doctrines.

[2] W. R. Ward, *The Protestant Evangelical Awakening* (Cambridge University Press, 1992), esp. pp. 54–92.   [3] Walsh, '"Methodism" and the Origins', pp. 22–6.
[4] Marcus Loane, *Cambridge and the Evangelical Succession* (London, Lutterworth, 1952), pp. 67–170.

Evangelicals were disliked by many in the Anglican church, especially in the early decades. The heart of the movement, belief in justification by faith, seemed to depreciate the importance of good works as agents of salvation – even though Evangelicals tried to stress the need for them as features of the Christian life – and was a lasting source of suspicion. So was the Calvinist doctrine accepted by many Evangelicals that God's grace, or justification, was accessible only to the elect, not in some sense to all men and women, as Arminians believed. The Evangelical movement was itself split on the question; Wesley was himself an Arminian, but many Methodists were Calvinists. Calvinism was antipathetic to many Anglicans, and accusations that they adhered to it tended to be levelled at Evangelicals who did not, such as, within Cambridge, the famous Charles Simeon. He was also caught up in what has been described as 'the chief theological controversy of the early and mid-nineteenth century':[5] the regenerative efficacy of baptism, a tenet of Anglicanism, seemed to be denied by Evangelical trust in conversion.

Many Evangelicals' pressing sense of mission led them, particularly the Methodists, to involve lay people in the task of conversion, and to their practice of itinerancy, or touring the land to preach where they might. John Wesley was himself an itinerant of prodigious energy, and the best-known reference to the practice in literature also concerns a Methodist, Dinah Morris, who in Chapter 2 of *Adam Bede* comes to the village of Hayslope to preach under a maple tree on the village green. Preaching by a lay woman seemed especially destructive of society's hierarchies, but Anglicans were also perturbed when as sometimes happened Evangelical clergymen stepped outside their own parish to preach in another's without permission. Simeon's friend John Berridge of Everton, Bedfordshire, often itinerated in the 1770s, for which the Bishop of Ely upbraided him:[6] 'Well, Berridge, they tell me you go about preaching out of your own parish. Did I institute you to the livings of Abbotsley, or Eaton Socon, or Potton?' After Berridge defended his action, '"Poh!" said his lordship, "I tell you, you have no right to preach out of your own parish: and, if you do not desist from it,

[5] Bebbington, *Evangelicalism in Modern Britain*, p. 9.
[6] *Evangelical Magazine*, February 1794, quoted in Smyth, *Simeon and Church Order*, pp. 261–2.

you will very likely be sent to Huntingdon gaol".'[7] The way in which charges of itinerancy were levelled at Evangelical Anglicans who abjured it, such as, once more, Charles Simeon, was a good example of the tendency to portray them as stereotypes in hostile fashion that the movement suffered from in its early decades, notably within the university.

THE CAMBRIDGE METHODISTS

> Brother William and mother exceedingly zealous for the Lord of Hosts. William has raised up a party for God in Cambridge. They are already stigmatized for Methodists.[8]

So wrote Charles Wesley to his brother John in January 1738, concerning the activities of William Delamotte and others in Cambridge, in the first known example in the university of the Evangelical renewal of the 1730s. A small number of undergraduates from diverse backgrounds came together to form a society for common devotion and spiritual exercises. Their experiences paralleled those of many men and women in this mysterious revolution. For many the preaching of John Wesley brought the warmth and heartfelt conviction they were seeking; and the eventual size of Methodism and its institutional separation from the Established Church have led to its being awarded too great an importance in some accounts of the revival's early years. In fact in the case of the Cambridge 'Methodists' Wesley was only one of several influences.

The founder of the Cambridge group, Francis Okely, was born in 1719, the son of a Bedford barber. After schooling at Charterhouse, and while waiting at home to go up to Cambridge, he experienced a spiritual awakening. He animated his mother and neighbours to 'a new zeal', and together they formed a little group which 'endeavoured to pursue religion in the greatest strictness and purity of it, according to the best devotional tracts of the Church of

---

[7] Berridge was in due course threatened with ejection from his parish, but escaped because Thomas Pitt, First Baron Camelford and MA of Clare (Berridge's college), persuaded a nobleman of his acquaintance to intervene with the bishop: see Smyth, *Simeon and Church Order*, p. 263.

[8] Quoted in John Walsh, 'The Cambridge Methodists', in Peter Brooks, ed., *Christian Spirituality. Essays in Honour of Gordon Rupp* (London, SCM, 1975), pp. 256–7. What follows is indebted to this essay, and to John Walsh, 'The Origins of the Evangelical Revival', in G. V. Bennett and J. D. Walsh, eds., *Essays in Modern English Church History in Memory of Norman Sykes* (London, A. & C. Black, 1966), pp. 132–62.

England'.[9] Their society seems like one of the many that arose in the last quarter of the seventeenth century, for the most part fervently Anglican in their usage and loyalties and keen students of the devotional works of High Churchmen like Robert Nelson. Many of these societies were exposed to the Evangelical revival. In June 1736 Okely matriculated at St John's, and soon founded a little society like the one he had left in Bedford, consisting of undergraduates. One of the few members whose names we have was William Hammond, Okely's friend at Charterhouse and now his roommate in college. As a child he had experienced powerful religious 'drawings', like many Evangelicals. In his *Narrative of the Life of William Hammond* he described how when young he heard 'a sermon in which the minister treated largely of the conversion and salvation of men, saying that those who were born Christians must be saved by their works, but such as were heathen born, by faith alone'. He continued, 'O how often have I ardently wished that I might have been a heathen, that I might thereby be entitled to that justification that is procured alone by faith.'[10]

The Cambridge group was smaller than the wide and overlapping circles of Evangelicalism at Oxford; and since it lacked, it seems, the support of any dons it could not hope for the strength that the Wesley brothers brought in Oxford.[11] But the Cambridge men undoubtedly knew of doings at Oxford, through the pamphlet *The Oxford Methodists* (1733) and certainly through some personal contacts. One was William Delamotte. As an undergraduate at St John's College, Cambridge, he was converted by Charles Wesley and Benjamin Ingham, a member of the Holy Club in Oxford, in the summer of 1737. He was the 'brother William' mentioned in the epigraph to this section, and by Michaelmas 1738 at the latest Okely's group joined Delamotte's little 'party for God', and were said to have 'all received the then three capital and distinguishing doctrines of the Methodists, viz. Original Sin, Justification by Faith and the New Birth'.[12] When Ingham visited Cambridge in

---

[9] Quoted in Walsh, 'The Cambridge Methodists', pp. 252–3.
[10] Quoted in Walsh, 'The Cambridge Methodists', p. 254.
[11] V. H. H. Green, *The Young Mr Wesley. A Study of John Wesley and Oxford* (London, Arnold, 1961), pp. 145–201; Richard P. Heitzenrater (ed.), *Diary of an Oxford Methodist, Benjamin Ingham, 1733–1734* (Durham, N.C., Duke University Press, 1985), pp. 1–47.
[12] Quoted in Walsh, 'The Cambridge Methodists', p. 258, and pp. 258–9 for the next quotation.

December 1738 he wrote that 'the gownsmen seem to be in good dispositions, seeking and striving to be better, and there is a great deal of love and freedom amongst them'. They were visiting the prisoners in the Castle Hill gaol, just as members of the Holy Club were ministering to the inmates of the Bocardo prison in Oxford. From our brief Cambridge sources we learn little of their spiritual life, but we may get some sense of their régime from the Oxford diary of the man who so much approved of their activities, Benjamin Ingham.

At Queen's College from October 1730 onwards, Ingham kept a diary which is preserved in the Methodist Archives. For Tuesday 9 April, a typical day, Ingham recorded:[13]

> 4 Rose; dressed. 4.15 Business and virtue; ri.[14] 4.30 Private prayer. 4.45 Chapter. 5 E;[15] read Country Parson[16] on resignation. 6 E; read Country Parson, motives to resignation; ri. 7 E and private prayer. 7.15 Public Prayers. 8 E; went to visit the sick woman, religious talk of frequenting the Holy Sacrament, and the church; of daily examination and private prayer; questioned her how she designed to amend her life; exhortation to her and several other women that were there; read prayers for the sick; ri; called at the Workhouse, and at Smith's.

So much achieved, yet the day for most undergraduates was doubtless just beginning. For Ingham the morning and afternoon were filled with devotional practices, with a little physical exercise but, on this day at least, no scholarly course-work. For the last few hours of the day Ingham recorded:

> 6 Supper; ri; no flesh. 7 Divided the Servitors'[17] wages; ri. 8 Went to Smith's, he was engaged; came home. 8.30 Wrote diary; read Norris' first Beatitude;[18] ri. 9 E; wrote diary. 9.15 Private prayer. 9.30 [bed]
> Blessings; rose; recollected 6 times; fervent in private prayer; zealous in conversing with sick woman; serious resolutions in reading the Country Parson.
> Sins: dead in Public Prayers; vain and unchaste thoughts; dissipated.

---

[13] Heitzenrater, *Diary of an Oxford Methodist*, pp. 157–8.
[14] A notation that refers to spiritual recollection.
[15] Abbreviation for 'ejaculatory prayers'.   [16] The *Country Parson's Advice* (1680).
[17] An Oxford equivalent to sizars, with whom it appears Ingham had some administrative function.
[18] John Norris, *Practical Discourses Upon the Beatitudes of Our Lord* (1728). The first discourse is 'Christian Blessedness' on Matthew 5:3.

It is unlikely that this last word had anything like its usual current meaning. Ingham retired to bed when for many in Queen's College the evening was just beginning. It was most probably due to austere conduct like Ingham's that the Cambridge group were disdained by other students. Delamotte's public preaching was disrupted by undergraduates; some students were warned by their tutors for associating with him, and one college forbade his entry. We hear no more of the Cambridge Methodists after Okely, Hammond, and Delamotte went down in 1739 and 1740, to take part severally in the years to come in what their historian has called a 'spiritual odyssey' that demonstrates the inchoate nature of early Evangelicalism: by different routes they all joined the Moravian Brethren.

We do not know of any like associations until Rowland Hill drew friends round him in St John's in the 1760s,[19] though in view of the research that has shown Oxford to have contained more devotional gatherings than just the Wesleys' Holy Club it is possible that other cells will be uncovered in the sister university.

THE MAGDALENE EVANGELICALS

In the 1770s and 1780s Magdalene was transformed into an Evangelical college, and the process illustrates the power that determined individuals might possess over the small institutions that most colleges then were.[20] The prime mover was Samuel Hey, a Yorkshireman, Ninth Wrangler in 1771, soon elected a fellow; he became tutor and in due course president, or vice-master. Barton Wallop, master till 1781, was largely non-resident and always unconcerned, and he allowed Hey to transform the college. Wallop's successor was Peter Peckard, an ex-soldier with an interest in heterodox religion; he was a quasi-Unitarian of the sort familiar in Cambridge. His religious views and Hey's were sharply opposed, but a bond uniting Rational Dissenters and Evangelicals was detestation of slavery,[21] and in addition Peckard had great respect for the

---

[19] Loane, *Cambridge and the Evangelical Succession*, pp. 92–107.
[20] What follows is based on John Walsh, 'The Magdalene Evangelicals', *Church Quarterly Review*, 69 (1958), pp. 499–511, Cunich, Hoyle, Duffy, and Hyam, *A History of Magdalene College*, pp. 185–93 – chapter 7, by Eamon Duffy.
[21] As Vice-Chancellor in 1784 Peckard set as the subject for a Latin prize-essay competition the lawfulness of slavery. A young graduate of St John's, Thomas Clarkson, was drawn to the

academic and disciplinary régime that Hey established; he allowed Hey to continue his work of conversion, in which Hey was assisted by another Yorkshireman, Henry Jowett from an Evangelical family in Leeds, and William Farish from Carlisle, Senior Wrangler in 1771 and famous in Cambridge annals as Jacksonian Professor and for his lectures on natural philosophy (in effect, engineering).[22]

These serious Evangelicals gained the attention of the Elland Society, a group of Yorkshire Anglicans anxious to promote the education of young men who would add to the Evangelical ranks in the Established Church; often from humble origins, their pensioners were given some Latin and Greek, and sometimes some social polish, before going to university. Truly welcoming colleges were hard to find; Hey's Magdalene was a godsend. An old student described his achievement in 1795: 'In this College discipline had been much neglected when the learned and reverend Samuel Hey was appointed tutor: he immediately began by enforcing a proper degree of attention to study, regularity in attendance on lectures, chapel, etc.'[23] The first Elland pensioner entered Magdalene in 1778, the year Hey became president, and in 1782 the secretary of the society explained to Lord Dartmouth, a prominent Evangelical, that pensioners 'have hitherto been sent without exception to Cambridge, where Mr S. Hey of Magdalen has exceedingly befriended them; and the tutors Farish and Jowett are both serious men ... we have not any rule against sending them to Oxford, but the advantage they have at Cambridge has prevailed in its favour'. Soon Magdalene was thought amongst Evangelicals to be 'the general resort of young men seriously impressed with a sense of religion'. Many were from Evangelical households and schools in Yorkshire, for example, Hull Grammar School, whose headmaster was Isaac Milner's brother Joseph. By 1796–7 there were twelve Elland pensioners at Magdalene, as well as other Evangelicals; since there were only about fifteen undergraduates at the college altogether[24] it is clear that Evangelicalism dominated it.

anti-slavery cause by reading for the prize, which he won; Clarkson went on to become a leading abolitionist.

[22] For Farish as Jacksonian Professor, see chapter 6, pp. 220–1. Farish was also vicar of St Giles, where he erected an acoustic sounding-board.

[23] Quoted in Walsh, 'Magdalene Evangelicals', p. 503, and pp. 502 and 503 for the next two quotations. [24] Christopher Wordsworth, *Social Life*, p. 640.

The lives of Magdalene Evangelicals were strictly controlled. Ellard pensioners had to promise to obey their guardians (dons appointed by the society) in all things lawful. Guardians monitored their dress and behaviour and their academic and spiritual record. Samuel Knight, a one-time Elland pensioner himself and afterwards a fellow of the college, reported on George Barrs: 'Exceedingly serious and diligent – makes a good progress and wou'd do much more work than his Tutor cou'd find time to overlook – as to religion rather at a low ebb – in danger from literary pride, but considered upon the whole as a ... rather good young man.'[25] At times pensioners were punished for extravagance, or the range of cheeky offences suggested by the accusation against W. H. Deverel, dismissed from the Elland Society in 1798, that he had 'put on a Fellow Commoner's gown, and given at different times much uneasiness to the Society'.[26] The examining chaplain to the Bishop of Ely said to two Magdalene ordinands: 'I generally find men of your College ... better informed in divinity than most others'; in the first twenty-three years of the Norrisian Prize for Divinity (1781–1803) Magdalene men won it thirteen times.[27] The first friends and followers of Charles Simeon, the great Cambridge Evangelical, came from Magdalene. Many years afterwards he said: 'Forty years ago, I had none but Magdalen men at my parties. I hope religion in that College may be like leprosy in a house – impossible to be got out again without pulling it all to pieces.'[28] But a reputation for saintliness did Magdalene no good among more worldly circles in Cambridge. They were described as 'rippish quizzes' – in other words, prigs, or self-conscious eccentrics. J. F. M. Wright, detailing the particularities of Cambridge colleges in the 1820s, remarked that though Magdalene's special piety had long departed and that wine was now drunk there as copiously as anywhere else, 'the "Maudlin men" were, at one time, so famous for Tea-drinking, that the Cam, which licks the very walls of the college, is said to have been absolutely rendered unnavigable with Tea-leaves'.[29]

---

[25] Quoted in Walsh, 'Magdalene Evangelicals', p. 506.

[26] Quoted in Walsh, 'Magdalene Evangelicals', p. 506, and p. 503 for the following quotation. Nevertheless, Deverel graduated in 1802.

[27] Not fifteen as is stated by Walsh: Tanner, *Historical Register*, p. 312.

[28] Quoted in Walsh, 'Magdalene Evangelicals', p. 503.

[29] *Alma Mater*, vol. II, pp. 201–2.

Magdalene's Evangelicals tended to have self-contained and carefully protected lives. Three – Cocker, Jerram, and Thomason – occupied all the rooms over the library in the early 1790s, 'so that we were never disturbed or interrupted in our studies or social intercourse by others whose habits, taste, or pursuits differed from our own'.[30]

> Our terms of intimacy were so familiar we were constantly in the habit of using each other's rooms, books, or whatever either of us wanted, that the other had, without the least ceremony. Pleasanter days than these I never spent; they remind me of that happy state when the first Christians had all things common, parted their goods as each of them had need, and continued daily with one accord eating their bread with gladness and singleness of heart and praising God.[31]

With others of like mind these three men

> formed among ourselves two or three parties of religious persons, for the purpose of reading together some portion of the Greek Testament – discussing some topic given out at a previous Meeting for consideration, – and concluding the whole with singing a hymn and prayer. These meetings and exercises I found peculiarly useful and interesting. They served to keep alive the spark of personal religion, which was in danger of being quenched by the uncongenial pursuit of mathematical subjects, or the impure mythology and profane poetry, which constitute the daily routine of study.[32]

These young men were sententious, proffering pietistic opinions on matters usually regarded in a more worldly way. The following letter written in December 1796 by Samuel Settle, an Elland pensioner contemporary with Jerram, disparages Cambridge competitiveness not because he was indolent or uninterested in a fellowship, or because of the arid nature of the tripos course, but because spiritual attainment was a worthier goal than examination success.

> I have been busy in attending lectures; but the term ended yesterday, and now I must be up to the head and ears in reading for the schools.

[30] James Jerram (ed.), *The Memoirs and a Selection from the Letters of the Rev. Charles Jerram* (London, 1855), pp. 81–2. [31] J. Sargent, *The Life of the Rev. T. T. Thomason* (London, 1833), p. 39.
[32] *Memoirs of Charles Jerram*, pp. 83–4.

My neglect of reading in the summer has thrown me into deep confusion. However, there is divine reading which cannot, or at least, ought not to be omitted. But alas, we are purblind; present objects engage our view, and we lose sight of that which is invisible. Custom has a powerful influence on the mind, and we cannot brook the idea of being exceeded by those whose abilities are only equal or perhaps inferior to our own. But this is a weak argument when placed in competition with the affairs of the soul. Inferiority is no disgrace provided religion be kept in the heart. We ought to labour for an immortal crown, and I wish it were my concern in a far greater degree. 'Can a man walk on coals and not be burnt?'[33]

On the other hand the manuscript diary of Romaine Hervey, an Elland pensioner who came up in 1796, shows that the lives of some Magdalene Evangelicals were far from solemn. He and his friends swam at Queens' bridge, fished, in the winter skated at Chesterton, and played battledore and shuttlecock in the college hall. They were facetiously hearty – quite a common Evangelical characteristic. On 6 November 1797: 'Evening went to see the squibs and rockets in the market place.[34] Batley brought home serpents and fired them in Barrs' room which burnt Barrs' face most dangerously.' Two weeks later, 'Green attempting to pull Dornford's nose in Hall had a scuffle with him.'

> 1798. March 19. Supped with Paine where Hartley and Porter quarreled. The challenge was given but made up. As I went away Paine threw a mug of ale downstairs after me, as they had done a bason of water on Barrs and Foster before . . . May 10. Supped with a large party at Gilmore's, sung and romped till 12 o'clock, when Farish who was on the look out chased (me) to my room. May 16. Supped with Hartley of Trinity, made horrible noise with post horns etc.

Like so many Magdalene Evangelicals Hervey became a clergyman in due course, serving as a curate in Lincolnshire.

'These Magdalene Evangelicals were unquestionably the most significant group ever produced in the College, and had an impact on British and even world history in the early years of the

---

[33] Thomas Hervey, *Life of the Rev. Samuel Settle* (Colmer, Hants., 1881), p. 40.
[34] These quotations are taken from Walsh, 'Magdalene Evangelicals', p. 507. It seems that Bonfire Night was celebrated one day late.

nineteenth century quite disproportionate to their numbers.'[35] The most famous were the Grant brothers, Robert and Charles, the sons of a director of the East India Company; both matriculating in 1795 they were linked to Magdalene through fellowships until 1814. Charles became Lord Glenelg and Secretary of State for the Colonies, his Evangelical conscience revealing itself in his concern for native rights. Robert became Governor of Bombay, and also wrote the hymn 'O worship the King, all glorious above'.

Evangelicals like Wilberforce and the Magdalene fellows Farish and Richard Hey (Samuel's brother) promoted the spread of the Gospel to newly discovered lands in Africa and the Pacific; and it was natural for them to turn to Magdalene for missionaries, such as the five Magdalene men, recruited as undergraduates in the 1780s and 1790s, who were among the first Protestant evangelists in India, Australia and New Zealand. This movement, writes the college historian Ronald Hyam, was 'one of the foremost exertions of the western world from the 1790s'; and 'at no other point in more than five centuries has the College intersected so influentially with the main current of national and indeed world history'.[36]

However, Evangelical domination of Magdalene lasted only a few decades, though the sect retained a presence of sorts till the 1820s. The coming of new men to the top of the college hierarchy was crucial in effecting change. Samuel Hey was replaced as president by Thomas Kerrich, a distinguished antiquarian and artist, and from 1797 the University Librarian. His dislike of Evangelicalism was shared by Thomas Gretton, in 1797 appointed Master of Magdalene. Discouraged by the attitude of these new men Evangelicals began to send their pupils and sons to other colleges.

Chief among them was Queens', whose Evangelical ethos was created by one man, as it had been at Magdalene.[37] The driving force at Queens' was Isaac Milner, who matriculated in 1770 and was elected a fellow in 1776 and master in 1788 at the age of

[35] Eamon Duffy in Cunich, Hoyle, Duffy, and Hyam, *A History of Magdalene College*, p. 191, and pp. 191–4 for what follows.
[36] Quoted in Cunich, Hoyle, Duffy, and Hyam, *A History of Magdalene College*, p. 192.
[37] In a later generation the Evangelical Charles Clayton, tutor of Gonville and Caius from 1848 to 1865 and vicar of Holy Trinity, provided another example of how one man could influence a society dramatically; Caius was in his day the leading Evangelical college. See Christopher Brooke, *Gonville and Caius College*, pp. 218–19.

thirty-eight.[38] Until then Queens' was not Evangelical in spirit; there is for example not a hint of it in Philip Yorke's many letters concerning his life there in the 1770s. Milner is said to have been the only student in the college who refused to sign the petition against subscription to the Thirty-nine Articles in 1772, but in 1786 he had made his views quite plain in his act for the BD degree, on the theme of justification by faith alone. It remains a mystery why a man of such opinions, whose dictatorial character was certainly known to his colleagues, was elected master three years later by men mostly renowned for their liberalism. At all events, very quickly Milner transformed the college into an Evangelical stronghold, using his power as master to fill tutorships and by his ruthless and determined character forcing fellows who disagreed with him into college livings or resignation; the intolerant atmosphere of the early 1790s, which Milner could exploit to represent his own reactionary opinions as the best defence against revolutionary atheism, also worked in his favour. Gunning, whose portrait of Milner as a self-absorbed, gluttonous yet hypochondriacal despot is skilful but one-sided, remarks that 'after a few years, no one thought of offering the slightest opposition to his will'.[39] As Magdalene had been before it Queens' became the leading Evangelical college, a position it held until after Milner's death in 1820. Milner was not, however, the *spiritual* head of Cambridge Evangelicalism: the man who by his ministrations and preaching added notably to the number of Evangelicals in the university, and to whom they looked for guidance, was Charles Simeon. His prominence in the movement warrants detailed consideration, and to him we now turn.

CHARLES SIMEON

Charles Simeon was a fellow of King's and perpetual curate of Holy Trinity, from 1782 to 1836, and a hero to men like Jerram and Thomason.[40] 'He laid great stress in his preaching upon the depravity of human nature, the divinity and atonement of Christ,

---

[38] Much is said about Milner in chapter 11, pp. 417–18. What follows is based on Twigg, *A History of Queens' College*, pp. 170–8, including the quotations.

[39] *Reminiscences*, vol. 1, p. 263, and pp. 257–76 generally.

[40] What follows draws upon William Carus, *Memoirs of the Life of Charles Simeon* (London, 1847), Henry Carr Glyn Moule, *Charles Simeon* (London, 1892), and Smyth, *Simeon and Church Order*.

the justification of a sinner exclusively through the merits and righteousness of the Redeemer, the necessity of the agency of the Holy Spirit to restore the divine image, and final perseverance.'[41] The son of a Reading attorney, Simeon became an Eton colleger, and thus automatically a scholar at King's, then still an Etonian preserve. Its undergraduates were entitled to graduate without examination,[42] and at King's we hear of Simeon's studying Aristotle's *Ethics* rather than the stringent mathematical course required for the Senate House Examination. As a scholar of King's Simeon was entitled to a fellowship, which he might retain for life provided that he did not marry. In the event he did not, and so Simeon was a fellow until the age of eighty-seven, as a result of his election at Eton in childhood – a striking example of an anomaly in Old Cambridge.

Simeon's background was Anglican, though not markedly devout; yet within three months of his coming to King's in January 1779 he experienced a religious conversion of the sort characteristic of Evangelicals. It is necessarily hard to explain, the process appearing to be stimulated by a summons from the college authorities to take Holy Communion in three weeks' time. Realising that spiritual preparation was essential,

> without a moment's loss of time, I bought the *Whole Duty of Man* (the only religious book that I ever heard of) and began to read it with great diligence;[43] at the same time calling my ways to remembrance, and crying to God for mercy; and so earnest was I in these exercises, that within the three weeks I made myself quite ill with reading, fasting, and prayer. From that day to this, blessed, for ever blessed, be my God, I have never ceased to regard the salvation of my soul as the one thing needful.

The task of preparation led to self-scrutiny and intense awareness of his sinfulness, the usual Evangelical phenomenon, and like others experiencing the spiritual awakening Simeon seems to exaggerate through his vehemence the nature of the sins he is bewailing. 'I continued with unabated earnestness to search out, and mourn over

[41] From an obituary sermon by Samuel Thodey, a Dissenting minister of Cambridge, quoted in Hugh Evan Hopkins, *Charles Simeon of Cambridge* (London, Hodder & Stoughton, 1977), p. 180.

[42] For the exceptional character of King's College at this time see chapter 3, pp. 86–8.

[43] Carus, *Charles Simeon*, pp. 6–7, and pp. 7–9 for the following quotations. The *Whole Duty of Man* (1658) is a devotional work which discusses in detail man's duties towards God and his fellow men.

the numberless iniquities of my former life; and so greatly was my mind oppressed with the weight of them, that I frequently looked upon the dogs with envy; wishing, if it were possible, that I could be blessed with their mortality, and they be cursed with my immortality in my stead.' This unhappiness continued for three months, until in Easter week, as he wrote, 'I sought to lay my sins upon the sacred head of Jesus; and on the Wednesday began to have a hope of mercy ... and on the Sunday morning (Easter-day, April 4) I awoke early with those words upon my heart and lips, "Jesus Christ is risen to-day; Hallelujah! Hallelujah! Hallelujah!" From that hour peace flowed in rich abundance into my soul.'

Ordained deacon in May 1782, Simeon was given charge of Holy Trinity in November, when he was twenty-three and one of the very few Evangelical clergymen in Cambridge. For many years this man of striking physiognomy (at Eton he was given the nickname 'Chin' Simeon) was a familiar figure in Trumpington Street – his dress often exceptionally fine for a don, and inseparable from his umbrella. Blessed with exceptional energy, he habitually rose early and applied himself to the mastery of the scriptures that was apparent in his sermons; his learned guide to the composition of sermons, in twenty-one volumes, sold in quantity and brought him £5,000, an unusual sum even in a pietistic age.

Through the ministrations of his many disciples Simeon's influence spread at home and abroad. Simeon was active in promoting foreign missions, particularly in India. His curates Henry Martyn and Thomas Thomason were among the many followers who went there as missionaries. Simeon's adroit organising ability created a permanent Evangelical presence in key parishes like Cheltenham; he set up the Simeon Trust in 1817 to purchase rights of patronage. The 1851 religious census showed that in Simeon Trust parishes 44 per cent of parishioners attended church on the crucial day, as against 25 per cent in nearby parishes of unknown churchmanship.[44] This difference is a tribute to the more effective pastorate of their clergy, and to Simeon's own work as the most important single influence on many generations of Cambridge ordinands.

[44] Bebbington, *Evangelicalism in Modern Britain*, pp. 32, 108.

His personality was dominating and intrusive, and certain to create strong reactions, both favourable and hostile. James Stephen, himself an Evangelical, remarked that Simeon was too aware 'of the advantages of his figure'.[45] There is a hint of vanity in the balanced and sympathetic portrait by Abner Brown, a Northamptonshire clergyman who had known Simeon well at Cambridge, and found in him 'the courtly polish of the old school',[46] but also a shrewd helpfulness which made him 'cheer the drooping young Minister with an encouraging promise out of the Word of Truth, or with some pithy remark, grounded on a common-sense view of the circumstances of his Ministry!' Though Simeon was prone to irritability, it quickly subsided, and was balanced by 'the warm and eager manners of a foreigner, with an English heart beneath them', which made him express affections openly – a common Evangelical characteristic.

A key to his ascendancy was his power as a preacher. The Evangelical Francis Close, perpetual curate of Cheltenham and later Dean of Carlisle, recalled one sermon in his obituary address.[47]

> He was preaching upon those striking words: 'All day long I have stretched forth my hands unto a disobedient and gainsaying people' (Rom. 10: 20, 21). And after having urged all his hearers to accept the proffered mercy, he reminded them that there were those present to whom he had preached Christ for more than thirty years, but they continued indifferent to a Saviour's love; and pursuing this train of expostulation for some time, he at length became quite overpowered by his feeling, and he sank down in the pulpit and burst into a flood of tears, and few who were present could refrain from weeping with him.

For John Stoughton, a Dissenting minister with knowledge of many preachers, the chief impression of Simeon was of a man 'not penetrating like dew, but coming down like "hailstones and coals of fire". I was struck with the preacher's force, even vehemence. He spoke as one who had a burden from the Lord to deliver – as one

---

[45] James Stephen, *Essays in Ecclesiastical Biography* (5th edn, London, 1867), p. 575. From 1849 to his death James Stephen was Regius Professor of Modern History: see chapter 6, pp. 243–9.
[46] Abner William Brown, *Recollections of the Conversation Parties of the Rev. Charles Simeon* (London, 1863), pp. 32–41.   [47] Quoted in Hopkins, *Charles Simeon*, p. 66.

who, like Paul, felt, "Woe unto me if I preach not the Gospel!"[48] Still, as his usually enthusiastic biographer records, Simeon's idiosyncratic style, the gesticulations accompanied by 'the usual fervid moulding of his face', disconcerted many.[49]

> Occasionally indeed his gestures and looks were almost grotesque from the earnestness and fearlessness of his attempts to illustrate or enforce his thoughts in detail . . . At that time such manifestations of feeling were very unusual in the pulpit; and it is therefore highly probable, that the opposition and ridicule he encountered, in the earlier part of his ministry, may be attributed as much to the manner as to the matter of his preaching.

When he went to Holy Trinity in 1782, Simeon faced great suspicion as a 'Methodist', even though he declared that 'he did not merely deem the Church preferable to Nonconformity, but honestly believed the Church right, and the principles of Dissent wrong'.[50] His parishioners elected his predecessor's curate, John Hammond, to the Sunday afternoon lectureship, so that Simeon could preach only on Sunday morning, a bad time for servants. He therefore began a Sunday evening service, an innovation that 'attracted some attention. In the college chapels it was no novelty; but in a parish church it conveyed at once the impression, that it must be established for the advancement of . . . what the world would call, Methodism.' In any case, the church was soon locked against him, and he had to wait till 1790 to get the churchwardens' permission to restore the evening service.

Undergraduates disturbed Simeon's preaching. Gunning wrote:[51]

> For many years (I speak from my own personal knowledge), Trinity church and the streets leading to it were the scenes of the most disgraceful tumults. In vain did Simeon, with the assistance of persons furnished with white wands, exert themselves to preserve order in the church; in vain did Professor Farish, who as Moderator was well known and popular with the undergraduates . . . station

---

[48] J. Stoughton, *Religion in England* (2 vols., London, 1884), vol. I, p. 124. See also Georgina King Lewis, *John Stoughton D.D. A Short Record of a Long Life* (London, 1898).

[49] Carus, *Memoirs*, pp. 53–4, and pp. 63–4 for the next quotation.

[50] Abner William Brown, *Recollections of Simeon's Conversation Parties*, p. 12. For what follows, see Carus, *Memoirs*, esp. pp. 40–6, and p. 88 for the quotation.

[51] *Reminiscences*, vol. II, p. 147.

himself at the outside door to prevent improper conduct to the persons leaving the church.

It was comparatively easy to proceed against non-students in the disturbances through the city authorities,[52] but 'university-men were amenable only to their own statutes, and punishable only in their own court'; for some time tutors ignored Simeon's complaints, but eventually the Vice-Chancellor was helpful 'far beyond my most sanguine expectations'.[53] Offenders were made to read a public apology during service at Holy Trinity. This seems to have prevented further trouble.

But for many years Simeon faced the hostility of Herbert Marsh, a fellow of St John's and one of the most learned theologians in the university, whose word was bound to be heeded if not assented to; in 1807 he became the Lady Margaret Professor of Divinity in recognition of his talents. In 1805 he preached a series of sermons before the university, attacking the doctrine of justification by faith alone, and alleging that the depreciation of good works that it entailed gave a licence to immoral living. These animadversions on Calvinism were directed against Simeon and Milner and by no means did justice to their assessment of the value of good works.[54] The dispute grumbled on for years, and became absorbed into a lengthy wrangle over the Bible Society. Founded in 1804, the society was based on co-operation between Dissenters and some Anglicans for the limited purpose of disseminating Bibles. Marsh's objections were to the co-operation itself, and to the circulation of Bibles unaccompanied by Prayer Books, which he thought a disparagement of the Anglican liturgy. He made further accusations of Calvinism too, in his many contributions to this war of sermons and pamphlets in 1811.[55] A subsidiary dispute was the proposal by 200 undergraduates (to be equated with the following that Simeon had by this time built up in the university) to found a branch of the Bible Society in Cambridge itself. Made at one of the most anxious

---

[52] Carus, *Memoirs*, pp. 89–93 for these lines.
[53] It is not possible to discover who this Vice-Chancellor was.
[54] J. E. B. Mayor, ed., *History of the College of St. John . . . by Thomas Baker* (2 vols., Cambridge, 1869), vol. II, pp. 775–6. Baker, 1656–1740, was an eminent antiquarian; his MS history of the college was unpublished until Mayor edited it and added much material.
[55] Carus, *Memoirs*, pp. 293–320, and Hopkins, *Charles Simeon*, pp. 76–9. Many of the sermons and pamphlets generated by this dispute are listed in Mayor, *Baker's St. John's*, vol. II, pp. 809–64.

periods of the Napoleonic Wars, and arousing fears of the contamination of undergraduates by subversive French ideas, the proposal 'met with strong opposition from the leading members of the University, who considered that if the young men assumed the character of a deliberating body, it would be productive of great mischief to the discipline of the University'.[56] The undergraduates were persuaded to act only with the concurrence of their seniors, and in due course a meeting was held in the Town Hall under the chairmanship of the Earl of Hardwicke. Dr Marsh continued his contentions, but as Gunning remarks 'this unprotestant mode of opposing the meeting disgusted many persons who were not originally friends to the Society'. The attacks on Simeon seem to have ceased at about this time, thirty years after his coming to Holy Trinity.

Meanwhile despite obstacles Simeon had been ministering to his congregation. Very soon after his coming to Holy Trinity he added prayer meetings to the scheduled services, and in 1796 he divided the 120 followers he then had into six religious societies, meeting each of them once a month. He took this idea from the Methodists,[57] who found such meetings useful 'for the keeping of their respective members in one compact body. Where nothing of that kind is established, the members of any church are only as a rope of sand, and may easily be scattered with every wind of doctrine, or drawn aside by any proselyting sectary. What influence can a minister maintain over his people, if he does not foster them as a brood under his wings?' If he did not, 'they would infallibly go to the dissenting meetings'.[58]

Through regular meetings Simeon attracted a large following among 'gownsmen' intending to take Holy Orders.[59] Every Friday evening at 6 pm sixty or more would assemble in his rooms in King's in a circle round him, 'every one asking what questions he would, and receiving an answer longer or shorter as might be', on scriptural and church matters, the talking being 'as much as possible left to Simeon himself'.[60] It is a measure of Simeon's wide influence

---

[56] Gunning, *Reminiscences*, vol. II, p. 278, and p. 279 for the next quotation.
[57] Carus, *Memoirs*, pp. 138–9.   [58] Carus, *Memoirs*, pp. 45–6.
[59] Details are given in Abner W. Brown, *Recollections of Simeon's Conversation Parties*, pp. 42–55.
[60] Pp. 53–4, and p. 47 for what follows.

that very unusually for a parochial clergyman of modest ecclesiastical status he had an annual meeting for twenty or thirty clergymen from many parts of Britain; they discussed 'scriptural and parochial subjects' in Thomas Thomason's house in Little Shelford.

Through these several sorts of gathering Simeon was a guide to men who took the Evangelical message into many parishes. George Eliot's Amos Barton, whose 'Christian experiences had been consolidated at Cambridge under the influence of Mr Simeon', was the curate of Shepperton, in 'a flat ugly district' of coalmines and handloom weavers, recognisable as North Warwickshire, that George Eliot recalled from her youth, 'a troublesome district for a clergyman'.[61] Patrick Bronte was just such another poor and devout Evangelical whose religious principles were consolidated by Simeon. Coming from County Down to Cambridge in 1802 with a view to becoming ordained, he matriculated at St John's; it was the college of his Evangelical friend in Drumballyroney, the Reverend Thomas Tighe, and it was also able to admit him to a sizarship, without which a Cambridge education would have been impossible for him.[62] The tutor of St John's, James Wood, was himself an Evangelical, and so was Henry Martyn, a fellow, who for some time was to be Simeon's curate at Holy Trinity. The survival of correspondence enables us to see how Patrick Bronte's meagre funds were supplemented by gifts from prominent Evangelicals, in ways probably enjoyed by other young men.

Learning of Bronte's acute poverty Martyn wrote immediately to John Sargent early in 1804.[63] In the eighteen months since Bronte entered St John's, Martyn wrote,

> he has received *no* assistance from his friends who are incapable of affording him any – Yet he has been able to get on in general pretty well by help of Exhibitions &c which are given to our sizars. Now however, he finds himself reduced to great straits & applied to me just before I left Cambridge to know if assistance could be procured for him from any of those societies, whose object is to maintain pious young men destined for the ministry.

[61] 'The Sad Fortunes of the Reverend Amos Barton', chapter 2, in *Scenes of Clerical Life* (1858).
[62] Juliet Barker, *The Brontes* (London, Weidenfeld, 1994), pp. 1–14.
[63] Juliet Barker, *The Brontes*, p. 11. Sargent was an Etonian and at the time of writing had just graduated BA and gained a fellowship. He fell under Simeon's influence in Cambridge and was a prominent Evangelical; he became rector of Graffham, Sussex.

Sargent contacted Henry Thornton, another leading Evangelical, and Thornton's cousin William Wilberforce; each man agreed to give Bronte £10 annually. Without this help it is unlikely that Bronte could have continued in St John's.

A contemporary of Patrick Bronte, and from an equally humble background, was another St John's sizar, Henry Kirke White.[64] Born in 1785 the son of a Nottingham butcher, he began in his fifteenth year, when he was an attorney's clerk, a prodigious course of bookish self-advancement, like the famous achievement of the cobbler Thomas Cooper. Overwork was attended by religious turmoil; White was 'converted' from deism by an Evangelical friend. Like Cooper a generation later he wished to go to Cambridge, and unlike Cooper he succeeded. A book of verse brought encouragement from Robert Southey, and admission to St John's. Kirke White was to die of consumption at the start of his second year, but meanwhile his sizarship was supplemented by Simeon, an act typical of the support he gave to many struggling Evangelicals. Kirke White wrote of his mentor, 'his conduct towards me has ever been fatherly'.[65]

Simeon built up a circle of adherents in Cambridge. To some extent they were set apart from the generality of undergraduates. In his shrewd and clever survey of the dozen social types of 'Cantabs' – the reading, boating, sporting, and 'Unionic' Cantabs and so on – John D. Lewis in the middle of the century distinguished the 'ultra-Evangelical Undergraduate, or "Sim"' from those professing other sorts of piety.[66] Forgetful of Simeon's own precepts 'on universal benevolence and philanthropy' the charity of 'Sims', 'appears to consist in condemning every one but themselves; who tell you that the theatre is the workshop of Satan; the ball room, a rendezvous for lost spirits; novels, the literature of hell'. The Sim, with his 'peculiar jargon, borrowed from the sacred Scriptures . . . speaks of A. as "a young man actuated no doubt by highly benevolent motives, but a sad *worldling*" . . . ; of B. as "one who has not yet experienced the *saving change*"; of C. as "one of the

---

[64] What follows is taken from the biographical notice by 'C.B.W.' of Trinity College in pp. i–xvi of *The Remains of Henry Kirke White* (rev. edn, Cambridge, 1839).
[65] Henry Kirke White to his brother Neville, 12 August 1806, in *Remains*, pp. 344–5.
[66] 'John Smith', *Sketches of Cantabs*, pp. 127–49.

unconverted" ... A. is a Tractarian perhaps, B. has been seen in a theatre, C. at a race-course.' An example of the way in which in its extreme form the Evangelical sensibility jarred on most Cantabrigians is given to us in Kirke White's comment on Tom Moore's chaste lyrics:

> I think Mr Moore's love poems are infamous, because they subvert the first great object of poetry – the encouragement of the virtuous and the noble, and metamorphose nutritious aliment into poison. I think the muses are degraded when they are made the handmaids of sensuality, and the bawds of a brothel.

While avoiding such extreme judgements Simeon declared that 'English literature is only partially of value to the student here; use it cautiously, and step as with your toes in mud.' Prose was much more help to students than poetry, while 'mathematics *are* important; they will enable us to think clearly'.[67] Simeon was clever, shrewd, articulate, and infinitely learned in the scriptures. But his mind was narrow and closed, and above all, incurious and instinctively hostile to new ideas. Seeing his beliefs as utterly unproblematic, he felt no need to defend them against critics. Invited by atheists to a public disputation he advised his students to 'go not near the unholy place. Let not unhallowed curiosity tempt you.' It was necessary not to ask questions about the 'butchery' in the Old Testament, since 'the natural tendency of the Old Testament is to make us sceptics, if we come in pride to the reading of it'.[68] After the notable French palaeontologist Cuvier published his views on the great antiquity of the earth in 1827 Simeon, without giving evidence of knowing much about them, had 'no doubt' that the 'airy systems of Cuvier' would be found 'to be erroneous'. 'The *literal* meaning of Scripture will be discovered to be the true solutions of creation and of geology.' While Whewell was wrestling with scientific discoveries and seeking to accommodate them to his Anglicanism, Simeon advised those attending his 'conversation parties' to 'beware of feeding upon science, lest your souls be starved'.[69] In these characteristics Simeon was typical of

---

[67] Abner W. Brown, *Recollections of Simeon's Conversation Parties*, p. 194.
[68] Abner W. Brown, *Recollections of Simeon's Conversation Parties*, pp. 329–30, and p. 133 for the next quotation.   [69] Abner W. Brown, *Recollections of Simeon's Conversation Parties*, p. 326.

many Evangelicals, in being intellectually 'narrow and naively reactionary. The wider problems of faith and reason did not trouble' them. They scarcely looked beyond the Bible. 'Philosophy, science and the arts were things intrinsically of this world, and of no consequence for eternity.'[70]

Simeon died in his rooms in King's on 13 November 1836, and the size of the congregation at his funeral six days later showed how great a following had been created since his early days in the university. Joseph Romilly observed:[71]

> some hundreds of A.M. [i.e. MAs] & underg[raduate]s all in deep mourning: there were so many that tho' walking 4 abreast the procession reached round 3 sides of the great Quadr[rangl]e: it was very touching to see the way in w[hi]ch the inside of the Chapel was thronged by those who had been habitual attend[an]ts at his church:- a large proportion was women and all were in deep mourning.

On Sunday 20 November Romilly heard a funeral sermon from James Scholefield, the Regius Professor of Greek and Simeon's most devoted adherent among the dons. At 6 pm there was a 'huge crowd' at Trinity Church; to get a seat Romilly 'went into the Vestry to Carus & put myself under his guidance'.

Prominent as they were, however, Evangelicals were not the only varieties of Anglican in Cambridge; to the others we now turn.

[70] Reardon, *Religious Thought*, pp. 29–30.
[71] Bury, *Romilly's Cambridge Diary 1832–42*, p. 106.

Chapter 10

CAMBRIDGE RELIGION: THE MID-VICTORIAN YEARS

THE ORTHODOX TRADITION

PARTIES WITHIN THE CHURCH OF ENGLAND, 1830–1870

'It has been the fate of the Church of England from the beginning to be divided into parties', remarked J. B. Marsden in 1856,[1] and between 1800 and 1830 two chief groupings were to be discerned, the Evangelicals and the High Church or Orthodox. They were united in loyalty to the Established status of the Anglican church, the Protestant character that it owed to the Reformation, and its hierarchical episcopal structure. They accepted the doctrines of justification by faith and the authority of Scripture, as they did the Thirty-nine Articles and the Book of Common Prayer. Within this consensus there were differences of emphasis which led sometimes to acrimony, for example Herbert Marsh's long campaign against Simeon and the Evangelicals. The Orthodox valued the authority of the church and its function to interpret the Bible; they were greatly attached to episcopacy and distinguished between continental Protestants (above all the Lutherans) who had retained it and the Dissenters who had not. Evangelicals, on the other hand, emphasised the importance of an individual's apprehension of scripture, and sometimes welcomed links with the Dissenting churches.

In the period 1830–70 Anglican unity was put under great strain by two developments that were quite distinct, indeed sharply

---

[1] Quoted in Peter Nockles, 'Church parties in the pre-Tractarian Church of England 1750–1833: the "Orthodox" – some problems of definition and identity', in John Walsh, Colin Haydon and Stephen Taylor, eds., *The Church of England c. 1689–1833. From Toleration to Tractarianism* (Cambridge University Press, 1993), p. 334. What follows is based on this essay, esp. pp. 334–44, and Paul Avis, *Anglicanism and the Christian Church. Theological Resources in Historical Perspective* (Edinburgh, T. & T. Clark, 1989), pp. 157–88.

opposed – Tractarianism and the Broad Church movement. The Broad Church was in part an attempt to come to terms with a third development, the growth of disbelief in Christianity, at least as it had usually been represented. These diverse and contradictory tides of opinion are examined in this chapter. Originating in Oxford, Tractarianism took a different shape in Cambridge, and the Cambridge Camden Society and its architectural emphasis is the subject of one section. Two more look at leading Cambridge dons to suggest attitudes within Orthodoxy. William Whewell was very much in the tradition of Waterland and Hallifax. He set Revelation above natural religion, and, despite his great eminence in science, regarded the scientific discoveries of the age as confirming the truths of Revelation rather than conflicting with them. Whewell was not tempted by Tractarianism. Nor was the other don to be considered in detail, Julius Charles Hare. A deeply ambivalent figure who offered incompatible views simultaneously, Hare's career suggested the strains within Anglicanism, but also its breadth, its willingness to embrace a wide variety of opinions yet stay a united church beneath the grumbling and the tension. Hare's life reveals indeed the limited utility of the notion of 'party' with respect to Anglicanism; it was subject to contention, but it was not polarised. On the one hand intensely suspicious of 'Romanising' tendencies and often sympathetic towards Evangelicals, Hare was also a prophet of Christian unity, and an innovator in biblical criticism, an element in the growth of scepticism and the Broad Church. His medley of sentiments was influenced by the equally paradoxical Coleridge, whose presence broods over these pages and cannot be ignored in any assessment of Cambridge Anglicanism. Lastly, the growth of unbelief is considered with particular respect to two Cambridge men, Charles Darwin and Leslie Stephen.

TRACTARIANISM AND THE CAMBRIDGE MOVEMENT

On 14 July 1833 a fellow of Oriel College, John Keble, gave the annual assize sermon in Oxford, choosing the theme 'National Apostasy'. The sermon discussed the interference of the state in the affairs of the Church of Ireland: that is, the Irish Church Temporalities Act that suppressed some bishoprics to provide augmentation for poor livings in Ireland.[2] The act was paralleled by the plans of successive governments in the 1830s and 1840s to rationalise the church's resources in England and Wales. The programme seemed sensibly pragmatic to some clerics and laymen at the time, but to others, notably High Churchmen, it was gravely offensive. High Churchmen valued the close union of church and state, seeing the state's role as protective, but now it seemed in 1833 that the Whig government was intent on an Erastian policy, to make the church the state's creature.

John Henry Newman later wrote: 'I have ever considered and kept the day, [of Keble's sermon] as the start of the religious movement of 1833.'[3] It stimulated a discussion in Oxford on the true nature of the Church of England, in which besides Newman two other High Churchmen, Keble and Edward Pusey, were prominent. High Churchmen stressed the church's function as a guardian and interpreter of doctrine; informed by a deep sense of history, they saw the Church's authority as derived from the Protestant Reformation. Newman and his associates came to see the roots of the Church of England as more remote, in the Middle Ages. In a series of *Tracts for the Times* they emphasised its Catholicity; Newman's aim, it has been written, was to 'de-Protestantise' the Anglican church. Eventually he came to believe that his rightful place was in the Roman Catholic Church; he 'went to Rome' in 1845. At different times so did others, though not Keble and Pusey, or indeed more than a minority of the Tractarian movement as a whole.

Historians have often omitted Cambridge from their accounts of the movement. Yet there was a 'Cambridge Movement' too, and springing from the same roots. The most prominent member during its early years was John Mason Neale, an undergraduate at Trinity from 1836 to 1840; a brilliant classicist, he failed the Senate House Examination and so had to be content with a poll degree, yet another victim of the tyranny of mathematics.[4] Like Newman he

---

[2] These lines are based on Ian Ker, *John Henry Newman. A Biography* (Oxford, Clarendon, 1988), pp. 80–336, and Avis, *Anglicanism and the Christian Church*, pp. 189–238.

[3] Quoted in Ker, *John Henry Newman*, p. 80.

[4] For what follows see Leon Litvack, *John Mason Neale and the Quest for Sobornost* (Oxford, Clarendon, 1994), pp. 1–62, A. G. Lough, *John Mason Neale – Priest Extraordinary* (Newton Abbot, A. G. Lough, 1975), pp. 1–29, Michael Chandler, *Life and Work of John Mason Neale* (Leominster, Gracewing, 1995), pp. 1–50, and James F. White, *The Cambridge Movement*, pp. 1–116.

came from an Evangelical home, and like him too he moved away from Evangelicalism during his undergraduate years. Neale, a modern historian has written, 'was amazingly quick off the mark and would hit upon something new and have the scheme or the book underway in no time'; he had 'a great many ideas and the impetuous energy, and the needful equipment, to set about to convert the ideas into realities'.[5] During 1839 he came to long for a return to the purity he discerned in the English church in the Middle Ages. He began to date his journal entries according to its festivals, fasted on Fridays, and with his friends began rising at 4.15 to say lauds. Hearing William Carus, Simeon's protégé, preach in Holy Trinity, he recorded 'I thought it a poor sermon... Oh how my taste has changed.'[6] His conversion was largely due to his avid reading of *Tracts for the Times*. To his Trinity friend Edward Boyce he wrote in 1839 'Confine yourself to the O.T. [Oxford *Tracts*] and – so far as I have read them, and that is very nearly all – heart and soul, entirely and completely, do I join with them.'[7]

Neale, Boyce, and Benjamin Webb, another Trinity undergraduate, were active in the formation of the Cambridge Camden Society in May 1839. By 1845 the society had 800 members: 140 were undergraduates, and about the same number were BAs who had, one assumes, joined while they were undergraduates a few years before. In 1850 there were 1,753 undergraduates in the university (Appendix IB), and perhaps it is safe to assume that rather fewer than one in ten joined the Cambridge Camden Society. Of its members, 390 were MAs or doctors; unfortunately there is no way of knowing how many were resident dons, but some fellows were certainly active supporters; among them might be mentioned F. W. Collison of St John's and William Hodge Mill of Trinity, who in 1848 became Regius Professor of Hebrew. The society consisted very largely of Cambridge men, but many (perhaps most) were at any one time non-residents. Neale was typical of many in staying active in the society after graduating and moving to church livings away from Cambridge. In addition, 130 Camdenians were not members of the university, and they included some of the 2

[5] Adam Fox, quoted in Litvack, *John Mason Neale*, p. 14.
[6] Quoted in Litvack, *John Mason Neale*, p. 10.
[7] Quoted in James F. White, *The Cambridge Movement*, p. 26.

archbishops, 16 bishops, 31 peers and MPs, 7 deans or chancellors of dioceses, and 21 archdeacons and rural deans who lent their names in the first few years.

The thrust of the society was architectural, but there was a wide spread of interests and motives among its members. Some members were drawn to the history of Gothic, which the writings of Whewell and Rickman were making one of the epoch's great concerns. Dons like Adam Sedgwick and Samuel Lee, the Regius Professor of Hebrew from 1831 to 1848, were as devout Protestants keen to improve church buildings, but by no means accepted the devotional agenda that Neale and his associates proved to have. In *Church Enlargement and Church Arrangement* (1843) Neale wrote:[8]

> A Church is not as it should be, till every window is filled with stained glass, till every inch of floor is covered with encaustic tiles, till there is a Roodscreen glowing with the brightest tints and with gold, nay, if we would arrive at perfection, the roof and walls must be painted and frescoed. For it may safely be asserted that ancient churches were so adorned.

This statement embodies the beliefs of the most committed Camdenians that architecture reflected the piety of the society creating it, that the most devout age for the English church was the fourteenth century, and that its characteristic architectural style, Decorated, should be adopted when churches were constructed or restored because it would re-create the spirituality that it had originally expressed.[9] Their programme for the English church, developed at length in the *Ecclesiologist* and many other publications, embraced however far more than stone and brick; Neale is now chiefly known for his translation from the Latin of many hymns that he hoped would inspire Anglican congregations with the glories of medieval piety. Whereas the Tractarians were interested above all in doctrine, the Camdenians were drawn to its expression in building and worship: 'though Oxford had for the most part provided the letterpress of the movement, Cambridge was furnishing the illustrations'.[10]

The constitution of the Cambridge Camden Society left effective

[8] Quoted in Litvack, *John Mason Neale*, p. 12.
[9] Neale and other ecclesiologists referred to Decorated as the 'Middle Pointed' style.
[10] E.A. Towle, quoted in Litvack, *John Mason Neale*, p. 7.

power in the hands of a small committee, in which Neale and a few like-minded men were salient. Among them was A. J. Beresford Hope, son of the virtuoso Thomas Hope, while Benjamin Webb, co-founder with Neale, acted as secretary of the society throughout its life, 1839 to 1868. The president of the society in its early years was Thomas Thorp, a fellow of Trinity and Archdeacon of Bristol. He was more measured in his utterance than the young men (Neale above all) who in the society's first few years were responsible for the society's exceedingly dogmatic writings, and he tried, usually without much success, to soften their prescriptive advice concerning church building.

This was most notorious in their attacks in the first issue of the *Ecclesiologist* on a new church, St Paul's, in a rapidly growing district of Cambridge.[11] It was denounced 'as a conspicuous red brick building, of something between Elizabethan and debased perpendicular architecture', its flat roof 'as gay as the roof of the saloon in a first-rate steamship', and above all lacking both an altar and a chancel – often omitted from Protestant churches, but essential for Camdenians. St Paul's was a place where 'the sacraments can scarcely be decently and rubrically administered, and which possibly presents to the unlearned parishioner no mark of distinction from some neighbouring conventicle'. In 1844 George Gilbert Scott was denounced in the *Ecclesiologist* for agreeing to build a Lutheran church in Hamburg:

> How must we characterize the spirit that prostitutes Christian architecture to such an use? If this art means anything,– if it is not a hollow mocking of beauty,– a body without a spirit,– then it symbolizes the whole substance of Catholick teaching, the whole analogy of the Faith. How absurd then, in the first place, to apply it to those who reject that teaching and that faith! . . . Truly absurd is this, in an aesthetical point of view; and what in a moral? . . . We do earnestly trust that Mr Scott's example will not be followed. We are sure that the temporal gains of such a contract are a miserable substitute indeed for its unrealness, and,– we must say it,– its sin.

Neale and his Camdenian friends always denied that they were tempted by Roman Catholicism; they were English Catholics,

[11] For what follows, including the quotations, see White, *The Cambridge Movement*, pp. 117–27.

reviving the traditions of the church of the High Middle Ages. They very often used the term 'Catholic' (or 'Catholick') as a vague term of praise meaning 'invested with sweetness and light'. 'You will always find a love of flowers co-existent with a Catholick state of feeling in a nation', wrote Neale in *Hierologus: or, the Church Tourists* (1843), his most romantic work written when he was twenty-five; he also described a forest as a 'grand Catholic oakwood' and found 'Catholick feeling' in a 'Camdenian field-day' and Trinity College Chapel.[12]

It was inviting dispute to say these things in a nation whose Established Church thought of itself as Protestant, and where inveterate hostility to Popery was being galvanised by Newman's *Tracts*. The harshest criticisms of the society came from Evangelicals,[13] such as James Scholefield, the Regius Professor of Greek and Simeon's chief disciple. Francis Close, a graduate of St John's and in the 1840s perpetual curate of Cheltenham, ran a sustained campaign against the Camdenians. Its tenor is shown by the title of his sermon, *The Restoration of Churches is the Restoration of Popery: Proved and Illustrated from the Authenticated Publications of the 'Cambridge Camden Society'* (London, 1844); it purported 'to show that as Romanism is taught *Analytically* at Oxford, it is taught *Artistically* at Cambridge – that it is inculcated theoretically, in tracts, at one University, and it is *sculptured, painted,* and *graven* at the other'.

1845 was a year of crisis for the Oxford Tractarians and the Cambridge Camdenians. W. G. Ward's book *The Ideal of a Christian Church* (1844) was in fact a eulogy of the Roman Catholic Church, and in February 1845 the Oxford authorities condemned it and revoked his degrees. Meanwhile it was plain that Newman had virtually ceased his career as an Anglican clergyman; he was received into the Roman Catholic Church in October.[14] In Cambridge there was a 'mass exodus of patrons' from the Cambridge Camden Society, including the Chancellor and many bishops, who were perturbed by the society's Catholic tendencies. Because its activities had led to dissension within the university the committee suggested the dissolution of the society, intending to

[12] James F. White, *The Cambridge Movement*, p. 34.
[13] For what follows including the quotations, see James F. White, *The Cambridge Movement*, pp. 135–44. [14] Ker, *John Henry Newman*, pp. 257–315.

found another body not in the academic milieu; but when balloted most members proved to be against dissolution, and legal opinion was that their wishes made continuance necessary.[15] The highly contentious Sixth Anniversary Meeting (or as we would call it the AGM) was held on 8 May 1845, and in the Town Hall because the usual meeting-place, the Philosophical Society's rooms, was too small for the 300 or 400 attending.[16] They included many dons, clergymen from surrounding counties, and architects with a professional interest in the society's utterances. The long meeting was tangled, and must have been as mystifying to members at the time as its copious record makes it appear to us. There were two main disputes, constitutional and religious. The committee had decided that the society's public meetings

> rendered the continuance of their functions injurious to academic order. They felt that under the existing circumstances of the church, there were many matters which made it not right that the Society should be a sort of nucleus, around which the junior members of the University might form a body, the existence of which might be disagreeable to some persons in high station in the University.[17]

They therefore suggested that the society should continue but without public meetings, so as to prevent such frictions, and that the committee should devise new rules for its activities.

At this point, however, Professor Samuel Lee intervened to suggest that the society was too offensive to be allowed to continue at all:[18]

> Young men might very properly spend a portion of their time at Cambridge in the study of Church architecture, with a view to rescuing the parishes in which they might hereafter be located, from the obloquy of having Churches like barns and houses in which they could not reside ... But he could not help thinking there was something more than architecture involved in the proceedings and objects of the committee ...; young men could not avoid being misled by such views as are put forward in the *Ecclesiologist* into arguments in favour of certain church principles, and into certain symbolism which was not Church symbolism, but which had arisen

---

[15] James F. White, *The Cambridge Movement*, pp. 144–9.
[16] The account that follows is based on the full record of the meeting in the *Ecclesiologist*, 4 (1845), pp.1–28. [17] P. 12. [18] Pp.16–17.

out of the Roman Catholic doctrine of the Eucharist. (Hear, hear, and cries of 'Question'.)

Adam Sedgwick, as so often in Cambridge meetings, made a long, rambling and highly emotional speech. He did not agree with Lee that it was 'necessary to smother the society like a mad dog', though 'amputation or depletion might be useful'.[19]

> He was an old member of the Society, and had stuck to it through good report and evil report: he hoped at one time that certain appearances which had manifested themselves on the face of it were like pustulary eruptions of a temporary character, but was sorry to say that those eruptions had now assumed the form of a violent scurvy, damaging the whole constitution and requiring a strong and active remedy.— (Laughter, in which the Professor joined.) . . . Everybody knew that men connected with the Society had sent forth books, the language and principles of which no consistent member of the Church of England could possibly approve of . . . He had attended one meeting of the Society in which the subject of Ecclesiastical Architecture was properly discussed, but afterwards there was a paper read in the course of which it was broadly stated that Cranmer, Latimer and Ridley had suffered death or martyrdom, he knew not which, as a judgment for having consented to the confiscation of monastic property. (Ironical cheers.) This was permitted to go on, and the man who uttered such a detestable insult to the Church of England proceeded without being called to order by the chair. (Confusion.)

The President, Archdeacon Thomas Thorp, asked if notice had been taken by the chair.

> Professor SEDGWICK: I assert that no notice was taken.
> The PRESIDENT: And I assert that Professor Sedgwick is mistaken (hear, hear): that paper was stopped. If a chairman was to stop all irrelevant matter, perhaps we should not have had this discussion; but (*emphatically*) I stopped the reader of that paper. (Prolonged cheers.)

Thorp 'was far from defending all that the Society had done, and all that its members had published, but he did not come before that meeting to accuse people who had done injudicious acts; he had

---

[19] Pp. 20–1.

accused them to themselves'.[20] He wanted to defend the functions the society had adopted, 'in originating, exciting, he might say creating, activity in various departments of art,– in advising upon the furniture and decorations of churches, &c. . . . and it was undeniable that church restoration had been encouraged in places where it would perhaps have been scarcely thought of had it not been for the Society'. His speech 'concluded amid very loud applause', and in due course the meeting approved his wish that a committee should be elected to devise fresh rules for the society. At this point Sedgwick intervened again, much to the irritation of the meeting.[21] When S. N. Stokes, who had graduated at Trinity the previous year, was proposed for the committee Sedgwick 'asked if he was the author of the *Ecclesiastical Calendar*', which he described as 'an insult to the Church and University'.[22]

> Professor SEDGWICK: I believe I know that he is the author, and I denounce him as such before this meeting. (Sensation.)
> The PRESIDENT: I must have some authority here, and I do say that it is as very indecent thing to bring forward a matter which has no bearing except on the personal character of a member of the Society. (Cheers.)
> Professor Sedgwick said that the author of that publication was unfit to be a member of the Society at all.
> The PRESIDENT said if that were the case the Society would not elect him on its Committee . . . [Professor Sedgwick] must, however, stop these somewhat indecorous proceedings. (Applause.)

The impression that emerges from this long and detailed account is of a split in the university like the Oxford quarrels over Tractarianism. Several hundred enthusiasts for medieval English Catholic ritual and architecture denied any leanings towards Roman Catholicism, and were bitterly opposed by men of Protestant views who disbelieved them. S. N. Stokes was elected to the committee: but Sedgwick proved to be right about him after all,

---

[20] Pp. 12, 16.   [21] Pp. 21–3.

[22] Sedgwick was referring to *A Christian Kalendar for the Use of Members of the Established Church Arranged for the Year of Our Lord God MDCCCXLV*, 'by a Lay member of the Cambridge Camden Society' (Cambridge, 1845). This effusion of Roman Catholic sentiment contains the names of many saints not in the Book of Common Prayer, and recommends confession of sins 'to a learned and discreet Priest' – a phrase that in the 1840s would be taken by some to be a touchstone of Popery.

since soon after the fateful meeting Stokes became a Roman Catholic. So did another committee member, F. A. Paley.[23] As a result of the 1845 crisis 121 members, out of a total of 800, left the society by September.

The new committee moved the society to London and renamed it the Ecclesiological Society. It remained faithful to its principles and inspired much church restoration and the Ritualist movement that was active between 1845 and 1900. John Mason Neale was among the first of many clergymen who fell foul of their bishop for Ritualist practices. In 1846 appointed warden of Sackville College, an almshouse in East Grinstead, Neale set up a rood-screen in the chapel and adorned the altar with a cross and candlesticks. A complaint by an Evangelical clergyman to the Bishop of Chichester led to a visitation in 1847. The bishop admonished Neale for the 'frippery with which ... [he had] transformed the simplicity at Sackville College into an imitation of the degrading superstitions of an erroneous Church', and called Neale's innovations 'spiritual haberdashery'. Until 1863 Neale was prohibited from conducting services within the diocese of Chichester.[24]

WILLIAM WHEWELL AND THE USES OF NATURAL THEOLOGY

On Thursday 21 April 1842 Joseph Romilly, a fellow of Trinity, heard the master, William Whewell, preach in the college chapel:[25]

> Sacrament in the College Chapel; I assisted – The Master preached from Proverbs XV.3 'The eyes of The Lord are in every place, beholding the evil & the good'. –:– for the benefit of the Freshmen there was a long passage about the Oedip. Colon.,[26] & the inability of ancient philosophy to show how an offending creature could be reconciled to God: ... There was an eloquent passage where Whewell descanted on the majesty with w[hi]ch Law invested itself,

[23] The grandson of the philosopher. F. A. Paley resigned his St John's fellowship upon his conversion, became a tutor to several Catholic families, and in due course returned to Cambridge as a private classical tutor. He had perhaps a more prolific pen than any other don ever, writing more than fifty books on topics as various as Aeschylus, earthworms, and Gothic architecture.

[24] Litvack, *John Mason Neale*, pp.21–3.

[25] Pickles and Bury, eds., *Romilly's Cambridge Diary 1842–1847*, p.6.

[26] *The Oedipus at Colonus*, by Sophocles.

& that its highest force was derived from its reference to Religion (– by Oathes). – But the sermon was in parts hard and too metaphysical.

Whewell's creative fecundity as a mathematician and natural philosopher and the diverse subtlety of his observations upon these concerns make it easy for us in the late twentieth century to consider him as a scientist of a familiar modern type, and as though his mind were secularised; but it is necessary to remember that he thought of himself first as a clergyman, whose additions to knowledge were inevitably subordinate to, or at least not inconsistent with, the truths of his devout Anglicanism. These enjoyed moral and intellectual priority.

Whewell was an Orthodox Anglican in the tradition of Waterland and Hallifax; he was not Evangelical and nor was he persuaded into Tractarianism in the 1830s. Like many – though not all – in the Orthodox Anglican mainstream Whewell was a Tory whose political beliefs had a doctrinal sanction,[27] which he explained with considerable subtlety in a lengthy statement of his credo written a few months after the sermon just quoted.[28] Whewell declared that 'the truth, which is really true' must 'include and rest upon that which has been true up to the present time'. Fundamental truths 'on which man's well-being, as to his soul, depends ... have been disclosed to former generations, and at one great epoch so fully disclosed, that all our main light must be borrowed from that one Revelation'. No development of our ideas that we might manage could 'obliterate the great leading conditions of the relation of man to his Maker, on which all our spiritual hopes depend. No development of our views, however lively and luminous, can make our catechism false, which we learnt as child, if it were ever true.' And we have to acknowledge that any change which occurs must be slow if it is to be true.'Providence, if He gives *us* the means of discovering truths speculative and practical, has given like means to former generations, and has never withheld them from any generation.' And so, 'there is a great deal of truth already in the

---

[27] On this point see J. C. D. Clark, *English Society 1688–1832: Ideology, Social Structure and Political Practice during the Ancien Régime* (Cambridge University Press, 1985), pp. 387–93.
[28] What follows draws on Whewell's letter of 27 December 1842 to James Garth Marshall of Leeds, in Stair Douglas, *Whewell*, pp. 279–83.

world, and a great deal of it embodied in the frame of society'. Whewell meant by this certain principles 'necessary for the existence and development of men . . . and which are never shaken, except in certain convulsive disorders to which man's career is liable. Such are marriage, property, contracts, government; constitutional government, that is, liberty.' He continued, 'I believe in our National Constitution and in our National Religion. I believe that these embody more of the truth, are better approaches to the true form of Church and State, than have ever yet been established.' But they were accepted

> not as mere formulae, but as living things, as the most essential part of the social and political life of the nation. Therefore that in which I believe is not a dead, stationary, immovable thing, but something which is developed and expanded and renewed with the development and expansion of men's social and political workings. I cannot believe in any Church or State which is not constantly unfolding, enlarging, and renewing itself – which must not have from time to time Reform and Reformation – except we are happier still, and keep up, constantly alive, a formative spirit that makes *reform* unnecessary.

This is Whewell's familiar voice: sounding quite radical but with a profoundly conservative meaning, and advocating changefulness as a means of avoiding real change. And at the root of this sophisticated conservatism is his belief in the religious basis of society.

Much about Whewell reminds us of an earlier Cambridge savant, William Paley; they were alike in being pious Anglicans who used religious arguments in the service of a conservative philosophy, and diverse scientific knowledge in the service of religion. But their versions of religious truth were very different: Whewell was firmly opposed to Paley's ideas, and his opposition goes to the heart of Whewell's Anglicanism.[29] Like others of his generation who were influenced by Coleridge he regarded the system of utilitarian ethics composed by Paley and Bentham as being quite implausible. Its calculus balanced incommensurable sorts of pain and pleasure against each other, so that carried to its full logic a sinful act might be

---

[29] What follows draws on John Hedley Brooke, 'Indications of a Creator: Whewell as Apologist and Priest', in Fisch and Schaffer, *William Whewell. A Composite Portrait*, pp. 149–73. On Paley, see chapter 8, pp. 295–313.

justified if it was thought to bring a net gain of pleasure. Whewell declared that morality leads to happiness, not vice versa, and that 'the morality which depends upon the increase of pleasure alone would make it our duty to increase the pleasures of pigs or geese rather than those of men, if we were sure that the pleasure we could give *them* were greater than the pleasures of men'.[30] The test of morality was conscience, provided that this divinely given faculty were informed by religious instruction based on Revelation: 'reason is not enough . . .; it is religion which gives the hope and reality of a power of enlightenment' to the conscience.

Whewell's career coincided with immense advances in scientific knowledge, to which he greatly contributed. He saw no contradiction between religion and science. The laws of nature were effects of the divine Will, 'rules of his operation and production'.[31] Religion had nothing to fear from enquiries into the natural world, since 'how can this ordering and reasoning be conceived except we suppose an Intelligent Ruler employed in deducing, from the laws, the facts . . . from which we, reversing this course of deduction, can, to those containing principles ascend again'. So Whewell often used the idiom of the natural theologians, for example in his contribution to the *Bridgewater Treatises* (1833).[32] But in arguments of great subtlety he makes clear that the truths of natural theology are necessarily subordinate to the truths of Revelation, and once again that is because reason is an inadequate agent; it prompts the asking of questions, but it does not lead to all the answers. As scientific knowledge increased the area of apparent ignorance increased too: 'as we discover new laws the laws of these laws become more and more mysterious and lose themselves in the darkness which surrounds the throne of light'.[33] Reason cannot explain the purpose of Creation, which was 'another evidence of the infinitely limited nature of the human mind, when compared with the Creative or Constitutive Divine Mind'. Whewell therefore declared that 'it would be presumptuous to suppose that we can enter into [God's purposes] to any but a very small degree'.

[30] Quoted by J. H. Brooke, 'Indications', p. 156, and p. 157 for the next quotation.
[31] Quoted in J. H. Brooke, 'Indications', p. 151, and for the next quotation.
[32] Following a bequest from the Earl of Bridgewater, the *Treatises* were composed by eight authors to demonstrate 'the Power, Wisdom and Goodness of God, as manifested in the Creation'.
[33] These quotations are taken from J. H. Brooke, 'Indications', pp. 166–8.

Like other Victorians Whewell had profound doubts, but about science, not religion. What could science, by its very nature, ever explain? In his examination of Whewell's sermons John Hedley Brooke was struck by one that raised the question 'why the appearances of nature – a starlit sky or the effusive glow of the rising sun – have such a palpable effect on the human spirit. The impression, Whewell insisted, was one "which no mere laws of material nature can account for – which no science can explain".'[34] Whewell 'wished to invest the whole material universe with spiritual significance', but 'no argument from design could meet that requirement'. So

> his appeal was to a divine agency which, directly or indirectly, worked on the human spirit. In this respect the limitations of natural theology were associated with the limitations of science itself: 'as no natural causes, no material agencies, no physical laws, can explain such an operation, we have still, in spite of all the discoveries of natural science, a wide and varied region left to us, in which God's work produces upon our souls, impressions mysterious and inexplicable'.

Whewell talked of science *confirming* faith derived from elsewhere; it might 'feed and elevate ... devotion when it exists'. It was not his purpose to suggest 'new proofs of religious truths', or to remove 'the objections of those who seek in their doctrines an exercise of the reason only without ever referring to their heart and conscience'.[35] While advancing arguments from the natural theologian's repertory Whewell sometimes exhibited a sense of unease, as though he feared seeming to press their claims further than he would wish. In his Bridgewater Treatise, for example, his reservations are shown by the frequency with which he employed the interrogative mode, or double negatives, or sometimes both together: 'What are the habits of thought to which it can appear possible that this could take place without design, intention, intelligence, purpose, knowledge?' Whewell's doubts about the function of natural theology, like the obscurity of diction that they gave rise to, are very far removed from the certainty and clarity of Paley's utterance.

---

[34] J. H. Brooke, 'Indications', pp. 167–8.
[35] These quotations from Whewell are taken from J. H. Brooke, 'Indications', pp. 162–3, and the next quotation from p. 154.

JULIUS CHARLES HARE: FROM WEIMAR TO HERSTMONCEUX

A contemporary of Whewell at Trinity, and like him in the Orthodox centre of the church, was Julius Charles Hare (1795–1855), perhaps the most bookish and erudite Cambridge man of his day. 'The whole house was a library', wrote A.P. Stanley about the rectory at Herstmonceux in which Hare lived for the last twenty years of his life.[36] 'The vast nucleus which he brought with him from Cambridge grew year by year, till not only study, and drawing-room, and dining-room, but passage, and antechamber, and bedrooms were overrun with the ever-advancing and crowded bookshelves.' In the 12,000 volumes on the classics, theology, philosophy, and history, German works predominated: 'No work, no pamphlet of any note in the teeming catalogues of German booksellers escaped his notice.' Though lacking a catalogue Hare 'knew where every book was to be found', and 'for what it was valuable'. He did not wear his learning lightly; his printed sermons were overburdened with notes, and he was marked down as an exceedingly learned don even when many miles distant from Cambridge.

A fellow of Trinity from 1818 to 1844, Hare was non-resident after 1832, as the rector of Herstmonceux in Sussex. Hare's religious views were a puzzling and complicated mixture. Esteeming the Protestant character of the Church of England, he was opposed to Tractarianism and Romanising tendencies. His personal sympathies lay with the Evangelicals, but he differed from them over the nature of religious faith and biblical inspiration, matters that point to Hare's originality as a churchman. He was the first man in Cambridge to be influenced by the philosophical writings of Samuel Taylor Coleridge (and one of the very first in Britain). Coleridgean ideas were not, however, totally integrated into the more traditional repertory of orthodoxy: there was a contradiction between Hare's vehement anti-Popery and his expressions favouring tolerance and church unity that were greatly influenced by Coleridge. As F. D. Maurice's teacher he introduced to Coleridge's ideas the man who was to diffuse them more widely in the Church of England than anybody. So Hare has

---

[36] 'Archdeacon Hare's Last Charge', *Quarterly Review*, 97 (June 1855), pp. 8–9.

plausibly been regarded as one of the first 'Broad Churchmen', and yet he was more Orthodox than most given that title.

Hare came from a Sussex landed family.[37] His parents eloped and spent many years on the Continent; during residence in Italy and in Germany (at Weimar) Julius began to acquire the knowledge of foreign tongues for which he was famous. Between 1806 and 1812 he was at Charterhouse, where he came to know a fellow-pupil, Connop Thirlwall, whose career was closely to parallel his; they were to co-operate in one highly significant venture, a translation of Schleiermacher's study of St Luke's Gospel.[38] In 1812 Hare matriculated at Trinity, where his enthusiasm for letters and disinclination for mathematics led to a poll degree; but as was to happen to Macaulay in 1824, his classical gifts brought him a fellowship in 1818. Disliking the idea of holy orders, for a time Hare studied law in London,[39] but his aversion to law helped to take him back into residence in Trinity in 1822, and to active college work and to ordination. Classical and modern literature was an abiding enthusiasm, and he was one of the few Cambridge dons of the day to be at home in the metropolitan literary scene. He was also one of very few British people of the time to be especially well versed in German literature, and he published translations from the German, including La Motte Fouqué's Gothic tale *Sintram*. With Thirlwall he began in 1831 the *Philological Museum*, devoted, Hare wrote, to 'every subject that concerns antiquity, and can be treated philologically';[40] reflecting the predilections of the Cambridge classical circle, this fruit of their scholarly zeal was too specialised to command a wide enough market, and it soon folded.

The following year, 1832, Hare became the rector of Herstmonceux. His nephew Augustus, who lived close to him in Sussex, described the emotional and unpredictable behaviour of his lovable and infuriating uncle.[41]

> The rugged, almost uncouth presence of the master of the house pervaded everything. The eagerness with which he called for

[37] What follows is based on N. Merrill Distad, *Guessing at Truth. The Life of Julius Charles Hare* (Shepherdstown, W. Va., Patmos, 1979), pp. 3–34. There is an excellent essay on J. C. Hare by his nephew Augustus J. C. Hare in the *DNB*.

[38] See John Connop Thirlwall, *Connop Thirlwall. Historian and Theologian* (London, SPCK, 1936), pp. 1–18.   [39] Distad, *Guessing at Truth*, pp. 35–115.

[40] Distad, *Guessing at Truth*, p. 75.   [41] From Augustus J. C. Hare's essay in the *DNB*.

sympathy over every passing event of public interest, his uncontrolled vehemence where he detected any wrong or oppression, his triumphant welcome of any chivalrous or disinterested action, his bursts of unspeakable tenderness, the hopeless unpunctuality of everything, especially of every meal, the host often setting off on his long evening ramble just as the dinner-bell was ringing, gave a most unusual character to the daily life.

In his memoir of Hare, E. H. Plumptre wrote that he entered on his pastoral duties 'with zeal and eagerness'.[42]

What he had learnt from Wordsworth, in the world of poetry, – reverence for their joys and griefs, the endurance and the devotion of English peasant life,– now became a reality in the range of his own experience. When he found what he recognised as a living faith and love in some girl dying of consumption in a cottage, or an old woman bedridden for life with a broken limb, he looked at them with an enthusiastic admiration, and a desire to sit at their feet and learn from them.

But Hare could never quite conquer 'the original defect of training ... His thoughts and theirs ran in different grooves. He would sit by them, almost weeping in his sympathy, and yet found it hard to say the words they wanted, to talk to them about their ailments, to meet their religious difficulties.' He was often 'silent and embarrassed' in their houses.

When preaching he talked too much, giving point to A. P. Stanley's remark that a 'curious disregard for congruity ... more than any other single cause, marred his usefulness in life',[43] and to his nephew's comment in his *DNB* essay that his sermons were 'over the heads' of his Sussex parishioners, 'who used to say: "Mr Hare, he be not a good winter parson," which meant that he kept them so long in church that they could not get home before dark'. His parishioners thought he was talking down to them, and they misunderstood his homely illustrations. 'He spoke of the danger of men "playing at ninepins with Truth", and they thought he was warning young labourers against beer and skittles.'[44] But his

---

[42] E. H. Plumptre, 'Memoir of J. C. Hare', in J. C. and A. W. Hare, *Guesses at Truth by Two Brothers* (rev. edn, London, 1866), pp. xxxii–xxxiii.

[43] 'Archdeacon Hare's Last Charge', p. 17.

[44] E. H. Plumptre, 'Memoir', p. xxxiv, and pp. xlv–xlvi for what follows.

pleasure in the company of the Cambridge and literary friends he frequently entertained in his rectory suggests that in spirit he never left the university. 'In the midst' of friends like Whewell, Sedgwick, Thirlwall, Herschel, Carlyle, and Max Müller the conversation would be 'genial and unrestrained', Hare 'now listening with delight, now talking with enthusiasm, now reading from the pages of some favourite author, now darting off to fetch some volume from his library, and turning to some passage, known to few others, that bore on the point under discussion'.

In 1840 Hare became Archdeacon of Lewes. He took his duties seriously and discharged them with an efficiency that one might not have expected,[45] pursuing drunken, libidinous and non-resident clergymen, and becoming an enemy of pew-rents like many another archdeacon anxious about the failure of the poor to attend church. 'Uncle Julius', wrote his nephew, 'as soon as he became Archdeacon, used to preach a perfect crusade against pews, and often went, saw and hammer in hand, to begin the work in the village churches with his own hands.'[46] The impression of mis-placed energy that these words convey is confirmed by Edward Plumptre's feline ironies, reminding us that Hare, only too used to preaching to rustics in Herstmonceux and longing for the learned MAs who had endured many a prolix sermon from him in Great St Mary's, leapt at the chance to take on the don's mantle again.[47] Giving his archidiaconal charges to 'numerous and, at least, patient listeners', he then turned to the work 'he most delighted in . . . reading round and round them, and bringing them out in print with copious and elaborate notes'. In this way he tackled all the ecclesiastical questions of the day. 'But', remarked another com-mentator, 'they were less read than they would have been' if Hare 'had not delayed the publication of them till the topics of which they treated had lost their immediate interest'.[48]

In 1849 he was ambitious to return to his 'beloved University' as Regius Professor of Divinity.[49]

[45] Distad, *Guessing at Truth*, pp. 141–7.

[46] Augustus J. C. Hare, *The Story of My Life* (6 vols., 1896–1906), vol. I, p. 113.

[47] E. H. Plumptre, 'Memoir', pp. xl–xli.

[48] F. D. Maurice, 'Introduction' to J. C. Hare, *Charges to the Clergy of the Archdeaconry of Lewes . . . 1840 to 1854* (3 vols., Cambridge, 1856), vol. I, p. i.

[49] Distad, *Guessing at Truth*, pp. 190–1, quoting Hare's letter to Whewell, 31 October 1849.

The many testimonials of gratitude & affection w[hi]ch I have received from students of divinity at Cambridge encourage me to think that, if I were living amongst them & opening my heart and mind to them, I might render them service in helping them to steer among the quicksands by w[hi]ch theological speculation in these days is beset. And it might be of some use to show them that one may admit and recognize whatever is true and valuable in German Theology, and yet retain a positive conviction of all the positive truths of the Gospel.

Whewell and Sedgwick encouraged Hare, while warning him about the 'jealous fears of German Theology, Rationalism & what not' that might greet his candidacy.[50] Hare, though undeterred by these fears, in the end did not stand because he wished to retain his Herstmonceux living in case his uncertain health forced him to resign the Regius chair. Whewell told him that that expedient was unacceptable, no doubt knowing only too well that reform was in the air in Cambridge and that the Graham Commssion was about to descend on the university.

COLERIDGE AND HARE: THE MISSION OF THE VINDICATOR

Hare was proud to acknowledge his reverence for Wordsworth and Coleridge, whose work he defended when it was unfashionable.[51] He dedicated the second edition of *Guesses at Truth*, the volume of aphorisms and spiritual reflections he wrote with his brother Augustus, to Wordsworth, 'My honoured friend': 'For more than twenty years I have cherisht the wish of offering some testimony of my gratitude to him by whom my eyes were opened to see and enjoy the world of poetry in nature and in books.' Hare continued, associating with Wordsworth

> the name of one to whom we [that is, Julius and Augustus Hare] felt an equal and like obligation,– a name which, I trust, will ever be coupled with yours in the admiration and love of Englishmen,– the name of Coleridge. You and he came forward together in a shallow, hard, and worldly age,– an age alien and almost averse from the

---

[50] Distad, *Guessing at Truth*, p. 191, quoting a letter of unclear provenance.
[51] Distad, *Guessing at Truth*, pp. 39–40, 155–7.

higher and more strenuous exercises of imagination and thought, – as the purifiers and regenerators of poetry and philosophy . . . It was a great aim; and greatly have you both wrought for its accomplishment. Many, among those who are now England's best hope and stay, will respond to my thankful acknowledgement of the benefits my heart and mind have received from you both.[52]

The bond between Hare's beliefs and Coleridge's was complicated and indeterminate. Hare's reverence cannot be discounted: Coleridge's profound and poetic utterance inspired Hare thoughout his life, and sometimes Hare took ideas directly from him. In particular, Hare's striking combination of a profound desire for Christian unity with vehement anti-Popery paralleled a similar duality in Coleridge in an uncanny way. But Hare was no mere conduit who transmitted Coleridge's ideas to others. Hare was one of the very few persons in the Britain of his day who was as well versed as Coleridge himself in the German idealist philosophers from whom both men's ideas largely derived, and he seems to have arrived at a conception of faith similar to Coleridge's from his independent study of Kant. Hare was also capable of detachment and criticism. Coleridge, he wrote, 'is often hindered from seeing the thoughts of others . . . by the radiant flood of his own; . . . often, like the sun, when looking at the planets, he only beholds his own image in the objects of his gaze'. Hare pointed to Coleridge's needless obscurity. 'His chief failing as a critic was his fondness for seeking depth below depth, and knot within knot: and he would now and then try to dive, when the water did not come up to his ancles.'[53]

Coleridge was aged forty-five when Hare met him first, in about 1817.[54] Behind him lay the great poems published in *Lyrical Ballads* (1798), the radical and Unitarian beliefs of his youth, and intense spiritual crises in which despair was deepened by opium addiction. Though his life was always scarred by turmoil and unhappiness, by 1814 Coleridge regained his belief in Trinitarian Christian orthodoxy and was trying to lead a more balanced and productive life.

---

[52] Julius Charles Hare and Augustus W. Hare, *Guesses at Truth by Two Brothers* (2nd edn, first series, London, 1838), pp. v and vi. Hare ended preterites and participles with t rather than ed, but like his other spelling 'reforms' they did not catch on.

[53] J. C. and A. W. Hare, *Guesses at Truth* (rev. edn., 1866), pp. 190–1.

[54] For this paragraph, see Rosemary Ashton, *The Life of Samuel Taylor Coleridge* (Oxford, Blackwell, 1996), pp. 1–318, and Distad, *Guessing at Truth*, pp. 39–40, 155–7.

Hare and Coleridge became close friends, and when after the poet's death in 1834 De Quincey ferociously attacked him Hare was quick to spring to his defence in the *British Magazine*.

'Our author's mind', wrote Hazlitt of Coleridge, 'is (as he himself might express it) *tangential*. There is no subject on which he has not touched, none on which he has rested.'[55] Many themes and pregnant ideas are to be found in Coleridge's disordered and often opaque philosophical writings.[56] Describing in chapters 5, 6, and 7 of *Biographia Literaria* (1817) his disgusted rejection of the associationist psychology on which so much eighteenth-century thought was erected, Coleridge denied that we learn solely through the senses. They had their important part to play, in what he called Understanding, 'the faculty of judging according to sense', or 'the science of phenomena', which has as its province measurement and analysis, abstraction and classification. The higher functions of the mind Coleridge called Reason, a compound of intellect, intuition, and imagination, 'the Power of Universal and necessary Convictions, the Source and Substance of Truths above Sense, and having their evidence in themselves'. To learn anything both intellectual functions need to be harnessed to the Will, the essential determining feature of the human mind, its capacity for originating action – which the associationists forgot. Religious faith is to be attained not through 'evidences' of the sort Paley adduced but by exercising the Will to gain it over time through our experience, or as we might say, existentially; faith is a function of personal commitment, acting upon the Reason and deep feeling. In a letter to Wordsworth Coleridge wrote that 'the philosophy of mechanism' was fatal to 'everything that is most worthy of the human intellect', idly demanding 'conceptions where intuitions alone are possible or adequate to the majesty of the Truth'.

Coleridge's hero was Luther, 'this dear man of God, heroic Luther'.[57] Luther worked by Reason as Coleridge defined it, seizing

[55] 'Mr Coleridge', in *The Spirit of the Age*, first published 1825 (Oxford University Press, World's Classics edn, 1904, p. 36).

[56] For what follows, see in particular Reardon, *Religious Thought*, pp. 63–72, from which the quotations are taken; see also James D. Boulger, *Coleridge as Religious Thinker* (New Haven, Conn., Yale University Press, 1961).

[57] For what follows, see Avis, *Anglicanism and the Christian Church*, pp. 239–44, and for the quotations from Coleridge.

on the essential principle of justification by faith intuitively: 'O how the painted mist of mock-rationality dissolves before him – the hollowness of self-procured gradual self-reformation by force of prudential reflections and enlightened self-interest.' Luther was also 'this Christian Hercules, this heroic cleanser of the Augean Stable of apostacy': in other words, the man who overthrew Antichrist, embodied in the Papacy. Much in the later Coleridge reads like straightforward anti-Popery of the familiar British Protestant sort, though some of his modern biographers ignore it, in effect removing a dimension from him and making him seem more modern than he was.

Yet in this most paradoxical of thinkers there was an ecumenical and eirenic strain that conflicted with his anti-Popery, and is much more often emphasised by commentators.[58] Coleridge envisaged the National Church as 'all the so-called liberal arts and sciences, the possession and application of which constitute the civilization of a country, as well as the theological'; so those key people in society, 'the clerisy' charged with guarding and disseminating the nation's spiritual and cultural heritage, included lay persons as well as clerics. The Christian church was part of this National Church, but it had a special function amidst the rapid economic and technological advance that Britain was experiencing, which Coleridge distrusted as a threat to happiness and a balanced social order.[59] The Christian church was 'the sustaining, correcting, befriending opposite of the World'; the message that it spread through worship and schooling was all-important. He had a sense of the universality of the Christian church, and the comparative unimportance of theological differences in the face of it.

In his most famous sermon, delivered in Great St Mary's on Advent Sunday 1828, Hare developed Coleridge's argument that ratiocination is a superficial and inadequate instrument. He confused the discussion by employing the term Reason in the customary way, that is, in the contrary sense to Coleridge's; thus Hare confines it to the 'logical faculty or the power of drawing inferences'. Still,

---

[58] For what follows, see Reardon, *Religious Thought*, pp. 84–9, from which the quotations from Coleridge are taken.

[59] Coleridge's ideas on modern capitalism in *The Constitution of the Church and State* (1829) in some ways prefigure Ruskin's remarkably.

the Coleridgean nature of his contentions is clear indeed, as is the way in which they were directed, at a time when parliamentary and other reforms were in the air, to a political purpose of which Coleridge, the prophet of conservativism, assuredly approved.[60] Reason, because not 'continually refresht and replenisht by influxes from the Imagination, and from the Heart . . . has given our age its revolutionary character. We have asserted that *we are light*, and that *we were darkness*', a denial of the truth that complete Reason (in the Coleridgean sense) conveys to us: 'that all human improvement must be gradual,– that we can only advance step by step,– that there is no absolute beginning upon earth, – that the law of continuity cannot be infringed'. So in Britain men have been guilty of 'infatuation', in other words plans for radical change, 'the wild and dreary daydreams of our political system-mongers . . . short roads to universal knowledge, the multifarious panaceas against moral and political evil'. The folly of basing religious faith on our logical faculty alone was discussed by Hare elsewhere, notably in a series of sermons delivered in Cambridge in 1839. He confuted those (Paley was undoubtedly in his mind) who argued that faith was 'an intellectual assent to certain truths, beyond the reach of reason . . . delivered by inspired witnesses, whose inspiration is proved by the evidence of miracles'.[61] Humankind needed to employ in conjunction the Understanding (here Hare used the word in its Coleridgean sense) and the Will:

> Every genuine act of Faith is the act of the whole man, not of his Understanding alone, not of his Will alone, but of all three in their central aboriginal unity. It proceeds from the inmost depths of the soul . . . It is the act of that living principle, which constitutes each man's individual, continuous, immortal personality.

ARCHDEACON HARE: CHURCH UNITY AND ANTI-POPERY

In Hare's life as a don and a country clergyman two threads were intertwined for many years: a desire for church unity, and powerful

---

[60] 'The Children of Light', in Julius Hare, *Sermons Preacht on Particular Occasions* (Cambridge, 1858), pp. 4, 12–14 for the quotations. For Coleridge's animadversions on the Great Reform Bill, alleged to threaten revolution, see Ashton, *Coleridge*, p. 398.

[61] 'Faith, the Victory that Overcometh the World', pp. 15–24, and 'Faith, a Practical Principle', pp. 37–8, in Hare, *The Victory of Faith and Other Sermons* (Cambridge, 1840).

anti-Catholic instincts that were in the last resort incompatible with it. In an archidiaconal charge delivered in 1842, the 43 pages of text and 119 of notes on 'The Means of Unity', are instinct with Coleridgean notions on the necessity of unity. Christ assured us that we would be led 'to the whole truth', but[62]

> this promise was only to be fulfilled collectively in the whole Church, not in any one individual. Every living member of Christ is to have a portion of truth breathed into him, sufficient to form a ground of union with the rest of the body; but no member, except the Head, is to have all. Moreover every member is to recognize those portions of truth ... wherewith the other members are animated, and not to reject them as alien from Christ, because they are different from his own.

It is perhaps more significant that Hare showed a tolerant spirit with his curates.[63] In 1844 he wrote to Edmund Venables, whose appointment he was contemplating, 'that he should hold the doctrine of Justification by Faith; that he should be a lover of the Reformation; that he should not be one of those who reject and revile the name of Protestant'. On the other hand he did appoint Venables despite his High Church views, because he valued the theological learning that High Churchmen brought to parochial work. Hare wrote:

> In the Church at large I am anxious that the utmost range, compatible with the retention of the fundamental truths of Christianity, would be left open for diversities of opinion; and in my own parish I should rather wish, than object, that there should be as much diversity as can well co-exist with harmony and unity and hearty co-operation.[64]

Hare's eirenic spirit was not however always in evidence, as may be seen in his highly complex attitude towards the chief controversy among churchmen of his day: how should the Church of England react to Roman Catholicism and to 'Romanising' tendencies within the Anglican body? As it happened, during the 1840s his

[62] 'The Means of Unity', in Hare, *Charges*, vol. I, p. 10. See also 'The Unity of Mankind in God' (1848), in *Miscellaneous Pamphlets* (Cambridge, 1855).
[63] Distad, *Guessing at Truth*, p. 170, and pp. 125–6 for the quotations that follow.
[64] A. J. C. Hare, *Memorials of a Quiet Life*, 13th edn (3 vols., London, 1876), vol. III, pp. 250–1, quoted in Distad, *Guessing at Truth*, p. 126.

colleague in the second archdeaconry in the diocese was Henry Manning, a leading Tractarian who in 1851 was to convert to Rome.[65] Soon after Manning became archdeacon in 1840 he and the Hare family became close friends, but Julius and he were often locked in argument because of their doctrinal differences. Much discussion was good-natured enough, since both men enjoyed fencing without wounding, and Hare avowed that disagreement 'will not interfere in our concurrence in higher things ... and you know I love *unity* without *uniformity*, which is the bane of unity ... I belong to a generation & a university that cares less about such matters, & the habits of my life & my own feelings have strengthened my indifference'.[66]

But Hare's instinctive anti-Papist feelings kept breaking out. F. D. Maurice wrote of Hare that a visit to Rome 'left him a stronger Protestant than it found him. "I saw the pope", he used to say, "apparently kneeling in prayer for mankind; but the legs which kneeled were artificial; he was in his chair. Was that not sight enough to counteract all the aesthetical impressions of the worship, if they had been a hundred times stronger than they were?"'[67] Differences with Tractarians went deep and sometimes drew blood. Hare was especially irritated by Newman, antipathies of personality being compounded by doctrinal dispute. In 1838 Newman published *Lectures on Justification by Faith*, criticising Luther for allegedly basing all Christianity on this single doctrine which Newman believed was unwarranted by the Scriptures and the writings of the Christian Fathers.[68] For the next seven or eight years Hare was obsessed by the issue. As with Coleridge Luther was a hero for him, and clearing his reputation from the allegations in Newman's caricature became entwined with the question of Tractarianism, the Romanising of the Church of England, and the many conversions to Roman Catholicism, notably of Newman himself in 1845. He accused Newman and his associates of glamourising the early Christian epoch and the Middle Ages and so approaching the Reformation in a very unhistorical way – a fault that especially

---

[65] For these lines, see Distad, *Guessing at Truth*, pp. 139–41.
[66] Quoted in Distad, *Guessing at Truth*, p. 140.
[67] F. D. Maurice, 'Introduction' to Hare, *Charges*, p. xxvi.
[68] For what follows, see Avis, *Anglicanism and the Christian Church*, pp. 253–8, Distad, *Guessing at Truth*, pp. 164–6, and E. H. Plumptre, 'Memoir', pp. xxxvii–xxxviii.

irritated Hare, alive from his reading of the German historians to the need to treat every age on its own terms, not ours.

Hare wrote harshly, while at the same time baffling his audience with calls for tolerance. Being the Select Preacher at Great St Mary's in 1839 gave him an an opportunity to 'protest against what he believed to be a step backwards towards the theology of Rome, a re-assertion of the great truth of which Luther had borne witness'.[69] Hare's sermons linked the doctrine of justification by faith to the teachings of St Paul and showed that it had had its place in Christian theology since its early days.[70] The themes were resumed in sermons preached in Cambridge in 1840, and making additions to them with a view to publication

> became the main subject of his studies. The exegesis of every text was elaborately pursued through the whole range of Patristic, Anglican and German commentators ... The notes overshadowed the text at once by their number, and the greater interest of their subject-matter. One of them (the famous Note W, running through not fewer than 22 closely-printed 8vo. pages) stood then, and will probably remain for ever, the longest treatise calling itself a note in the English language.[71]

The note in question was eventually published in 1846.[72]

Henry Manning was received into the Roman Catholic Church in April 1851, and Hare reacted angrily to the 'defection and desertion of one whom we have long been accustomed to honour' and 'to reverence'.[73] 'I can only wonder at the inscrutable dispensation by which such a man has been allowed to fall under so withering, soul-deadening a spell, and repeat with awe, to myself and to my friends, *"Let him who thinketh he standeth take heed lest he fall"*.' The bulk of the charge from which these words are a quotation was a ferocious attack on 'the superstitions and idolatrous corruptions' of the 'subtile, insidious adversary' of the Church of

---

[69] E. H. Plumptre, 'Memoir', p. xxxvii.
[70] The sermons were published as *The Victory of Faith*.
[71] E. H. Plumptre, 'Memoir', p. xxxviii.
[72] *The Mission of the Comforter* (2 vols., London, 1846). The first volume, the text, contains 386 pages, and the second, notes, 1,027. The quotation from Note W occurs in vol. II, pp. 703–4. An expanded version of Note W was published in 1855 as *Vindication of Luther Against his Recent English Assailants* (Cambridge, Macmillan, 1855).
[73] 'The Contest with Rome', in *Charges*, vol. III, p. 11, and p. 43 for the next quotation.

England. Manning's conversion, wrote Hare's memoirist, 'cast its shadow over the rest of his life'.[74] It seems to have been in part responsible for his ill-health in the 1850s and his death in 1855 at the age of sixty.

HARE AND CONNOP THIRLWALL: BIBLICAL CRITICISM AND THE CYCLICAL VIEW OF HISTORY

One of the most momentous labours that Hare was concerned with was biblical criticism, and once again his views paralleled Coleridge's. When Hare graduated in 1816 it was very widely – perhaps almost universally – held among orthodox Christians that the Bible was divinely inspired, and many took the further step of believing every detail of it to be true. This view is, for example, very obvious in accounts of Simeon's conversation parties. To give examples of the growth of scepticism, it has also to be said that learned students of the texts were ready to adopt a more flexible argument on the question of divine inspiration, while the geologists were already giving reasons for doubting the accuracy of the chronology that men like Archbishop Ussher had constructed from the diverse and confusing indications in the Pentateuch.[75] But in 1798 and 1799 Coleridge studied the writings of Wilhelm Gottfried Lessing and gained from them a sense of the problematic nature of the biblical texts: they were the product of varying stages of historical development, some primitive and some advanced.[76] They could not be read as though they were all dictated by an infallible intelligence, and to attempt to do so was to mount a defence that could not be sustained. It was necessary to abandon indiscriminate reliance on each and every detail, while trusting to the spiritual truths that the Bible could be discovered to contain. But the Scriptures could only impart what the receptor had the capacity to assimilate. Coleridge's stress on the need for inner readiness or spiritual preparation is akin to his description of the existential process by which faith itself may be gained, and is why he is regarded by some as a singularly modern philosopher.

[74] E. H. Plumptre, 'Memoir', p. xlii, and Distad, *Guessing at Truth*, pp. 194–7 for what follows.
[75] See chapter 6, pp. 212–17.
[76] Reardon, *Religious Thought*, pp. 81–4, and for the quotations.

Though Herbert Marsh, the Lady Margaret Professor, had touched on German biblical criticism in his translation of J. D. Michaelis, *Introduction to the New Testament* (1793–1801),[77] a more substantial contribution came from Hare and Connop Thirlwall; they made available to British scholars recent German views on the extent of divine inspiration in the Scriptures. Hare, who had persuaded Thirlwall to learn German in the first instance, introduced him in 1823 to Friedrich Schleiermacher's critical study of St Luke's Gospel, published two years earlier. Thirlwall translated it, while Hare provided him with almost all the materials he required for the long introduction he wrote to his volume.

Schleiermacher dealt with the problem of the synoptic Gospels, the narratives of Matthew, Mark, and Luke. Their common elements were usually explained by postulating borrowings from each other, or a source-Gospel, an *Urevangelium*. Schleiermacher argued that it was more likely that many different versions of the life of Christ would have been composed as the Christian religion spread, and that this 'extraordinary treasure of detached narratives' would have been 'collected by diligent research' by Matthew, Mark, and Luke and used in their Gospels.[78] If the notion of an *Urevangelium* made the orthodox uneasy because it implied a questioning of divine inspiration of the Gospels, the idea that there might have been scores of such heretical documents was greatly offensive. While defending the translation that Hare and he had effected, Thirlwall admitted that[79]

all the hypotheses we have mentioned are equally and decidedly irreconcilable with that doctrine of inspiration once universally prevalent in the Christian church, according to which the sacred writers were merely passive organs or instruments of the Holy Spirit. This doctrine however has been so long abandoned that it would now be a waste of time to attack it. When I say it has been abandoned, I mean of course only by the learned; for undoubtedly it is still a generally received notion.

[77] For what follows see Distad, *Guessing at Truth*, pp. 86–92, and Terrence N. Tice, Editor's Introduction to Friedrich Schleiermacher, *Luke: A Critical Study*, translated by Connop Thirlwall (Lampeter, Dyfed, Edwin Mellen, 1993).

[78] Distad, *Guessing at Truth*, p. 87.

[79] Connop Thirlwall, 'Introduction by the Translator', *Luke: A Critical Study* (1993 edn, ed. Terrence N. Tice), pp. xi–xii.

The doctrine was certainly not abandoned by Hugh James Rose, the vicar of Glynde, Sussex, who in May 1825 attacked German theologians, particularly Schleiermacher, from the pulpit of Great St Mary's where he was Select Preacher.[80] He rebuked Schleiermacher again in a review in the *British Critic* in 1827. Thereafter the work, important though it was, was given very little attention in Britain for many years, a phenomenon that is as difficult to explain as most negatives. It may reflect the inaccessibility of Thirlwall's tightly packed introduction, described by Maria Hare, as 'quite bewildering, and enough, I think, to turn any one disbeliever in the inspiration'.[81] But memories did linger. In 1848 Caroline Fox, the Quaker diarist, showed F. D. Maurice some translations of Schleiermacher's sermons that she had prepared. He warned against their publication. Because of a rumour that Thirlwall was to be made archbishop 'all the most revolting passages' of his *St. Luke* 'have been carefully hunted out and paraded in the newspapers as exhibiting' Thirlwall's 'deep-seated rationalism and blasphemous temper'.[82]

For Hare the historical process itself had a religious significance. Hare and Thirlwall were members of a group of historians later called by J. S. Mill the 'Germano-Coleridgeans', a name that neatly encapsulated the two chief sources of their approach. The German historian who most inspired them was Georg Niebuhr, author of the *Römische Geschichte* (1812).[83] Like their kinsmen who studied biblical texts, the German historians practised strict evaluation of sources. Though scepticism has been a virtue of historians from Herodotus onwards, the German philosophy of history was novel in arguing that it was essentially cyclical, and that the intelligible field of study was the nation. Nations were like individuals, passing through youth, maturity, and decay, and so exhibiting at their several stages different patterns of behaviour. These views were in part a reaction against the associationist psychology of their

---

[80] Rose was a graduate of Trinity and a High Churchman; later he was sympathetic to the Tractarians. His four sermons on German theologians formed his *Discourses on the State of Protestantism in Germany* (London, 1825).

[81] Augustus J. C. Hare, *Memorials of a Quiet Life*, (2 vols., London, 1872), vol. I, p. 328. Maria Hare was the widow of Julius's brother Augustus.   [82] Quoted in Distad, *Guessing the Truth*, p. 89.

[83] These lines draw upon Duncan Forbes, *The Liberal Anglican Idea of History* (Cambridge University Press, 1952), esp. pp. 12–86.

Enlightenment, which conceived human nature as very much the same in all epochs, and its optimistic faith in progress and human perfectibility. In contrast, the Germano-Coleridgeans were pessimistic, or at least sceptical, about the future.

In *Guesses at Truth* Julius Hare included essays on history whose target is plainly the rationalist historians of the Enlightenment who assumed that Progress was a basic feature of the human chronicle.[84] 'The natural life of nations, as well as individuals, has its fixt course and term. It springs forth, grows up, reaches its maturity, decays, perishes.' Britain had already reached the stage of decadence: the material advances around Hare as he wrote were masks for inner decay, and threatened social and spiritual crisis.

> All the doters on steam-engines, and cottonmills, and spinningjennies, and railroads, on exports and imports, on commerce and manufactures,– all who dream that mankind may be ennobled and regenerated by being taught to read, – all these, and millions more ... who fancy that happiness may be attained by riches, or by luxury, or by fame, or by learning, or by science, – one and all may be numbered among the idolaters of the golden calf: one and all cry to their idol, *Thou are my god! ... thou wilt lead us to the Canaan of light and joy.*

Humankind's increasing control of its external world, Hare believed, led it to assume 'that the greater amount of knowledge implied a proportionate improvement in the faculties by which the knowledge is acquired'. But 'a man's clothes are not himself', and 'the notion of his perfectibility is as purely visionary, as the search after an elixir of life', unless we rely on 'the doctrine and means of perfectibility we have', which is based on the only view of human nature 'which is not incompatible with all experience'; that is, not on 'its perfectibility, but its corruptibility'.

The cyclical view of history, in the twentieth-century form offered by a writer in some ways curiously like Hare, Oswald Spengler, is pessimistic and gloomy; decay is inevitable, and the system of ideas is determinist. Hare often seems determinist too, but he is uneasily aware of it, and proffers a way out – Christianity. Faith alone can alter the future and convert the cycle into a helix.

[84] For what follows, see J. C. and A. W. Hare, *Guesses at Truth* (1866 edn), pp. 169–71 and 305–9, from which the quotations are taken.

> Only through Christianity has a nation ever risen again: and it is solely on the operation of Christianity that we can ground anything like a reasonable hope of the perfectibility of mankind; a hope that what has often been wrought in individuals, may also in the fulness of time be wrought by the same power in the race.

So Hare's view of history gave urgency to his sense of Christian mission; the boundless optimism of the rationalists had to be abandoned, but it might be replaced by the cautious optimism implied by the doctrine of redemption.

Hare did not attempt the practice of history, being perhaps diverted from it by the multiplicity of his interests. He did however collaborate with Thirlwall in a translation of seminal works, volumes I and II of Niebuhr's *Römische Geschichte*.[85] These tasks were among the last completed by Hare while in residence in Trinity. Niebuhr's work was greeted by Macaulay as 'an era in the intellectual history of Europe', and in future decades it influenced the approaches of ancient historians, renowned in their day, such as Thomas Arnold, Charles Merivale, Thirlwall himself, and George Cornewall Lewis. The translation of Niebuhr attracted a hostile notice in the *Quarterly Review*, attacking his political liberalism and his questioning of biblical texts, and linking him with the rioting of German university students. Hare replied with his usual over-long defence.[86]

A willingness to ask questions about sources was natural in a learned don, and in 1845 he welcomed the publication by his friend Christian Karl Josias von Bunsen of the first volume of a critical analysis of Old Testament chronology, which had long been discounted by savants the world over.[87] Hare wrote that *Ägyptens Stelle in der Weltgeschichte* 'seems to me destined to form an epoch in the science of Primeval History ... I do not know how to controvert the evidence w[hi]ch Bunsen's book collects to prove the great antiquity of the world'. Bunsen's orthodoxy was impugned by E. B. Pusey, the Regius Professor of Hebrew at Oxford, and Hare published 'A Vindication of the Chevalier Bunsen' in the

---

[85] Distad, *Guessing at Truth*, pp. 105–15 for what follows, including the quotations.
[86] *A Vindication of Niebuhr's 'History of Rome' from the Charges of the Quarterly Reviewer* (Cambridge, 1829). These sixty pages were followed by a three-page postscript by Thirlwall. The pamphlet was known in Cambridge as 'Hare's bark and Thirlwall's bite'.
[87] Distad, *Guessing at Truth*, pp. 168–9, and for the quotations.

British Magazine and Monthly Register in September 1846. He argued
that Bunsen's

> direct object is to show that the book of Genesis does not contain
> sufficient information on which to construct a chronology for the
> early history of mankind . . . a person may believe that the Scriptures
> are inspired, that they are a revelation of Divine truth, and yet may
> conceive it possible that the inspiration does not extend to such
> things as dates; and it is the most unjustifiable to assert that he who
> questions the correctness of the chronological statements, does not
> believe the facts; and that too when his argument shows that he does
> believe them, one of his reasons for questioning the chronological
> statements being their apparent inconsistency with these facts.

Bunsen's enquiry involved 'that most weighty, but most difficult
and troublous question concerning the nature, the mode, and the
extent of inspiration in the composition of the Scriptures'. On that
question Hare 'would not presume to speak publicly' unless he
'could hope to set it forth calmly and fully, without needlessly
disturbing and shocking the minds of simple believers'.

Hare's position was in fact doubly precarious. To Tractarians and
Evangelicals any probing into biblical authenticity was deeply
suspect, while beneath his scholarly questioning Hare was himself a
conservative and conventional Anglican, hoping and expecting,
like Coleridge, that in essentials the divine inspiration of the Bible
would continue to be apparent; though 'the question of Inspiration
. . . was one from which Hare characteristically shrunk, in the hope
of one day being able to deal with it more thoroughly, there is
enough to indicate in what fashion he would have treated it'.[88] But
questioning similar to his led to conclusions that he could not
accept. For example, he rejected the views expressed in the *Leben
Jesu* of David Strauss (1835), brought to a British audience by
George Eliot's translation in 1846. Strauss, while conceding that
Christ was an historical person, regarded the miraculous and
supernatural incidents essential to him in the Gospels as myths; in
other words, he denied Christ's divinity.[89]

Hare was anguished when his close friend and one-time curate at

[88] E. H. Plumptre, 'Memoir', p. xlviii.
[89] Edwina G. Lawlor, *David Friedrich Strauss and His Critics* (New York, Peter Lang, 1986), pp. 39–45.

Herstmonceux, John Sterling, adopted Strauss's views, so much more radical a refutation of the idea of divine inspiration than Hare could accommodate.[90] In the memoir with which Hare prefaced his posthumous collection of Sterling's *Essays and Tales* (1848) Hare tiptoed around Sterling's sceptical views, and was plainly uneasy about the entire matter. Hare 'felt it a solemn duty to speak of my Friend's errors' because he did not wish to be guilty of falsehood. 'It may be thought that the story of Sterling's life is a warning to refrain from all speculation. But this would be to misread and pervert it.' Any man who after intellectual endeavours like Sterling's could say 'he has never been shaken or troubled in the calm composure of his faith', was free to 'cast a stone at Sterling: I cannot'.[91] But 'the publication of this *Memoir* gave a new prominence to Sterling's name, and furnished a handle of attack to the controversialists who looked on Hare as one of the foremost leaders of what has since come to be known as the Broad Church School'.[92] In the December 1848 issue of the *English Review* an Oxford High Churchman, William Palmer, published an article, 'On Tendencies towards the Subversion of Faith', which criticised Hare because he had expressed admiration for Sterling, an 'infidel', and because he had helped to create interest in Britain for German theology.[93] However pointed, these criticisms were mildly expressed, but drew from Hare an intensely indignant reply, *Thou Shalt Not Bear False Witness Against Thy Neighbour* (Cambridge, 1849).[94] Fifty-nine pages are spent attempting to rebut charges that Hare said branded him 'as a wretch who ought to be cast out of all honorable society'; but there are few substantive arguments, probably because Hare realised that within the terms of the narrowest orthodoxy Palmer's accusations were true. They had touched a raw nerve in Hare; the incident was a sign of the strain that theological novelty imposed on one thoughtful Cambridge cleric.

---

[90] For these lines, see Distad, *Guessing at Truth*, pp. 166–70, 174–83.
[91] J. C. Hare, 'Sketch of the Author's Life', in *Essays and Tales by John Sterling* (2 vols, London, 1848), pp. ccxix, ccxxvii–ccxxviii.
[92] E. H. Plumptre, 'Memoir', p. 1.
[93] Distad, *Guessing at Truth*, pp. 176–7.
[94] Reprinted in J. C. Hare, *Miscellaneous Pamphlets*. The quotation comes from p. 2.

FAITH AND UNBELIEF

THE GROWTH OF UNBELIEF

Charles Darwin recalled that after his unsuccessful period at Edinburgh University his father decided in 1828 to send him to Christ's College, Cambridge, to become a clergyman.[95]

> I had scruples about declaring my belief in all the dogmas of the Church of England; though otherwise I liked the thought of being a country clergyman. Accordingly I read with care Pearson on the Creeds and a few other books on divinity; and as I did not then in the least doubt the strict and literal truth of every word in the Bible, I soon persuaded myself that our Creed must be fully accepted.

At Cambridge Darwin accepted as entirely plausible the logic of Paley's arguments on Design, and indeed was more impressed by his *Evidences* and *Moral Philosophy* than by any other works in the Cambridge curriculum. He left the university content with his faith, if unreflective, and when in 1836 he went round the world on the *Beagle* he was 'quite orthodox', and remembered 'being heartily laughed at by several of the officers (though themselves orthodox) for quoting the Bible as an unanswerable authority on some point of morality'. But between 1836 and about 1840 his beliefs were transformed.

After his marriage his wife gently prompted him to examine his beliefs. Firstly, Darwin traversed the ground trodden by many sceptics in the previous century, and came to disavow many details in the Bible: 'its manifestly false history of the world, with the Tower of Babel, the rain-bow as a sign. &c., &c.'. Miracles were plainly incredible, and the Gospels inconsistent and too removed in time from the events they purported to describe. He also found Christianity morally repugnant, since it attributed to God 'the feelings of a revengeful tyrant':

> Thus disbelief crept over me at a very slow rate, but was at last complete. The rate was so slow that I felt no distress, and have never since doubted even for a single second that my conclusion was

---

[95] For what follows see Darwin, *Autobiographies*, ed. Gavin de Beer, pp. 31–50, and pp. 31, 49 and 50 for the quotations; see also Michael Bartholomew, 'The Moral Critique of Christian Orthodoxy', in Gerald Parsons (ed.), *Religion in Victorian Britain: II, Controversies* (Manchester University Press, 1988), pp. 174–82.

correct. I can indeed hardly see how anyone ought to wish Christianity to be true; for if so, the plain language of the text seems to show that the men who do not believe, and this would include my father, Brother and almost all my best friends, will be everlastingly punished.[96]
And this is a damnable doctrine.

Though like many Victorians Darwin kept some of the outward observances of conventional Anglicanism and refrained from parading his disbelief, it was not shaken, and a common Victorian tragedy reinforced it: in 1851 the Darwins' daughter died when she was ten.

So Darwin's rejection of Christianity antedated the working out of his views on natural selection, brought to the world in the *Origin of Species* (1859). Their bearing on the argument on Design is constant and close, but a little ambiguous. Darwin concludes the *Origin* thus:[97]

> There is grandeur in this view of life, with its several powers, having been originally breathed by the Creator into a few forms or into one; and that, whilst this planet has gone cycling on according to the fixed law of gravity, from so simple a beginning endless forms most beautiful and most wonderful have been, and are being, evolved.

But for the most part the tendency of his discourse is quite different, as Michael Bartholomew explained:[98]

> Species of plants and animals, including humans, are as they are because accidental minor variations in the structure of their ancestors conferred on them a fitness in the contest for food, for mates, for survival in hostile environments. Species are temporary survivors in an incessant and relentless struggle for existence. The theory depicts nature as a site of general death and extinction, with accidental variations determining the victory of the handful of survivors. Presented like this, the theory is the very antithesis of the providential, benign account of the living world that Darwin had found in Paley's *Evidences* at Cambridge.

[96] No doubt many did believe in the total damnation of those without faith, but it was not an *essential* Christian doctrine, being controverted by much in the Bible.

[97] *On the Origin of Species by Means of Natural Selection* (Oxford University Press, 1929), p. 441. This edition in the World's Classics Series is a reprint of the 2nd edition of 1860. The phrase 'by the Creator' does not appear in the 1st edition.

[98] Michael Bartholomew, 'The Moral Critique', pp. 178–9, 181.

Thus 'either God stands remote from the processes that shape the living world, or he is continuously present in them. If the former, his existence is of no great consequence: if the latter, He is involved in some pretty shady dealing.' The critique of Christianity that biology implied for Darwin was essentially *moral* in character, and fortified the objection to it that was raised by the death of his daughter.

Despite Darwin's unique stature his spiritual odyssey was similar to those of many Victorian intellectuals between 1830 and 1860. There was a revulsion from the apparent cruelty of Christianity, at least as it was conventionally represented, intertwined with a scorn for those who accepted the Bible as divinely inspired, literally true, and textually unproblematic.[99] It was becoming impossible without self-delusion to reconcile the picture of Creation in Genesis with the findings of the geologists, while the Unitarians Charles Hennell and Francis Newman (the cardinal's brother), drawing on German biblical criticism and writing from within a sceptical and questioning tradition that most Anglicans refused to regard as Christian at all, published works that contributed greatly to the 'unsettlement of faith'. 'Between them these books questioned the date and authorship of books in both the Old and the New Testaments; recognized the piecemeal and composite nature of books in both Testaments; questioned traditional notions of inspiration and the miraculous; and generally tended towards rational and naturalistic explanations.' 'I shuddered at the notions which I had once imbibed as part of religion', wrote Francis Newman, 'and then got comfort from the inference, how much better the men of this century are than their creed. Their creed was the product of ages of cruelty and credulity; and it sufficiently bears that stamp.' George Eliot, who so often registered the changing opinion of the era, wrote very critically in the *Westminster Review* about a work by an Evangelical preacher, John Cumming. 'She resents', comments Michael Bartholomew, 'Cumming's imputation that unbelievers are sinful and stupid.' On the contrary, 'it is Cumming who should be adjudged morally odious and intellectually imbecile'. His knowledge of geological

---

[99] For what follows including the quotations, see Bartholomew, 'The Moral Critique', pp. 168–74, and Gerald Parsons, 'Biblical Criticism in Victorian Britain: From Controversy to Acceptance', in *Religion in Victorian Britain, II, Controversies*, pp. 239–44.

theory and biblical criticism is weak, and above all 'she is offended by his dwelling on divine retribution to the exclusion of divine love and mercy'. George Eliot, that is to say, was seeking to rescue from shipwrecked dogma an ethical system that would look remarkably like New Testament morality, though it might be called 'humanism'. Walking round the Fellows' Garden at Trinity with F. W. Myers many years later she put matters thus: 'she, stirred somewhat beyond her wont, and taking as her text the three words which have been used so often as the inspiring trumpet-calls of men,– the words *God, Immortality, Duty*, – pronounced, with terrible earnestness, how inconceivable was the *first*, how unbelievable the *second*, and yet how peremptory and absolute the *third*'.

The sceptics mentioned had one thing in common: they were not Anglican clergymen. The church had to concede that unbelief existed as an external enemy, but was horrified when its essential doctrine was challenged by an enemy within. Though the full implications of Thirlwall's writing in an earlier generation might be passed over, the challenge presented by Frederick Maurice could not be.[100] Maurice had been Hare's pupil at Trinity, and Hare had led him to Coleridge. The ideas of Coleridge on the unity of humankind and the sovereign value of Christ's helpfulness to the individual were of continued importance to Maurice though the anguish caused by his attempts to realise exactly what their importance was, and indeed exactly what Maurice might really be thinking about anything, is attested by his tortured, impenetrable, cloudy utterance. In 1853, when he was a professor at King's College London, he published *Theological Essays*, described by Owen Chadwick as 'filled with literary head-scratching'.[101] Dr Jelf, the Principal of King's College, grasped after hard reading that Maurice did not believe in hell's everlasting torment, one of the touchstones of Anglican orthodoxy, and one of the doctrines repudiated by the humanists, not to mention most laymen. After full consideration by the college council Maurice was dismissed.

A similar assault was mounted against the leading Broad Churchman of the epoch, Benjamin Jowett of Balliol College, Oxford,

---

[100] For these lines see in particular Reardon, *Religious Thought*, esp. pp. 158–85.
[101] Owen Chadwick, *The Victorian Church*, Part 1 (London, A. and C. Black, 1966), p. 545, and pp. 545–50 for what follows.

because of his commentary on the Pauline Epistles.[102] His 'principle was to discard previous interpretations and to grapple directly with the text' so as 'to penetrate the mind of St Paul'. In an essay showing his profound debt to Coleridge, Jowett wrote that 'Christianity is not a philosophy but a life . . . we return to Scripture, not to explain it away, but to translate it into the language of our own hearts, and to separate its accidents from its essence.' Another essay by Jowett asked for the comparative study of religion, since revelation was not confined to Jews and Christians who had in any case borrowed from each other; however acceptable today, this was a startling suggestion in the 1850s. Most striking was the repugnance he expressed for the idea of substitutionary atonement. Jowett, recently appointed Regius Professor of Greek, was subjected to the indignity of being made to subscribe again to the Thirty-nine Articles. Courageously, in 1859 he published a second edition in which he made a more direct attack on the penal theory of Atonement: 'God is represented as angry with us for what we never did . . . He is satisfied by the suffering of his Son in our stead.' Jowett and others were attempting to respond to the challenge posed by the honest doubters to the Anglican intellect and sense of moral justice. He prepared for the second edition of *The Epistles* another essay that was not ready in time. Instead, it appeared in the most momentous publication of the Anglican Broad Church, *Essays and Reviews* (1860).

Jowett's essay 'On the Interpretation of Scripture' was the most searching and most durable of the seven studies in the volume; Basil Willey has described it as the book's 'centre of gravity'.[103] The authors were mostly Oxford dons or graduates; only one, C. W. Goodwin, an ex-fellow of St Catharine's, was from Cambridge. The seven were often regarded by their enemies as conspirators who had polished their utterances to produce maximum wounds on Christian orthodoxy: they were not, but it is true that despite their differences of approach, intellectual weight and, above all,

---

[102] *The Epistles of St Paul to the Thessalonians, Galatians and Romans: With Critical Notes and Dissertations* (2 vols., London, 1855). For what follows see Josef L. Altholz, *Anatomy of a Controversy: The Debate over 'Essays and Reviews' 1860–1864* (Aldershot, Scolar, 1994), pp. 6–7, including the quotations from Altholz and Jowett himself.

[103] 'Septem Contra Christum', in Basil Willey, *More Nineteenth Century Studies. A Group of Honest Doubters* (London, Chatto and Windus, 1956), p. 154. The account that follows is based on pp. 137–60 and Altholz, *Anatomy of a Controversy*, pp. 9–33.

imaginative reach, they tended towards the same end – the 'demythologising' of religion, the removal of encrustations and glosses that many centuries had deposited on the essential truth, and which now had to be removed if it were to convince English men and women. One influence common to many of the authors was the notion that Coleridge had advanced in *Aids to Reflection*, that the core of religion was existential – though they envisaged in the search for the essence a much greater loss of Anglican doctrine than Coleridge had. Jowett declared that it would be a great folly if[104]

> in the present day the great object of Christianity should be, not to change the lives of men, but to prevent them from changing their opinions; that would be a singular inversion of the purposes for which Christ came into the world. The Christian religion is in a false position when all the tendencies of knowledge are opposed to it . . . No one can form any notion from what we see around us, of the power which Christianity might have if it were at one with the conscience of man, and not at variance with his intellectual convictions.

Those who still accepted the Mosaic cosmogony or biblical literalism must abjure them, yet the 'eternal import' or 'true basis' would remain.

The book aroused great controversy, which became intertwined with the parallel case of J. W. Colenso's denial of the Mosaic authorship of the Pentateuch, and its factual accuracy.[105] Very widely reviewed, it was widely condemned by Anglicans and Dissenters too because of its alleged heretical statements, and in due course 45 per cent of the Anglican clergy in England, Ireland, and Wales signed a declaration that in effect criticised it in the strongest terms. Though it is true that such arrays of signatures can be factitiously assembled, the percentage is remarkable when one considers that many essentially agreeing with the declaration withheld their signatures because of technical objections. Some clerics sympathised with the authors, or at least doubted the wisdom of punishing them. Notably, F. D. Maurice published in their support *The Mote and the Beam*, described as 'vintage Maurice,

---

[104] Quoted in Willey, 'Septem Contra Christum' in *More Nineteenth Century Studies*, pp. 156–7.
[105] Altholz, *Anatomy of a Controversy*, pp. 35–128. On Colenso, one-time fellow of St John's and Bishop of Natal, see chapter 3.

prophetic but not precise, not meeting arguments but transcending them, "a tract which probably failed to convince anyone as a piece of argument but which lifted the issues onto a higher plane"'.[106] But two of the seven, Williams and Wilson, were prosecuted in the Court of Arches, which had to adjudicate not on the truth or error of their asseverations, but on the narrower ground of whether they were in conformity with the doctrines of the Church of England as declared in its Articles and Formularies. On some charges they were acquitted, but on others convicted. But on appeal to the Judicial Committee of the Privy Council, which had to consider the case on the same terms as the lower court, Williams and Wilson were acquitted. One battle then ended, but hardly the war.

These transactions may seem to take us too far from King's Parade for this book's purpose, but it is hoped that they will assist understanding of the religious development of one Cambridge don, Leslie Stephen.

LESLIE STEPHEN: MR RAMSAY WHEN YOUNG

What he said was true. It was always true. He was incapable of untruth; never tampered with a fact; never altered a disagreeable word to suit the pleasure or convenience of any mortal being, least of all his own children, who, sprung from his loins, should be aware from childhood that life is difficult; facts uncompromising, and the passage to that fabled land where our brightest hopes are extinguished, our frail barks founder in darkness (here Mr Ramsay would straighten his back and narrow his little blue eyes upon the horizon), one that needs, above all, courage, truth, and the power to endure.[107]

Virginia Stephen was born in 1882, when her father was fifty. Her portrait, of the agnostic who valued above all things fidelity to truth and the will to submit to it, transmits to us the impression which Leslie Stephen in his late middle age made on her as a young woman. Although barbed with resentment and irony, it reflects his self-image well enough. But he had not always possessed this

---

[106] Altholz, *Anatomy of a Controversy*, quoting in the last two clauses Ieuan Ellis, *Seven against Christ: A Study of 'Essays and Reviews'* (Leiden, 1980), p. 131.
[107] Virginia Woolf, *To the Lighthouse* (London, Hogarth, 1927), Part I, *The Window*, chapter 1.

certainty that there was no God, nor had he attained it without suffering.

His spiritual odyssey, from a sufficiency of faith to an abundance of doubt, had been undertaken as a young don in Trinity Hall in the 1860s when *Essays and Reviews* was being much discussed, and it suggests a course perhaps common to many others. Unfortunately, Stephen said less about it than he might. In 1901 Stephen was asked by William James, engaged on the lectures which in due course became *The Varieties of Religious Experience*, to give an account of his own religious experience. Stephen replied:[108]

> I can only say that if you could cross-examine me viva voce you might possibly attract some ideas. But left to myself I can say no more than 'Story, God bless you, I have none to tell'. I seem to myself to have had no spiritual history whatever, except that I gradually shed some old formulae and did not regret them because I had never much believed in them. It is all too painfully common-place to supply even a sentence – not a paragraph – in a lecture. And now I find myself becoming more commonplace than ever.

Leslie Stephen wrote that his 'father's fine taste and his sensitive nature made him tremblingly alive to one risk. He shrank from giving us any inducement to lay bare our own religious emotions. To him and to our mother the needless revelation of the deeper feelings seemed to be a kind of spiritual indelicacy.'[109] Yet the home was deeply religious, with daily prayers and a 'full allowance of sermons and Church services', and it was 'pervaded by an air of gravity', which, Stephen wrote, 'became the law of our natures, not a law imposed by external sanctions'. Many influences in this household led Leslie towards the church, and, writes his biographer, 'from the moment when he entered Trinity Hall [he] regarded the clerical profession as one which was not unlikely to be his'.[110] There were hopes of a fellowship for Leslie, and the college statutes would lead him towards either the church or the law. He had little desire to be a barrister. His father wanted one of his sons to be a clergyman, 'the noblest and happiest' of vocations, and fondly hoped that his

---

[108] Quoted in *Sir Leslie Stephen's Mausoleum Book*, with an introduction by Alan Bell (Oxford, Clarendon, 1977), p. xvii, from a Harvard MS.
[109] Leslie Stephen, *James Fitzjames Stephen*, pp. 61–3.
[110] For what follows, Maitland, *Leslie Stephen*, pp. 130–1.

own religious doubts would be dispelled by his son's 'theological erudition': what in the event happened makes this wish a strange irony. When his brother Fitzjames chose the law the church was left for the younger brother, and perhaps it was suited to him for another reason: he was thought to be lacking in robustness. Stephen's prodigious physical exertions in his twenties and later showed this apprehension to have been erroneous, but it suggests that in the 1850s it was assumed that a fellowship and a clerical career would not be particularly arduous.

Stephen pursued the usual mathematical course, which was to give a lasting twist to his family conversations: 'He would ask what was the cube root of such and such a number; for he always worked out mathematical problems on railway tickets; or told us how to find the "dominical number" – when Easter falls was it?'[111] At all events he became Twentieth Wrangler in 1854; a fellowship followed, one of the two in Trinity Hall that necessarily entailed taking holy orders. Stephen also became a tutor in 1856. He was ordained deacon in 1855, and priest in 1859. 'Some of those who knew Leslie and were interested in his future thought that he was making a mistake and warned him.'[112] Stephen wrote, much later,[113]

> I took this step rather – perhaps I should say very – thoughtlessly. I was in a vague kind of way a believer in Maurice or in what were called 'Broad Church' doctrines. My real motive was that I was very anxious to relieve my father of the burthen of supporting me. By taking the tutorship I became independent and after taking my degree I never cost my father anything. I was, for a time, very much attached to Cambridge. I had many friends, as you may partly see from my life of Fawcett; I was popular with my pupils,[114] being young ... and very anxious to avoid the fault of 'donnishness' ... My chief means of keeping up familiarity with the undergraduates was my interest in the boat-club and in various athletic pursuits.

'As an undergraduate', Maitland averred, 'Leslie was, I imagine, being gently and kindly, and perhaps almost without his knowing it, impelled towards the church.'[115] It seems likely that his story was

---

[111] Virginia Woolf, 'A Sketch of the Past', in *Moments of Being*, ed. Jeanne Schulkind, revised and enlarged edition (London, Hogarth, 1985), p. 111.   [112] Maitland, *Leslie Stephen*, p. 132.
[113] *Sir Leslie Stephen's Mausoleum Book*, p. 5   [114] Stephen taught mathematics.
[115] *Leslie Stephen*, p. 131.

typical of many young men of much talent but no very certain and focused ambition, who gave no thought at twenty to the need to resign a fellowship if they married, and to the need to consider other means of support, should they marry, than a clerical living that their college would be sure to supply. As it happened Stephen did not marry till he was thirty-five, somewhat older than the age for most ex-fellows.

A key question for historians is in what sense such men 'believed' when they were clerical fellows because we know that some ceased to do so, and it is natural to assume some shallowness or self-deception before the loss of faith. Men around them accepted Anglican doctrine as true, and they might be no more tempted than we are to question the conventional wisdom of their society, especially since the theological training given at Cambridge in the 1850s was not particularly intensive or challenging. In articles written many years after the event Stephen stated that he did not discover 'that my creed was false, but that I had never really believed it. I had unconsciously imbibed the current phraseology; but the formulas belonged to the superficial stratum of my thought instead of to the fundamental convictions.'[116] We are further led towards accepting that the clerical state was as easily acquired as it was to be discarded by Stephen's attempt, in a volume of ambiguous ironies, to convince us that the Cambridge man of his day cared 'little for abstract disquisition', was marked by 'rough, vigorous, common sense', and so was sharply different from the Oxonian, who admired 'metaphysics and general principles' and was 'apt to be, in our opinion, rather too hairsplitting and refined for practice'.[117] So 'the movement led by Dr Newman scarcely stirred our sober minds. *Essays and Reviews* have not seriously troubled our repose.' Combination rooms were disturbed by bitter quarrels over the American Civil War (Stephen was a Northern partisan) but 'it was only necessary to turn the conversation upon theology to smooth the troubled waters ... The one thing that can spoil the social intercourse of well-educated men, living in great freedom from unnecessary etiquette, is a spirit of misplaced zeal.'

---

[116] Leslie Stephen, *Some Early Impressions* (London, Hogarth, 1924), p. 70. This volume reprints articles first published in the *National Review* in 1903.
[117] Leslie Stephen, *Sketches from Cambridge*, pp. 138–41.

But as Maitland shrewdly observed, 'If you have to "discover" or to "become convinced" that you never really believed the story of Noah's flood or of Jack the Giant-killer, then you have really believed it, however baseless and superficial . . . the belief may have been.'[118] Certainly, 'his doubts accumulated but slowly', since in 1859, four years after his diaconate, he was ordained priest. The only one of the twenty-five sermons he preached that survives (he later destroyed all he could find) is 'commonplace' but has 'no trace of heretical pravity'. Still, with his reading of sceptical authors his doubts grew. The process caused him far more anguish than he admitted, and he discussed matters with his great friend Henry Fawcett, also a fellow of Trinity Hall. Sedley Taylor, who knew Stephen well at Cambridge, felt that his account of his 'deconversion' did not comport with what Fawcett had reported: 'Fawcett said that he was with Stephen late one night discussing the position and that when he quitted him Stephen's state of mind was such that Fawcett entertained serious fears he might cut his throat during the night.'[119]

At all events in 1862 Stephen resigned his tutorship which gave him special moral responsibilities towards undergraduates, and which neither his conscience nor some of his colleagues would wish him to retain. But till his marriage in 1867 he held on to his fellowship; the Cambridge view was that fellowships were prizes for intellectual achievement, and Fawcett persuaded his colleagues, and doubtless Stephen too, that under the statutes then obtaining there was no need for Stephen to resign his; he had to be in holy orders to retain his fellowship (which it will be recalled was clerical in nature), but as the law then stood he could not by his own act disavow them or the disabilities attached to them. 'Had all this occurred a few years later', when it became possible to abjure clerical status, 'he might have taken a somewhat different view of the situation and have touched no penny that, however faintly, bore the taint of a test. As it was, he had done enough to earn the gratitude of all honest men. He is one of our liberators.' Henry Sidgwick and others did not resign

---

[118] *Leslie Stephen*, pp. 134–9 for these lines including the quotations from Maitland.

[119] Quoted in John W. Bicknell, 'Mr Ramsay was Young Once', in Jane Marcus, ed., *Virginia Woolf and Bloomsbury. A Centenary Celebration* (Basingstoke, Macmillan, 1987), p. 58. This letter was most probably the basis for Maitland's hint to Virginia Stephen that her father had contemplated suicide: 'A Sketch of the Past', p. 108.

their fellowships until 1869.[120] The highly complex matters here summarised throw into relief the dilemmas that were posed for individuals and colleges by the decay of the religious belief that had been presumed when rules and conventions were constructed.[121]

A series of articles written from his standpoint of unbelief a few years after he left Cambridge made Stephen's views on religion crystal clear.[122] Taking an absolutist stand, Stephen equated Christianity with the dogmas and doctrine it had cost him so much anguish to repudiate a few years before. So the Broad Church school were abolishing Christianity itself:[123]

> The Atonement is spiritualised till it becomes difficult to attach any definite meaning to it whatever. The authority of the Bible becomes more difficult to define and to distinguish from the authority of any other good book. Everlasting punishment is put out of the way by the aid of judicious metaphysical distinctions. The sharp edges of old-fashioned doctrine are rounded off till the whole outline of the creed is materially altered. Phrases that once seemed perfectly definite turn out to have no meaning, and to become mere surplusage.

Broad Churchmen were self-deceiving: they turned away from the plain results of their enquiries, a sort of benign agnosticism, and pretended that they were Christians still, and what was worse, that their ideas were well expressed in the Thirty-nine Articles after all, thus enabling them to commit the intellectual dishonesty of sheltering behind the strictly legal defences offered by the Judicial Committee of the Privy Council:

> They protest, and I doubt not with perfect sincerity, that they throw aside all considerations except the simple desire of discovering the truth. And yet their investigations always end in opinions which are at least capable of expression in the words of the most antiquated formulae. It is as if a man should say that he always steered due north and yet his course should invariably take him safely through all the

---

[120] Maitland, *Leslie Stephen*, pp. 139–42; Leslie Stephen, *Henry Fawcett*, p. 126.
[121] Stephen renounced his clerical status in 1875, as permitted by an Act of Parliament of 1870.
[122] What follows is based on 'The Broad Church', 'Religion as a Fine Art', and 'Are We Christians?', which are among the papers gathered into Stephen's *Essays on Freethinking and Plainspeaking* (London, 1873); and also on 'Ritualism', *Macmillan's Magazine*, 17 (1867–8), pp. 479–94, 'Mr Matthew Arnold and Church of England', *Fraser's Magazine*, NS 2 (October, 1870), pp. 414–31, and 'Mr Voysey and Mr Purchas', *Fraser's Magazine*, NS 3 (April, 1871), pp. 457–68.
[123] 'The Broad Church', p. 31, and p. 18 for the next quotation.

shoals and tortuosities of the Thames and land him conveniently in Lambeth stairs.

Honesty demanded that men said what they really believed, 'in the plainest possible language', which would enable us to discover 'the new doctrines which will satisfy at once our reason and imagination'. Honesty also entailed a free market in ideas, and hence Disestablishment: 'if a religion is to prevail by its powers of persuasion, it should be as free as possible from association with the State'.[124]

But as Noel Annan points out, lacking imagination Stephen defined religion too narrowly, as merely 'Belief'. 'When Stephen called the doctrine of the Atonement repulsive he saw a clear concept, the theory of penal substitution; he did not see the mystical purification through suffering which Dostoevesky beheld.'[125] Impatient with the vague and tentative enquiries of Maurice and the Broad Churchmen he did not grasp that much that was vital would be made out of them, often in his own university.[126] In her perceptive and subtle memoir his daughter recalled, among his many estimable qualities, a 'strong mind', but 'an impatient, limited mind; a conventional mind entirely accepting his own standard of what is honest, what is moral . . . a black and white world'.[127]

Much of Leslie Stephen's life after he left Cambridge looks like an attempt to find substitutes for religious sanctions for morality, and for the personal fulfilment that religious faith might have been expected to bring him. Men who, like him, renounced their religion yet stayed as dons found in the rewards of scholarship – above all in the direct service to others that teaching means – compensation for the loss of faith. For Stephen the search was harder, and more diffuse. The writings of Comte and Darwin convinced him that society was evolving progressively, or at least that it might be made to do so if enlightened men steered it in the right direction.[128] So he became committed in the 1860s to political

[124] 'Religion as a Fine Art', p. 71, and 'Mr Matthew Arnold and the Church of England', p. 426.
[125] *Leslie Stephen*, pp. 256–7.
[126] See for example Christopher Brooke, *History of the University of Cambridge*, pp. 147–50, on Charles Raven.   [127] 'A Sketch of the Past', p. 115.
[128] For these lines, see in particular Jeffrey Paul Von Arx, *Progress and Pessimism. Religion, Politics and History in Late Nineteenth Century Britain* (Cambridge, Mass., Harvard University Press, 1985), pp. 10–63.

action, only to become disenchanted with its waste and ineffic-
iency. 'Some', he wrote in the American journal the *Nation* in April
1869, 'were disgusted with the parliamentary system of government', and thought that 'Parliament should use its power and
knowledge to conduct business, instead of frittering away time on
party struggle.'[129] In 1872 he named Bismarck as an effective
national leader, and compared his methods with the 'timidity,
shuffling and underhand flirtations of that which calls itself our
Liberal party'. Himself the epitome of Victorian moral rectitude,
Stephen vainly tried to find justification for right conduct in the
evolutionary process itself; ethics were those principles which
assisted progress.[130] But

> when Stephen applies the principle of Natural Selection to human
> conduct, he is unaware that he is faced with a choice: are we to
> concentrate on the brutal competition of the process or on the
> advantages which society gains from this process of change? When
> Stephen says that right and wrong are names given to rules that
> existed before man had a moral sense, is he saying that it is right for a
> tribe faced with starvation to migrate and pillage the territory of
> another tribe?

But in fact Stephen

> was making the social sciences do the work of religion. Evolution
> replaces God. Evolution is the Creator, Man his child; Evolution is
> an Immanent God or Process at work within the world... It is this
> desire to find metaphysical sanctions which gives Victorian agnosti-
> cism the appearance of a new nonconformist sect. The power of
> religion over the very minds which denied it emerges nowhere
> more subtly than in Stephen's evolutionary ethics.

In the end Stephen found most satisfaction in the same way as
some of the dons he left in Cambridge – scholarship, and loyalty to
truthfulness in its pursuit. His greatest achievement was the
Dictionary of National Biography. It was 'the most troublesome
undertaking in which I was ever involved', but it had 'one
advantage: that is, I could feel that I was taking part in a really useful

---

[129] Von Arx, *Progress and Pessimism*, pp. 30–1.
[130] Noel Annan, *Leslie Stephen. The Godless Victorian* (London, University of Chicago Press, 1986),
pp. 286–90, including quotations.

undertaking ... the facilitation of historical inquiry'.[131] Because of Stephen's efforts, the *Dictionary* is superior in range and penetrating judgement to any like production from other hands. He devised its scope and nature, edited 26 of its 63 volumes, ensured that they appeared with a regularity that far more liberally staffed agencies might now emulate, and wrote 378 biographies himself, including many of its most thoughtful and enduring essays.

[131] Leslie Stephen, *Some Early Impressions*, pp. 155, 167. See also Annan, *Leslie Stephen*, pp. 83–9.

Chapter 11

THE UNIVERSITY AS A POLITICAL INSTITUTION, 1750–1815

THE UNIVERSITY IN PARLIAMENT: THE DUKE OF NEWCASTLE AS CHANCELLOR

THE UNIVERSITY AS A PARLIAMENTARY CONSTITUENCY

The important contest for this University, which has so long been looked forward to with intense anxiety throughout the country, commenced on Tuesday last, the Candidates being Sir John Copley, Attorney-General, Lord Palmerston, Mr Bankes, and Mr Goulburn. During the whole of Monday, the members of the Senate kept pouring into the town, and by night the streets of the town, the halls of the colleges, and their groves were completely thronged with the sons of science, many of whom had not visited the scenes of *Alma Mater* for several years. The business was commenced at the usual hour, but with this difference, that the votes after being tendered and accepted by the Vice Chancellor, were all entered in a poll book.[1]

Cambridge and Oxford were the only places where elections were held for three parliamentary constituencies at once: the county, the borough, and the university, each seat of learning being given the right to return two MPs by James VI and I in 1603.[2] Unlike other members, the university representatives did not have to own landed or personal property; the only essential qualifications were membership of their university itself and a place on their college's boards, which they had to be careful to retain; uniquely, they represented their constituency in a very strict sense.[3] The universities also had a powerful if vague feeling of the qualities needed in their MPs;

[1] *Cambridge Independent Press*, 17 June 1826.
[2] Representation was reduced to one member in 1885 and abolished in 1948.
[3] Daniel Cook, 'The Representative History of the County, Town and University of Cambridge, 1689–1832' (University of London PhD thesis, 1935), pp. 209–11.

386

intellect, standing, and concern for university interests were desired, and their alleged lack led to complaints like Professor Richard Watson's to the Duke of Grafton in 1771 about his nominee's lack of substance.[4] The Cambridge electors were all MAs and doctors, qualifications always fully registered; disputes over entitlement of the sort so common in other places seem to have been rare. Unsurprisingly, given the character of the university, most electors were in holy orders – 3,171 out of 6,221 in 1879, and a higher proportion a century earlier. Since non-residents were allowed to vote a familiar sight at contests was clergymen toiling to Cambridge from remote livings, though sometimes friends would 'pair' to save trouble. Travelling expenses were sometimes paid by candidates, as in 1826 when a record number of clergymen came up to vote on the Catholic Emancipation question – 1,293 electors out of 1,800; Palmerston the Emancipation candidate likened their advance along King's Parade to the charge of the Black Hussars. Attempts to outlaw the payment of expenses as bribery were very unpopular, as the thin end of the wedge to confine the franchise to residents. Far-flung graduates valued the link with their alma mater.[5]

Quite different in qualification from the freeholders in the county or the freemen in Cambridge borough, the university electors also voted in an unusual way. Instead of declaring their choices to an officer on the hustings, they voted in the Senate House on slips of paper, writing their names and those of the preferred candidates.[6] They then handed the slips to the Vice-Chancellor who placed them in a box, an early prefiguring of the modern ballot except that there was no guarantee of secrecy; indeed the Esquire Bedell sometimes printed pollbooks.[7] This voting procedure prevented the state of the poll being known during the eight days of the election, which elsewhere added to the excitement of contests.[8]

---

[4] Richard Watson, *Anecdotes*, pp. 47–8.
[5] Cook, 'Representative History', pp. 211–12, 312–18.
[6] The usual formula was 'A (degree) Coll. XXX eligit B in Burgensem huius Academiae in Parliamento'.
[7] The voting procedure is fully described by Henry Gunning, *Ceremonies Observed in the Senate House of the University of Cambridge* (Cambridge, 1828), pp. 230–3.
[8] During the heated contest of 1826 the Vice-Chancellor changed procedure to permit the state of the poll to be assessed. Electors delivered their slips to a Proctor who read them aloud while a clerk copied them into a pollbook. The traditional practice was, however, soon resumed. Cook, 'Representative History', pp. 213–14.

University elections were conducted with dignity and decorum. Open bribery would have been thought outrageous, though government patronage was often expected in the Newcastle years. Canvassing was sometimes intense, but it was bad form to attempt it in the street, while public speeches by candidates were also too blatant. Lord Henry Petty, candidate in 1806, wrote from Cambridge: 'I cannot urge too strongly, that all unnecessary show of electioneering bustle, etc., should be avoided even in town, & upon the road, & much more here, for the grave people here are nice [that is, fussy], & perhaps not improperly so upon that subject.'[9]

In the eighteenth century, men often described themselves as 'Whigs' or 'Tories', terms whose meaning has occasioned much debate among historians in recent generations. Until about 1965 scholars were much influenced by Sir Lewis Namier's view, first enunciated in 1929,[10] that such labels denoted no ideological content, being masks for groupings based on the possession or hope of office, and on electoral interests and relationships with kinsmen and friends. In the last thirty years, however, the reality of ideological differences between Whigs and Tories has increasingly been accepted, albeit with continued recognition that Namier's taxonomy was also important.[11] Fundamental differences in attitude began in bitter disputes after 1680, and in some respects recognisably persisted until the late nineteenth century although inevitably subject to great modification over the passage of time. Early in the eighteenth century Whigs were inescapably attached to the Revolution Settlement of 1688 which implied, at least, a polity validated by popular consent; they revered the Protestant Succession and its post-1714 incarnation, the Hanoverian dynasty; they had an erastian (or 'Low Church') view of the status of the Established Church and they respected the toleration that Trinitarian Protestants were granted in 1689. Tories, by contrast, were distinctly unenthusiastic about 1688 and the new royal family and,

[9] Kenneth Bourne, *Palmerston: The Early Years 1784–1841* (London, Allen Lane, 1982), p. 62.

[10] See *The Structure of Politics at the Accession of George III* (London, 1929).

[11] These lines are based on J. C. D. Clark, *English Society*, esp. pp. 30–3; Linda Colley, *In Defiance of Oligarchy* (Cambridge University Press, 1982), esp. pp. 85–145; Geoffrey Holmes, *The Making of a Great Power. Late Stuart and Early Georgian Britain 1660–1722* (Longman, 1993), esp. pp. 334–66; Geoffrey Holmes and Daniel Szechi, *The Age of Oligarchy. Pre-industrial Britain 1722–1783* (London, Longman, 1993), esp. pp. 39–54.

while accepting that history could not be reversed and that it would be folly to take up arms as Jacobites, often regarded the ousted Stuart dynasty as the legitimate dynasty. While such differences between the parties did not rule out a common set of values about a hierarchical society, their attitudes towards religion, the great touchstone, were sharply opposed. Tories, the Church party, were hostile to Dissent, hated its apparent growth, and spoke as though they would have liked to end toleration; they tended to have High Church views, in other words that the Established Church should be in partnership with lay authority, not crudely subordinate to it.

It is clear that these contrasting religious principles were relevant to Oxford and Cambridge, which were at the same time both clerical and political institutions. The party affiliations of the two universities diverged in the eighteenth century. Oxford was always predominantly High Church in sentiment and returned Tory MPs. Cambridge, while possessing a larger contingent of High Churchmen than is sometimes argued, was in large measure Low Church and was the home of the leading erastian apologists.[12] Still, in 1715 Cambridge returned Tory MPs, and as was shown during the contest for the Chancellorship in 1748, a strong Tory element remained later; some colleges, notably Emmanuel and Gonville and Caius, were strongly Tory throughout the first half of the century. But the Whigs, in power in Britain with the Crown's support from 1715 till the 1760s, were aided in Cambridge by the university's ability to confer honorary doctorates giving the franchise. In 1726, for example, 110 honorary degrees were conferred, and in 1728, 286;[13] a straw in the wind was the conversion to Whiggism of Sir Thomas Gooch, Master of Caius and the one-time Tory leader in the university.[14] From the late 1720s the university was as a parliamentary constituency little more than a Whig pocket borough for a half-century, an ascendancy that Newcastle's position as Chancellor reinforced; the constituency was uncontested from 1734 to 1771. Cambridge borough was a

---

[12] See chapter 8, pp. 277–86.
[13] Cooper, *Annals*, IV, p. 197; Richard Romney Sedgwick, ed., *The History of Parliament: The House of Commons 1715–1754* (2 vols., HMSO, 1970), vol. I, p. 202. There was no such royal prerogative at Oxford. [14] Christopher Brooke, *Gonville and Caius College*, pp. 163–70.

Whig seat too, uncontested between 1737 and 1774. Landowners like the Bromleys of Horseheath and the Yorkes of Wimpole kept the Whig interest paramount with the aid of election money from the secret service fund, while the county seats were held by Whigs without contest from 1737 to 1780; the Yorkes of Wimpole shared influence with the Manners family, Dukes of Rutland, until well into the nineteenth century.

From 1727 two Whig members were returned for the university (usually unopposed) till they retired, Edward Finch in 1768 and Thomas Townshend in 1774. Both were archetypal Court Whig placemen, holding office under the administration.[15] Finch, of Kirby Hall, Northamptonshire, the fifth son of the second Earl of Nottingham and member of a large Whig family, served as a diplomat in the 1720s and 1730s, mostly in Sweden, and during that time is recorded as having voted only once, aptly against the Place Bill of 1740.[16] Horace Walpole described him as combining the 'unpolished sycophancy' of the Russian court with 'the person and formality of a Spaniard'.[17] Finch nimbly transferred his allegiance to successive administrations till his retirement. His colleague Townshend came from an even larger and more influential clan that insinuated itself into many governments; he was Newcastle's nephew, and the son of Walpole's brother-in-law. Though one of his family's less talented and energetic members, his father procured for Townshend a life-sinecure, as teller of the Exchequer, that was worth £7,000 a year, or perhaps £1,000,000 in modern terms. A regular attender at the Commons, he defended his university's interests in debate; fittingly, his last known speech was against the motion to abolish subscription to the 39 Articles at the universities – a great topic of argument in Cambridge in the 1770s.[18]

---

[15] Court Whigs were the groups monopolising government; the friends and kin to whom they gave offices were much resented by Tories and Whigs out of power.

[16] The place bill was intended to restrict the number of government office-holders permitted to sit in the Commons.

[17] Horace Walpole, *Memoirs of the last ten years of the reign of George the Second* (3 vols., London, 1846), vol. II, p. 120.

[18] R. R. Sedgwick, *The History of Parliament*, vol. I, pp. 200–2; vol. II, p. 32. L. B. Namier and J. Brooke, eds., *The History of Parliament: The House of Commons, 1754–1790*, 2nd edn (3 vols., London, Secker & Warburg, 1985), vol. I, pp. 218–20; vol. II, p. 424; vol. III, p. 554.

NEWCASTLE AS CHANCELLOR OF THE UNIVERSITY

'I saw all the Heads except the Vice-Chancellor, who happened to be out when I called, and the Master of Queens' who is in a bad state of health . . . The harmony, which appears among the king's friends, . . . gave me pleasure, and the spirit and determined firmness, which they have all shewn, has strengthened their own party and discouraged their adversaries.'[19]

So wrote Lord Dupplin to his patron the Duke of Newcastle on 5 August 1748, giving him news of the battle to secure Newcastle's election as Chancellor of the University. Newcastle, Secretary of State and from 1724 to 1766 pillar of successive Whig governments, energetic, insecure, emotional, and fussy,[20] had since 1737 been the university's High Steward, an honorific post usually regarded as leading to the Chancellorship. He began to campaign for this office months before his slowly expiring predecessor died, and while for a time he was afraid that the Prince of Wales might be a candidate, Newcastle faced in the event no opponent. The election was therefore somewhat hollow, but he was rewarded by an unusually large attendance at the Senate in December 1748. One hundred and ninety voted for Newcastle and none against, though the diehard Cambridge Tories abstained: 'all the Fellows of pure Emanuel, the three or four tories they still have at Peterhouse, all of the same stamp at King's, one or two of Trinity and Pembroke, several of Caius, and Dr Rutherforth and some few of St John's'.[21]

Newcastle was Chancellor till his death in 1768. He was proud of his office; as part of the British Establishment of church and state the university conferred great honour on its titular head. Newcastle was a generous benefactor, beginning the custom of the award by the Chancellor each year of gold medals to the two men 'who, having obtained senior optimes in philosophical [that is, mathematical] learning, shall pass the best examination in classical learning'.[22] He

---

[19] BL Add. MS 32716, fol. 17, quoted in Winstanley, *Eighteenth Century*, pp. 45–6. From this lengthy account much of what follows is taken.

[20] See the most recent study by Reed Browning, *The Duke of Newcastle* (New Haven, Conn., Yale University Press, 1975), esp. pp. 84–6.

[21] BL Add. MS 32717, fol. 443, quoted in Winstanley, *Eighteenth Century*, p. 48.

[22] BL Add. MS 32926, fol. 99, quoted in Winstanley, *Eighteenth Century*, p. 222. The restriction to the mathematically proficient was abolished in the nineteenth century.

also took a keen interest in the rebuilding of the Old Schools frontage by Wright that we now possess, and he contributed £1,000 to the appeal needed to raise its £10,500 cost.[23] Newcastle visited the university frequently, staying in his old college, Clare, and he wrote voluminously to his many supporters in Cambridge. It soothed both his vanity and his anxiety to know what was going on, and to try to influence events. As a constituency returning two MPs to the Commons the university was an important focus of political influence, and it was natural for Newcastle to want it to be in Whig hands. Naturally the university offered many opportunities for patronage to the foremost political arranger of the age; and Cambridge men themselves were quick to solicit help from him in an age when it was common to use friends for advancement.

In 1922 a leading historian of the university, D. A. Winstanley of Trinity, published a book which despite its title – *The University of Cambridge in the Eighteenth Century* – was entirely a study of Newcastle's involvement with the university as Chancellor, concentrating on his attempts to win friends and influence people, and to get his own way.[24] The relationship offers a fascinating psychological study worthy of Samuel Richardson. Newcastle was a fusspot and found it difficult not to interfere; on the other hand, he had great respect for his university. Cambridge itself was eager to please its Chancellor, usually, but touchy about its autonomy, rights and privileges.

Shortly after he became Chancellor Newcastle irritated many of the dons in the university, in a dispute that revealed, incidentally, how difficult it was to effect real change in an institution like Cambridge whose constitution might have been designed to prevent it for ever. Government anxiety about the two universities was stimulated by attitudes towards the 1745 rebellion in Oxford. The Jacobite cause gained no real support there, but the largely Tory dons showed their resentment of the Whig régime by not signing the declaration of support for the Hanoverian monarchy, which was in the event approved by an embarrassingly small number of Whig dons. At anniversaries of the Forty-Five some drunken Oxford

---

[23] Winstanley, *Eighteenth Century*, p. 226. See also chapter 1, pp. 17–18 above, for Wright's work.
[24] It was also the first study of the sort later called 'Namierite', examining eighteenth-century patronage networks using dense evidence from original sources.

undergraduates toasted 'the king over the water'. The university, sensibly deciding not to make a fuss, gave them large chunks of classical translation as a punishment and stopped them from graduating for a year.[25] Still, government nerves were irritated, and reacted very badly to a provocative speech, at the opening of the Radcliffe Camera in 1749, by William King, the Tory Principal of St Mary Hall. Some Whigs, among them Hardwicke, the Lord Chancellor, suggested a parliamentary visitation of the universities – an echo of the abortive Whig bill of 1719, and perhaps an omen of another full-scale attack on university autonomy in the interests of Whig hegemony; such was the fear expressed in Horace Walpole's pamphlet, *Delenda est Oxonia*, that the pamphlet was seized at the printers on government orders. Newcastle was anguished by his colleagues' attitudes, since any attack directed against Oxford was bound to affect Cambridge too: 'but I can never admit, That if the late and notorious, Conduct of the University of Oxford, should make a Visitation, or Enquiry there adviseable, That will be any reason for the same at Cambridge whose Behaviour is as meritorious, as the other is justly to be censured'.[26] The visitation proposed also attracted the intervention of Frederick, Prince of Wales, a notable opponent of the Whig administration. In April 1749 the prince got pledges of support for the defence of Oxford from more than 100 MPs. This threat, and Newcastle's doubts about the wisdom of the venture, led to the dropping of the proposal.

But the idea was bubbling in the background of university affairs for several years, and helped to stimulate the thinking of Newcastle and others on the subject of discipline at Cambridge.[27] Student misbehaviour irritated and worried him, and when he learnt in 1749 that the Vice-Chancellor and heads of house were drawing up new regulations for the university he took the opportunity to revise and amend the draft with the help of two clerics with Cambridge links – Thomas Herring, the Archbishop of Canterbury, and Thomas

[25] For these lines, see Sutherland and Mitchell, *The Eighteenth Century*, pp. 120–7, and John Gascoigne, 'Church and State Allied: The Failure of Parliamentary Reform of the Universities, 1688–1800', in L. Beier, D. Cannadine, and J. Rosenheim (eds.), *The First Modern Society: Essays in English history in Honour of Lawrence Stone* (Cambridge University Press, 1989), pp. 401–29.

[26] BL Add. MS 32718, fol. 31, 21 January 1747, quoted in Sutherland and Mitchell, *The Eighteenth Century*, p. 123.

[27] What follows is based on Winstanley, *Eighteenth Century*, pp. 199–222, a very detailed account.

Sherlock, Bishop of London.[28] The Chancellor himself added a regulation to the list that was so obnoxious to every interest in Cambridge that it was speedily withdrawn; it required an account of the character and behaviour of every member of the university to be sent to the Chancellor – a threat of political interference that not even the 1980s brought.[29] The remaining regulations forbade undergraduates and BAs to be out of college after 11 pm, to keep a servant or a horse without permission, to frequent coffee houses or places of amusement in the morning, or to dice and play cards in taverns. They were also ordered to attend sermons in the university church and to refrain from rioting and extravagant dress. Penalties that ranged from fines to expulsion from the university were laid down for infraction of the regulations. They were faithful to the spirit, and sometimes the letter, of earlier rules, and perhaps the failure of Newcastle and his associates to predict or comprehend the opposition they aroused may be understood.

In May 1750 the regulations were introduced in the Senate, which had to approve them; they were prefaced by a heavy-handed letter from the Chancellor that assumed concurrence with his wishes and aggravated opposition. Members of the Senate felt that a committee representing them and the principle of university democracy should have shared in the drafting. Tutors and deans felt that they knew more about the practicalities of discipline than did the heads of house. At the congregation on 11 May Jonathan Lipyeatt of St John's proposed that anyone punished for breach of the regulations should be able to appeal to the Senate. This was a recipe for endless dissension. When Lipyeatt's grace was vetoed in the Caput by the Master of Caius, Newcastle's ally Sir Thomas Gooch, members of the Senate were convinced that 'the liberties of the university were in danger and the Heads were aiming at new powers in these regulations'.[30] The regulations were opposed line by line and half of them were voted down. After intensive lobbying by the Vice-Chancellor, Edmund Keene the Master of Peterhouse, the regulations were passed by small majorities on 26 June.

---

[28] Though he was a Tory, Sherlock became a bishop (successively holding the sees of Bangor, Salisbury and London) because of the patronage of Queen Caroline: see Christopher Brooke, *Gonville and Caius College*, p. 164. [29] Cooper, *Annals*, IV, p. 281.
[30] BL Add. MS 32720, fol. 383, quoted in Winstanley, *Eighteenth Century*, p. 207.

Within months, however, the dispute was revived by a spectacular disciplinary dispute. It involved a breach of the regulation requiring students to return to college before 11 pm. On Saturday 17 November 1750 the Senior Proctor, James Brown of Pembroke, heard his college clock strike eleven before he set out for the Three Tuns tavern, a quarter-mile away.[31] In the tavern Brown found the Westminster Club dining; the club comprised members of the university educated at Westminster School, and they were celebrating the anniversary of their foundress, Elizabeth I. The company, amounting to about forty, included Thomas Francklin, the Regius Professor of Greek, at least two other dons (Thomas Ansell of Trinity Hall and Samuel Crew of Trinity), and many young men of less than MA status. When Brown ordered them to return to their colleges Francklin, Ansell and Crew got into an argument with him; harsh words were spoken to a chorus of cheers and laughter from the undergraduates.

All forty were charged by the Proctor with insulting him in the execution of his duty, and the Vice-Chancellor[32] decided to prosecute them in his court, a procedure rarely inflicted on senior members. On the day the Law Schools were crowded with undergraduates. Ansell directed his speech towards them, and they applauded him. After this indignity Keene swore in thirteen pro-Proctors for the next day and threatened expulsion to anyone guilty of disorder. In due course Francklin and Crew and the undergraduates were sentenced to be reprimanded, and Ansell was deprived of his degree. Ansell wished to appeal, but the Vice-Chancellor denied his right to it. In reply the tenacious opponents of Newcastle and Keene over the appeals issue, about forty in number and forming therefore a very large fraction of the resident Senate, were able to vote down supplicats for bachelor's degrees. The appeals matter was in contention for twenty-one months before, in March 1752, the Senate agreed to refer it to six arbitrators. They never reported: nor did they need to, the reference to them being merely a formal recognition that the two sides were

---

[31] The Three Tuns stood on the corner of St Edward's Passage and the market, where the Midland Bank is now.

[32] Edmund Keene, who was re-elected to the office for a second term in the same month at Newcastle's request; the Chancellor wished to retain the help of someone he could rely on.

deadlocked. The opposition in the Senate had proved that it could bring the university's essential business to a standstill.

The point was not lost on Newcastle, who never again attempted anything as high-handed as the change in regulations. Sometimes he still overstepped the mark. Hoping to continue his link with congenial Vice-Chancellors, he was given to suggesting that the heads of house should re-elect them for a second year. They obliged several times but, wanting to share the honour among themselves, much preferred single terms. Eventually they rebelled, and Newcastle's friend John Green, Master of Corpus, refused to consider re-election in 1758. The mixture of firmness and courtesy in his letter (of 3 November) is typical:

> I beg leave to acquaint your Grace that this morning I resigned the office of Vice-Chancellor in the usual form. As I was well apprized of your sentiments as to the expediency of continuing for two years, and think it would be much for the advantage of this place, I used the precaution of calling together your Grace's friends to consult about this matter and to offer my service for another year if it should be thought an advisable measure. After a due consideration of the affair it was not judged proper to attempt it at present, as it would not probably be done without an opposition.[33]

Newcastle also irritated the university over the matter of mandate degrees, so called because they were granted by royal mandate to candidates lacking the usual qualifications. Though sometimes justifiable – as the very similar MAs given to university lecturers coming from other universities are now – mandate degrees had been made very disreputable by James II. Soon after 1688 the university agreed with the Crown that mandate degrees would only be awarded after a petition from the Chancellor, upon the initiative of the heads of houses. So anger was aroused in Cambridge by Newcastle's practice of instigating petitions himself and seeking the approval of the heads of houses for them as a mere formality, and for unsuitable candidates such as Samuel Hill, a fellow commoner of St John's of one year's standing and aged only seventeen. The heads of houses agreed to his requests, but there was friction between

---

[33] BL Add. MS 32885, fol. 212, quoted in Winstanley, *Eighteenth Century*, p. 179; for the issues of Vice-Chancellors' tenure and mandate degrees see pp. 160–80.

them and the Chancellor because of a clash of assumptions. Newcastle, after all, was behaving no worse than seventeenth-century Chancellors had, but the university was groping towards a much more modern concept of academic autonomy and appropriateness. A result of this new attitude was a grace of 1781 requiring the assent of the Senate as well as of the heads of houses for petitions for mandate degrees.[34]

On the whole Newcastle handled the university and college authorities with sufficient tact.[35] He tried to work through intermediaries, heads of house like John Green of Corpus and Lynford Caryl of Jesus, who favoured him and his politics, and he knew that blatant partisanship might offend university sensitivities. In any case, more than one of his friends might be candidates. This happened, for example, in the election for the Regius Professor of Divinity in 1748; if Newcastle had openly supported John Green or George Rooke he would have lost the friendship of the other. The third candidate, Thomas Rutherforth of St John's, had supported the candidacy for the Chancellorship of Frederick, Prince of Wales, Newcastle's political enemy, and Newcastle's hostility to Rutherforth was too obvious to need publicising. The electors did not even consider him, and chose Green. Newcastle was gratified without needing to intervene. Within a few years Rutherforth had made his peace with Newcastle, who favoured him therefore when the Regius Professorship next fell vacant, in 1756, though again without openly admitting his support. Rutherforth was a substantial scholar, and deserved serious consideration. Edmund Law, the Master of Peterhouse, was equally distinguished, but was dissuaded from standing by a hint from a friend that to do so would disoblige the Chancellor. In the event the electors decided for Rutherforth.

The issues Newcastle faced when endeavouring to control Cambridge elections are most graphically illustrated by the complex events that accompanied the approach to death of John Newcome, Master of St John's and Lady Margaret Professor of Divinity. Newcome was a supporter of Newcastle and one the Chancellor greatly valued, since the master of the largest college had great influence in the university, while Newcastle had a frictional

---

[34] Cooper, *Annals*, IV, p. 406; the grace was unopposed in both houses of the Senate.
[35] Winstanley, *Eighteenth Century*, pp. 180–93, for what follows.

relationship with the second largest, Trinity.[36] Newcome being in frail health, competition to succeed him was evident in 1758. The three most likely contenders for the mastership in the event of Newcome's death were the two tutors of St John's, Zachary Brooke and William Samuel Powell, and Thomas Rutherforth the Regius Professor of Divinity. Both Brooke and Powell had substantial support in the college fellowship, but Rutherforth's backing was slight. In 1758 Brooke and Rutherforth were in the Newcastle camp and Powell a supporter of the Chancellor's great enemy the Earl of Sandwich; the task of supporting Brooke for the mastership without offending Rutherforth caused Newcastle much anguish. It is plain that it was hard for Newcastle to win friends and influence people in this small and close-knit society, riven by frictions while bonded by affections. Fortunately the aged Newcome recovered his health and the immediate crisis passed.

In the long term the problem remained. In 1764 matters came to head; Newcome was obviously failing, and the allegiances of Powell and Brooke changed dramatically. The reasons are not altogether clear, but seem to have been linked to the contest for the high stewardship of the university. Newcastle's candidate, his political colleague the Earl of Hardwicke, was challenged by the Earl of Sandwich. It appears that Powell offered his support to Newcastle on condition that he received his backing for the mastership, that this deal was struck, and that Brooke thereupon moved to Sandwich's camp in anger. As Newcome's life slipped away in the autumn (he died on 10 January 1765) much time was expended by Newcastle and others on the complexities of two imminent and inter-related elections, for the mastership and the professorship; one lasting result is many hundreds of letters in the Hardwicke Papers in the British Library. Brooke was a candidate for both posts, and Powell for the mastership, as were several other fellows. Another serious candidate for the Lady Margaret chair was Edmund Law, the Master of Peterhouse and a supporter of Newcastle; his ambition caused additional difficulties for the Chancellor, who felt constrained to back him but knew that the St

[36] The paragraphs that follow are based on Winstanley, *Eighteenth Century*, pp. 240–65; I am also very grateful for Christopher Brooke's comments on these episodes and the sources for our knowledge of them.

John's fellows he was relying on in the mastership election would want a candidate from their college for the professorship.[37]

Newcastle wished above all things to prevent Brooke from becoming master, since that would greatly add to Sandwich's power in the university. Anxious that William Powell might have a clear run and therefore that the anti-Brooke vote should not be split, Newcastle wanted to persuade Rutherforth not to stand, but without alienating him. He wrote:

> The very sincere regard and esteem which I have for you and your merit, and the grateful sense I have of the many obligations which I have received from you, make me take the liberty to trouble you . . . As Dr Powell has been so lately Tutor there, and I believe has long had a view to the mastership, I doubt not but he has kept up such connections with his pupils and with the college as must give him a very fair chance of succeeding, provided we with all our force do assist him. If not, I should fear Dr Brooke might carry it, and then the three great colleges, St John's, Trinity and King's united, would undoubtedly fling the university absolutely into Lord Sandwich's hands.[38]

The electors for the mastership were the forty-five foundation fellows of St John's. Powell was likely to get more votes than any other candidate, but if he failed to obtain twenty-three the election would devolve to the senior fellows; the outcome was uncertain. Newcastle's determination to leave no stone unturned may be judged from a letter he wrote to the Archbishop of Canterbury on 18 January:

> If your Grace should think proper so far to interfere as to direct your chaplain to write to Dr Murray to influence his curate to vote for Dr Powell to be Master of St John's upon the present vacancy, I should be very much obliged to you. But if your Grace thinks such an application will be improper, or has the least objection to it, I beg you would forgive the liberty I have taken in troubling you upon it.[39]

---

[37] All doctors and bachelors of divinity were electors to the Lady Margaret Professorship, and in 1764 there were 102 electors; 36 were in St John's, the largest group in any college, and St John's had come to think of the chair as rightfully theirs.

[38] BL Add. MS 32964, fol. 303, quoted in Winstanley, *Eighteenth Century*, p. 253.

[39] BL Add. MS 32965, fol. 242, quoted in Winstanley, *Eighteenth Century*, pp. 262–3. Dr Murray was Vicar of Gainsborough from 1761 to 1778, and his curate was William Plucknett, a fellow of St John's.

In the event the issue was settled by compromise within the St John's fellowship. Powell discovered that there was a certain majority against Law for the professorship, and not a certain majority for him for the mastership. He therefore agreed to support Brooke for the chair on condition that Brooke backed him for the mastership. Brooke became Lady Margaret Professor, and Powell was unanimously elected master on 25 January 1765. Newcastle, chagrined at Law's defeat, attacked his Cambridge associates: 'You only are afraid of disobliging everybody, and by that means will evidently let in the enemy.'[40] But at the price of much ink and intrigue Newcastle had not done too badly; his man was now Master of St John's. The college did well too; Powell proved an admirable reforming master, and perhaps some sense of his talents had led the fellows to back him.

The transaction at the heart of this election – Newcastle's working to secure the mastership for Powell in return (or so it seems) for his support in an election elsewhere – points to an aspect of the letter-writing duke that he has been much reproved for, his undoubted willingness to further the ambitions of his political friends. A chief critic was the Cambridge historian David Winstanley, who wrote 'it was good to be a whig in those days, but better still to be a Cambridge whig', and gave examples of heads of houses who were promoted to bishoprics after serving the duke's interests in Cambridge. Their 'shamelessness' in soliciting posts was matched by Newcastle's in favouring them. The university itself became implicated in the 'disgusting' work of this 'seemingly contemptible person', as Winstanley put it in the full heat of Edwardian indignation about 'unreformed' eighteenth-century iniquity.[41] It would be foolish to deny that Newcastle sought to reward his political supporters through his patronage; one example from many is the appointment of John Green, the Master of Corpus, to be dean and then Bishop of Lincoln. But modern scholars are inclined to view Newcastle and his Cambridge associates in a more balanced and less censorious way than Winstanley.[42] Naturally filling vacancies with

---

[40] BL Add. MS 32965, fol.268. The letter was addressed to Lynford Caryl, the Master of Jesus.
[41] Winstanley, *Eighteenth Century*, esp. pp. 11–12, 35–6.
[42] For what follows, see Stephen J. C. Taylor, 'Church and State in England in the Mid-eighteenth Century: The Newcastle Years 1742–1762' (University of Cambridge PhD thesis, 1987), pp. 87–122; also Richard Middleton,'The Duke of Newcastle and the Conduct of Patronage

heads of house in Oxford and Cambridge, the only two gatherings of ecclesiastical talent in the land, Newcastle's prescription was not always partisan. He certainly required a correct political attitude, but he had in mind unwavering support for the Hanoverian succession rather than loyalty to a narrow clique of politicians: his desideratum was natural enough in the middle years of the century when Jacobitism still seemed a threat, and it was compatible occasionally with Tory principles. In 1752 Newcastle recommended William Richardson, the Tory Master of Emmanuel, for a royal chaplaincy, and secured a canonry of Christ Church for Richard Newton, the Principal of Hertford College, Oxford who had been 'always wt they call a Tory, but never a Jacobite'.[43] Some of Newcastle's bishops were irregular in attendance at the House of Lords or opposed the government at times when they were there, as Thomas Secker[44] for example did over place and pension bills. But in 1750 he was awarded a deanery of St Paul's nevertheless, Newcastle's associate Hardwicke writing that 'it shows that Desert will meet with Regard, notwithstanding some little Court-Objections'.[45] For ecclesiastical preferment, piety and concern for Christian witness and pastoral care were as essential as political soundness. Thus Archbishop Herring averred in 1749 that the qualities needed in the new bishop of Lichfield were 'as much Goodness, & Learning, & Prudence & Courage, as one would wish to find in the character of a Xtian Bishop, & at the same time, as good an Heart towards the King, as your Grace has'.[46] These criteria do not seem incongruous when assessing the Cambridge ecclesiastics whom Newcastle preferred, however much modern sensibilities are offended by their outspoken allegiance and the open soliciting that attended the promotion process.

If Newcastle had ever been sufficiently detached from his life to write an autobiography he would have recorded the concern that,

during the Seven Years War, 1757–1762', *British Journal for Eighteenth-Century Studies*, 12 (1989), pp. 174–86.
[43] BL Add. MS 32730, fol. 182, quoted in Taylor, 'Church and State', p. 93.
[44] Bishop of Bristol (1735–7) and Oxford (1737–58), and Archbishop of Canterbury (1758–68).
[45] BL Add. MS 32722, fol. 108, quoted in Taylor, 'Church and State', p. 100. The deanery of St Paul's was held in plurality by successive bishops from 1740 to 1849. When Secker became Archbishop of Canterbury in 1758 the deanery was passed on to his successor as Bishop of Oxford: see J. Le Neve, *Fasti ecclesiae Anglicanae, 1541–1857*, compiled by Joyce Horn (London, Institute of Historical Research, 1969), pp. 6–7.
[46] BL Add. MS 32719, fols. 326–7, quoted in Taylor, 'Church and State', p. 112.

for good and ill, he had as Chancellor shown for his beloved university's affairs. His successor, the Duke of Grafton, a landowner in west Suffolk, was a very different sort of Chancellor; though he kept the office till he died in 1811, he mentions Cambridge only twice in his austere autobiography, and he was not much concerned to help it.[47] In any case, he was not able to. First Lord of the Treasury when elected Chancellor in 1768, he was out of office by 1770 and held no post of consequence afterwards. He could not, like Newcastle, bring to Cambridge gifts and posts to cement his power. Still, in 1771 he succeeded in pushing his friend Richard Croftes, a Norfolk landowner, into the university seat, despite some grumbling from dons at his lack of necessary weight, and in 1774 Croftes was elected unopposed with Charles Manners, Marquis of Granby; Granby's being heir to the Duke of Rutland and the family's estates in the county made him a very suitable member for the university, as his father had been for the shire.[48] The Duke of Grafton also helped to get his son, the Earl of Euston, elected as the university's MP in 1784.

REFORM, WAR, AND REVOLUTION

RATIONAL DISSENT IN CAMBRIDGE

The political stability that had kept Newcastle in power for so long vanished in the 1760s. George III, coming to the throne in 1760, was determined not to suffer the powerlessness that the Court Whigs had inflicted on George II; breaking their monopoly of office, he chose his ministers widely, from the many factions jostling for power in parliament. The many groups of 'Whigs' professed love of liberty and religious toleration. While the Tory party of George II's time collapsed in the 1760s, its principles of support for Anglicanism and authority and dislike of Dissent and foreigners remained powerful in British politics.[49] Confusion was aggravated

---

[47] Winstanley, *Unreformed Cambridge*, pp. 7–8, 282. Sir William R. Anson, ed., *Autobiography and Political Correspondence of Augustus Henry Third Duke of Grafton* (London, 1898), pp. 3 and 235, briefly recording Grafton's time at Peterhouse and his election as Chancellor. The family's link with Cambridge is recalled by the name of a 1980s shopping mall, the Grafton Centre.

[48] Namier and Brooke, *History of Parliament*, vol. I, p. 218.

[49] Linda Colley, *In Defiance of Oligarchy: The Tory Party 1714–60* (Cambridge University Press, 1982), pp. 110–15, 130–1, 290–2; Holmes and Szechi, *The Age of Oligarchy*, esp. pp. 277–82; Paul Langford, 'Old Whigs, Old Tories and the American Revolution', in P. Marshall and G. Williams,

by new pressures: growing militancy from Dissent in the 1760s; the conflict with the Thirteen Colonies and the imperial dismemberment that resulted from military defeat; unrest in Ireland; and the campaigns for parliamentary reform that these events stimulated. Amidst such vicissitudes, the Court Whigs evolved into the Rockingham Whigs, a nascent party in the modern sense, with rudimentary discipline and a programme, advanced in opposition, that aimed to circumscribe the monarch's prerogative by forcing on him a party government commanding a Commons majority – a novel concept. Meanwhile, the Whigs were divided, like other groups, on issues of the day such as parliamentary reform, the abolition of the slave trade, and the removal of Dissenters' disabilities. Events at the university reflected these strains and cross-currents.[50]

Before 1760 such political conflict as existed in Britain was largely limited to parliament and the few elections that were contested. After 1760, however, it often moved outside these boundaries and embraced newly politicised groups. In many towns they were encouraged by newspapers profiting from the growth in literacy and giving publicity to issues and contention. John Wilkes, maverick adventurer and propagandist of genius, drew support from many in the middle and lower ranks of urban society by his exploitation of grievances as diverse as the power of the executive, the partiality of justice, and high food prices. He stimulated and at times supported the cause of parliamentary reform, which aimed to secure fairer representation through the redistribution of seats and a widening of the franchise. This call became louder during the American War of Independence, which broke out in 1776. Sympathy for the colonists' cause and outrage at the incompetence that brought stunning British defeats and the threat of French invasion, combined in campaigns to make the government more amenable to electoral pressure.[51]

eds., *The British Atlantic Empire before the American Revolution* (London, Frank Cass, 1980), pp. 106–30.
[50] Frank O'Gorman, *The Emergence of the British Two-Party System 1760–1832* (London, Edward Arnold, 1982), pp. 1–22; Holmes and Szechi, *The Age of Oligarchy*, esp. pp. 315–17.
[51] Edward Royle and James Walvin, *English Radicals and Reformers 1760–1848* (Brighton, Harvester, 1982), pp. 13–31; H. T. Dickinson, *Liberty and Property. Political Ideology in Eighteenth-Century Britain* (London, Weidenfeld, 1977), pp. 195–321; John Brewer, 'The Wilkites and the Law, 1763–74: A Study of Radical Notions of Governance', in John Brewer and John Styles, *An*

Sometimes Protestant Dissenters were at the centre of these reforming activities. Certainly they had reason to oppose the Establishment; they were excluded from all offices of central and local government by the Test and Corporation Acts, and Lord Hardwicke's Marriage Act of 1753 forced them to go through the ceremony in an Anglican church. Still, many Dissenters, traditionally very loyal to the Protestant Hanoverian state, seem to have been politically inactive, getting on with their lives and businesses within their enclosed devout communities, as *Silas Marner* and the novels of Mark Rutherford relate for their grandchildren. By contrast, political activism characterised the so-called Rational Dissenters, men often of Presbyterian confession and tending in the eighteenth century to various forms of Unitarianism. Such men, strongly imbued with Enlightenment rationalism and its habits of sceptical enquiry, naturally questioned the anomalies of their society, while their profound sense of human equality before God led them towards political egalitarianism. The optimism, indeed millennianism, that marked their religious vision gave them combative self-confidence. Joseph Priestley and Richard Price are the most famous of these radical Dissenters. In popular constituencies with many Dissenting electors their radicalism was a powerful force during the crisis caused by the American wars.[52]

Dissenters were by law excluded from Cambridge. Nevertheless, there were some nominally Anglican dons who approached Rational Dissent in their theology, men exemplifying the Cambridge Latitudinarian tradition that emphasised natural religion and hence simplicity of doctrine. Chief among them was John Jebb, tutor and mathematical lecturer at Peterhouse (he was Second Wrangler in 1757). Several colleges forbade the attendance of undergraduates at his lectures on the Greek Testament because of

Ungovernable People (London, Hutchinson, 1980), pp. 128–71; John Brewer, *Party Ideology and Popular Politics at the Accession of George III* (Cambridge University Press, 1976), pp. 163–200.

[52] John Seed, 'Gentlemen Dissenters: The Social and Political meanings of Rational Dissent in the 1770s and 1780s', *Historical Journal*, 28 (1985), pp. 299–325; James E. Bradley, *Religion, Revolution and English Radicalism. Non-Conformity in Eighteenth-Century Politics and Society* (Cambridge University Press, 1990), pp. 195–430; John A. Phillips, *Electoral Behavior in Unreformed England. Plumpers, Splitters and Straights* (Princeton University Press, 1982), pp. 253–311.

their manifest unitarianism.[53] In his radical propensities Jebb was like Priestley and Price; his dynamism repelled his Cambridge colleagues, and Jebb eventually left academic life in frustration. William Cole, Cambridge antiquarian and diehard Tory, denounced him as one of 'a restless generation who will never be contented till they have overturned the Constitution in Church and State'.[54] Jebb was a protégé of Edmund Law, Master of Peterhouse from 1756 to 1768, whose theological views influenced many in his college towards political and religious reform. They included John Disney, who became Law's chaplain on his translation to Carlisle; eventually he was Jebb's biographer. Other Cambridge men who in varying degrees imbibed reforming ideas at university retained them on leaving it, and were linked through friendship or kin. They included Francis Blackburne, Archdeacon of Cleveland, and his son-in-law Theophilus Lindsey, one-time Fellow of St John's.[55] Like Jebb and Disney, Lindsey at length abandoned the Church of England and became a Unitarian; he founded the first Unitarian chapel in England, in Essex Street, London, attracting to it many of radical religious and political views.

Associated with these Anglicans was the most prominent Rational Dissenter in Cambridge, Robert Robinson, the minister of the Particular Baptist chapel in the Stone Yard, St Andrews Street. A barber's apprentice in London, Robinson was in 1752 'converted' by Whitfield, the Calvinist Methodist evangelist. Nine years later, well known for his skills as a preacher, he came to the troubled Stone Yard. Very soon his energy and intellectual depth was attracting congregations of 600, among them many members of the university; the Professor of Music, John Randall, composed hymn tunes for them. Very largely self-educated, Robinson surpassed many college fellows in his learning and powers, and was donnish in his habits of life and thought. Master of seven or eight languages, he was extraordinarily well read, getting access through his friends to the rich stocks of the University Library, to which his

---

[53] Disney, *The Works of John Jebb*, vol. 1, esp. p. 28; see also the entry in the *Dictionary of National Biography*, by Alexander Gordon.

[54] Quoted in John Gascoigne, 'Anglican Latitudinarianism and Political Radicalism', p. 37. The paragraph that follows is based on this article.

[55] Disney married another of Blackburne's daughters. Frend, the Jesus radical of the 1790s, married Blackburne's granddaughter.

own considerable output was eventually added. Steeped in Milton and Locke, his writings argued cogently for religious freedom and toleration, while he travelled from the Calvinism of his youth to one of the many subtle varieties of Unitarianism that the age professed. His biting tongue and bawdy wit marked him as a Cambridge character.[56]

THE SUBSCRIPTION CONTROVERSY

Cambridge radicals are prominent in the record. Men of more conservative attitude were more numerous and more powerful, sometimes calling themselves Tory and sometimes Whig. One typical Tory, expressing trenchantly the views of his party on Church and Dissent, was Samuel Hallifax. Third Wrangler in 1754, fellow at Jesus and then at Trinity Hall, Hallifax was a distinguished lawyer, becoming Regius Professor of Civil Law in 1770. Learned too as a theologian, Hallifax wrote among many things a masterly introduction to Butler's *Analogy of Religion* which was often reprinted.[57] He became bishop of Gloucester and later of St Asaph. Described by some as courteous and unassuming, and by others as 'languid' and 'servile',[58] Hallifax was ferocious in his defence of the British constitution, 'which, though not absolutely perfect is perhaps possessed of as much perfection as the times will bear'.[59] The Established Church and its doctrines needed to be guarded by Test Acts to exclude Dissenters from office. Those eager to alter settled institutions really wanted to return to the seventeenth century when their kind, 'a filthy brood of Enthusiasts' were able 'to

---

[56] See George Dyer, *Memoirs of the Life and Writings of Robert Robinson, Late Minister of the Dissenting Congregation, in St Andrew's Parish* (London, 1796), Graham W. Hughes, *With Freedom Fired: The Story of Robert Robinson, Nonconformist* (London, Carey Kingsgate Press, 1955), and James E. Bradley, 'Religion and Reform at the Polls: Nonconformity in Cambridge Politics, 1774–1784', *Journal of British Studies*, 23, 2 (1984), pp. 55–78. To illustrate the need for religious innovation Robinson suggested some pamphlets with odd titles. Among them are *A High Heeled Shoe for a Dwarf in Christ*, and *An Effectual Shove for a Heavy-Arsed Christian*; see Ursula Henriques, *Religious Toleration in England 1787–1833* (London, Routledge, 1961), p. 47.

[57] Joseph Butler, *Works. To which is Prefixed … some Account of … the Character and Writings of the Author, by Samuel Hallifax* (2 vols., Oxford, 1820), vol. I, pp. vii–xlvii.

[58] Edmund Henry Barker, *Parriana: Or Notices of the Rev. Samuel Parr, LL.D* (2 vols., London, 1828), vol. II, pp. 383, 400–7; Brydges, *Autobiography*, vol. I, p. 59.

[59] Samuel Hallifax, *A Sermon Preached before the … House of Commons … on Monday, January 30, 1769; Appointed to be Observed as the Martyrdom of King Charles I* (Cambridge, 1769), pp. 12–13.

overturn the monarchy of Charles'.[60] Nowadays the enemies of religion (Hallifax meant Jebb and his friends) were 'now clad in the flimsy vest of French philosophy and critique; now cloaked in the solemn garb of abstract speculation and enquiry; and now again, which is its usual form, in a disavowal of every moral principle, by an open and bare-faced naturalism'.[61] Keen to preserve the status quo in Cambridge too, in 1774 Hallifax contended against Jebb's examinations reforms.[62] Curiously, he was Jebb's first cousin, and early in life they had been friends.

They crossed swords over plans to give greater religious toleration. These owed much to the natural philosophy that was associated with Cambridge; as scientific knowledge of the universe expanded, the truths dependent on revelation appeared to shrink, and belief in supernatural mysteries was undermined. A simpler and less dogmatic creed seemed more fitting, as it seemed too to those trusting in scriptural authority, like Francis Blackburne, whose work *The Confessional* was a powerful Tolerationist text. Also influential were arguments, ultimately derived from Milton, about the necessarily direct relationship between a believer and his God and the evil of interposing between them; while Locke's claims that truth was best discovered in freedom and that liberty of thought was a natural right may be seen reflected in a host of Cambridge pamphlets.[63]

In the 1770s there were calls for the lifting of religious disabilities from both Anglicans and Dissenters. In July 1771 Anglican clergy and laity met at the Feathers Tavern, in London, to petition parliament to relieve Anglican clergy (and laymen) from the need to subscribe to the Thirty-nine Articles. The petition had many Cambridge supporters, including besides Jebb and company two heads of house, Edmund Law of Peterhouse and Robert Plumptre of Queens', all the fellows of the latter college, William Paley the Christian apologist, and James Lambert the Regius Professor of Greek. The spectre of seventeenth-century Puritan attacks on the

---

[60] Hallifax, *A sermon* (1769), pp. 11–12.
[61] Samuel Hallifax, *Three Sermons Preached before the University of Cambridge, Occasioned by an Attempt to Abolish Subscription to the XXXIX Articles of Religion* (Cambridge, 1772), p. 3.
[62] Disney, *The Works of John Jebb*, vol. I, pp. 62–4.
[63] Anthony Lincoln, *Some Political & Social Ideas of English Dissent 1763–1800* (Cambridge University Press, 1938), pp. 182–200; Henriques, *Religious Toleration*, pp. 18–32.

church raised by Sir William Newdigate, member for Oxford University, was enough to kill the petition by 217 votes to 71 in the Commons, but the attempt stimulated leading Dissenting ministers to campaign for relief from their need to subscribe, some of the most powerful pages in support coming from Robert Robinson.[64] Self-evidently more justifiable by natural right than the claims of the Anglican petitioners, the Dissenters' bill passed the Commons, but failed in the Lords in April 1773.[65]

Relief from the need for university students to subscribe was one purpose of the Feathers Tavern petition. Unlike at Oxford, matriculants at Cambridge had never been required to subscribe, but from 1616 onwards all graduands had been obliged to declare that the sovereign was the supreme Governor of the Church and that the Book of Common Prayer and the Thirty-nine Articles were in accordance with the word of God. In the seventeenth century naturally regarded by the Establishment as a necessary defence of the truths that it was the university's task to propagate, in the eighteenth the requirement seemed harder to defend. Subscription meant that Dissenters were prevented from proving their competence in mathematical learning that was approved by all Christians; Thomas Blackburne's son, at Peterhouse, was denied his BA for refusing subscription. Not all graduates became clergymen, and subscription seemed an absurd requirement for those, for example, becoming physicians. As Wedderburn the Solicitor General himself remarked, 'He could not conceive but a prescription was equally efficacious and proper to be followed, whether the physician had signed the Articles or not'.[66] On the other hand many dons disliked the thought of Dissenters in the Senate, altering the university's clerical character, while Hallifax lamented that 'the approved customs of the University are to be set aside, and the honest frankness of our youth abused, to serve the purposes of a despairing faction'.[67]

---

[64] Henriques, *Religious Toleration*, pp. 45–52. The freedom given by the Toleration Act of 1690 could only be enjoyed by Dissenters who subscribed to thirty-four of the Thirty-nine Articles.

[65] Lincoln, *English Dissent*, pp. 202–35. Dissenting ministers were given the relief they wanted in 1779, in the worst crisis of the American War of Independence, the government being too weak to counter Opposition Whig pressure.

[66] Quoted in Winstanley, *Unreformed Cambridge*, p. 308; see pp. 299–316 for this paragraph in general.

[67] Hallifax, *Three sermons* (1772), pp. 19–20.

Undergraduate opinion was aroused against subscription. Early in 1771 Jebb published four letters urging them to read very carefully the Articles that they would have to subscribe to. The suggestion was taken up by Charles Crawford, a turbulent fellow commoner of Queens' who had just begun a long harassment of university authority by threatening to throw the senior fellow of Pembroke out of the window.[68] He promoted a petition asking for undergraduates to be relieved from subscription on the grounds that they were too busy studying to have time to master the Articles. Nothing could have been less true for Crawford, who was not even taking a degree, but as so often with student protest the antics of some belied the seriousness of many. Many undergraduates signed the petition. When the Feathers Tavern petition was debated in the Commons in February 1772 several speakers distinguished between clergy and laity, and argued that the universities should themselves end subscription. The two university MPs wrote to the Vice-Chancellor that 'it seemed to be the general sense of those they had conversed with that something should be done by the Universities, and also that it should be confined to lay degrees'.[69] University counsel advising that Cambridge had the power to amend subscription,[70] ten graces for abolition were proposed, one for each variety of degree the university awarded. All were non-placeted, which suggests that many dons sympathised with Dr Johnson's declaration 'that our Universities were founded to bring up members for the Church of England, and we must not supply our enemies with arms from our arsenal'.[71] The largest majority, 55:13, was against relieving intending doctors of divinity, and the smallest, 40:32, against altering the qualification for the BA, which had no necessary religious significance. University feeling was more conservative than the Commons, and being warned of the need to do something the Senate agreed to a compromise grace that permitted BAs merely to declare their membership of the Church of England 'as by law established' instead of having to subscribe to every item of doctrine. The concession eased consciences, but it did not apply to degrees

---

[68] On Crawford, see Winstanley, *Unreformed Cambridge*, pp. 218–24, 306–7.
[69] Quoted in Winstanley, *Unreformed Cambridge*, p. 308.
[70] Subscription was originally enforced by letters from James I, and some believed that royal letters had the authority of statutes and therefore could not be altered by the university.
[71] Boswell, *Life of Johnson*, p. 463; Saturday 21 March 1772.

other than the BA (including the MA that gave membership of the Senate) and it meant the continued exclusion of all unwilling to call themselves Anglicans. Though relief was by grace extended to four other degrees[72] in 1779, there was no further change till the next century, an attempt in 1787 to end religious tests for the BA proving too unpopular in the university.

THE AMERICAN WAR OF INDEPENDENCE AND PARLIAMENTARY REFORM

By the mid-1770s Jebb was deeply frustrated by the failure of the campaigns to abolish subscription and reform the university's examinations and curriculum, and his progress towards Unitarianism made his position in Peterhouse hard to defend. He left Cambridge, and in a strikingly courageous change of career studied medicine at St Bartholomew's Hospital and after receiving an MD from St Andrews set up in practice in London.[73] His political activism remained. As with others, belief that the war against the American colonies was a folly committed by a government unresponsive to public opinion led him to propose parliamentary reform; Jebb with his calls for manhood suffrage was in the advance guard of that movement and a member of the Society for Constitutional Information. Others were led to espouse reform by anger at British defeat, a more shallow and temporary reaction. Most reformers in any case favoured much less extensive change than Jebb. Their spokesman was the Reverend Christopher Wyvill, whose Cambridge background gives a reason to call parliamentary reform a Cambridge movement. A graduate of Queens', Wyvill had been influenced by its liberal fellows and was a Feathers Tavern petitioner.[74] During the American war the Yorkshire Association, whose inspiration he was, favoured strengthening gentry power against the executive by adding to county seats and reducing the period between general elections. In 1780 when the shame of British defeats seemed blackest these

---

[72] Bachelors of law, physic, and music, and doctors of music.
[73] Disney, *Works of John Jebb*, vol. I, pp. 44–128.
[74] Ian R. Christie, *Wilkes, Wyvill and Reform. The Parliamentary Reform Movement in British Politics 1760–1785* (London, Macmillan, 1962), esp. pp. 70–4.

proposals were taken up in more than a dozen counties as well as London, but only there and in Yorkshire did enthusiasm last. In Cambridge 'a prodigious motley horde of all sorts' that included many undergraduates gathered in Senate House Yard in March 1780 to hear John Wilkes and others talk of reform. A petition for reform was signed by 1,000 freeholders in a few days, and Richard Watson, the Regius Professor of Divinity and another Latitudinarian Anglican, prepared a plan for a Cambridge Association on the Yorkshire model. But another meeting in April was small enough to fit into Shire Hall. Two years later the county Association had only forty members.[75]

Though there were few reformers in the university, the American War divided combination rooms. Soon after the war's inglorious start with the battle of Bunker Hill, Oxford urged the king to continue it instead of conciliating American opinion. Cambridge followed, an address being proposed in the Senate by the Vice-Chancellor Richard Farmer, Master of Emmanuel, Tory, bibliophile, Shakespearean scholar, and bon viveur.[76] Urged on by Rockingham, the leader of the parliamentary opposition, government critics fought the address in the Senate. They were defeated in both houses, in part because the government, anxious about expressions of opinion from the university, sent down Cambridge MAs, 'ministerial troops ... from the Admiralty, Treasury & etc.' to vote.[77] Some sense of the passions aroused in the university by the war policy of the North government is conveyed by the confusions of the 1780 parliamentary election. The sitting members were Croftes and James Mansfield,[78] one-time scholar of Eton and like almost all such a fellow of King's; Mansfield was university counsel and embarked on a distinguished legal career. He was guaranteed a large vote among dons, despite his husky voice and ungraceful delivery. In addition he enjoyed the full weight of government support, and his election was not in doubt.

[75] Christie, *Wilkes, Wyvill and Reform*, pp. 113–14. Richard Watson, *Anecdotes*, pp. 77–81. Cooper, *Annals*, IV, pp. 393–8.
[76] His *Essay on the Learning of Shakespeare* (1767) is an important piece of criticism.
[77] Richard Watson, *Anecdotes*, pp. 54–8.
[78] He had been elected at a by-election in 1779.

The university as a political institution

At the 1780 election there were four candidates for the second seat, all of them against the North administration. The most assiduous was the youngest, William Pitt, barely of age when votes were cast and only recently graduated from Pembroke.[79] Pitt started to canvass support a year before the election, taking close advice from his friend the Duke of Rutland, who had been MP for the university from 1774 to 1779, and getting a list of MA graduands whose votes might be requested. Pitt wrote as many as 400 letters in one week, but still came bottom of the poll with 142 votes. Mansfield got 277. the second place went to John Townshend, kinsman of the earlier university representative, a poet much admired in his day, and a political associate of Fox.[80]

Pitt wanted the distinction of sitting for his university one day. Immediately, he was returned for the pocket borough of Appleby and won golden opinions (not least from George III) for his parliamentary performances. Dismissing in 1783 the Fox–North coalition that had been wished on him a few months before, the king put Pitt in power instead, and called a general election in March 1784. Standing for the university, Pitt had his brilliant reputation and his authority as Prime Minister in his favour, as well as royal support. William Ewin, a Cambridge brewer,[81] wrote to Hardwicke:

> let Mr Pitt send down the Purse of the Exchequer which is the emblem of his office – and hang it in the Senate House and we should as naturally put our vote into it as Catholicks dig their fingers into the Pan of Holy Water – with this difference that we should mark our foreheads with P in room of the X.[82]

Pitt had supporters among the country clergy out-voters, and correspondents among them helping with his canvass. College loyalties counted. Pembroke's 18 electors voted solidly for Pitt and Lord Euston, the other government candidate and the son of the

---

[79] Pitt, a fellow commoner, had taken his degree without examination.
[80] Cook, 'Representative history', pp. 271–6.
[81] Ewin graduated from St John's in 1753, but is not recorded in Venn and Venn, *Alumni Cantabrigienses*. There is a detailed entry in the *DNB*.
[82] 25 March 1784: BL Add. MSS 35627, fol. 22, quoted in Cook, 'Representative history', pp. 278–9.

university's Chancellor, and 107 of Trinity's 137 for Euston, a member of the college. Magdalene voted solidly for Pitt and Euston too. Other combination rooms were split.[83] Overall Pitt and Euston won a crushing victory. Pitt sat for Cambridge till his death over twenty years later. His period as MP was the only time that the university was represented in parliament by the Prime Minister.[84] Euston remained member until 1811.

Pitt was supported by MPs normally inclined to favour an administration with the Crown's confidence. Their backing stiffened after the war with France began in 1793; Pitt became 'the pilot who weathered the storm'. His supporters eventually formed the new Tory Party, its principles being the respect for monarchy, authority, and the Anglican church that the struggle against revolutionary France had helped to arouse. Meanwhile, the Whigs suffered. Hated by George III for their attitude to the American War and the 'influence of the crown', they were deeply divided in their response to the French Revolution and the war, and on some it was easy to pin the charge of defeatism and lack of patriotic feeling. Nor were they united on much. The Foxite Whigs favoured civil liberty and opposition to religious disabilities, but these had few backers in the 1790s.[85]

Even as Prime Minister, Pitt kept links with his college, Pembroke, attending feasts and presenting plate. His tutor, George Pretyman, served as his private secretary; as a mathematician he was useful in Treasury matters. Eventually he wrote the jejune official life.[86] In 1787 Pitt got him appointed Dean of St Paul's and Bishop of Lincoln, concurrently; Pitt's power of preferment meant that he was much sought after in Cambridge and London by ambitious dons.[87] As MPs for the university Pitt and his colleague Euston were

[83] Cooper, *Annals*, IV, p. 412 prints an analysis of the poll.

[84] John Ehrman, *The Younger Pitt. The Years of Acclaim* (London, Constable, 1969), pp. 149–50; Cook, 'Representative history', pp. 278–80. In 1784 another long tenure started, the borough representation being captured by the Rutland interest allied with the unscrupulous Cambridge banker John Mortlock. Through manipulation of corporation powers Cambridge remained a Rutland pocket borough till 1832. See the articles by Helen Cam in *Proceedings of the Cambridge Antiquarian Society*, 40 (1944), 1–12, and *Cambridge Historical Journal*, 8 (1944–6), pp. 145–65.

[85] H. T. Dickinson, *Britain and the French Revolution, 1789–1815* (London, Macmillan, 1989), esp. pp. 21–59.

[86] Described by Macaulay as 'the worst biographical work of its size in the world'.

[87] Ehrman, *The Younger Pitt*, vol. I, pp. 13–14, 578, 590.

challenged only once, in 1790 by Lawrence Dundas, whose canvass was denounced by his opponents as treating the university 'like a mere common borough'.[88]

THE FRENCH REVOLUTION AND THE UNIVERSITY

WILLIAM FREND; THE REPRESSION OF DISLOYALTY

We may approach the impact of the French Revolution in the university by looking at the life of William Frend, a Canterbury wine merchant's son who came up to Christ's in 1775; taught by William Paley, he was Second Wrangler in 1779, and was afterwards elected to a fellowship at Jesus. Quickly appointed a tutor, he taught Thomas Malthus, later the population prophet. Taking holy orders, he became vicar of Madingley, and like so many combined clerical and scholastic functions by dint of early rising on Sunday mornings and feats of endurance on horseback. A successful Cambridge career seemed predictable. But another fellow of Jesus was Robert Tyrwhitt, a Hebrew scholar and a convinced Unitarian. (In 1772 Tyrwhitt had proposed in the Senate the graces to abolish subscription to the Thirty-nine Articles.) Talk with him aroused doubts in Frend. In 1787 he became a convert to Unitarianism, and resigned his Madingley living. He supported the unsuccessful campaign to abolish the need to declare on graduation one's membership of the Church of England.[89] Frend vigorously announced his Unitarian views,[90] an indiscretion that led to the loss of his tutorship.[91]

Frend regularly attended Robert Robinson's meetings in the Stone Yard chapel, and through it came to be intimate not only with the small group of dons in his circle, but also with the

---

[88] R. G. Thorne, ed., *The History of Parliament. The House of Commons 1790–1820* (5 vols., London, Secker & Warburg, 1986), vol. IV, p. 33.

[89] The 'declaration' had replaced the more elaborate formula of subscription in 1772. Moves fifteen years later to abolish it were linked with the Dissenters' unsuccessful attempts, between 1787 and 1790, to abolish the Test and Corporation Acts.

[90] See his *An Address to the Inhabitants of Cambridge and its Neighbourhood, Exhorting Them to Turn from the False Worship of Three Persons to the Worship of The One True God* (St Ives, Cambs., 1788).

[91] Frida Knight, *University Rebel. The Life of William Frend (1757–1841)* (London, Gollancz, 1971), pp. 17–60.

close-knit world of Unitarian activists outside Cambridge, men like Theophilus Lindsey and Joseph Priestley; and he was drawn into their campaign of 1787–90 to abolish the Test and Corporation Acts.[92] For such men the extension of religious liberty and political power were linked, and these common concerns were discussed at the quarterly meetings of the Cambridge Society for Constitutional Information, when after dinner Robert Robinson preached 'civil and religious liberty, and often, when tea comes, theology, – not points, but general, and, I judge, useful truths'.[93] The society celebrated the anniversary of the Glorious Revolution of 1688. It was natural for them to regard the French Revolution, or at all events its early moderate stages, as a move towards the sort of parliamentary government that Britain had praised herself for since 1688, and which radicals were now seeking to improve; Britain, once a model for France, might indeed now learn to take France as her model. The effect of events in Paris on Cambridge reformers may be gauged from some words by John Tweddell, a Trinity undergraduate aged twenty in 1789,[94] who in November 1790, in a declaration in Trinity College chapel ostensibly devoted to praising the character and memory of William III, recorded his joy at the progress of the French Revolution:

> Liberty has begun her progress, and hope tells us, that she has only begun. She has already unveiled the charms of her august countenance to the fortunate inhabitants of the western world; she is now combining in glorious concert the Polish king with the Polish people, and re-kindling in the breasts of modern Gauls an emulation of their free and hardy progenitors. Soon will she deign to visit the Spaniard and the Hollander, the Prussian and the Swede, the German and the Turk, nor shall the sovereign of all the Russias be able to prevail against her.[95]

[92] See W. Frend, *Thoughts on Subscription to Religious Tests, and a Letter to the Rev H. W. Coulthurst* (St Ives, Cambs., 1788).

[93] Dyer, *Memoirs of the Life and Writings of Robert Robinson*, pp. 193–4, 228–32; Knight, *University Rebel*, pp. 60–103.

[94] Elected a fellow of Trinity in 1792, Tweddell was a keen classicist who toured Greece recording antiquities. He died of fever in Athens in 1796 and was buried in the Theseum, a block of marble from the Parthenon being erected over his grave at Byron's suggestion.

[95] *Remains of John Tweddell ... being a Selection of his Correspondence ... Prolusiones Juveniles ... Some Account of the Author's Collections ... Preceded by a Biographical Memoir of the Deceased ... by the Rev. Robert Tweddell A.M.*, 2nd edn augmented (London, 1816), pp. 109–10 (of *Prolusiones Juveniles*). The declamation was awarded the Greaves book prize.

The Revolution polarised opinion in Britain. Societies calling for radical political reform (usually called Corresponding Societies) grew in London and manufacturing cities such as Sheffield and Norwich, though not, in fact, in Cambridge. By 1795 there were at least eighty, containing a higher proportion of artisans than the middle-class groups such as the Robinson circle in Cambridge.[96] Significant though the Corresponding Societies are in the modern British radical consciousness, and much as they have been discussed by its historians, they were a far smaller movement than the Tory reaction. Public opinion was in 1789 benignly disposed towards the apparent onset of constitutionalism in France, but in the early 1790s it became hostile following the deposition and execution of Louis XVI, the massacres of September 1792 and the Terror, and attacks on religion. The declaration of war against Britain in 1793 aroused long-standing patriotic feelings. It was easy to represent French ideas as potentially subversive of the British state and church, and British reformers as a fifth column for French invaders. Abundant books and pamphlets reflected these sentiments, and the virtue of loyalty to the established order – the mood of publications being well conveyed by the title of one with Cambridge origins, *Reasons for Contentment* by William Paley, Frend's old tutor.[97]

In Cambridge the university presented a loyal address to the King reprobating 'the wicked attempts of the enemies of our happy Constitution', and in December 1792 town and gown joined in forming an Association for 'preserving liberty and property against Republicans and Levellers', typical of more than 1,000 such societies, comprising perhaps a quarter or more of British adult males. In December a town-and-gown mob, whose cry was 'God save the King', broke the windows of reformers and Robinson's Stone Yard Chapel, and toured the city with the effigy of a radical Cambridge grocer, Gazam, with a halter round its neck. Some fellows of St John's joined in dispersing the mob, but George Whitmore, tutor of that college, called its actions 'a laudable ebullition of justifiable zeal'. Standing outside Emmanuel gate

---

[96] Dickinson, *Britain and the French Revolution*, p. 70.

[97] Robert R. Dozier, *For King, Constitution, and Country. The English Loyalists and the French Revolution* (Lexington, Ky., University Press of Kentucky, 1983), pp. 76–102; Dickinson, *Britain and the French Revolution*, pp. 103–25; J. C. D. Clark, *English Society*, pp. 247–76.

when Gazam's effigy was brought past, the master, Richard Farmer 'laughed heartily; he gave the men who carried it five shillings, and desired them to shake it well, "opposite Master Gazam's house"'. Just before Christmas over 100 publicans promised to inform on any customers discussing or reading sedition, and on New Year's Eve an effigy of Tom Paine, salient in loyalist demonology, was burnt on Market Hill.[98]

The Vice-Chancellor at this time was Isaac Milner, a leading Tory in the university and certainly one of its most powerful presences: 'his sonorous voice predominated over all other voices, even as his lofty stature, vast girth, and superincumbent wig, defied all competitors'.[99] Milner had come up the hard way. Of humble stock and a weaver from the age of ten, he educated himself in classics and mathematics while at the loom. Rescued by his brother Joseph,[100] and given a sizarship at Queens', his gifts brought him the highest honours. Senior Wrangler in 1774, he was elected President of Queens' fourteen years later. Milner was a man of puzzling contradictions. Despite his energies, he was something of a hypochondriac, as Vice-Chancellor journeying in a closed carriage and reluctant to venture abroad for fear of the cold.[101] Popularity came from his kindly disposition, entertaining discourse, and a liking for the burlesque that made his lectures uproarious,[102] yet he ruled Queens' with a rod of iron. A key is his devout Evangelical faith: a close friend of Wilberforce, he helped to effect his conversion. He transformed Queens' into an Evangelical college by forcing the election of like-minded fellows. Like many Evangelicals he was a convinced Tory, and a desire to be Master of Trinity (a Crown appointment) made him keen to show his loyalism.[103]

Many others in the university believed that there was a plot to

---

[98] Gunning, *Reminiscences*, vol. I, pp. 278–9; Cooper, *Annals*, IV, pp. 443–7.

[99] James Stephen, *Essays in Ecclesiastical Biography* (2 vols., London, 1853), vol. II, p. 362. On Milner, see Mary Milner, *Isaac Milner*; R. I. W. and Samuel Wilberforce, *The Life of William Wilberforce* (5 vols., London, 1838) – many references; Gunning, *Reminiscences*, vol. I, pp. 90–3, 254–76.

[100] Born 1744, died 1797. Educated at Catharine Hall, Joseph lacked his younger brother's mathematical bent, but did become Third Senior Optime. A clergyman, he became in 1770 an ardent Evangelical, and helped to spread the new faith in Hull. As headmaster of the town grammar school he gave Isaac the post of usher that took him from the loom at the age of eighteen.

[101] Gunning, *Reminiscences*, vol. I, p. 270.

[102] Milner was the first Professor of Natural Philosophy; he also lectured on chemistry.

[103] See in particular the revealing letter to Wilberforce in Milner, *Isaac Milner*, pp. 161–2.

accomplish revolution, and evidence was said to come in a pamphlet by Frend published in early 1793,[104] just weeks after the execution of Louis XVI and the start of the war. With typical energy Frend rushed to attack the notion of war and the burden it would place on the poor. There was also a call for parliamentary reform – and criticism of religious tests and establishments. There was no revolutionary or subversive intent. Nevertheless, the university proceeded against him, Milner (who would be judge in any legal action in the Vice-Chancellor's Court) most improperly permitting twenty-seven dons to meet in his lodge at Queens' to discuss an attack on Frend. An indictment was promoted in the Vice-Chancellor's Court by Dr Kipling of St John's, whose pomposity and imperfect Latin were much derided by Gunning. The court (consisting of the heads of houses) decided that in issuing his pamphlet Frend had broken a university statute, but when called upon to recant Frend replied that 'he would sooner cut off his hand than sign it'. The Vice-Chancellor therefore pronounced sentence of banishment from the university. On a strict interpretation of statutes and procedures Frend would never have been convicted, but Milner overrode all his arguments. Undergraduates in the gallery of the Senate House, says Gunning, 'were unanimous in favour of Mr Frend, and every satirical remark reflecting upon the conduct and motives of his prosecutors was vociferously applauded'. One culprit was S. T. Coleridge, who was at that time an undergraduate of Jesus and influenced by Frend, who had converted him to Unitarianism. Slipping into the crowd, Coleridge escaped capture by the Senior Proctor, Farish.[105]

Meanwhile, Jesus College had acted too. One week after the pamphlet was published five fellows of Jesus resolved that it appeared to have 'the evil intent of prejudicing the clergy in the eyes of the laity, of degrading in the publick esteem the doctrines and rites of the Established Church, and of disturbing the harmony of Society'. At a meeting, the master and six fellows (a majority of those present, though not of the fellowship) voted to exclude Frend from the college – a penalty of very doubtful legality, for an offence that was alleged by pointing not to specific passages but merely to

---

[104] *Peace and Union Recommended to the Associated Bodies of Republicans and Anti-Republicans* (St Ives, Hunts., 1793). [105] Gunning, *Reminiscences*, vol. 1, pp. 280–308.

the pamphlet's 'general tendency'. Frend's appeal having been dismissed by the Visitor (the Bishop of Ely) he was excluded from Jesus, in the Long Vacation the gate being chained against him. The college did not however venture to attack his fellowship, whose emoluments Frend enjoyed till his marriage (to Archdeacon Blackburne's granddaughter) in 1808.[106] While hankering now and then for a return to Cambridge (he even competed for the Lucasian chair when Milner was given it) Frend was a freelance writer and teacher in London till in 1806 he became actuary to the newly created Rock Life Assurance Company. Throughout life he remained an active reformer, dying in 1841.[107]

Though Frend was punished far more lightly than others in these years – another Cambridge Unitarian, Thomas Fyshe Palmer, was transported to Botany Bay for expressing similar views[108] – his case shows the power of Tory feeling in the university. Milner even averred, in a letter to Wilberforce in 1798, that 'I don't believe Pitt was ever aware of how much consequence the expulsion of Frend was. It was the ruin of the Jacobinical party as *a university thing*, so that that party is almost entirely confined to Trinity College' – Milner making clear that he hoped to become Master of Trinity as a reward for his services, and to effect repression there.[109] But as Gunning, a radical with a strong prejudice against Milner, scathingly remarked: 'there never existed, or was supposed to exist, a Jacobin party in the University'.[110] Nor did Frend's banishment end discord. Gunning and Frend's companion Richard Reynolds of Paxton were among those who in November 1795 protested in Senate House Yard at the continuance of the war and new legislation to suppress sedition.[111] This group of dissentients was served by the *Cambridge Intelligencer*, one of the most remarkable journals of the era, that Benjamin Flower, of the Hertfordshire brewing family, published in Bridge Street from 1793 to 1803. A Unitarian much influenced by Robert Robinson, Flower made his newspaper 'a sort of nation-wide congregational magazine for Rational Dissenters', printing contri-

[106] Gray and Brittain, *A History of Jesus College*, pp. 125–8.
[107] Knight, *University Rebel*, pp. 173–308.
[108] Palmer, an ex-pupil of Jebb at Peterhouse, and a Unitarian minister in Dundee, was convicted at Perth in September 1793, in the notorious series of Scottish treason trials.
[109] Milner, *Life of Isaac Milner*, pp. 161–2.
[110] *Reminiscences*, vol. I, p. 309.   [111] Cooper, *Annals*, IV, pp. 456, 459.

butions by Frend, Dyer, and Gilbert Wakefield as well as poems by Coleridge, alongside calls for peace, parliamentary reform, and Catholic Emancipation.[112] He was allowed to publish by Pitt's government, suffering for his opinions only once, with six months in Newgate for calling Richard Watson, the Regius Professor of Divinity and one-time reformer, now Bishop of Llandaff, 'the Right Reverend time server and apostate'. At a time when a provincial newspaper usually had a circulation of some hundreds, the *Cambridge Intelligencer* sold over 2,000 a week in the mid-1790s. Reaching Scotland and South Wales and most places between, the paper was, however, bought by few people in Cambridge itself, and its editorials are not to be regarded as reflecting the opinions of more than a small minority in the university – and there are parallels here with more recent publications.

For the university, as for other parts of Britain, the war was a necessary struggle, and expressions of dissent were regarded as unpatriotic. When in 1798 invasion threatened the university, colleges and dons gave nearly £7,000 of the £11,000 raised in Cambridge. Busick Harwood, Professor of Anatomy, became captain of the corps of volunteer soldiers raised in the city. In 1803 invasion threatened again, and the university community, besides subscribing once more, raised its own corps of volunteers; 180 served, tutors permitting one hour each day for drill, and the wearing of military dress.[113] We can derive some impression of life in this detachment from the pen of Edward Daniel Clarke, a young fellow of Jesus, well known for having dispatched from the college grounds a hot-air balloon carrying a kitten, and returning from his extensive travels with abundant classical artefacts and enough memories for six volumes. The restless wanderer threw himself into the university volunteers. He wrote that he had

> just come from practising the light infantry manoeuvres, over all the hedges and ditches, towards Madingley; wet, muddy, and oozing at every pore... At present nothing is talked of in Cambridge, but the drill – who shoulders best; and who trod down Beverley's[114] heels in

---

[112] Michael J. Murphy, *Cambridge Newspapers and Opinion 1780–1850* (Cambridge, Oleander Press, 1977), p. 26, and pp. 24–40 for the following paragraph.

[113] Cooper, *Annals*, IV, pp. 451, 461–2, 475–80.

[114] Of Christ's College, Esquire Bedell.

close marching. Yesterday we had a sort of sham fight, on Parker's Piece, and they all allow we do better than the Town Volunteers ... We paraded through the streets, from Clare Hall to Parker's Piece, with a full band of music. The corps is intended as a nursery of corps, to supply the nation with officers and drill serjeants.[115]

PALMERSTON REPRESENTS THE UNIVERSITY

On the death of William Pitt in January 1806 the university constituency was contested by three young aristocrats, all destined to reach high office, while one, the third Viscount Palmerston,[116] would appear in any short list of Great Victorians. Among his achievements was to be the representative of the university for over twenty years – though his tenure did not start in 1806. Between Harrow and St John's, Palmerston spent two and a half years at Edinburgh, learning mathematics, bookkeeping and the art of fluent and rapid composition that sustained him as Foreign Secretary. He always reckoned that his Cambridge acquirements were less useful in life. As a nobleman, he did not take the university examinations, and his college studies seem not to have inspired or stretched him (though he usually was in the First Class in the St John's examinations). He thought Cambridge dons complacent and self-satisfied, by contrast to Edinburgh's lively professors. Still, he enjoyed the collegiate life and made lifelong friends. He was always loyal to Cambridge, and particularly to St John's, and he came forward quickly in 1806. His old tutor, James Wood, was his manager in the elaborate canvass.[117]

His chief opponent, Lord Henry Petty, son of the Marquess of Lansdowne, was only twenty-five, but he had been an MP for the family seat of Calne for four years. A Foxite Whig, he had the backing of the new (albeit brief) Ministry of All the Talents, and could hold out the lure of government patronage to dons avid for it; and on the great moral question of the day, the abolition of the slave

---

[115] William Otter, *The Life and Remains of the Rev. Edward Daniel Clarke, Professor of Mineralogy in the University of Cambridge* (2nd edn, 2 vols., London, 1825), vol. II, pp. 211–12. In 1808 Clarke became Professor of Mineralogy. His lectures were entertaining but inaccurate, like his classical scholarship. Highly credulous, he was deluded, so Gunning alleged, into regarding the bones of a rat and a mouse, accidentally united, as the skeleton of a new species of miniature kangaroo. See Gunning, *Reminiscences*, vol. II, pp. 202–15.

[116] He had succeeded to the title in 1802, aged seventeen.   [117] Bourne, *Palmerston*, pp. 1–51.

trade,[118] he was more convincing than Palmerston, even attracting some Evangelical votes traditionally solidly Pittite. Palmerston came bottom of the poll, behind even the tongue-tied Viscount Althorp.[119] He was not disheartened, standing again for the university at the 1807 general election. As a Tory, he had the backing of the new Portland ministry, but Euston, so long a university MP, was successful again with Sir Vicary Gibbs, a Kingsman and Attorney-General. Protestant feeling damned Petty, a supporter of Catholic Emancipation. Samuel Parr of Emmanuel heard 'the yell of "No Popery": on the walls of our senate house, of Clare Hall chapel, and of Trinity Hall, I saw the odious words, in large characters'.[120]

Through family influence, Palmerston captured the pocket borough of Newport (Isle of Wight). Nevertheless, he stood again for the university in 1811 when the Duke of Grafton died and Euston succeeded to the title. In 1806 Isaac Milner had said 'He is but a lad';[121] five years later Palmerston had had four years experience in government, two of them as a very hardworking and hard-pressed administrator at the War Office.[122] He had also, as one historian has put it, 'nursed his dons over whist and punch'.[123] This time Palmerston was successful, beating Euston's nephew Henry Smyth, a Trinity graduate of Whig sympathies, favouring Catholic Emancipation. In 1812, however, Palmerston and Smyth, with somewhat different political allegiances, were returned unopposed, and this compromise, so common in their day, lasted till Smyth's death in 1822. Palmerston himself continued to represent the university till 1831, his twenty-year tenure almost equalling Pitt's.

[118] Abolition occurred in 1807.   [119] Bourne, *Palmerston*, pp. 50–61.
[120] Quoted in Thorne, *History of Parliament*, vol. II, p. 34; pp. 32–6 for these paragraphs generally.
[121] Quoted in Bourne, *Palmerston*, p. 61.
[122] Palmerston was Secretary at War, responsible for much army finance, from 1809 to 1828.
[123] Thorne, *History of Parliament*, vol. II, p. 35.

Chapter 12

THE BACKGROUND TO UNIVERSITY REFORM, 1830–1850

THE UNIVERSITIES OF THE BRITISH ISLES

Few Cambridge writers mentioned, or at all events valued, the other universities in the British Isles – apart from Oxford and perhaps Trinity College Dublin. But the ancient universities of Scotland, and new foundations in England and Ireland, were prominent in national discourse on the purposes of education and the best ways to organise it. They offered models that contrasted with Cambridge's collegiate tuition and narrow honours curriculum; at least compelling Cambridge to justify its ways, they excited debate and influenced its terms. Though their effect upon the reform movement is hard to measure, it was no less important for that.

The ancient universities of Scotland were in some fundamental ways quite different from Oxford and Cambridge. There were four (or strictly speaking five) universities,[1] in Edinburgh, Glasgow, St Andrews, and Aberdeen.[2] They were 'non-collegiate' in structure, apart from St Andrews, whose two colleges did not possess the endowments and power familiar in Cambridge. While the medical schools of Oxford and Cambridge were moribund in the eighteenth century, those in Edinburgh and Glasgow were famous for combining advanced scientific instruction with clinical experience in local hospitals. And while Cambridge's few outstanding contributions to scholarship were in the traditional field of classics, Scotland's intellectual adventurousness was famous; some leading

---

[1] The two Aberdeen colleges, Marischal and King's, were separate universities until their amalgamation in 1860.

[2] What follows is based on Laurance James Saunders, *Scottish Democracy 1815–1840* (Edinburgh, Oliver and Boyd, 1950), pp. 307–71, and R. D. Anderson, *Education and Opportunity in Victorian Scotland. Schools and Universities* (Oxford, Clarendon, 1983), pp. 26–69.

figures in the European Enlightenment were professors, most notably Adam Smith, who was a professor at Glasgow.

Most students came up to read arts courses, and they were very different from the specialised curricula of the honours degrees at Oxford and Cambridge, being attached to the generalist tradition of the Renaissance that the English universities were moving away from. The Scots first degree, the MA, entailed the study of six subjects for different periods over four years: Latin, Greek, mathematics, logic, moral philosophy, and natural philosophy (physics). Some students enrolled for a few classes and did not take a degree; the classic example was Walter Scott, who attended Edinburgh classes in Latin, Greek, and logic between 1783 and 1785, aged between twelve and fourteen, before becoming apprenticed to his father.[3] Universities' endowments and professors' stipends were meagre; their income depended very largely on class fees. Professors conducted all the teaching, by lecture or class; sometimes groups contained more than 100 students. Written work or extensive questioning was in fact more common than we might suppose, but the lack of equivalents to Cambridge tutors limited what could be achieved. Even so, students were not merely passive sponges soaking up professors' thoughts; like the Wordsworth brothers, they brought a bookish and thoughtful culture to university – it may be discerned for example in the Edinburgh career of Thomas Carlyle – and a distinctively speculative character was given to college life by the largest element in the arts course, philosophy; it encouraged in other disciplines arguments about principles, such as 'the comparative excellence of Homer and Virgil' rather than 'the merits of rival emendations to corrupted texts',[4] usual in England. James Bryce, a student at Edinburgh in the 1850s, found the lectures of Robert Buchanan the philosophy professor tedious. But he recorded that

> the atmosphere of College life was highly stimulating, more so than I found that of Oxford afterwards. The class work kept us on the 'qui vive' and nearly the whole class wanted to learn and enjoyed learning. Whenever we had a chance we talked about our work,

[3] J. G. Lockhart, *Life of Sir Walter Scott* (10 vols., Edinburgh, 1882 edn), vol. I, pp. 163–78 (Chapter 4).

[4] George Elder Davie, *The Democratic Intellect. Scotland and Her Universities in the Nineteenth Century* (Edinburgh University Press, 1961), p. 15.

discussing the questions that came up, an incessant sharpening of wits upon one another's whetstones. We spoke very little about theology and much about politics, and though we cared about classics the ambition of most of us would have been to be metaphysicians.[5]

Universities were what are now termed 'open access' institutions. Boys came up at sixteen, sometimes as young as fourteen, from grammar schools or even on occasion the elementary schools, and the generalist curriculum and introductory teaching of Scots universities were fitting complements to what in English terms was inadequate preparation for a student's task;[6] many of the Scottish universities' 'feeder' schools could not easily have provided more intensive teaching. At university there were no religious tests, and little supervision, young as students were.[7] Graduating was not always a spur to effort; often the gathering of certificates of attendance sufficed. The greatest difference from Oxford and Cambridge was the cost of university education. At Glasgow fees, accommodation and board might cost only £25 a year, or even as little as £13 if a student lived very frugally; costs elsewhere were similar, and bursaries were available.[8]

The breadth of their arts courses and their ease of entry have encouraged a belief in the popular character of the Scots universities, one aspect of the faith in the superiority of Scotland's educational provision generally. College is thought to have been open to the 'lad o'pairts' from a humble background, like Thomas Carlyle, the stonemason's son from Dumfriesshire who walked to Edinburgh in 1809, at nearly fourteen years of age:

> They had no one to look after them either on their journey or when they came to the end... They found their own humble lodgings, and were left entirely to their own capacity for self-conduct. The carriers brought them oatmeal, potatoes and salt butter from the home farm, with a few eggs occasionally as a luxury. With their

[5] Quoted in Anderson, *Education and Opportunity*, p. 33. Bryce became a statesman, and Lord Bryce.
[6] Still today the roles of school and university are interpreted differently in Scotland and England. The Scottish first degree (MA) is longer, and students begin it at seventeen, not eighteen, after only one year in the sixth form. To some extent the degree is still 'general' in scope.
[7] At St Andrews and Aberdeen attempts were made to enforce church attendance, though in the nature of things they were not always effective. [8] Saunders, *Scottish Democracy*, pp. 361–2.

thrifty habits they required no other food. In the return cart their linen went back to their mothers to be washed and mended.[9]

Thus to the royal commissioners in 1826 Francis Jeffrey endorsed

> on the whole the justice of the reproach that has been levelled against our general national instruction — that our knowledge, though more general, is more superficial than with our neighbours ... but I think it is a great good on the whole, because it enables relatively large numbers of people to get ... that knowledge which tends to liberalise and make intelligent the mass of our population, more than anything else.[10]

Recently we have been urged not to exaggerate the democratic openness of Scottish education.[11] Overall her educational achievements were not dramatically superior to England's, nor her schools much less influenced by class and hierarchy. There were few 'lads o'pairts' in universities; and, as far as the delphic statistics allow us to judge, it seems that entry was disproportionately weighted towards the landowning and professional classes. Still, Scotland was very different. The cheapness of the universities encouraged the entry of sons of tradesmen and skilled artisans for whom there was little Cambridge parallel. Above all, Scotland had a much higher ratio of university places to population, although her universities were more akin to sixth-form colleges than to Oxford and Cambridge.[12] Her universities offered a contrasting model of higher education that profoundly affected the debate on the future of Oxford and Cambridge.

In the period 1820–60 university reform was if anything even more widely debated in Scotland than England. There were various proposals for entrance and honours examinations, increased atten-

---

[9] J. A. Froude, *Thomas Carlyle. A History of the First Forty Years of His Life, 1795–1835* (new edn, 2 vols., London, 1895), vol. I, p. 21.

[10] Quoted in Davie, *The Democratic Intellect*, p. 27. Jeffrey was an advocate at the Scots bar, and the first editor of the *Edinburgh Review*.

[11] The following argument is based on R. A. Houston, *Scottish Literacy and the Scottish Identity. Illiteracy and Society in Scotland and Northern England, 1600–1800* (Cambridge University Press, 1985), esp. pp. 244–55; W. M. Mathew, 'The Origins and Occupations of Glasgow Students, 1740–1839', *Past and Present*, 33 (April, 1966), pp. 74–94; T. C. Smout, *A History of the Scottish People. 1560–1830* (London, Collins, 1969), esp. pp. 472–3, and *A Century of the Scottish People. 1830–1950* (London, Collins, 1986), esp. pp. 216–18.

[12] In the 1860s Scotland's ratio of places to population was 1 : 1000 as compared with 1 : 5,800 in England.

tion to classics, and the introduction of a tutorial system in some form, that reflected admiration for the English colleges, and also the ambition of the Scottish middle class – to some extent in conflict with the 'open access' ideal as voiced by Jeffrey and others. In a lecture in 1857 comparing Oxford and Edinburgh, J. S. Blackie, a classicist anxious to raise Scotland's academic standing, declared against the 'impertinent' idea that 'Universities ought to be regulated mainly for the sons of the poorest classes . . . The middle classes certainly and the rich have as great a claim.'[13] The legislation that in 1858 resulted from these contentions introduced, through the medium of executive commissioners, optional entrance examinations and honours courses, without however damaging open access and the generalist MA.[14]

The Scottish universities strongly influenced the notion of what, in 1825, the poet Thomas Campbell called 'a great London University', for 'multifariously teaching, examining, exercising, and rewarding with honours in the liberal arts and sciences, the youth of our middling rich people, between the ages of 15 or 16 and 20, or later if you please'.[15] The thrust behind the foundation of University College in 1826 came from men opposed to the leading features of the ancient universities – their religious exclusiveness, intellectual narrowness, inadequacy in training for the professions, and expensive and wasteful patterns of instruction. The need to break through these limitations brought together men who were liberal in politics such as Campbell, Henry Brougham, and James Mill,[16] often in the circle of Jeremy Bentham and Utilitarian in philosophy, and also Dissenters with their own special reasons for desiring more opportunities for higher education. There were also some Anglican and Roman Catholic supporters who welcomed the fresh intellectual openings the college made. The Cambridge architect William Wilkins was chosen to design the college, and from the first it had some Cambridge men among its teachers

---

[13] Quoted in Anderson, *Education and Opportunity*, p. 56. This paragraph is based on this book, pp. 36–74.

[14] The 1858 Act also reformed the universities' constitutions, which were as obsolete as Cambridge's.

[15] *The Times*, 9 February 1825, quoted in Hugh Hale Bellot, *University College, London, 1826–1926* (University of London Press, 1929), p. 52. The following account is based on this work, pp. 1–84.

[16] A politician playing a minor role who should be mentioned in view of his later importance in the university question was Lord John Russell.

including the mathematician Augustus De Morgan, but the principles on which it was based were Scottish – many of its founding fathers having experience of Edinburgh or Glasgow – with some influence too from German universities and Jefferson's University of Virginia, itself owing something to Scotland. University College imposed no religious tests and was not residential,[17] had a wide curriculum for its four-year course but like Edinburgh admitted students to single courses, and laid great stress on the professional education of lawyers and doctors. Teaching was professorial; that is, by lecture, and there was no place for the indolent scholars of the sort who attracted William Wordsworth's scorn at St John's; professors were in the main remunerated directly by students' fees for their courses. And the college was cheap; the average annual cost for a student nominated by a proprietor (that is, someone investing capital) was £22 7s 6d.

The first Anglican backlash against the 'godless' institution in Gower Street seems to have come from Cambridge, in the form of a sermon preached in Great St Mary's on Commencement Sunday by the Revd Hugh James Rose, in July 1826.[18] There followed a series of attacks on irreligious education in the Conservative and Anglican press, and in due course a meeting in June 1828 to inaugurate a rival establishment at which the Duke of Wellington took the chair and the two archbishops were present, together with many other Anglicans, clerical and lay. King's College London resulted.[19] The founding of the University of Durham in 1832 reflected a similar Anglican impulse.[20] Both institutions were modified versions of the ancient universities rather than 'open-access' foundations on the Scottish model, and this was especially true of Durham. It was endowed from the see of Durham but partly modelled on Christ Church, Oxford, which was also linked to a cathedral; it had fellows and in due course Proctors, and was residential in nature so as to

---

[17] One reason for its lack of residence was the wish to avoid any scrutiny of students' religious habits. Fear of contention also led to the omission of any theological instruction.

[18] *The Tendency of Prevalent Opinions about Knowledge Considered* (Cambridge, 1826). Rose, Fourteenth Wrangler in 1821, was a fellow of St John's from 1824 to 1838. From 1837 to his death in 1873 he was rector of Houghton Conquest, Bedfordshire.

[19] F. J. C. Hearnshaw, *The Centenary History of King's College London 1828–1928* (London, Harrap, 1929), pp. 33–101, for this account.

[20] C. E. Whiting, *The University of Durham 1832–1932* (London, Sheldon Press, 1932), pp. 30–113 for what follows.

reinforce student discipline. At both Durham and King's attendance at Anglican prayers was obligatory, and Durham did not admit Dissenters at all. But both colleges had broader curricula than the ancient universities and stressed professional education. Durham prepared men for the Anglican ministry more thoroughly than its southern exemplars, and its zeal to establish an engineering school (the first at a British university) outran demand. At King's the medical school was important. Both colleges, too, enjoyed the economies of scale that came from professorial teaching, and were cheaper than Oxford or Cambridge. Still, neither departed so far from the ancient tradition as to be approved by the writers who clamoured so long for university reform. They showed the strength of the Anglican Establishment that was the reformers' chief target, and also how Oxford and Cambridge might usefully be modified without substantial change. They did not however provide evidence for defenders of the ancient universities, who tended to look only at themselves.

The Irish university colleges at Belfast, Cork, and Galway were founded by Peel's government in 1845 and federated to form the Queen's University by Russell's administration in 1850; they were the first such institutions created by the state in the British Isles in modern times, and were by design very different from the Cambridge of the 1840s.[21] The only Irish university at that time, Trinity College, Dublin, was an episcopalian foundation and in many respects like Oxford and Cambridge. Though it admitted Roman Catholics to degrees, they could not be given bursaries or fellowships. Nor could Presbyterians, numerous in Ulster, who for many generations had gravitated to the Scots universities. The new colleges, therefore, owed their origin to the desire, adverted to by the eminent Roman Catholic layman Thomas Wyse, that 'the national intellect, waste but fertile, should be brought into cultivation';[22] and to Peel's hope 'of weaning from repeal [of the Union with Britain] the great body of wealthy and intelligent Roman Catholics by the steady manifestation of a desire to act with impartiality'. Attempting

[21] What follows is based on T. W. Moody and J. C. Beckett, *Queen's, Belfast 1845–1949. The History of a University* (2 vols., London, Faber, 1959), vol. I, pp. xxv–lxvii, 1–83, and W. E. Vaughan (ed.), *A New History of Ireland, vol.* v, Ireland under the Union 1801–70 (Oxford, Clarendon, 1989), pp. 186–7, 235–6, 396–8.

[22] Quoted in Moody and Beckett, *Queen's, Belfast*, p. liv, and p. 1 for the quotation from Peel.

to steer between the mutual suspicions of the three denominations, Peel trusted to a structure welcoming all sects while giving control to none; the episcopalian prescription of Trinity and its English exemplars had to be eschewed. Thus the colleges owed much to the Irish National Education scheme that Grey's Whig government had founded in 1831 for state-supported elementary schooling.[23] As in the Scottish universities and University College, London, there were no religious tests – though Irish zeal meant that students were under the supervision of their church, which was not true in the British institutions mentioned. In the great range of subjects necessary for graduation Scotland and the London colleges were models, as they were for the professorial pattern of teaching, the lack of residential colleges, and the cheapness of instruction. A student paid £28 for the three-year course at one of the colleges, while the cost of four years at Trinity College, Dublin was £84. The three colleges at Belfast, Cork, and Galway were united in one degree-granting university in 1850 owing much to the structure of London University, though more closely federated.

Founded by Peel, the colleges were built and recruited staff and students while Russell was in power. At the same time as moving towards royal commissions to speed up change at Oxford and Cambridge, Russell had to consider strong sectarian hostility to the principle behind the Irish colleges, which culminated, on the part of the intransigents in the Roman Catholic Church, in the rejection, at the Synod of Thurles in 1850, of the idea of 'mixed education' that the Queen's Colleges embodied, and eventually to the founding of the Catholic University of Ireland in 1854. When the catastrophe of the Great Famine was striking Ireland, Russell's government had also to try to cope with Cardinal Cullen, William Whewell, and the orthodox Presbyterians of Belfast: the Irish colleges were on his mind as he grappled with the reform of Oxford and Cambridge.

TOWARDS REFORM: THE ECCLESIASTICAL COMMISSION

Many events brought about the appointment in 1850 of royal commissions to enquire into the state of Oxford and Cambridge,

---

[23] Donald H. Akenson, 'Pre-University Education, 1782–1870', in Vaughan, *Ireland under the Union, 1801–70*, pp. 523–37.

and the reform of the universities to which they led. One particularly important agency is described in this section: the Ecclesiastical Commissioners for England and Wales, which made the reform of the universities in the long run inevitable.

In 1835, Peel, Prime Minister in a brief Conservative government, set up the Ecclesiastical Commissioners in response to a widely perceived need to reform the administration of the Church of England; the commissioners, consisting of clerics and lay churchmen, set about a systematic campaign to effect change, through enquiry and recommendation that led to legislation, and through the executive powers the commissioners themselves in due course acquired.[24] Bishops' stipends were equalised, more or less, and age-old anomalies in diocesan boundaries redressed; sinecures in cathedral chapters were removed and the money generated used to benefit poor parochial clergy, and leasing-policy for church lands improved, to the lessors' advantage. The labour was intricate, laborious, and time-consuming, and took many decades to complete. The commissioners faced bitter and tenacious opposition from vested interests and their allies on the political Right, and from radicals and Dissenters who wanted the Church of England not reformed but disestablished. But support came from Conservatives and Liberals alike, anxious to protect the Establishment, and as Peel declared in his 'Tamworth Manifesto' (1834) 'to remove every abuse' that could 'impair its efficiency', and 'to extend the sphere of its usefulness, and to strengthen and confirm its just claims upon the respect and affections of the people'.

Much in this process seemed highly pertinent to Oxford and Cambridge dons at the time, and remains so to their historian today. While professing Newton or Thucydides was very different from the varied tasks of a parochial clergyman, church and college concerns were intermingled; many graduates and the majority of fellows took holy orders, and countless *DNB* biographies show movement from fellowship to college living and back again, perhaps to a headship of house. Sometimes the university was

---

[24] These paragraphs draw on G. F. A. Best, *Temporal Pillars. Queen Anne's Bounty, the Ecclesiastical Commissioners, and the Church of England* (Cambridge University Press, 1964), esp. pp. 273–398, and Owen Chadwick, *The Spirit of the Oxford Movement* (Cambridge University Press, 1990), pp. 63–85.

immediately interested in the Ecclesiastical Commissioners' ideas and contributed to the debate – for example over plans to suppress canonries at Christ Church and Ely cathedrals so as to sustain theological teaching for those intending ordination, an issue much in the minds of those promoting Anglican renewal.[25] At high table in forty colleges, the spectacle in the 1830s and 1840s of a closely parallel institution, the Church of England, being steadily reformed was certain both to raise hopes and also cause dismay, its great potential for good being deepened, while its undoubted faults were diminished at the cost of discomfort to vested interests. Most ripe for reform were cathedral chapters, overstocked with prebends and canonries that shared income from the capitular estates in return for insubstantial tasks. What their reform portended for college fellowships was obvious, and many apprehensions were laid bare in the plea of the Revd J. W. Blakesley, a fellow of Trinity, that the church should consist of more than parochial clergy and bishops. There was a need to retain channels 'by which every valuable talent has flowed into the Church . . . We can as little dispense with the scholar, the metaphysician, and the antiquary, as with the preacher.'[26]

Geoffrey Best has discerned a range of attitudes towards ecclesiastical reform in the early 1830s. At one extreme was the 'bold reformism' of Charles Blomfield, Bishop of London, and at the other the 'cavalier young conservatism of the early Tractarians'. Between was 'a rather timid conservatism, bowing somewhat to the storm around them, and hoping that a show of reforming readiness might buy off all but the most implacable of the establishment's foes';[27] Christopher Wordsworth, the Master of Trinity, was in this group. Dons' views on university reform varied in just the same way, and given the overlap between the two sets of institutions, the cultures they embodied and the challenges they faced, that is not surprising. Thus Bishop Blomfield, ex-fellow of Trinity College, Cambridge and moving spirit in the Ecclesiastical Commission, had an exact parallel in John Graham, ex-Master of Christ's College and chairman of the Cambridge Royal Commission of Enquiry of

[25] Richard Brent, *Liberal Anglican Politics. Whiggery, Religion, and Reform 1830–1841* (Oxford, Clarendon, 1987), pp. 210–11.
[26] *Thoughts on the Recommendations of the Ecclesiastical Commission . . . A Letter to W. E. Gladstone* (1837), quoted in Best, *Temporal Pillars*, p. 338.   [27] *Temporal Pillars*, pp. 274–5.

1850. But the two reform movements were linked by more than similarities of personnel, attitude, and issue. Changes in ecclesiastical structures in the 1840s, however slow and incremental, made it less and less likely that the universities would not be induced to change. Also, the use for church reform of commissioners chosen from within the institution itself guaranteed the conservative and sympathetic character of the changes they effected. It provided a model for the university reforms, which however much anguish they caused in the 1850s and 1860s were in fact remarkably gentle and moderate.

THE DEBATE ON UNIVERSITY REFORM

'On a fine morning about the middle of October', wrote Thomas Joyce in 1841 about a Cambridge matriculant, 'behold our young aspirant at the door of the White Horse, Fetter Lane. He will be surrounded with ten or twelve more on the same errand, all laden with huge bales of luggage and with admonitions paternal and maternal, the one not to study too little, and the other not to study too much.'[28] In the pages that follow we are taken through 'the routine and rusty usages' that beset the novice: his entrance test was a farce, Cambridge tradesmen bandits, his dinner disgusting, compulsory chapel a disservice to religion, and college lectures 'often exceedingly good' but unable to 'supply the wants of the most advanced'. Because of their very nature Cambridge examinations encouraged 'cramming', incompatible with 'real improvement', while the host of disciplinary regulations would have been most irksome if canny undergraduates had not learned to evade them. Among some real scholars and gentlemen there were too many cynics, drunkards, 'rowing men',[29] and playboys who talk and laugh well and 'can do anything but study'. Young men are tempted into dissolute habits by the lack of any real moral guidance, beneath the dense fabric of minute regulation which had been devised for schoolboy seminarians centuries ago, and was easy for men of nineteen to dodge. Joyce's wide-ranging critique is typical of many

[28] Thomas Joyce, 'College Life at Cambridge', *Westminster Review*, 35 (April, 1841), pp. 457–8. The following quotations are from pp. 461–81.
[29] That is noisy men, perhaps hooligans, but not boaters.

in its attitude though by no means the most vehement in its utterance. Criticism of the English universities began at the beginning of the century, with attacks in the *Edinburgh Review* on the obsolete character of their scholarship and the narrowness of their curricula.[30] Comment broadened and became more intense about 1830, and one writer was sure of the reason: 'This is the age of reform.- Next in importance to our religious and political establishments, are the foundations for public education; and having now seriously engaged in a reform of "the constitution, the envy of surrounding nations", the time cannot be distant for a reform in the schools and universities which have hardly avoided their contempt.'[31] A common theme is the outmoded nature of Oxford and Cambridge, bypassed by nineteenth-century progress. 'On the whole',[32] Joyce continues in the article already cited, considering

> how few concessions have been made to time and circumstance, it is wonderful that the good is as great as it is; as to the evil, it is impossible to calculate it . . . how many characters have been ruined, how many false notions have been instilled into the breast. . . Nor will many of the evils be remedied as long as the government of the colleges is confided to those who have spent their lives within their walls; men originally distinguished for nothing but an accurate knowledge of the mathematical ideas of others, the refuse of wranglers, who have been too lazy or too stupid to enter on the more active and exciting business of the world. There is a moral unfitness supposed in their choice of life, and this unfitness is increased tenfold by the habits and ideas acquired in their seclusion, and by the want of that necessary intelligence which their seclusion prevents them from acquiring. The only qualification at present required for the man who is to direct the characters and perhaps fix the fates of the youth of our country is, that he should have been one of the first twenty wranglers twenty years ago, and should never have quitted his college since.

[30] See the reviews of La Place, *Traité de Méchanique Celeste* in *Edinburgh Review*, 11 (1807–8), pp. 249–81, the Clarendon edition of Strabo's geography, in *Edinburgh Review*, 14 (1809), pp. 429–41, and Richard Edgeworth's *Essays on Professional Education* in 15 (1809–10), pp. 40–53.
[31] 'On the State of the English Universities, with more especial reference to Oxford' (June, 1831), pp. 386–7, reprinted in William Hamilton, *Discussions on Philosophy and Literature, Education and University Reform* (London, 1852), pp. 386–434.   [32] 'College Life at Cambridge', pp. 480–1.

Another writer, taking up the theme of unpracticality, focused on the Revd Theophilus Mudge,[33] the son of a parson, an ex-fellow of St John's, who introduced his son to Euclid at the age of ten and 'inoculated' him 'with Differential Calculus'. At St John's in his turn, the son lacked 'imagination and invention, whether in classics or mathematics'. But he learned to write out his bookwork fast, and 'translated Thucydides with that awkward accuracy which none but English scholars could admire'. This 'ossified scholar' became Eighth Wrangler and got a second class in the Classics Tripos. After a fellowship, he went to a college living 'among the woolcombers and corn-factors of Bumble-borough-on-the-hill', a 'rude and sharp-witted population' who had acquired hatred of the aristocracy and the Church of England at the Chartist Club and the Tabernacle. But knowing nothing of the mental world of his assailants, Mudge was both 'helpless and contemptuous', and had to suffer 'the shameless impudence of braggart ignorance to triumph unrefuted'. He became despised, and 'in this case, the world at large ... is much of the mind of Bumbleborough, and looks with deserved suspicion at a system where ... the Mudges can succeed in carrying away its emoluments and honours'.

One of the chief impressions one gains from these critics is of the very extensive common ground between them and the most enlightened apologists for the ancient universities. They share J. H. Newman's dislike of merely useful or practical education, and the need for a university to be 'liberal' in its purpose and curricula, dedicated, the Trinity MA J. M. Kemble wrote, to the 'cultivation of the imaginative and the intellectual faculties', and thus to 'the development of their character as men'. Unhappily, 'the *means* have been erected into an end'; the competitiveness that mathematical examinations especially foster has become 'idolatry'. 'For this evil course Cambridge is deeply responsible, – much more so than Oxford... The schoolboy intended for Cambridge becomes habituated to the consideration of a fellowship as the goal towards

---

[33] C. J. Bayley, 'University Reform', *Edinburgh Review*, 89 (April, 1849), pp. 499–517. The quotations that follow are taken from pp. 504–5.

which he is to strive, and which he can only attain by passing over the necks of his competitors.'[34]

On the other hand another keen reformer, Charles Lyell the eminent geologist, praised the competitiveness of the nineteenth century for at least increasing 'zeal and emulation... The preparation for fellowship examinations has thus become a powerful incentive to industry after graduation'.[35] Lyell's qualities were characterised by Darwin as 'clearness, caution, sound judgement and a good deal of originality... The science of geology is enormously indebted to Lyell, more so, as I believe, than to any other man.'[36] Lyell, a graduate of Exeter College, Oxford, first wrote on university reform in 1827, and again in 1845. He wrote as an Englishman, but explicitly drew upon the characteristics of Scottish and Continental universities – making salient the differences between them on the one hand and Oxford and Cambridge on the other. While yielding to no one in his concern for a sound liberal education, Lyell pointed out that for an Englishman it comprised a much narrower range of subjects than in Scotland and elsewhere in Europe. There was much complacency on this issue in England. Also, the *liberal* might turn out to be *useful* after all. In a travel memoir Lyell averred

> that it is often the boast of writers who extol our university system above that of other countries, that we promote *liberal* studies, and do not condescend to qualify students for a lucrative profession or trade. But what is the real fact? Do not the majority of the ablest students toil at Latin, Greek and mathematics, with purely professional objects? Are they not preparing themselves for becoming private tutors, schoolmasters, and college-tutors; expecting to combine these avocations with fellowships, or with clerical duties?[37]

A liberal education should also comprise far more than the classical and narrowly mathematical curricula of Oxford and

[34] J. M. Kemble, 'British and Foreign Universities: Cambridge', *British and Foreign Review*, 5 (July, 1837), pp. 179–81. Kemble, a member of the theatrical clan, was the brother of Fanny Kemble and nephew of J. P. Kemble and Mrs Siddons. At Trinity he was a friend of Tennyson, and according to William Hunt in the *DNB*, 'read much, but would not follow the course of study prescribed by the university'. He became a noted Anglo-Saxon scholar, and edited the *British and Foreign Review* from 1835 to 1844.

[35] Charles Lyell, 'State of the Universities', *Quarterly Review*, 36 (June, 1827), pp. 258–9.

[36] *Autobiographies*, pp. 58–9.

[37] Charles Lyell, *Travels in North America* (2 vols., London, 1845), vol. 1, pp. 289–90.

Cambridge, as it did indeed in Scotland and abroad. In promoting the claims of the natural sciences Lyell was typical of many reformers, conscious of the rapid advances around them in the civilised world, but neglected in two of its greatest universities. Physical science, like traditional subjects, might 'contribute to perfect the moral character', because 'conflicting evidence may be tried fairly by its own strength, and the judgement formed by an habitual practice of examining proofs with an unbiassed desire of discovering truth'. The principles of reasoning fostered 'are not limited in their operation to philosophical inquiries alone, but conduce both to the moral and the intellectual advancement of society'.[38] In a passage reminding us greatly of the Snow–Leavis 'Two Cultures' debate of the 1960s Lyell declared that 'if we confine elementary knowledge on this subject to a small circle in society ... the beneficial effects above alluded to are enfeebled in energy, and retarded in their progress; and, secondly, very serious inconveniences arise from the unequal rate at which the intellectual improvement of different parts of the same community advances'. Lyell was among the most vigorous of many advocates of a scientific curriculum. He also alleged that the length of a liberal education, lasting to the age of twenty-two in Oxford and Cambridge, was unique in Europe, and that as a result men of modest means intending to be lawyers or doctors did not resort to them. In addition, the purely *professional* education of lawyers and doctors, though keenly pursued in medieval Oxford and Cambridge, had languished there compared to Paris and Padua.[39]

Thomas Jefferson Hogg, Shelley's friend and biographer whose special reasons for disliking the ancient universities lent bitterness to his comments,[40] like other writers attacked the laziness and non-residence of fellows, and the waste of wealth, 'greatly exceeding the sum of all the possessions of all the other learned bodies in the world'; but 'not a single shilling of their enormous income is truly applied to the purposes for which it was designed'. The universities' 'spiritual constitution' is alleged to be the 'mischief' that 'annuls'

[38] Lyell, 'State of the Universities', pp. 221–3, and p. 223 for the next passage.
[39] 'State of the Universities', pp. 221–37.
[40] He was sent down from Oxford with Shelley in 1811 for helping him to write *The Necessity of Atheism*. What follows is based on his article, 'The Universities of Oxford and Cambridge', *Westminster Review*, 15 (July, 1831), pp. 56–69. The quotations that follow are taken from pp. 60–1.

their academic purpose; it 'converts establishments that ought to be schools of learning, into race-courses and amphitheatres'; in them 'competitors and gladiators . . . struggle, or collude, to get possession of livings'. This problem was by many restated as one of *colleges* as against the *university*, and one such critic was John Conington.[41] Colleges, inward-looking and selfish institutions, had since the Reformation 'engrossed' (the word was often used) the university itself, the representative of or spokesman for, wider interests – scholarship, intellectual progress, and the nation. Originally, 'they were merely charitable foundations, without any academical power'; but now 'they have engrossed all the students, and a large portion of the instructors', so that the university is dominated by 'the rules of a rigid and narrow ecclesiasticism'. Thus Conington and Hogg, responding to Cambridge's polymorphous nature, used different terms to describe a concern that fundamentally they saw in the same way.

The Anglican character of the university that its constitution protected, and the exclusion of Protestant Dissenters and others that it led to, was the greatest single complaint of the reformers, and (for whatever numbers may mean) seems to have produced more writing, both for and against, than any other – with most, it appears, being against. Strongly in favour of the universities was a piece by William Sewell,[42] tutor of Exeter College, Oxford, friend in their early Tractarian days of Newman, Keble, and Pusey, and the man who tore up and burned J. A. Froude's *Nemesis of Faith*. Sewell's article rehearses the arguments used by Tories in the 1837 debates on the issue of Anglican exclusiveness.

Sewell's writing thus had the vehement and unreasoning tone of the *ex parte* sectarian statement and was certain to stiffen the faithful rather than convert anybody. That was also true of many of the reformist articles. An exception was thirty pages by William Empson and Francis W. Newman that appeared at the height of the late 1840s controversy.[43] Empson was Professor of Law at the East India College, Haileybury, and editor of the *Edinburgh Review*.

---

[41] Conington, 'The English Universities', pp. 169–201; the quotations that follow are taken from p. 192. Conington was aged twenty-five in 1850, and a fellow of University College, Oxford; in 1854 he became Professor of Latin.

[42] 'The Universities', *Quarterly Review*, 59 (October, 1837), pp. 439–83.

[43] 'Academical test articles', *Edinburgh Review*, 88 (July, 1848), pp. 163–93.

Newman was brother of the famous Oxford convert to Roman Catholicism. Francis moved away early from his brother's influence and in 1830 resigned a Balliol fellowship because he could not subscribe to the Thirty-nine Articles; he was, says an unidentified writer in the *DNB*, 'zealous for intercommunion of all protestants'. When the article in question appeared he was Professor of Latin in University College, London. Complex and sometimes involved utterance, the article is a scrupulous philosophical defence of a university's essential intellectual diversity,

> in contrast to practical societies, which are all necessarily Sectarian. The former are peculiarly ennobled by being devoted to advance and perfect knowledge; the latter proceed *from* established results, and, as institutions, have no power or business to search for truth at all. They are, therefore, inferior in dignity to the former, as the hand is to the eye.[44]

While truth is immutable, our conception of it evolves, and tests devised to guard the intellectual status quo do not in fact guarantee uniformity of opinion, as a glance at Oxford and Cambridge confirmed, while 'in lecturing on Thucydides or Newton's Principia, no deficiency will be felt from the speaker's imperfect belief of the University Test Articles'. But tests do tempt hypocrisy, while 'a preference of things spiritual to things material', qualities such as the love

> of knowledge rather than of gain . . . sentiments, not propositions . . . are the elements which distinguish better from common minds. Yet if all these were framed into a creed, to exact subscriptions to it would still be ridiculous . . . and it is the *intensity* of these sentiments which has in every age constituted the true hero, saint, and martyr, not the being able to subscribe sincerely to Nicene, Tridentine, Augsburghian or Anglican formularies.

Empson and Newman, like others, recommended laicising colleges, and so the universities themselves. Unusually for this era, they even urged that divinity professors should not be fettered by a system implying 'that every thing was settled for ever by *somebody* three centuries ago; yet who the somebody was, nobody can truly say'. But 'the same considerations then apply to professors of

---

[44] P. 176, and pp. 170 and 174 for the next quotations.

Divinity, as of Physiology. The person who is invited to occupy the teacher's chair should not be subject to dictation. Where is his superior in knowledge? – who can decorously claim to enact conclusions for him?'[45] The divinity dons should possess an assured place, perhaps indeed an enhanced place, in the reformed prescription, but one where their true function as seekers after religious truth was to be the criterion for inclusion, and their utterance was to rely upon persuasiveness rather than edict. Above all, their roles as tutors and parochial clergy were no longer to be confused. Theology might be composed in college, but not to the neglect of parish duties, and no value was to be attached

> to a modern theory, on which great stress has been laid, – that a Tutor has the undergraduates of his college for his parishioners; and we are told by some tutors, that unless they are allowed to account themselves *pastors* to their pupils . . . they will feel it opposed to their ordination vow to hold the place of Tutor at all. There could not be a broader acknowledgement of their false position; for they are ordained not on their tutorship, but on their fellowship. If the theory is worth any thing, every theological fellow, not every Tutor only, is a parish priest to the young students . . . The remedy for the false position of the Tutors is not to be found in . . . a theory which cripples the Universities for their proper intellectual ends, but in rescinding the College Statutes which constrain the Fellows to take Orders.[46]

Like every serious commentator on the nature of the university, Empson and Newman inevitably touched on the functions of tutors – even though they began by considering a different topic. This was the heart of the university question: who should teach, and upon what terms? The focus was on the issue, Professors or Tutors? – but it was always a discussion about balance, not between absolutes: a point that it is necessary to stress, since John Henry Newman alleged that it was a struggle between partisans of professorial and tutorial teaching – Newman naturally supporting the latter. In his *Historical Sketches*[47] he wrote that the

---

[45] P. 177.   [46] P. 183.
[47] J. H. Newman, *Historical Sketches* (3 vols., London, 1872), vol. I, pp. 181–2. It is only fair to add that Newman was 'for both views at once', and thought 'neither of them complete without the other'. But he does not say that the 'professorial party' were of the same opinion, at least in Cambridge.

dispute ... carried on at intervals in the British Universities for the last fifty years ... began in the pages of the *Edinburgh Review*, which might at that time be in some sense called the organ of the University of Edinburgh. Twenty years later ... it was renewed in the same quarter, and lately it was going on briskly between some of the most able members of the University of Oxford.

The point at issue was 'whether a University should be conducted on the system of Professors, or on the system of Colleges and College Tutors'. J. H. Newman continued,

> The party of the North and of progress have ever advocated the Professorial system ... and have pointed in their own behalf to the practice of the middle ages and of modern Germany and France; the party of the South and of prescription have ever stood up for the Tutorial or collegiate system, and have pointed to Protestant Oxford and Cambridge, where it has almost or altogether superseded the Professorial.

Now while it is true that the weight of Cambridge opinion favoured college teaching, it is not true that reformers were anti-tutorialists, advocating professorial teaching exclusively, as we may see by examining the writings of Sir William Hamilton, Professor of Civil History in the University of Edinburgh until 1836, and of Logic and Metaphysics thereafter. Hamilton was regarded by Newman as the chief opponent of the tutorial system.

Hamilton, from Glasgow merchant stock, like other Scots went up to Oxford after university classes at home. At Balliol a negligent tutor forced him to organise his own studies, but nevertheless Hamilton gained a first in *literae humaniores* (classics) in 1810. Afterwards Hamilton also studied medicine and law in Edinburgh; a man of omnivorous reading, and 'subtle in thought, vehement in argumentation, precise in speech, ardent in nature',[48] Hamilton was an inspiring lecturer, and a vigorous controversialist, whose 'one great practical interest' was higher education, on whose history and the means of reform he amassed 'a wonderful accumulation of knowledge'. Because of the copiousness of his

---

[48] John Veitch, *Memoir of Sir William Hamilton* (Edinburgh, 1869), p. 218, and pp. 163–4 for the quotations immediately following.

writing on the matter and the attention Newman paid to him, he is the most famous reformer, though the title given to him by a twentieth-century historian, the 'Father of University reform',[49] underplays the contributions of many others, perhaps most notably Sir Charles Lyell. In the most salient of his essays[50] Hamilton first discussed at length his interpretation of Oxford's history – which was that the true and original function of the university had been usurped by the colleges, which meant that 'public utility, and the interests of science' were 'sacrificed to private monopoly'. Hamilton's very determined argument for the revival of professorial teaching reflects his Scottish background (hence Newman's dig at 'the party of the North and of progress') but he also declared that 'we are no enemies of collegial residence, no enemies of tutorial discipline', and 'a tutorial system in subordination to a professorial (which Oxford formerly enjoyed) we regard as affording *the condition of an absolutely perfect University*'.[51] The great majority of reformers, at least, were of a similar opinion. In his second essay on university reform, a brief though pregnant contribution, Francis Newman averred that[52]

> at the Universities themselves a certain consciousness pervades the younger Masters, – Tutors and Fellows, – that their relation to the Public Professors is essentially unsound. The Professors ... are at present reduced to ciphers by the collegiate and tutorial system. To remove this anomaly – to use both Tutor and Professor, each in his own place – this is the great problem for all University reformers.

But 'if some modification of the system added a new impetus to Professorial exertion, – there is no reason why Oxford and Cambridge might not become centres in which all the highest knowledge of the age is accessible'.

A few months later, when the Graham Commissioners were meeting and reform of the universities was a prominent but

[49] A. I. Tillyard, *A History of University Reform 1800 A.D. to the Present Day* (Cambridge, Heffer, 1913), p. 67.

[50] Hamilton, 'On the State of the English Universities', reprinted in William Hamilton, *Discussions on Philosophy and Literature, Education and University Reform* (London, 1852), pp. 386–434. References that follow to Hamilton's essays are to this volume, the first occurring on p. 389.

[51] 'On the State of the English Universities', in *Discussions*, p. 402.

[52] Francis W. Newman, 'University Reform', *Prospective Review*, 5 (February, 1849), p. 8.

undetermined issue, the mood of uncertainty was repeated in the gloomy coda to John Conington's article.[53] 'The Commercial element', he wrote, 'is now becoming the chief power' in English life, and 'as it rises' the old universities 'are likely to decline'. No reforms they might carry out would counteract the disadvantage of a very high age of graduation: 'school is the only time that the young manufacturer, who is destined to add to the fruits of his father's industry, and not merely to enjoy them, will have for the undisturbed cultivation of learning', while a man in that very much larger group in some way 'engaged in the grand mêlée of competition' should pause before going to Oxford or Cambridge. Giving up the chance of 'becoming a more refined intellectual being' would be outweighed by 'the acquisition of an independence' to 'enable him to fight the battle of life'. The learned professions themselves, for so long closely linked to Oxford and Cambridge, but now affected by 'the industrial spirit', might well turn to institutions that offered more useful professional education to younger students, and did not make classics or geometry desiderata. Supposing them abandoned, 'provincial University-towns are not likely to have all the advantages that professional students desire. The London University will have greater inducements to offer than its elder sisters', and 'if we lose the old Universities, we may have local institutions, suited to every calling ... and capable within their own sphere of every perfection'.

After further stoical ruminations Conington concluded 'we have written with considerable hesitation... It is easy to assume the mantle of prophecy, but difficult so to wear it as not to have cause to repent of the assumption.' He hoped 'to scrutinize attentively any forthcoming demonstration' from Oxford and Cambridge that they grasped the extent of the difficulties they faced. While Conington's reflections show how precarious the position of the ancient universities seemed to one experienced observer, the views that were commonly expressed in Cambridge suggest a more complacent and assured set of attitudes.

---

[53] Conington, 'The English Universities', pp. 169–201. The quotations that follow are taken from pp. 194–201.

CAMBRIDGE ATTITUDES TO REFORM

A CONSERVATIVE UNIVERSITY

This survey of five Cambridge writers begins with the most prominent don of the period 1840–60, William Whewell, who offered a lengthy defence of Cambridge as it was, while conceding the need for change of a strictly limited kind that would not affect what he saw as the fundamental nature of the university. Considered next are two moderate reformers, George Peacock and Adam Sedgwick, and lastly two radicals, Albert Henry Wratislaw and Benjamin Dann Walsh.

Such a discussion may give a static picture of opinion, yet it is important to suggest both movement over time and the variety of attitudes towards different issues. Attracting significant support first was the movement to abolish religious tests, a grievance growing since the eighteenth century; their only defence was that the universities were rightly Anglican monopolies. In 1834 about one-third of Cambridge dons were in favour of abolishing the tests. In the majority on that issue, Whewell also spoke for almost all dons on the curriculum question in the 1830s; mathematicians and classicists all, they nodded their heads in admiring agreement of his trenchant defence of the status quo. By 1848 majority opinion had moved in favour of curricular reform, after intense criticism from writers in the heavyweight journals and the growing realisation in Cambridge of the need to find useful employment for the professors. But on the university's collegiate structure, so often excoriated in the journals, there was no discernible movement at all in Cambridge until long after the middle of the century.

Perhaps the most helpful analogy for Cambridge attitudes to reform would be the skins of an onion, the religious tests being on the outside and most easily discarded and the university's collegiate structure being the irreducible core. It is because of this background that the timing of reformist utterances is seen to be highly important: one must ask not merely, What did he say? but also, When did he say it? Peacock was an early reformer, but his wishes were modest indeed compared with those of Wratislaw and Walsh. Wratislaw, however, published his tract late, in 1850. In contrast,

Walsh was not only the most extreme of reformers, with his outspoken criticism of almost everything in the university, but also the first, publishing *A Historical Account* in 1837. Nobody seems to have bothered to reply to this most disenchanted author. It is not surprising that Walsh left Cambridge in 1838 for an entirely new life on the plains of Illinois.

WILLIAM WHEWELL

William Whewell towers over the Cambridge of the day. Luminous in his intelligence and forbidding in his fluency and propensity to offer judgements, he expressed opinions on most matters, and certainly had much to say on university organisation. A profoundly conservative reformer, he envisaged changes linked to, and justified by, his complex educational philosophy. Whewell was one of the very few Victorian dons who gave utterance to such a philosophy. In turn, it was derived – at all events apparently – from his philosophy of science and knowledge.

The best-known words about Whewell are Sydney Smith's: 'Science is his forte and omniscience his foible',[54] and they suggest the exceptional range of his achievements. A key to it was his superabundant energy, manifested in his massive physique; according to a Cambridge legend mentioned by Leslie Stephen in his *DNB* essay, a prizefighter remarked about Whewell 'What a man was lost when they made you a parson!' Thomas Woolner, the sculptor of the 'fine seated statue of Dr Whewell' which is now in the Trinity antechapel, caught a characteristic impression of his powerful presence, 'seated in his Master's gown and cassock, and with outstretched hand holding before him upon the seat a large book, while, gravely and full of thought, he looks forwards, a type of earnest meditation in the act of judgement'.[55]

Whewell, the son of a Lancaster master carpenter, won an exhibition to Trinity College, where he matriculated in 1812 at the age of eighteen. Academic success quickly followed; he was Second

---

[54] Todhunter, *William Whewell, D.D.*, vol. I, p. 410. The following account of Whewell is based on this work, on Stair Douglas, *The Life* and on the essays in Fisch and Schaffer, *William Whewell*, esp. Becher, 'William Whewell's Odyssey: From Mathematics to Moral Philosophy', pp. 1–29.
[55] F. G. Stephens, 'Thomas Woolner, R.A.', *The Art Journal* (1894), pp. 84–5.

Wrangler in 1816, and became a fellow of Trinity in 1823, remaining there until his death in 1866. From 1841 he was master, appointed by Sir Robert Peel to a position for which his talents made him a natural candidate. But most probably he would not have been chosen by his colleagues. It has been said:[56]

> Those who disliked him thought him a bully, aggressive, pompous and over-confident; and even his friends, while recognising the quality of his mind, the depth of his affections, and the extent of his generosity, acknowledged faults of temperament for which allowance had to be made. Self-conscious, probably, rather than self-confident, he had not the serene contentment of mind which may breed charm and a sense of humour.

It is revealing that while Whewell was likely to be at ease with close friends and pupils, one of whom said 'he was anything but dictatorial, and . . . perfectly accessible to proposal of objections', he was quick to resent criticism from colleagues, and apt to be authoritarian, after a prolonged examination of his conscience told him what was the right course to follow. Whewell possessed the arrogant manner that comes from the conquest of inner doubt, and he could be very overbearing indeed; he thought that fellows ought not to have keys to their own college and, though most Victorian males sat wreathed in tobacco clouds, that they should not smoke in the combination room. As Vice-Chancellor, the most famous instance of Whewell's imperiousness concerns his decision to rearrange certain nude paintings on the walls of the Fitzwilliam Museum in 1855, on the grounds 'that it should be possible to pass through the gallery without looking at such pictures'.[57] He had no warrant for his action, which much offended his old friend Thomas Worsley the Master of Downing and as a syndic responsible for the original disposition of the paintings. Whewell, as convinced of the soundness of his aesthetic judgement as he was over ideas, was unconciliatory even when a majority of the syndics resigned in protest.

Whewell was an intellectual giant, a polymath. 'Whewell composed a symphony of learning', says a recent writer, adverting

---

[56] Robert Robson, 'William Whewell, F.R.S. (1794–1866). I: Academic Life', in *Notes and Records of the Royal Society of London*, 19 (1964), pp. 168–76. What follows draws upon this essay, from which the quotations are taken.

[57] Quoted in Winstanley, *Early Victorian Cambridge*, p. 141; these lines are based on pp. 139–47.

to his blending of many themes throughout a lengthy progression, and it is the difficulty of doing justice to a career at once a unity yet so various that explains the paradox of his historiography – that he lacks a proper biography. Darwin, a far more original man, is easier to explain because his achievement was monothematic. In the Cambridge tradition that he lauded, Whewell retained a lifelong interest in the classics, and translated many of Plato's *Dialogues*. Drawn to poetry from childhood onwards, as an undergraduate he won a Chancellor's Medal for 'Boadicea'; as a fellow he adapted part of Carlyle's *Chartism* into English hexameters, and translated Goethe's *Herman and Dorothea* into the same form. These effusions revealed breadth of interests rather than inspiration, and they would not by themselves have brought Whewell into the *DNB*. His contributions to architectural history would. Whewell's interest in the topic began early in life, and he soaked himself in the details of the medieval structures of Germany in energetic travels, most notably with Thomas Rickman, whose many Gothic revival achievements include the New Court of St John's. Whewell applied scrupulous scientific techniques to his observations, remarking that 'any sound speculation must be founded on the accurate knowledge of an extensive collection of particular instances'.[58] The fruit of his researches was *Architectural Notes on German Churches*, published in 1830 and later in two revised versions. It described the character of German Late Romanesque and the transition to Gothic more expertly than any German work of the day. In some respects his history has still not been superseded, despite the constant reassessment of the subject by later scholars.

The two dominant themes in Whewell's life were mathematics and Anglicanism. He was always a wrangler, and though he added little to the science of mathematics, he played a large part in its politics, getting some (though not too much) analysis added to the Senate House Examination – a complex and time-consuming task that exploited his syndicate skills to the full.[59] His mathematical cast of mind may also be seen in his achievements in other sciences. In economics he has been 'lauded' by its historians as 'the first

---

[58] Quoted in Pevsner, *Some Architectural Writers of the Nineteenth Century*, p. 46. These lines are based on Pevsner's detailed analysis of Whewell's work, pp. 45–51.
[59] See chapter 5, pp. 171–4.

mathematizer of the Ricardian model', the pioneer in transforming 'some of the leading principles of classical economics into mathematical equations';[60] his aim was, however, in a sense profoundly anti-Ricardian, since he was concerned to refute, through his equations, the pessimistic belief of Malthus and others in the classical school that population growth would in due course cause misery – an idea that, Whewell said, 'shook and startled the minds of pious and benevolent men, and seemed like an oppressive and disquieting thought forced in among their belief and trust in God's goodness'.

In 1828 Whewell was elected Professor of Mineralogy. The field was contested by natural historians classifying minerals by their external characteristics and chemists who looked to their chemical composition. Whewell rejected the first approach, and thought the second inadequately mathematical. Critical of the mere aggregation of data, Whewell advanced with the cutting edge of theory that data seemed to confirm but might at a future stage cause to be modified: truth was reached dialectically, and he might be proved wrong (which did not prevent his arguing his own case forcefully). In four years Whewell provided 'a nomenclature, a taxonomy, and a simple mathematical foundation for crystallography', and in 1832 he resigned his chair to his protégé William H. Miller, content that the progress he had stimulated should now be left to others.[61] Another endeavour, to explain the laws governing the world's tides in fifteen articles published between 1833 and 1850, showed how his intrepidity might outrun the hypotheses to hand. Realising the gaps in available data, Whewell vigorously set about getting it collected from many parts of the world, and then constructed cotidal maps, linking points with simultaneous high water. But an explanation that embraced myriad differences of detail proved impossible, in part because Whewell's mathematical expertise was too limited. On the other hand, better mathematicians of the day such as the Lucasian Professor G. B. Airy were not able to provide a totally satisfactory model either.[62]

---

[60] Becher, 'William Whewell's Odyssey', pp. 9–12, and p. 11 for the next quotation.
[61] Becher, 'William Whewell's Odyssey', pp. 3–4, and in the same volume Simon Schaffer, 'The History and Geography of the Intellectual World: Whewell's Politics of Language', esp. pp. 218–22.
[62] Becher, 'William Whewell's Odyssey', pp. 13–14, and in the same volume Michael Ruse, 'William Whewell: Omniscientist', esp. pp. 96–8.

Whewell's ambitious reach led to his greater achievement, two works on the history and philosophy of the inductive sciences, published in 1837 and 1840. Highly complex and subtle, the result of long endeavour, they departed from Enlightenment writers in stressing not merely the part played by rationality in making sense of discrete facts through induction, but also the role of the scientist's creative talents in acting positively to organise sense-impressions. The scientist must have imagination, the ability to grasp the Fundamental Ideas, 'those inevitable general relations which are imposed upon our perceptions by acts of the mind, and which are different from anything which our senses directly offer us'.[63] On these Ideas, Space, Time, Number, Cause, and others, was based all knowledge in the sciences. Great advances in science are made by great minds, and influencing them are the qualities of their age and the unfolding of Divine Providence. Whewell's subtle and complex discourse profited from his knowledge of the writings of Immanuel Kant and other giants of German Idealism, whom he discussed with two other fellows of Trinity, Julius Hare and Connop Thirlwall; these three men, fluent in German, were far from the type of English intellectual, insulated from continental ideas, that George Eliot satirised in Edward Casaubon.[64]

Intellectually Whewell was at once adventurous and profoundly conservative, characteristics that help to explain his ascendancy in the Cambridge of his day. We may see this powerful combination in his attitude to the controversial topics of the epoch, geology and evolution, that he strove to reconcile with his devout Anglicanism,[65] and to the demands for university reform. Whewell offered a principled yet subtle defence of the status quo.

Fundamental Ideas, it is important to note, were to be found in morality too. In his tenure of the Knightbridge Professorship of Moral Philosophy from 1838 onwards, Whewell made clear his belief that there was no 'essential difference between the nature of

---

[63] *The Philosophy of the Inductive Sciences* (2 vols., London, 1840) quoted in Michael Ruse, 'William Whewell: Omniscientist', p. 90.

[64] See three chapters in Fisch and Schaffer, *William Whewell*, Michael Ruse, 'William Whewell: Omniscientist', esp. pp. 87–95; Geoffrey Cantor, 'Between Rationalism and Romanticism: Whewell's Historiography of the Inductive Sciences', in Fisch and Schaffer, *William Whewell*, pp. 67–86; and Richard R. Yeo, 'William Whewell's Philosophy of Knowledge and its Reception' in Fisch and Schaffer, *William Whewell*, esp. pp. 175–84.

[65] Whewell's religious views are treated in Chapter 10, pp. 347–51.

truth, or the mode of seeking it, in morals and in physics'.[66] Morality was a science, its Fundamental Ideas Humanity, Justice, Truth, Purity, and Order. Whewell's belief in Fundamental Ideas was of vast importance for his vision of the university. Fundamental Ideas are active in the minds of some, and latent in others; they only become evident as minds come to attain a certain culture:

> One idea after another, of those which constitute the basis of science, becomes distinct, first in the minds of discoverers, then in the minds of all cultured men, till a general clearness of thought illuminates the land; and thus the torch of knowledge is handed forwards, thousands upon thousands lighting their lamps as it passes on; while still from time to time some new Prometheus catches a fresh light from heaven, to spread abroad among men in like manner.[67]

These words are taken from Whewell's first systematic study of the educational implications of his philosophy; it was, he wrote, 'suggested by a long and somewhat laborious course of researches',[68] but it was also a riposte to the criticisms of Hamilton and others, and to the parliamentary campaigns of Radnor, who in 1837 tried unsuccessfully to get a royal commission appointed to investigate college statutes.[69] Whewell's essay presented a counter-model – a Cambridge Idea of a University – to the sort of institution the critics had in mind. Whewell's elaboration of his beliefs a few years later was also in part a reaction to threat: he wrote in 1845 that he could see 'tolerably plain indications that the old Universities are not to expect a continuance of the protection they have been accustomed to receive at the hands of Government'.[70] His new work[71] contained suggestions for such few changes as Whewell thought advisable, and accounts of those he very definitely thought were not. The second edition of 1850 had more details in both categories. An aura of the immediate and pressing suffuses these texts.

[66] From *Two Introductory Lectures in Moral Philosophy* (Cambridge, 1841), quoted in Richard Yeo, 'Whewell's Philosophy of Knowledge', p. 186, on which, pp. 185–8, this paragraph is based. See also Perry Williams, 'Passing on the Torch', in the same volume, pp. 122–3.

[67] *On the Principles of English University Education* (London, 1837), pp. 26–7. I acknowledge my debt, in much that follows, to Perry Williams, 'Passing on the Torch', and to Harvey W. Becher, 'William Whewell and the Preservation of a "Liberal Education" in an Age of Challenge', *Rocky Mountain Social Science Journal*, 12 (1975), pp. 59–70.   [68] *Principles* (1838), p. 1.

[69] See Winstanley, *Early Victorian Cambridge*, pp. 186–9.

[70] Winstanley, *Early Victorian Cambridge*, p. 198.   [71] *Of a Liberal Education* (1845).

On the title pages of all three there is a picture of a hand passing a flaming torch to another, while beneath is an epigraph from Plato's *Republic*, lampadia ekhontes diadosousin allelois:[72] carrying torches they pass them on to one another. English universities concerned with liberal education – Whewell often made clear that he was not discussing professional or vocational instruction, and distinguished Oxford and Cambridge from other sorts of universities, for which he did not hide his disdain – 'have to transmit the civilisation of past generations to future ones, not to share and show forth all the changing fashions of intellectual caprice and subtlety'.[73] Almost always this civilisation came from ancient Greece and Rome. The Fundamental Ideas of their mathematics (above all, Euclidean geometry) and their literature made them Permanent Studies,[74] and necessary therefore for any liberal education worthy of the name. Properly studied, a very important reservation, classical literature reveals to us 'powers and properties' of Language 'in their most complete form' making possible the most accurate and telling utterance and giving imperishable standards of excellence; while mathematics, 'in which truths respecting measurable quantities are demonstrated by chains of the most rigorous reasoning', educates our capacity for thinking.[75] Both had to be insisted on, even if an undergraduate dislikes one or the other.

> It is said . . . that the seeming of mathematical prowess, or of classical learning, which we wring by force from ungenial and unwilling minds, is of no real value, and is no real culture. But to this we reply, that if men come really to understand Greek or Geometry, there is then, in each study, a real intellectual culture, however unwillingly it may have been entered upon. There can be no culture without some labour and effort; to some persons, all labour and effort are unwelcome; and such persons cannot be educated at all, without putting some constraint upon their inclinations.[76]

Distinguished from the Permanent are Progressive Studies, which are, briefly, everything else, whose forms were still changing:

---

[72] *Republic* I 328 a.3. Hamilton chose a very different epigraph for his 1852 *Discussions*, 'Truth, like a torch, the more it's shook it shines.'   [73] *Principles* (1838), p. 128.

[74] The terms Permanent and Progressive Studies were first used in 1845 though their meaning is in *Principles* (1837).

[75] *Of a Liberal Education* (1845), p. 12.   [76] *Of a Liberal Education* (1845), pp. 106–7.

modern languages and literatures, history, philosophy, and all sciences that have arisen, at least very substantially, since ancient times. It is good to study them, or even take a degree in them, but only after men have been connected

> with the most gifted and most cultivated portions of their species which have hitherto existed. When they have arrived at such an apprehension, but not till then, they may go on to sympathize with the most gifted and cultured minds of their own time... But the former step must be a portion of Education, in order that there may be an intelligence as to the present... Attempts at progressive knowledge can have no value or real result, in the minds of those who have not been prepared to understand what is still to do, by understanding what has already been done.[77]

Here we may turn aside to notice Whewell's method of argument. He does not discuss or demonstrate; he asserts, and perhaps it is the vehemence with which he does so that has prevented commentators from asking awkward questions. How can he be so sure that Sophocles is superior to Shakespeare, or that one is essential and the other merely advisable, or that geometry does immeasurable good even if you hate it? Horace Walpole, Macaulay, and Charles Bristed confute him from the consumer's standpoint. The categories of Permanent and Progressive are fabricated, and Whewell himself had difficulty in deciding which one to put some sciences in. In the *History of the Inductive Sciences* (1837) he seems to argue that all the inductive sciences were 'progressive'; but in *Principles* (1837) astronomy and mechanics were regarded as 'permanent', dependent on Fundamental Ideas ascertained by the Greeks, while in *Liberal Education* (1845) astronomy, optics and harmonics are once more described as 'progressive'.[78] In straitjacketing knowledge Whewell got into a morass; Whewell on the nature of the German Gothic or the inductive sciences is on a higher intellectual plane than Whewell the educational philosopher. Newman, who also wrote on the character of liberal education in a work deservedly more enduring that Whewell's, avoided his errors by stressing the purpose for

[77] *Of a Liberal Education* (1845), p. 21.
[78] Richard Yeo, *Defining Science. William Whewell, Natural Knowledge, and Public Debate in Early Victorian Britain* (Cambridge, 1993), p. 217.

which education was undertaken rather more than the areas of study that constituted it. Thus the *Idea of a University* might concern every university, not merely the Dublin university college it initially addressed, while Whewell's writings could not be about anywhere remote from Great St Mary's. It is extraordinary that after pondering the nature of university education Whewell concludes that the Cambridge curriculum of 1840 is ideal. He is aiming at the men, inside the university and out, who were seeking to alter its essentials.

Whewell thought that there were two sorts of teaching – 'speculative' or 'professorial' on the one hand, and 'practical' on the other. Whewell uses words in a puzzling way, like a modern deconstructionist, and the first sort might have been more closely described as 'expository' and the second as 'tutorial'; today 'interactive' describes best the way it constantly involves the student. Both kinds of knowledge, it is averred, may be treated by professorial teaching, but 'practical teaching is applicable only to a limited range of subjects; – those, namely, in which principles having clear evidence and stable certainty, form the basis of our knowledge'.[79] At first this perplexes us, since progressive knowledge, because uncertain, might be thought the more suited to tutorial teaching. But it is essential to recognise that with respect to fundamental knowledge Whewell does not have in mind a joint search for truth. In the 'practical' session the student's understanding and acceptance of principles is tested: 'a distinct possession of the fundamental ideas enables a student to proceed to their applications, and to acquire the habit of applying them in every case with ease and rapidity'. Since in progressive subjects there are no certainties to test, there is no point in having practical teaching for them. Practical teaching is superior: 'When the education is practical teaching, it is a genuine culture, tending to increased fertility and vigour', whereas under speculative teaching 'men's minds ... lose that force and clearness on which intellectual progression depends'.[80] Thus the reform of the European universities on the right lines was 'the Vital Question of Civilisation', on which would depend whether the continent would go into intellectual decline like the later Roman Empire or

[79] *Principles* (1837), p. 9, and for the next quotation.
[80] *Principles* (1837), p. 25, and pp. 25–6 for the next quotation.

'exhibit that ... constant effort at real improvement, which has characterized this quarter of the globe for the last three hundred years'.

'You are to recollect that the intention of obeying the rules constitutes your duty, and that the College officers are to judge of this intention.'[81] Whewell's university was highly authoritarian, sharply distinguished from the 'free system' which he contemptuously compared with it, and inseparable from the collegiate organisation, the 'small world', that made close tutorial discipline possible. Students must not be guilty of actions

> inconsistent with the condition of persons under discipline. Such are, for example, all acts of a political kind, as meetings or organizations for political purposes, public petitions, or public discussions on the agitated questions of the day, and the like. Under the discipline system, the student cannot act at the University, except in the capacity of a pupil. In like manner, public and tumultuous exhibitions of opinion by the cries of a crowd ... cannot, in any calm view of propriety, be reconciled with the pupil's position. Indeed, the exaggerated and insatiable manner in which public applause is given by bodies of students, is of itself an evidence that in such cases, they feel that they are not merely expressing an opinion, but are also gaining a victory over some expected restraint by the mode of expression.[82]

We are not surprised to read that fellows, charged with the welfare of their college, ought not 'openly declare themselves against the College system'. Public expressions of dissent would be a 'great evil'.[83]

Whewell granted the case for new triposes in the Natural and Moral Sciences,[84] and indeed played a large part in initiating them, but candidates for them were only to be able to proceed if they were at least junior optime (the lowest honours category in the Mathematical Tripos), and the separation of that examination into two parts (the first part to give the junior optime qualification) was designed to make the threshold easier for the examiners to arrange – and also to make possible the increased 'geometrisation' of the first

---

[81] *Principles* (1837), p. 96, and pp. 78–127 for this paragraph generally.
[82] *Principles* (1837), p. 125.   [83] *Principles* (1837), p. 120.
[84] See *Of a Liberal Education* (1845), pp. 135–227.

part of the test; it was therefore to an extent a conservative proposal.[85] So was his suggestion that private tutors should be subordinated to college teaching, the strengthening of the collegiate dimension of the university being very much Whewell's desire.

GEORGE PEACOCK

In the 1840s George Peacock, already prominent in the university's affairs, became known as a 'reformer'. Though he seemed to embrace change, rather than, as Whewell, to concede it, Peacock like the other occupied the middle ground. He accepted the collegiate dominance of the university and proposed changes at the margins.

Like so many Cambridge men Peacock came from a clerical family, his father being for fifty years perpetual curate of Denton in the county of Durham.[86] There were seven other children, and means were scanty, but George Peacock was admitted as a sizar to Trinity in 1809, at the age of eighteen, his mathematical and classical preparation for the university having been intense during eighteen months' stay in Tate's school in Richmond (Yorkshire).[87] Second Wrangler and Second Smith's Prizeman in 1813, he was immediately elected a fellow of Trinity, and became a tutor in 1823, in which role he was exceptionally successful. He showed far more sympathy with his pupils than was then usual among official tutors, and his ex-pupil W. H. Thompson remarked in his funeral sermon[88] that

> his inspection of his pupils was not minute, far less vexatious, but it was always effectual ... His insight into character was remarkable, and, though he had decided preferences in favour of certain qualities and pursuits over others, he was tolerant of tendencies with which he could not sympathise, and would look on the more harmless vagaries of young and active minds rather as an amused spectator than as a stern censor and critic.

These words suggest a temperament radically different from that of Whewell, his Trinity colleague; their careers as university math-

---

[85] Whewell's views on the mathematical examination are treated in more detail in chapter 5.
[86] These paragraphs are based on the obituaries in *Fraser's Magazine*, 58 (1858), pp. 741–6, and *Proceedings of the Royal Society of London*, 9 (1859), pp. 536–43.
[87] Tate had been fellow of Sidney Sussex. His private school was famous.
[88] Quoted in J. W. Cox's essay on Peacock in the *Dictionary of National Biography*.

ematicians and men of business were often in contrast, though also often in parallel.

As young dons they were enthusiasts for the new analytical approach, and as moderator in 1816–17 Peacock's examination questions were said by Whewell to 'have made a considerable outcry... He has stripped his analysis of its applications and turned it naked among them.'[89] Peacock's riposte to discontent was uncompromising, and helps us to understand his later attitudes on university reform:[90]

> I shall never cease to exert myself to the utmost in the cause of reform... It is by silent perseverance only that we can hope to reduce the many-headed monster of prejudice, and make the University answer her character as the loving mother of good learning and science.

Peacock played a large part in furthering analysis at the university in following years, and published a treatise on algebra in 1830. But though Peacock defeated Whewell in a contest for the Lowndean Professorship of Astronomy and Geometry in 1836,[91] he made much less of it than, it is certain, Whewell would have done; he never attempted to emulate his rival's productivity as a natural philosopher, though he did have one great achievement as a scholar, a biography, twenty years in composition, of Thomas Young, physician, physicist, and pioneer in the deciphering of hieroglyphics.

Active in the Senate on many concerns, Peacock took a leading part in the protracted debate on the architecture of the new university library. Strongly in support of C. R. Cockerell's successful classical design, Peacock was in aesthetic conflict with Whewell, a partisan of Rickman's Gothic extravaganza, for whose failure in the competition we can only be grateful.[92] Perhaps Peacock's greatest work was architectural, the restoration of Ely

---

[89] Whewell to J. F. W. Herschel, 6 March 1817, quoted in Todhunter, *William Whewell, D.D.*, vol. II, p. 16. The introduction of analysis is described in Chapter 5, pp. 168–73.

[90] *Proceedings of the Royal Society*, pp. 538–9.

[91] Harvey W. Becher, 'William Whewell's Odyssey', p. 16, where it is stated that Peacock owed his election to the vote of his friend Lord Monteagle.

[92] See George Peacock, *Observations on the Plans for a New Library ... by a Member of the First Syndicate* (Cambridge, 1831), and William Whewell, *Reply to Observations on the Plans for a New Library. By a Member of Both Syndicates* (Cambridge, 1831). For the new library question, see chapter 1, pp. 24–8.

Cathedral from the 'squalid and forlorn' state[93] in which he found it when appointed dean in 1839. To its improvement he gave his energies in the years that followed, while however continuing to retain his professorship and its stipend; he was not rich, and he had lost in unwise investments. But as his lectures declined in quality and in due course ceased altogether, it is not surprising that Peacock was unpopular in the conscientious culture of 1840s Cambridge, especially since he was known as 'a "Reformer" by temperament and conviction'. A 'shrewd man of business' and 'brilliant talker', his idiosyncratic features and manners were often mimicked unkindly at university wine-parties.[94]

Peacock's suggestions for reform are contained in an erudite work of historical research still of great value to the historian, a careful and detailed elucidation of the ancient statutes that constrained university and colleges.[95] Purporting to lay down in minute detail the organisation of life and studies, the statutes were often obsolete and unenforced, except where the common interest of dons had preserved them, and they did not cover changes introduced since they were framed in the sixteenth century; thus the mathematisation of studies since 1730 was contrary to the statutes. Yet altering them would entail great difficulty, even supposing that dons could agree on what was wanted. Peacock's recommendation, itself for some a revolutionary idea, was that the statutes should be revised and separated into two categories, those prescribing the constitution and government and therefore resting on parliament's authority, and those regulating detail and so, Peacock thought, amenable to change by Cambridge agencies. This pattern was in fact to be the eventual result of the process of reform.

The most important of Peacock's proposals for substantive change concerned degree studies.[96] He envisaged shortening the BA course from eleven terms to nine,[97] with corresponding reductions in the content of the Mathematical and Classical Triposes. Also affected would be private tuition, whose cost he estimated at £52,000 a year, 'or more than three times the sum paid

---

[93] *Fraser's Magazine*, p. 745.   [94] *Fraser's Magazine*, pp. 742–3.
[95] *Observations on the Statutes*, pp. 3–74, 106–39 for what follows.
[96] *Observations on the Statutes*, pp. 146–51.
[97] Courses for higher degrees would also be abbreviated.

to the whole body of public tutors and professors'. The changes he envisaged would make this 'evil of the most alarming magnitude' less necessary, 'as a means of artificial and forced preparation for the very varied forms which an examination may assume'.[98]

Peacock thought that the imposition of the mathematical degree upon everybody seeking honours was too rigid:

> There are many students who possess very considerable powers of memory or imagination, and who are frequently accomplished classical or general scholars, who experience the greatest difficulty in appreciating or comprehending the most simple principles of mathematical reasoning ... and though it may be quite true that there is no class of students in the university who would derive greater benefit from the cultivation of those severe studies, which are so well calculated to strengthen the sinews of the intellect, and to prepare men for the business of life, yet it is not desirable to close the avenues to our degrees and to their consequent advantages, to men whose attainments, in other departments of knowledge, would do honour to their place of education. The failure of such candidates (of which some remarkable examples have lately occurred) is, in fact, more discreditable to the system of the university than to those who are unhappily its victims ... the only expedient of an obvious kind which presents itself, is a commutation of the mathematical parts of the examination (either in whole or in part) for a classical examination of considerable range and severity.

This is a key passage. Peacock also urged that time should be devoted after the first degree to professional education, so that the university 'would be enabled to retain within her bosom large classes of students, who are now compelled to draw the draughts of knowledge from other fountains than those which she offers to her sons'.[99] He also made some important administrative recommendations: the appointment of a university bursar to assist the Vice-Chancellor, the abolition of the individual veto within the Caput, the setting up of permanent syndicates to supervise the main university institutions including the entire academic course, and the amalgamation of the two houses within the Senate.[100]

These proposals, from the man more than any other known as a

[98] *Observations on the Statutes*, pp. 153–5, and p. 163 for the next quotation.
[99] *Observations on the Statutes*, p. 166.   [100] *Observations on the Statutes*, pp. 135–45.

university reformer, are remarkable for what they propose to leave alone rather than for what they seek to alter. The essential structure of the university, the centrality of collegiate membership and teaching, is accepted. In tone it is a long way from Sir William Hamilton's 'professorial' and anti-collegiate bias; in fact Peacock attempts an historical justification of the colleges' role – that their assumption of teaching in the sixteenth century was a necessary act, not a usurpation as Hamilton contended, and the result of the decline in the number of regents at the Reformation.[101] Alike in venerating their university, Whewell and Peacock suggested programmes that were complementary rather than antagonistic. Their one important point of conflict was Peacock's willingness to make classics and mathematics alternatives, while Whewell wished to insist on junior optime qualification in mathematics for everybody. It was a sign of the government's desire to effect 'conservative reform' in the university that Peacock was appointed to the Royal Commission of Enquiry in 1850. Adam Sedgwick was also a member of the commission, for the same reasons.

ADAM SEDGWICK

Adam Sedgwick's background[102] was very similar to Peacock's, his father being perpetual curate of Dent in the West Riding of Yorkshire;[103] after schooling at Dent and Sedbergh grammar schools he went up to Trinity as a sizar in 1804, aged nineteen. He graduated Fifth Wrangler, obtained a Trinity fellowship, and in 1818 was elected Woodwardian Professor of Geology, a subject of which he at that time knew little but to which he thenceforth gave himself vigorously. Geology became his life's work for which he is justly famous.

Sedgwick was a paradoxical man whom at this distance it is hard to fathom. He was genial and relaxed in company yet was subject to depression. He was inordinately fond of the society of young women

---

[101] *Observations on the Statutes*, p. 34.
[102] These details of Sedgwick's life are taken from Clark and Hughes, *The Life and Letters of Adam Sedgwick*, one of the best biographies of a Victorian don. Colin Speakman, *Adam Sedgwick. Geologist and Dalesman, 1785–1873* (Heathfield, Sussex, Broad Oak Press, 1982) is a brief sketch but adds some material to Clark and Hughes.
[103] Dent, in the far north-west of the ancient county, is now in Cumbria.

yet never married, while the zeal with which as Senior Proctor he prowled along the Barnwell footpath in search of streetwalkers – committing seven young women to the Spinning House on one day in January 1828 – suggests a darker side to his nature.[104] He lived to the age of eighty-eight and was immensely strong, yet throughout life complained of ill-health; plainly in large measure psychosomatic in origin, it only assailed him in Cambridge, and not on his beloved geological field-trips, as he strode across the fells: 'listless as he was at Cambridge, the moment he got to Dent he became a different man'.[105] Though he wrote many scientific papers of seminal importance, he never gathered his findings into a definitive volume as his fellow-geologists Lyell and Murchison did. But as a lecturer he was superb, drawing audiences to geology long before it was examinable, with the vigour of his utterance and skill in exposition. 'I sat rapt', wrote Richard Wilton, an undergraduate at St Catharine's from 1847 to 1850. 'His lectures are a rich mine of strong, rugged and picturesque English, and I am confident Tennyson has worked in it assiduously. I could quote many passages to prove that he has studied and imitated Sedgwick's grand, nervous style.'[106]

A Discourse on the Studies of the University, first published in 1833, illustrates the cumbrousness that afflicted so much of Sedgwick's writing. Hurriedly composed as a sermon in Trinity College chapel in December, it was expanded to twice its length for publication. Sedgwick's justification for studying Newton complements Whewell's, valuing rather more than geometry's inculcation of abstract thought Newton's demonstration of the truths of natural religion, the harmony and order of the universe; Sedgwick was a devout churchman.[107] Sedgwick's vindication of the classics re-proves Cambridge's stress on linguistic refinement, stressing the insights that literature gives into emotions, ideas, and history.[108] Though much of the volume is a rambling and repetitious attack on Locke and Paley for ignoring the innate capacities of the human

---

[104] See Adrian Desmond and James Moore, *Darwin* (London, Michael Joseph, 1991), p. 54.
[105] Clark and Hughes, *The Life and Letters of Adam Sedgwick*, vol. I, p. 132; see also vol. II, pp. 494–501 for this paragraph.
[106] The first quotation is from a letter dated 6 November 1849, and the second from Wilton's diary; both sources are in the Sedgwick Museum, and quoted in Speakman, *Adam Sedgwick*, p. 87.
[107] *A Discourse* (1833), pp. 9–19. Dons and students, it has to be said, seem to have seen Newton as a mathematician, not as a theologian. [108] *A Discourse* (1833), pp. 28–39.

mind,[109] Sedgwick revealed his willingness to question Cambridge's received ideas, as he also very clearly did in 1834 over the issue of religious tests.

A Discourse on the Studies of the University went through further editions, becoming less of an integrated essay meriting its title as Sedgwick added material on the collateral matters. The final edition was the fifth (1850), in which *A Discourse* itself was dwarfed by a 'preface' of 430 pages largely dealing with the tendencies of the age to which Sedgwick was very opposed, notably the growth of materialist explanations of the universe, to which his opposition is most apparent in his attack on Darwin's *Origin of Species*. But forty-three pages in the preface discuss directly university issues, and show how conservative a reformer Sedgwick was, like his colleagues Whewell and Peacock. His pages are instinct with his sense of the university's capacity for the most fruitful self-change, witnessed by the improvements that have taken place in his lifetime and, above all, inspired by its noble history:

> It is impossible for any young man to be so dead to historical sentiments as not to feel some sense of moral obligation when he sits down every day in a Hall decorated with the portraits of Bacon, Newton, Barrow, Russell, Ray, Coke, Cowley, Dryden, Bentley ... whose names will ever live ... in the glorious annals of their country. We have a noble intellectual ancestry; nor can any power on earth take this honour from us; nor can any new institution share it with us; and this thought is in itself a true element of security and public good – All our studies and forms and fashions are historical. There are many customs amongst us which, in a new institution, might be thought burdensome, unreasonable, or ridiculous. But we should be far more unreasonable and ridiculous were we to abolish them: for they are the links that connect the past with the present; they tell us of stirring times in the by-gone days of literature and science; and they remind us also of past struggles in the cause of civil freedom, and of noble deeds done in behalf of religious liberty by those who went before us, and once filled the very stations in which it has been the will of Providence now to place us.[110]

So had Sedgwick thought that the new triposes would have the effect of displacing 'our stern mathematical studies ... from that

---

[109] Pp. 39–69. [110] *A Discourse* (5th edn, 1850), Preface, pp. ccclv–ccclvi.

high place' he would 'have been almost willing to cross England barefoot to record my vote against them. But ... our highest prizes will still be carried off by those who reap their honours in the Mathematical and Classical fields.'[111] The new provision for the Natural and Moral Sciences was intended for men 'by nature little fitted to gain distinction from the study of Mathematics', but if they progress in these 'more humble and less exact studies' the new 'Tripos of Honour' was open for them. Also, Sedgwick did not expect, and certainly did not wish, the university to cease to be an Anglican institution as a result of abolishing religious tests. Deeply attached to the ancient constitution, he would 'grieve to see the Caput abolished altogether', desiring just a modification of the veto and the addition of some extra members.[112] It seems certain that Sedgwick urged the retention of the essential collegiate university on the Prince Consort when he stayed at Osborne in 1847, in his capacity as the Chancellor's Cambridge Secretary, a position that has not left evidence of its possessing any great importance.[113] He had a later opportunity to press the case for his sort of reform as a member of the Graham Commission.

ALBERT HENRY WRATISLAW

A very different commentator from Whewell and Peacock was Albert Henry Wratislaw, a man of unusual background for a Cambridge don, prominent in the history of three public schools, university reform, and Bohemian studies in Victorian Britain. Wratislaw was descended from an aristocratic family of the Habsburg Empire, the Counts of Wratislaw von Mitrovicz. His grandfather, Marc Mari Emanuel Wratislaw, was an attaché at the Austrian embassy in Paris for a time (he was present at Marie Antoinette's marriage) but came to England in 1770 and taught French in King Edward's School, Birmingham, and at Rugby School from 1784 to 1796. All five sons went to Rugby, and two became masters there. Another, William Ferdinand, was a solicitor in the town, and A.H. was his son, born in 1822.[114] In 1829 he

---

[111] *A Discourse* (1850), preface, p. cccxxv, and p. cccxxvii for the next quotation.
[112] *A Discourse* (1850), pp. ccclviii–ccclxi.
[113] Clark and Hughes, *The Life and Letters of Adam Sedgwick*, vol. II, pp. 120, 136.
[114] Michael Craze, *History of Felsted School* (Ipswich, Cowell, 1955), p. 151.

entered the school but left in 1836, probably because his father quarrelled bitterly with Thomas Arnold over the headmaster's attempt to diminish the right of local boys to free tuition at the school.[115] In his mature life, A.H. Wratislaw seems to have looked to the paternal role-model, tough controversialism, but his memories of Rugby itself seem to have been happy enough since he introduced its idiosyncratic form of football to Felsted immediately on becoming headmaster in 1852.[116]

Put at first to the law, Albert Wratislaw disliked it, and matriculated at Trinity in 1840. Migrating to Christ's in April 1842, he graduated senior optime and Third Classic in 1844. A fellowship followed, and he became a tutor. He also became increasingly drawn to his roots. His ancient family was originally Czech: he was 'connected with the Bohemian Slavonians in no distant degree by blood and name, and a member of their oldest, once their royal family',[117] and at the same time that he was angered by Whewell's pronouncements on the university expressed equal indignation about the oppression that since the seventeenth century his people had suffered at the hands of Austrians and Magyars, and the Bohemian Protestants had suffered from Jesuits. He spent at least one long vacation in Prague, acquired fluent Czech, and published a volume of his translations 'from an almost entirely unknown literature ... I have thought it a sacred duty to make myself personally acquainted with their language, their feelings and their strivings, and as far as my isolated efforts can avail, to make them known in the country of my birth and education'.[118] To this task Wratislaw gave a great deal of energy in the next forty years and published much as a result.[119]

[115] T. W. Bamford, *Thomas Arnold* (London, Cresset, 1960), pp. 128–42. W. F. Wratislaw was a prominent Rugby radical, interested in the right of free tuition for local boys for reasons of principle as well his self-interest. Such local rights were common in ancient grammar schools, but men like Arnold were keen to diminish them to encourage entry by fee-paying boys reckoned more likely to desire the classical education ambitious headmasters thought it was their special function to impart.   [116] Craze, *Felsted School*, p. 158.

[117] A. H. Wratislaw, *Lyra-Czecho-Slovanska. Bohemian Poems, Ancient and Modern, Translated from the Original Slavonic, with an Introductory Essay by A. H. Wratislaw* (London, 1849), p. vii, and pp. vii–xxxi for what follows.   [118] *Lyra-Czecho-Slovanska*, p. vii.

[119] For example: *Patriotism: An Ancient Lyrico-epic Poem, Translated from the Original Slavonic* (London, 1851), *Historical and Statistical Sketch of the Slavonic Protestants, in the North of the Austrian Empire* (London, 1861), *Adventures of Baron W. Wratislaw of Mitrowitz. What He Saw in the Turkish Metropolis, Constantinople; Experienced in His Captivity ... Literally Translated from the Original Bohemian* (London, 1862). *The Native Literature of Bohemia in the Fourteenth Century. Four Lectures Delivered before the University of Oxford on the Ilchester Foundation* (London, 1878).

In the late 1840s Wratislaw's loyalties were focused on the issues of Bohemian nationalism, and it is perhaps not surprising that he seems to have been increasingly irritated by the equivocations and ethical complexities of Cambridge that men more fully at home in it were able to ignore: in particular, the paradox, much more apparent in 1850 than now, that the university one had sworn to uphold had been almost entirely absorbed and reconstituted by seventeen other institutions, purporting to serve it but in fact different in their qualities and purpose. Wratislaw, engaging vigorously in the details of internal reform in the late 1840s, mounted the most vehement attack on the college system, controverting Whewell's arguments directly. Firstly, the professors ought to be 'a body directing and superintending the higher education and studies of the University';[120] but the 'Professorial Staff', was 'a mere hodge-podge of independent and sometimes capricious foundations'. This was because the colleges were in control, and

> almost every subject of Professorial lectures is unanimously ignored by the Colleges, and it is mere waste of time for a student wishing to obtain a Fellowship to pay the slightest attention to them . . . Where any symptom of the Professorial system is found, every development of the principle of competition, so unsparingly applied to the students, is sedulously suppressed and exterminated.

Colleges were good at disciplining students, but bad at teaching them: hence the expensive extra, private tuition. 'I have no hesitation in asserting the average run of College Lectures to be rarely above, and generally far below, the level of the lessons of the head class in a well-conducted Public school, depressed as such Lectures necessarily are, owing to the mixed classes of ignoramuses and proficients lectured together under the College system.' Specialised teaching was needed, but colleges could not provide it because of the limited resources they could, or chose to, provide; there were not enough college tutors. In a clear reference to the marriage bar and the way it denied permanent employment Wratislaw pointed out that most college lecturers were very young, and moved on to public schools for higher stipends and security 'at

[120] A. H. Wratislaw, *Observations on the Cambridge System, Partly in Reply to, Partly Suggested by Dr Whewell's Recent Educational Publications* (Cambridge, 1850), p. 30, and pp. 29–31 for the quotations that follow.

the very age when they begin to be most useful'. Wratislaw's comments remind us that there was professional urgency, in addition to a concern for individual desires, behind the attempt of the Christ's College reformers to abrogate the celibacy rule. In fact the collegiate basis of the university contained 'evils which the University cannot remedy by any revision or reformation of her Statutes', wrote Wratislaw, calling for more external interference than anybody else in the university.

> She has no control whatever over the individual Colleges. If any College were to stop Lectures entirely to-morrow, close its Chapel, or perform any other antic, the University would have no power of interfering. These evils arise from the relation between the Colleges and the University, and can be remedied only by *the compulsory application of a portion of the revenues of the separate Colleges, at present wasted upon non-residents, to the higher purposes of the University.* They can therefore only be remedied by the State and the two Houses of Parliament. Under these circumstances, and until such State interference takes place, it only remains for every individual engaged in the Public Tuition of the Colleges to do his utmost to alleviate the evils, which he may lament, but cannot cure.

BENJAMIN DANN WALSH

'The spirit of innovation has always been most loudly deprecated in our Universities, and there is no place where the attachment to old usages is so strong. But these are not times in which it is safe to remain far in the rear of improvement.'[121] These are words typical of the Cambridge don who must be judged the most advanced of internal reformers: his programme was more detailed and searching than Wratislaw's, and (a testing criterion) he published it first – four years before Peacock, and thirteen before Wratislaw. The antithesis of Whewell, he is an appropriate person with whom to end a survey of university attitudes to change.

Benjamin Walsh was born in 1808; his father, a stockbroker, was MP for the rotten borough of Wootton Bassett from 1808 to 1812, having purchased his seat as an expedient to avoid arrest for debt. In 1809 the Stock Exchange expelled him, as the House of Commons

---

[121] Walsh, *A Historical Account*, pp. 105–6.

did in 1812 for attempted fraud.[122] Benjamin Dann Walsh attended St Paul's School, and entered Trinity in 1827 as a sizar, a reflection probably of his family poverty; in 1830 he became a scholar, and in 1831 he graduated Fifth Classic. A fellowship followed in 1833. In 1837 he published the first volume of what was planned as a complete metrical translation of Aristophanes' comedies,[123] an augury, it might seem, of a conventional career in British society for a man who had as his brothers a clergyman and a writer on horses, dogs, and field sports.

Benjamin Walsh and the Trinity fellowship did not find each other congenial. In January 1835 the normally tolerant and easy-going diarist, Joseph Romilly, recorded 'that a few days ago after a long symposium somewhere about 3 in the morning Kemble kicked our fellow Walsh out of the Comb. room – Walsh is an ill mannered disgusting person, but kicking is rather a strong measure'.[124] One reason for these frictions was explained by Walsh many years later in a letter to the American scientist Le Conte:

> The shabbiest tricks I ever had played on me in my life were uniformly at the hands of parsons. They are like monks – isolated from the rest of the community & not bound by the laws of honor. As a class, I hate despise & eschew them. Nine tenths of them are rascals – believing no more of what they preach than you & I do; and a large portion of the remaining fraction are fools. I have lived 12 years in the English Factory (Cambridge) where they manufacture this kind of ecclesiastical beast & having mixed familiarly with them on terms of social equality, I know all about them. I have known very few honorable & honest clergymen – Prof. Henslow Late Botanical Professor at Cambridge, & Prof. Sedgwick, the English Geologist. But they are the exception & not the rule.[125]

We are not surprised to learn that Walsh drew the attention of the Trinity students' protest against compulsory chapel, the Society for the Prevention of Cruelty to Undergraduates. Between 17 Febru-

[122] Thorne (ed.), *History of Parliament*, vol. v, pp. 475–7.
[123] The publication of 'the remaining two volumes' of Aristophanes was announced for 'early in the October Term' 1837 on the end-page of *A Historical Account*.
[124] Bury, *Romilly's Cambridge Diary 1832–42*, p. 66.
[125] From an unpublished letter of 19 March 1869 in the library of the American Philosophical Society. I owe this reference to Carol Anelli Sheppard of the Department of Biology, University of Scranton; and the text of the letter and permission to quote from it to Beth Carroll-Horrocks of the American Philosophical Society.

ary and 24 March 1838 Walsh did not appear in chapel once, and was condemned by the society 'to write out 150 lines of the *Aves* of Aristophanes (omitting the indecent parts)'.[126] Walsh's anti-clericalism is reflected in his reformist pamphlet, as is in addition his resentment at being passed over for an assistant tutorship by the High Church Master of Trinity, Christopher Wordsworth.[127] No doubt these tensions, and perhaps also those aroused by the pamphlet itself, led to Walsh's departure from Trinity in the summer of 1838, though he did not resign his fellowship until 1841 and continued to receive a rent allowance during those three years when in fact he was on the other side of the Atlantic.

Walsh gave up Cambridge for a career that could scarcely have been more different. He emigrated to Illinois, which had been a state of the Union for only twenty years. He became a farmer, describing his experience in a letter of 1864 to Charles Darwin whom he had known at Cambridge.[128] 'I was possessed with an absurd notion that I would live a perfectly natural life, independent of the whole world . . . So I bought several hundred acres of wild land in the wilderness, twenty miles from any settlement that you would call even a village, and with only one neighbor.' After working 'like a horse, raising great quantities of hogs and bullocks' and 'doing everything from mending a pair of boots to hooping a barrel', he nearly died of malaria, sold his land at a loss, and found that he was $1,000 poorer than when he began twelve years before. From 1851 onwards Walsh was in the lumber business in Rock Island, Illinois, making enough by 1858 to buy houses and live off the rents.[129] Thenceforth he devoted himself to entomology, for

[126] I owe this reference and the details below concerning the termination of Walsh's residence at Trinity to Diana Chardin of the Wren Library. [127] *A Historical Account*, pp. 110–33, 145.

[128] Quoted in F. Darwin and A. C. Seward, eds., *More Letters of Charles Darwin* (2 vols., London, 1903), vol. II, pp. 248–9. A later letter (pp. 249–50) reveals that after reading *The Origin of Species* in 1861 Walsh became a convinced evolutionist. He contended with anti-Darwinians in the USA such as Louis Agassiz.

[129] The following details of Walsh's American career, and the quotations, are taken from Leland Ossian Howard's article in the *Dictionary of American Biography*. See also Clark A. Elliott, *Biographical Dictionary of American Science: The Seventeenth through the Nineteenth Centuries* (London, Greenwood, 1979). Walsh's 'prodigious contributions' to *The Practical Entomologist* are discussed by Carol Anelli Sheppard, 'A Brief History of *The Practical Entomologist* and its Contributions to Economic Entomology,' *Entomological News*, 100 (1989), pp. 212–23, and Edward H. Smith and Carol Anelli Sheppard, 'A Heritage of Distinguished Journals', *American Entomologist* (Spring, 1990), pp. 7–17. I owe these references to Carol Sheppard.

which he is best known in the United States, and the fruit, it is said, of an interest acquired in Cambridge. As editor of the *Practical Entomologist* this 'mature, cultivated and far-seeing man' was one of the first to warn American farmers of the likely increase in pest infestation, and to suggest for insect control 'the introduction of foreign parasites and natural enemies of imported pests'. His many substantial scientific papers led to his appointment as the state entomologist for Illinois in 1867, two years before his death in a rail crash.[130]

His *A Historical Account of the University of Cambridge* had appeared over thirty years previously. It was intended to provide information for those participating in the Earl of Radnor's 1837 campaign to secure the appointment of a royal commission of inquiry into the English universities,[131] and it was plainly written at great speed to appear when it did. Yet it is not a brief and superficial tract, but a lengthy work replete with much recondite detail, and the product of a great deal of thought and study; for example, Walsh was at least as knowledgeable about the imbricated process by which the university statutes were composed as Peacock was to show himself to be.

A Historical Account reads like a Cambridge version of Hamilton's Oxford-centred polemic. Walsh presses the 'usurpation' argument: the predominance of colleges and the heads of houses within Cambridge was essentially illegitimate since it resulted from the wresting of authority from the university in the sixteenth century; power had been transferred from a public institution to a series of private and self-interested ones, and from academic democracy to a corrupt oligarchy, controlling the university and the colleges by fiat assisted by patronage – 'the means of promoting their obedient followers . . . in their several Colleges; . . . few unprejudiced persons will, I think, dispute my position, when I assert, that the power of the Heads has been increased by usurpation, is maintained by tyranny, and ought to be diminished by legislative enactments'.[132] The heads controlled the Caput, and so their powers, 'always exercised for the suppression of beneficial change . . . weigh like an

[130] Walsh's entomological collection was destroyed in the Chicago fire of 1871.
[131] *A Historical Account*, p. 1.   [132] *A Historical Account*, p. 57, and pp. 32–55 and 110–19 generally.

incubus upon the talents of every member of the senate, able and willing to propose measures of a really advantageous nature'.[133]

> The collegiate structure of teaching was disastrous. What can be more absurd, than for a small foundation, with some 15 or 20 undergraduates on its boards, of three or four distinct years, with distinct studies, and distinct degrees of talent, application, and acquirements, to have its private and peculiar lectures, mathematical and classical; each lecture being necessarily attended by not more than half a dozen at furthest? . . . It is exactly as if a man were to hire the Italian Opera-house, and insist upon the performers exhibiting to a select party, consisting of his own private family . . . How could Madame Pasta work herself up to the requisite pitch of excitement, if she were displaying her abilities to such an audience?[134]

Walsh regarded small-group teaching, at all events in the form it had in Cambridge – 'conveying instruction by word of mouth' – as 'the least calculated to produce beneficial results'. Fear of interrupting prevented pupils from asking questions (this is a very dubious assertion), while on the other hand there was 'none of the generous enthusiasm, and high-hearted emulation' resulting from the 'mutual collision of intellect with intellect'.

Walsh's remedy, buttressed with a quotation from Adam Smith on the benefits of market forces and competition in the academic world, was inspired by the medieval Cambridge system of 'Regency',[135] and by contemporary Scottish universities. For college fellows there was to be a fixed stipend of £200 a year – even Walsh realised the political difficulty of abolishing fellows' property rights altogether – but Walsh would give to 'every M.A. the ancient statutable privilege of lecturing for any fixed fee, upon any subject'. As in Glasgow and Edinburgh, students would be free to attend or not; thus 'the remuneration obtained' would be 'precisely proportioned to the goodness of the article furnished'.[136]

Contrasting with Walsh's criticism of almost everything else in

---

[133] *A Historical Account*, p. 32.
[134] Pp. 129–30, and p. 130 for the quotations that follow immediately.
[135] The obligation on MAs to give public tuition in the university after graduation. In the Middle Ages one or two years were required; by the 1570 statutes the obligation became five years, though Regency was by then nearly defunct anyway: Damian R. Leader, *Cambridge: The University to 1546*, pp. 22, 243–5.   [136] Pp. 68–72, 130–1.

Cambridge was his rapture over written examinations, a Cambridge invention that was a 'high-pressure engine in the world of the mind'.[137] It was impossible to design a plan 'more admirably adapted ... to call forth and develope the talents of young men'. To it Cambridge owed 'its glory and renown as the cradle of genius and the temple of literature and science ... our statesmen and our schoolmasters, our ambassadors, and our apothecaries, our barristers, our officers, naval and military, [and] clerks in public offices' should have 'to pass a Cambridge examination in the difficult kinds of knowledge required for their different duties'. Cambridge's great invention would then be an agent in the radical reform of Britain, 'because a free competition in the market always raises the standard of excellence, while at the same time it lowers the scale of remuneration'.

Meanwhile, the curriculum that Cambridge actually examined was far too narrow, expansion being limited by a 'senseless clamour against innovation'.[138] Walsh proposed adding more examination subjects than any other mid-century reformer, and more in fact than found their way into the tripos list until this century. The additions were to be grouped in five triposes:

1st. Ancient and Modern History, Political Economy, Moral and Political Philosophy, and the History of the Human Mind.
2ndly. Natural History in all its branches.
3rdly. Geology, Mineralogy, Chemistry, Electricity, &c.
4thly. The principal Oriental Languages, and
5thly. The principal languages of modern Europe; doing away at the same time, with the present necessity for obtaining a Mathematical Honour, before the student can sit for a Classical one.[139]

Walsh averred that 'these are not times in which it is safe to remain far in the rear of improvement'. But these new subjects would help the university to 'become the great nursery of statesmen, orators, diplomatists, philosophers, and linguists, and the focus of all the various departments of practical knowledge, which are now principally cultivated in the metropolis'.[140]

[137] Pp. 80–1.   [138] P. 98, and pp. 98–110 for this paragraph generally.
[139] P. 109.   [140] P. 106.

Outside Cambridge the ideas of Walsh and Wratislaw brought nods of agreement from the university's sternest critics. But inside Cambridge the two men contributed nothing to meaningful debate: they were too far outwith the boundaries of what was regarded by the community of dons as acceptable terms of discourse. Because their ideas were far-reaching and adventurous they are merely historical curiosities, although ironically in due course they have all been implemented.

Chapter 13

CAMBRIDGE AND REFORM,
1815–1870

CONFLICTING ATTITUDES AND THE ELECTIONS OF 1826 AND 1831

'The friends of freedom in Cambridgeshire have to contend', wrote Weston Hatfield in his newspaper the *Cambridge Independent Press* in 1832, with 'all the influence of the Aristocracy, the Church, the Squirearchy, and of every class of corruptionist'.[1] With the foundation of the *Independent Press* in 1819 Weston gave a fresh hearing to the tradition once expressed by Benjamin Flower. He was the enemy of the Rutland interest in borough and county and of the oligarchical corporation it manipulated; he condemned the acts of repression, such as the suspension of Habeas Corpus in 1817, with which the government met the postwar slump and demands for parliamentary reform. Representing the militant Dissenters of Cambridge, Weston opposed the privileges of the Established Church in university and society and called for Catholic Emancipation.[2] Another common radical demand that Weston voiced was for Corn Law repeal; though he recognised that in a farming area such as Cambridgeshire 'our views on this subject may be somewhat unpopular among the class of society in which our paper perhaps most generally circulates'.[3]

These views were opposed by the *Cambridge Chronicle*, the Tory newspaper in the region. The *Chronicle* also regarded itself as the university journal, carrying much news of Senate votes and anxious to guard the university's interests as Conservatives saw

---

[1] Quoted in Michael Murphy, *Cambridge Newspapers and Opinion*, p. 62; pp. 58–73 for these paragraphs in general.
[2] The right of Roman Catholics to sit in Parliament. It would chiefly affect Irish politics. Roman Catholics might already become electors, if otherwise qualified.
[3] Quoted in Michael Murphy, *Cambridge Newspapers*, p. 63.

them. In the years of slump after the Napoleonic Wars the *Chronicle* advised the poor to trust to the charity of their betters for relief, and by no means to resort to violence, like the machine-breakers of the Midlands; the 'outrages of the Luddites ... proceeded from a spirit of insubordination, created, fostered and inflamed by the periodical press'.[4] This was largely in the hands of the 'Ultra-Whigs and the Radical Reformers, the knife and cautery men' who wished to exasperate the people against the government. Their prescription, parliamentary reform, was unnecessary and dangerous. The *Chronicle* supported 'the present constitution of affairs in Church and State'. Because he 'most firmly and undisguisedly' was of this opinion too the *Chronicle* backed William J. Bankes at the university parliamentary by-election of November 1822.[5] Bankes pledged 'the most steady and decided opposition to any measures tending to undermine or alter the established church'.[6] These words referred to proposals to enact Catholic Emancipation, which in the 1820s became an increasing point of contention, notably within the university where several hundred clerics debated the future of Anglican exclusivity and privileges. The Senate regularly petitioned against the granting of Catholic relief, though there was a large minority of dons favourable to the Catholic claims.[7] At the by-election in December 1822 Bankes was elected by a large majority to sit for the university, against two 'Catholics'.[8]

The issue divided the Tory government itself, and there was a gentleman's agreement that its members might hold their own views on it. Palmerston had been known to favour Catholic Emancipation ever since he had sat for the university, and in the 1826 general election, in which the Catholic question was every-

---

[4] *Cambridge Chronicle*, 22 November 1816, quoting the *Quarterly Review* with approval.
[5] 22 November 1822. Bankes, of a Dorset landed family, was at Trinity with Byron, whose lifelong friend he became. After graduating in 1808, he became MP for Truro. Samuel Rogers remarked that Bankes outshone Sydney Smith as a wit: 'I have seen him at my own house absolutely overpowered by the superior facetiousness of William Bankes': Alexander Dyce, ed., *Recollections of the Table-talk of Samuel Rogers* (New Southgate, 1887), p. 291. Bankes was known to the literary world because of his travels in the Near East.
[6] *Cambridge Chronicle*, 8 November 1822.
[7] Cooper, *Annals*, IV, pp. 517 (May, 1817), 524 (April, 1819), 530 (March, 1821).
[8] Cooper, *Annals*, IV, p. 539, where the voting figures for each college are given. Bankes got 419 votes, and Lord Hervey and James Scarlett 281 and 219 respectively. The by-election was caused by the death of J. H. Smyth. The other MP was Palmerston.

where fought over, his views created difficulties for him.[9] Besides Bankes, the other sitting member, the other two candidates were members of the government itself – Sir John S. Copley the Attorney-General and Henry Goulburn the Chief Secretary for Ireland. They were both 'Protestants'. Palmerston wrote that it was 'unusual . . . that an official man should find himself endangered in a seat which he has held for fourteen years, by the undisguised competition of two of his colleagues in office'.[10]

Dons debated the issues in letters in the local press in May. 'A. B.' defended the right of clergymen to discuss Catholic Emancipation in the pulpit: it 'intimately' involved 'the eternal interests of mankind. Why then is a Protestant minister, anxious for the welfare of his people, to be prohibited from cautioning them . . . against the dangerous errors of Popery?'[11] These letters were replete (some were 2,000 words in length) with accusations of casuistry, misreporting, and quotation out of context: there were excerpts from Cicero and urgings to read informative books. 'Let your correspondent', wrote 'Anti-Romanist', 'read with care . . . *Accusations of History against the Church of Rome* . . . let him thence learn both what Catholics have been and *are*: let him try his fallible judgment upon the facts, and ask himself if [he can] give them the right hand of fellowship'.[12]

A letter written by Adam Sedgwick on Palmerston's behalf at the end of 1825 (the university campaign had effectively started six months before the vote) suggests the way that personal feelings added to the election's complexity:

> Strange things come to pass. I am now in the Committee room of a Johnian, a Tory, and a King's Minister; and I am going to give him a plumper. My motives are that he is our old Member, and a distinguished Member, and that I hate the other candidates – I mean with public and political hate, without private malice. Bankes is a fool, and was brought in last time by a set of old women, and whenever he rises makes the body he represents truly ridiculous. Copley is a clever fellow, but is not sincere, at least when I pass him I

---

[9] In the Cambridge borough election the anti-Catholic speeches of the Tory Trench were greeted with 'immense cheers'; Pryme, the reform and Emancipation candidate, received only 4 votes against 24 and 23 for his two opponents. Michael Murphy, *Cambridge Newspapers*, p. 72.

[10] Quoted in Bourne, *Palmerston*, p. 244.

[11] *Cambridge Chronicle*, 19 May 1826.   [12] *Cambridge Chronicle*, 12 May 1826.

am sure I smell a rat. Goulburn is the idol of the Saints, a prime favourite of Simeon's, and a subscriber to missionary societies. Moreover he squints. Now, my good fellow, though I believe you have the liberality of a great Inquisitor, yet I think you will hardly vote against your own college, your own friends, and the cause of common sense.[13]

Like all observers, Palmerston was unsure what would happen in this intelligent, wayward, and unpredictable constituency. He feared the 'rural reverends' most, the MAs who if they were to 'come up in mass against me', would form a charge as 'formidable as that of the Black Hussars'.[14] Candidates paid the travelling expenses of non-resident MAs, and during Monday 12 June, the day before the poll opened, 'the members of the Senate [kept] pouring into the town'.[15] On the following morning,

at the instance of two non-resident Masters of Arts, the Bribery Oath was administered to every member who voted, a circumstance which excited a very strong feeling of indignation among the Voters, who considered it not only as a personal insult upon themselves individually, but also as casting a most unmerited stigma upon the Senate as a body. Towards night the ebullition of feeling to which this gave rise, displayed itself in so strong an outcry against the practice, that the Vice Chancellor found it necessary to suspend the business, and for a full half hour the Senate House exhibited a scene of perhaps unprecedented uproar.

Eventually, the administration of the 'obnoxious oath' was withdrawn by the two men responsible.

At the close of poll on Tuesday, Copley and Palmerston were ahead. On Wednesday the polling, from 8 am to 3 pm and 5 pm to 10 pm, was 'particularly animated', a spurt by Bankes being balanced when 'a body of 13 gentlemen of King's College came up, and voted for Lord Palmerston, and thus gave him an advantage which he kept'. At the close of the poll, at 1 pm on Friday 16 June, Copley and Palmerston were ahead. The final vote was Copley 772,

---

[13] Clark and Hughes, *The Life and Letters of Adam Sedgwick*, vol. I, pp. 268–9. The letter was written to William Ainger, who as the pollbook reveals voted for Copley and Bankes despite Sedgwick's efforts.

[14] Quoted in Bourne, *Palmerston*, pp. 245–6. Much of this account is based on pp. 242–7, and on the files of the *Cambridge Chronicle* and *Cambridge Independent Press* for May and June 1826.

[15] *Cambridge Independent Press*, 17 June 1826, and for the next two quotations.

Palmerston 631, Bankes 508, and Goulburn 437.[16] Palmerston came top of the poll in both St John's and Trinity, and was praised by the Tory journal as being, 'with one exception . . . admirably qualified for the station which he has so ably filled for a long period of years'.[17] Personal qualities plainly counted a lot. So did the lustre that Palmerston brought to his university by representing it, as Pitt had done in an earlier generation. It is true, however, that the preponderance of votes for anti-emancipation candidates shows that there was wide support among MAs for the monopoly of Anglican power to be maintained.

Palmerston's fear, quoted earlier, of the effect of the 'rural reverends' on his chances, may well have been justified, but it would certainly not be right to suggest that non-resident MAs *as a whole* were less liberal than fellows, the residents. Analysis of the 1826 pollbook shows that the two groups voted very similarly.[18] Of the total of fellows 50 per cent voted for Palmerston, while 49 per cent of non-fellows did. The small numbers in most colleges mean that their individual percentages are not significant. But it is interesting to look at the figures for Trinity and St John's. At Trinity 22 fellows out of 36 (61 per cent) voted for Palmerston, and 202 non-fellows out of 349 (58 per cent). At St John's the corresponding figures were 38 out of 46 (83 per cent) and 156 out of 260 (60 per cent): much the highest percentage for any fellowship, and for MAs a higher percentage than for any college apart from Magdalene with its small sample. These striking percentages presumably reflect college loyalty to a distinguished St John's graduate.

Sentiment was mostly Conservative in 1826; the election points to battles lying ahead, when the Anglican structure of the university was strongly challenged inside and outwith the university. Meanwhile, Palmerston's experiences in 1826 helped soon to lead him into the Whig camp where he spent most of his political life, and the immediate issue of Catholic Emancipation was conceded as a political necessity by the Tory government in 1829.

Palmerston became Foreign Secretary in the government that the

---

[16] Cooper, *Annals*, IV, p. 552.   [17] *Cambridge Chronicle*, 23 June 1826.
[18] See appendix XI for the analysis. The pollbook does not distinguish fellows from mere graduates, or in other words 'residents' from 'non-residents', and they have been separated for the analysis by collating the pollbook with college entries in the *Cambridge University Calendar* for 1826. Further details are given in the appendix.

Whig leader Earl Grey formed in 1830. Grey and his colleagues were committed to a measure of parliamentary reform, and Palmerston met the strength of Tory anti-reform opinion at the crucial election of May 1831 when the electorate served judgement on the Reform Bill that Lord John Russell had introduced two months previously. In the contest for the two Cambridgeshire county seats reformers were returned unopposed, Lord Charles Manners, of the Duke of Rutland's family, retiring early when he saw that the Tory cause was certain to lose because of the desire for change that the freeholders of Cambridgeshire manifested.[19] In the university constituency, representing 'that large and important class of the community, the members of the three great professions, and of the educated gentlemen of England',[20] some dons felt that the Reform candidates Palmerston and William Cavendish should be supported;[21] the bill, favoured by most respectable people, was needed to avert 'the greatest of all calamities – a Revolution'; moreover, Cavendish, a kinsman of the Duke of Devonshire, moved 'in too high a station to attempt anything like republican innovation'.[22] Palmerston throughout his twenty years as the university's 'long-tried and faithful representative' had shown 'the greatest attention, and zeal, and ability'. But in the four days of polling in the Senate House[23] most electors heeded the warning of one of the Tory candidates, Henry Goulburn, that the proposed extension in the franchise and in the number of constituencies represented was 'pregnant with danger to many of the best interests in this country, and tending ultimately to the subversion of the Constitution'.[24]

There was much excitement in Cambridge during the poll, 'unusual in the annals of university elections'.[25] 1,450 MAs attended

---

[19] Michael Murphy, *Cambridge Newspapers*, p. 76.   [20] *Cambridge Chronicle*, 29 April 1831.
[21] Cavendish (1808–91) graduated Second Wrangler and Eighth Classic at Trinity in 1829. He was the great-grandson of the fourth Duke of Devonshire and was to succeed his cousin to become the seventh duke in 1858. He was the university's great benefactor in the 1870s; the physics laboratory and Cavendish College were named after him.
[22] See the letter of 'A Moderate Tory M.A.', in *Cambridge Independent Press*, 30 April 1831, and the letters of 'An Independent M.A.' and 'A Member of the Senate' for the next sentence.
[23] It was interrupted by the conferment of degrees on Friday morning, 5 May.
[24] See his letter in the *Cambridge Chronicle*, 29 April 1831. Goulburn's Tory colleague was William Yates Peel, younger brother of Sir Robert Peel.
[25] *Cambridge Independent Press*, 6 May 1831, and for the following quotations.

to vote, or 157 more than at any previous contest. More than 1,200 were non-residents. At the declaration at noon on Friday 5 May 'the junior members of the University, who thronged the galleries in vast numbers (all townsmen being excluded), amused themselves with giving three cheers for the party they espoused', while when the candidates left the Senate House 'Trinity Street was completely thronged with a dense crowd, testifying in front of the respective committee rooms . . . by cheering or hissing.' Goulburn and Peel received over 800 votes, and Cavendish and Palmerston over 600.[26] Palmerston got only 99 votes in his own college, St John's, as against over 200 each for the Tories, though at Trinity about 250 MAs voted for the 2 reformers out of 450. 'The residents are equally divided', wrote 'A Churchman' from Trinity halfway through the poll:[27]

> the majority in Trinity being reformers. The London voters are generally for the old members; but a cloud from Norfolk, Suffolk, and especially *Suffolk*, has overspread us. It is of little moment that the University has cast away a reputation for sense, *which it never deserved*. It is absolutely of no importance that it has made a second ineffectual effort to arrest the course of political improvement. But it is painful to see the church thus broken down by the hands of her own ministers, and to witness the stupid exultation with which they deal their blow.

Once again, analysis of the pollbook shows little difference in voting-pattern between fellows and the aggregate of non-fellows; 51 per cent of fellows voted for anti-Reform candidates, and 56 per cent of non-fellows.[28] Adam Sedgwick wrote to Charlotte Murchison that he was 'mortified by the result more than I can find words to express'.[29] The strength of diehard opinion was shown once more two years later, over the refusal to admit non-Anglicans to membership of the university.

[26] The poll is analysed in Cooper, *Annals*, IV, p. 570: Peel 805, Goulburn 804, Cavendish 630, Palmerston 610.

[27] *Cambridge Independent Press*, 6 May 1831. 'A Churchman' may well have been Adam Sedgwick.

[28] See appendix XI.

[29] Clark and Hughes, *The Life and Letters of Adam Sedgwick*, vol. I, p. 376. At her death in 1869 Sedgwick wrote that 'for many many years Lady Murchison was one of the dearest of those friends whose society formed the best charms of my life'. Her husband was Sir Roderick Impey Murchison, the geologist.

COUNTY AND BOROUGH AFTER 1832

The 1832 Reform Act added new groups to the electorate: in the boroughs householders whose properties had an annual value of £10, and in the counties various categories of tenant farmers. It has recently been calculated that the act increased the electorate by about 45 per cent, 200,000 electors being added to the existing 440,000, 'a discernible and a significant difference but scarcely the stuff of which political revolutions are made'.[30] The effect of the act, however, varied greatly between constituencies. In the county of Cambridgeshire there were 4,013 electors in 1836. Of these 2,813 freeholders and 39 office-holders and others would have qualified before the Reform Act, while 1,161 men were newly enfranchised.[31] Between the electors and the landlords there were strong bonds, based on influence and sentiment; the county tended to choose Conservative representatives who supported agricultural protection, and as before 1832 MPs were often from the great landowning families. From 1832 to 1878 the Hardwickes supplied one Cambridgeshire member continuously, while the Rutland family did also, with one short break, from 1847 to 1874. In the county the great electoral changes came after the Reform Acts of 1867 and 1884–5, and the enactment of secret ballot in 1872.[32]

In the borough of Cambridge, by contrast, the growth in the constituency was dramatic. After the Reform Act there were 79 freeman electors, qualified on the pre-1832 franchise, and 1,490 newly qualified £10 householders.[33] The tiny close borough of pliant freemen had disappeared. On the other hand the larger electorate was open to various improper influences. Intimidation was one, and Cambridge being a sort of 'company town' the

---

[30] Frank O'Gorman, *Voters, Patrons and Parties. The Unreformed Electoral System of Hanoverian England 1734–1832* (Oxford, Clarendon, 1989), pp. 180–2.

[31] PP 1837–8, HC xliv (329): *A Return . . . from Every County, City and Borough in England and Wales, of the Number of Electors Registered . . . 1836 and 1837*, p. 3. The new electors consisted of 572 copyholders, 564 £50 tenants-at-will, and 25 leaseholders. The county now returned three MPs instead of two.

[32] H. J. Hanham, *Elections and Party Management: Politics in the Time of Disraeli and Gladstone* (London, Longmans, 1959), esp. pp. 3–38; David Cresap Moore, *The Politics of Deference* (Hassocks, Sussex Harvester, 1976), esp. pp. 45–102, 304–7 (on Cambs.); *VCH Cambs.*, III, p. 418.

[33] PP 1833, HC xxvii (189): *Number of Electors Inrolled in Each County, City, Borough or Place . . . Under 2 William IV, c.45*, p. 111.

university was particularly guilty of it, at all events immediately after the Reform Act. Many dons could lean on college servants and tradesmen, and the Vice-Chancellor had power over publicans and the 200 or 300 licensed lodging-house keepers. This university influence was exercised for Conservative candidates. In 1832 the Vice-Chancellor removed from two Liberal booksellers their contract to supply writing-paper to the university, and the dismissal of the gardener employed by the President of Queens' for voting for the Liberal Spring Rice was a *cause célèbre* at the 1834 election. In 1835 the Vice-Chancellor sent his butler to tell publicans that he wished them to vote Conservative; he also postponed the day that lodging-house licences were to be granted, until after the election. At St John's 'the feeling of all the tutors' was 'decidedly opposed to the liberal interest', and only one servant voted for them.[34] One Liberal estimate was that such tactics were worth 200 votes to the Conservatives in 1835, out of their total poll of 688. Many dons thought such pressures were immoral, or at least undignified. The Trinity fellows 'made it understood among the servants, that they were at liberty to vote as their principles might suggest to them', and 50 dons protested that 'every species of undue interference' with the 'sacred trust' of the franchise was 'a gross breach of public and private morality'.

After 1835 dons exercised their influence less grossly, if at all, as a result of the adverse publicity brought by the select committee's proceedings. But the university was still involved with city elections in a surprising fashion: both sides spent money like water between 1835 and 1853, and undergraduates helped to spend it.[35] Both sides wooed the new electorate by a lot of treating in public houses, by hiring men for 5s or 10s a day for nominal jobs as messengers, and by spending on 'matters of a decorative character, such as flags, banners, processions, etc.'[36] Undergraduates were hired as 'watchmen' for the Conservatives; they wore gowns and false moustaches and were blacked up,

---

[34] PP 1835, HC viii (547): *Report from Select Committee on Bribery at Elections*, p. 12, pp. 1–23 for these lines. generally, and pp. 9–10 for the next quotation.

[35] What follows is based on *Report of the Commissioners Appointed ... to Inquire into the Existence of Corrupt Practices in the Borough of Cambridge together with the Minutes of Evidence* (London, 1853), esp. pp. v–xviii, from which the quotations are taken. This document is not a Parliamentary Paper.

[36] P. vi.

perhaps to disguise themselves from the Proctors, who seemed in fact to take no notice whatever.[37] One meeting in the Black Bear public house during the 1841 election was said to be for the Conservative Mechanics' Assocation, but consisted very largely of undergraduates gathered together to be briefed on their duties as messengers and the like.[38] There was a great deal of direct bribery too, by the Conservatives who were anxious to gain advantage in a balanced constituency; the Liberals very rarely bribed in turn. The Cambridge Conservative had an agent who scrutinised the electors' list minutely, learnt who was bribable,

> and left him to be operated on when required ... After a voter had once received a bribe, the proceedings became very much simplifi-ed. It was obvious that no delicacy was necessary in applying to him on future occasions. A voter once bribed might be calculated upon as bribeable ever after; and the bribed voter himself became also an agent for the procuring of other bribed voters among his friends and connexions.[39]

Bribers took care to avoid detection. The chief briber, Samuel Long, became so accomplished that he could 'send voters to the poll by merely looking at them with a peculiar expression of counten-ance, or ... by merely leaving a message with the wife that Long had called'.[40] Or a voter might be told 'Go and do the thing that is right, and I will see it right.'[41] The £5 or £10 came later, surreptitiously. Remarkable as it may seem, some undergraduates were involved in these sleazy transactions, flitting about the streets of Cambridge as go-betweens. Their names were not known, or at least not usually divulged to the committees of enquiry; but Charles Burdon of Trinity was named as a link-man in the 1841 election, securing a vote in return for his promise to get a 'bill' paid – which was done. £13 1s 6d and 'threepence in halfpennies' were handed over.[42]

---

[37] PP 1843, HC vi (316): *Minutes of Proceedings ... Select Committee of the Cambridge Borough Election Petition*, p. 47. The watchmen's task was to see that the Liberals did not bribe electors. Treating undergraduates was not likely to influence Cambridge electors, nor could they become electors themselves. Their being hired is evidence of how recklessly money was spent in borough elections.
[38] PP 1843, HC vi (316), p. 118. [39] *Report* (1853), p. vii. [40] *Report* (1853), p. viii.
[41] PP 1852–3, HC ix (185): *Minutes of Evidence ... Select Committee on the Cambridge Borough Election Petition*, pp. 40–1.
[42] PP 1843, HC vi (316), p. 29. The name is puzzling. There was a Charles Burdon at Trinity, the son of the Deputy Lieutenant of Northumberland, but he did not matriculate until Lent 1842.

Candidates were not told, and were shrewd enough not to ask, where the cash they gave was going to. No dons can be discerned among the solicitors, surgeons, and shopkeepers that managed electoral finance for the Cambridge Tories, but the group did include a well-known private tutor – Thomas Coward, a BA of Queens' in 1837, and the Tyrwhitt Hebrew scholar in 1838; unfortunately his exact role in this shadowy and half-lit world cannot be discovered.[43] Though there were never more than 200 bribed electors, they were sufficient to turn the scales in a borough in equipoise. Select committees of the House of Commons aired all the evidence in 1840 and 1843, the Conservative candidate in the 1839 election was unseated, and Samuel Long was imprisoned. But bribery grew worse. The 1852 election cost Cambridge Conservatives over £3,000 (half coming from the candidates) and much of it went on corruption. After another select committee had investigated matters and it was clear that Cambridge borough was one of the most notorious constituencies in the United Kingdom, the Home Secretary, Palmerston, appointed a commission of enquiry consisting of three barristers; the 700 pages of evidence they collected, which have been quoted here, may be regarded as definitive. In 1854 a bill was introduced into the Commons to disfranchise 122 named Cambridge electors guilty of giving or receiving bribes. It was withdrawn, Cambridge being one of the constituencies that prompted the Corrupt Practices Act (1854) with its stringent penalties for electoral malpractice.

At the first election after the Reform Act the borough electorate returned two Whigs.[44] Thomas Spring Rice, of Anglo-Irish gentry stock, was a graduate of Trinity College, Cambridge, and represented Limerick from 1820 until his election for Cambridge borough. A very capable man, Spring Rice served in several government offices, rising to be Chancellor of the Exchequer in 1835. He was too cautious to please the Radicals on the government benches (or in Cambridge either) while his natural warmth of manner, as Lord Sumner wrote in the *DNB*, 'involuntarily ... raised in many quarters hopes of preferment which it was not in his power to

---

[43] PP 1852–3, HC ix (185), p. 69.

[44] Details of elections and MPs for borough and university are taken from F. W. S. Craig, *British Parliamentary Election Results 1832–1885* (London, Macmillan, 1977), pp. 76–7, 611–12.

satisfy'. Ill at ease in the Commons, Spring Rice resigned in 1839, becoming Lord Monteagle.

George Pryme, also elected in December 1832, had a longer connection than Spring Rice with the borough of Cambridge, and was one of the few dons ever to represent it in the Commons. Pryme, a resident MA of Trinity, attended a public meeting in Cambridge about 1812 and apologised

> as a member of the University, for taking part in the affairs of the Town . . . This remark was greeted with approbation by some of the principal inhabitants of the Town, who said they wished that such participation by University men in their affairs was of more frequent occurrence. I was soon after elected a Paving Commissioner, and took an active part in all local matters.[45]

Pryme's character, wrote his daughter, was

> a very peculiar one, unlike, as a whole, any other that I have known . . . his manners and his mind were fashioned in the formal mould of the last Century, yet he entered thoroughly into the progress and energy of this one. Deliberate in thought, and slow to generalise, he was, perhaps for that very reason, before his time, and had not unfrequently to be overtaken by quicker and more enthusiastic spirits. He always kept sincerity and directness in view, avoiding all kinds of exaggeration, and speaking of 'the delicious delight of reposing one's mind upon truth'.

Pryme was born in 1781, the son of a Hull merchant of Huguenot stock. Like so many undergraduates of the day he attended private schools conducted by clergymen, and he was also for two years a pupil of the Reverend Joseph Milner (brother of the President of Queens' College) at Hull Grammar School; again like others he prepared for Cambridge mathematics by spending the summer before matriculation with an expert coach – in his case the celebrated John Dawson of Sedbergh, who had also taught Adam Sedgwick. Graduating Sixth Wrangler in 1803, Pryme was elected to a Trinity fellowship, while reading for the bar, and 'found the life of a fellow, mixed though it was with the melancholy of disappointed views', highly agreeable.[46] He vacated his fellowship on marriage in 1813, but continued to reside in Cambridge, in

---

[45] Pryme, *Autobiographic Recollections*, p. 104, and pp. 356–7 for the quotation in the next paragraph. The account that follows is based on this work.   [46] Pryme, *Autobiographic Recollections*, p. 86.

Barnwell Abbey. He practised successfully as a provincial barrister, and also began in 1816 to give lectures on Political Economy in Cambridge, the first such course in a British university. Very ignorant of this subject as a young graduate, his interest in it had been sparked by the debates in the 'Academical', a debating society he joined while at Lincoln's Inn in 1804; he bought the *Wealth of Nations* and mastered it, and continued his studies in later years. The annual course of lectures he began to give in 1816 were at first regarded warily by the heads of houses, who gave permission for them only on condition that they were not given before midday, lest they interfered with college tuition. In 1828 the Senate conferred the title of 'Professor' on Pryme, but he was paid no more than £30 a year in lecture fees, and the chair did not cease to be merely personal until it was established by the Senate in 1863, on Pryme's resignation from his professorship.

Rejected by the tiny borough electorate in 1820 and 1826, Pryme had a majority of 439 over the Tory candidate (the total poll being 1247) in December 1832.[47] As a Whig and a supporter of the Grey and Melbourne administrations, Pryme was especially interested in the abolition of slavery, law reform, and reform of the universities. In December 1833 he proposed in the Senate two graces 'for appointing syndicates to consider the propriety of abolishing or modifying subscription on graduation'.[48] They were rejected by the Caput. On 24 March 1834 Pryme supported in the Commons the anti–Subscription petition which Sedgwick and others had organised, and which Spring Rice presented to the house. In 1837 he took the momentous step of proposing a commission of enquiry into Oxford and Cambridge, Pryme being particularly concerned over the celibacy issue and the territorial limitations on many fellowships.[49] The limitations were rapidly ceasing to be of consequence in practical terms, and were less prominent in the reform literature than in Pryme's consciousness. Perhaps Pryme was not immersed in the university question, on which he did not write; at all events he withdrew his motion when on this occasion Russell opined that the time was not ripe,

[47] Cooper, *Annals*, IV, p. 575.
[48] Cooper, *Annals*, IV, p. 579. The question of subscription to Anglicanism is dealt with in this chapter below.   [49] *Autobiographic Recollections*, pp. 252–6.

and did not make the suggestion again. Pryme supported the memorial by Oxford and Cambridge graduates asking in July 1848 for a commission of enquiry. But by that time he had ceased to be an MP, resigning for reasons of health in 1841; and he was no longer to a great extent involved with university matters (though his lecture course in the Lent Term continued). In 1847 he made a crucial move to an estate he bought in Wistow in Huntingdonshire: 'I wished to lead a more tranquil life than I could do in Cambridge, and to look more after my property.'[50] Pryme died in 1868.

Cambridge borough did not have a permanent 'natural' Liberal majority.[51] Though there was a strong Dissenting tradition, which was politically Liberal, Conservative attitudes were equally entrenched in its electorate and were encouraged by its powerful university presence: notably veneration for the social hierarchy, the landed and agricultural interest, and the Church of England and the institutions associated with it. These attitudes were more important long-term in bringing electoral victory than corruption, spectacular though this was on some occasions. The Liberals lost both seats in 1841. Conservative disarray over Corn Law repeal in 1846 led to bad organisation and voters' dissatisfaction, and the Tories' defeat in 1847. Systematic bribery five years later marked an attempt at a comeback, but it rebounded with the unseating afterwards of Macaulay and Astell, the successful Conservatives, while the Liberals won in 1854. Yet three years later the Conservatives had recovered, and they won every contested election between 1857 and the Reform Act of 1867. The much larger electorate that was then created voted in the Liberals in Cambridge.

THE UNIVERSITY AFTER 1832

In contrast to Cambridge borough, 1832 had no effect whatsoever on the university as a parliamentary constituency. The qualification for the franchise remained the same, possession of the MA degree,

---

[50] *Autobiographic Recollections*, p. 315.
[51] What follows draws upon Jeremy C. Mitchell and James Cornford, 'The Political Demography of Cambridge, 1832–1868', *Albion*, 9 (1977), pp. 242–72.

and therefore membership of the Senate, and the retention of one's name on the college boards; non-residents were not excluded, as they were in some constituencies with popular pre-reform electorates, with dramatic effect on numbers.[52] There were about 2,200 qualified Cambridge MAs in 1831 and 2,400 in 1835.[53] The increase in the size of the university in the mid-Victorian years raised the electorate to 5,212 by 1865. The 1867 Reform Act made no difference to the university constituency, just as the preceding act had not, and by 1870 there were 5,572 electors.[54]

Henry Goulburn, elected MP for the university in 1831, held his seat uninterruptedly until his death in 1856, and with only two contested elections. Intelligent, upright, and possessing firm Anglican sympathies, Goulburn was just the sort of man to attract continued support from university electors, and he was one of the most distinguished representatives the university has ever possessed. Educated at a private school in Sunbury (Middlesex) and graduating from Trinity College in 1805, Goulburn entered the Commons in 1808, as member for Horsham. Quickly rising up the ladder, he served as Chief Secretary to the Lord Lieutenant in Ireland, where his pronounced anti-Catholic views gave him an Orange reputation that commended him to university diehards. In 1828–30, and again in 1841–6 under Peel, he was a successful Chancellor of the Exchequer. Goulburn and Peel became acquainted as young MPs, and soon became very close friends, and 'almost inseparable' in their opinions.[55] Self-effacing, a poor speaker, and with a limited personality, he was in Peel's shadow, and in need of his encouragement. But he was 'completely honest, and unswervingly loyal', and 'the perfect foil to his more nervous and brilliant companion'.[56] Goulburn's colleague J. W. Croker remarked that he was 'a most

---

[52] The Statutes of 1858 laid down that MAs and Doctors who had on admission to their degree declared themselves to be members of the Church of England were members of the Senate. Members remained on the Register if they paid 12s a year in university dues, either to their college or to the Registrary. In 1865 there were 104 members in this last category, 'not on the boards of any college'. The 1858 Statutes also limited the roll for elections to the Council to members of the Senate residing within one and a half miles of Great St Mary's; but the parliamentary roll still included non-residents. See *Cambridge University Calendar*, 1865, pp. 2, 432–4.

[53] *University Pollbooks*: 1831, p. 2; 1835, p. 2.

[54] *University Pollbooks*, 1865, p. 484; 1870, p. 532.

[55] The words are Norman Gash's, in *Mr Secretary Peel* (London, Longman, 1961), p. 80. Much of what follows is based on this book, esp. pp. 371, 375, and 578, and on the same author's *Sir Robert Peel* (London, Longman, 1972), esp. p. 286.   [56] Gash, *Mr Secretary Peel*, p. 80.

excellent and honourable man, with high principles both moral and political'.[57] Goulburn was pall-bearer at Peel's funeral.

The university had seven other representatives between 1832 and 1870: Charles Manners-Sutton (1832–5), Charles Ewan Law (1835–50), L. T. Wigram (1850–6, 1857–9), Spencer Walpole (1856–82), Charles Jasper Selwyn (1859–67), Alexander Beresford Hope (1868–87), and G. Denman (1856–7). They were usually returned without contest, a reflection of the university's predominant Conservatism. Denman, who served for the shortest time, was the only Liberal. They came from patrician or upper-middle-class professional families: Denman and Law were sons of Lords Denman and Ellenborough, the distinguished lawyers, and Selwyn's father was a lawyer too, and a writer on legal matters; Manners-Sutton was the son of the Archbishop of Canterbury; Beresford-Hope's father was Thomas Hope the writer on classical art and collector of its treasures, and his stepfather was Field-Marshal Beresford.[58] Spencer Walpole's great-great-uncle was the famous Prime Minister and his family had included numerous politicians, diplomatists, and writers; he was also a kinsman of Spencer Perceval and Nelson.

The Walpoles were a large Cambridge clan, fifteen members being at Cambridge between 1750 and 1900;[59] Spencer Walpole's father was among them. Of the other six MPs, four were the sons of Cambridge graduates, and Law was in addition the grandson of the Master of Peterhouse, Edmund Law. Three of the MPs were alumni of Eton, one of Harrow, and one of Winchester – a larger proportion from Great Schools, other samplings in this book suggest, than among the generality of Cambridge undergraduates. Wigram was educated in Richmond (Surrey) and Denman, unusual in several respects, attended Felsted and Repton, which in his day were country grammar schools like Hawkshead, Wordsworth's school. All were graduates of Trinity except Law, who went to St John's. Denman was remembered by a contemporary as 'perhaps the most respected' undergraduate of his year, combining 'classical capacity with power of muscle and endurance . . . for he was both Senior Classic of his year [1842] and Stroke Oar

[57] J. W. Croker, *Correspondence and Diaries* (3 vols., London, 1884), vol. III, pp. 59–61, from a letter to Lord Brougham, 4 February 1846.   [58] On Thomas Hope see chapter 1, pp. 21–2.
[59] Venn and Venn, *Alumni Cantabrigienses*.

of the University crew ... warily looking after his own boat crew, the First Trinity, and joining their rollickings in order to keep them within bounds, but doing hard mental work at other hours.'[60] He continued to write classical verse during his legal career, translating Gray's *Elegy* into Greek and the First Book of Pope's *Iliad* into Latin – unusual pleasures for a High Court judge. Described by William Carr in his *DNB* essay as 'more distinguished as a graceful scholar than as a strong lawyer', Denman's career suggests dilettantism. There is certainly no hint of such a trait in the committed professionalism of the other six. No fewer than five were lawyers, a reflection probably of the desire of barristers to become MPs; the sixth, Beresford Hope, was a dedicated Anglican and ecclesiologist, who devoted much of his great wealth to church-building. All Saints, Margaret Street, Butterfield's polychromatic interpretation of Anglo-Catholicism, was his most spectacular benefaction.[61]

Manners-Sutton became Speaker of the Commons and Selwyn Solicitor-General, while Walpole was Home Secretary for three periods between 1852 and 1868. Their careers look like lesser versions of Goulburn's, displaying reliability, hard work, and intelligence, but none of the luminous quality of Pitt the Younger, an earlier MP for the university, or W. E. Gladstone, Oxford's most distinguished representative. For the most part Cambridge's electorate, the most intellectually gifted in the country, chose as their members men of solid background and abilities rather than outstanding talent. The choice may perplex us, since in the years in question the university and the state were often in conflict, and it might have seemed an advantage to have more thrusting advocacy of its case in the House of Commons than the university's MPs proffered. Whewell, had he been its MP, would certainly have given a more vigorous defence; on the other hand, the Commons would have laughed at it. Perhaps the truth of the matter was that Cambridge preferred to mould 'reforms' to its patterns through the syndicate room and the Senate House, rather than attempt vainly to defeat them by high-profile argument.

---

[60] Francis Galton, *Memories of My Life* (London, Methuen, 1908), p. 74.
[61] For Beresford Hope's contribution to the Cambridge Camden Society, see chapter 1, pp. 37–9.

THE ELECTION OF 1847

We may derive an impression of the style of university electioneering and the concerns of the constituency in the mid-Victorian years from a close study of the campaign of July 1847, one of the few contested elections Goulburn was engaged in. It aroused greater interest than any university election since 1826 or 1831. The *Cambridge Chronicle* gave it an unprecedented coverage, including in its issue of 7 August a statement of the poll at every half-hour during the five days of voting.

The election came at a time of great political confusion. The previous year Peel had split the Conservative party by pushing the repeal of the Corn Laws; Goulburn followed Peel, while his colleague as member for the university, Evan Law, remained in the majority grouping in the party, the Protectionists; the two men were opposed in the election campaign. J. G. Shaw-Lefevre, one time Senior Wrangler and fellow of Trinity, was a Whig and though he was a Repealer party loyalties kept him apart from Goulburn. Viscount Feilding also stood.[62] He was twenty-four and much the youngest candidate; his candidature inevitably meant that Feilding was compared with an earlier representative of the university, Pitt the Younger. Most observers found the comparison implausible. His participation in the campaign was regarded as an affront to the learned constituency by the *Cambridge Independent Press*.

The candidates' utterances were almost entirely concerned with the two institutions which dons felt most earnestly involved with, and whose future seemed at risk from common dangers, the Church of England and the university itself. Feilding was the most Conservative; considering 'the union of Church and State' as 'essential', he was hostile to 'all connexion with and concession to Romanism ... the endowment of the Romish Church in Ireland ... as well as all attempts to establish an intercourse with the Court of Rome'; finally, Feilding would 'spare no exertions to uphold your best interests, as identified with the Church of England'.[63] While Feilding showed his opposition to recent talk of university

---

[62] Feilding was born in 1823, and after three years in Trinity as a nobleman graduated MA in 1844. He was the son and heir of the Earl of Denbigh, whom he succeeded in 1865.

[63] The candidates' addresses were printed in the *Cambridge Chronicle*, 19 June 1847.

reform, and to the subsidy that Peel's government had given to Maynooth College, Shaw-Lefevre, who was in favour of both, promised to prove his 'attachment to the University by a steady and unremitting endeavour to promote its best interests', which was coded support for university reform; Shaw-Lefevre came bottom of the poll, and never seemed likely to rise above that position. The addresses of Goulburn and Law were similar to Feilding's, and the contest was throughout between these three men.

The campaign was in stark contrast to the Eatanswill excesses usual in contests for the borough seats, where the parties' 'messengers' could hardly walk after drinking solidly for eight hours in the 'Old English Gentleman' at the candidates' expense.[64] In the university election there were no meetings, and indeed no public attempt to persuade the constituency apart from the addresses and letters in the *Chronicle*. These were long, literary,[65] and contentious though usually courteous. 'A Member of the Senate' warned his colleagues to think of 'the members of a National Church, who as a body cannot record their opinions, but who look to you with anxious solicitude, to uphold in its integrity the principles of the Reformed Church'. The three Conservative candidates were 'tolerably equal' in qualifications, but Goulburn did not inspire confidence. 'I hate *trimming* to circumstances, as much as I admire consistency: I hate the abandonment of principles.'[66] These were references to Goulburn's vote for the Maynooth grant, the Dissenters' Chapel Bill, and the consolidation of the bishoprics of Bangor and St Asaph, 'in opposition to the petitions of the Senate'. On 3 July the *Chronicle* took a column to detail Goulburn's objectionable votes in the Commons, and the Reverend Christopher Benson, BA Trinity 1812, Prebendary of Worcester, and the first Hulsean Lecturer, wrote that he could not consider 'the increased grant to Maynooth to have been a measure calculated to obtain "the blessing of Divine Providence"', while the Dissenters' Chapels Bill 'gave to Unitarian teachers, what the law as it stood would have withdrawn from them, the power of preaching at their

---

[64] PP 1843, HC vi (316): *Select Committee on the Cambridge Borough Election Petition*, pp. 1–155.

[65] The *Chronicle*, maintaining its position as the 'University journal', had a stock of Greek type and printers able to set it accurately.

[66] For these lines, see *Cambridge Chronicle*, 26 June 1847. See also the letter of 'A Late Fellow' in the same issue.

ease doctrines contrary to the Divinity and Atonement of our blessed Lord'.[67]

Of the other correspondents who made clear their determination to abandon Goulburn, the only one to identify himself was James Scholefield, the Regius Professor of Greek, and a prominent Evangelical.[68]

> Believing the present to be the most important and critical (if not the last) opportunity we may have of making a stand in defence of our most valued institutions, I should feel bound to support any respectable [man] who would represent our principles and feelings upon this point, and I am doubly thankful that a candidate has come forward ... possessing such high positive recommendations as, in my judgment, Lord Feilding does.

Scholefield joined Feilding's committee. Though he was disadvantaged by looking like an undergraduate, Feilding commended himself by the vigour of his anti-Catholicism. '*As long as Rome is what she is*', wrote 'A Member of the Senate of Cambridge', 'if England is not to be shorn of her strength, the Protestant character of her Church must be vigorously maintained; and the Church of England would not be what she is – a faithful witness of Catholic truth – *unless* she protested against the errors and corruptions of Rome.'[69] In a lengthy leading article the *Chronicle* asked Conservative dons voting for Law to pledge their second votes to Feilding, a man 'of the highest promise and of the best principles', responsible for 'sentiments so elevated and noble' at a time 'of low expediency and heartless political economy': views supported by letters from 'Almae Matris Filius Observantissimus' and others.[70] On the other hand, 'A Correspondent' urged dons to reflect that whatever Goulburn's faults, he was 'the ablest servant and defender the University can produce,' and so entitled to Conservative support. 'A Tory' asked his university colleagues to remember that they were removed from the exigencies of political life, and that for fifty years '*no statesman of any pretensions*, Whig or Tory, has appeared to object' to the Maynooth Grant. 'Private judgment run mad, that is, which takes no account of the judgment of others, is confessedly a weak

---

[67] *Cambridge Chronicle*, 24 July 1847.   [68] *Cambridge Chronicle*, 31 July 1847.
[69] *Cambridge Chronicle*, 17 July 1847. The italics are in the original.
[70] *Cambridge Chronicle*, 3 July 1847.

prop in religious matters; and so, *I* think, it is also in political matters.'[71]

These views counted in the long run. On the first day's poll Feilding was second to Law, but on the remaining two Goulburn passed him. The growth of the Senate, the excitement raised by the issues at stake, and the convenience of the new railway linking London and Cambridge, produced a larger turnout than at any earlier election. At the close of the poll Law and Goulburn were victorious; the latter was just 42 votes ahead of Feilding, and Shaw-Lefevre trailed badly.[72] A comparison of the two largest colleges, Trinity and St John's, shows a markedly different pattern. St John's was more Conservative, 'Protestant', and anti-reform, its electors giving more support to Law and much less to Shaw-Lefevre.[73] 'There is no doubt', it was commented, 'but that Mr Goulburn owes his return to the friends of Mr Lefevre ... in a very large measure.'[74] The election was a parallel to what at this time was occurring in the university over its reform. Those favouring substantial change were very much in a minority, and perforce co-operated with men wanting very much less, or perhaps scarcely any change at all. In Cambridge reformers rarely got all they wanted. On the other hand if Protestant dons had won a more striking victory they would not have been happy for long. In 1850 Feilding was received into the Roman Catholic Church.

THE DISPUTE OVER RELIGIOUS TESTS, 1834

In March 1834 some members of the Senate met in the rooms of Cornwallis Hewett, the Downing Professor of Medicine, and with Adam Sedgwick in the chair it was decided to petition both Houses of Parliament, 'not as coming from the body at large [that is, the Senate itself] but as expressing the opinions of certain individuals'. The petitioners suggested 'the expediency of abrogating by legislative enactment every religious test exacted from members of the

[71] *Cambridge Chronicle*, 24 July 1847. Italics are in the original.
[72] The vote was Law 1,486, Goulburn 1,189, Feilding 1,147, Shaw-Lefevre 860: Cooper, *Annals*, IV, p. 696, and also for the college figures given in the next footnote.
[73] The votes were: Law, T 334 and St J's 402; Goulburn, T 483 and St J's 179; Feilding, T 243 and St J's 292; and Shaw-Lefevre, T 397 and St J's 103.
[74] *Cambridge Chronicle*, 7 August 1847.

University before they proceed to degrees, whether of bachelor, master, or doctor, in Arts, Law, and Physic'.[75] So began a dispute over the religious tests that divided the university community deeply and showed that on some fundamental issues a majority of MPs disagreed with a majority of dons. Though on the immediate issue the weight of university opinion won because of the power of the House of Lords, the controversy was a bad omen for Cambridge reactionaries.

The issue of religious tests on graduation had last been seriously contested in Cambridge in 1772.[76] The abolitionists were defeated, but the Senate replaced the need to subscribe on graduating in Arts to the Three Canons of 1604[77] with a declaration of membership of the Church of England. This briefer subscription, easier to slide through[78] than the three canons, was extended in 1779 to Bachelors of Civil Law, Medicine, and Music and to Doctors of Music. Graduands in divinity had to subscribe to the Three Canons still, and all holders of offices or fellowships in college or university had by the Act of Uniformity of 1662 to conform to the liturgy of the Church of England.[79] Oxford had even more onerous requirements. The universities' function as the educators of the Established Church's clergy was held to justify the church's grip on them, but it was hard for institutions that were national to offer the Anglican Establishment as a reason to exclude non-Anglicans. The repeal of the Test and Corporation Acts in 1828 allowed non-Anglicans to hold offices under the Crown and be members of corporations from which they had previously been excluded, while Catholic Emancipation in 1829 opened the House of Commons to men who had previously been specifically excluded from it. The exclusion of non-Anglicans with conscientious scruples from Oxford and Cambridge, was now outstanding as a disability.[80] In England and Wales

---

[75] Clark and Hughes, *Adam Sedgwick*, vol. I, pp. 418–20 for these sentences.
[76] See chapter 11, pp. 406–10.
[77] The subscription issue, with the texts of the various oaths, is treated in PP 1852–3, HC xliv [1559]: *Graham Commission Report*, pp. 38–43. The three canons asserted that the sovereign was the Supreme Governor of the Church of England, that no foreign prince or prelate had any ecclesiastical or spiritual jurisdiction within the kingdom, and that the Prayer Book and Thirty-nine Articles were in accordance with the word of God.
[78] For C. A. Bristed's evasive action in 1845 see chapter 16, p. 590.
[79] Winstanley, *Early Victorian Cambridge*, p. 84.
[80] The Anglican monopoly on the ceremonies of marriage and burial, and the liability of all to pay tithe and church rates, were also powerful grievances.

it was felt chiefly by Protestant Dissenters, who outnumbered Roman Catholics, particularly, it is probable, within the middle classes likely to covet a Cambridge degree; in any case Roman Catholics, unlike Dissenters, did not usually seek education in institutions their church did not control.[81] Most Scots were not Episcopalians, but Scotland had its own universities anyway.

The Reform Act of 1832 was a watershed. The electorate was substantially increased, in large measure to the advantage of the urban middle class which included many Protestant Dissenters. The general election that followed confirmed the power of the Whigs, the friends of the Dissenters, though they proved less helpful in practice than the Dissenters hoped. Still, in the early 1830s there seemed to be hope for those aggrieved by the Established Church of England, its rights and privileges. It seemed also that university religious tests might be undermined from another direction. London University, recently founded, was pressing for a royal charter to give it the power to award degrees, and in 1833 the government was discussing whether to grant one. If it did, the Anglican church's monopoly in higher education in England would be breached.[82]

In December 1833 George Pryme, a leading university liberal, active in the Dissenters' cause, attempted to get syndicates to enquire into the tests' value, but this move was vetoed in the Caput by the Vice-Chancellor, Joshua King, the President of Queens'. In February 1834 Cornwallis Hewett proposed a syndicate to examine the case of religious tests for medical students, but King vetoed this suggestion too.[83] The background to Hewett's move was that while Oxford and Cambridge had a monopoly of medical degrees in England the professional instruction they offered was quite inadequate, and notably inferior for example to the medical schools of Edinburgh and Glasgow. Faced with growing pressures for improvement, the new Regius Professor of Physic, John Haviland, began regular courses in pathology and the practice of medicine in 1819, and in February 1829 the Senate passed a grace that recast the medical curriculum and examinations and so laid the foundations of

---

[81] Vincent Alan McClelland, *English Roman Catholics and Higher Education* (Oxford, Clarendon, 1973), esp. pp. 175–218.   [82] Bellot, *University College, London*, pp. 56–7, 219–22.
[83] Winstanley, *Early Victorian Cambridge*, p. 88.

the present medical school.[84] In 1834 Hewett knew that the College of Physicians, in London, had already petitioned to be allowed to grant degrees, and so there was a very real risk that promising candidates might be drawn away from the university by the religious freedom offered elsewhere. Efforts that were being made to improve Cambridge medicine might prove pointless.

London University's bid for a charter was opposed in Cambridge. In 1831 the Senate by large majorities in both houses petitioned for the inclusion in the charter of a clause 'declaring that nothing therein should be construed as giving a right to confer any academical distinctions designated by the same titles or accompanied with the same privileges as the degrees then conferred by the Universities of Oxford and Cambridge'. Three years later, in March 1834, the Senate reaffirmed its stand.[85] In other words, the Senate argued that non-Anglicans should be unable to take degrees at either Cambridge or an institution designed for them; the Anglican monopoly should remain inviolate. It was after this second petition, following Joshua King's vetoes in the Caput, that Sedgwick and his associates decided on their move.

Sedgwick was one of a group of fellows of Trinity – George Peacock, J. W. Blakesley, and Connop Thirlwall being others – whose misgivings about the tests were not merely expedient. They had pronounced theological objections. Stressing the complementarity and concordance of Reason and Revelation, they were very much in the Cambridge Latitudinarian tradition. They gave priority to essential scriptural truths that seemed to unite Christians – or at least Trinitarian Protestants – while regarding as comparatively unimportant doctrinal differences and refinements that separated them from each other. The Oxford theologian Hampden, very much at one with Sedgwick and his associates, wrote that 'religion consists of those truths which are simply contained in the Divine Revelation with the effects, dispositions and actions suggested by them. Theological opinion is the various result of the necessary action of our minds on the truths made known to us by the Divine word.' By contrast, formularies and creeds were at best 'a collection of negation; of negations ... of all ideas imported into

---

[84] Langdon-Brown, *Some Chapters*, pp. 76–7.   [85] Cooper, *Annals*, 4, pp. 568, 580.

Religion beyond the express sanction of Revelation'.[86] These ideas encouraged at least toleration of Dissent and perhaps something more.

Meeting in Hewett's rooms the anti-subscriptionists drew up a petition affirming their attachment 'to the doctrines and discipline of the Church of England as by law established', and urged 'the expediency of abrogating by legislative enactment every religious test exacted from members of the University before they proceed to degrees, whether of Bachelor, Master, or Doctor in Arts, Law, or Physic'. Degrees in divinity were not included, naturally. Any intention was disclaimed of interfering 'with the private statutes and regulations of individual Colleges, founded as these Colleges are on specific benefactions and governed by peculiar laws'. This was a reservation natural to loyal Cantabrigians, however reformist, but less so to liberals outside, and it was shortly to cause trouble. The petitioners also declared that they were only 'asking for a restitution of their ancient academic laws and laudable customs', since subscription had been imposed by James I 'against the wishes of many of the then members of the Senate', and against 'the true principles of Christian toleration'.[87] The petition lay in the rooms of Thomas Musgrave, like Sedgwick a fellow of Trinity.[88] It collected sixty-two signatures from resident members of the Senate;[89] two were heads of houses – Davy of Gonville and Caius and Lamb of Corpus Christi – and nine professors, while there were also several tutors.[90] One signatory was Joseph Romilly. A few hours after sealing, as Registrary, the petition against London University's charter and dining with the judges in Cambridge for the Lent Assizes, Romilly, acting in his private capacity as fellow of Trinity, 'At 10 1/2 left the Judges & went to Musgrave's to put my name to a Petition to Parliamt. to emancipate our degrees (except the Div[init]y) from religious tests – At 11 T.M. & I went to Sedgwick's, had tea & smoked a cigar.'[91]

---

[86] Quoted by Richard Brent, *Liberal Anglican Politics*, p. 171, on which, pp. 144–83, this passage is based.   [87] Cooper, *Annals*, IV, pp. 581–2.

[88] Fourteenth Wrangler, 1810. He was Lord Almoner's Reader in Arabic 1821–37, a sign, like Sedgwick's geology, of the willingness of men qualified in mathematics to turn to other sciences. After some years as Bishop of Hereford, he became Archbishop of York in 1847.

[89] And just one from a non-resident: Winstanley, *Early Victorian Cambridge*, p. 89.

[90] Clark and Hughes, *The Life and Letters of Adam Sedgwick*, vol. I, pp. 418–19.

[91] Bury, *Romilly's Cambridge Diary 1832–42*, pp. 51–2. Friday 14 March 1834.

The 62 petitioners were soon shown to be in a minority of the 180 resident members of the Senate, and probably far more greatly outnumbered among non-residents. The controversy drew in almost all residents: 110, including 11 heads of houses and the 3 divinity professors, protested against the petition, while it was said that it

> must have the effect of admitting into the several colleges persons whose religious opinions are avowedly adverse to the tenets of the Established Church, and possibly opposed to the truth of Christianity itself: and that under such circumstances, the maintenance of any uniform system of wholesome discipline, or sound religious instruction, would ... be utterly impracticable.

These words are from a petition that was signed by 258 members of the Senate, the majority being non-resident. When Hewett, using King's tactics of a few weeks before, vetoed the petition in the Caput, it was set out for signatories in the hall of Queens' College and eventually attracted over 1,200.[92] This total suggests the non-residents' hostility to any loosening of the university's religious framework.

On 14 March Sedgwick wrote to Thomas Spring Rice, a graduate of Trinity and Pryme's colleague as MP for the borough of Cambridge, that he was 'cooking up a *petition to Parliament* for the abrogation of all religious tests', and asking him to 'drum up some of our good Cambridge liberal friends to give us a lift out of our present illiberal slough with which our lights are half put out and even half choked'.[93] The anti-subscription petition was in the event presented to the Commons on 21 March by Spring Rice and to the Lords by the Prime Minister Earl Grey, who thereby signified his government's support for the Cambridge liberals. On 17 April, however, G. W. F. Wood, a Unitarian and member for South Lancashire, introduced a bill to grant to 'His Majesty's subjects generally' the right to be admitted to the English universities and to take their degrees, except those in divinity.[94] This by implication

---

[92] Thus I interpret the ambiguous description in Cooper, *Annals*, IV, pp. 582–3. See also Winstanley, *Early Victorian Cambridge*, pp. 91–2.

[93] Brent, *Liberal Anglican Politics*, p. 189, quoting from a letter in the Monteagle Papers in the National Library of Ireland.   [94] Winstanley, *Early Victorian Cambridge*, p. 92.

abrogated the rights of the colleges to admit whomsoever they chose and to impose discipline on them, and it was not what Sedgwick and his allies wanted, as he made clear on 27 April in a letter to Bishop Blomfield, a stern critic of Wood's bill. After wishing 'heartily the getting up of the Bill had not been with a Dissenter', Sedgwick declared 'We wish no man to be forced on the University . . . A man is not to come up as a Dissenter; he is not to be considered as such by any official college act; he must conform to discipline, and we give him a degree without exacting subscription. A bigot – a man who would haggle about organs and surplices – will and must keep away, and we do not want him.' Candidates were not to enjoy '(as far as our wishes are concerned) any right of admission which is not sanctioned by the voluntary acts of the admitting officers'.[95]

Anxious to conciliate those within the university and outside it who feared that Wood's bill was the first step in a Dissenting design to effect Disestablishment, the Cambridge liberals worked with people in government who were equally anxious to get it amended. On 11 April Musgrave conferred with Peacock, Sedgwick and Romilly on the terms of the bill, and afterwards persuaded Wood to agree that the right of admission should be limited to those of 'good moral character', of 'competent knowledge', and 'willing to conform to the regulations established by the executive authorities of the several colleges'.[96] After scrutiny, the bill still seemed ambiguous on the crucial issue of the colleges' control of their admissions, and Musgrave enlisted Spring Rice's help in amending it so as to make it certain that Dissenters could not demand entry. Wood did not object to these changes.

In debates on Wood's bill liberals stressed their attachment to the Established Church and the fact that it was not intended to abridge it, or the church's hold on Oxford and Cambridge. Dissenters would not, for example, be eligible for fellowships. 'These were founded for members of the Established Church, and those who were not members of the Established Church had no more right to claim that they did [*sic*] participate in the pecuniary advantages which belonged to that church, than a member of that church had

---

[95] Clark and Hughes, *The Life and Letters of Adam Sedgwick*, vol. i, p. 422.
[96] Brent, *Liberal Anglican Politics*, pp. 190–1, and for these lines generally.

to share in the endowments founded at Highbury.'[97] The bill proposed an act of justice about the right to be admitted to national institutions. Melbourne avowed the government's support for the bill, 'for the sake of general peace and union, and for the sake of bringing together those who had been excluded so long'.[98] Those opposing their admission were also opposed to London University's charter: were Dissenters to be denied degrees everywhere? Their admission should not disturb the religious life of colleges, any more than at Cambridge it did already. On the other hand, some feared that perhaps the granting of a right would not in practice lead to many more Dissenters, since the colleges, whose control of admissions was conceded, might well not admit them. 'The doubt which he entertained with respect to the present measure', said Brougham, 'was . . . that it would not be efficacious – for that which was done, if he might so say, against the grain, was not very likely to be of much practical benefit in its operations'.[99]

Connop Thirlwall, a Trinity don eager for the admission of Dissenters, argued that any who entered would fit very easily into the usual sort of collegiate religion. Colleges were 'not theological seminaries . . . among all the branches of learning cultivated in them there is none which occupies a smaller share of our time and attention'.[100] Religious instruction was confined to some part of the New Testament, plus Paley's *Evidences*, which were in any case often treated from a literary or historical viewpoint. 'Branches of learning which may very properly be admitted into a plan of liberal education' would not need to be refocused if Dissenters sat with Anglicans. Those intending to become clergymen naturally needed to undertake a special course of reading *privately*. Wood's bill would make little practical difference. But it would do so, insisted another fellow of Trinity, William Whewell, 'feeling oppressed and griev-ed' at having to publish his opinions on what was a 'domestic matter', an intra-college dispute.[101] Whewell's argument went to the heart of the dispute between the supporters and opponents of

---

[97] *Hansard*, 3rd series, vol. 25, p. 866, Lord Brougham.
[98] *Hansard*, 3rd series, vol. 25, p. 843.   [99] *Hansard*, 3rd series, vol. 25, pp. 864–5.
[100] Connop Thirlwall, *A Letter to the Rev. Thomas Turton . . . on the Admission of Dissenters to Academical Degrees* (2nd edn, Cambridge, 1834), p. 6, and p. 27 for the next quotation.
[101] William Whewell, *Remarks on Some Parts of Mr Thirlwall's Letter on the Admission of Dissenters to Academical Degrees* (Cambridge, 1834), p. 3, and p. 18 for the next quotation.

Wood's bill, but seems detached from the realities of collegiate life. He declared that colleges were Anglican institutions assuming a community of belief and feeling and rightly employing discipline to maintain it; the introduction of Dissenters would disrupt these bonds of sympathy.

> Our course of study is not constructed for the year, it is not framed in an accidental and arbitrary manner, it is not that which one person, at a particular time, happens to have a fancy for; it is that of which the origin goes back to the origin of our College: which has been deliberately continued, deliberately improved and altered in detail, as literature and science have altered their phases, but with no change of spirit or principle. On this it is that we have hitherto relied for producing an effect which we could not hope from our own skill and zeal: under this discipline a community of study spreads along the innumerable lines of social intercourse and sympathy; . . . the caprices of individuals are borne along by the momentum of ages and multitudes; and we have a unity of purpose, which, produced by such agencies, is itself, in my judgement, a means of inestimable benefit.

A young fellow of Trinity, Christopher Wordsworth, added that the result for the Church of England of 'admitting Dissenters to degrees and thence to Collegiate endowments' would be 'the national recognition of a sectarian ordination and ministry as co-existing and co-equal with its own'.[102] The writer's father, Christopher Wordsworth the Master of Trinity, asked Thirlwall to resign his office of assistant tutor – the appointment of tutors being the responsibility of a head of house. The internal affairs of a college here intersecting with the politics of a wider world, Wordsworth forced Thirlwall's resignation but at the cost of a bitter quarrel within Trinity.[103]

Tories did not accept the Liberal contention that Wood's bill, if passed, would make little practical difference. W. E. Gladstone, at that time a leading young Conservative, thought that it was certain to 'lead to great dissension and confusion, and eventually to endless applications and legislation in that House'. It was better to maintain the Anglican monopoly, and the universities' character as seminar-

---

[102] Christopher Wordsworth, *On the Admission of Dissenters to Graduate in the University of Cambridge. A Letter to the Rt. Hon. Viscount Althorp M.P.* (Cambridge, 1834), p. 28.
[103] Winstanley, *Early Victorian Cambridge*, pp. 74–8.

ies for the clergy. The universities 'were undoubtedly national institutions, but only in so far as they were connected with the National Church'.[104] The doctrines of the Church of England, declared the Duke of Wellington, the Chancellor of Oxford, were inseparable from the education given in the universities, and the admission of Dissenters 'would be completely destructive' of it.[105] Tory speakers assumed that the universities had a crucial place in the Anglican Establishment, and so in the constitution itself. 'From the moment' that the Anglican character of the universities was relaxed, said the Duke of Gloucester, 'might be dated the separation of Church and State, and the overthrow of the Throne and the Constitution'.[106] At all events, though the bill was approved by 164 votes to 75 at its third reading in the Commons on 28 July, it was defeated in the Lords on 1 August, by 187 to 85.

This was not the end of the subscription issue. The Whig government had very similar aims to Sedgwick and Thirlwall; they wished to retain the Anglican character of Oxford and Cambridge while making it legally possible for others to enter the national institutions and to take degrees in them, and they had compatible policies in their dealings with Durham and London, new universities whose governance was much discussed in the 1830s.[107] Durham, founded in 1831 as an Anglican university of the North, with the same subscription tests as Cambridge, applied for a charter, needed to grant degrees. Though Lord John Russell, the Home Secretary, felt unable for political reasons to make the admission of Dissenters a condition for conceding the charter, through complex negotiations he got Durham to agree to issue attendance certificates to Dissenters and London to agree to accept them as sufficient qualifications for its degrees. In London the government recognised the need for the non-denominational college founded in 1826, and of course the claims of its Anglican rival King's College. But conceding to 'an avowedly irreligious body' the authority 'to distribute titles hitherto recognised as badges of a Christian education' would antagonise Oxford and Cambridge opinion, and

[104] *Hansard*, 3rd series, vol. 25, pp. 635–6.
[105] *Hansard*, 3rd series, vol. 25, p. 837.   [106] *Hansard*, 3rd series, vol. 25, p. 831.
[107] For these paragraphs see Whiting, *The University of Durham*, pp. 71–3; Bellot, *University College, London*, pp. 240–6; and Brent, *Liberal Anglican Politics*, pp. 195–204.

seem 'a step towards the separation of church and state', something it was anxious not to imply.[108] The government performed a neat balancing act. Both King's College and University College (as its rival was henceforth termed) were given charters, but degree-granting powers were reserved to a new institution, London University, created in 1836 to service both colleges. At the end of the decade Russell suggested a cognate structure for English and Welsh elementary schools, acknowledging sectarian separateness but enforcing co-operation in the interests of the nation as a whole. But this proposal was defeated.[109]

Immediately after the defeat of Wood's subscription bill in August 1834 Melbourne remitted the matter to a Cabinet committee for consideration, but after an autumn spent gathering information the fall of the government in November prevented any further move at that time. In June 1835, however, the Earl of Radnor, who had spoken in favour of Wood's bill, introduced an anti-Subscription measure of his own into the House of Lords. Radnor was a lifelong supporter of advanced opinions and popular rights – the friend of Cobbett and the enemy of the Corn Laws – whose interest in university reform deserves mention.[110] His long speech, a well-informed survey of the issue, did not persuade their lordships, who defeated the bill by a very large majority of 106 on its second reading.[111] Tests for all degrees save divinity were abolished in 1856, but until 1871 they remained necessary to qualify for university and college office and membership of the Senate, and were a live issue throughout the intervening years. Writing in the 1930s D. A. Winstanley opined that Sedgwick and company 'by premature action' might 'have retarded progress towards religious liberty' since 'the very bitter resentment which their action evoked' gave the supporters of the tests 'the glamour of defending the University from external interference'.[112] This judgement reads like one of the jokes in F. M. Cornford's *Microcosmographia Academica* and could

[108] Bellot, *University College, London*, p. 240.
[109] James Murphy, *The Religious Problem in English Education. The Crucial Experiment* (Liverpool University Press, 1959), esp. pp. 174–201, and D. G. Paz, *The Politics of Working-Class Education in Britain 1830–50* (Manchester, 1980), pp. 61–87.
[110] The only study, Ronald K. Huch, *The Radical Lord Radnor: The Public Life of Viscount Folkestone, Third Earl of Radnor (1779–1869)* (Minneapolis, Minn: University of Minnesota Press, 1977), does not mention the university question.   [111] *Hansard*, 3rd series, vol. 29, pp. 496–537.
[112] *Early Victorian Cambridge*, pp. 94–5.

scarcely be less helpful. The demand for access was there, and growing; Sedgwick was right to attempt to meet it. However understandable, the universities' resolve to permit no breach in their Anglican bastions allied them with one political party against the firm desires of the other and made their controversial status certain. A concession would not have altered their character very greatly, but it might have taken them, a little anyway, out of the political limelight. But of course these words benefit from knowledge of the next twenty years that was denied them.

THE MOVEMENT FOR SELF-REFORM

On 1 September 1866 Adam Sedgwick, aged eighty-two, wrote to his friend the Reverend J. Edleston, 'In early life I used to count much upon this day, for I was a keen sportsman till I became a professed Geologist. So soon as I was seated in the Woodwardian Chair I gave away my dogs and gun, and my hammer broke my trigger. My sporting days ended with the autumnal season of 1817.'[113] Sedgwick was prone to exaggerate crises, but his election to the chair was indeed a turning-point in his life, for reasons important in the life of the university itself. As is well known, Cambridge professors did not in the eighteenth century lecture very much. In fact, professors that did, like John Symonds, whose lectures Philip Yorke attended in the 1770s, are often not mentioned, while those that did not are mentioned very often, the most famous being Richard Watson, Regius Professor of Divinity from 1771 to 1816, while others attacked are William Lax, Lowndean Professor of Astronomy from 1795 to 1837, and Francis Barnes, Knightbridge Professor of Moral Philosophy from 1813 to 1838.[114] Sedgwick's predecessor, John Hailstone, held the chair from 1788 onwards but gave 'No *systematic* Lectures', though he attended 'to demonstrate and explain the subjects of this Branch of Natural History to such curious persons, whether residents or strangers', who were 'engaged in the study of them', words that suggest an easy assignment even for the modest stipend of £100.[115]

[113] Clark and Hughes, *Adam Sedgwick*, vol. I, p. 152.
[114] Winstanley, *Early Victorian Cambridge*, p. 175.
[115] Clark and Hughes, *The Life and Letters of Adam Sedgwick*, vol. I, p. 197, quoting the *Cambridge University Calendar for . . . 1803*. On Hailstone, see also p. 212.

But as Winstanley has pointed out, a change in university sentiment occurred during the 1810s, which was a sign that Cambridge did respond, however tentatively, to pressures for reform. On Hailstone's resignation a syndicate was appointed 'to consider what rules and orders should be framed for the development of Doctor Woodward's intentions'. The syndicate decided that in future the stipend would not be paid unless a course of lectures had been given, and that another £100 would be paid if in due time an additional course were offered.[116] Sedgwick was one of three strong candidates for the chair, and lost ground at first because his statement of intent failed to make clear his determination to lecture, while his opponents' promise to do so was 'considered by their supporters as greatly in their favour'. Sedgwick drew ahead when he gave an explicit undertaking since 'there was a general feeling throughout the University in his favour' because of his 'reputation for thoroughness in whatever he did', which he fully vindicated in his long tenure of the chair. Sedgwick was the most striking example of the revolution in professorial diligence. Another was J. S. Henslow, appointed Professor of Botany in 1825, when, as he later remarked, there were 'no stipulations as to lectures, and my predecessor [had] delivered none during the last 30 years of his life', whereas Henslow gave a course of twenty every Easter Term from 1826 onwards.[117]

In April 1837 Lord Radnor moved the second reading of his bill for the appointment of a commission of enquiry into the statutes and revenues of Oxford and Cambridge colleges. Though the bill failed, his opponents had to counter his arguments, which they did by pointing to the colleges' power to reform their statutes. Radnor then proposed a committee to enquire into whether colleges really did have the power to reform themselves, an adroit move; if such a committee reported that there were no such powers then the case for state intervention would be stronger, yet if Radnor's motion were opposed a bad impression might be created. The two university Chancellors did in fact stall Radnor's move, by declaring that the

---

[116] Clark and Hughes, *The Life and Letters of Adam Sedgwick*, vol. I, pp. 197–8, and pp. 153–65 for what follows.
[117] PP 1852–3, HC xliv [1559]: *Graham Commission Evidence*, p. 113. Thomas Martin had however lectured from 1762 to 1796: see Tanner, *Historical Register*, p. 90.

desire for self-reform was strong: so one way or another Radnor might very well win anyway.[118] The few attempts at reform indeed showed how feeble the wish to embrace it was. County restrictions were sometimes removed, obsolete provisions as to discipline, studies, and stipends omitted, and wording sometimes brought into conformity with existing practice, for example sanctioning the custom of paying dividends. But the new codes were not forward-looking, as their adherence to Latin utterance shows.[119] More dramatic change was desired by some fellows of Christ's and the master, John Graham. The revisions which they asked the Crown to approve in 1838 would have permitted fellows to marry and opened college offices to non-Anglicans. But some fellows appealed to the Visitor, who ruled that he must be consulted before any attempt to alter the statutes, and the changes were not effected.[120]

At Trinity the revision of the statutes coincided with the first years of Whewell's mastership. He made sure that it was in the hands of himself and the Seniors, without reference to other fellows, and set down his view 'that the changes made should be the smallest which will truly answer the purpose of bringing about an accordance between our laws and our practices; and that we ought to preserve the existing statutes whenever we can without manifest inconvenience'.[121] It may be said that the revision did just that. Prayers were no longer set for members of the college on rising and retiring to sleep, and misbehaving undergraduates were no longer to be birched; but spears, swords, and daggers were still not to be carried in college or town except by permission of the master, and the statutes were still written in Latin. 'None of the changes made were of fundamental importance, and no regard had been paid to the more serious criticisms of the outside world, such as those directed against fellowships tenable for life if Holy Orders were taken.'[122]

In 1838 the heads of houses appointed a committee of four to revise the university statutes. Graham, the Master of Christ's,

---

[118] Winstanley, *Early Victorian Cambridge*, pp. 186–8.
[119] See, for example, Bendall, Brooke, and Collinson, *Emmanuel College*, chapter 15. See also Gray and Brittain, *Jesus College*, pp. 155–6, Miller, *Portrait of a College*, pp. 83–4, and Twigg, *A History of Queens' College*, p. 224. Pembroke and Peterhouse also revised their statutes in a highly conservative fashion.   [120] Peile, *Christ's College*, pp. 279–80.
[121] Stair Douglas, *The Life*, p. 255.   [122] Winstanley, *Early Victorian Cambridge*, pp. 195–6.

favoured thorough reform. The others favoured doing nothing. When Whewell was Vice-Chancellor (1842–4) and ex officio a member, he 'endeavoured to obtain meetings of this committee, with a view of promoting the progress of the measure'. He 'succeeded in obtaining one such meeting, but failed entirely in procuring a second or in having any other step for this purpose taken'.[123] Not until 1849, nearly eleven years after its initiation, did the committee report, and it did no more, remarked John Graham, than 'consolidate the more important laws of the University into one code, which should present in a moderate compass and connected form the system as it is now in actual operation';[124] in other words, it scarcely began to meet the needs of the hour.

[123] From a draft in the Whewell papers dated 26 May 1851, quoted in Winstanley, *Early Victorian Cambridge*, p. 196; this paragraph is based on pp. 196–7.
[124] From a letter to Colonel Phipps, the Prince Consort's secretary, 29 January 1849, quoted in Winstanley, *Early Victorian Cambridge*, p. 197.

Chapter 14

THE GRAHAM COMMISSION AND ITS AFTERMATH

Whereas, we have deemed it expedient for divers good causes and considerations that a Commission should forthwith issue for this proposal of enquiring into the State, Discipline, Studies, and Revenues of Our University of Cambridge and of all and singular the Colleges in Our said University.

Royal Commission dated 31 August 1850

THE GRAHAM COMMISSION, 1850

LORD JOHN RUSSELL AND THE PRINCE CONSORT

The appointment of Lord John Russell as Prime Minister in 1846 and the election of Prince Albert, Queen Victoria's Consort, as Chancellor of the University of Cambridge, brought university reform nearer and affected the way it was accomplished. Russell's restless temperament and reforming tendencies made him responsive to the clamour for change at the universities, and dissatisfied with the leisurely pace that they thought it fitting to employ. The Chancellor was also keen to effect change and used his position as Chancellor to press for it, but he was more anxious than Russell to work with the university if possible; he restrained Russell from pressing ahead with a royal commission at least once, but in the end failed to influence the Prime Minister, who was after all far more powerful than the Queen's Consort, however intelligent and perceptive Albert might be.

Russell was unusual among British (or at least English) politicians in not having spent any time at either university. His elder brother, the Marquess of Tavistock, had received only a 'pretended education' at Cambridge,[1] and their father, the Duke of Bedford,

---

[1] Quoted in Spencer Walpole, *The Life of Lord John Russell* (2 vols., London, 1889), vol. 1, p. 44, from which (pp. 43–50) this account and its quotations are taken.

declaring that 'nothing was learned in the English universities', sent John Russell to Edinburgh. He lived in the house of John Playfair, Professor of Natural Philosophy, and enjoyed his lectures and those of another eminent scholar, Dugald Stewart, on moral philosophy; he was also elected Praeses of the student debating society, the Speculative. He left Edinburgh without graduating, as did many others, but looked back fondly on his three years there, while never it seems having much time for the ancient English universities. In his spare and reticent memoir he says of his encounters with Oxford and Cambridge in the late 1840s over reform: 'The ancient Universities of Oxford and Cambridge required only amendments and reforms in conformity with the spirit of their institutions, and with a view to those liberal studies which must from time to time be made suitable to the spirit of the age.'[2] His comments at the time, as deposited in *Hansard* and the Royal Archives, suggest a more troubled and frictional involvement.

The Prince Consort, who for several years was to be linked with Russell in an uneasy partnership for reform, was an obvious choice to succeed the Duke of Northumberland as Chancellor when he died in February 1847. Quite apart from his high position, he was intelligent, serious-minded, and known to be interested in higher education.[3] Whewell asked him to stand, which Albert did, after being misleadingly assured that the university's invitation was unanimous. Some fellows of St John's proposed the Earl of Powis, a member of their college, for twenty-three years a Tory MP for Ludlow, and a High Churchman who had won praise for opposing the merger of Bangor and St Asaph into the new bishopric of Manchester. An election committee for Powis containing several heads of houses was publicly established. The Prince Consort thought that withdrawal would be the most dignified course, but was dissuaded from it by Sir Robert Peel. Still, he refrained from any campaign. He was supported by three-quarters of resident MAs, but the overall majority was smaller, 953 to 837, an indication of the weight of Tory feeling among the university's graduates.

---

[2] John, Earl Russell, *Recollections and Suggestions 1813–1873* (London, 1875), p. 372.
[3] For this paragraph see Theodore Martin, *The Life of His Royal Highness the Prince Consort*, 5th edn (5 vols., London, 1875–80), vol. I, pp. 385–99, and Robert Rhodes James, *Albert, Prince Consort* (London, Hamish Hamilton, 1983), pp. 172–7.

Victoria and the Prince Consort visited the university in July 1847, when he was installed as Chancellor in glorious weather and with high ceremony, though the Public Orator's Latin speech 'was too long for the occasion (lasting near an hour) and was frequently interrupted by marks of disapprobation'.[4]

The prince lost no time in involving himself in the business of the university. He quickly came to know the Vice-Chancellor, Henry Philpott, the Master of St Catharine's. Without being at all original in his thoughts Philpott was a very efficient and meticulous man of business, with a very wise sense of what it was necessary for the university to do. At his death in 1892 (until 1890 he had been Bishop of Worcester) it was said by *The Times* that Philpott had 'insight into men and affairs which enabled him to forecast the result of a debate', and that 'there is not a department in the University whose records do not show abundant traces of his painstaking skill in the form of papers and minutes of the most lucid character'.[5] The prince soon came to trust his judgement. In October 1847 he asked Philpott to let him have 'a comprehensive table, showing the scheme of tuition in the Colleges separately and the University for the ensuing year'.[6] Philpott's detailed reply showed that most of the professors were lecturing, but it was pointed out by Peel, to whom Albert showed it, that since the lectures were voluntary and rarely linked to degree courses, not many students were necessarily attending: 'Does not the devotion of time to other pursuits, in which great progress is requisite to ensure academical distinctions and advantages, discourage attention to those objects which are valuable only for themselves?'[7]

Peel, now an advisor to the prince on academic matters, was also greatly repelled by a memorandum that Whewell submitted to Albert on possible changes in the university's curriculum. Whewell, more pessimistic than he had seemed in *Liberal Education* two years

---

[4] From Joseph Romilly's diary, 5 July 1847, in *Victoria and Albert at Cambridge* (Cambridge University Library, 1977), an unpaginated transcription of the diary entries relating to the two royal visits of 1843 and 1847. The installation ode was composed by Wordsworth, but he was seventy-seven and his fears of lacklustre verses proved justified. It was thought in the university that his nephew Christopher Wordsworth, fellow of Trinity (later Bishop of Lincoln), had assisted in their composition. The chief author was in fact the poet's brother-in-law Edward Quillinan.

[5] *The Times*, 11 January 1892.

[6] Theodore Martin, *The Prince Consort*, vol. II, p. 116, 14 October 1847.

[7] Theodore Martin, *The Prince Consort*, vol. II, pp. 119–20, letter of 2 November 1847.

before, suggested the infinite difficulty impeding change in Cambridge:

> It does not appear likely that any legislation will take place within the University, of such a nature as to modify materially, the existing system. The University would not be likely to agree in selecting any new subjects of study which should be placed side by side with the old ones; and if laws to this effect were made it would be difficult to find examiners, and to establish habits of examining and being examined in the new subjects, without offering some special inducement.[8]

Without examinations and rewards additional subjects would not be studied, just as professorial lectures were neglected in Cambridge at the time. So Whewell suggested giving scholarships and prizes on examination results in subjects such as law and natural history where lectures were already given, in the hope that in the fullness of time new qualifications would attract prestige and fellowships. He appeared resigned to very slow progress, and more eager to devise audiences for professors (a besetting problem) than new degree courses. With scathing comment Peel responded to the spirit of the memorandum rather than the letter:[9]

> I think Dr Whewell is quite wrong in his position – that mathematical knowledge is entitled to *paramount* consideration, because it is conversant with indisputable truths – that such departments of science as Chemistry are not proper subjects of academical instruction, because there is controversy respecting important facts and principles, and constant accession of information from new discoveries – and danger that the students may lose their reverence for Professors, when they discover that the Professors cannot maintain doctrines as indisputable as mathematical or arithmetical truths.
>
> The Doctor's assumption, that *a century should pass* before new discoveries in science are admitted into the course of academical instruction, exceeds in absurdity anything which the bitterest enemy of University Education would have imputed to its advocates. Are the students at Cambridge to hear nothing of electricity, or the speculations concerning its mysterious influence, its possible

---

[8] Royal Archives: Letters of the Prince Consort as Chancellor of the University, memorandum of 8 March 1847. (CUL MS 3547, microfilm.)

[9] Theodore Martin, *The Prince Consort*, vol. II, pp. 117–18, letter of 27 October 1847.

connection with the nervous system and with muscular action, till all doubts on the subject are at an end? . . . If the principle for which Dr Whewell contends be a sound one, it will be difficult to deliver a lecture on theology. But the fact is, that adherence to the principle, so far from exalting the character of Professors and Heads of Houses, would cover them with ridicule.

Some weeks after this letter, with which he agreed, the prince invited Philpott to Windsor to discuss reform at Cambridge.[10] In his stay of a few days Philpott agreed that 'the offer of any lectures on other sciences [in addition to mathematics and classics] will lead to no result, unless the system of examination be altered, and those sciences added to the cyclus in which students are examined'. But Philpott said 'that the University attaches such *veneration* to the study of Mathematics, that any invitation tending (as they imagine) to lessen the attention to this science is viewed with the greatest suspicion. Moreover, the College tutors and private tutors would not be able to teach or to examine in anything else.' Philpott suggested a plan to add the natural sciences to the degree list by incremental stages, or even by stealth. Philpott was replying to a note from Lord John Russell announcing the Crown's intention to 'appoint a Commission to inquire into the state of schools and colleges of Royal foundation, in order that Her Majesty might be informed how far the benevolent views of her predecessors had been carried into effect, and what improvement could be made either by Royal authority or by Parliament'.[11] Though at this stage Russell was contemplating an enquiry into no more than Trinity (Cambridge), Christ Church, Eton, and Westminster, it would have been impossible to confine it so narrowly, as Russell and the prince were fully aware. Albert was therefore pushing on two fronts, to persuade Philpott and others to carry out reforms, and meanwhile to persuade Russell 'to pause with the recommendation of a Royal Commission of Inquiry, till we have seen whether any good can be effected in the way now proposed to be followed'.[12]

[10] The details and quotations that follow are taken from a letter of the Prince Consort to Lord John Russell, 13 November 1847, in Theodore Martin, *The Prince Consort*, vol. II, pp. 121–4.

[11] Theodore Martin, *The Prince Consort*, vol. II, pp. 120–1. The letter is there dated 12 December but Winstanley redates it to 12 November.

[12] Prince Consort to Lord John Russell, 13 November 1847, in Theodore Martin, *The Prince Consort*, vol. II, pp. 123–4.

Aware in Cambridge of the urgency of matters, Philpott ascertained that his successor as Vice-Chancellor, Robert Phelps, Master of Sidney Sussex College, was willing to see changes, and at the end of the year he put a detailed plan to Phelps on paper, pressing the need to broaden the curriculum and to maintain the confidence of the higher orders of society who sent their sons to the university; the letter reflected Philpott's shrewd sense of what was politically expedient.[13]

THE UNIVERSITY RESPONDS

The Vice-Chancellor raised the question of reform at a meeting of the heads of houses on 1 February 1848; it was agreed to ask the Senate to approve a grace for the appointment of a syndicate. The Vice-Chancellor, by custom entrusted with the nomination of persons to a syndicate, also consulted Philpott; Phelps would be an ex officio member, and Philpott, Whewell, John Graham (the reforming Master of Christ's), and William French (Master of Jesus) were proposed together with eleven others, including four professors.[14] These persons, thought Philpott, 'have both the desire and the ability to devise improvements', and their names would 'secure the confidence of the University'.[15] The grace was agreed in a very small congregation, by 13 to 4 by Non-Regents, and 13 to 3 by the Regents.[16] Phelps wrote to the Prince Consort that he feared 'very strong opposition to any important alterations',[17] and the prince replied that 'while Parliament is sitting, and the enemies of the University may any moment take the initiative, there is *periculum in mora*'.[18]

---

[13] Royal Archives: Letters of the Prince Consort as Chancellor of the University, letter of H. B. Philpott to R. Phelps, 30 December 1847 (CUL MS 3547, microfilm). Phelps was later an ultra-reactionary.

[14] The names are given in Cooper, *Annals*, IV, p. 705. The four professors were James Challis (Plumian, Astronomy), John Haviland (Regius, Physic [Medicine]), Henry Maine (Regius, Civil Law), and Alfred Ollivant (Regius, Divinity). The other members were Henry G. Hand (Vice-Provost of King's), William Hopkins (MA, Peterhouse – the famous private tutor), Charles Merivale (tutor of St John's), John Mills (tutor of Pembroke), John James Smith (tutor of Gonville and Caius), William Henry Thompson (tutor of Trinity), and Edward Warter (tutor of Magdalene).

[15] Philpott to the Prince Consort, 4 February 1848, in Theodore Martin, *The Prince Consort*, vol. II, p. 126.   [16] Cooper, *Annals*, IV, p. 702.

[17] In a letter of 10 February 1848 in the Royal Archives, quoted by Winstanley, *Early Victorian Cambridge*, p. 207.

The syndicate reported in April, in their preamble 'admitting the superiority of the study of Mathematics and Classics over all others as the basis of general education, and acknowledging, therefore, the wisdom of adhering to our present system in its main features';[19] the syndicate nevertheless desired to afford 'greater encouragement to the pursuit of various other branches of science and learning which are daily acquiring more importance ... and for the teaching of which the University already possesses the necessary means': it had ostensibly been set up to foster the disciplines that had professorships. The most momentous recommendations were that two new triposes should be set up, moral sciences and natural sciences,[20] and that all who had qualified for a bachelor's degree in arts, law, or medicine should be eligible. All candidates for the ordinary degree, for a first degree in law,[21] and for the Voluntary Theological Examination, were to be obliged to attend the lectures of appropriate professors. Lastly, the mathematical professors, together with the examiners and moderators for the tripos, were to constitute a Board of Mathematical Studies – the first step towards a faculty board of which there are now so many dominating life for dons.[22]

The report's kinship with the suggestions for reform that Whewell had made in 1845 is apparent: this was conservative reform, and as Philpott wrote to Colonel Phipps, 'it is as much as there is the slightest chance of passing the Senate'.[23] In the spring it was known that a campaign was under way to secure a royal commission of enquiry, and that government support for it was being withheld to give the university an opportunity for self-reformation. As the Congregation planned for 31 October approached, reformers such as Wratislaw, Philpott, and Whewell (named in descending order of eagerness) argued in favour of the five graces intended to give effect to these changes. 'Circumstances at the present time', wrote Philpott, 'have rendered absolutely

[18] Prince Consort to Dr Phelps, 16 February 1848, in Theodore Martin, *The Prince Consort*, vol. II, pp. 126–7.

[19] Cooper, *Annals*, IV, p. 702, and pp. 702–5 for what follows.

[20] Moral Sciences included moral philosophy, political economy, modern history, and law, and Natural Sciences, anatomy, physiology, chemistry, botany, and geology – in all of which subjects there were professors. More is said about these triposes in chapter 6.

[21] Highly qualified candidates were to be exempted from this latter requirement.

[22] Boards of studies proliferated in the late nineteenth century. They were called faculty boards after 1926. [23] Letter of 10 April 1848 quoted in Winstanley, *Early Victorian Cambridge*, p. 209.

necessary, on the part of all well-wishers to the University, a careful consideration of our mode and processes of study ... Persons, high in authority, have declared their opinion, that the state of Education in Oxford and Cambridge presents matter worthy of the deepest consideration and inquiry.' Mathematics, classics, and theology 'form the only sufficient and complete basis of a liberal Education', and their position would be protected in the proposed dispensation (this was Whewell's argument too) but the university could not continue to ignore other studies regarded by 'persons well experienced in the active business of life ... as indispensable requisites in the course of a complete and generous Education'.[24]

Diehards made their views known in the *Cambridge Chronicle*. Francis Whaley Harper, classical lecturer at Sidney Sussex, having had 'the benefit of even the present minimum of requisition for mathematical honours, and ... truly grateful for the salutary compulsion of the University which enforced it', suggested making honours in each subject necessary for honours in the other, and deferring new triposes till the MA, 'for those who should then choose to compete for them'.[25] J. R. Crowfoot of Gonville and Caius also favoured the MA option, 'declaring in the face of a hurried and hurrying generation that there cannot be a railroad to sound learning', while 'A Member of the Senate' thought it 'most *undesirable* to encourage ... "general knowledge" during the time when every student should be in a course of *training* by means of those studies, Classics and Mathematics, which are admitted to be superior to all others for this purpose', and 'H.C.B.' feared that 'the studies of the place' might 'become as diversified and shallow as the contents of some popular "Family Library"'.

In the event all five graces on the proposed reforms were passed by clear majorities, the narrowest ratio of *placets* to *non-placets* being 60:40 in one of the Regents' votes. At the other end of the range the Non-Regents voted 101:40 on one grace.[26] 'My plan for a

---

[24] H. B. Philpott, *Remarks on the Question of Adopting the Regulations Recommended by the Syndicate Appointed February 9, 1848* (Cambridge, 18 October 1848), pp. 5, 9–11. Whewell's fly-sheet of 26 October offered similar arguments.

[25] Harper's letter is dated 25 October 1848, and appears in a volume of newscuttings in the University Library (Cam.c. 848.47). The other quotations are taken from this source.

[26] Cooper, *Annals*, 4, p. 706. There were two houses, for Regents and Non-Regents, and ten votes altogether. See chapter 2, pp. 52–4, on the constitution of the Senate.

reform of the studies at Cambridge is carried by a large majority', wrote the Prince Consort in his diary on 1 November.[27] But events were to show that difficulties still lay ahead in the negotiation of detailed changes; the block of 40 diehards in a total Congregation of about 150 that the 10 votes revealed would at least be able to delay change, though Lord John Russell waited restlessly for prompt action.

On 7 March 1849, four months after its crucial vote on the new degrees, the Senate appointed a syndicate to revise the statutes of the university.[28] The Revising Syndicate, as it came to be called, was prompted by the very conservative revision that the heads of houses had just suggested, but was thought likely to go much further, as indeed it did. It sat for many years and initiated many significant changes. Its secretary was William Bateson of St John's, who also became secretary of the royal commission, and its labours ran in parallel with the commission's and were to an extent prompted by it. Meanwhile, it held semi-weekly meetings from 14 March 1849 onwards. But as its sessions began another contentious issue arose, showing how hard it was to make changes smoothly. Outside observers proposed a university entrance examination to control the admission of undergraduates, as a means of raising the intellectual level.[29] The idea was taken up by John James Smith, the tutor of Gonville and Caius.[30] 'I must think', he wrote in 1846, 'that unless every effort is made to improve, to advance and to extend our system, our University will quickly suffer far more derogation from its importance and influence.' Only one college (Trinity) had a matriculation examination, and if other colleges began one 'it would exert a large and salutary influence over all the schools in the kingdom; and so produce a capability in the students, which would allow the University influence to be exercised much more largely for their benefit'.[31] In the Easter Term 1847 Smith approached the

[27] Theodore Martin, *The Prince Consort*, vol. II, p. 114.
[28] Cooper, *Annals*, IV, p. 707.
[29] See for example Thomas Joyce 'College Life at Cambridge', *Westminster Review*, 35 (April, 1841), pp. 456–81. The notion of centralised control of admissions arouses similar feelings today.
[30] Smith, the son of William Pitt's private secretary, was Tenth Wrangler in 1828. Editor of the *Cambridge Portfolio* (1840) and author of works on coins and college plate, he helped to found the Cambridge Antiquarian Society.
[31] J. J. Smith, *A Letter to the Vice-Chancellor* (Cambridge, 24 November 1846), pp. 1–2, 4. This letter is to be found at CUL, Cam. c. 846. 17.

Vice-Chancellor, Philpott, who despite his support for many reforms disliked Smith's idea. Smith then approached some heads of houses, but they refused help too, some on the grounds that Philpott was against it.

At the end of the year Smith spoke to the incoming Vice-Chancellor, Phelps, who, wrote Smith, 'informed me that the Heads were almost, if not altogether, opposed to my proposition: so that I saw no course was left for me but to drop the project altogether, or proceed at once upon my own responsibility'.[32] It was usual for graces to be proposed by the Vice-Chancellor, but Smith assembled a syndicate and moved a grace himself as constitutionally was his right, though it had still to be approved by the Caput before being put to the Senate. A paper battle took place early in December. The most persuasive pamphlet seems to have come from Francis Martin, the senior bursar of Trinity.[33] Admission was a college matter, and it was right for their academic standards to differ since the university's natural constituency was of varying talent:

> when we consider the nature of our University, and that it is the ordinary channel of admission to Holy Orders, great care must be taken not to exclude deserving persons, who, though ill-prepared at first, may probably by diligence and attention sufficiently improve themselves, and so attain an object of great importance, to be debarred from which for a year or two longer might be attended with extreme disadvantage.

And there would be too many candidates – 400 in Michaelmas alone: 'At least four Examiners would be required.' Also, 'great jealousy between the Tutors of the different Colleges and the Examiners would probably arise, at the rejection of Students, of whom the Tutors . . . might have had reason to think well'. Though Whewell greatly approved of the pamphlet and Philpott thought its case incontrovertible, readers now may be struck by its failure to heed the reformers' arguments. It gives priority to the university's seminary function, and does not concede that colleges need to take

[32] J. J. Smith, *A Letter to the Vice-Chancellor on the Late Rejection by the Caput of a Grace Respecting an Examination Previous to Residence* (Cambridge, 14 December 1847), p. 2. These lines are based on this letter.

[33] *Some Reasons against the Expediency of Instituting a Public Examination of Students Previous to their Residence in the University*, 3 December 1847, which is reprinted in Whewell, *Of a Liberal Education*, 2nd edn (1850), Part 2, appendix, pp. 139–41.

account of wider interests, or that examiners might be recruited from a great body of fellows. At all events, Smith's further response was ineffective.[34] The Caput refused to put the grace to the Senate, and declined to give Smith any reasons for not doing so. In January 1849 Smith brought forward a similar grace, but it was rejected in the Non-Regent House by 29 votes to 11.[35] The strong feeling against the proposed change showed once more how unlikely it was that internal pressure alone would suffice to bring about reform, at all events at the pace that the Prince Consort and Russell thought necessary.

So did the way in which the question of Classical Tripos reform was handled in the spring of 1849. Now that recipients of an ordinary degree were to be allowed to take the Natural Sciences and Moral Sciences Triposes it was logical and equitable to permit them to take the Classical Tripos too. Though Philpott and others thought so and in the event succeeded in effecting the change,[36] Whewell fought the proposal strongly. He shrewdly pointed to the very narrow linguistic range of the Classical Tripos,[37] and here he was supported by the eminent classicist Lord Lyttelton. But uppermost in Whewell's mind was a feeling that the ordinary graduates, or at least the less talented, were 'dull of intellect, or idle or inert in study', and so were not likely 'to make any great figure in the general intellectual culture of the nation'.[38] It therefore hardly mattered if the university did not insist on a strong dose of mathematics for them. On the other hand the best classicists, potential prizemen, were 'the intellectual aristocracy of the land . . . The characteristic education of the nation is *their* education', which therefore had to contain a large element of mathematics. Whewell did not notice his inconsistency between objecting to an entrance examination while lamenting the dullness of the *polloi*. Eventually a messy and illogical compromise was agreed which loosened the restrictions without giving classicists parity with candidates for

---

[34] *Reply to Some Reasons against the Expediency of Instituting a Public Examination of Students Previous to their Residence in the University*, 6 December 1847. (CUL Zz. 39. 11/14.)

[35] Cooper, *Annals*, IV, pp. 697–8, 707. J. J. Smith, *A Letter to the Vice-Chancellor*, 14 December 1847.

[36] Winstanley, *Early Victorian Cambridge*, pp. 216–17.

[37] The institution of two parts in the Classical Tripos in the 1880s gave scope (in Part 2) for ancient history and philosophy, but the degree is still markedly more linguistic in emphasis than the Oxford Mods and Greats course.

[38] Whewell, *Of a Liberal Education*, 2nd edn (1850), Part 2, pp. 7–43 for this section and quotations.

Natural and Moral Sciences.[39] Even so three heads of houses including Whewell and two Regius Professors refused to sign the syndicate's report. Reform generated purely *within* the university would certainly be slow.

RUSSELL DECIDES TO ACT, APRIL 1850

In July 1848 a petition was presented to Lord John Russell, the Prime Minister, calling for a 'Royal Commission of Inquiry into the best methods of securing the improvement of the Universities of Oxford and Cambridge'.[40] The universities' system was 'not calculated to advance the interests of religious and useful learning to an extent commensurate with the great resources and high position of those bodies' and their constitutions prevented them from introducing the necessary changes. The petition, it is said, was drawn up by Arthur Stanley, Bonamy Price, and James Heywood.[41] Stanley did not sign the petition. The other two did. Heywood was in this context the most important member of the trio, if only because from August 1847 to March 1857 he was MP for North Lancashire and so in the best position to press the government. Heywood, the son of a banker, and born in 1810 in Liverpool,[42] was educated at Trinity College, where he became Twelfth Senior Optime in 1833; unable to take his BA because of the theological test, 'he, however, continued to keep his name on the college books till better times', and graduated in 1857 after the abolition of tests for degrees. Prominent in educational advance, Heywood founded the Manchester Athenaeum, was one of the leading progenitors of Owens College Manchester, and for fourteen years (1874–88) maintained a public library in Notting Hill at his own expense.[43]

[39] See *Of a Liberal Education*, 2nd edn (1850), Part 2, pp. 111–14.

[40] The printed petition, with marginal notes by J. W. Clark that draw on Joseph Romilly's notes in the 'Registry Cuttings Book' is in the University Library (Cam. a. 500. 5/124). Details that follow are taken from this copy.

[41] Stanley and Price were Oxford graduates. At this time Stanley was a fellow of Balliol; he had published his biography of Thomas Arnold in 1844. Price was classical master at Rugby School.

[42] There is no *DNB* entry concerning Heywood. The following details are taken from Frederic Boase, *Men of the Time* (7 vols., Truro: Netherton and Worth, 1892–1921), vol. v (1912), and from Joseph Thompson, *The Owens College: Its Foundation and Growth* (Manchester, Cornish, 1886), esp. pp. 659–60.

[43] Thomas Kelly, *A History of Public Libraries in Great Britain 1845–1965* (London, The Library Association, 1973), p. 154.

The older universities, especially Cambridge, remained however his chief concern.

The petition was signed by 133 Cambridge graduates, 62 Oxonians, and 29 Fellows of the Royal Society. The Cambridge signatories included Erasmus and Charles Darwin, Augustus De Morgan, Thackeray, Charles Babbage, A. W. Kinglake (author of *Eothen* and future historian of the Crimean War), Tom Taylor the playwright, Sir David Brewster the Principal of St Andrews University, and J. M. Kemble the Anglo-Saxon scholar. There were 27 Cambridge MPs, and 18 erstwhile or non-resident fellows, but only one resident fellow, Charles Eyres of Caius, and one professor, J. S. Henslow, about whom Romilly notes 'but he is *non-resident*'.[44] The contrast in attitudes revealed by these figures between resident and non-resident members of the university, or in more modern terms its staff and its graduates, could not have been more telling. In standing with Heywood and others when presenting the memorial to Lord John Russell on Monday 10 July Edward Bunbury, MP for Bury St Edmunds and an ex-fellow of Trinity, pointed out that the study of many subjects taught by professors had been virtually abandoned because of tripos pressures; he

> spoke of the great disproportion between University and collegiate funds – the constitution of the academic body as opposing great obstacles to reform – the absolute veto of any member of the Caput, and the want of all power of discussion or amendment of Graces of the Senate. The object of the memorialists was not to urge specific measures of reform but to obtain preliminary enquiry by means of a royal commission.[45]

The petition reminded Russell of the contrast between the desire for reform among Cambridge's friends outside the colleges, and the dilatoriness within. In the months that followed, the handling of the issues of an entrance examination and the Classical Tripos underlined dons' reluctance to change. Action was finally triggered by Russell's learning that Heywood intended to move for a royal commission in the House of Commons, and the government's deciding to support it. Heywood linked Oxford, Cambridge, and

---

[44] Henslow gave his lectures, but normally lived in his rectory in Hitcham, Suffolk, where he botanised.   [45] J. W. Clark's marginal notes on Cam. a. 500. 5/124.

Trinity College, Dublin in his indictment.[46] Russell eschewed any detailed plans, while arguing that a central problem was the need to bring professorial and collegiate teaching into harmony. But 'the restrictions which are imposed by the original foundations and deeds of endowment of separate colleges'[47] made it hard for universities to be effective without the state's help, which, Russell pointed out, had been given to the Church of England and the Scottish universities by means of royal commissions. Inglis and Goulburn, members for the two English universities, opposed the motion, Goulburn taking the line that was to be very common in Cambridge in coming weeks: a royal commission would be illegal,[48] and no analogy with Scotland was helpful, 'for the Crown had a legal power of interfering with the Scotch universities, which did not apply to those of England'. Heywood withdrawing his motion, Russell's for English commissions was accepted, Russell doubting 'whether it would be convenient to include' Trinity College, Dublin, at a time when the charter of the new Irish university was being composed.[49] The Attorney-General rebutted the charge of illegality, and hinted that a statutory commission might eventually be imposed on the universities to give effect to recommendations of the commission of enquiry. Indeed there is not much doubt that from the beginning the government planned a statutory *executive* commission.

Russell did not let the Chancellor know of the government's plans until the morning of the Commons debate. The Prince Consort wrote in a tone of dignified regret, and the Queen noted in her diary that Russell had behaved 'in his strange way ... No-one feels more strongly than we do that improvements are necessary, and no-one has given and does give himself more trouble than my beloved Albert; therefore not to consult him ... is wrong and imprudent on Lord John's part.'[50] The universities were far angrier, and were not placated by Russell's letter to the Chancellor,

---

[46] *Hansard*, 3rd series, 110, pp. 691–765 for the debate.   [47] P. 750.

[48] P. 760. Goulburn did not give grounds for regarding the commission as illegal. The usual reason, as advanced by Gladstone in the Commons on 18 July, was that it was set up by 'the simple act of the Executive; the noble Lord has shown no anxiety to be advised by the House of Commons'. *Hansard*, 3rd series, 112, p. 1500.

[49] *Hansard*, 3rd series, 110, p. 765.

[50] Winstanley, *Early Victorian Cambridge*, p. 222.

amplifying his Commons statement.[51] Russell argued, correctly, that there could be no question of an enquiry commission's being illegal, and that one was needed to gain knowledge of 'the obstacles which are interposed by the wills of Founders, the retention of Customs, and the decisions of competent authority, to the full development of that large and improved system of study which the Universities have sought to establish'. Russell expressed his desire 'to bring the aid of the Crown, and if necessary, of Parliament, to assist' in the completion of the changes required, and clearly believed that sufficient reform could not be achieved without legislative authority. That would itself require a statutory agency to carry its decisions into effect. His belief was encouraged by Cambridge's own complaints at the burden of the statutes. Only so much progress could be made through *internal* activity.

This was not however the general view in the university. In May an address was presented to the Vice-Chancellor by members of the Senate.[52] It asked for time to undertake changes, and for revised statutes to be submitted to the Crown by university and colleges. It averred 'that a Royal Commission sent to Colleges or to either of the Universities, and claiming power to regulate the affairs of those bodies in a way different from that prescribed by their statutes, is illegal and unconstitutional'. This memorial was signed by 14 heads of houses, 12 professors, and 131 other members of the Senate, a total of 157 out of 221 resident members of the Senate, including, wrote Adam Sedgwick, 'many Liberal members with whom I have long been in the habit of acting'.[53] The address is very revealing: even dons who strongly desired reform more strongly wanted the university to be left to get on with it. In forwarding the address to the Chancellor Cartmell wrote that a royal commission would 'be felt as an affront and an indignity'.[54] In a further letter Cartmell wrote that since 'the Duke of Wellington [the Chancellor of Oxford] has identified himself with the authorities at Oxford, and has allowed it to be understood that he shares in their feelings, something of the same kind appears to be desired here'.[55]

[51] Printed in Cooper, *Annals*, v, pp. 11–12.   [52] Printed in Cooper, *Annals*, v, pp. 12–15.
[53] Quoted in Winstanley, *Early Victorian Cambridge*, p. 228.
[54] Cartmell's letter of 14 May is printed in Cooper, *Annals*, v, pp. 15–17.
[55] The letter, of 25 May, is quoted in Winstanley, *Early Victorian Cambridge*, p. 230.

The Prince Consort was in a peculiar difficulty, anxious not to compromise the Queen's constitutional relationship with her government, but also to dissuade anybody at Cambridge from refusing to co-operate with the commission, which naturally the government could not now abandon. The Chancellor wrote[56] that he had 'felt that it was not unnatural on the part of the University to look with apprehension at the proposed measure, as affording a means to those who may be ill disposed towards these venerable institutions to vent their hostility against them, and also to regard it as a proof of want of confidence in their ability or inclination to carry out useful reforms'. The government, however, had told the Chancellor that 'nothing could be farther from their intention than to cast such a slur upon the University', and that they were eager to show goodwill by their choice of commissioners. He therefore recommended 'the authorities of the University not to meet it with opposition, but rather to take it as the expression on the part of the Crown and Parliament, of a natural desire to be accurately informed'. The Chancellor urged dons 'to take a pride in shewing to those who have indulged in attacks against them, that they have conscientiously and zealously fulfilled the great task entrusted to them'. Probably this very judicious letter played a part in lessening the university anger, more especially as Russell replied: 'Oh, no: I don't promise to postpone the Commission', when asked to do so by Gladstone on 31 May,[57] and the Earl of Carlisle showed with equal firmness on 13 June that there was no point in continued opposition.

Russell had promised in his letter of 8 May to choose commissioners who were 'well qualified' and likely to inspire 'confidence and respect', and in the event he selected five eminent members of the university. John Graham, at one time the reforming Master of Christ's and now Bishop of Chester, became chairman of the commission which is therefore often named after him. Sir John Romilly, cousin of the university Registrary, was a Liberal MP, and newly appointed Attorney-General; he was a graduate of Trinity. Sir John Herschel, one of the most distinguished scientists of the day, was Senior Wrangler in 1813, a founder of the Analytical

---

[56] See Cooper, *Annals*, v, pp. 17–18.
[57] *Hansard*, 3rd series, 111, p. 491, and pp. 1151–3 for Carlisle's statement.

Society, and a fellow of St John's from 1813 to 1829. The remaining two were dons in residence, George Peacock and Adam Sedgwick, who were willing to undertake reform but were essentially moderates and known to be very loyal to the university. A sequence of letters reveals Sedgwick's response to Russell's invitation, on 29 May, to serve on the commission.[58] His immediate reaction was reluctance: 'it might deprive me of some of my most valued friendships'. He regretted that the government had not postponed the commission to see what the university might do 'spontaneously'; like many other dons, Sedgwick exaggerated the possible results of autonomous action. He felt, however, that the government could not now back down, and that 'if a friendly Commission be not appointed now, before long an adverse Commission might be sent down to us'. Accordingly, when the Chancellor pressed him twice to serve, Sedgwick agreed, but without enthusiasm.

THE GRAHAM COMMISSION IN CAMBRIDGE

'After having ascertained from high legal authority, that the University Commission is without the form of law, and is, moreover, regarded as unconstitutional, and of a kind that was never issued except in the worst times, I feel obliged by a sense of public duty, to decline answering any of the questions which I had the honour to receive from you a short time ago.'[59] So wrote the Vice-Chancellor, the arch-Tory G. E. Corrie, on whom D. A. Winstanley commented that 'the last ditch was his spiritual home'. He also declined to co-operate in his capacity as Master of Jesus, as did the Master of Clare, William Webb, while Whewell and Benedict Chapman, the Master of Caius, stood stiffly on their dignity. Other heads were more helpful, though they did not always provide all that was requested; for example, Corpus Christi and St Catharine's failed to give any details of fellows' remuneration in the copious information they supplied.[60] Still, a vast amount of oral and written evidence is collected in the 460 pages of the volume, concerning very numerous aspects of university life and business as

[58] For what follows, see Clark and Hughes, *The Life and Letters of Adam Sedgwick*, vol. II, pp. 172–81.
[59] PP 1852–3, HC xliv [1559]: *Graham Commission Report and Evidence* (separately paginated), *Evidence*, p. 2, and pp. 2–12 for what follows.   [60] *Graham Commission Report*, p. 167.

they were in the middle of the century – much the richest single source on the university. It is fully listed in a table of contents, but not indexed or provided with cross-references, so that it was no doubt as difficult for contemporaries to find their way through as it is for historians a century and a half later. The report is even more opaque. Badly organised, 'it moves along in slow and ponderous style, dropping no doubt many pearls of wisdom by the way, but these have a knack of running into dark and unsuspected corners . . . It contains no summary of recommendations to aid the tired reader.'[61] The commission's secretary was W. H. Bateson, who as senior bursar of St John's from 1846, and as master from 1857, proved a skilful and far-sighted administrator.[62]

The commission praised the work of the Revising Syndicate, whose reports appeared just before the commission's were published in November 1852. But its recommendations went far beyond the syndicate's, perhaps most notably in tackling head-on the religious tests, which had for long been a sore grievance for so many. The commission recommended outright abolition of the tests: the university greatly influenced 'the intellectual, moral and social character of the nation', but its ability to do so 'fully and completely must depend on its keeping pace with the progress of enlightened opinion . . . It is one of the noblest characteristics of our times that the barriers, which long excluded so many of our fellow subjects from the equal enjoyment of civil rights . . . have happily been removed. . . The University will be placed . . . in a false position, if it estranges itself from this great movement of liberal progress.'[63]

On another contentious issue, additions to triposes, the commission suggested modern languages, law, engineering, and theology,[64] besides commending the Natural Sciences and Moral Sciences degrees already scheduled. In each tripos there should also be an ordinary examination, to open up opportunities for 'that numerous class of Students, who are contented with an ordinary Degree, not

---

[61] Tillyard, *History of University Reform*, p. 112. There is a summary in Cooper, *Annals*, v, pp. 75–89, under 127 headings; but it follows the order in which the recommendations occur in the report and so mingles matters large and small. The commission also published three volumes of Cambridge University documents in 1852. Reflecting a remarkable amount of research they are at least as valuable as the *Report* itself.   [62] Miller, *Portrait of a College*, pp. 82–94.
[63] *Graham Commission Report*, p. 44.   [64] *Report*, pp. 28, 90–1.

feeling themselves to be fitted to embark in the competition for Academical Honours', but at present unable to take an ordinary degree in any subjects but mathematics and classics, 'in which ... most of this class of Students did not possess the desire or the aptitude to excel'.[65]

All these changes would entail new provision for teaching, and the commission recommended increasing the numbers of professors by ten, and tightening regulations so that professors should be compelled to reside for at least six months each year and forfeit stipend if they failed to deliver their scheduled lectures.[66] University lecturers were also to be appointed, more numerous than professors so that students would no longer have to resort to private tutors, and unlike college fellows they were to be 'unfettered by the ties of celibacy and Holy Orders'.[67] Though it was envisaged that college tutors should continue to teach for the Previous Examination (that is, the first two terms of the first year) tuition after that would be undertaken by the professors and lecturers – a move intended to wrest such teaching from the colleges' hands, and a momentous break with Cambridge tradition that alone among the commission's recommendations has not come to pass. A very significant proposal was the taxing of colleges to support the new teachers and other university purposes, and a necessary step for the mid-Victorian years in view of the university's income which was quite inadequate for additional stipends.[68] Lastly, a recommendation that contained the germ of the modern university administration was the creating of boards of studies for six subjects examined in triposes, actually or potentially – classics, law, medicine, moral sciences, natural sciences, and theology; the model was the Board of Mathematical Studies, recently formed to supervise the oldest and grandest tripos. 'We have recommended', the commission added, 'that a Council should be instituted ... to report to the Senate upon all matters which relate to the public instruction of the University, and to give unity of action to the Boards who preside over its several departments.' Provisions as to the composition of the Council followed – the inclusion of professors and others by right, and other members of the Senate

---

[65] *Report*, pp. 27–8.   [66] *Report*, pp. 102–3.   [67] *Report*, p. 81.   [68] *Report*, p. 82.

'according to a specified cycle'. The Council here sketched was a prefiguration of the General Board.[69]

One may summarise much by saying that the commission was kind to the university and kinder still to the colleges. 'The moral discipline of the University', averred the commission, is 'sustained by the internal system of the several Colleges. The domestic constitution of a College contains in itself a combination of the most wholesome and beneficial influences for this end.'[70] They did not believe that a Cambridge education was unduly expensive, and did not follow the Oxford commission's lead in proposing that 'non-collegiate' status might be allowed, an omission that disappointed the Chancellor, who was attracted to the 'plan of admitting any numbers who like to come, without belonging to any college, or being under the ordinary restraints of academic discipline – just as at Edinburgh and the foreign universities'.[71] When the expedient was adopted in Cambridge in 1869 it considerably reduced the cost of residence. The commission also wished that the Cambridge fellowships that had to be filled by men in holy orders or intending to take them should continue to bear that requirement, and they offered some puzzling reasons in support. If fellows did not choose a profession, 'the sinecure character of Fellowships would soon become such as to demand some very sweeping measure of reform',[72] while the clerical profession had been envisaged by benefactors. Also, celibacy 'cannot in our opinion be conveniently separated from the Collegiate system', while the commission did not even think it expedient 'to attempt to recal the severity of ancient statutable regulations in respect to residence', since fellowships were 'rewards for successful industry and talent'. The core of the university would continue to consist of celibate clerical fellows, though they would be complemented by the professors and lecturers on whom celibacy would not be imposed.[73]

The commission also had much to say about the many fellow-

---

[69] *Report*, p. 104. The full title was to be the General Council of Studies. Its functions were to be very similar to those of the General Board of the Faculties set up in 1882. The present Council (until 1994 called the Council of the Senate) is the university's supreme decision-making body, and was created in 1856 to replace the Caput Senatus abolished by the Cambridge University Act.

[70] *Report*, p. 16.   [71] Clark and Hughes, *The Life and Letters of Adam Sedgwick*, vol. II, pp. 223–4.

[72] *Report*, pp. 171–2 for these lines.

[73] A few years later the Statutory Commissioners were to take a more relaxed view of celibacy: see pp. 542–3 below.

ships and scholarships that were nominally restricted to candidates from specified kin, regions, or schools. Noting that the greater number of restrictions upon fellowships had been by usage or statute abolished by colleges, and that many scholarships had also fallen into desuetude, the commission recommended the removal of all remaining such provisions, save that a school's entitlement to scholarships would be retained in a much reduced form.[74]

Enough detail has been quoted to show that the Graham Commissioners' report was not radical enough to satisfy Russell. The university's own efforts at internal reform, which had been drawn up while the commission was sitting, were even less far-reaching.

THE REVISING SYNDICATE

The Revising Syndicate, which met for the first time on 14 March 1849, continued to sit regularly for three years; concurrent with the Graham Commission, it had the same Secretary, William Bateson of St John's, and naturally knew what the royal commissioners were discussing and deciding a few hundred yards away. The syndicate's motives were mixed and changed according to issues, timing, and personalities. At times they anticipated the commissioners by resolving to end ancient anomalies that in the middle of the nineteenth century no one could possibly defend, and whose toleration for so long was itself an indictment of the university. On other occasions the syndicate was noticeably forward-looking, while on others very resistant to the idea of change, as though the Graham Commissioners might still be subverted. By no means a sort of puppet administration, the syndics reflected the university's tenacious independence of spirit, existing before Lord John Russell and continuing long after him, and at all times exciting admiration and anger.

Matters that commanded general assent need not long detain us.[75] It was recommended that in future undergraduates should

[74] *Report*, pp. 160–5, 184. Scholarships would be commuted to exhibitions, bursaries given to matriculants from the school in question and conferring no corporate rights on their holders, as scholarships did.

[75] The work of the Revising Syndicate was dealt with in great detail by D. A. Winstanley, on whose account in *Early Victorian Cambridge*, pp. 237–57, these paragraphs are based.

reside for at least two-thirds of a term for it to count as having been kept. Candidates for degrees in law and divinity might be examined *viva voce* rather than by Latin disputation. The opportunity of acquiring a degree as a Ten-Year man, for some time a vexatious issue, was to be abolished. Permission to qualify for a doctorate in divinity *per saltum*, an odd loophole indeed, was no longer to be possible. Another proposal meant that it was no longer to be assumed on little evidence that certain MAs were reading for divinity degrees and might thereby be required either to perform religious duties or pay fines in default: this had been a source of harassment and friction. So had the practice of exacting extra fees from graduands with incomes from land above a very low threshold on admission to their degrees; that too was to be ended.[76] Though this list does not exhaust the anomalies removed by the Revising Syndicate, perhaps no more need be mentioned to show that for too long the university had been bemused by ancient rights and rituals. Its inertia is understandable – other institutions, notably the law, were similarly cumbered. It is also easy to see that deep divisions led the syndicate to suggest a timid compromise over religious tests.[77]

Even making allowances for the inward-looking character of the university, however, it is difficult to explain the syndicate's refusal to do anything about its finances, which were solely the responsibility of the Vice-Chancellor of the day, even in slight details. In his reforming suggestions of 1841 George Peacock pointed out that tasks of 'academical government' were given to men 'not sufficiently experienced and vigorous to guide them', and that as a result the finances were 'neglected and mismanaged, and the general interests of the university very seriously and permanently injured'. The appointment of a bursar was Peacock's sensible suggestion.[78] But

---

[76] This matter, whose complexities are not fully dealt with even by Winstanley's detail (pp. 249–50), is a good example of the way antique lumber had for centuries cumbered an *academic* corporation. The forty-ninth chapter of the Elizabethan Statutes, itself based on even older provisions, set the threshold at forty marks, or £26 13s 4d, an amount made obsolete by inflation three centuries later but applied to certain lands and not to others and not to investment income. One reason for the retention of this anomaly had been the dependence of the Proctors and other officers on fee income.

[77] Subscription was to remain for all degrees, but with the exception of degrees in theology all other graduands were to be required to give the modified declaration agreed for bachelors of arts in 1772. See Cooper, *Annals*, v, p. 39.

[78] Peacock, *Observations on the Statutes*, pp. 136–7.

nothing was done. Something was at least attempted over the Caput Senatus, the small executive committee whose unrepresentative character and dictatorial powers, best exemplified in the right of veto possessed by every member, angered members of the Senate;[79] the vast majority of dons hated outside interference yet might want to effect some change through the Senate itself, while the Caput had for centuries been a source of inertia.

In the syndicate a long struggle centred on this 'tribunitarian' power of veto,[80] defended by Whewell, one of its few real friends, as needed as a defence 'against the most rash and unadvised proposals, and the most flagrant violations of the statutes', precisely because the Senate itself had no power of debate[81] – which was itself a source of resentment among reformers. There was a general desire to abolish the right of veto for all members of the Caput save the Vice-Chancellor, provided that his ceased to be an absolute power. Various measures to check his authority having failed, largely because of Whewell's violent opposition, 'the majority of the syndicate preferred retaining the negative power in the individual members, as a kind of check upon that of the Vice-Chancellor'.[82] Compromise failing, the syndicate had to admit in their report of December 1851 that they could not agree on a Caput recommendation. A numerously signed memorial asking for the question to be reopened, it was remitted to a sort of arbitration panel consisting of three heads of houses and three others. Among these were William Bateson and Godfrey Sykes of Downing College. Sykes and Bateson produced a shrewd compromise: the retention of the veto in the Caput but the transfer of almost all its powers to a new representative elected body, the Council.[83] But by the autumn of 1852 the report of the Graham Commission appeared imminent, and the Revising Syndicate delayed submitting its recommendations to the Senate, so as to take account of the commission's findings. Altering their proposals in the light of the commission's

[79] On the Caput and its powers see Chapter 2, pp. 53–4.
[80] Much of what follows is based on the thorough discussion in Winstanley, *Early Victorian Cambridge*, pp. 238–42, 253–6.
[81] *Of a Liberal Education*, 2nd edn (1850), Part 3, pp. 62–3.
[82] A. H. Wratislaw, a member of the syndicate, quoted in Winstanley, *Early Victorian Cambridge*, p. 239.
[83] The direct ancestor of today's Council.

comments on some relatively unimportant matters, the syndicate put them to the Senate in February 1853, four years after it had first met. All the significant graces were placeted, but the reforms suggested – which in any case were not as far-reaching as all that – could not be considered as evidence of 'internal' reform since over the syndicate's proceedings lay the shadow of the Graham Commission, and the greater threat of a statutory commission to give effect to the state's desires.

THE STATUTORY COMMISSIONERS

THE CAMBRIDGE UNIVERSITY ACT, 1856

When the reports of the universities' commissioners were discussed in Parliament Russell was not Prime Minister, having been succeeded by Derby in 1852. Russell took office, however, in the government formed by Aberdeen at the end of the year. After the briefest of spells at the Foreign Office, he became Leader of the House of Commons, and in that capacity introduced on Monday 4 April a debate on education, always one of his chief interests. Russell,[84] as he had on earlier occasions, declared the government's willingness to act upon suggestions for reform made by the universities themselves, but made clear that they would be expected to fulfil four conditions – and in detailing them Russell implied that the Graham Commissioners had greatly disappointed the government in not fully following them: there was to be a more effective and representative form of government, fellowships were to entail tasks of teaching or research, and students were to be able to attend 'the teaching of the University ... by means other than those of belonging to, or residing in, colleges'. Also, Russell expected 'the removal or modification of the restrictions which now exist in regard to the attainment of the rewards and honours of the University to a particular county or locality;[85] and ... the application of some part of the endowments and property of the colleges to the purpose of instruction in the University, which are not now

[84] *Hansard*, 3rd series, vol. 125, pp. 543–9 for Russell's words on universities.
[85] Russell might have noted that this particular change was well in hand and that the Graham Commission had encouraged it.

given for any purposes of instruction whatever'. Finally, Russell declared that if the universities were willing to meet these objectives, 'and carry them into effect as far as they can, and apply to Parliament for powers to carry them out still further, we shall be happy ... but ... if there are persons who are still deterred by their prejudices from making any, even the most useful, alterations, it will then be our duty ... to bring in such measures as we may think absolutely necessary for the expediency of the case'. Russell's words were opposed unimpressively by two university MPs, Inglis for Oxford and Wigram for Cambridge, and supported by other members. In December Palmerston, the Home Secretary, wrote to the Prince Consort, as Cambridge's Chancellor, spelling out Russell's principles in greater detail, asking for the nature of the university's response, and threatening further legislation.[86]

The university did not meet these firm challenges with wisdom, its inadequate response reminding one of the lacklustre efforts of the Revising Syndicate. The colleges declared almost all Russell's objectives to be too objectionable or unnecessary, while the syndicate set up to formulate answers to the questions about university government and non-collegiate students responded by remarking that the first was adequately met by the scheme for a council,[87] while the second threatened to weaken discipline, the guaranteed result of the college system.[88] A Studies Syndicate did propose, in March 1854, to meet the wishes of the Graham Commission for Boards of Studies (on the model of the Board of Mathematical Studies created in 1848) for Classics, Law, Medicine, Moral Sciences, and Natural Sciences Triposes, and theology; it also proposed a Theological Tripos and allowing men achieving honours in it and in the Classical, Moral Sciences, and Natural Sciences Triposes to be awarded the BA.[89] But the Senate, while agreeing this concession for classicists, refused it for the others as it also non-placeted the Theological Tripos and Boards of Studies for the new triposes too. One reason given by Philpott was an 'unwillingness of the Senate to put any other studies on the same

[86] Cooper, *Annals*, v, pp. 135–7.   [87] Government opinion did not agree.
[88] The government's other objectives were strictly speaking the immediate concern of colleges rather than the university.
[89] That is, after passing the Previous Examination. The proposal would have removed the obligation to pass the ordinary degree examination.

531

footing as the old established studies of mathematics and classics' – a recurring problem.[90] Whewell, wise enough to see despite his earlier attitude that accommodation with the government's wishes was essential, called the decision 'a very unfortunate reverse in our progress ... a manifestation of this feeling in that manner and with such an utter disregard of consequences, is certainly as childish a proceeding as well can be imagined, and very little suited to give other persons a belief that we are fit to manage such matters for ourselves'.[91]

Despite moves quickly made to accomplish the changes, it was clear that the university had sacrificed its last chance, which in any case had not perhaps been very great, to avert the direct intervention of the State. In the spring of 1854 the government finally decided to set up statutory commissioners to oversee the reform of Cambridge, and a bill was drafted on the model of the Oxford bill, approved by both houses of parliament in 1854, allowance in this new venture being made for Cambridge's rather different circumstances, and help over details being given by Philpott, Ainslie, and Cookson, determined to co-operate with the State's inescapable reforms.[92] A bill introduced into the House of Lords in 1855 progressed so slowly that it reached the Commons too late, and had to be abandoned. A new bill, very like the old, was introduced in the Commons on 14 March 1856. At the committee stage at the end of May Pleydell-Bouverie, the Vice-President of the Board of Trade, asserted the incontrovertible right of parliament to interfere with one of the 'great national institutions ... enjoying great privileges by Act of Parliament, receiving annually grants of public money, and virtually intrusted with the education of the clergy of the Established Church'.[93] Adverting to the university's ancient and cumbrous constitution, the undemanding nature of the ordinary degree, and the neglect of professional education and modern subjects which were essential features of a gentleman's culture, Pleydell-Bouverie argued that while Cambridge's resources 'were of the highest description, the result

[90] Royal Archives: Letters of the Prince Consort as Chancellor of the University, letter of Philpott to Colonel Grey, 3 May 1854 (CUL MS 3548, microfilm).
[91] Stair Douglas, *Whewell*, p. 408, quoting a letter to Adam Sedgwick of 12 May 1854.
[92] For these lines, see Winstanley, *Early Victorian Cambridge*, pp. 273–86.
[93] *Hansard*, 3rd series, 142, pp. 803–26.

produced was comparatively very small'; he stated that the income of the university (including the professors' endowed stipends) was £24,500, and of the seventeen colleges £185,000. In a crude calculation of the expense of a Cambridge education, he asserted of the 205 men who had in 1850 passed the Voluntary Theological Examination 'that the cost before ordination of each of these clergymen during their residence in the University would be more than £1,000'.[94]

The bill was accepted in principle by other speakers, including Spencer Walpole, MP for the university.[95] But many clauses were contested; for example, Walpole and his colleague L. T. Wigram wished to amend clause 27 so as to prevent colleges from disregarding the wishes of their founders when framing statutes – a reactionary proposal – while James Heywood tried to alter the same clause to exempt students from the obligation to worship in the college chapel. Both attempts, like others, were unsuccessful.[96] Only two significant amendments were carried, in each case owing to Heywood's tenacious opposition to religious tests. Students were not to be obliged to take an oath on the award of a scholarship, while clause 44, abolishing tests for all lay degrees, was broadened so that membership of the Senate was not to be subject to tests either.[97] But this amendment was overturned in the House of Lords, and to prevent further delay the Commons accepted in July the bill as altered.[98] Tests for membership of the Senate were not abolished until 1871.

An Act to make further Provision for the good Government and Extension of the University of Cambridge was given the royal assent on 29 July 1856.[99] The ancient constitution of the university, with its contradictory elements of democracy, anarchy, and oligarchic centralism, was replaced by representative government; the Caput disappeared in favour of the Council of the Senate, which was to be elected by resident members of the Senate,[100] and to contain four

---

[94] The equivalent of at least £50,000 in 1995, or considerably more than current costs in real terms.
[95] *Hansard*, 3rd series, 142, pp. 823–43.   [96] *Hansard*, 3rd series, 142, pp. 1198–211.
[97] *Hansard*, 3rd series, 143, pp. 309–19.   [98] *Hansard*, 3rd series, 143, pp. 1042–5.
[99] P.G. 19 & 20 Vict. c. 88 is printed in Cooper, *Annals*, v, pp. 221–38, from which the following details are taken.
[100] Sections 5–21. 'Residence' was to be within one and a half miles of Great St Mary's – a dramatic indication of the tiny spread of the essential university.

heads of house, four professors, and eight other members of the Senate, plus the Vice-Chancellor, a far better balance of the different university interests than previously. The Council was to decide all matters by majority, including the approval of all graces to be submitted to the Senate; thus the capricious individual veto enjoyed by Caput members disappeared. The powers of the heads of houses were also reduced, the nomination to vacant offices being transferred to the Council by Section 21 of the act. Another significant innovation was the abolition of religious tests for all degrees save divinity,[101] though by virtue of the compromise agreed in the Commons in July membership of the Senate and tenure of university offices was still to be confined to those declaring their membership of the Church of England.[102]

THE COMMISSIONERS AND THEIR NEGOTIATIONS

As important as these changes were those contemplated by the eight statutory commissioners, who were named in Section 1 of the act. All were members of the university. John Graham, Bishop of Chester, had been chairman of the inquiry commission of 1850, and George Peacock a member. The others were John Lonsdale, Bishop of Lichfield; Edward Henry Stanley, usually called Lord Stanley, a Conservative politician who became fifteenth Earl of Derby at his father's death in 1869; Matthew Talbot Baines, Liberal MP for Leeds; Sir William Page Wood, another Liberal and a Chancery judge; Sir Laurence Peel, first cousin of the Conservative statesman and a distinguished lawyer; and the Reverend Charles John Vaughan, Headmaster of Harrow, whose disreputable conduct there would certainly have excluded him from the commission and like bodies had it been known.[103] The Bishop of Lichfield served only briefly and was replaced in May 1858 by Sir George James

---

[101] Section 45.

[102] It was possible to take the MA without oaths or declaration. 'But those who intend being Members of the Senate must declare: – so I divide each page of M.A.s into 2 sets of Declarants and Non-declarants.' Diary of Joseph Romilly (Registrary), Friday 10 September 1856: CUL MSS. Add. 6836. I owe this reference to Mrs M. E. Bury.

[103] Vaughan was guilty of homosexual love affairs with pupils. In 1859 he was forced to resign from Harrow under the threat of public exposure when the father of John Addington Symonds discovered the truth: see Phyllis Grosskurth, *John Addington Symonds* (London, Longmans, 1964), pp. 30–40.

Turner, another Chancery judge, and a Conservative. On Peacock's death in November 1858 his place was filled by Horace Waddington, at one time a barrister and since 1848 Permanent Under-Secretary at the Home Office.

The commission thus had pronounced legal strengths, valuable in the complex negotiations they undertook. Until the end of 1857 the Council and the colleges were able to submit to the commissioners proposals for the modification of their statutes; and after that the commissioners had the power to frame proposals of their own to be presented to the Privy Council for ratification, although the Cambridge authorities if acting by substantial majorities might secure further revision.[104]

For about two years the commissioners, the Council, and the Senate were engaged in a complex process of negotiation.[105] There were certainly differences of attitude, with the Senate markedly more conservative than the commissioners, as we might expect, while the Council acted as a wary intermediary. Public hostels occasioned one of the most notable conflicts. Sections 23–5 of the act authorised the university to set up public hostels for undergraduates desiring non-collegiate and therefore cheaper residence in Cambridge. The Council framed statutes which did not require the principals of such hostels to be Anglicans or their students to attend Anglican worship, sensible provisions since Dissenters might well find open-access hostels attractive. Anglican diehards in the Senate induced many non-resident MAs to travel to Cambridge to throw the proposed statute out. The commissioners reversed this vain gesture. But disputes were briefer and less intense than they had been in the preceding decade between Russell and the Cambridge intransigents. Dons could no longer delude themselves that the state's wishes might be frustrated.

The result of these labours was a university shorn of ancient and redundant officers such as Scrutators and Taxors, the Heresy Board to exclude the wayward from the pulpit of Great St Mary's, and the 'ten-year men', intending clergymen able to take degrees even though non-resident. The period of residence required of under-

[104] Sections 26–31, 35, 39–43, 52.
[105] What follows is based on the very full account in Winstanley, *Early Victorian Cambridge*, pp. 314–38.

graduates 'to keep their terms' was lengthened, from half of each term to two-thirds; and the number of terms' residence required for the ordinary degree was reduced from ten to nine. Professors and other university officers were obliged to be resident, the privileges enjoyed by undergraduates of higher rank under the Elizabethan statutes were very much reduced, and the two houses of the Senate, Regents and Non-Regents, amalgamated. Above all, the university was freed from the trammels that Elizabeth I and later legislators had fixed upon it, and given a constitution that was workable and allowed Cambridge to make changes – though never as quickly as some wished.

The commissioners failed in one major respect, however, to effect in the university statutes a change they desired. The Graham Commission had recommended that colleges should contribute to university funds so as to support professors and lecturers; one mechanism suggested was that 20 per cent of fellowships should be suppressed.[106] The Statutory Commissioners rejected this idea, and thought of a levy of 5 per cent upon the distributable income of each college, to increase the stipends of nine existing professors and to create endowments for ten new ones.[107] 'This proposal, however, though accepted by Trinity, St Peter's, and Christ's Colleges, was rejected by all the other Colleges, and in consequence fell to the ground.' In contrast, in two traditional fields of study, theology and mathematics, the commissioners were able to raise the number of chairs from three to four in each case by redirecting existing university endowments.

The question of revenues linked university and colleges in the Statutory Commissioners' negotiations, and was one of the most contentious items within them.[108] It is plain from the commissioners' report that college matters gave them far more trouble than university matters; dealing with seventeen separate and differently constituted societies added further complexities to a base of acute conflict over principles. In terms of the onion simile, the *university* reforms were the outside skins most dons were willing to concede,

[106] *Graham Commission Report*, p. 85.
[107] What follows is based on PP 1861 HC xx [2852]: *Report of the Cambridge University Commissioners*, pp. 5–8.
[108] What follows is based on PP 1861, *Report of the Cambridge University Commissioners*, pp. 9–32.

while the *college* matters that nobody was willing to concede were the innermost ones. College affairs attracted the most intense loyalties; indeed some active university reformers were among the most vehement opponents of college changes.

Section 27 of the Cambridge Act authorised the commissioners to seek to amend college statutes to improve college government and the terms on which fellowships and undergraduate scholarships might be filled and enjoyed, and to redistribute college revenues, in particular in favour of 'the benefit of the University at large'. Some items, it has to be said, caused hardly any argument at all, the chief of these being the scholarships and fellowships that were linked to named localities and schools, or even to particular families. The Graham Commissioners had suggested removing these restrictions, save where the scholarship rights of some schools were involved, and the Statutory Commissioners followed their lead. For many years colleges had been ignoring these restrictions where meritocratic considerations conflicted, and they were more than happy to consent to new statutes that abrogated restrictive particularities. In no college were they more numerous than at St John's, and changes now meant 'the merging into the general property of the college the numerous separate endowments (including the Platt endowment) of fellowships and scholarships, exception being made only for some funds maintaining awards attached to certain schools, which were retained to support closed exhibitions ... all county and other qualifications for fellowships and scholarships were abolished'.[109]

The Cambridge Act required colleges to submit draft revised statutes to the Statutory Commissioners by the end of 1857, and they did so to varying degrees of completeness, and satisfactoriness to the commissioners. The prospect of offering the same sorts of comments to each college in turn seemed so wasteful that in the summer of 1857 the commissioners circulated some 'General Principles'. 'At the same time we endeavoured to guard ourselves from the appearance of laying down peremptory rules, by expressly stating that the propositions thus transmitted were not to be regarded as final conclusions, but only as indicating the views of the

---

[109] Miller, *Portrait of a College*, pp. 85–6.

Commissioners.'[110] Their views on fellowships were very contentious. By the end of the century fellowships were linked to specific tasks of teaching, administration or research.[111] But in the 1850s the predominant view was of fellowships as prizes for intellectual distinction, or opportunities to pursue scholarship or to prepare for a career untrammelled by material cares,[112] and to an extent the commissioners shared it. Still, they knew that a life fellowship hardly gave a stimulus to preparing for a job, and at the same time they like others were feeling their way towards the notion of the *professional* don.[113] Taking a significantly more adventurous line than the Graham Commissioners, they wanted to open up the self-perpetuating celibate clerical college. By the university statutes of 1570 all fellows had to be unmarried, while college statutes reserved 87 per cent of fellowships for men in holy orders or intending to take them.[114] Freedom to marry, at all events after some years as a fellow, might encourage men to devote their careers to college service, 'while the effect of the rule [of ordination] in tempting young men, who were otherwise unwilling, to undertake the grave responsibilities of the clerical profession, appeared to us injurious alike to the Church and the Colleges'.[115] On the other hand, 'the simple removal of the condition, so as to render all Fellowships tenable for life, without distinction of profession, subject only to be vacated by marriage or by the acceptance of a benefice, appeared to us likely to exercise an injurious effect upon the Colleges, by materially diminishing the number of vacancies, and, consequently, the chances of a succession to a Fellowship'.

Accordingly, the commissioners suggested limiting tenure to ten years, except for a proportion of dons performing specific tasks (such as professor, tutor, or bursar), who might retain them for life, and marry if they chose. The proportion of clerical fellowships was

---

[110] PP 1861, *Report of the Cambridge University Commissioners*, p. 12; pp. 12–20 for the General Principles and the following details.

[111] Christopher Brooke, *History of the University of Cambridge 1870–1990*, esp. pp. 88–9.

[112] One of the most ardent defenders of the 'prize' conception of fellowships was the radical Henry Fawcett, who saw them as egalitarian agents, assisting bright men from modest backgrounds: Leslie Stephen, *Henry Fawcett*, pp. 105–6.

[113] Christopher Brooke, *History of the University of Cambridge 1870–1990*, pp. 1–19.

[114] See chapter 3, pp. 101–3. Trinity Hall, Gonville and Caius, and Downing had substantial numbers of lay fellowships.

[115] PP 1861, *Report of the Cambridge University Commissioners*, p. 18, for these quotations.

to be reduced, and fellowships 'thrown open to the competition of the whole University, after public notice and examination'.[116] Similarly, 'in the election of a Master' the choice 'should be free and unrestrained within the limits of the University'. Nor should it be confined to men in holy orders. There were some relatively uncontentious proposals about instituting scholarships, to increase opportunities for the impecunious. Perhaps most opposition was aroused, however, by the suggestion that 'a portion of the divisible revenues' of a college should be appropriated 'to University purposes'.

Colleges differed in their constitutions and the composition of their fellowships, and the issues themselves were exceedingly complicated; the balance of sentiment varied from item to item and governing body to governing body. Within the Senate as a whole there seems to have been a minority, sometimes very vocal, that approved of the general drift of the commissioners' intentions; notable members of this group were John Grote and J. Llewellyn Davies, both of Trinity. Still, on most issues 'the greater part of them [that is, fellows] differed widely from our views upon some of the leading points ... especially with regard to the opening of Fellowships to the University generally, and to the limitation of their tenure'.[117] Fearing protracted negotiations, the commissioners therefore decided to settle matters with Trinity and St John's next, since as issues were resolved with them so would they be settled with the smaller colleges. Accordingly the commissioners drafted statutes for the two largest colleges, using where possible the colleges' own suggestions but nevertheless producing versions very different from the colleges. This move made friction worse, since the two college masters 'communicated the proposed Statutes to the members of other Colleges', and ushered in a collective debate. After a concerted campaign, the Vice-Chancellor, Philpott of St Catharine's, called a meeting on Tuesday 26 October 1858 for members of all governing bodies; it was unprecedented in the university.[118] Three members of the Senate who were not fellows

---

[116] *Report*, pp. 12–13 for these quotations.
[117] PP 1861, *Report of the Cambridge University Commissioners*, p. 13, and p. 14 for the next quotation.
[118] *Cambridge Chronicle*, 10 July and 30 October 1858. The Senate was open to a wider constituency, and in any case did not allow discussion.

were asked to leave – an early example of the presumption of conflict between university and colleges.

Celibacy aroused less dissent than other issues, even Whewell, while passionately conservative in everything else, admitting that unless fellows were allowed to marry it would be difficult for colleges to retain tutors, on whom the college structure largely rested.[119] But the commissioners' proposal that fellowships should be open to competition throughout the university implied that there was in the commissioners' minds 'an utter dislike of the existing state of things', as Whewell said at the meeting of 26 October 1858.[120] Though some supported the small colleges' right to recruit talented graduates from outside their society, Heath of Trinity Hall spoke for many in viewing the proposal as a restriction of freedom, not its extension: a conspiracy 'to confiscate the Colleges, and convert them into a congeries of University prizes', and in other words a backdoor attempt to mulct the colleges to pay for university purposes. As to the commissioners' plans for financial contributions, Whewell like others thought them 'the only way in which the needs of the University could be supplied. But he objected to a percentage, and was in favour of a contribution by agreement among the Colleges, administered by representatives of the Colleges [and] . . . in proportion to the property of the College.' Differences over how a contribution might be levied was one reason for the undermining of the commissioners' plan, but there was also outright opposition. Campion of Queens'

> defended the administration of College funds under the present system as remarkably free from abuse. The only argument he had ever heard in favour of this proposed contribution was, that the income-tax would shortly be removed, and it would make no difference if they paid to the University the money which they had been paying to the government. The fact that the income-tax, from its unequal pressure, had proved a failure, showed that they ought not to follow the example set. The Act of Parliament might give power to take the money; but he hoped that many would refuse to give it up, and have the credit of guarding the finances which had come down to them.

[119] See William Whewell, *Remarks on Proposed Changes in the College Statutes* (Cambridge, 23 September 1857).
[120] *Cambridge Chronicle*, 30 October 1858, on which these paragraphs are based, and from which the quotations are taken.

Martin (Trinity) was 'in favour of a contribution for the encouragement of the residence of a learned body of Professors, and did not
object to the mode proposed by the Commissioners ... As to the
argument that it was contrary to the statutes, they must not shut
their eyes to the fact that they were living under changed
circumstances.' Nevertheless, resolutions against the financial and
fellowship proposals were carried by large majorities.

As to the commission's plans to reduce college clericalism,
Perowne of Corpus 'could not conceive anything more prejudicial
to the religious character of the students than that they should be
allowed to absent themselves from all religious worship ... [The
scheme] did tend to interfere with what had always been the
brightest and greatest ornament of this University', while G.
Williams of King's saw in the St John's draft statutes 'an attempt to
admit by the back-stairs, not only Protestant Dissenters, but persons
who did not even profess to be Christians'. The feeling of many of
those who had called for a meeting, said the *Cambridge Chronicle*,
'was far stronger on the religious than on the secular or social
interests at stake', and few agreed with one interrupter, 'A
Gentleman in the Gallery', whose speech was summarised thus:
'This was a national University, and should be devoted to national
purposes, without distinction of creed.' Most contention, however,
seems to have surrounded the limitation of fellowship tenure.
Those erstwhile reformers William Bateson and Adam Sedgwick
led the call for life-tenure. Bateson, the Master of St John's,
remarked that 'it was not the amount of the emolument, but the
knowledge that a man was provided for – placed, as has been said,
on an island, where the waters could never overwhelm him which
was the great attraction in a Fellowship'. Re-election on condition
of filling an office 'might corrupt the administrators of the election;
and destroy the freedom of the Fellow ... people would be invited
to follow a course of obedience and acquiescence', but 'able men
were not commonly persons who assented to the opinions of those
around them'. For Adam Sedgwick it was 'a proud day' when he
became a fellow of Trinity. 'He felt that he possessed something
which he had gained honourably, and which he could look forward
to as bearing upon his success in life ... he could not conceive
anything more degrading than to make it a terminable annuity.' A

lifelong fellowship gave him secure prospects in his impoverished youth, and would pension him after he resigned his professorship. 'He believed that . . . the same sentiments applied to many around him', and 'that the proposition of the Commissioners would tend to the moral degradation of the different societies'. J. Llewellyn Davies 'differed with reluctance from the Vice-Master of his own College', but he wanted to be shown why the proposition would be 'ruinous', and 'that had not been done'. There were a few other dissentients, but a resolution against terminable fellowships was passed overwhelmingly.

Faced with a virtually united collegiate front on these crucial issues, the commissioners in effect climbed down. Their statutory deadline approached, and they had to get by parliamentary approval an extension of their powers till the end of 1860; and they did not wish to spend yet more time, and risk major parliamentary battle, by fighting for the 'General Principles' to the limit.[121] The opening of all fellowships to general competition and the idea of a financial contribution were dropped, and fellowship tenure and the ordination requirement were settled by negotiation college by college. The results varied greatly in detail, being affected by the requirements of the original college statutes, modifications suggested by governing bodies, and the interaction of these proposals with the commissioners' desires. At the two largest colleges, Trinity and St John's, with which the commissioners' negotiations were most tense and protracted, life-tenure for fellowships remained, as did the obligations on fellows to take holy orders and to remain celibate. These requirements might be dispensed with, however, for specified groups though they would almost certainly amount to a minority of fellows: holders of professorships and 'public lectureships' or a few important posts in the university or college, men who after holding such positions for ten years had given them up, and lastly 'any person eminent for science and learning, whether a member of the University or not'.[122] At Jesus College 'the conditions of tenure of Fellowships' remained 'unaltered' and at Sidney Sussex, nearly so; while at six others – Christ's, Corpus Christi, Emmanuel, Pembroke, Peterhouse, and St Catharine's –

---

[121] For what follows, see PP 1861, *Report of the Cambridge University Commissioners*, pp. 15–32.
[122] For these lines, see PP 1861, *Report of the Cambridge University Commissioners*, pp. 15–32.

the structure also stayed very much the same, with exemptions from celibacy like those at Trinity and St John's, though covering fewer categories. At these six colleges, however, there was an overall reduction in the number of clerical fellowships.

Greater changes were accepted at other colleges. There was a 'willingness to accept the general rule of limited tenure, if coupled with an extended relaxation of the condition of celibacy',[123] at Clare, Gonville and Caius, Trinity Hall (for the lay fellows only),[124] Queens', and with modifications at Magdalene and Downing; at these six colleges tenure was normally for ten years but might be extended to life for holders or ex-holders of college or university offices, these special groups being similar to those exempted from celibacy at Trinity and St John's. At these six colleges too the total of clerical fellowships was reduced. We might sum up, therefore, by saying that for many Cambridge fellows the rules changed little as a result of the Statutory Commissioners' labours. Very surprisingly, there was no attempt to tighten provisions for residence, the commissioners being so much in thrall to the 'prize' conception of fellowships that they 'with the consent of the several Colleges, expunged from their Statutes ... the provision enforcing the residence of the Fellows ... allowing all Fellows not holding College Offices to absent themselves from the College at their pleasure'.[125]

At King's, fellowships continued to be tenable for life on condition of celibacy, though as elsewhere professors might be exempted from it. The reform of the college's unique constitution had been in progress for some time. Richard Okes, Provost from 1850 to 1888, with wisdom welcomed the Graham Commissioners and later worked with fellows, notably Austen Leigh, to loosen the bonds with Eton that had previously excluded entrants from other schools. The new college constitution of 1861 was for a foundation of 46 fellows and 48 scholars, only 24 scholarships being specifically reserved for Etonians. Pensioners might also be recruited from other schools. The first non-Etonian pensioner came in 1865 and

---

[123] PP 1861, *Report of the Cambridge University Commissioners*, p. 20.
[124] At Trinity Hall the trade-off was organised by Henry Fawcett through skilful manipulation of voting preferences: see Leslie Stephen, *Henry Fawcett*, pp. 109–10.
[125] PP 1861, *Report of the Cambridge University Commissioners*, p. 17.

the first scholar in 1869, while the first non-Etonian fellow was elected in 1873: momentous changes in the pattern of four centuries, even though Eton remained disproportionately represented in the college for many decades.[126]

[126] Morris, *King's College*, pp. 45–6; Christopher Brooke, *A History of the University of Cambridge 1870–1990*, pp. 33–5; PP 1861, *Report of the Cambridge University Commissioners*, pp. 29–30.

Chapter 15

THE UNDERGRADUATE
EXPERIENCE, I: PHILIP YORKE
AND THE WORDSWORTHS

PHILIP YORKE

A FELLOW COMMONER AT QUEENS' COLLEGE

I have now finished the Book of Homer, that I was doing before the Holidays ... I hope to be able when I come home at Whitsuntide, to show your Lordship the Verses and Themes, that I shall have done since Easter, & hope that your Lordship sometime or other, will have an Opportunity to try me in some Book. Your Lordship was so kind as to hint to me to translate a Paper in the Spectator into Latin, which I hope to be able to show your Lordship at Whitsuntide.[1]

So wrote Philip Yorke, aged fourteen, from Harrow School to his guardian, the second Earl of Hardwicke of Wimpole Hall, Cambridgeshire. Philip, the son of the earl's younger brother, Charles, had come into the earl's charge in 1770 on his father's death.[2] As the typical letter that is quoted above indicates, Philip Yorke's years at Harrow were spent in intensive scholarship. Schoolboy scrapes were few, and rather touchingly apologised for to his redoubtable guardian – as was, indeed, any slight delay in picking up his quill to respond to Hardwicke's insistent letters. Philip turned to authors his uncle pressed on him, and sent his classical verses and themes to Wimpole for comment, which was sometimes adverse. In addition to his regular Harrow lessons Philip worked with a private tutor, Samuel Weston (a fellow of St John's), and pursued with him a special course of study. In March 1772 he was reading parts of

---

[1] BL Add. MS, 35377, fol. 5, 23 April 1771. The following paragraph is based on folios 1–58 of this MS. Philip Yorke was born on 31 May 1757.

[2] Charles Yorke was briefly Lord Chancellor before his death. His father, called Philip like many of the Yorkes, was Lord Chancellor 1737–56; created Baron Hardwicke in 1733, he became the first earl in 1754; he bought Wimpole in 1740.

Herodotus, Thucydides, and Theocritus with his Harrow master, and with Weston Livy on the Punic War, 'a french book concerning the Grandeur & fall of the Roman Empire',[3] and Fortin's sermons on Sunday.

Since Weston was not slow to mention any slight lapse to Hardwicke, Philip had a harder life than any modern schoolboy of fifteen years, at Harrow or elsewhere. In November 1772 he wrote: 'I will endeavour to be more attentive to french than I have been; the reason I have rather neglected it is, that I could hardly find time for so many employments, as school lessons & exercises, attending on Mr Weston, & making myself previously acquainted with the books I read with him; all these consume so much time.'[4] When released from Harrow by a school epidemic he studied, with Dr Robert Plumptre,[5] Virgil, the Greek Testament, Clarke's exposition of the catechism, and some 'Geography & Chronology'.[6] Still, Philip Yorke seems to have flourished under pressure. In February 1774, aged seventeen, he was enjoying the *Cyropedia* of Xenophon[7] and offering some shrewd comments on it. He left Harrow a few weeks later, certainly more versed in Latin and Greek than the great majority of sixth-formers today. He was also fairly fluent in French, and had a patchy knowledge of history, having read a few French textbooks and part of Robertson's *Charles V*. His English utterance, it should be said, was sophisticated and accurate, putting many modern sixth-formers (and even undergraduates) to shame. On the other hand his knowledge of mathematics was tiny.

Philip Yorke was admitted to Queens' College as a fellow commoner in April 1774, a few weeks before his seventeenth birthday; Hardwicke (who had himself been at Corpus) chose Queens' because of his close acquaintance with the president, Plumptre. Yorke's undergraduate career was very unusual for its day. Fellow commoners were commonly exempted from college lectures, the toughest of the degree hurdles, and rigorous discipline; they could spend their days at Cambridge in amusement and diversion, or worse. Thus Philip Yorke's younger brother, Charles,

[3] Fol. 20.   [4] Fol. 39.
[5] President of Queens' College from 1760 to 1788, and rector of Wimpole and so well known to Hardwicke.   [6] Fol. 8.
[7] The *Cyropedia* is a fictionalised life of the Persian king Cyrus. It was translated by W. Baker (*c.* 1560) but Yorke read it in the original.

was responsible for a serious affray in May 1781 while a fellow commoner at St John's. He got into a quarrel with bargemen while boating near Magdalene Bridge; leading a dozen friends armed with bludgeons he returned to fight the bargemen, and when defeated proposed to fight again with larger bludgeons. A riot was averted by Weston's intercession.[8] The behaviour of Charles Crawford, a fellow commoner at Queens' in the 1760s, was even more reprehensible, as Winstanley details for us. Fellow commoners were given a bad press in the eighteenth century, and have fared no better since.[9]

Philip Yorke was certainly treated very lightly by his college. Though he attended some college lectures, he was not placed under a heavy academic obligation by Queens'; nor did he often see his college tutor. The president introduced him to the Vice-Chancellor a few days after his arrival, and showed him special attention thereafter, and Yorke dined with Sir John Cotton and Soame Jenyns, as befitted the nephew and heir of the mightiest aristocrat in Cambridgeshire. But his two years at Queens' were anything but frivolous, and his industry and conduct were exemplary. He suffered an even harsher régime at Hardwicke's hands than he had at Harrow, at all events when he was actually in Cambridge. Samuel Weston accompanied him to university, taught him as a schoolboy still, and reported progress to Hardwicke, whose attitude was reminiscent of familial relationships in an earlier age, for instance Agnes Paston's ferocious control of her son Clement, at Cambridge in the 1450s.[10] Philip Yorke was unusual in another respect. Though he was merely the grandson of one Whig aristocrat and the nephew of another, he was given the privilege accorded to noblemen's sons, of taking his degree after just six terms' residence and without any academic tests at all. In effect, he was given an honorary degree.[11] No doubt this concession was arranged by Hardwicke and Plumptre before he matriculated.

In eighteenth-century Cambridge the teaching-period was shorter than the term, or in other words 'term' existed for some time

---

[8] He had acted as private tutor to Philip Yorke some years earlier.
[9] Winstanley, *Unreformed Cambridge*, pp. 198–200, 215–25.
[10] See John Warrington, ed., *The Paston Letters*, Everyman's Library (2 vols., London, Dent, 1956), vol. I, p. 127.   [11] Fol. 306.

both before and after the weeks when teaching took place. The same is true today, though the teaching season is longer. In Yorke's day undergraduates were in residence for the teaching-period and not usually outside it, although some were also around at times when today students have gone. Thus when Philip Yorke left Queens' on 22 December 1775 for the family house of Titten-hanger, he left 'some of our friends at Cambridge about to enjoy their usual Christmas feastings'.[12] Gunning, who came up to Christ's in 1784, records in his memoirs that 'When the Term ended, the University was far from being deserted. No college was entirely without resident members during the long vacation.' After the first long vacation, Gunning wrote,

> I returned to college towards the end of September, and, by the advice of Hartley, I left my gun in the country. I applied very closely to study . . . He and I, with Mr Adam Wall, the Senior Fellow, were the only residents till the middle of October, when the election of college officers took place, which brought up several of the Fellows. I had thus six clear weeks for reading, as lectures did not commence until after the division of Term.[13]

When in October 1774 Yorke returned to Cambridge after the Long Vacation, he wrote: 'I found the University much emptier than I expected; there were but three come in this college, but it begins to fill now [i.e. 30 October] very fast, & I dare say will be almost full again in a fortnight.'[14] On 19 November 'the colleges have not been long full', and Professors Symonds and Hallifax had been lecturing for a few weeks.[15] They ceased to do so about the middle of December, and resumed in the middle of February, finishing at the beginning of April. In the Easter Term they lectured in May and early June. Thus, since May was not then disrupted by tripos examinations[16] the total period of university teaching was only slightly less than now – eighteen weeks as against twenty – while college teaching took place in the same weeks, and lasted for a similar period.[17]

Hardwicke, the eldest son of the first earl, the famous Lord

---

[12] Fol. 246.   [13] Gunning, *Reminiscences*, vol. I, pp. 29–30.
[14] Fol. 122.   [15] Fol. 132.
[16] Until the changes of the early 1880s they occurred in January, outside the teaching period.
[17] Today, of course, much teaching occurs outside full term, especially college teaching.

Chancellor, inherited the title in 1764.[18] The Hardwickes were the most important aristocrats in the county, and Wimpole Hall, which the first earl bought in 1740 from the second Earl of Oxford, was its most imposing mansion. The second earl had a fitting sense of his family's status; thus his father's tomb, which he caused to be constructed in Wimpole church, is far more grandiose and ostentatious than its subject had desired. Hardwicke was unpopular with some in Cambridgeshire, including the Reverend William Cole, the Milton antiquarian, who wrote in 1778:

> Lord Hardwicke's little enmities and meannesses are not unknown to this county. I heard the master of a college say in public company last year, and before some of his particular friends who endeavoured to defend him, that when he and his brethren paid their annual dining visit, they were always glad to get into their coach, for if he said nothing offensive, which was sometimes the case, his behaviour was so chilling and forbidding that, was it not for the disrespect, he would never go again.[19]

Philip Yorke, the concern of these pages, was the obvious heir to the earldom from an early age since his guardian had no sons. It was therefore natural for Hardwicke to take a keen interest in his ward's education, and the weight and thrust of the guidance he received were given a distinctive character by Hardwicke's leanings and dominating temperament. He did not explain why he was imposing the particular pattern that he did, but his insistence on Yorke's studying law and history, which in the eighteenth century were regarded as valuable for the future statesman, shows that he had the usual Yorke career in mind.[20] Hardwicke, however, was himself drawn far more to scholarly and artistic pursuits than to politics. Very learned in the classical tongues, he composed as an undergraduate, with the help of others, a work that was remarkably popular for the rest of the century, the *Athenian Letters*.[21] In later life to his

---

[18] For what follows, see in particular David Souden, *Wimpole Hall* (n.p., National Trust, 1991), pp. 26–8.

[19] Wilmarth Sheldon Lewis (ed.), *Correspondence of Horace Walpole*, vol. II (1937), pp. 118–19. The letter is dated 3 September 1778.

[20] For much of what follows, see George C. Brauer, *The Education of a Gentleman. Theories of Gentlemanly Education in England 1660–1775* (New York, Bookman Associates, 1959). esp. pp. 52–113.

[21] The supposed letters of an agent of the king of Persia residing in Athens during the Peloponnesian War; they drew extensively on Thucydides at a time when there was no good English translation.

classical interests were added political history, landscape design, and art; Hardwicke published a series of State Papers from previous centuries, brought Capability Brown to Wimpole to refashion its grounds, and covered its walls with paintings.

Endeavouring to reproduce his own tastes in his nephew, he sent him to tour Holland for three months as an undergraduate, and on the Grand Tour, the usual preparation for a life as a virtuoso, after he graduated.[22] In these respects Hardwicke's prescription adhered to a common eighteenth-century aristocratic pattern, as did his comparative lack of interest in mathematics; Philip Yorke's attention to mathematics at Queens' (which in any case was not very great) seems to have owed nothing to his uncle's pressure. In contrast, Hardwicke showed an intense and unaristocratic zeal for classical learning. He did not share the gentlemanly anxiety that it should be lightly worn, or the belief that a reading knowledge of the ancient tongues was sufficient; while his ward was at Queens' Hardwicke occasionally got him to write his letters in Latin. Perhaps Hardwicke's dual concern, for both scholarship and the pursuits of a virtuoso, helped to give a schizophrenic quality to the régime he imposed. During Philip Yorke's long periods away from Cambridge he was permitted to jog along with his books, while in the term he was ordered to work unremittingly. It has to be added that no hint of irritation at his uncle's most pressing commands ever entered his letters. Philip Yorke fully accepted his uncle's role, and his.

The correspondence between uncle and nephew was sustained by the excellent horse-post that brought letters across country in a day or two. Philip Yorke wrote 400 words to Hardwicke at least once a week; and the sometimes scarcely legible replies – the quill forced across the paper by an indignant hand – came quickly too. Delay or lack of detail were reproved, and Hardwicke asked for letters in French (returning them with errors corrected), recommended books to read and lectures to attend, insisted on Philip Yorke's sending his lecture notes for checking, and required Philip to ask his permission to study Italian and to attend lectures *he* wanted, and to leave Cambridge at the end of term. He also gave his views on the direct method of teaching foreign tongues (he was

---

[22] Philip Yorke was the first member of his family to go on the Grand Tour.

against it), and was always concerned lest his hapless nephew was trying to steal a march on him, as we shall see over the vexed question of Professor Symonds's lectures. Winstanley's opinion that Hardwicke 'was an over-anxious guardian' is meiosis indeed.

In answer to an enquiry from Hardwicke, Yorke gave details of his timetable in a letter of 1 May 1774:[23]

Rise at 7: Chapel from half past seven till 8.
8 to 9. Breakfast and Demosthenes by myself: 9 to 10. Demosthenes
    with Mr Weston. 10 to 11. Classical Lecture.
11 to 12. Euclid.
        abt 3 hours & half in Morning Study.
12 to 1. Walk & dressing time.
1 to 2. Dinner and Combination Room.
2 to 3. Friends rooms.
3 to 5. Correspondence, or private reading.
From half past 5 to 6. Chapple – NB – an awkard time for Chapple.
6 to 7. Visits, Tea drinkings.
7 to 9. Xenophon & mathematics.
        5 hours Study.
9 to 11. Friends' rooms, or Company at home.

Yorke's letter concludes, 'I have sent it you as it really is, perhaps, not as it ought to be.' Hardwicke was dissatisfied with five hours of study a day, and reproved his nephew for having visited Newmarket races (even though Yorke had said that they gave him little pleasure):

I am glad to hear you have got into a regular Method of employing your Time; but am doubtful whether you employ as many Hours in Study, as you did at Harrow, & wish to know how that Matter stands. You should consider the University as a Place, where you are to lay in a Stock of Knowledge for the rest of your Life, & without a good foundation, there can be no handsome Superstructure.

As you have satisfied your Curiosity about Newmarket, I presume that you will not be in haste to make another Excursion there. The Mischief done by Gaming at that Place, is more than a Ballance for the Service it is of in the Breed of Horses. I am sorry to hear that some of the Young Men at the University keep Racers, a thing never practised in my Time.[24]

---

[23] Fols. 69–71.   [24] Fol. 75.

Though Yorke attempted a defence of his work schedule his guardian's pressure for more hours of study was repeated. In December 1774 Yorke reported that his studies took up 'I believe one day with another between six & seven without reckoning a common english book or the hour with my french Master 5 times a week.'[25] A few months later he sent a detailed timetable to Hardwicke. Like the one quoted earlier as devoting three or four hours to study in the morning, it differed from it in setting aside five hours more, instead of two, after 6.0 pm.[26]

But Philip Yorke spent his days differently when he was away from Cambridge. Coming up to Queens' in the middle of April 1774 he worked very hard till the middle of July when he went to Tittenhanger. There, he wrote, 'Mr Weston & I continue our studies though not within the walls of a college: I do not read much more than four hours a day, exclusive of such Books as Pope.'[27] Returning to Queens' towards the end of October, after a gap therefore of more than three months, he remained there continuously till 8 April 1775 (apart from a Christmas break of a week or two). He resumed residence at the beginning of May, but left again on 13 June. Towards the end of July he sailed for the Hague without Samuel Weston, for what was in effect a three-month holiday. He read Tacitus for a while with a Dr Richardson, and had some lessons in French and fencing; but for three and a half months he did little more than dine with Dutch notables and his kin and other expatriate Britons, enjoy balls and the theatre, and visit art galleries, museums, and libraries (to gaze, not read). Returning to Cambridge on 12 November, he wrote: 'I ... do not find that the agreable and different manner in which I have passed my vacation, has given me any distaste to study, but rather hope that it will become more agreable by the contrast.'[28] The pattern of residence resumed. Hardwicke would not allow him to leave for Tittenhanger till 22 December, and after his usual lighter holiday stint Yorke came back to Queens' about four weeks later. For the next five months Yorke studied hard with just a fortnight's break in April, until he finally left Cambridge in July; thus his graduation in May was not a terminus to effort as it most certainly

[25] Fol. 143.   [26] Fol. 153.   [27] Fol. 99.   [28] Fol. 226.

is for current students. On the other hand Yorke had no examinations to pass.[29]

In May 1774 Hardwicke wrote: 'I should be glad to know who the young men are, with whom you converse chiefly; & whether you have made any Acquaintance with Mr. Hyde & his Brother[30] of St John's; They have both very good Characters'.[31] 'My acquaintances are but few,' replied Yorke, mentioning several names; 'these are very genteel men but there are some of this College whom I should be extremely sorry to be acquainted with, any more than being civil to them'.[32] Hardwicke's concern nevertheless continued: Yorke was anxious to reassure him about his friends' gentle status, the chief of them being Ponsonby of Trinity, Lord Bessborough's nephew, 'a very sensible young man, & a good Scholar'.[33]

PHILIP YORKE'S PLEASURES

Yorke's pleasures were restrained: 'I usually spend my idle time in fishing, walking, or playing at Bowls, riding sometimes, & when it is too hot for any of these, I read some Book.'[34] (Yorke read much English poetry, and was fond of a now-forgotten blank-verse epic, *Leonidas* by Richard Glover.) He also took up fencing, and one winter he skated along the river to Ely. Once, he managed to go to the assizes ball at Hertford. He was among many undergraduates in enjoying riding.[35] Contemporary with him in Cambridge was a horse-keeper called James Barrow, who between 1773 and 1786 made £3,000 by letting and selling horses to students. The prices for horses ranged from £18 to £120, and the hiring fees varied too, from 4s 6d for 'a common ride' to £1 5s for fox and stag hunting; a ride on 'the hills' (presumably the Gogs) cost 10s 6d, and hire for a day at Newmarket twice as much. Riding was clearly a pastime for the rich. University authorities were uneasy about the pursuit, regarding it as likely to cause indiscipline; the abortive 'Orders and

[29] Fol. 306.
[30] Thomas Villiers Hyde was the eldest son of Baron Hyde, and was admitted to St John's as a nobleman in 1771. (It is not clear why he called himself 'Hyde' rather than by his family name of Villiers.) He graduated MA in 1773, which Hardwicke does not seem to have been aware of. His younger brother John Villiers was admitted to St John's as a fellow commoner in 1774
[31] Fol. 75.   [32] Fol. 78.   [33] Fol. 261.   [34] Fol. 86.
[35] Much of what follows is based on Christopher Wordsworth, *Social Life*, pp. 140–80.

Regulations' of 1750 proposed to forbid it. The driving of carriages was more frowned on, as liable to cause congestion and disorder in Cambridge's narrow streets: in 1798 it was prohibited by a decree reinforced in 1807. As to another of Yorke's pleasures, fishing, Gunning, who was at Cambridge a few years after Yorke, remarks: 'I do not think there were ten men in the University who were regular anglers'; but perhaps many fished occasionally, in view of the pleasures he describes:

> A very common practice, during the spring and summer months, was for a party to divide into two sets, one on a shooting scheme, and the other on a boating and fishing expedition, both parties agreeing to meet and dine at Clayhithe. There was a public-house on each side of the river,[36] where fish were dressed to perfection; the charges were very moderate, and the ALE very good. The fishing-party (who frequently went as far as Upware, and occasionally to Dimmock's Court) scarcely ever failed to get an abundance of fish.[37]

In contrast, George Pryme states that mere rowing, in the modern sense, 'was not then the custom'.[38]

Yorke occasionally visited a coffee house between 4 and 5 in the afternoon.[39] They had been popular in Cambridge for over a century. William Paley, at Cambridge a decade before Yorke, used to attend Dockerell's in Trumpington Street, where MAs used to occupy the upper floor and undergraduates the lower.[40] Dockerell would set up a temporary house at Stourbridge Fair and sell excellent milk punch there. There was a coffee house specially for reading men, the 'Caryophylli', and perhaps this was the one Yorke went to. Another, opened next to Emmanuel College in 1763, offered a pleasant garden, lessons, and conversation practice in foreign tongues, particularly French, and pictures on the walls to encourage 'Innocency and Virtue by exposing Vice and the Folly of Intemperance'; though strong drink was served, the Emmanuel coffee house concentrated on 'harmless Tea, Lacedemonian Broth, and invigorating Chocolate, comforting Cakes with cooling Tarts and Jellies, &c.'[41] This house does not seem to have lasted very long.

---

[36] One remains, on the west bank. Clayhithe is five miles from the centre of Cambridge.
[37] *Reminiscences*, vol. I, pp. 42–3 and 116.   [38] Pryme, *Autobiographic Recollections*, p. 43.
[39] Fol. 153.   [40] Meadley, *Memoirs of William Paley* 1st edn, (1809), p. 12.
[41] Cooper, *Annals*, IV, pp. 328–9.

In contrast, the Union coffee house in Bridge Street, opposite the Round Church, existed for at least fourteen years from 1788.[42] It is described in a set of tripos verses from that year. Among the company were a parson looking in the newspapers for vacancies, a questionist waiting for tomorrow's 'act' and drawing mathematical diagrams on the table with a spill, a 'lounger' wearing a large old-fashioned wig and playing with a toothpick, a dissolute riding-man talking of horses, and two sportsmen boasting of nights spent in the Fens otterhunting. The rednosed landlord watches the company keenly from among his mugs. Eventually its less reputable members go off to the Bear Tavern (where Whewell's Court of Trinity now stands).[43]

Taverns and alehouses were often the location of student rowdiness, of course, and the most celebrated disturbance of the eighteenth century occurred in the Tuns Tavern in 1750. The occasion was the annual meeting of the Westminster Club, for old boys of the school (dons as well as undergraduates) who met on 17 November to celebrate the anniversary of the accession of their foundress, Queen Elizabeth. Trouble with the Proctors and the Vice-Chancellor followed, and became a Cambridge *cause célèbre*.[44]

Such an association, and its counterpart the Charterhouse Club, necessarily had a long life. More transient were clubs like the one founded in the 1790s by Henry Champneys, whose career as a fellow commoner of Christ's, supported by 'a liberal allowance from a fond and indulgent mother', was very different from Philip Yorke's; when Champneys took his nobleman's degree the Public Orator, instead of complimenting him, censured his dissipated habits. His club had twelve members,

> and they adopted a most remarkable livery. The coat, I remember, was of bright green, lined and bound with buff silk, with buttons made expressly, and upon which *Sans Souci* was elegantly engraved; the waistcoat, curiously adorned with frogs, was buff, with knee-breeches of the same colour.
>
> The members met at each other's rooms one evening of the week, when they played for very high stakes; also they dined

---

[42] Its premises were swept away when the new chapel of St John's was built in the 1860s.
[43] Christopher Wordsworth, *Social Life*, pp. 141–2; Pryme, *Autobiographic Recollections*, p. 43.
[44] See chapter 11, pp. 395–7.

together once a month, when each member was allowed to invite a friend; and in conclusion, they had a grand anniversary.[45]

At the end of the century, George Pryme recalled, there was a True Blue Club, a hard-drinking group of Trinity men whose name suited its apparel and its principles. Very different was the 'Speculative', named after an Edinburgh debating society, and consisting of twenty members.[46]

These diversions continued into the following century, but shooting, though popular with many in the eighteenth century, did not last into the next. Gunning had a passion for shooting wildfowl in the Fens near Cambridge:

> you met with great varieties of wildfowl, bitterns, plovers of every description, ruffs and reeves, and not unfrequently pheasants. If you did not go very near the mansions of the few country gentlemen who resided in the neighbourhood, you met with no interruption. You scarcely ever saw the gamekeeper, but met with a great number of young lads, who were on the look-out for sportsmen from the University, whose game they carried, and to whom they furnished long poles, to enable them to leap those very ditches which intersected the Fens in every direction.[47]

When Gunning reminisced in the 1850s, however, the Fens were drained and the wildfowl had departed.

YORKE'S STUDIES AT CAMBRIDGE

Yorke's course of study was quite unlike that required for the Senate House Examination. Coming up knowing very little of mathematics, he did not add dramatically to his knowledge at Queens'. By the end of June 1774 the end of Euclid's first book was in sight; 'but there still remains the hardest proposition, the forty seventh, which is by far more difficult, than any in the book. I begin to find that Euclid improves my attention and will I fancy be of great service to me in that respect.'[48] By August, after a vacation in which Euclid was ignored, he was getting into the second book, as Weston wanted, but wrote with an air of wonderment 'the first book is for

---

[45] Gunning, *Reminiscences*, vol. II, pp. 152–4.   [46] Pryme, *Autobiographic Recollections*, p. 117.
[47] *Reminiscences*, vol. I, p. 41.   [48] Fol.89. The 47th proposition is Pythagoras' theorem.

the most part about triangles, the next about squares & four sided figures: & the third seems to be about circles, but of this last I know nothing at present'.[49] His study of geometry in fact took up little of his time and progress was slow. In May 1775 Yorke wrote 'I have begun Saunderson's Algebra with Mr Weston and shall go thro' those parts of it which he thinks immediately useful. I must own I am rather slower at Mathematics than I expected.' But other studies were 'equally useful, & more entertaining'.[50] Since mathematics was not pressed by Hardwicke it is not surprising that Yorke's study of it petered out, though probably he learned enough to gain an ordinary degree in the Senate House Examination had he taken it.

About half Yorke's time was spent doggedly working through, with Mr Weston's constant help, the list of classical authors insisted on by his guardian Hardwicke. It was slanted towards preparing him for a statesman's career. In addition to the historians Thucydides, Xenophon, Tacitus, and Sallust he read the orators and rhetoricians, Demosthenes, Cicero, and Quintilian. Among modern works he studied Montesquieu and Voltaire's *Louis XIV*; and in English, Eachard's history, More's *Utopia*, Locke (which Weston helped him to understand), and volumes in law by Sullivan and Blackstone. On Sundays, again with Weston by his side, he read Burnet's *de fide Christiano*, Beattie on truth, Barrow's sermons, and Butler's *Analogy*, the famous defence of Christianity against the eighteenth-century deists that was studied by many generations of Cambridge undergraduates. Yorke critically remarked: it 'seems to require a tolerable share of attention both to understand & retain: we have made but a small progress in it so I am not a judge of it by any means; his stile appears rather rough & unharmonious'.[51] No imaginative modern literature was prescribed, save for Boileau's *Satires*, so favoured as an arbiter of taste by Augustan critics, and Voltaire's *La Henriade*, an epic poem on the career of Henry of Navarre. Among the tragedies that we think of as pre-eminent in classical literature Yorke read only one, and that in English, West's translation of *Iphigenia in Tauris*.

The official college teaching played little part in Yorke's life at Queens', competing as it did with so many demands on his energies.

---

[49] Fol. 101.   [50] Fol. 177.   [51] Fol. 236.

By contrast, he gave much time to the lectures of two university professors, John Symonds and Samuel Hallifax, whom he started to hear in November 1774. Of Symonds' first three lectures he wrote:

> the first was merely introductory, in which Dr. S. gave some account of history in general, and recommended a method of reading it: he explained the great use it was of, & shewed in some measure the plan he intended to follow: in the second he gave an account of the four empires, and in the third he expatiated considerably on the Roman: I am impatient for him to begin upon modern history which he takes up at the time of Charlemagne. He pronounces his lectures without book, & has a few notes lying before him to refresh his memory: his manner is slow and his pronunciation very affected, both which circumstances are a disadvantage, and make many people dislike the lectures, which is unjust, as they are very clever in themselves.
>
> Dr Hallifax began with giving an account of the civil law & then explains each article in the same order as they are in the syllabus. He reads his lectures from manuscript, but with such rapidity that it is impossible to take down notes: however his manner and voice are pleasing, & there is as much propriety in his reading, as in anybody that I ever heard. I am afraid I shall not be able to take so many notes at his as at Dr Symonds' lectures.[52]

For more than a year – until in fact shortly before he took his degree – Yorke attended or was otherwise concerned with these lecture courses. In their several ways they gave him much trouble, despite the professors' expressed willingness to help him privately with difficulties, and his going to their lectures for a second round. In Michaelmas 1775 he breathed a sigh of relief when Hallifax cancelled his sessions to preach at Lincoln's Inn, 'for I fill up the omissions that were unavoidably made last year, & by that means shall make my notes tolerably perfect'.[53] His notes on Symonds also caused problems. He wrote as he laboured over them at Tittenhanger on New Year's Eve:

> The Lectures upon the Saracens have retarded me considerably, for there are many parts of them that I cannot make out so that I think it better to pass them over till I can get some light into them either from other notes that have been taken or from the Professor himself;

[52] Fols. 131–2.   [53] Fol. 236.

and proceed with the lectures that are farther on when I can go on more smoothly both from their being more interested [*sic*] in themselves, & from my being more acquainted with the subject.[54]

In the middle of February 1776 his lecture notes were still giving acute anxiety. For the previous three weeks, he wrote,

> I have given about two hours a day to the decyphering my notes from Dr Symon's [*sic*] Lectures, & have transcribed at the rate of above twenty pages per week. I shall send them to your Lordship in about ten days, by which time I hope to have written a very handsome quantity. I believe Dr Symon's Audience is much the same as to numbers this Course, as it was the last. He has about five or six & twenty names on his list, and of those there are fifteen or sixteen who attend regularly. I have not been able to procure any assistance from my acquaintance who attend those Lectures, for there are scarcely any who have taken any Notes at all, & those who have, have done it in so desultory a manner that they cannot make out anything from them. I have still got twelve or fourteen Lectures of Dr Hallifax to transcribe, viz. those upon the different Courts where the civil law is now in use; but I meant to stay till he came to that part again which he will do in a few months, that I might have them more complete.[55]

Perhaps there was a worthwhile increment in understanding as a result of this feverish activity, but we may doubt it since it was undertaken to provide Hardwicke with the full record he exacted. The Saracens gave Yorke as much bother as they did to Richard the Lionheart. When in March Yorke sent his notes, Hardwicke scrutinised them carefully and suspected his nephew of using a crib 'abridgement' to fill the gap. In several lengthy replies Yorke was driven to explain how he had used respectable and detailed histories as aids, endeavouring it seems to conceal the fact that his attention, and others', had strayed during Symonds's sessions.

In this dutiful record few paragraphs suggest real intellectual excitement. In Lent 1776, however, he attended the college lectures on astronomy given by Isaac Milner, the new tutor, and was 'extremely well pleased with Mr Milner's manner of giving them: his method is reckoned very judicious & his way of explaining

---

[54] Fol. 246.   [55] Fols. 267–8.

himself is so clear & intelligible that it is scarcely possible not to comprehend his meaning'.[56] Reinforcing his understanding by daily sessions with the faithful Weston, he reported: 'I assure your Lordship I have been more entertained with the Study than with anything of the Sort that I have ever gone through.'[57] In the Easter Term Milner was lecturing on optics, which Yorke found almost as 'entertaining' as astronomy,

> for though the Elementary parts are not so amusing as those of Astronomy, yet one becomes acquainted with the principles of several things that are of daily observation, and is able to account for common appearances. I was highly pleased with the dissection of an Eye... Superior contrivance is nowhere more fully displayed than in the different humours ... of the Eye.[58]

Shortly afterwards Philip Yorke took his degree – his guardian complaining at the expense – and some weeks later he left Cambridge.

Yorke's connection with the university did not end in the summer of 1776; he became High Steward in 1806, and LLD in 1811. These were episodes in a distinguished career, in which he displayed a temperament different from his uncle, whom he succeeded as third earl in 1790. He was active politically, first following Fox but from 1794 onwards (like so many Whigs) supporting Pitt. For six years till the death of Pitt he was Lord Lieutenant of Ireland, quietening the discontent produced by the Act of Union of 1801, and becoming himself converted to the cause of Catholic Emancipation.

His chief claim on posterity's regard, however, is his artistic sensibility, and in particular his patronage of John Soane. While in Italy surveying antiquities he wrote to his uncle in January 1779, describing a recent expedition to Paestum: 'The three temples... are magnificent buildings and I was astonished to find how perfect they are. An English architect by name Soane who is an ingenious young man now studying at Rome accompanied me thither and measured the buildings.'[59] Soane was then largely unknown, and

---

[56] Fol. 275.   [57] Fol. 288.   [58] Fol. 298.
[59] Quoted in Dorothy Stroud, *Sir John Soane, Architect* (London, Faber, 1984), pp. 36–7; from this source comes much of what follows. See also Souden, *Wimpole Hall*, pp. 29–34.

most of his plans, such as those for Ickworth, had come to little. Philip Yorke was only twenty-two, and his discernment of Soane's promise suggests that his aesthetic judgement had been developed by his classical education. In the 1780s Soane designed alterations to Yorke's Hertfordshire house, Hamels – plans in which Soane introduced the elements he later elaborated at Wimpole. These Soane was commissioned to undertake in 1790, as soon as Yorke became Earl of Hardwicke. They included such ventures in opulent neo-classicism as the Yellow Drawing Room, with its look of the Villa Madama that Raphael had built in Rome, and an essay in the aristocratic pastoral, the Wimpole Model Farm, which Philip Yorke's study of Theocritus at Harrow may have helped to originate.

Philip Yorke's degree course was exceptional. For the great majority the route to the BA was the mathematical tests in the Senate House. How these were regarded by two students in the late eighteenth century, the brothers William and Christopher Wordsworth, is one theme of the following pages.

WILLIAM WORDSWORTH

WORDSWORTH AT HAWKSHEAD AND ST JOHN'S

> It was a dreary morning when the chaise
> Rolled over the flat plains of Huntingdon
> And through the open windows first I saw
> The long-backed chapel of King's College rear
> His pinnacles above the dusky groves.
> Soon afterwards we espied upon the road
> A student clothed in gown and tasselled cap;
> He passed – nor was I master of my eyes
> Till he was left a hundred yards behind.
> The place as we approached seemed more and more
> To have an eddy's force, and sucked us in
> More eagerly at every step we took.
> Onward we drove beneath the castle, down
> By Magdalene Bridge we went and crossed the Cam,
> And at the Hoop we landed, famous inn.[60]

[60] William Wordsworth, *The Prelude*, 1805 text, Book Third, ll. 1–15.

With these lines William Wordsworth recalled, eighteen years later, his journey to Cambridge on 30 October 1787, aged seventeen, to be admitted as an undergraduate at St John's College. The Third, Fourth, and Fifth books of *The Prelude* are his reflections upon his sojourn at Cambridge, and testimony unique from a major English poet.[61] Exceptional too is the diary of residence at Trinity in 1793–4 compiled by his younger brother Christopher. The brothers' differing reactions to Cambridge are the theme of the next two sections.

In 1779, after their mother's death, William (aged nine) and Christopher (aged five), became pupils at Hawkshead Grammar School, boarding with Mrs Ann Tyson in her cottage.[62] Especially after their father died in 1783 it was effectively their home, and Ann Tyson a new mother, to whom Wordsworth paid loving tribute in *The Prelude*. From her he heard stories of the ordinary people in the locality that later were to nourish his poems of common life, while his adventures on the hills and Lake Coniston with his school friends found a place in *The Prelude*. Hawkshead helped to shape his life, and the school prepared him well for academic work at Cambridge. In this respect, it is worth noting, it was an above-average but not unique grammar school: since Hawkshead was typical of some other institutions responsible for preparing young men for Cambridge we may assume that his experiences at university were like others' too, however unique his utterance. Hawkshead had about 100 pupils, most of them boarders, and four or five assistant masters.[63] In Wordsworth's time there were four headmasters: James Peake (1766–81), Edward Christian (1781–2),[64] William Taylor (1782–6), and Thomas Bowman (1786–1829; he had been usher from 1784).[65] All had Cambridge degrees, and all save Peake had high honours and fellowships, the three men being respectively Third, Second, and Sixth Wrangler. Taylor and

---

[61] It may be compared with John Betjeman's account of his Oxford years in *Summoned by Bells* (London, 1960).

[62] This paragraph draws upon Stephen Gill, *William Wordsworth. A Life* (Oxford University Press, 1989), pp. 14–36.

[63] See appendix IV, 'Hawkshead Grammar School and the New Library', in T. W. Thompson, *Wordsworth's Hawkshead*, edited by Robert Woof (Oxford University Press, 1970), pp. 342–3.

[64] Brother of the *Bounty* mutineer Fletcher Christian, and later a famous Cambridge lawyer.

[65] The entry in Venn and Venn, *Alumni Cantabrigienses* confuses Thomas Bowman with an Oxford namesake, but plainly he was the headmaster of Hawkshead.

Bowman were enthusiasts for English literature and Bowman in particular seems to have introduced Wordsworth to many books, in this way strengthening the taste for reading to which he gave much time and energy when he was an undergraduate. Bowman's son many years later recalled Wordsworth's debt to his father:

> it was books he wanted, all sorts of books; Tours and Travels, which my father was partial to, and Histories and Biographies, which were also favourites with him; and Poetry – that goes without saying. My father used to get the latest books from Kendal every month, and I remember him telling how he lent Wordsworth Cowper's 'Task' when it first came out, and Burns' 'Poems' ... my father also introduced him to Langhorne's poems and Beattie's 'Minstrel' & Percy's 'Reliques', and ... it was in books or periodic works my father lent him that he first became acquainted with the poetry of Crabbe & Charlotte Smith & the two Wartons.[66]

The formal instruction at the school was excellent, as Stephen Gill comments:

> unlike in many other schools, a good grounding did not mean wearisome rote learning and exercises in verse composition in Latin and Greek. Wordsworth was taught in a humane way, to judge from this recollection: 'Before I read Virgil I was so strongly attached to Ovid, whose *Metamorphoses* I read at school, that I was quite in a passion whenever I found him, in books of criticism, placed below Virgil. As to Homer I was never weary of travelling over the scenes through which he led me. Classical literature affected me by its own beauty.'[67]

More important as apprenticeship for honours at Cambridge was the very high quality of the mathematical instruction at Hawkshead. Taylor and Bowman, the headmasters with most influence on the school in Wordsworth's day, knew the demands of the Cambridge degree course intimately, and prepared their pupils expertly for it. From the three or four men that went up to Cambridge from Hawkshead each year there were, between 1789 and 1793, five who were Tenth Wrangler or higher, including one Senior Wrangler and one Second. Wordsworth admitted that 'I had a full twelve-

---

[66] Quoted in T. W. Thompson, *Wordsworth's Hawkshead*, p. 344.
[67] *William Wordsworth*, p. 27. Wordsworth's words are a note to the *Ode to Lycoris*.

month's start of the freshmen of my year.'[68] At school he immersed himself in Newton's ideas enthusiastically. In 1885 the son of Wordsworth's headmaster recalled a story that his father used to tell him about Wordsworth. His father left Wordsworth

> in his study once for what he thought would only be a minute or two, telling him to be looking for another book in place of the one he had brought back. As it happened he was kept half an hour or more by one of the school tenants. When he got back, there was W. poring over a book, so absorbed in it he did not notice my father's return. And 'what do you think it was' my father would say, or 'you'll never guess what it was'. It was Newton's 'Optics'. And that was the book Wordsworth was for borrowing next.[69]

That Wordsworth's mathematical record at Cambridge was disappointing was not the fault of the grounding he had been given at school.

It was natural for Wordsworth to enter St John's, where he was a sizar. Hawkshead Grammar School had been founded by a Johnian, Archbishop Sandys, and there were sundry scholarships and prizes at the college for Cumbrian boys.[70] When Wordsworth went up his uncle, William Cookson, and his old headmaster, Edward Christian, were both fellows, and might be expected to help him. Cookson filled the Cumberland slot in the fellowship, but was likely soon to vacate it on marriage (as indeed he did in 1788). Wordsworth might reasonably hope to succeed him in his county place, if he became a wrangler. He would be able to use the stipend to study for the legal profession, which we know he was thinking of entering as he went up to Cambridge.[71] Christian, a lawyer, could be relied on for support; as it happened he was then appearing for the Wordsworth family in their lawsuit against Lord Lonsdale for the payment of a debt.[72]

[68] Quoted in Ben Ross Schneider, *Wordsworth's Cambridge Education* (Cambridge University Press, 1956), p. 5.

[69] T. W. Thompson, *Wordsworth's Hawkshead*, p. 344.

[70] What follows is based on Schneider, *Wordsworth's Cambridge Education*, pp. 1–17, and Mary Moorman, *William Wordsworth. The Early Years 1770–1803*, corrected 1st edn (Oxford University Press, 1965), pp. 90–2, 123–4.

[71] Ernest de Selincourt and Chester L. Shaver, eds., *The Letters of William and Dorothy Wordsworth: Vol. I, The Early Years 1787–1805*, 2nd edn (Oxford University Press, 1967), letters 1 and 2, pp. 4 and 7.

[72] Wordsworth's father was Lonsdale's agent in Cockermouth. On his death his children applied to Lonsdale for £4,500 that he was found to owe their patrimony. The claim was not settled till 1804,

Wordsworth needed a fellowship for financial security. He was an orphan, and had no independent means or prospects of them. Nor did his four siblings, apart from the eldest, Richard (b. 1768), who would inherit the small family estate at Sockbridge, near Penrith. For the costs of his education William was dependent on his uncles. His position was unenviable, and they did not make it easier. In December 1790 his Uncle Christopher wrote to his nephew Richard: 'I am sorry to say that I think your Brot. William very extravagant. He has had very near £300 since he went to Cambridge which I think is a very shameful sum for him to spend, considering his expectations.'[73] By this time his uncle knew that William was not taking honours and that his expectations were indeed meagre. But William was hardly spendthrift, given the cost of Cambridge residence. From his uncles he had just over £100 a year, and there was in addition about £20 each year from a Foundress's scholarship that his tutor, Frewen, gained for him, no doubt because of his knowledge of Euclid, within a week of his arrival. Wordsworth owed money to his tutor, James Wood, when he went down, and £10 was still outstanding in 1803.

Two boys had come up from Hawkshead Grammar School to St John's in 1786, a year before Wordsworth: his close friend John Fleming, and William Penny. Another came up with him and two others came up in 1789. Other Hawkshead pupils senior to Wordsworth were at other colleges. Most of these ex-schoolfellows were achieving academic distinction, showing Wordsworth what might be gained if their school's intellectual inheritance were exploited with hard work. Wordsworth did not lack for friends at Cambridge, despite *The Prelude*'s sentiment that solitude enhanced his consciousness of his mission to poetry. Like most undergraduates many friends were from his own college. With one, Robert Jones, he went on his Alpine walking tour in the Long Vacation of 1790; they remained intimate friends throughout life. Other Cambridge acquaintances were at Pembroke, and they included a man from Hawkshead Grammar School, William Raincock.

by Lonsdale's family: see Stephen Gill, *William Wordsworth*, pp. 34–5. For Lonsdale's very similar treatment of James Wood, tutor of St John's, see chapter 4, above.
[73] The quotation is taken from Moorman, *Early Years*, p. 124.

In his first-term college examination[74] Wordsworth gave promise of high honours if he worked hard. The examination was on portions of Horace and Xenophon, and some theology; he was placed in the first class. The examination of June 1788 concerned the first three books of Euclid, plus some algebra, and Tacitus' *De Moribus Germanorum*. From a freshman group of 40, 10 did not present themselves, while 14 got firsts, 4 seconds, and 12 thirds. For Wordsworth, with extensive natural talent that had been well cultivated at Hawkshead, a first in the college examinations (plainly not such a great achievement as it is now) would have been attainable without exorbitant effort. But he gained a second – a very lacklustre result. At the end of 1788 he sank even further, being unclassed since he did not complete the mathematical examination while doing well in the classical part; the prescribed reading for it was Sophocles' *Oedipus Coloneus*. In the spring of 1789 he was unclassed again. He did not attempt the examination in mechanics (levers, inclined planes, friction, and so on) but did well, the examiners reported, 'in the classic'; this was to do with the twenty-first book of Livy's *History of Rome*, which concerned Hannibal's invasion of Italy.

By this time indeed Wordsworth had decided (if that does not give too precise an impression of the mental process involved) not to read for honours – a conclusion that put paid to the family's hopes for a fellowship and without doubt caused disappointment to them. In his detailed scrutiny of Wordsworth's spurning of honours B. R. Schneider gives great weight to the allegedly repellent atmosphere of the university. 'Cambridge men habitually conducted their affairs', he writes, with 'unprincipled expediency'; while Wordsworth's northern origins and accent, and his lowly status in the collegiate hierarchy as a sizar, exposed him to insult. The absurd exaggeration in the first statement makes us uneasy, as does the thinness of the corroboration offered for the second – none of which in fact concerns Wordsworth himself. (Schneider also asserts elsewhere that at that time it was a positive *advantage* in Cambridge to come from the North.)[75] He also manipulates evidence from *The Prelude*, taking criticism of Cambridge at face value but averring that

---

[74] What follows draws on Schneider, *Wordsworth's Cambridge Education*, pp. 28, 95–6, 105–6.
[75] Pp. 6–7, 24, 40–1.

Wordsworth could not really have meant certain lines of praise.[76] Mary Moorman's briefer account[77] of the Cambridge years is far more balanced and perceptive.

The first version of Wordsworth's autobiographical poem was completed, though not published, in 1799. He was then twenty-nine, and had contributed the major share of a slim and anonymously published volume, *Lyrical Ballads*.[78] But he had no reliable income and, an observer might think, no talent to acquire one. Nevertheless, the poem's purpose was to demonstrate that he had a vocation to become a great poet, and that his dominant experiences – childhood, schooling, awakenings to Nature and religion – confirmed this calling and deepened his understanding of it. This teleological design remained through successive modifications of the utterance, to thirteen books in 1805, and fourteen by 1839.[79] As perhaps need not be said at length, *The Prelude* was not planned as a chronicle of a life's externality; it stands at the other extreme from, say, that most banal record of a university career, James Woodforde's diary of his years at New College, Oxford.[80] To assist the strategy of *The Prelude*, there is much compression of events and time; the three and a half years at Cambridge are treated in 800 lines, and much less is said about the later terms than the first. Still, *The Prelude* gives us the subtle responses to Cambridge of a highly intelligent and imaginative man who was well prepared for academic life, yet found it sadly wanting in some respects while fulfilling in others.

Wordsworth's first impressions were of the colour, variety, and fascination of Cambridge life at the start of a new academic year:

> I was the Dreamer, they the Dream; I roamed
> Delighted through the motley spectacle;
> Gowns grave, or gaudy, doctors, students, streets,
> Courts, cloisters, flocks of churches, gateways, towers:

[76] Pp. 48–50.   [77] Mary Moorman, *Early Years*, pp. 86–127.
[78] For this paragraph, see Gill, *William Wordsworth*, pp. 1–10.
[79] The poem was not published until 1850, immediately after Wordsworth's death, being given by his widow and executors the title by which it is known, *The Prelude: Growth of a Poet's Mind*. Cambridge is mentioned first in the 1805 version.
[80] W. N. Hargreaves-Mawdsley, ed., *Woodforde at Oxford 1759–1776* (Oxford Historical Society, new series, 21, 1969).

> Migration strange for a stripling of the hills,
> A northern villager.[81]

Welcomed by the other students around him, Wordsworth was loaded with 'Questions, directions, warnings and advice'. Imagining himself 'A man of business and expense', he visited shop after shop, buying 'splendid garb, with hose of silk', and a 'lordly dressing gown' – 'signs of manhood that supplied\ The lack of beard'. In those hectic first weeks there were 'invitations, suppers, wine and fruit'. But in view of the frugal character that we know Wordsworth's years at St John's possessed, we should beware of exaggerating the expense of these early weeks; he was no free-spending aristocrat.

His room was in the first court of St John's, and as befitted someone on a stringent budget was 'a nook obscure' above the kitchens, whence came

> A humming sound, less tuneable than bees
> But hardly less industrious, with shrill notes
> Of sharp command and scolding intermixed.[82]

Nearby was Trinity's clock, chiming insistently every quarter-hour and signalling each hour lengthily, 'with a male and female voice'. But also nearby was Trinity chapel, which Wordsworth could see from his window. Inside was the statue of his hero Isaac Newton

> with his prism and silent face,
> The marble index of a mind for ever
> Voyaging through strange seas of Thought, alone.[83]

The statue may be regarded as a symbol of what Wordsworth most admired about Cambridge. He very quickly came to despise the competitive teaching and examination process which, in Wordsworth's day, was what Newton's thought had been brought to serve. In the crowded college undergraduates were prepared for

> Examinations, when the man was weighed
> As in a balance! of excessive hopes,
> Tremblings withal and commendable fears,

---

[81] *The Prelude* 1850, Book Third, ll. 30–5.   [82] 1850, Book Third, ll. 50–2.
[83] Ll. 61–3. We may compare the veneration for 'Euclid's Elements' expressed in Book Fifth, ll. 71–140. Note that it does not say, as it sometimes assumed, that he could see the *statue*. It would have been invisible from his window.

Small jealousies, and triumphs good or bad...
Such glory was but little sought by me,
And little won.[84]

Wordsworth's momentous decision to abjure honours is thus very quickly mentioned in *The Prelude*. Fortunately we have some other words of his that reveal his dislike of intellectual competitiveness (which he termed 'emulation'). At Cambridge there was just one occasion when he felt envy. 'This once was in the study of Italian, which I entered on at College along with—I was his superior in many departments of mind, but he was the better Italian scholar, and I envied him.' Wordsworth added: 'The annoyance this gave me made me feel that emulation was dangerous for *me*, and it made me very thankful that as a boy I never experienced it. I felt very early the force of the words "Be ye perfect as your Father in heaven is perfect".'[85] Wordsworth felt guilty because he disappointed his family's ambitions for a fellowship, but he did not renounce his decision. He took an ordinary degree in January 1791. Unfortunately we know nothing of the labours it entailed, although we have his nephew's authority for believing that in the previous week he read Richardson's *Clarissa*.[86]

The contrast between Wordsworth's scorn for the mathematical examination and his reverence for the natural philosophy that underlay it, reflected his attitudes towards Cambridge as a whole. Such ambivalence has perhaps always been usual among sensitive alumni, especially since the 'mathematisation' of the university sharpened its competitive ethos and opened up so many opportunities for the ambitious. Despite his Anglicanism he had a great dislike of compulsory chapel.[87] He was also very critical of dons, most of whom had no tutorial or other affective contact with undergraduates. The 'grave elders' were

men unscoured,[88] grotesque
In character, tricked out like aged trees

---

[84] 1850, Book Third, ll. 69–75.   [85] These words are quoted in Moorman, *Early Years*, p. 56.
[86] Christopher Wordsworth, *Memoirs of William Wordsworth*, vol. 1, p. 48.
[87] *The Prelude* 1805, Book Third, ll. 416–25. He still declared his dislike in the revised version of 1838–9, even though he was then a determined Conservative and his brother was Master of Trinity, and much berated for his insistence on compulsory chapel.
[88] A puzzling word. Perhaps Wordsworth meant that they were dirty, or unbrushed, or untidy.

> Which through the lapse of their infirmity
> Give ready place to any random seed
> That chuses to be reared upon their trunks.[89]

He denounced Cambridge itself for its

> Feuds, factions, flatteries, enmity and guile;
> Murmuring submission, and bald government.[90]

Yet disarmingly Wordsworth adds that

> Of these and other kindred notices
> I cannot say what portion is in truth
> The naked recollection of that time,
> And what may rather have been called to life
> By after-meditation.[91]

And we should also take into account Wordsworth's confession that

> Of many debts which afterwards I owed
> To Cambridge and an academic life,
> That something there was holden up to view
> Of a republic, where all stood thus far
> Upon equal ground, that they were brothers all
> In honour, as of one community –
> Scholars and gentlemen – where, furthermore,
> Distinction lay open to all that came,
> And wealth and titles were in less esteem
> Than talents and successful industry.[92]

Another contradiction that persists in *The Prelude* is within Wordsworth's character and inclinations. One impulse led to the convivial life, in which he and his companions talked in the small hours, drifted through Cambridge streets, read trivial books, and spent their energies in galloping through the countryside or sailing on the river.[93] But, Wordsworth claims, he did not communicate to his friends his 'deeper pleasures ... *Caverns* there were within my mind which sun\ Could never penetrate.'[94] The more he mixed, too, the more he became aware of 'dissolute pleasure' that he had no

---

[89] *The Prelude* 1805, Book Third, ll. 574–8. The words are little changed in the 1850 text.
[90] 1850, Book Third, ll. 604–5.   [91] 1850, Book Third, ll. 612–16.
[92] 1805, Book Ninth, ll. 227–36. The sentiments remain in the later text. This is the passage which Schneider maintains Wordsworth could not have meant.
[93] See 1850, Book Third, ll. 251–8.   [94] Ll. 238–47.

desire to indulge in.[95] Another inclination was for ruminative solitude, for example evening walks along the Backs near St John's, 'through hours of silence'.[96] Such pleasures are presented as morally superior, or at least as more creatively fruitful, since they led to the communion with Nature that strengthened his vocation as a poet. Wordsworth's several reservations about Cambridge student life encourage us to envisage him as set apart from his fellow students by consciousness of his calling to poetry (and perhaps by a priggish sense of rectitude). But an anonymous writer in the *Gentleman's Magazine* for March 1794, recollecting that he had 'seen him once or twice while I was his contemporary at Cambridge', gave an impression of someone gregarious and fully engaged with the society about him: 'The only time indeed, that I have a clear recollection of having met him, I remember his speaking very highly in praise of the beauties of the North; with a warmth indeed which at the time appeared to me hardly short of enthusiasm.'[97] Perhaps we may conclude that Wordsworth appeared to his Cambridge contemporaries to be more like them than is implied in *The Prelude*: and that his response to the university – even the oscillation between solitude and conviviality which is after all common with undergraduates today – was far more typical than for special reasons he later encouraged us to believe.

WORDSWORTH AND CAMBRIDGE'S INFORMAL CURRICULUM

Eighteenth-century Cambridge offered men of talent only one way to shine in university examinations, but it allowed them to devise entirely independent courses of study if they wished. Such permissiveness seems today like neglect (perhaps not even 'benign neglect') and antipathetic to the purpose of a university, but Wordsworth argues tentatively for the creative potentiality of the freedom the university offered. After the first-year decision not to attempt honours he passed some months in 'loose indifference . . . duty and

---

[95] 1805, Book Third, ll. 535–9. He warns against 'unworthy pleasures or pursuits' in a letter of March 1804 to Thomas de Quincey, who had just gone up to Oxford: de Selincourt and Shaver, *Letters . . . Early Years*, pp. 453–4.   [96] 1850, Book Sixth, ll. 68–72.

[97] Quoted in Moorman, *Early Years*, p. 91. The review appears to be the only independent witness to Wordsworth's years at Cambridge.

zeal dismissed'.[98] 'By a more just gradation' it led on 'to higher things'. He turned to a teacher who gave his genius far more than it would have gained from desiccated Newtonian geometry. This was Agostino Isola, who taught him Italian and Spanish.[99] Isola taught outside the formal curriculum, but he was appointed and encouraged by the university – an example of the way the alternative Cambridge redeemed the most visible one. The university statutes of 1724 required the Professors of Modern History 'to maintain with sufficient Salarys, two Persons, at least, well qualified to teach in writing and Speaking' Italian and Spanish. Isola was appointed in 1764 by the Regius Professor, Laurence Brockett, and his tenure was renewed in 1768 by Brockett's successor Thomas Gray, the poet, and again in 1771 by John Symonds.[100]

Isola was born in Milan in 1713, and his Cambridge appointment therefore came in middle age, not long in fact after he fled to Britain for political reasons. His new job was not a piece of unconsidered charity. Isola was a scholar and teacher of great distinction, who won respect and affection in the university. Thirty years after his death Charles Lamb wrote that in Cambridge Isola's 'memory is almost venerated'. He 'was generally beloved', writes Gunning, 'particularly by his pupils, who were very numerous'.[101] Their names are mostly irrecoverable, but one was William Gooch, who having become Second Wrangler in 1791 was appointed astronomer on Vancouver's voyage; he was advised by the Board of Longitude to learn Spanish. To his parents in Brockdish, Norfolk, he wrote: 'I'm now reading Spanish agreeable to Dr. Maskelyne's Wish with Mr Isola who is himself an Italian, but is reckon'd an excellent Spanish Master as well as an Italian Master; – (There isn't a Spaniard in Camb.) – I'm about to begin Don Quixote in the Original.' Isola seems to have inspired him with a liking for Cervantes; he carried copies in Spanish, English, French, and Italian to the South Seas, and it was the only novel he took.[102] Isola was then seventy-eight, and had been teaching in Cambridge since he

---

[98] 1850, Book Third, ll. 327–9, and ll. 530–1 for the next quotation.
[99] What follows is indebted to June Sturrock, 'Wordsworth's Italian Teacher', *Bulletin of the John Rylands University Library of Manchester*, 67 (1984–5), pp. 797–812. Quotations are taken from this valuable article unless otherwise noted.
[100] Philip Yorke attended Symonds's lectures: see this chapter, pp. 558–9.
[101] *Reminiscences*, vol. II, p. 75.   [102] Christopher Wordsworth, *Scholae Academicae*, pp. 326–9.

was fifty-one. One landmark in his career was his publication in 1778 of *Pieces Selected from the Italian Poets by Agostino Isola and Translated into English Verse by Some Gentlemen of the University*, who presumably were his students. Their names are not announced, but pencilled notes in the margin of Wordsworth's own copy (now in the Fitzwilliam Museum) that are possibly in Wordsworth's hand tell us that among the many contributors were the following Cambridge men: William Collier (Trinity), William Lort Mansell (Trinity), Thomas James Mathias (Trinity), and Jacob Mountain (Caius). The last three men were undergraduates from 1770 to 1774, and Collier from 1758 to 1762. Gunning writes that Collier was 'particularly well versed in modern languages (at that time a very rare accomplishment in the University)', words that suggest that Isola's influence was more than ordinarily strong on him.[103] Isola also seems to have had a lasting effect on Mathias, who lived in Italy from 1817 to his death in 1835 and is said by W. P. Courtney, in his *DNB* article, to have been 'the best English scholar' in Italian 'since the time of Milton'. Apparently we must discount as legend the claim that William Pitt was a pupil, but we certainly glimpse a man remembered and respected by generations of pupils, so that on his death in 1797, as Gunning tells us, 'there was a great desire, to do something for his son', a graduate of Emmanuel. Charles Isola was thereupon elected Esquire Bedell by 94 votes to 42, though his qualifications for the office were not as extensive as his opponent's.[104]

One of Isola's pupils was William Hayley, an undergraduate at Trinity Hall from 1762 to 1767; he did not take a degree. Isola imparted to him an enthusiasm for Italian and Spanish literature, and it led him to compose his *Essay on Epic Poetry*, of which Southey wrote that 'a greater effect was produced upon the rising generation of scholars' by the notes to the *Essay on Epic Poetry* 'than by any other contemporary work', Percy's *Reliques* alone excepted.[105] Hayley also aided the spread of knowledge of Dante in Britain by his translation of parts of the *Inferno*, from which only brief passages had

[103] Gunning, *Reminiscences*, vol. I, p. 119. Collier, Regius Professor of Hebrew 1771–90, is also said by Gunning to have been dissolute and gluttonous.
[104] *Reminiscences*, vol. II, p. 75.
[105] 'Hayley's Life and Writings', *Quarterly Review*, 31 (1825), p. 283.

earlier appeared in English. Hayley's example helped to persuade H. F. Cary to undertake his enormously influential translation of the entire *Divine Comedy*. Nor, as June Sturrock points out, does this exhaust the debt that British literary pursuits owed to Isola, through the capillaries of teaching and inspiration – quite apart from his notable effect on Wordsworth.

Isola published four other books, in addition to *Pieces Selected*. They included *Italian Dialogues* (1774), a student's aid to learning Italian which shows Isola's teaching methods to have been remarkably modern. Quite unlike the rigid formal instruction usual in contemporary teaching of Latin and Greek, Isola's dialogues aimed to teach idiomatic Italian through practice: 'as the rules of grammar are taught by translation, so is speech by exercise', he states. So the dialogues concern everyday situations (at least for educated males), and include the weather, travel, taking a walk, hunting, and the beauty and virtue of a lady; they employ a basic vocabulary.

Wordsworth became a pupil some time in 1788–9, and no doubt learnt Italian partly through the medium of these dialogues. Isola's chief gift to him, however, was literary, and we may get some sense of it from Dorothy's famous letter of 26 June 1791 to Jane Pollard, in which she says of her brother (just six months after his graduation):

> William you may have heard lost the chance, indeed the certainty of a fellowship by not combating his inclinations, he gave way to his natural dislike of studies so dry as many parts of the mathematics, consequently could not succeed at Cambridge. He reads Italian, Spanish, French, Greek and Latin, and English, but never opens a mathematical book. We promise ourselves much pleasure from reading Italian together at some time, he wishes that I was acquainted with the Italian poets.[106]

Wordsworth's involvement with Italian poetry, as a result of Isola's teaching, lasted throughout his life. He translated Ariosto, Tasso, and others and quotes readily from them too, while his poems often show the influence of Italian models; such parallels are particularly evident between *Orlando Furioso* and *Peter Bell*, as June Sturrock convincingly reveals.

The accident of Isola's involvement with a major poet has drawn

---

[106] De Selincourt and Shaver, *Letters . . . Early Years*, p. 52.

the research spotlight to him, but we know of others who offered fruits to be plucked by students wanting to replace or supplement mathematics. For example, tuition in French was available at a coffee house that opened next to Emmanuel College in 1763.[107] It is said that about 1750 'young men were imbibing a taste for modern languages, and that among those who were proficient therein were numbered many who were also skilful in the ancient tongues'.[108] One of their teachers was René La Butte (or Labutte) who was introduced to Cambridge by Conyers Middleton. La Butte was a printer and compositor, who also taught French from about 1742 until his death in 1790, with great reputation, it is said. His French grammar was published in 1764, and again in 1790.[109] In addition to this informal provision was the instruction in the classical languages offered by colleges and the lectures, such as they were, of the professors of modern history, Hebrew, and so on.[110] But this official tuition should be distinguished from the efforts of Isola and his like in one important respect, in that lacking the sanction of students' private fees it did not necessarily amount to what undergraduates most desired.

There was loss as well as gain when Oxford and Cambridge were reformed. J. Barton, writing about the teaching of law at Oxford, remarks that because of the 'very unexacting character of the old degree examinations' at Oxford, the university might require the Vinerian scholars to take a degree in civil law without fearing that candidates would be distracted from the study of common law. 'With the introduction of examinations which were a genuine test of attainment the ambitious undergraduate was less able to afford the time to embark upon a serious study of a subject which was not examined, and the unambitious undergraduate was no more inclined than before to embark on a serious study of anything.'[111] At Cambridge too there was a narrowing of perspective as honours courses became more demanding for the intellectually vigorous.

While there is positive testimony to Isola's legacy, there is very little to other results of Wordsworth's Cambridge years, for example the possible links between his reading or contacts at

---

[107] See pp. 554–5, above.   [108] Christopher Wordsworth, *Scholae Academicae*, p. 150.
[109] Christopher Wordsworth, *Scholae Academicae*, p. 153.   [110] See chapter 6, pp. 233–6.
[111] Sutherland and Mitchell, eds., *The Eighteenth Century*, p. 605.

university and his radicalism in the 1790s. We must be cautious, especially since most members of the university seem to have been conservative patriots in the 1790s. Wordsworth asserts in *The Prelude* that the university's intellectual egalitarianism predisposed him to welcome the French Revolution in 1791–2,[112] but of course residence in France meant that so much which he experienced there stimulated his radicalism. In estimating the effect of university education the difficulty is always that of distinguishing undergraduate experiences from earlier or later ones, a problem that renders the task of measuring Cambridge's impact on its society peculiarly intractable.

CHRISTOPHER WORDSWORTH

THE POET'S YOUNGER BROTHER

Christopher Wordsworth (b. 1774), went up to Trinity College as a pensioner in 1792. Ahead lay a distinguished though on balance probably an unhappy life, especially in the twenty-one years he spent after 1820 in the master's lodge at Trinity. At Trinity Wordsworth was a strict disciplinarian somewhat lacking a sense of humour and the arts of social address, unpopular with fellows and undergraduates alike.[113] Yet he had an active and enquiring mind and was an energetic innovator, being for example largely responsible for the building of the New Court at Trinity and the setting up of the Classical Tripos. A biography, at present lacking, might exploit the copious materials available at Cambridge and Lambeth and present a more rounded and complex man than the rigid 'high and dry' cleric usually suggested to us.

In their mature lives he and William, though they often corresponded on political matters (they were both ardent Conservatives) were never intimate. William wrote that Christopher gave him 'not more I think than twenty minutes at the very utmost when I saw him in town'. When invited to write Christopher's biography William replied that he was quite unfitted for the task, for 'as I grievously lament, we have had very, very little personal inter-

---

[112] 1805, Book Ninth, ll. 227–36; 1850 text also.
[113] For his unsuccessful period as master see chapter 3, pp. 92–3.

course'.[114] Yet for some time the brothers had been schoolboys together in Hawkshead, and in lines apparently intended at one time for *The Prelude* the poet refers to the bond of early experiences in common, despite a later divergence, for

> My playmates! brothers! nurs'd by the same years,
> And fellow-children of the self-same hills,
> Though we are moulded now by various fates.[115]

Some light is thrown on the nature of their youthful transactions by a manuscript notebook (discovered about 1950) filled with jottings compiled at Hawkshead by Christopher between 1788 and 1791, when he was between fourteen and seventeen years of age. They show him immersed in the same literary culture as his brother, in which classical writers and eighteenth-century British poets such as Thomson and Goldsmith were prominent; he was pondering themes later exploited in poetry by William. We know that after 1787, when William went up to St John's, the brothers met in the Lake District during summer vacations, and also corresponded frequently.[116] We should see the brothers in these years as engaged in a sort of unequal partnership, in which Christopher dogged the footsteps of his infinitely more gifted brother and tried to emulate him. One result of his ambition is the prose synopsis of a Latin poem that Christopher produced in 1792 shortly before going up to Trinity, and its pedestrian and laboured nature suggests why he found his muse less compelling than William's. It is interesting that when in February 1793 Dorothy compared the two brothers, she mentioned similarities of temperament and sensibility, but also differences in drive:

> He is like William: he has the same traits in his Character but less highly touched, he is not so ardent in any of his pursuits but is yet more particularly attached to the same Pursuits which have so irresistible an Influence over William, which deprive him of the

---

[114] Quotations are from Mary Moorman, *William Wordsworth. A biography. The Later Years 1803–1850* (Oxford University Press, 1965), p. 424.

[115] Quoted in Z. S. Fink, *The Early Wordsworthian Milieu* (Oxford University Press, 1958), p. 13. Much of what follows is based on this work, esp. pp. 10–19.

[116] De Selincourt and Shaver, *Letters . . . Early Years*, p. 37. This letter, written by William to Dorothy on 6 September 1790 from Switzerland, mentions that he and Christopher had been 'almost upon terms of regular correspondence' (i.e. in England).

Power of chaining his attention to others discordant to his feelings. Christopher is no despicable Poet, but he can become a Mathematician also, he is not insensible of the Beauties of the Greek and Latin Classics, or of any of the charms of elegant Literature but he can draw his mind from these fascinating studies to others less alluring; he is steady and sincere in his attachments, William has both these Virtues in an eminent degree.

There was a hint, too, of the characteristic that in middle age led to Christopher's reclusive habits: 'his Modesty is so extreme as almost to amount to absolute Bashfulness'.[117]

CHRISTOPHER WORDSWORTH AT TRINITY

Dorothy's assessment suggests some reasons why the brothers' responses to Cambridge were so greatly contrasted, and hence, to some extent, why the channels they later cut in life were so different. The historian naturally seeks a commentary from Christopher to match *The Prelude*; but unfortunately his manuscript diary for parts of his second year at Trinity lacks reflectiveness, or reference to his inner life and motives for action.[118] A brief document of 5,000 words, it describes the surface of daily life. Perhaps the lack of a perceived audience, in his own imagination or the world outside, led Wordsworth to discontinue his entries on 15 November 1793 after only five weeks. When after a gap of nearly four months he resumes them, he writes, 'Sunday Evening. March 9. 1794. Have lately been reading Boswell's Johnson: to w[hi]ch perhaps I may impute the resumption of my plan of keeping a Diary.' The special interest of these words lies in their implication, first that literary pleasures were a powerful influence at this stage of Wordsworth's life, and second that he had no compulsion to write; so it is not surprising that six weeks later he finally abandoned the diary.

But its great merit is that it entirely lacks the idealised gloss we may suspect in journals composed with others in mind. We may

[117] De Selincourt and Shaver, *Letters . . . Early Years*, p. 87.
[118] The diary (Trinity College MS 0.11.8) covers two periods, 9 October–15 November 1793, and 9 March–22 April 1794. A selection of entries, amounting to nearly 40 per cent of the original, were printed by the diarist's grandson, Christopher Wordsworth, in *Social Life*, pp. 587–94, and quotations from this selection are distinguished in footnotes

believe what he says – and he tells us about a pattern of life, at all events in his second year, characterised by only the most modest amount of effort; we would not guess that a wranglership and a life of dedicated toil as a churchman and don lie ahead of him. He often rose late and missed chapel, doing so for example on at least four mornings, including Sunday, in the week beginning 3 November. He worked on that Sunday and Wednesday morning, and on Thursday, Friday, and Saturday, the first days of lectures, he spent several hours each morning at them; on Friday evening he also spent some time reading about ratios and variable quantities. His labours in the week appear to have amounted to no more than fifteen hours altogether. In the preceding ten days Wordsworth had put most of his effort, such as it was, into writing and memorising a Latin declamation, but after dinner on Saturday 2 November he found that four particular friends 'had taken possession of my rooms with[ou]t invitation. Sat with me till chapel-time. To this I in p[ar]t impute it that I c[oul]d not repeat my dec[la]m[atio]n as perfect as I ought to have done.'[119]

These words are an epigraph for his Michaelmas and Lent terms. Typically, a few hours of work were complemented with a wine or supper party (and sometimes both) with three or four friends from Trinity; and the evenings, which in theory were spent in solitary toil, were given over largely to conversation. In fact such groups gathered on forty-five of the seventy days for which Wordsworth gives us details of his activities after dinner, while the attention given to these events in the diary suggests that social intercourse, rather than intellectual effort for the degree, was the focus of his life as a second-year undergraduate. In this respect Christopher Words-worth seems to have been typical of many, and his diary, brief though it is, therefore has great value for us.

Often the topics under discussion were literary, and here we see surfacing that interest that we know Christopher Wordsworth brought with him from Hawkshead School. An early entry in the diary shows his fascination with the idea of discussion:

Thursday, 24. [October 1793] Went to the library to consult some books on my Declamat[io]n subject. Met Bilsborrow there. Went

[119] Fol. 2v.

with him to his lodgings. Tells me Dr Darwin[120] got more knowledge in th[a]t way fr[o]m Kaim's[121] Essay on Criticism th[a]n from any book he ever read. He has seen a l[ette]r fr[o]m Dr Priestly[122] much to the same purport. Dr Darwin & a few friends meet every evening. Whatever be the subject of their conversation they divide, half & half; each gives his sentiments on the side allotted; & when all have so done; they change again, each having to defend the side he before condemned.[123]

In the event the notion of a formal society came from elsewhere.

Tuesday. 5. [November] Roused about 9 o'clock by Bilsborrow & Le Grice with a proposal to become member of a literary society. The members they mentioned as having already come into the plan. Coleridge: Jes[us].[124] Satterthwaite. Rough. & themselves Trin[ity] C[ollege] and Franklin, Pembroke...; was to have gone to Coleridge's to wine, to consult on the plan had I not been engaged at home with the Howeses & Strickland. Went with them to the coffee house. On my going out met Bilsborrow; returned back with him. Soon after came in Le Grice, Coleridge & Rough. Got all together into a box (& having met with the monthly review of my B[rother]'s Poems) entered into a good deal of literary & critical conversation on Dr Darwin. Miss Seward.[125] Mrs Smith.[126] Bowles.[127] and my B[rothe]r.[128]

We are told that the society met on four occasions in the following week. Coleridge read some of his poems, Wordsworth showing the effects of his literary education by noting in his diary a Shakespearian allusion and a couplet 'w[hi]ch, by the bye, is borrowed f[ro]m an epigram of Plato'.[129] On Saturday 9 November there was a long discussion (whose nature cannot however easily be derived from

---

[120] Erasmus Darwin (1731–1802), physician and poet, grandfather of Charles.
[121] Henry Home, Lord Kames (1696–1782), Scots jurist and writer, published *Elements of Criticism in Three Volumes* in 1762.
[122] Joseph Priestley (1733–1804), Nonconformist writer and scientist, the discoverer of oxygen.
[123] Fol. 1r; *Social Life*, p. 588.
[124] Samuel Taylor Coleridge entered Jesus in 1791 but left in 1794 without taking his degree.
[125] Anna Seward (1747–1809) of Lichfield, poet and friend of Erasmus Darwin.
[126] Charlotte Smith (1748–1806), novelist and poet.
[127] William Lisle Bowles (1762–1850), clergyman, published in 1789 the work for which he is now remembered, *Fourteen Sonnets*; it was much admired by Coleridge, who dedicated his *Poems* to him in 1796
[128] Fols. 2v and 3r; *Social Life*, p. 589.
[129] Thursday 7 November, fol. 3v; *Social Life*, p. 589.

Wordsworth's rambling account) of Erasmus Darwin's theory of laughter:

> Ax[iom]. 'No man can feel strongly & act strongly at the same time'. Why we bite our lips when chagrined, soldiers put bullets in their mouths &c &c. 'Pleasure & Pain very nearly & strongly allied'. The emotion which we feel from humour, wit &c w[oul]d by its excess become painful, were it not (ax[iom]. 1.) kept down by 'acting' i.e. laughter, th[a]t it may not be entirely destroyed the laugh is intermittent ha! ha! ha!

The pleasure of tears, Wordsworth reported, might be derived from the same source: 'the pleasure of riot, break[in]g tables, chairs, bruising, even one's head or hand, in a paroxysm of rage. &c &c' Wordsworth then turned to another preoccupation – literary composition and publication – in which his brother's experience is plainly in his mind.

> No author ought I think, with[ou]t he enters the world with considerable advantages, to begin with publishing a very elaborate work; however, not a work upon w[hi]ch tastes may very considerably vary. e.g. my B[rother]'s Poems. If *he* had had his reput[atio]n raised by some less important & more *popular* poem, it would have ensured from petty critics a diff[eren]t reception to his 'Descrip[ti]ve Sketches' & 'Evening Walk'. – Chapel.[130]

The society devised a formal constitution, members to take it in turn to produce an 'essay' for delivery. Ominously, when his turn came on 13 November Coleridge failed to produce his essay and read some more of his poems instead. Within days Coleridge disappeared from Cambridge until April 1794.[131] Perhaps the loss of a leading light led to the demise of the society. The cessation of Wordsworth's diary makes it impossible to know; certainly, when he resumed it in March there is no mention of it. However, the friends continued to meet, as this typical entry shows:

> Tuesday April 1st. Rose to chapel. read Astronomy till 10. lectures. Rough & Vaughan called at 1/4 after 11. Walked till 1/2 past 12:

---

[130] Fols. 3v and 4r; *Social Life*, p. 589.
[131] See Richard Holmes, *Coleridge: Early Visions* (London, Hodder & Stoughton, 1989), pp. 51–9. During his months of absence Coleridge volunteered for the army and was a private in the 15th Light Dragoons.

called on Satterthwaite. sat with till 1/4 before two. Drank wine at Braithwaite's St John's – present Rhodwell St John's, Satterthwaite Trin[ity]: R shewed a goodness of heart, an honest bluntness & openness which was very pleasing... A great admirer of the ancients. We had a long argument on the comparative excellence of the Grecian & English drama And ancient & modern oratory: & on the inference he wished to draw from his own ideas of it, in favour of the Athenians when compared with the English as a polite & virtuous nation... Chapel. Met Tilt. Lounged with him till 1/2 past 6 at Lunn's & Merrill's. Met Maud in our court, the first time since his arrival in C. In the Evening read the British critic for March. Bed.[132]

But lest we assume that all discussion was of an elevated tone fitting for intending clergymen, it should be recorded that some was what Wordsworth called 'rude'. (It was omitted from his grandson's selection.)

Sunday March 16... Towards the latter part of the afternoon a great while was taken up in solving [?] Owen's supposed celibacy: in offers to send girls to his rooms &c &c very rude, & to indifferent persons very unpleasant. During the whole afternoon in Gleeds behaviour to Owen I observed most markedly that of a Senior boy to a Junior: w[hi]ch was their situation, at Winchester. Whatever Ow: said G. was ready to contradict or turn into ridicule.[133]

In the Michaelmas Term 1795 Wordsworth worked furiously for his disputation and the Senate House Examination, abandoning the easy-going régime of his second year; from Monday 7 September 1795 to Saturday 2 January 1796 he read on average nine and three-quarter hours a day, with one holiday, 17 December, Commemoration Day. His longest day was Friday 18 December; from 10.30 am to 3.0 pm on 'Newton', from 5.15 pm to 10.30 pm on mechanics, with his friend Malcolm, and from 10.30 pm to 1.30 am on problems. The following day he was examined by Sheepshanks, a fellow of Trinity – presumably to be given a preliminary classification for the Senate House Examination. In that examination he became Tenth Wrangler – a measure of success that would not have been possible on his second-year routine. Christopher

[132] Fols 18r and 19r.   [133] Fol. 10r.

Wordsworth's schedule reminds that while intensive effort was required for a wranglership it was not necessarily long-continued.[134] The behaviour of William Thomson (the future Lord Kelvin) at Peterhouse fifty years later was very similar, and he became Second Wrangler.

In the diary forty-seven acquaintances are named, most of them a few times merely. Ten are mentioned twelve times or more, as having foregathered with Wordsworth, and often each other, at a variety of social contexts from breakfast to supper. These were Wordsworth's closest companions at Trinity. Their biographies reveal some differences, but for the most part remarkable homogeneity. All were undergraduates of Trinity, and all were admitted as pensioners save one, Thomas Young, a sizar; Young came from Hawkshead Grammar School and had known Wordsworth there. There was another Cumbrian, James Satterthwaite, the son of a lieutenant-colonel, who (Dorothy Wordsworth wrote) 'lives at Cockermouth in the house where my Brothers and I were born and where our Father died'.[135] Perhaps this striking coincidence brought Wordsworth and Satterthwaite together; at all events the two men were inseparable, Wordsworth meeting his friend for a walk, wine or conversation at least once a day, far more often than he encountered anybody else. Satterthwaite was an Etonian, as was William Tilt, the son of an auctioneer. Edward Vaughan was educated at Rugby, William Rough at Westminster, and Gilbert Malcolm at Edinburgh High School. The others came from grammar or private schools in Hackney, Houghton-le-Spring, Newcastle, and Norwich. The geographical spread was wide, within Britain, as perhaps was the social spread (to the extent that schooling in the 1790s reflected it) within the gentle middle class. As the lack of any hint of scandalous, rackety or even wayward conduct suggests, at least most of the group were 'reading men'; of the total of 11, 6 became wranglers (including Wordsworth himself) and 3 others senior optimes. A question mark hangs over Rough and Tilt; presumably they took poll degrees. Rough, as it happens, was the

---

[134] This paragraph is based on details in Christopher Wordsworth, *Social Life*, pp. 594–5, which are derived from a manuscript by his grandfather which has since been lost.

[135] The letter, of 7 August 1805, is given in De Selincourt and Shaver, *Letters ... Early Years*, pp. 615–18.

only one whose career was coloured by the unconventional and offbeat. He became a colonial judge, quarrelled with the Governor of Demerara over questions of principle, and was vindicated by the Privy Council; he also published now-forgotten dramas on Lorenzino de Medici and the Conspiracy of Gowrie, and a collection of John Wilkes's letters, having married his illegitimate daughter. Henry Reynolds also became a lawyer, ending as Chief Commissioner of the Insolvent Debtors' Court. Nine became clergymen. In addition to Wordsworth, who became Master of Trinity and had considerable intellectual achievement, eight men became parish clergymen and led lives of conscientious conventionality. None, incidentally, touched mathematics for long after graduation, apart perhaps from George Howes and Young, who were college tutors for some years. For Cambridge undergraduates their uniformity of vocation narrowed horizons, and inhibited differences of temperament that might have fostered growth. It is not surprising that the verdict of *The Prelude* is ambiguous.

Chapter 16

THE UNDERGRADUATE EXPERIENCE, II: CHARLES ASTOR BRISTED AND WILLIAM EVERETT

CHARLES ASTOR BRISTED IN NEW YORK, YALE, AND TRINITY

'Late in October, 1840, a young New Yorker was losing himself among the impracticable streets, and admiring the remarkable edifices of Cambridge.'[1] These words introduce the most detailed and the most thoughtful memoir of Cambridge undergraduate life ever penned. It was written by an American, Charles Astor Bristed, and is considered in this chapter with the reminiscences of another American, William Everett, who followed Bristed to Cambridge (and to Trinity College) in 1859.[2] Both men combined American citizenship and patriotism with sympathy for much in British, especially English, life – the life of the comfortable and cultivated upper-middle class whose attitudes and culture were so often scarcely distinguishable from their own circles' in the North-eastern United States, and whose bookshelves were filled, as theirs were in New York and Boston, with the works of Scott, Dickens, and Emerson. Both men were less critical of Cambridge and of Britain than, shall we say, a Kansas cowboy is likely to have been in the improbable event of his becoming a Trinity undergraduate. But it also gives their occasional criticisms the peculiar force that comes from intimate knowledge, like the perceptive judgement of a brother. One particularly turns for enlightenment to Bristed, the more informative and reflective man.

A British reviewer[3] – probably W. G. Clark – criticised his undue censure of Harvard and Yale, his 'sweeping condemnation' of

---

[1] Bristed, *Five Years*, vol. I, p. 4. All references to Bristed's book are to this edition.
[2] Everett, *On the Cam*. Everett gave his lectures in the Lowell Institute, Boston, in 1864.
[3] 'Cambridge Life according to C. A. Bristed', *Fraser's Magazine*, 49 (1854), pp. 89–100.

585

Oxford on the most perfunctory acquaintance, and his allegation of undergraduate fornication. (On the first two points Bristed was certainly at fault, and on the last the evidence is hard to interpret, as we might expect.) But for the most part the reviewer approves of Bristed's attitudes, as indeed we should expect, since they were usually very much in Cambridge's favour. More telling is the reviewer's praise of Bristed's accuracy over details: 'generally his descriptions are so faithful as to convince one that the sly "chiel" must have been "takin notes" all the time'.[4] The reviewer recalls Bristed speaking at the Cambridge Union, and gives us the sense of a man emitting contradictory signals that is a mark of Bristed's Cambridge career. Bristed sported a moustache (when they were very unusual in Cambridge) and clothes of foreign cut and audacious colours, yet 'over all was thrown the gown of a Trinity fellow-commoner, heavy with silver lace. The outward man was thus anything but democratic, and did not prepare us for the tone of his speech ... a brilliant eulogium of the Pilgrim Fathers and the great republic which they founded.'[5]

Bristed's grandfather was an Anglican clergyman in Dorset. Following an education at Winchester College, his father, John, supported himself by his pen after attempting medicine and the law. In 1806 he emigrated to the United States. Perhaps it was his writing that brought him into contact with John Jacob Astor, the China merchant, fur trader, and dealer in real estate. In 1820 he married Astor's daughter, Magdalen, and Charles Bristed was born the same year. The marriage soon collapsed. After some wanderings John Bristed became an Episcopal clergyman in Bristol, Rhode Island, where he is said to have been a 'devoted churchman'.[6] After his mother's death in 1832 Charles Bristed was brought up by his grandfather on his country estate at Hell Gate, at what is now the Upper East Side of New York City. There he acquired some distinctive attitudes; one influence on him was the Anglophile Washington Irving, his grandfather's friend.[7] 'Ever since my early boyhood', Bristed wrote in *Five Years*, 'it had been a leading idea

---

[4] P. 95.   [5] P. 98.
[6] These details of John Bristed's life are taken from Sarah Bowerman's article in the *Dictionary of American Biography*, vol. III (Oxford University Press, 1929), p. 54.
[7] His Anglophile ideas are offered in *The Sketch Book of Geoffrey Crayon, Gent.* (1819–20). Hell Gate Farm was situated at what is now East 87th Street, between York and East End Avenues.

with me that the great branches of the Anglo–Saxon family, distinguished by their language, by their ethical principles, by their judiciously liberal political institutions, from the rest of the world, ought to work harmoniously together.'[8] Astor, very fond of his grandson, paid for Bristed at Yale and Trinity, and in his will left him considerable wealth, including his house on Broadway.[9] Bristed was thus able to live as an independent man of letters. In his many occasional writings he displayed much knowledge of classical and modern literatures, his zeal being most aroused by questions of accuracy, prosody, and linguistic nicety – in which he confesses to the lasting influence of the Classical Tripos.

Devoted to humane letters, he was apt to attack the American education system for not sufficiently inculcating them, and he was inclined to criticise many other things about America too. 'Thackeray wrote a book on English snobs', declared Bristed in 1858, 'and showed up a great many of the institutions of his fatherland in very large type. We think we see him writing a book about the Snobs of America and some of the said snobs reading it.'[10] At his death in 1874 a friend wrote that Bristed 'left a sincere mourner in every one who knew him well. Of those there are not many, for he was in no sense of the word a popular man... His liking he always showed; his disliking he was too outspoken to conceal, except by avoiding occasion of offence. He was too sincere for many friends.'[11] Bristed himself suggests the truth of this frank obituary in a thinly disguised self-portrait he offers in a collection of sketches published in 1852. 'Carl Masters' is a young gentleman of independent means with an estate on the wooded bank of the Hudson; lacking manual dexterity and business sense, he is bookish and haunts his library, is tactless, painfully sincere and truthful,

[8] Vol. I, p. 36. Bristed was uneasy about the divergence between British and American spelling that was occurring in the middle of the century. He denounced Noah Webster, the American lexicographer, as 'no authority at all among scholars', but nevertheless chose the 'or' form of certain nouns 'because the practice of good writers varies sufficiently to leave their orthography an open question': *Five Years*, vol. I, p. 5.

[9] Kenneth Wiggins Porter, *John Jacob Astor. Business Man* (2 vols., Cambridge, Mass: Harvard University Press, 1931), vol. II, esp. pp. 1035–6 and 1053–4.

[10] Charles Astor Bristed, *Pieces of a Broken-Down Critic. Picked Up by Himself* (4 vols. in 1, Baden-Baden, 1858–9), Book 1, pp. 283–93, a review of the *Ajax* of Sophocles.

[11] Richard Grant White, 'Charles Astor Bristed', *The Galaxy. A Magazine of Entertaining Reading*, 17, 4 (April 1874), pp. 473–84.

dresses in a subdued English fashion, carefully protects his private self, and hates the Irish, French, Roman Catholics, Southern slaveholders, and entrepreneurs who deface the Hudson valley with railroads. 'He wrote for elegantly and thoroughly educated men, such as had been the associates of his youth, and found few of his countrymen to read, and fewer to understand him.'[12]

Bristed wrote some sketches about Cambridge life as soon as he returned to the United States in 1846:

> two different Magazines at different times began to publish them, but were very soon afraid to go on, because I did not pretend to conceal our inferiority to the English in certain branches of liberal education. I then resolved to refrain, not merely from publishing, but from writing any more, until as many years as I passed in England had elapsed since my return thence... I can truly say that my opinions on all the matters discussed in it have undergone no important change for the last five years; all my observation has tended to confirm them.[13]

His motives in writing *Five Years* were mixed – to express his strong views, but also to convey to his countrymen, whom he described as relying upon 'popular novels and other light literature' for their knowledge of the English universities, a lot of solid detail that is very unusual in a personal memoir. It is a slightly odd medley of calendar and credo. A second edition followed the first in the same year, 1852. In his engaging work William Everett is clearly in awe of Bristed's lengthier and altogether more earnest one, and would not have attempted to speak, he says, had not the plates of *Five Years* been destroyed in a fire at Harpers', the publishers.[14] Presumably continuing demand led Bristed to publish a third edition in 1873. Apart from its format (one volume instead of two) it is remarkably similar to its predecessors of twenty-one years before. There are a few changes of expression, the addition of a few pages to bring matters up to date, and the omission of about thirty more that had

[12] Charles Astor Bristed, *The Upper Ten Thousand: Sketches of American Society* (London, 1852), pp. 276 and 259–88. Bristed first published these sketches in *Fraser's Magazine*, under the name Frank Manhattan. His attacks on rascally hotel-keepers and squalid newspapers (he keeps mentioning *The Sewer*) remind us of Dickens's satire in *Martin Chuzzlewit*.

[13] *Five Years*, vol. I, Preface, p. vi.

[14] *On the Cam*, p. 7.

been bypassed by events. None of these changes materially altered the sense of the argument.[15]

John J. Astor sent Bristed to Yale when he was fifteen. Bristed thought the régime there far too easy-going, and that after five years' residence (he graduated after four years and stayed up for another) his knowledge was wide but shallow. He arrived at Trinity College in October 1840. At first he was a fellow commoner, but in his third year became a pensioner, because he needed to save money, be eligible for a scholarship, and for his health's sake to eat simpler fare than was supplied to the 'upper table'.[16] Possessing much in common with the English Anglican gentlemen around him, Bristed nevertheless found that English clothes did not fit, and that food was monotonous and taste in wine barbarous. He was irritated by the rampant Toryism ('Jacobitism' he calls it) of many undergraduates, the frequent drunkenness, and the habit – common even among those intending to be clergymen – of patronising the Barnwell brothels. In fact, Bristed was Anglophile on the East River but felt himself to be an American on the Cam. He was nettled by the attitudes of some Tories:

> The general bearing of such Tories, and that not merely young men or Dons at Cambridge but Londoners, was very civil to me personally, but mingled with a sort of implied pity for my belonging to a country where a gentleman was out of place ... For with the English Tory I found it a fixed idea that all our 'Upper Ten' are bullied and plundered by the mob, just as it is with the American Radical, that all the mass of the English people are miserable serfs, and all the landed aristocracy bloated tyrants. With men of this sort I took a very summary course, neither more nor less than the ordinary American dodge of stoutly asserting and imperturbably maintaining our national superiority in morals and intelligence. Take the following as a specimen. *B.* at the Dean's table ... Enter (rather late) Strafford Pope, a young aristocrat with £30,000 a-year,[17] and a large

[15] Except the dropping of four pages that in the 1st edition admitted the educational value of geometry (though not algebra), and asked for it to be retained as a compulsory study up to the Previous Examination. These pages were probably omitted from the 3rd edition because in 1854 mathematics had ceased to be obligatory after the Previous for intending classicists. The omission of these pages had the effect of strengthening the impression of Bristed's hostility to mathematics.

[16] Bristed, *Five Years*, vol. 1, pp. 157–8.

[17] Bristed probably means Frederick Peel, Sir Robert's son; Bristed's exact contemporary at Trinity, he was Fifth Classic in 1845.

assortment of the most antediluvian politics. *P.* has heard that *B.* is an American, and takes a seat alongside him half intentionally; *B.* knows *P.* by reputation as one of the few reading Fellow-Commoners. They strike up a conversation in the pauses of the dinner; by and by the discourse takes a political turn.

P. A republic may be very well when we can make all men angels, but till then it can't answer.

B. Why, we make one answer very well, though our men don't pretend to be angels, and only some of our women.

P. Answer very well! You have no law – or, at least, no means of enforcing the law, you know.

[An Englishman always appends 'you know' to the very thing you *don't* know, and won't admit.]

B. Oh, that's altogether a mistake on your part. I can see how it arises very naturally. You look around on your own lower orders and think how unfit they would be for political power; and so they are now, no doubt. But wait till virtue and intelligence are diffused among your people as generally as they are among ours, and then you will be ripe for a republic and will have it too.[18]

Fortunately, Bristed was able to escape to the relaxing company of the Trinity 'bachelor scholars', – graduates in residence to read for a fellowship – finding their intelligence, cultivation, and literary conversation very alluring.

Appalled by the success of Polk in the presidential election of 1844 Bristed and his associates in New York saw themselves 'given up to the mercy of Irish aliens and rampant slaveholders . . . In short, a large proportion of the wealthiest, best-educated, and most estimable men in our State seemed verily to have despaired of the Republic.'[19] Expecting to qualify for his BA in January 1845, he intended at first not to take his degree because of the need to swear the oaths of allegiance and supremacy. Dismayed by news from home he resolved to graduate, so as to become eligible for a fellowship and perhaps even become a British subject. The swearing was perfunctory, each graduand merely kissing a Testament as it was passed around a group of a dozen in the Senate House, while the oath of allegiance was read to them. Bristed passed the Testament along without kissing it, a subterfuge that still caused

[18] Bristed, *Five Years*, vol. 1, pp. 39–40. [19] Bristed, *Five Years*, vol. 1, pp. 334–5.

much remorse years later. 'Let every young man beware how he violates his integrity or deviates from a straightforward, honest course in the smallest matter.'[20] Early in 1846 he returned home anyway. His explanation is blurred, as no doubt his mind was at the time. He feared that war between Britain and America was inevitable over the Oregon boundary dispute. But news from home was like 'news from abroad', and he felt that he was going native in Cambridge. 'I would rather have been a Fellow of Trinity than anything which I could rationally hope to be in my own country, and there was a chance, though a very remote one, of getting a Fellowship... It was like tearing myself up by the roots to leave Cambridge.' Still he took his name off the college boards, and proposed at the Cambridge Union that 'the American claims in Oregon were just and reasonable', a motion that was lost by a narrow margin. Proud to the last of his exotic cuisine, he entertained his friends to *bisque d'écrevisse* and chocolate pudding, and 'on a fine May morning I took my last walk in the grounds of Trinity'.

WILLIAM EVERETT, ANGLOPHILE

For four of the years that Bristed was at Trinity the American Minister in London was Edward Everett, a Bostonian and an Anglophile. An Everett, he remembered, had emigrated from England in the 1630s. Dignified, courteous, and restrained in manner, he was fonder of aristocratic ways than republicans at home thought fitting; he even painted the Everett arms on his hired carriage. Though sometimes critical of John Bull's foreign policy he was fêted by British political and literary society, meeting Macaulay often and staying with Whewell in the master's lodge at Trinity. 'He made upon us', wrote Sydney Smith, 'the same impression he appears to make universally in this country: we thought him (a character which the English always receive with affectionate regard) an amiable American, republican without rudeness, and accomplished without ostentation.'[21] It was natural for his son William,

[20] Bristed, *Five Years*, vol. I, p. 339.
[21] Quoted in Paul Revere Frothingham, *Edward Everett. Orator and Statesman* (Port Washington, N.Y., Kennikat Press, 1971, repr. of 1925 edn), p. 220; the rest of this paragraph draws on this source.

when he had graduated from Harvard, to proceed to Cambridge. After he had been there two and a half years his father wrote to Sir John Coleridge:

> My boy continues to be much gratified with his residence, both as to society and study. He is at Trinity, where his maternal ancestor in the seventh generation (John Cotton, famous in our ecclesiastical annals and even in our civil history, for our Boston was named in honor of him, as Vicar of Boston in Lincolnshire), was a student at the close of the sixteenth century. Dr Whewell writes me the best accounts of him . . . the Prince of Wales has honored him with the most condescending attentions.[22]

A few years later William Everett began his lectures on his Cambridge years by telling his Boston audience that he was to impose upon them 'a frequent, though I hope not undiscriminating, eulogy of the Old Country'.[23] 'It is our boast that we love to cut deeper, year after year, the inscriptions on the graves of our ancestors, and trace with eagerness in English soil the roots and stock which have brought forth the branches of American learning and civilisation.' The American Union itself was inspired by the example of the English collegiate universities – indissoluble federations of sovereign societies. And Everett's praise of Trinity was effusive indeed. His only serious criticism of Britain was of her alleged partiality towards the Confederacy in the recent war – Everett and his father being Unionists.[24]

After Cambridge Everett followed interests like Bristed's, and where, once again, the influence of the Classical Tripos may be discerned. He took a PhD in philology at Harvard, and lectured in classics. In 1907 he returned to Trinity to give the Clark lectures, shortly before his death. His publications were not as numerous as Bristed's, however, and there is more than a hint of the dilettante about him, his kinsman Paul Frothingham remarking that 'With all

[22] Quoted in Frothingham, *Edward Everett*, p. 439. Edward, Prince of Wales was studying in Trinity (and in residence at Madingley Hall) in 1861.

[23] *On the Cam*, p. 2, and p. 5 for the next quotation.

[24] His criticism brought an irritated rebuke from his Cambridge editor: the British government was 'just and impartial', and since Britons could not understand the rights and wrongs of the quarrel, 'we watched the fight much as we might a pugilistic encounter in the street'. Sympathy for the South was 'nothing more than the admiration we instinctively feel for a plucky little boxer who is overmatched': p. 2.

his brilliant mental gifts William Everett lacked the precious quality of perseverance.'[25]

THE DAILY ROUND, 1840–1870

In his memoir Bristed wrote:

> The Cantabs' garb generally consists of a not too new black coat (frock or cutaway), trousers of some substantial stuff, grey or plaid, and a stout waistcoat, frequently of the same pattern as the trousers. Straps are unknown to him, and instead of boots he wears easy low-heeled shoes, for greater convenience in fence and ditch jumping, and other feats of extempore gymnastics which diversify his 'constitutionals'. The only showy part of his attire is the cravat, which is apt to be blue or some other decided color, and fastened in front with a large gold-headed pin. During the middle of the day this outfit is completed by a hat of the average ugliness of English hats, but before 12 a.m., and after 4 p.m., you must superadd the academical costume. This consists of a gown, varying in color and ornament according to the wearer's college and rank, but generally black, not unlike an ordinary clerical gown, and a square-topped cap, which fits close to the head like a truncated helmet, while the covered board which forms the crown measures about a foot diagonally across. It is not by any means a *sine qua non* that the cap and gown should be in good order and condition; the latter is often sadly torn and faded, while the former retains but few traces of its original form ... In one thing only is the Cantab particular – the one nicety of every English gentleman, however clumsy or shabby the rest of his dress may be – his linen is always faultless. A dirty shirt, or even a badly got up one, is a phenomenon in the University.[26]

So begins Bristed's description of the undergraduate's daily life, the most detailed we possess and one with which all our other sources for the period 1840–70 in essentials agree.

Bristed's gyp called him at 6.30, just as Christopher Wordsworth's had fifty years before, for chapel that began at 7.00. At 6.50 the bell started to toll, quickening its pace at 6.55; but for three or four minutes after the clock struck the hour the chapel gates were

---

[25] *Edward Everett*, p. ix.
[26] Bristed, *Five Years*, vol. I, pp. 5–6 and pp. 19–29 for the following paragraphs, for which see also Everett, *On the Cam*, pp. 100–16, John Venn, *Early Collegiate Life*, pp. 269–71, and Shipley, *"J." A memoir of John Willis Clark*, pp. 26–34.

A Breakfast Party.

14 A Breakfast Party, drawn in 1859.

open to allow the latecomers to squeeze in. At 7.30, the service finished: 'it is the custom to take a fifteen minutes walk in the college grounds, for the purpose of affording the bed-maker time to get the rooms in good order, and of giving the student an appetite for his breakfast'.[27] This was eaten before the sitting-room fire (an open coal fire, naturally) and was generally a simple meal: for Bristed rolls, butter, and tea, though John Venn, at Gonville and Caius in the 1850s, managed bacon and eggs. The food was ordered from college kitchens or buttery, and tea or coffee prepared by the student. Exceptionally, lavish breakfasts were ordered – perhaps from grocers outside the college. Everett's neighbours at Trinity would occasionally eat fried soles, grilled fowl or curried sausages.

[27] Bristed, *Five Years*, vol. I, p. 23.

594

COLLEGE FARE

Dinner in Hall. Trinity College.

15 Dinner in Hall, Trinity College, drawn in 1859.

Lunch, such as it was, was a snack of bread and cheese, and supper was simple too, except for the greedy. These meals were eaten privately. Dinner was the main meal of the day, and taken communally, in the college hall, as it had been since medieval times. The hour had advanced over the centuries. By the middle decades of the nineteenth century it was 4.0 or 5.0 pm.

Despite the antiquity of dining together, and the special function of collegiate bonding attributed to it, hall had less dignity (at least for pensioners) than it has now, when it is supposed to be informal and less freighted with significance. Fellows, fellow commoners and scholars ate separately, had better food and more courses, and perhaps sat longer at table. For pensioners dinner lasted forty-five minutes, and consisted, at least by way of official college provision, of joints of beef, mutton, and pork (ducks and geese were added on saints' days), plain vegetables, and beer *ad libitum*. Soup, cheese, and puddings were extras that might be 'sized for' – ordered from the kitchens by note, although Everett notes that at any rate by the 1860s pies and puddings were part of the set meal – a step towards the lavish undergraduate fare of the twentieth century. There were no napkins, and no assigned places. Hungry students tried to get a seat near a joint, and there was a lot

595

of pushing, at least at Trinity with its large number of students. (In the 1860s a dining club was started, the Anti-Dining-in-Hall-on-Sunday-because-of-the-Squash, or ADIHOSBOTS; it met at the Lion Inn.) There was a veritable army of servants about, bedmakers acting as waiters in bonnet and shawl, but the pensioners themselves carved the meat, or hacked at it to grab as much as possible while the waiters tried to prevent them, since any meat left over was servants' perquisites. 'The college hall of Trinity', wrote Everett, was 'pretty dismal, except for a very hungry man'. For once his Cambridge editor agreed with him: an undergraduate 'really ought to dine like a gentleman, not be fed like a pig'.[28]

Dinner was the pivot of the day. Before it there were two long sessions – morning for classes in college and with private tutors, and afternoon for hard exercise (about which more is said below). After dinner students strolled in the college grounds, or read newspapers in the Cambridge Union, or entertained each other with parties, drinking wine and eating oranges and cake. If the party was held in lodgings the host might engage one of the bands that toured the Cambridge streets looking for work; the musicians (they always included a harpist) sat on the stairs. At 6.0 pm the chapel bell rang again, and after the service the serious private study occurred for perhaps four hours, at least for 'reading men'. Effort was sometimes lightened by supper parties, the frugal entertaining friends with bread and jam, while in some rooms there was heavy drinking. Teetotallers were rare, and pointed out to the curious. Friends from other colleges had to hurry home before 10.0 pm, when college gates closed, and be sure to take their academical dress lest they be intercepted by the Proctor and his bulldogs in the Cambridge streets, and fined. After 10.0 pm, too, fines were payable for entry to colleges (unless you knew a way to climb in), and after midnight admission would mean an interview with your tutor the following morning.

Undergraduates' resources varied greatly, and so did the rooms available for them to rent. Sets of rooms for Trinity fellow commoners might be palatial, while at the other extreme were some sets at Caius in the 1850s.

---

[28] Everett, *On the Cam*, p. 101.

I should doubt if a single bedroom had a fire-place, except where an original entire chamber had been converted into a bedroom. Sometimes the sleeping apartment had been obtained by making a sort of hutch in the corner of the sitting room, separated off by a lath and plaster partition; sometimes a whole neighbouring chamber had been annexed for the purpose; sometimes one of the ancient 'studies' in the corner of the main room was retained. There was one bedroom in which, literally, a man of six feet could not stand up; another, in which he could hardly lie down; in several, a bath was impossible unless you balanced it on the bed. In my case, in the ancient Perse Buildings, a top attic – once doubtless shared between two students – had been set apart for a bedroom; so that I went up two pairs of stairs to bed. It was under the tin sloping roof, with one window to the north. In the terribly severe winter of 1854–5 the water in the jug was frozen apparently into a solid block for several weeks, and my sponge became as a brickbat. Such washing as could be effected was carried on over the sitting-room fire.[29]

John Venn also reminds us that movable hip-baths were the only ones available (as of course in private houses) and the water was not laid on to individual rooms but drawn from pumps in college courts.

To carry water and coal a college needed a host of servants, who surrounded students constantly.[30] A 'gyp' (from the Greek word for vulture) was a personal servant for up to twenty undergraduates; he called them in the morning, brushed their clothes, carried parcels, and notes, and waited at parties. The blacking of shoes and boots was carried out by another functionary altogether. A bedmaker was usually female, and there was one to every staircase of eight rooms. In addition to their obvious tasks they carried coal and water and set out breakfast and tea in their students' rooms, usually ordering from the buttery far more than was needed so as to claim their perquisites. Similarly, the glass, china, and crockery of an outgoing tenant became their property. They possessed keys to their charges' rooms and knew all their movements since they hovered about the staircase most of the day. 'You are hopelessly in their power, and have your choice of submitting quietly to their ultra-despotic rule,

---

[29] John Venn, *Early Collegiate Life*, pp. 271–2.
[30] This topic is also discussed in chapter 4, pp. 142–6.

or of carrying on a constant warfare.'[31] Bedmakers had the duty to inform the tutor if any undergraduate failed to occupy his room overnight, and this task made them a threat to the dissolute.

For what their utterance is worth, even chaste and abstemious witnesses seem to have disdained or disliked college servants. At least by custom enjoying security of tenure, they demarcated their functions and added to their numbers by engaging supernumeraries. On Everett's staircase the bedmaker, a young woman of thirty-five, employed her father, aged seventy-seven, to do all the hardest work such as drawing water. Everett thought the gyps even more disreputable: 'most of them are entirely too old and worn out, or young, impudent and thievish ... the whole set may be defined as leeches'.[32] He thought the Trinity porters as bad, because of their practice of collecting all college mail from the post office and charging a halfpenny per item for delivery to a college room. It was very difficult to decline services pressed on one – although Everett's Cambridge editor tells of an undergraduate who extracted from his tutor a certificate, which he framed on his wall, declaring: 'I hereby certify that Mr F. is at liberty to have his dirty linen washed by any laundress he pleases.' Gratuities were exacted each term, and on special occasions like success in the Senate House, after which servants knocked on the victor's door: '"The porters, sir, wish to congratulate you on getting your scholarship;" and that means money,– hard, sterling coin, in silver, aye, or gold, according to the rank of the official.'[33] In Caius in the 1850s it was usual to give tips in the form of beer-cheques to be drawn on the buttery. 'As some of them (e.g. the boot-black) came, to every man every term, for this purpose, the results were undesirable. I once asked that functionary how ever he managed to get through it. He could only reply, "We works it off, Sir, we works it off."'[34] But perhaps it might be said, by way of commentary, that most such stories come from large colleges with a large proportion of rich undergraduates whom it was natural for servants to exploit in the low-wage and high-unemployment early Victorian economy. Much of the blame should be attached to

[31] Everett, *On the Cam*, p. 221 and pp. 220–7 for this paragraph generally, for which also see Bristed, *Five Years*, vol. I, pp. 18–19.

[32] *On the Cam*, p. 223, and pp. 224–5 for the next quotation.

[33] Everett, *On the Cam*, p. 225.   [34] Venn, *Early Collegiate Life*, p. 271.

Trinity Cloisters, between 2 and 4, on a wet day.

16 Trinity Cloisters, between 2 and 4, on a wet day, drawn in 1859.

college bursars for not instituting proper controls long after the Treasury had shown the way.

If Cambridge seemed very busy during the terms, they were short and the vacations long and comparatively quiet; and this was especially true of the Long Vacation, effectively from the middle of June to the middle of October. 'So attractive is the Vacation-College-life, that the great trouble of the Dons is to keep the men from staying up during the Long', wrote Bristed – reminding us once more that some things have not changed in Cambridge in the last 150 years.[35] Scholars and sizars were by statute permitted to reside all year, and these formed the bulk of the 200 undergraduates (out of 1,800) that stayed up in the summer. They were more studious than most, and the city offered few distractions except the swings and travelling players at the Midsummer Fair; so Bristed, like others, read a great deal. His one regret was that ice

[35] Bristed, *Five Years*, vol I, p. 108; see pp. 105–9 and 272–8 for this paragraph generally, and also Everett, *On the Cam*, pp. 124–5.

cream was hard to come by; the confectioners would only make it to order. One year he joined a reading party consisting of four students and a tutor. Expecting to meet them in Dinan (Brittany) he found them in Jersey, and rapidly concluded that they had stopped there for the billiard halls, livery stables, and female company that it offered in abundance. Bristed was very sceptical about the academic value of most reading parties, since the holiday atmosphere of new scenery tempted men to 'lie on your back dreamily watching clouds sailing over head and ships gliding by on rivers'.[36] His words are more convincing than Everett's claim that 'in all cases, their plan, I am bound to say, faithfully carried out by almost all, is, to pass six or eight hours of each day in study, and the remainder in athletic pursuits'. Everett himself does not seem to have joined a reading party, and his Cambridge editor treats his description very ironically.[37]

THE ACADEMIC ROUND: CLASSICS AND MATHEMATICS

In early Victorian times it was usual to poke fun at the Cambridge 'reading man', who from his first months in college dedicated himself to examination success – eating little at dinner in case he was sleepy for his four hours of evening toil, despising novels as frivolous, and boasting among fast men that he too once shirked a lecture.

> He seldom reads an English work, and of the history of his native country is strangely, almost supernaturally, ignorant. Passing occurrences do not affect him. He doesn't care how many men are slaughtered on the banks of the Jhelum. *His* heart is at Marathon, his sympathies with the gallant Hannibal at Cannae. The fields with which he is best acquainted are not battle fields, but rectangular ones with mathematical properties, through which he fights his way to a solution over the carcases of x's and y's. Beautiful landscapes fail to delight him. He looks upon hills, and valleys, and rivers, as interesting or otherwise, according to their capabilities of furnishing a sum...
>
> The Rev. Mr G, Senior Wrangler of his year, and Fellow of St. John's College, went some time ago with a reading party into Wales. On his return a friend asked him if he had visited Snowdon.

[36] Bristed, *Five Years*, vol. I, p. 273.   [37] *On the Cam*, p. 125.

'Snowdon', he replied, 'what is that?' 'Why the great mountain; don't you know?' 'Oh! ah! yes to be sure, so it is', said he, 'Why no; the fact is we had a little hill behind the house where we were lodging, *quite high enough for all practical purposes.*'

The worthy Senior Wrangler did not conceive it possible that a man should inspect a mountain with any other intention than that of taking its altitude.[38]

We can of course recognise the fun and parody in this sketch. Nevertheless, there is truth in it. The early Victorian years, from 1830 to 1870, were the pinnacle of Cambridge competitiveness, at all events for the reading man who entered into its spirit;[39] and it entailed great effort and specialisation of consciousness, at least in the last four terms before the tripos. As the numbers of candidates and papers in the Mathematical Tripos were growing steadily larger the labour exacted by the spirit of emulation was increasing too, while the introduction of the Classical Tripos in the 1820s had added another spur to effort for undergraduates wishing to excel at literary pursuits. A competitive atmosphere was created, in the years between matriculation and the degree, by college examinations and contests for a variety of university and college scholarships and prizes. Colleges held their examinations in the Easter Term – hence their name, the 'Mays' – while the other contests were scattered throughout the year. College Mays were taken seriously by reading men, and were, like the triposes, exacting tests of stamina. In Bristed's first year his 'May' lasted for four days, each containing two papers each of four hours (9.0 am–1.0 pm, and 4.0 pm–8.0 pm). Occasionally there were papers of five hours' duration. Less important was the Previous Examination, or Little-Go, held in the Lent Term of the second (Junior Sophister) year, the only other hurdle for the degree itself apart from the Senate House Examination; for a serious reading man the 'Little-Go' was an irritant rather than a worry.

The competitive spirit was most active in the two largest colleges, Trinity and St John's. The number and prestige of their fellowships

---

[38] 'John Smith', *Sketches of Cantabs*, pp. 5–8. The 'Rev. Mr G.' was William Nathaniel Griffin, Senior Wrangler and First Smith's Prizeman 1837 and fellow of St John's from 1837 to 1848. He is said by Venn to have been a 'very successful private tutor'.
[39] The following paragraphs are based on Bristed, *Five Years*, vol. 1, pp. 83–156.

excited it, and Trinity also had many scholarships, awarded annually, that were striven for too. The large colleges had for many years captured a large proportion of 'firsts', and the presence in the colleges of many highly qualified graduates meant that their keen undergraduates had ready access to the best coaches, who gave their pupils an advantage in the race by arousing the desire for contention. Certainly the reminiscences of John Venn suggest that at his comparatively small college (Gonville and Caius) in the 1850s passion for a wranglership at first visited individuals, rather than the society as a whole.[40] Still, despite the disdain that Bristed and his like evinced, many small-college men did become wranglers, and indeed leading wranglers.[41] Examination rivalry pervaded the entire university, not just a few colleges.

In most contests both classics and mathematics were examined – the Little-Go, the Mays, and the college scholarships. (The *university* scholarships, on the other hand, were largely classical in nature.) There was no literary test in the Senate House Examination,[42] nor in the contest for the two Smith's Prizes that were linked with it; but they were exceptional, if very important. Hard and precise knowledge was demanded as much from classicists as from mathematicians. The number of texts set for a May examination was small, but they needed to be supported by 'a vast heap of collateral and illustrative reading'.[43] This knowledge was tested not by essays, as we might naturally expect, but by a host of small questions, filling four printed sides of paper for one four-hour session. Their character is shown by these first few questions, about one twenty-fifth of the entire examination paper, set at Trinity College in June 1841.

Thucydides, Lib. IV

(1) What do we learn of the life, station and character of Thucydides from his own writings? (2) What is assigned as the date of his birth?

---

[40] *Early Collegiate Life*, p. 265.
[41] For example in 1845 the small colleges took 17 wranglerships out of 38, including 6 of the first 15. On the other hand 5 of the 6 firsts in the Classical Tripos were from Trinity, and the other was from St John's. Eighteen of the twenty-four men gaining honours in that tripos were from the two large colleges.
[42] In the middle of the century the mathematical test was usually called the Senate House Examination (its original name) while the classical was termed the Tripos. Strictly speaking they were both triposes, and they were both taken in the Senate House.
[43] Bristed, *Five Years*, vol. 1, p. 92.

(3) What account is given of his first vocation to write history, and with what probability? (4) Is it probable that he survived the end of the war? (5) What opportunities had he of acquiring information? (6) What period of time is embraced by his history? (7) By whom was it continued; and from what writers do we derive our knowledge of the history of Greece down to the time it became a Roman province?[44]

Exactitude indeed is expected from candidates for such papers, and quantity too; despite the four hours allotted to each of them it contained more questions than even the speediest undergraduate could answer. But mere length did not suffice; some men in the fourth or fifth class wrote as much as the firsts, but failed to produce the polish and elegance required for an accolade. Because of the huge number of facts predicated in a perfect script 300 or 400 marks were allocated to each paper, or 3,000 altogether, and the best candidate might achieve 2,400; the last, the bottom of the ninth class, would get 50, and below him would be two or three more out of the 130 Trinity freshmen. These dunces or idlers were said to be 'posted', and those posted twice were asked to leave the college. So the spectrum of talent and industry in the candidature was enormous, as in almost every Cambridge examination. The attainments of those at the top we may justly admire, but they did not include (or at least were not obliged to include) powers of reflective and imaginative judgement such as we take for granted.

Men desiring classical honours, as Bristed did, were under a grave disadvantage in early Victorian Cambridge, where the rules were set by mathematicians until the 1850s.[45] Classicists had to take the mathematical examination and achieve at least junior optime, and as we have seen some accomplished literary scholars (such as Macaulay) could not. The Classical Tripos was taken very soon after the Senate House Examination, and so candidates for it had to carry a double load of revision, in very different subjects: 'Double Firsts' distinguished themselves indeed. There was an additional handicap.

---

[44] The first page of the paper (about six times the length of this quotation) is printed in Bristed, *Five Years*, vol. I, pp. 89–91.

[45] In 1850 it became possible to take the Classical Tripos after qualifying for an ordinary degree in the Mathematical Tripos, and in 1854 the threshold for classicists was lowered, the Previous qualifying them for entry to their degree.

Two gold medals, the Chancellor's,[46] were awarded to the classicists who were senior optimes. Sometimes, as in 1843, 1844, and 1847, the two top classicists were also medallists, but more often than not that was not the case. In 1841 the medals were not awarded at all. Seven men, all likely candidates for the first class in classics, failed miserably in the Senate House Examination. The first class in the Classical Tripos (never more than a dozen or so at this time) had only five members. The first three were only junior optimes and the last two put up such a mediocre performance in the medal examination that they were held not to deserve them.[47] The bias against classicists was a standing grievance. Nevertheless, it is interesting that William Everett, whose scholarly concerns were very similar to Bristed's, took the Mathematical Tripos *voluntarily* before the Classical in 1863, presumably for reasons of prestige. Everett, like Bristed, achieved junior optime in the Mathematical Tripos and a good second class in the Classical.

For two years Bristed was dogged by misfortune. For long periods he had trouble with his heart and his eyes, and could not work for an extended time. 'In this strait an opportunity was afforded me to test the value of English friendship, and obtain an insight into the best side of English character which otherwise I might not have done.'[48] Undergraduates and fellows visited regularly to cheer him. Then the failure of the Bank of Pennsylvania created money problems for him, and Bristed was grateful to his tutor, John Grote,[49] for giving him much credit. After these vicissitudes Bristed had to work very hard to attempt both honours examinations, and he followed the Cambridge custom of 'putting on two coaches for the last Long'.[50] Bristed was a partisan of private tuition, and not always a convincing one. He argued that intensive teaching, thrice weekly or as often as every day, was the only way to enable freshmen from very different backgrounds to fill in the gaps in their schooling: Etonians and others from the leading public schools who were ahead in classics but knew little mathematics, the pupils from elsewhere who had been groomed for

[46] The medals were instituted by the Duke of Newcastle in 1751 and have been continued by later chancellors.
[47] These details have been taken from Tanner, *Historical Register*.
[48] Bristed, *Five Years*, vol. I, p. 111.
[49] The younger brother of the historian of Greece.
[50] Bristed, *Five Years*, vol. I, p. 200, and pp. 199–214 for much of what follows.

Cambridge mathematics but knew little Latin or Greek, and unfortunates who might not know much at all. Also, private tutors were on far more friendly and familiar terms with their pupils than regular dons, who were separated from undergraduates by college protocol. But there was much special pleading here, personality being more important in relationships than position, and intensive teaching being the proper function of the college itself. Bristed seems really to be putting a case for the reorganisation of Cambridge that was eventually to occur.

The aim of a good tutor was not to spoon-feed, but to prepare pupils for examinations by forcing them to work on their own to the highest standards of accuracy.

> The daily or ter-weekly attendance has a beneficial effect in making the pupil work regularly, nor is the tutor in most cases at all slow to blow up any of his team who give signs of laziness. Indeed this was an acknowledged requisite of a good coach. 'I am afraid of going to T—', you may hear it said, *'he doesn't slang his men enough'*.[51]

In mathematics, pupils continually wrote out the basics, 'book-work', in their own and their tutors' rooms, to get examination speed as well as accuracy; textbooks were relied on, supplemented with the manuscript guides that some tutors thought preferable. For most of the time, however, pupils worked at examples and problems. Procedures were similar with classics tutors, pupils writing out translations from and into Latin and Greek both in their own rooms and their tutor's, and then comparing their corrected scripts with the tutor's models. It was also the tutor's 'business to make selections of hard passages from authors whom the student may not have time or inclination to read the whole of, and to point out proper books for "cram"[52] and philological information'.[53]

> In working up a clever man whose previous training has been neglected, in cramming a man of good memory but no great brilliancy, in putting the last polish to a crack man and quickening his pace, so as to give him a place or two among the highest in either

---

[51] Bristed, *Five Years*, vol. 1, pp. 203–4.
[52] Bristed defines 'cram' as 'All miscellaneous information about Ancient History, Geography, Antiquities, Law, etc., all Classical matter not included under the heads of Translation and Composition' – this last being translation *into* the classical tongues.
[53] Bristed, *Five Years*, vol. 1, p. 204, and pp. 199–200, 204, and 226–7 for the following quotations.

Tripos – in such feats a skilful tutor will exhibit consummate jockeyship; he seems to throw a part of himself into his pupil and work through him.

Attaching secondary importance to mathematics Bristed tells us little about his private tutors, apart from one who was 'a great refuge of Classical men, who had a wonderful reputation for putting through incapables, and worked some thirty or forty pupils regularly'. He tells us about three classical tutors; one, a 'large and dignified' Johnian, nicknamed 'Jupiter', 'one of the best natured and one of the laziest of mortals: his end and occupation and pleasure seemed to be to lie all day on a sofa, writing Greek and Latin verses, which he did beautifully, or reading English poetry'. It is not possible to say who 'Jupiter' was. A second was 'the oracle of the Shrewsbury men',[54] who was 'not backward in *slanging*'. He would give Bristed the common classicist's task of translating English verse into Latin and Greek. 'Once I let some verses fall into the fire, and was going to pick them out. "Let them go!", quoth he, "that's the best place for them."' Bristed tells us most about a third man, who made the most impression on him as a person and to whom he owed a great deal. It has been possible to identify this man from clues Bristed plants. He was Tom Taylor, undistinguished junior optime in 1840 but also Fifth Classic, the sort of person whose academic success was mentioned in vindication of Cambridge, because of the opening that the examination grind gave to talent. Taylor came from a modest school (he had also spent two terms at Glasgow University) and his father was a self-made Durham brewer who began as a farm labourer. In 1842 Tom Taylor was elected a fellow of Trinity, but soon he became in succession Professor of English at University College, London (1845–7), a barrister, and a civil servant at the Board of Health. He is however chiefly known as a prolific writer and journalist (editing *Punch* for a time) and above all as the most successful of Victorian dramatists, the author or adaptor of scores of plays of all types, perhaps the most famous being the melodrama *The Ticket-of-Leave Man*.[55]

---

[54] This was Richard Shilleto, on whom see p. 131.

[55] Winton Tolles, *Tom Taylor and the Victorian Drama* (Morningside Heights, N.Y., Columbia University Press, 1940), esp. pp. 26–34; Martin Banham, ed., *Plays by Tom Taylor* (Cambridge University Press, 1985), esp. pp. 1–21.

When Bristed first knew him he was a bachelor graduate, reading for his fellowship in a third-floor room in New Court, Trinity. Bristed joined him there one evening in a noisy dinner party of duck, grilled fowl, and lobster *au gratin*, with champagne.

> His fine person is not displayed to full advantage in a loose plaid shooting-coat, and his very intellectual but decidedly ugly features are far from being improved by a black wool smoking cap of surpassing hideousness. Take him as he is, he is a rare fellow – with American versatility and English thoroughness ... a puritan might call him dissipated, but it is not wickedness aforethought, but an incurable passion for seeing *character* which drags him into all sorts of society – once he went off among the gypsies, Borrow-fashion, and stayed there long enough to learn their lingo.[56]

Blessed with superabundant energy, a ready wit and easy manner, and an aptitude for anger upon strong provocation,[57] Taylor was an ideal tutor, *of a certain type*: that is, for intelligent and industrious undergraduates. 'The intercourse between the private tutor and his pupil', writes Bristed, 'varies of course according to the character and age of both parties, but it is usually of the most familiar kind, the former seldom attempting to come Don over the latter. When they are personal friends, as is not unfrequently the case, it becomes very free and easy, sometimes blending amusement with instruction in a rather comical way.'[58] When Bristed had recovered sufficiently from illness to 'put on' Taylor again, Taylor used to visit him to save Bristed the trouble of climbing his stairs. Bristed gives us a very rare description of a tutorial session in progress, from which a fragment is quoted. Though perhaps in places a little embroidered, it suggests why such sessions were so successful in fostering knowledge of linguistic intricacies. Bristed and another pupil, Menzies, were studying Aeschylus' *Supplices*, a corrupt and difficult text that they thought a waste of time since it was scarcely ever set in examinations.

---

[56] Bristed, *Five Years*, vol. I, pp. 70–1. Taylor wrote about his gypsy experiences in the *Illustrated London News* in November and December 1851 under the name 'Roumany Rei'.

[57] See the comment of John Coleman in *Players and Playwrights I Have Known* (2 vols., London, 1890), vol. II, p. 133.

[58] Bristed, *Five Years*, vol. I, p. 206 and pp. 207–8 for the passage that follows, where the italics are in the original.

The manner of instruction is this: — the pupils construe five or six lines alternately, the construer stopping himself or being pulled up short by Travis, *at the end of every line, and a long discussion and annotation intervening between that line and the next, accompanied with consultations of some or all of the nine commentators. One of the sufferers has just been reading half-a-dozen lines of the almost unknown tongue, and takes a long breath before attacking the translation.*

TRAVIS.   Now then Bristed, go on.

B.   'But respect thy suppliants, O earth-holding, almighty Zeus, for the male race of Aegyptus, intolerable in their insolence;' *hybrin* an accusative with *kata* understood, isn't it?

T.   Don't say *kata* understood; call it *an accusative of reference.*

B.   'Pursuing me in a,' – can you say *hurriedly* for *dromoisi*, as you would for *dromo* in Herodotus?

T.   Yes; what's the construction of *meta*?

B.   Tmesis with *deomenoi*. 'Seek to take forcibly me a fugitive;' *biaia* adverbial, I suppose.

T.   Of course; go on *polythroois mataisi.*

B.   '*mataisi* is an *hapax legomenon*, isn't it?'

T.   No, I believe not.

[*A hunt for* mate *among the commentators and lexicons.* Menzies, *who has the* Linwood *nearest him, announces that it occurs also in the* Choephorae, *meaning a* crome, *and here means* wanderings.]

B.   'Noisy wanderings' – will that do?

T.   *maten* – *mataios*– it *may* mean *crimes*, or *rashness* here, perhaps. I thought it did. (*Scribbles down a memorandum for future reference on the margin of his book.*) I'll think of it. Go on, Menzies.

[Menzies *reads seven or eight lines; the first two or three are not very difficult, and he charges them with great determination.*]

M.   'The beam of thy balance is over all, and what without is accomplished to mortals? O! O! ah! ah!'

T.   Never mind the interjections.

[Menzies *makes a long pause.*] *hode marptis*, 'this snatcher', *naios*, 'at sea', *gaios* 'on land'. I'm at sea altogether myself.

T.   'This snatcher from the ship is now on land.' Don't go to sleep, Bristed. Well, Menzies.

M.   'May you labor for these things.'

T.   'Before these things, snatcher, may you perish,' that is, before you carry me off.

M.   *ioph om* is Egyptian, isn't it ?

T.   Probably; not Greek, at any rate.

In the Michaelmas Term of his third year Bristed decided to postpone taking honours till his fifth year of residence, as the regulations allowed, because of his ill-health.[59] So the agony of mathematics was prolonged, even if a better result might be in prospect. Eight years after starting algebra, he began again for the fourth time knowing as little as ever. Diverting himself with billiards (which he found so alluring that he gave it up), horse-riding, and the delights of the table (he claims to have introduced sherry cobbler to Cambridge), he persevered for two years, working away at his classics concurrently, of course. 'I never felt so thoroughly sick of everything like a Mathematical book as just before the "Great Go" . . . The feeling was exactly like that of eating sawdust.'[60] Feeling it necessary not to divert energy from algebra and trigonometry he resolved to keep his classics books in another room away from his study, and read 'old ballads and romantic poetry' for diversion. Still, as though confessing to secret drinking he writes of his adding Homer to them, and then of reading the *Republic* for an hour after breakfast to set him up for xs and ys.

Bristed would have liked the jokey ignominy of the Wooden Spoon, but instead was two places higher. Before the mathematical list was published he was hard at work for the Classical Tripos, little more than two weeks away. There were twelve papers, four each of three hours, two and a half hours, and one and a half hours: four of them were 'compositions', translating English verse or prose into Latin or Greek, and the rest required the translation of classical prose or verse into English.[61] Bristed took the second place in the second class. 'On hearing this double mediocrity of position assigned me, I had need of all my philosophy . . . I certainly was considerably sold by the final result.'[62] Eighteen years later William Everett, a man of very similar scholarly interests, achieved a nearly identical result; junior optime and head of the second class in the Classical Tripos.

But Cambridge was not just about the frustration of literary hopes by unsympathetic mathematicians – a theme for a Donizetti opera, perhaps. There were undergraduates who exulted in mathe-

[59] For what follows, see vol. I, pp. 223–36, 269–327, 345–56, 381–5.
[60] Bristed, *Five Years*, vol. I, pp. 289 and 298.
[61] The papers are printed in Bristed, vol. II, pp. 428–52.
[62] Bristed, *Five Years*, vol. I, p. 383.

matics – who thought it, as Newton had, the key to understanding the universe. One such man was a Scot, William Thomson, who as Bristed ate his sawdust was delighting in his gladiatorial struggle to be Senior Wrangler – though he too was disappointed of that supreme prize. The experiences of this undergraduate are considered in the next chapter.

EVERETT AND BRISTED: THEIR ASSESSMENTS OF
CAMBRIDGE

In his third and fourth lectures Everett offered his audience in the Lowell Institute a eulogy of Cambridge, with some criticisms:

> But taking man as he is, it is impossible that any one of ordinary powers, brought up in a classic atmosphere, contemplating classic models, and taught in classic literature, should fail in refinement and purity of thought, in conciseness and elegance of diction, or that he should be habitually the victim of the crudities and shallowness that so infest our untrained modern students. And on the other hand, no one can have truly devoted himself to the immutable foundations, and the ever-rising structure of mathematics, without having his mind imbued to the end of his life with these two all-conquering principles, – stability and progress. Such has been the history of Cambridge.[63]

Personal responsibility for one's own progress creates habits of work; competition breeds the rivalry not of enemies but of brothers (Everett being particularly vague on how this comes about). But somewhat inconsistently in view of his praise of Cambridge specialism and his attack on the 'crudities' of American students, he points out, like many others, that Cambridge failed to provide for the average student, and suggests that the university might take up the general curricula of American colleges:

> The defence of this system [that is, Cambridge] is obvious. It is said that they want to make fine scholars in each branch, not superficial jacks-of-all-trades. Very well; but how if a man cannot be a first-rate scholar in any one branch? How if his mind is essentially superficial and mediocre? Which is better, that in the vain struggle to be first or second in one subject, he should end by being thirtieth, or that he

---

[63] *On the Cam*, p. 95; pp. 49–97, 217–38 for these lines generally.

should be encouraged to take a good position in several subjects, and make up in width what he wants in depth? How is it in life? . . . The great lights elaborate a single speciality, – the average men know a little of everything, because they cannot know more than a little of anything. Therefore I think the plan pursued in our colleges of giving the inferior minds a chance to gain all the knowledge they can, be it wide and superficial, or narrow and deep, is well.[64]

Everett's most original criticism, and perhaps his most penetrating, is offered from a specifically American viewpoint: the atmosphere of inviolable tradition is stifling, an

> outrage on that feeling of pure independence which a young man in America so thoroughly enjoys. The life in Cambridge is like walking in a great and elegantly kept park or pleasure-ground. You may see and smell the flowers, but you cannot pick any of them; the fountains will play, but only just so, and at such times. You must only walk, or, perchance, must submit to be taken the grand round, from which you cannot deviate; so that, after getting through all the countless wonders and glories, you long for a ramble through a tangled forest.[65]

Charles Bristed gives a more considered and detailed assessment of Cambridge practice and behaviour.[66] His commentary on the principles behind Cambridge education is consistently encomiastic – more passionate and committed than Everett's. It is easy to see why he appears to have been far less popular in his own land than in Britain. In only one respect, he argued, were Yale and other American colleges superior to Cambridge – their teaching of fluency in English speech and writing – while in real scholarship, mathematics and the classical tongues, their teaching was notably inferior, in fact slipshod and inaccurate.[67] 'And from this combination of inaccuracy of detail with facility of expression results one of our great national faults, *a tendency to defend rather than prevent mistakes; plausibility in explaining away or glossing over an error rather*

[64] Everett, *On the Cam*, pp. 234–5.
[65] *On the Cam*, pp. 226–7.
[66] These paragraphs are based on Bristed, *Five Years*, vol. II, pp. 79–174.
[67] It was unfair to compare Cambridge with American colleges in this way since in the middle of the century their age-range was usually 15 to 19, in other words much more like the Scots universities or English public schools.

than caution in guarding against the probability of its occurrence.'[68] Regarding the natural sciences, modern languages, philosophy, and indeed any other subject as inferior to classics in their power to discipline the mind and inculcate habits of critical judgement and good taste, Bristed recommended the intensive cultivation of Latin and Greek,[69] in the competitive manner developed in Cambridge, to provide a common culture for American businessmen and men of affairs, and to counteract the tendencies to shoddy thinking and bad taste that resulted from the vulgarity of the American mob and the defective education of their betters.

> The critical habits induced by classical study, teaching condensation of thought by rejection of superfluities, purity of style and clearness rather than magniloquence of expression, are the best protection against the inroads of bad taste. Abolish the study of Greek and Latin entirely, and we should be delivered over to the Vandals of literature, the heroes of the stump and the penny paper.[70]

Bristed's account of his own land was more diatribe than description, and his panegyric of what we may call the Cambridge philosophy of education lacked sensitivity (and common sense). He swallowed it whole, and without reflection, and he was wrong-headed in pushing it in a society governed by a democratic ideal rather than the aristocratic one that best suited his philosophy. It is hard to resist the conclusion that it was a mistake to leave Trinity in 1846.

[68] Bristed, *Five Years*, vol. II, p. 111.
[69] He has very little to say about mathematics, and plainly regards it as less essential.
[70] Bristed, *Five Years*, vol. II, p. 148.

Chapter 17

THE UNDERGRADUATE EXPERIENCE, III: WILLIAM THOMSON

WILLIAM THOMSON BEFORE CAMBRIDGE

To thought and feelings seas and continents present no barriers... They roam at will to the uttermost parts of the earth. Though to those around me I appear to be seated in our little parlour at Knock[1] beside a blazing fire before which three apples are roasting and diffusing an agreable fragrance around ... in spirit I am with you in your solitary study, looking over your shoulder while you are unravelling the mazy intricacies of a mathematical problem. There you sit all absorbed, deep thought broods upon your brow. Now you pause and look with earnest eyes at the vacant wall, and now with sudden inspiration you turn to commit the happy thought to paper which lies before you. Your fire is almost out, your candle is unsnuffed, your once hot tea stands untasted before you on your table.[2]

So in October 1842 wrote Elizabeth Thomson, aged twenty-four, to her brother William, aged eighteen, an undergraduate in Peterhouse.[3] The letter reveals the intelligence and sensitivity characteristic of the family, and the close affection that bound its members together; it helps to explain the soaring trajectory of William's career at Cambridge and after. He was to become a famous scientist, and Lord Kelvin. There were six siblings, two girls[4] and four boys. Their mother, Margaret, died in 1830, when

---

[1] Near Largs, in Ayrshire.
[2] CUL Kelvin-Stokes Papers, Add. MS 7342: K61, Elizabeth Thomson to William Thomson, *c.* 31 October 1842. Elizabeth was soon to marry the Reverend David King.
[3] For what follows, see Crosbie Smith and M. Norton Wise, *Energy and Empire. A Biographical Study of Lord Kelvin* (Cambridge University Press, 1989), pp. 3–55; Silvanus P. Thompson, *The Life of William Thomson, Baron Kelvin of Largs* (2 vols., London, 1910), vol. 1, pp. 1–22; and Harold Isadore Sharlin, *Lord Kelvin, The Dynamic Victorian* (University Park, Penn., Pennsylvania State University Press, 1979), pp. 1–25.   [4] Another daughter died in infancy.

William was six. Their father, James, came from humble Ulster Presbyterian stock. At first largely self-educated, he proceeded like so many Ulstermen to Glasgow University; and after teaching at the Belfast Academical Institution he became Professor of Mathematics at Glasgow in 1832. He was remembered by a family friend as 'a good mathematician, an enthusiastic and successful teacher, the author of several valuable school-books ... laborious and precise and acute, destitute of the inventive, but largely endowed with appreciative faculties. Good-hearted, he was shrewdly alive to his interest without being selfish, and would put himself to some trouble, and even expense, to assist his friends.'[5]

An explanation of William Thomson's prodigiously successful career must give priority to his family background and his natural endowment. All his siblings were gifted, and their society helped to draw out the talents of each, just as with the Brontes. The strongest influence was their father, James, who emerges from Elizabeth's memoir as firm yet kindly and affectionate, although his letters to William at Peterhouse reveal, as a lesser side to his character, an authoritarian fussiness over trifles. His creed was a devout yet tolerant Protestantism, and an earnest support for intellectual endeavour, that characterised the Scottish Enlightenment. It was necessary for him to continue as a Glasgow professor his early habits of constant effort, if he was to sustain his large family's comfortable existence; his modest stipend had to be supplemented by textbook royalties and by fees from students his teaching skills attracted. Educating his children at home in their early years, he transmitted the work-ethic to them.

Within the family William was early singled out. Elizabeth cherished him as an infant, and his father (she says) made him a 'great pet ... partly, perhaps, on account of his extreme beauty, partly on account of his wonderful quickness of apprehension, but most of all, I think, on account of his coaxing, fascinating ways, and the caresses he lavished on his "darling papa"'.[6] Very surprisingly, to us, she goes on to say:

---

[5] John Nicol (Professor of English Literature at Glasgow, 1862–89, and son of J. P. Nicol, William's teacher, mentioned below) quoted in S. P. Thompson, *William Thomson*, vol. 1, p. 21.

[6] Elizabeth King, *Lord Kelvin's Early Home* (London, 1909), p. 87, and p. 88 for the next quotation.

17 William Thomson in 1840, aged sixteen, a drawing by his sister
Elizabeth.

I do not remember that any of us were ever in the slightest degree jealous of William on account of our father's making him a little more a pet than the rest of us. We were proud of him, and indeed we thought the child petted the father even more than the father petted the child, but we saw plainly that the fondling of his little son pleased him.

This looks like the prelude to a life as a spoiled wastrel, as another Branwell Bronte: but it was not so. Instead, his favoured upbringing seems to have added to William's self-confidence and dedication to effort. As was common in Scotland, the Thomson brothers began at university at a young age. Matriculating at Glasgow at ten, he attended classes in a variety of subjects, without however proceeding to the formality of graduation. He excelled at mathematics. Owing much to the teaching ability of his father, who was versed in continental advances in analysis as well as the geometrical tradition, William manifested very early an originality of mind that James lacked. It was stimulated by another teacher, John Pringle Nichol, Professor of Astronomy at Glasgow, whose classes Thomson, aged fourteen, attended in the session 1839–40. Many years afterwards Lord Kelvin recalled those youthful days:

> In his lectures the creative imagination of the poet impressed youthful minds in a way that no amount of learning, no amount of mathematical skill alone, could possibly have produced. For, many years afterwards, one of the most important affairs I have ever had to do with began with what I learned in the natural philosophy class in that session. I remember the enthusiastic and glowing terms in which our professor and teacher spoke of Fourier, the great French creative mathematician who founded the mathematical theory of the conduction of heat . . . I remember how my youthful imagination was fired with what I heard from my teacher . . . The benefit we had from coming under his inspiring influence, that creative imagination, that power that makes structures of splendour and beauty out of the material of bare dry knowledge, cannot be overestimated.[7]

Thomson began to display outstanding intellectual maturity about this time, winning a university medal for a lengthy essay, on the 'figure of the earth' – a sophisticated calculation of the extent the earth differs from an oblate spheroid, a conundrum that had

---

[7] 'Lord Kelvin and his first teacher in natural philosophy', *Nature*, 68 (29 October 1903), pp. 623–4.

exercised mathematicians since Newton. On the day Thomson received his medal for his essay he began to read Fourier's work on heat, having just been introduced to it, as we have seen, by J. P. Nichol. Fourier had published it eighteen years before, but it is a sign of the relative backwardness of British mathematics that it was very little known here; Thomson, young though he was, was among the first to become acquainted with it. Fourier demonstrated how mathematical reasoning could be used to measure a process, the movement of heat through solid bodies, that was not susceptible of measurement empirically. The approach could be used elsewhere, and became central to Thomson's thinking as a physicist and engineer – for example, in his calculations on the behaviour of electric current in cables and of ocean tides subject to gravitational forces. In his seventeenth year Thomson's grasp of Fourier's new ideas led to his first published paper, 'On Fourier's Expansions of Functions in Trigonometrical Series'. It was provoked by an attack on Fourier in a book by Philip Kelland, Professor of Mathematics at Edinburgh. His father submitted the paper anonymously to the *Cambridge Mathematical Journal*. Its editor, D. F. Gregory, showed it to Kelland, who agreed that he had been mistaken. The paper appeared in May 1841, before Thomson matriculated at Cambridge. A second article showed the correctness of a new mathematical relation that Fourier had employed but not verified.

These three papers demonstrate Thomson's originality of mind. A fourth, written in the summer of 1841 before he went up to Peterhouse, and published in the *Cambridge Mathematical Journal* in February 1842, manifested a leap in his creative imagination remarkable in a boy of seventeen. Discerning an analogy between phenomena not obviously akin, the conduction of heat and electrical attraction, he showed how Fourier's equations, devised to measure the first, might also be applied to the second. Though Thomson's perception had been in part anticipated by others,[8] neither its creative value nor the quality of intellect it revealed was lessened thereby. As Clerk Maxwell later wrote, it was one of the most valuable of 'science-forming ideas'.[9] Already very accomplished as a mathematician, William Thomson might add to his

[8] One of them being George Green, the Nottingham mathematician mentioned in chapter 5.
[9] Quoted in Sharlin, *Lord Kelvin*, p. 23.

understanding in only one university in Britain – in Cambridge, working intensively for the Senior Wranglership. His father had him entered on the books of Peterhouse in April 1841, in correspondence with the tutor, H. W. Cookson.

WILLIAM THOMSON: MONEY AND AMBITION

'Use *all economy* consistent with respectability . . . *You must contract no debts*, except through Mr Cookson', wrote James Thomson to William in the Lent Term 1842 – words that would have drawn agreement from many other parents, and are typical of the copious archive that illustrates William's years at Peterhouse more fully than those of any other undergraduate in our period.[10] In the three years October 1841 to October 1844 William Thomson spent (or had spent on him) almost exactly £900, comprising £90 from Peterhouse for the Gisborne scholarship and £32 in sundry prizes, and £774 6s 7d from his father. £144 of this was for private tuition, in the years 1842–4.[11] Whatever he protested to his father, Thomson's expenditure (excluding the costs of private tuition) was double that of an economical pensioner.[12]

James Thomson's income seems to have been about £800 a year (half coming from textbook royalties) and so supporting his son was a heavy load, since he was also responsible for three or four other children. Money was sent to William not in an annual allowance but as the need arose, his father waiting till his son had only 6s or 7s left. Disliking bank drafts because of the commission charges, James Thomson would send £10 or £20 in half banknotes, in separate envelopes to prevent postal theft. He was an exceptional parent in being worried about everything. A few weeks into his first term William proposed to buy ice-skates. His father replied,

I must require, that you ascertain the *perfect safety* of the amusement, before you participate in it: and, further, that it will not lead you into

---

[10] The section that follows is based on this correspondence in Add. MS 7342, particularly T.179–T.291, T.496–T.517, H.122–H.124, and C.132–C.140; and also on Smith and Wise, *Energy and Empire*, pp. 56–82, S. P. Thompson, *William Thomson*, vol. 1, pp. 23–112, and Sharlin, *Lord Kelvin*, pp. 26–42.

[11] T.274 and T.276, James Thomson to William Thomson 12 October and 18 October 1844; S. P. Thompson, *William Thomson*, vol. 1, p. 109.

[12] Costs are discussed at length in chapter 2.

company that will injure or relax your moral feeling... I find that Aytoun[13] goes to no wine parties, because of the excesses and other evils to which they lead. *At present*, I do not say, you should go to none, unless with fellows; but *you should scarcely go to any others*: and if you do go, observe the strictest caution, and always tell me about anything of the kind.[14]

Early in 1842 William submitted the accounts his father required. Confused in their arrangement, they irritated Dr Thomson by suggesting that his son had only 17s 7d left whereas he made the surplus nearly £1 more. 'And how do you require *two* pairs of shoes *about* 12/ each? Such a charge unless for very strong and excellent shoes, is quite too much.' He went on to raise as a dire warning the fate of William's old teacher J. P. Nichol. 'I feel the vast importance of your acquiring *accurate business habits* along with whatever else you may learn. Consider poor Dr Nichol, who for want of such habits, is a ruined man. His affairs turn out to be, I am satisfied, in irretrievable confusion. His debts ... turn out to be not less than about £5000!!!'[15] Pointing out that the college shoe-black system made two pairs necessary William apologised for forgetting where some shillings had gone and promised reformation. Yet friction continued. James Thomson's obsessiveness over financial detail was insatiable. In any case William had a healthy streak of independence. In February, writing 'to tell you, what I have no doubt will rather surprise you', he announced that he had with a friend bought a boat, 'built of oak, and as good as new', for only £3 10s each – 'a wonderful bargain' that had to be snapped up; there had therefore been no time to seek his father's permission, but 'I felt confident that you would not be displeased.'[16] At first enraged, but then mollified by praise of William's conduct and companions from Cookson (who certainly worked hard over the Thomson family) Dr Thomson eventually became reconciled to the boat, but within days was distressed again by William's quarterly account.

> I see, also, 'Barber 12/0', and 'Barber, 3/0' amounting to 15/0 – a sum that a gentleman present (when your accounts were examined)

[13] Roger St Clair Aytoun, a Scot, a pensioner at Trinity.
[14] T.186, James Thomson to William Thomson, 6 December 1841.
[15] T.191, James Thomson to William Thomson, 12 January 1842. Nichol spent money recklessly on scientific equipment.   [16] T.196, William Thomson to James Thomson, 19 February 1842.

of more than twice your years said he had never paid to a barber for all expenses of that kind during his life... Purchase no books but what are indispensable. In fact you must follow this latter rule in all cases. Even of *necessary articles*, too, let your *general rule* be to purchase as little as possible at Cambridge. Many articles you will get here greatly cheaper – clothes in particular. Are the sums you have paid to the gyp & etc, established & consuetudinal? If not so, do not pay them.[17]

It is unnecessary to detail the frequent further admonitions, and the explanations that followed from William. Yet William was denied no money he asked for. Despite his imperious letters, James Thomson was anxious to do everything needful to ensure that William became Senior Wrangler, and a professor too; and what is more he often turned to him for professional advice, as a more up-to-date and accomplished mathematician: this was a paradoxical fate for a university professor. 'I wish you could make out a solution for the question about the centre of gravity of a spherical triangle', he wrote a week or so into William's first term, and William obliged at length when he had time.[18] Such communications were typical of their correspondence, and sit oddly with the assumptions of filial dependence manifest in the same letters. When considering D. F. Gregory[19] for a chair at Glasgow Dr Thomson asked his son about his powers as a teacher: 'quietly look after this matter, and let me know what you gather on this subject either from your own observation or otherwise', to which query William gave a favourable reply.[20]

An opportunity to promote William to a chair at Glasgow seemed to be offered in the decline of William Meikleham, the frail Professor of Natural Philosophy (and friend of the Thomson family) though problems might arise if he were to die before William's tripos. Acres of letter-paper were covered with assessments of his health and of faculty attitudes – some Glasgow professors not favouring the appointment of a totally inexperienced son of a colleague. After Meikleham suffered a fall James

[17] T.204, James Thomson to William Thomson, 28 March 1842.
[18] T.180, 28 October 1841 and T.237, 20 April 1843.
[19] A Scot known to the Thomsons, a fellow of Trinity and editor of the *Cambridge Mathematical Journal*, Gregory died in 1844.
[20] T.184, 15 November 1841, and T.201, *c.* February 1842.

Thomson reported that 'his tenure of life is far more uncertain than ever... Keep the matter in mind therefore, and think on every way in which you might be able to get efficient testimonials.' Confident of his mathematical powers the ambitious twenty-year-old replied, 'I am very sorry to hear about Dr Meikleham's precarious state. I have now got so near the end of my Cambridge course that even on my own account I should be very sorry not to get completing it. For the project we have it is certainly very much to be wished that he should live till after the commencement of the next session.'[21]

William's tripos was then only eight months away. As January 1845 drew near Dr Thomson grew ever more concerned about whether William was doing everything possible to gain the Senior Wranglership. 'You say Fuller is to give you exams. "as soon as Hopkins gives up". Will Hopkins not rather increase his instructions till the great exams. take place? Get of course all possible instructions from all quarters... On *every* account do what you can to preserve your health, avoiding colds in particular.'[22] A fortnight before the tripos began James Thomson advised that, 'An illness such as John's or Robert's would knock up our expectations about your degree examinations; and I much doubt the propriety of your bathing out of doors on such a day as last Saturday was here.' He asked that during the examination itself, 'Can you continue to drop us a note each evening, telling us about your health, how you got on, etc; or to get someone else to do so?... I am told the best men often do worse than the inferior ones from having forgotten the earlier and more elementary subjects. Are you made up on those subjects?'[23] A few days later William Thomson was involved in the most intense contest ever for the Senior Wranglership, watched with interest by many in the university and of course by his kinsfolk in Glasgow, to whom frequent letters conveyed the news of each day's examination papers. In the event the depth of Thomson's interest in mathematical enquiry kept him from the highest place; he became Second Wrangler.

[21] T.256, James to William Thomson, 20 April 1844, and T.257, William to James Thomson, 22 April 1844.
[22] T.276, James to William Thomson, 18 October 1844.
[23] T.277, James to William Thomson, 18 December 1844.

INDUSTRY AND LEISURE

In the evening of Saturday 23 October 1841, a day or so after his father had left for Glasgow after escorting him to Peterhouse, William Thomson wrote to his sister Anna about his feelings of disorientation which many generations of freshmen have experienced. Nobody had told him what to read, yet he thought that he ought to be in a student routine: 'to make the time pass less heavily, I have been going out every now & then, & coming in again. I have plenty to see at Cambridge, but somehow I am not in a frame of mind for sight-seeing, as I consider that I should be walking about only between two & four'.[24] At the freshmen's dinner on the first evening nobody spoke except when addressed by Cookson, at the head of the table – who managed to create a conversation of sorts about mesmerism (the subject of a recent Cambridge lecture) and the college's neighbour, the Fitzwilliam Museum. 'By and by two or three older students dropped in, whom it was easy to know were not freshmen, from the comparative freedom with which they spoke.'

Within days he settled down, and into a regular routine of daily college morning lectures, varied by walking in the afternoons.[25] Freshmen had to read both classics and mathematics for the Previous Examination (or 'Little-Go') taken at the end of the Lent term; Cookson lectured on Euclid on Mondays, Wednesdays, and Fridays, while Freeman, the classics lecturer, took them through the set texts on the other two days. For each classical lecture Thomson and his college associates were expected to prepare seventy lines of the Greek text of *Prometheus Unbound*, and despite his comparative lack of classical talents he found this requirement well within his powers. In the mathematics lecture students followed the usual Cambridge practice of 'writing out' Euclidean propositions with simple deductions from them – explanations on paper being regarded as the only believable ones; but it was clear at the first session, concerned with the first six propositions of Book One, that some were going to find it impossible to keep up, since they

---

[24] B.182, William to Anna Thomson, 23 October 1841, from which the following quotation is also taken.
[25] These paragraphs are based on Add. MS 7342, T.179–T.233.

A Saunter on King's Parade on Sunday Evening.

18 A Saunter on King's Parade on Sunday Evening, drawn in 1859.

struggled to show how 'to draw from a given point a straight line equal to a given straight line'. With the aid of a blackboard and individual instruction as he toured the classroom, Cookson strove to help them. It was very like a sixth form containing a great spread of talent. Still, Cookson pushed on – students' academic efforts were after all not widely diffused – and within three weeks his class were into Book Three.

When he arrived in Peterhouse Thomson was widely known to

be an exceptional undergraduate because of his published papers and a forthcoming one, to be published in the *Cambridge Mathematical Journal*.[26] The editor, D. F. Gregory, met Thomson to discuss it, and late in November he and another fellow of Trinity, Archibald Smith,[27] called on him in Peterhouse – an unprecedented event in a freshman's life.

> They staid, I suppose nearly three quarters of an hour in my rooms, looking into my books & talking on various subjects, connected with them... They also entered into a long disquisition about a circle rolling along a parabola, or other curve, what it would do when it came to a point at which the radius of curvature is smaller than that of the circle, and got hold of my paper & drew no end of figures, regarding it.[28]

Thomson also received special attention from Cookson, who in his concern for the young Scots genius showed far more professional enthusiasm than is usually credited to college tutors in the Unreformed University. Cookson gave him extra test papers, and consulted William Hopkins, the distinguished private tutor, and member of Peterhouse, on how Thomson might best be assisted. The co-operation of Cookson and Hopkins shows how far some 'private' tutors were really integrated into the college system, though not all were: John Venn, at Caius ten years after Thomson, received no guidance from the college on what private tutors to resort to.[29] Hopkins's talents were greatly in demand, and the intervention of his college would help to secure them. In November Hopkins entertained Thomson and other prospective private pupils to supper at his home, 15 Fitzwilliam Street. Hopkins and his wife and daughter sang glees: 'and Mr Hopkins asked all of us whether we performed on any instrument, and when he heard that [we] did not, he said he was glad to hear it'. The gathering had a professional purpose; after supper he suggested privately to Thomson that he would examine him to diagnose his special needs, after Thomson had studied algebra on his own. A few weeks later, during

[26] 'On the Uniform Motion of Heat in Homogeneous Solid Bodies, and its Connection with the Mathematical Theory of Electricity': see above, p. 617.
[27] A Scot, a friend of the Thomson family.
[28] T.185, William to James Thomson, 21 November 1841, from which the next quotation also comes.   [29] John Venn, *Early Collegiate Life*, p. 263.

this examination, he put his finger on Thomson's weakness, a failure to 'write out' Euclidean propositions and their proofs (or 'bookwork') with enough economy; this was the element that made the Senate House Examination a test as much of speed and memory as of genius, and was to militate against Thomson in his great test in 1845. Hopkins and Cookson suggested that he should employ Fuller, a Peterhouse graduand, Fourth Wrangler in 1842. In October 1842 he began more intensive work each day with Hopkins himself. At first he was taught with four others. From May 1843 (after the Previous Examination) the pressure from Hopkins became greater, and Thomson saw him privately on three mornings a week in term, at 7.0 am. This pressure, which increased in Thomson's third year, lasted till the Senate House Examination in January 1845.

How much actual labour did Thomson undertake? – a question whose answer would help to give us a sense of customary student work-loads. The evidence conflicts. In his first year Thomson lost no chance to stress in his family letters his constant industry, apart from a few healthful and moral pursuits. On 27 December, from the Lincolnshire rectory where he was spending Christmas with a friend, he plaintively wrote, 'Every freshman but myself had left before I went away, and I think there were no second or third year men either. Of course all the fourth year men remain up for the examination. Every one, even the old porter, was so glad to hear that I was going to get a week's vacation.'[30] He proposed a demanding work-schedule for Lent:

Division of Time

Get up	5
Commence reading	5.15
till	8.15
Breakfast and finish dressing till	9
Lecture till	10
Read till	1
Exercise (including walking, boating and going to a gymnasium, where we can get all kinds of exercise for 2/6 a term) till	4

[30] T.188, William to James Thomson, 27 December 1841.

Hall, chapel, walking about and tea till	7.30
Read till	8.30
Go to bed at	9

I think this will not be so impracticable as at first sight it appears as I have been able, since I gave over morning chapel, to get up regularly at six, and light my own fire, which appears rather impracticable to most men.[31]

In February 1842 (as he admitted to buying the boat), he wrote, 'I have been going on reading steadily, about eight hours a day, & getting up *perfectly* regularly at a little before six o'clock'.[32]

Perhaps these resolves were seriously meant. But someone as talented as Thomson would not need such a régime for a modest examination like the Little-Go. At all events he did not keep to his plan in his second year, when the pressures on him were greater than in his first owing to the sessions with Hopkins. His routine then is shown by his manuscript diary for the period 13 February to 23 October 1843.[33] This intermittent record is very detailed on the days it does chronicle, and contains some 10,000 words. Though skimmed rather than exploited by Thomson's biographers, it is more candid about the habits of work and play of a mid-Victorian undergraduate than any other known document. Unfortunately, Thomson's comparatively few letters home from this time are silent on such matters and do not permit comparison of the private and family utterance.

The diary registers his frequent resolves to rise early, and his failures to do so. He wanted to work hard continuously but found it difficult before the Previous because cramming made him feel 'seedy'. After the examination, study was even more tedious. He certainly remained interested in mathematics, although far more in elaborating new ideas than in the tripos grind. Late in the evening of Monday 21 February, he records, 'read Lionville[34] till I got involved in some of my speculations on isothermal surfaces. No satisfaction yet however.'[35] Some days later, he wrote, 'Yesterday night I got foul of the orthogonal surfaces again, and sat till 12.30 with my feet

[31] T.187, William to James Thomson, 12 December 1841.
[32] T.196, William to James Thomson, 19 February 1842.
[33] Add. MS 7342, NB.29, Diary of William Thomson, 13 February–23 October. Apart from three October entries the diary ends at Sunday 14 May.
[34] A French mathematical journal to which Thomson subscribed.   [35] NB 29.

on the fender, but got no satisfaction. Today after coming from Hopkins I have got some new ideas, but not the ones I wanted.'[36] Eventually he did get the ones he wanted, however, and his paper on isothermal surfaces appeared in the *Cambridge Mathematical Journal* in May 1843 – one of ten articles that he wrote and published there as an undergraduate, an astonishing feat of creative fecundity.

He also felt the lure of competition that the Senate House Examination fostered. Writing at 11.45 pm on 15 February he reports:

> Papers looked over by Hopkins . . . All right but not in good form or according to manuscript.[37] Talked to Fischer[38] till 12.30. He seems to know everything of every subject, and still considers no subject as sufficiently 'got up'. I must therefore read very hard, and try at least to be as well prepared as he is. He has been reading all the parts in the 1st vol. of the Camb. Math. Journal on Geom. of 3 dimensions and . . . He knows 3 times as much of the subject as I do.

Eight days later he 'went to Hopkins at 10 and was maliciously glad to find that Fischer had not done all the problems'. But the following morning he 'did not get up till past 9, and just got breakfast over in time for lecture. I have been rather sleepy all day & very sleepy all evening. Fortunately Hopkins gave us only 3 easy examples. I have been sitting half asleep before the fire, for a long time thinking whether gravity & electrical attraction might not be the effect of the action of contiguous particles.'[39]

Thomson ruminated a great deal.

> This morning I got hold of my Math. Journal and spent an hour at least in recollections. I had far the most associations connected with the winter in which I attended the natural phil. and the summer we were in Germany. I have been thinking that my mind was more active then than it has been ever since, and have been wishing most intensely that the 1st of May 1840 would return. I then commenced reading Fourier, & had the prospect of the tour in Germany before me.[40]

---

[36] 5 March 1843.

[37] Hopkins lent his pupils manuscripts that elucidated problems.

[38] W. F. L. Fischer became Fourth Wrangler in 1845 and in 1847 a fellow of Clare. He was later Professor of Mathematics at St Andrews.

[39] NB 29, 23 and 24 February 1843.   [40] NB 29, 14 March 1843.

Strange though it might seem to us in view of his prodigious achievement a few years later, Thomson thought at this time that he might do badly (or at least not dramatically well) in Cambridge mathematics: 'I have pretty nearly determined to go to the Chancery bar, if something else do not succeed, though I cannot get over the idea of cutting mathematics.'[41] A month later he visited the assizes in Cambridge to experience the law for three hours: 'I think I could reconcile myself to the bar'.[42] One of the chief values of Thomson's self-revealing diary is that it suggests the effect of college life on some highly sensitive characters, in disturbing the equilibrium created by a tight upbringing, and allowing repressed sides of his nature to come forward. Thomson's latest biographers assume that the 'economy of time' for which in later life he was renowned was true of his Peterhouse years:[43] the self-doubt and disinclination of his second year show the superficiality of this view. Yet in the long run, after his digressions in 1843, Thomson returned to the tripos grind with renewed determination: time out did him good. One lesson of Thomson's diary (as of Christopher Wordsworth's fifty years earlier) is that the tripos did not demand continuous effort, and another is that this leniency was salutary for some.

Thomson discovered literature, reading the Shakespeare that he took as a first-year prize, and in April, not having read a novel for three years, took up Fanny Burney's *Evelina* in the evening of Saturday 22nd – an episode described in the diary in lines that vividly suggest his need for emotional relief from the mathematical intensity that had filled such a large part of his life. After an interlude spent drinking porter and port negus with friends, 'to a small extent', he read through the night, so enthralled by the romance that he did not notice the passage of time. When daylight came, he spent 'a long time looking at the sheep, and listening [to] the birds, whose singing filled the air'; he then went to bed for a few hours. Rising at 10.40 on Sunday, he bathed at Byron's Pool with friends for some hours, missed the university service at Great St Mary's, spent the rest of the day with wine, tea, and conversation, and finished *Evelina* at 2.20 on Monday morning, 24 April.[44]

[41] 21 February 1843.   [42] 24 March 1843.   [43] Smith and Wise, *Energy and Empire*, p. 72.
[44] NB 29, 24 April.

Another evening activity that at times spread into the small hours was practising the cornopean,[45] part of his obsession with music:

> After I had worked at Hopkins' problems till 11.30, I commenced practising and summoned Tom. About half past 12, after we had been for about half an hour practising We're a Noddin & Logie o'Buchan in the lowest keys we could devise, and when I was in the act of playing Adeste Fideles at my reading stand, and Tom playing Logie o'Buchan at the chimney piece a gentle tap was heard at the door. 'Come in,' shouted Tom, & in walked Mr Cookson. 'Perhaps you are not aware gentlemen how much noise these horns make.' 'We are very sorry etc.'[46]

The cornopean alternated with conversation when Thomson should have been working, sessions often taking place in the evening and aided by tea, milk punch, and porter. Topics included politics, astronomy, mathematics (sometimes), metaphysics, dreams, and ghosts, while the most popular one was the opposite sex, 'in which we all get interested'.[47] 'We talked politics again, till a letter from the Art Union turned us to pictures, and especially to one which is coming, of Titian's mistress. Thence to ladies bathing & modern bad taste & false delicacy in female dress & etc.'[48] The diary registers friends' keen interest in each others' love affairs: 'I cross questioned Stephen on his favourite subject.'[49] 'Jervis says Gisborne is in love. He is going to Brighton for 1 day.'[50]

In view of these hints of a powerful sex-drive it is not at all surprising that William Thomson appears obsessed with violent exercise in boats (walking satisfying him much less). Sculling in his one-man boat filled many hours, and his thoughts when he seemed to be otherwise engaged. On 2 April, after working at problems for Hopkins, reading Xenophon and *Punch*, hurrying to chapel (he was late), and talking to his friend Greenwood, he records, 'I have been thinking on the boat more than anything else, all day'.[51] Early in the

---

[45] An early name for the cornet. Thomson's involvement with the Cambridge University Musical Society is recounted in chapter 19.

[46] 5 March 1843.   [47] 16 April 1843.   [48] 21 March 1843.

[49] 21 February 1843. James Wilberforce Stephen was a pensioner at St John's, and Fourth Wrangler in 1844.

[50] Francis Gisborne (1840–5) and William George Jervis (1840–4) were pensioners at Peterhouse.

[51] NB 29. Boating at Cambridge is treated at greater length in chapter 18.

Easter term, succumbing at last to the temptation to row in a college crew (his father was against it), he reports on the 'bumps':

> The boat racing has commenced in earnest. On Wednesday we had not much racing but kept easily our place on account of the Johnians being bumped by Caius. Yesterday the odds were strongly in favour of Caius bumping us, but we astonished the university by keeping away. We had a glorious pull for it, and I shall remember for my whole life, the work of 7 minutes last night. My pleasure at keeping away was beyond anything I have ever felt.[52]

It is no wonder that, it was said, 'Cookson has got the idea I am idle.'[53] In the Easter Term, however, after the Previous Examination, Thomson began more intensive instruction with Hopkins that lasted for eighteen months, till the Senate House Examination in January 1845. He had less time to spare: the period of creative idleness was over.

THOMSON'S CIRCLE OF FRIENDS

Thomson's manuscript diary contains the names of many friends, fourteen of whom are mentioned seven or more times, in a variety of social and academic contexts. These close associates offer some interesting comparisons with the Trinity circle that Christopher Wordsworth touched on in his diary fifty years previously; they suggest, over time, more continuity than change, yet also some intriguing differences. Thus while all Wordsworth's circle were at Trinity, only half Thomson's were at Peterhouse; five were St John's undergraduates, and two were at Pembroke. The diary is artlessly unselfconscious, and does not explain acquaintanceship; but it may have been the habit of Peterhouse men, coming from a very small college, to find friends elsewhere. Pembroke is just over the road. Mathematics probably accounts for the St John's link; two of Thomson's St John's friends, G. W. Hemming and J. W. Stephen, were talented mathematicians and almost certainly known to Thomson very soon after he matriculated. Mentioned very often in the diary (39 and 22 times respectively) they were among Thomson's closest associates, and their discourse was certainly not

[52] 14 May.   [53] 11 April.

exclusively, or even mostly, mathematical. Some of his other friends showed little talent for mathematics or any other academic subject. Still, in 1844 Hemming was Senior Wrangler and Stephen Fourth Wrangler. Another friend, Wilhelm Fischer, was Fourth Wrangler in 1845. John Airey and Charles Gutch were wranglers too, and Thomas Field First Classic. There were also three senior optimes. The other five took ordinary degrees.

Fischer, a Pembroke pensioner, came from an unusual background. He was born in Magdeburg, the son of a merchant. Aged twenty-seven in 1841, Fischer struck Thomson with the depth of his reading: 'I went to Fischer and found him reading *Wilhelm Meister.*'[54] We also sense greater sophistication. It was his mathematical skills that made Thomson feel the goad of competition. James Wilberforce Stephen came from a famous family. He was Leslie Stephen's first cousin. The bond was not close. J.W.'s father was the lawyer George Stephen, whose coarse fibre is contrasted with his brother's sensitivity in a lapidary description by Leslie Stephen.[55] Among the ten others in Thomson's circle whose family we know something of, there were two fathers who were 'gentlemen', one merchant (in addition to Fischer's father), one captain (resident in Caen, presumably for reasons of economy) and no fewer than five clergymen.[56] We know about the schooling of ten, apart from Thomson. Two had been to Christ's Hospital, three to grammar schools in southern England, Stephen to King's College London, and Francis Osborne to King's College School. Thomas Shedden and William Stow had spent some years at Glasgow University; there were links with Professor James Thomson. The sample is small, but these pieces of evidence suggest, like the Christopher Wordsworth material, undergraduates who were gentlemen, and from the middle class.

Continuity with our impressions of the 1790s is most obvious in the group's later careers. Seven – half the group – became clergymen. But there are hints, in the brief biographies we have of these graduates in a usually conventional calling, of some uncom-

[54] NB 29, 16 April 1843.
[55] *Life of Sir James Fitzjames Stephen*, pp. 27–8. LS also contributed a memorable and pungent entry on his uncle to the *DNB*.
[56] Bainbridge Smith's father was also the headmaster of Horncastle Grammar School.

mon pursuits certainly without parallels in Christopher Wordsworth's circle, and implying attractively original or eccentric
personalities. Probably this difference between the 1790s and the
1840s is to be attributed to the contrast in character between
Wordsworth and Thomson, rather than any wide changes within
the university. After helping as an undergraduate to found the
Cambridge University Musical Society, William Blow was for
thirty years Rector of Layer Breton in Essex, but he was also a
distinguished amateur violinist and had the finest private collection of violins in Great Britain. Thomas Field was Vicar of
Madingley and other parishes in eastern England, but in the
mid-1850s he served in the crew of a cutter that in two summers
cruised the Baltic extensively; Field published an account of the
voyages, and many contributions to *The Antiquary* and *Lincolnshire
Notes and Queries*. He was also noted for his flowered silk
waistcoats. There was a restlessness about John Bainbridge Smith's
life that we do not associate with the Victorian clergy. After his
ordinary BA he was for seven years Professor of Mathematics at
King's College, Nova Scotia; then for more than a quarter-
century he was a country parson in Lincolnshire, only to throw up
this security to serve as chaplain in Smyrna for ten years in his
sixties. At the age of seventy he took a post in Christiania (Oslo) at
the other end of Europe.

Four became barristers, including Stephen and Hemming.
Hemming, one-time Senior Wrangler and First Smith's prizeman,
corroborated the hoary adage that the best Cambridge minds could
turn to anything; amid a sparkling legal career he wrote much on
mathematical and legal matters, and *Billiards mathematically treated*.
Stephen, emigrating to Australia, eventually became a judge of the
Supreme Court of Victoria, but it seems that his eager, nervous
temperament impeded an even higher climb. He possessed 'the
infirmity of saying unhappy things he afterwards regretted', says his
biographer.[57] Fischer was the only member of the circle, apart from
Thomson himself, who became a professional mathematician; he
was professor at St Andrews. The comparatively small legacy of so
much Cambridge mathematical effort is noticed elsewhere.

[57] A. T. Zainuddin in the *Dictionary of Australian Biography*.

WILLIAM HOPKINS, THOMSON'S PRIVATE TUTOR

William Hopkins was one of the most illustrious figures in the university system, a star producer of wranglers. A failed farmer, he sold his land to pay his debts in 1822, after the death of his first wife, and made a new start in life by entering Peterhouse in his thirtieth year. He became Seventh Wrangler, a distinction that would certainly have won him a fellowship had he not married again as an undergraduate. So began his career as a private tutor, in which he was immensely successful. Between 1828 and 1849 Hopkins had among his pupils 175 wranglers, 17 of them senior and 44 in the first three places.[58] Acting on hints from college tutors Hopkins chose potential wranglers as his pupils, and gave a supper party for his prospective class in the Michaelmas Term. At the party he would circulate a portfolio containing likenesses of his successes – a good way to arouse the emulative spirit.[59] Among his successes was Francis Galton the eugenist, who in a tribute to the interest he aroused by his teaching distinguished Hopkins from the dryasdust don of convention: 'Hopkins to use a Cantab expression is a regular brick; tells funny stories connected with different problems and is in no way Donnish; he rattles us on at a splendid pace and makes mathematics anything but a dry subject by entering thoroughly into its metaphysics. I never enjoyed anything so much before.'[60] Another pupil was Henry Fawcett, who cherished a lasting fondness for him and contemplated writing a memoir of his old friend till the pressure of work deterred him. The letter that Hopkins wrote to assist Fawcett when blindness struck him is a miracle of sensitivity and helpful sympathy; it reveals the generous warmth that drew people to Hopkins.[61]

Hopkins himself suggested £700 or £800 a year as the remuneration of a successful private tutor – a truly exceptional sum for a don not a head of house.[62] His earnings seem to have been even higher, and his charges were certainly greater than other private tutors'.

---

[58] Gunning, *Reminiscences*, vol. II, p. 359, quoting a letter from Hopkins dated 4 December 1849.
[59] Add. MS 7342, T.185, William to James Thomson, 21 November 1841.
[60] Karl Pearson, *The Life, Letters, and Labours of Francis Galton* (4 vols., Cambridge, 1914–30), vol. I, p. 163. Galton was a pensioner at Trinity from 1839 to 1844.
[61] The letter is quoted in full in Leslie Stephen, *Life of Henry Fawcett*, pp. 48–51.
[62] *Remarks on the Mathematical Teaching of the University of Cambridge* (Cambridge, c. 1854), p. 15.

Those of high reputation charged £75 for three terms and a Long Vacation.[63] Hopkins charged £102. He certainly worked very hard, in some seasons. He took five pupils from each matriculation, and taught them in their second and third years, and again in the Michaelmas Term of their fourth year.[64] He also had a six-week session in their last Long Vacation, at the end of the third year. Thomson's group went to Cromer, staying in a cliff-top cottage they called Jeopardy College, which has since fallen into the sea. In their second year he saw his pupils together every other day in the Michaelmas and Lent Terms, before their Previous Examination, but individually too on the intervening three days in the Easter Term, after the examination. This rhythm was kept up in the third year, and the Michaelmas Term of the fourth. (Thomson went for his private hour at 7.0 am, a requirement that drastically forced him to cure his habit of lying in bed late.) Thus at his maximum, in the Michaelmas Term, Hopkins seems to have been taking his classes for 9 hours a week, and his pupils individually for 30 hours in total each week. In Lent the totals dropped to 6 and 15, and rose to 6 and 30 in Easter.[65] Few Cambridge supervisors today would teach as intensively as that. But his teaching sessions were concentrated into half the year, or little more, even including the Long Vacation period, and Hopkins was not greatly burdened with administration, though he did have a modest official position in the university as Esquire Bedell.

Hopkins was a man of large and critical mind, uneasy about the system of private tuition in which he was so illustrious. He was sure that Cambridge should heed public criticism of the costliness of private tuition. Also, private tutors tended to follow the immediate needs of their pupils in their quest for examination success. He wished to convert them into 'public lecturers' for the university as a whole, believing that this role would encourage them to take a broader view of mathematics.[66] This was precisely the quality that bystanders thought 'conspicuous' in Hopkins's private tuition. 'He endeavoured to stimulate a philosophical interest in the mathemat-

[63] PP 1852–3, HC xliv [1559]: *Graham Commission Report*, p. 162, evidence of W. M. Gunson.
[64] The fee for this term was probably £24.
[65] See Add. MS 7342, T.223, October 1842, T.241, 5 May 1843, and T.259, 4 May 1844.
[66] See *Remarks on Mathematical Teaching*, esp. p. 40, and his evidence to the Graham Commission, in PP 1852–3, HC xliv [1559], pp. 245–6.

ical sciences instead of simply rousing an ardour for competition.'[67] Hopkins was also a research scientist (to use twentieth-century terminology) who contributed much, as did his close friend Adam Sedgwick of Trinity, to the nascent science of geology. Hopkins became interested in the topic when he observed the spectacular rock formations near Barmouth in 1832; very appropriately, he was conducting his Long Vacation session there that summer. Sedgwick helped to strengthen his interest. Many papers on geological science followed. Like the work of Sedgwick, they gave the new discipline a deep impression that came from Cambridge mathematics. Instead of the prevailing concern with rock taxonomies, the two men's vision was of 'mountain geometry' – the geometry of geological motions, the dynamics of spheral pressures, analogous to the celestial dynamics elucidated by Newton.[68] Exceptional among Cambridge dons, Hopkins became an accomplished landscape painter late in his life.

THE SENATE HOUSE EXAMINATION, 1845

Charles Astor Bristed, who just scraped an ignominious junior optime in 1845, offers testimony about the contest for the Senior Wranglership, which incidentally shows how fitting was the comparison of the Senate House with the Turf.

> The best man from John's is a candidate for Senior Wrangler pretty much as a matter of course, that College having a patent as it were for turning out Senior Wranglers, just as Trinity has for Senior Classics. This present year, however, one of the Small College men was a real Mathematical genius, one of those men who, like E—himself,[69] are said to be 'born for Senior Wranglers', while the Johnians were believed to be short of good men and owned it themselves. But now their best man suddenly came up with a rush like a dark horse, and having been spoken of before the Examination only as likely to be among the first six, now appeared as a candidate for the highest honors. E—was one of the first that had a suspicion of this, from noticing on the second day that he wrote with the

---

[67] Leslie Stephen, *Life of Henry Fawcett*, p. 26.

[68] See Crosbie Smith, 'Geologists and mathematicians: the rise of physical geology', in Harman, ed., *Wranglers and Physicists*, pp. 49–83.

[69] E— was Bristed's friend R. L. Ellis of Trinity, Senior Wrangler in 1840 and an examiner in 1845.

regularity and velocity of a machine, and seemed to clear everything before him . . . By-and-by it was reported that the Johnian had done an inordinate amount of problems, and then his fellow-collegians began to bet odds on him for Senior Wrangler. But the general wish as well as belief was for the Peterhouse man, who, besides the respect due to his celebrated scientific attainments . . . had many friends among both reading and boating men, and was very popular in the University. His backers were not disposed to give him up. 'One problem of his will be worth half a dozen of the other man's', said they; and there were grounds for this assertion, some of the problems being more difficult, and therefore marked higher than others, so that four on a paper may pay more than ten.[70]

Writing almost daily about the progress of the examination and enclosing the papers, William Thomson reported to his father on Sunday 5 January that his rival Stephen Parkinson 'has been getting on exceedingly well and so I must not be too confident. . . My health has stood out as well as possible.'[71] His father's anxiety may be imagined. Everybody had to wait till 9.10 am on Friday 17 January for the results to be published by the Proctors. Parkinson was Senior Wrangler, Thomson merely Second. Glasgow was informed by telegraph, and the following day Hopkins wrote: 'I confess that your son's not being senior wrangler is to me a very great disappointment. I can assure you however that the circumstance has not affected in the slightest degree the high opinion in which I hold both his talents and acquirements.'[72] This disappointment – which was general – at slipping by just one notch was as great as the loss of a coveted class might be today. It seems excessive, and justifies Leslie Stephen's aphorism that 'the Senior Wrangler is the winner of the Derby'.

Like the Epsom circuit, the Senate House tested speed, and Parkinson's speed was phenomenal:

It was said that the successful candidate had practised writing out against time for six months together, merely to gain pace. Mr Ellis, who examined that year, said it exercised quite a snake-like

---

[70] Bristed, *Five Years*, vol. I, pp. 318–19

[71] Add. MS 7342, T.281, William to James Thomson, 5 January 1845. Candidates were seated alphabetically, and so Thomson could certainly see Parkinson and get some sense of his progress. This chance increased the 'racetrack' factor.

[72] H.124, William Hopkins to James Thomson, 18 January 1845.

fascination on him to stand and see this young Johnian throw off sheet after sheet. He could scarcely believe that the man *could* have covered so much paper with ink in the time (to say nothing of the accuracy of the performance), even though he had seen it written out under his own eyes. There was a tremendous scene in the Senate House when the disappointed favourite took his degree.[73]

By contrast, Thomson wrote more slowly, yet revealed superior qualities of mind. That these counted less than speed in 'an examination so determinate in its character as our mathematical examination', as Hopkins remarked in his letter to Professor Thomson on 18 January:

> While others are simply *answering a question*, he will often be writing a dissertation upon it, admirable in itself, and indication of the fullness of his knowledge, but still not exactly what is asked for. It would be easy to set an examination of the highest order as to its philosophical and mathematical character, in which I have not the smallest doubt, your son would *distance* his opponent; but such examination would be ill adapted for the general body of students, and therefore for our University purposes.[74]

Many years later, when he 'was in a chatty mood', Thomson himself gave a similar explanation to his friend and biographer Silvanus Thompson:

> I asked him point blank how it occurred that he was not Senior Wrangler. His blue eyes lighted up as he proceeded to explain that Parkinson had won principally on the exercises of the first two days, which were devoted to text-book work rather than to problems requiring analytical investigation. And then he added, almost ruefully, 'I might have made up on the last two days, but for my bad generalship. One paper was really a paper that I ought to have walked through, but I . . . spent nearly all my time on one particular problem that interested me, about a spinning-top being let fall on to a rigid plane – a very simple problem if I had tackled it in the right way. But I got involved and lost time on it, and wrote something that was not good, and there was no time left for the other questions.'[75]

---

[73] The Reverend F. Arnold, *Oxford and Cambridge, their Colleges, Memories and Associations* (1873), quoted in S. P.Thompson, *William Thomson*, vol. 1, p. 98.

[74] H.124.   [75] S. P. Thompson, *William Thomson*, vol. 1, p. 110.

A week or so after the Senate House results were published the examination for the Smith's Prize took place, which 'required a more profound & philosophical view of the subject'.[76] The four examiners agreed unanimously that Thomson beat all his competitors by a wide margin, and proved himself a far more creative mathematician than the Senior Wrangler. Whewell, one of the Smith's Prize examiners, described him as 'much the greatest mathematical genius'.[77] Stephen Parkinson was Second Smith's Prizeman. For many years he was a fellow and tutor of St John's, and he wrote textbooks on mechanics and optics that for decades were standard works in Cambridge. He was also an active university administrator, serving on the Council of the Senate and as Senior Proctor.

WILLIAM THOMSON, SCIENTIST

Shortly after gaining the Smith's Prize Thomson was elected a fellow of Peterhouse. His career as a Cambridge don was short. In September 1846, after his own and his father's strenuous efforts, he was elected Professor of Natural Philosophy at Glasgow, a position he held until his retirement. Thomson, writes one of his biographers,[78] pursued a 'career of almost unparalleled fertility and honour, in which he published over six hundred papers on original research and scientific discussion, and patented seventy inventions including several of the most important produced in the nineteenth century'. The core of his work concerned the application of mathematics to elucidating the conduction of heat and of electricity, topics whose kinship he had the genius to grasp, and whose link with the researches of his youth was close. He was a leader in the new science of thermodynamics, or the convertibility of heat and work, that underlies modern industry, and he was largely responsible for solving the complex problems besetting the design of telegraph cables and for laying them under the Atlantic – an achievement for which he was knighted in 1866. In 1892 he was created Baron Kelvin of Largs. He dedicated a brilliantly practical

[76] Add MS 7342, C. 140, H. W. Cookson to James Thomson, 24 January 1845.
[77] S. P. Thompson, *William Thomson*, vol. 1, pp. 103–8.
[78] J. G. Crowther, *British Scientists of the Nineteenth Century* (London, Kegan Paul, 1935), p. 254.

imagination to the understanding of nature, and the advancement of industry and engineering. In the process he made his fortune, so that his grand yacht *Lalla Rookh*, a familiar craft on the Clyde, was a symbol of the wealth that his service to capitalism brought him.

In 1872, change in college statutes having removed the disability of marriage from fellowships, he was elected to one of the two life fellowships (they did not entail residence) founded at Peterhouse for men of distinguished achievement. He was offered the mastership of his college, and he was three times offered, yet declined, the Cavendish Professorship and the directorship of the laboratory.[79] Nevertheless, some slight reservations about his scientific personality may be found in the lengthy obituary notice composed by the Lucasian Professor, Joseph Larmor, in 1908.[80] Doing subtle and generous justice to Kelvin's greatness, Larmor commented on the *Treatise on Natural Philosophy* that he had written with P. G. Tait in 1867:

> He never had time to prepare complete formal memoirs. It was but rarely that his expositions were calculated to satisfy a reader whose interests were mainly logical; though they were almost always adapted to stimulate the scientific discontent and the further inquiry of students trained towards fresh outlook on the complex problem of reality, rather than to logical refinement and precision in knowledge already ascertained. Each step gained was thus a stimulus to further effort. This fluent character, and want of definite focus, has been a great obstacle to the appreciation of 'Thomson and Tait', as it is still to Maxwell's 'Electricity', for such readers as ask for demonstration, but find only suggestion and exploration. There is perhaps nothing that would contribute more at present to progress in physical thought than a reversion, partial at any rate, from the sharp limitation and rigour of some modern expositions to the healthy atmosphere of enticing vistas which usually pervades the work of the leaders in physical discovery. With increased attention to the inspired original sources of knowledge the functions of a teacher would be more than ever necessary, to point to the paths of progress and to contrast the effectiveness of different routes, as well as to restore valuable aspects which drop away in formal abstracts; science would thus adhere to the form of a body of improving doctrine rather than a collection of complete facts.

[79] S. P. Thompson, *William Thomson*, vol. II, pp. 628, 679, 694, 840–1.
[80] *Proceedings of the Royal Society of London, Series A*, 81 (1908), iii–lxxvi. The quotation is from p. lv.

There are echoes here, seventy years on, of Hopkins's comment that Thomson did not organise his material adroitly enough for tripos success, and also of the later criticisms of some of Thomson's Glasgow students that they couldn't make head or tail of his lectures. So maybe the examiners for the Mathematical Tripos in 1845 got it right after all. Yet one is naturally uneasy about a process that gave the first prize to someone who rose to be Senior Proctor, and the second to someone who was to link the Atlantic communities together by electric telegraph. We should not raise our eyebrows too far, since the limits on the reliability of timed examinations, especially for predictive purposes, were known at the time and scarcely need elaborating now. But if only because Cambridge played such a large part in devising the genre, we are right to ask: in striving with a large gathering of candidates to test what was readily examinable, how much were the examiners bound to get wrong at the same time as getting a lot of things right?

Chapter 18

GAMES FOR GOWNSMEN: WALKING, ATHLETICS, BOATING, AND BALL GAMES

WALKING AND ATHLETICS

WALKING

'The staple exercise is walking; between two and four all the roads in the neighborhood of Cambridge – that is to say within four miles of it – are covered with men taking their constitutionals.'[1] Until the invention of the safety bicycle in 1885 walking was the most common exercise in Victorian Cambridge, at least for reading men. They devoted the afternoon hours to it – the time always recommended for exercise, between the morning and evening stints of intellectual labour. The favourite route was the 'Grantchester Grind' – out from the college along the Trumpington Road, then turning west past Trumpington church, over the river past Grantchester mill and through the village back to Cambridge, taking the road or the river footpath. It was on such a walk one chill November afternoon that Olva Dune met and murdered Carfax in Hugh Walpole's novel of Edwardian Cambridge.[2] Most undergraduates walked in twos; conversation was part of the attraction of the exercise. 'These walks meant close companionship and exchange of views, and were in truth a valuable part of the varied processes that made up an University training.'[3] But as for the large numbers of non-reading men, 'the exercise was too humdrum to suit youths with no ideas to exchange and prone to intellectual rest'.

The walkers were time-conscious; they were fitting exercise into

---

[1] Bristed, *Five Years*, vol. II, p. 23; John Venn, *Early Collegiate Life*, pp. 276–9; Heitland, *After Many Years*, p. 115; Everett, *On the Cam*, pp. 133–4; *A Cambridge Staircase* (London, 1883), pp. 41–4.
[2] Hugh Walpole, *The Prelude to Adventure* (London, 1912), chapter 1.
[3] Heitland, *After Many Years*, p. 115 for these quotations.

a brief afternoon slot. They wore ordinary clothes, and did not change into rambling gear. For these reasons they stuck to recognised roads or paths, and did not usually scramble through hedges, even when farmers would have tolerated them.[4] Sundays gave more time for leisurely walks, but proctorial regulations enforced the wearing of cap and gown out of college on Sundays; so free rambling was still in effect interdicted. Students took extra long walks, true enthusiasts notching up fifteen miles in three hours, while 'the villages for ten miles round were familiar with the academic dress'.[5] Many wished to walk even further. 'Indeed', writes John Venn about the 1850s, 'there was a somewhat prevalent persuasion in my time that the proper thing to do was to walk to London in the day', and 'a considerable number of my contemporaries ... fulfilled this duty'. Some seem to have been nonchalant about it. In his laconic autobiography Herbert John Roby wrote of his acquaintance Cecil Monro that 'when, on his coming into my room about 1 o'clock on Sunday afternoon, I proposed to take a walk', he quietly replied, '"Yes, but I do not want a long one, as I walked from London last night"'.[6]

A Victorian panegyrist of the stout pair of boots ruefully admitted that 'walking does not carry its charm upon the face of it, say like making one of a party to climb the Matterhorn, or a day's shooting or fishing, or a game of golf and cricket'.[7] Lacking spontaneity and diversity, walking was not awarded a volume in the inclusive Badminton Library of sports and pastimes, to accompany its more adventurous cousins, athletics and dancing. A Cambridge theoretician of the pursuit, Leslie Stephen, praised its very predictability and lack of excitement. 'The true walker', not 'above a certain complacency in the physical prowess required', finds that 'the muscular effort of the legs is subsidiary to the "cerebration" stimulated by the effort'. He valued 'the intellectual harmony which is the natural accompaniment to the monotonous tramp of

---

[4] But note that Bristed remarks that students wore 'low-heeled shoes, for greater convenience in fence and ditch jumping': see chapter 16, p. 593.

[5] John Venn, *Early Collegiate Life*, p. 276, and p. 277 for the next quotation.

[6] H. J. Roby, *Reminiscences of My Life and Work, for My Own Family Only* (Cambridge, privately printed, *c.* 1912), p. 35. The only extant copy of this work appears to be in the library of St John's College, to which Cambridge University Press gave its file copy in 1968.

[7] Arthur Nevile Cooper, *Quaint Talks about Long Walks*, (London, 1904), p. 4.

his feet'.[8] Stephen, who 'boasted that every term I devised a new route' for walking the sixteen miles from the university to Ely, explained his love of walking in the Fens in a way that makes them seem even less captivating than they are: 'In a steady march along one of the great dykes by the monotonous canal with the exuberant vegetation dozing in its stagnant waters, we were imbibing the spirit of the scenery ... we felt the curious charm of the great flats'. Stephen's feelings while walking were often more exalted than that, but on the Cornish coast gazing at the Atlantic rather than at Mepal looking over the Hundred Foot Drain.

Leslie Stephen was appointed junior tutor of Trinity Hall in 1856, when he was twenty-four, and was in residence till 1864. He had been a delicate boy, and was sent by his father to a small college in the hope that he would not overtax his strength. But he turned himself into one of the most energetic men in the university, and as a young don was a force in various athletic activities. An undergraduate recalled his possessing, about 1860, 'a tall, almost gaunt body, devoid of all superfluous flesh and with muscles like steel'.[9] He needed more demanding exercise than the Grantchester Grind provided. Once he walked from Cambridge to London in twelve hours, after a breakfast of coffee and bread-and-butter, to dine with the Alpine Club.[10] On another occasion he walked with three other clergymen[11] from Bedford to Cambridge, passing a post marked 'Cambridge 30 miles' at 11.30 and reaching the back gates of St John's at 6 pm. 'Then the Vicar of Eaton Socon declared that his parish had been invaded by "four lunatics", who, he was told, were clergymen from Cambridge.'[12] He would sometimes walk a distance against time, in 1862, for example, 'covering six miles and three-quarters, less seventy-five yards, in the appointed hour'; in the following year, at the Trinity Hall sports, he undertook to walk two miles while a competitor ran three. Stephen won. Most of Stephen's Cambridge walks were not light-hearted races, but very earnest endeavours. His motives were mixed. In part walking seems

---

[8] 'In Praise of Walking', in *Studies of a Biographer* (4 vols., London, Duckworth, 1898–1902), vol. III, p. 256. The following quotation is from pp. 272–3.
[9] Quoted in Maitland, *Leslie Stephen*, p. 57; pp. 56–67.
[10] Stephen was a keen mountaineer.
[11] Stephen took holy orders in 1859, but ceased to regard himself as a Christian in 1865.
[12] Maitland, *Leslie Stephen*, p. 63 and pp. 61–5 for the next three quotations.

to have had the aim, natural in much vigorous exercise, of reducing Stephen's tenseness of mood. 'Their tutor', stated some ex-pupils to F. W. Maitland, 'was most at his ease when his legs were moving fast.' His walks also had a moral purpose, in which one may see a long-term effect of Stephen's Evangelical background. He would customarily take his students out for long walks on Sundays, after early chapel. It was reported to his biographer that he 'was always guarding his men against idleness and effeminacy,[13] and that these weekly tramps were organised for the better prevention of loafing. That the long walk is a moral agent of great power was an article of faith based upon personal experience.' Eventually undergraduates bought him a walking-stick 'in honour of his having outwalked them all'.

Stephen took his Cambridge habit into his London life as a man of letters, founding in 1879 the Sunday Tramps, whose leisure was stamped with the austerity Stephen regarded as the heart of the matter.[14] Their numbers restricted to ten, the Sunday Tramps consisted of metropolitan writers, lawyers, and scholars (all men); on alternate Sundays from October to June they took the train into the countryside, and walked twenty or twenty-five miles at four miles an hour, or even faster, to another station for the return journey. Stephen set the pace, pressing on through deluges and jocosely rallying stragglers. Conversation was not unknown, but inhibited by Stephen's reticence and celerity. He seemed to prefer the coldest pub for lunch, and the most frugal food; he stuck to bread and cheese himself when one Christmas some of his tramps ate turkey.

The story of the Sunday Tramps shows that the habit of walking, acquired at Cambridge, might last into later life. It did too for George Trevelyan, the most famous walker of a later Victorian generation.[15] Bringing to Trinity in 1893 a love of the pursuit he had learned from his Harrow housemaster, it became ingrained at

---

[13] This meant no more than a disinclination to intense physical exertion.
[14] These lines are based on James Sully, 'Reminiscences of the Sunday Tramps', *Cornhill Magazine*, new series 24 (1908), pp. 76–88.
[15] For what follows, see G. M. Trevelyan, *An Autobiography and other Essays* (London, Longmans, 1949), pp. 11, 25–6; G. M. Trevelyan, 'Walking' in *Clio, A Muse and Other Essays*, 2nd edition (London, Longmans, 1930), pp. 1–18; David Cannadine, *G. M. Trevelyan. A Life in History* (London, Harper Collins, 1992), pp. 145–8, 157.

Cambridge. Apart from brief forays, he took a weekly walk in term with his fellow-historian G. P. Gooch, and once walked from Cambridge to Marble Arch in twelve hours and three-quarters, thus almost equalling Leslie Stephen's earlier achievement.[16] As an established writer in the prime of life he continued this pleasure, sometimes in company but for his deepest satisfactions alone, in Italy or Northumberland walking up to forty miles a day. His 'ecstasy of body and mind' in walking, as he observed the 'goodness and harmony of things',[17] inspired him to play a leading part in founding the Youth Hostels Association in 1930 – the chief legacy outside the university of the Cambridge delight in walking.

ATHLETICS

'The public', wrote Montague Shearman in 1887, 'does not care for walking races, because when they go to see an athlete walk the probability is that they will see him shuffle, trot, or run.' The problem was 'that athletes, professional and amateur, have never yet arrived at a satisfactory definition, founded on a rational basis, of what fair walking is'. It was perhaps therefore not surprising that walking races never caught on at Oxford and Cambridge.[18] Still, it was natural for running to be taken up seriously in a university where perambulating was itself a serious pursuit, though it seems that, in contrast to rowing and football, Cambridge followed rather than initiated the popularity of athletics in the world at large. Athletics were not however popular early in the nineteenth century in the schools matriculants came from, and the other two pursuits were – hence the difference between them.

At all events athletics seem to have begun in Cambridge about 1855, about the same time as they did in boarding schools[19] – in other words about fifteen years after their growth in Britain generally, in the Victorian leisure boom. Leslie Stephen was an early enthusiast, as we might expect.[20] He was said as a young don to be

---

[16] But Stephen's exact terminus is not known, and perhaps he travelled a lesser distance. Trevelyan recommended starting from Cambridge at 5 am and eating a second breakfast at Royston at 8 am.
[17] 'Walking', p. 5.
[18] Montague Shearman, *Athletics and Football* (London, Badminton Library, 1887), pp. 122–3, 130.
[19] Shearman, *Athletics and Football*, p. 48.
[20] Maitland, *Leslie Stephen*, pp. 61–4 for this paragraph and the quotations.

'ready for a race of any sort at any time', and was remembered for 'tearing at full speed like a hunted stag through bushes and over ditches' on the Ditton bank of the Cam when racing against Burn of Trinity, 'trotting steadily' along the tow-path on the other side. Burn won. Stephen's deliberate testing of his exuberant energies explains why he became a legend, and was credited with 'being the founder of athletic sports at Cambridge'. They 'were at first very primitive and rough, even condescending to foolish and absurd antics'.

Evidence that athletic sports did not in fact begin in Trinity Hall comes from J. R. Jackson of St John's.[21] They began, he says, in 1855, when some St John's undergraduates 'got up what was facetiously called a "Johnian Derby", to be held on Fenner's ground.[22] A programme of "Events" was drawn up': flat and hurdle races, high and long jumps, throwing the cricket ball, 'sixteen hops', and putting a 14lb stone. Only Johnians competed. 'Thus the 19th November 1855 is the birthday, and St John's College is the birth-place of Athletic Sports in the University of Cambridge. This College held its second meeting in 1856; and other colleges held theirs first.' Elsewhere it is said that Emmanuel began in 1855 too, but for events small-scale and very informal in nature (contestants wore cricket shoes and flannel trousers), it is natural for disputes to occur over priority, especially in a university with intense collegiate loyalties. It is certain that the intercollegiate competition began in 1857 and that the Cambridge University Athletic Club was founded in 1863. Developments at Oxford were in parallel, and in 1864 the first inter-university match took place, on Christ Church cricket ground.[23]

In these early years Cambridge athletes were advised by a local solicitor, Macdonald, a keen miler, who 'had become generally familiar with the rising amateurs outside the 'Varsity'.[24] Through his influence 'questions of style came to be freely mooted', proper apparel was worn, and performances improved. Still, 'competitions

---

[21] 'The First Athletic Sports in Cambridge', *The Eagle*, 16 (1891), pp. 358–61, from which the details and quotations that follow are taken.
[22] The acquisition of Fenner's for cricket and athletics is described below, pp. 675–6.
[23] Shearman, *Athletics and Football*, pp. 48, 229.
[24] A. C. M. Croome, ed., *Fifty Years of Sport at Oxford and Cambridge* (2 vols., London, Southwood, 1913), vol. I, pp. 1–2.

between highly skilled and specialised performers were rare. The fact that a *victor ludorum* could be chosen at the University, of itself proves that specialisation in pursuit of the highest excellence was not then attempted.' A quarter-century after the events that are referred to here, Montague Shearman surveyed the state of athletics at the universities, and it is clear that in colleges they were still relaxed and uncompetitive, even though the academic year was marked out with a regular sequence of events. 'The season begins in the autumn with the "Freshers" *alias* the Freshmen's Sports, open to all who are in their first year at the university, and from these it is soon seen what new men will have a chance of their "blue" in the spring.' College meetings followed. Every college had its club. 'A college meeting itself is always a festive scene. It is not promoted for the benefit of the few cracks in each college. Men turn out for the handicaps who have never put on a shoe before, and in the level races the winners of previous years are penalised.'[25] After the college meetings came the university sports, held in the Lent Term at Fenner's, which the athletic club shared with the cricketers, using it during different terms.[26] On the results of the university sports were selected the representatives to meet the rival university at the 'Inter-'Varsity' gathering.

Every college had its own colours, and a man's status as a sportsman was defined by the caps, badges, and ribbons that he was entitled to wear.

Mere college colours, however, are considered to count for but little as compared with the dark or light blue colours which show that the wearer has represented his University in a contest against the rival University ... the Oxford or Cambridge runner looks forward, as the supreme goal of his ambition, to the right to wear a blue coat or cap. Only the winners of the nine events which are included in the programme of the Inter-University meeting are awarded this honour, and those who run as 'second' or 'third' strings in London only hold the 'half-blue' – that is, they can wear blue trimming upon their jerseys and knickerbockers when running, but may not sport the blue coat or cap.

[25] Shearman, *Athletics and Football*, pp. 230–3 for these paragraphs.
[26] The business manager was the Reverend E. H. Morgan of Jesus, the sporting enthusiast, on whom see below, p. 663.

The blue was a sign not only of sporting excellence, but also of moral fitness – a badge of amateur status, university participants being very definitely on that side of the great division in Victorian sport.

> This hierarchy of coat-wearers doubtless causes wonderment to the astonished stranger, but those who, from experience in other parts of the kingdom, know how soon a genuine sport can be corrupted by greed and money-making considerations, cannot see anything but good in a system which makes the chief distinction something which cannot possibly foster any undesirable quality except perhaps a little harmless vanity.

ROWING

PROFESSIONALS AND AMATEURS IN ENGLISH SPORT

In 1888 Walter Bradford Woodgate, a middle-aged Oxonian and a rowing fanatic, wrote that 'the sports and pastimes of a people are no insignificant product of its national spirit, and react to no small degree upon national character'. The most important of them was rowing, because it had 'played no inconsiderable part in great events of human history', and 'by reason of the pleasure and emulation to which it so readily ministers, as a healthful exercise and as a means of competitive effort requiring both skill and endurance'.[27] A similar enthusiast from Cambridge, Rudolph Chambers Lehmann, declared that when the oarsman 'joins the great army of "have-beens"', he would find that

> he has learnt what it means to be in perfect health and condition, with every sinew strong, and all his manly energies braced for contests of strength and endurance, and that he has bound to himself by the strongest possible ties a body of staunch and loyal friends whose worth has been proved under all sorts of conditions, through many days of united effort.[28]

When they wrote, rowing on the Isis and Cam had become far more than just messing about in boats or getting to the fishing-spot, as it had been to Gunning's generation a century before: for some it

[27] W. B. Woodgate, *Boating*, Badminton Library (London, 1888), pp. 2–3.
[28] R. C. Lehmann, Guy Nickalls, G. L. Davis, *et al.*, *Rowing*, Isthmian Library, no. 4 (London, 1898), p. 3.

was a life-absorbing pursuit, a source of fervent satisfaction and an object of the deepest loyalty. Many on rivers throughout England[29] were dedicated to it too, but their interest was focused on the ancient universities, which had boating fever more intensely than anybody.

One reason for the cult of games in the ancient universities was that matriculants had been converted at their boarding schools. Early in the nineteenth century schoolmasters were hostile to football and rowing, as the boys of Westminster discovered when they took to the river.[30] But from the 1840s onwards masters introduced organised games as disciplinary measures. Their pursuit became in time an end in itself; the effect of enthusiasts on the universities they moved on to was all the greater – so that by the end of the century Jesus College, Cambridge (to choose a particularly striking example) seemed to exist for the sake of the eights rowed and goals scored by its undergraduates.[31]

Outdoor pursuits flourished in the Victorian leisure boom, their popularity being recognised by the publication towards the end of the century of the Badminton Library – twenty-five volumes on Archery, Golf, and Yachting and much besides, often written by men who had learned their skills at Oxford or Cambridge.[32] The library addressed a readership in comfortable circumstances, and showed the popularity of physical recreations among the prosperous middle class, from which of course undergraduates at Oxford and Cambridge mostly came. But most enthusiasts for games actually were from the working class, which provided the players and the spectators for the new mass-pleasure, professional Association Football. Their interests were scarcely touched upon in the Badminton volume in question, which was enthusiastic about the gentlemanly players at the public schools but uneasy lest in making football a business professionalism might deprive amateur clubs of their talent. 'The longest purse must win the day, since it can command the services of the best players.'[33] Middle-class desires,

[29] Though not, it seems, in Scotland.
[30] Richard Holt, *Sport and the British. A Modern History* (Oxford, Clarendon, 1989), p. 75.
[31] J. A. Mangan, *Athleticism in the Victorian and Edwardian Public School: The Emergence and Consolidation of an Educational Ideology* (Cambridge University Press. 1981).
[32] Published by Longmans, the volumes sold for 10s 6d.
[33] Montague Shearman, W. J. Oakley, G. O. Smith, *et al.*, *Football*, Badminton Library, new edition

however, went further than the separation of amateurs and professionals. The bodies that set the rules for the new pursuits excluded manual workers or placed them in a subordinate class of membership. No group was more exclusive than the Amateur Rowing Association (ARA), *The Times* ironically commenting on its stance: 'outsiders, artisans, mechanics and such like troublesome persons can have no place found for them ... loud would be the wail over a chased goblet or a pair of silver skulls which a mechanic had been lucky enough to carry off'.[34] Yet it says much about the English pattern of class deference that by the 1880s the Oxford and Cambridge Boat Race excited more interest among ordinary Londoners and the newspapers serving them than almost any other sporting occasion.

From time immemorial much traffic within London, people and goods, went by river: this was the Thames described in *Our Mutual Friend* (1864–5), and it did not cease to be a major route until the coming of the electric railway and tram and the motor vehicle. Competitive rowing for financial gain (usually in the form of wagers) started among the river's huge navy of watermen at least as early as the eighteenth century, their most famous contest, which started in 1715, being for Doggett's Coat and Badge. Similar contests occurred on other waterways, such as the Tyne and the coast of Yorkshire. The Amateur Rowing Association was most anxious to exclude professional watermen from these areas when it was formed in 1879.[35]

Towards the end of the eighteenth century rowing was taken up as a pastime by gentlemen who did not earn their living in boats – men, that is, later called 'amateurs'; and early in the nineteenth century, when our knowledge becomes more definite, there existed on the London reaches of the Thames the Leander, Temple, and Eagle clubs; at Westminster School the Water Ledger begins in 1813, while at another riverine public school, Eton, the list of Captains of Boats starts in 1812. Competitive racing between these societies began soon afterwards, and was naturally taken to the

(London, Longmans, 1899), p. 183.
[34] Quoted in Holt, *Sport and the British*, pp. 74–117 for this paragraph, and p. 109 for the quotation, though the author does not seem to notice that *The Times* disapproved of the ARA's attitude.
[35] Christopher Dodd, 'Rowing', pp. 279–85, in Tony Mason, ed., *Sport in Britain. A Social History* (Cambridge University Press, 1989).

universities by matriculants from the two schools. At Oxford there may have been college races as early as 1815, and their existence is well attested by 1822.[36] At Cambridge college rowing seems to have started later, and was at first less competitive than it soon was to be. After a year or two of informal rowing, the St John's club, the Lady Margaret Boat Club, was founded in 1825. Rowing was at that time merely recreational, and carried on not for the whole term but only between certain fixed dates. There was no system of training, though members had to be efficient rowers. 'There were as yet no regular races, but impromptu trials of speed with other crews frequently took place.'[37]

These contests, more like *The Wind in the Willows* than anything else, were described many years later by Charles Merivale, the Dean of Ely, and an early member of the St John's club:

> In the summer of 1826 there were only two eight-oars on our water, a Trinity boat[38] and a Johnian, and the only idea of encounter they had was that each should go, as it were, casually down stream and lie in wait, one of them, I believe, sounding a bugle to intimate its whereabouts, when the other, coming up, would give chase.[39]

In a spirit that reminds us of the bucolic relaxation common on the Cam fifty years earlier, the St John's eight was also used in those early years for picnic excursions, the craft being capacious enough to hold crockery for nine, a canvas table, and a charcoal bag plus 'phosphorus box with blow-pipe' for tea-making – all contained within a 'tin panthermaticon'.

COMPETITIVE ROWING AT CAMBRIDGE: PLEASURES, PAINS, AND TECHNOLOGY

In 1827 a much more competitive spirit came with the foundation of the University Boat Club and the first organised inter-collegiate

---

[36] Woodgate, *Boating*, pp. 30, 313–14; Reginald P. P. Rowe *et al.*, *Boating and Punting*, Badminton Library, 1898, pp. 3–6. The publication of a second and completely new volume on aquatics in the Badminton Library only ten years after the first is evidence of the popularity of the pursuit.

[37] R. H. Forster, W. Harris, A. D. Stammers, and G. L. Day, *History of the Lady Margaret Boat Club, St John's College, Cambridge, 1825–1926* (Cambridge, Johnian Society, 1926), p. 2.

[38] The Trinity club was also founded in 1825.

[39] Quoted in George G. T. Treherne and J. H. D. Goldie, *Record of the University Boat Race 1829–1880* (London, 1883), p. x.

'bump'[40] races, in the Lent and Easter terms, at which times they have been held since then. In 1827 five colleges participated, Trinity with three boats competing against each other. Boat clubs were founded at the other colleges in the next decade or so.[41] The first university Boat Race was held in June 1829 at Henley, over a course of two and a quarter miles. It was written in 1884 that

> though boat-racing had not then the hold upon the public mind which it now boasts, Oxonians turned out on that day in far greater numbers than we see them even in these days... Through Bensington, down the steeps of Nettlebed Hill, and along the 'Fair Mile', came tandems, drags, and saddle-horses in strings. Cantabs, also, were there in force, though hardly in such numbers as their rivals, for the distance from headquarters was greater.[42]

Oxford won this first contest, and Cambridge the second. This did not occur till 1836, two proposals for races in the intervening years being abandoned, the first because of cholera in London, and the second because Cambridge thought the Henley course too remote. A course on the Thames, from Westminster to Putney, was used in 1836 because it was equally convenient for both universities. On this occasion Cambridge adopted its light blue colour for the first time, and by accident, Eton blue being selected at the very last minute. The third Boat Race occurred in 1839, and later ones nearly every year thereafter. The race was not in the 1840s what in 1883 was described as 'the greatest annual aquatic event on the face of the globe'; after the Henley Regatta was founded in 1839 the universities for twenty years put as much energy into competing there as they did in the Boat Race. Still, one way and another rowing and racing absorbed in these years an increasing amount of Oxbridge enthusiasm, and eventually the Boat Race was unchallenged at the pinnacle of publicity, public attention, and university patriotism. By 1900 Cambridge was far more likely to be known to the man in the street for its rowing than for its mathematics.

Rowing made an intense emotional impact on hundreds of undergraduates. The words of William Thomson, at Peterhouse

---

[40] Contests on the 'ladder' principle, points being scored by touching the tiller of the boat in front, 'bumps' are a convenient way of organising competition between many clubs on a narrow river.
[41] Forster and Harris, *Lady Margaret Boat Club*, pp. 3–28.
[42] Treherne and Goldie, *University Boat Race*, p. 6, and pp. 3–14 for these sentences generally.

from 1841 to 1846, enable us to trace the growth of its fascination for an impressionable and energetic undergraduate, highly intelligent and cultivated yet seeking an outlet for youthful vigour; the way in which he and his circle were drawn constantly to talk of women and love affairs suggests one reason why in celibate Cambridge he came to exhaust and to excite himself in boats. Within hours of arriving in Cambridge in October 1841 he was walking in the countryside, glad that an ankle injury suffered in Glasgow was no longer inhibiting free exercise. At his first hall, however, he was invited to a meeting of the boat club, the first of many such enticements. 'Of course I did not go', he wrote to his father, worried about everything and especially lest William should waste his mathematical genius.[43] In his first term Thomson was torn between the excitement and challenge of the boat club, and on the other hand fear of wasting time, which his Cambridge friend Grenside warned him against.

> He told me his brother (who belonged to this college, and took his degree last year) was a good deal injured by it, and he thinks it was that made him quit reading for honours. He joined it purely out of love for exercise, and, being a stout fellow, he was chosen among the boat's crew, and got plenty of rowing, but he got among an idle and extravagant set.[44]

Thomson took up rowing in 'funnys ... [two-oar skiffs] a very useful thing, as it gives some variety from mere walking, which alone, is not the best exercise'. Fortunately the 'dissipated men' rowed only in the college boat and were kept too busy in it to mix with Thomson and his friends. This is ingenious special pleading by Thomson that nevertheless implies many degrees of commitment to rowing.[45] Not being in the boat club, he has to hire his funny – a hint of what came in February 1842, when he purchased a funny for £7. This caused much anguish in Glasgow, his aunt urging him to break it up for firewood, until at last his family accepted it.[46] In the spring, dissatisfied with his rowing partner who several times damaged the funny, Thomson bought his half-share. He sculled over as much as fourteen miles in an afternoon: 'every one now says

---

[43] CUL Add. MS 7342: T.179, William to James Thomson, 26 October 1841.
[44] T.181, William to James Thomson, 30 October 1841.
[45] T.187, William to James Thomson, 12 December 1841.   [46] T.196–T.203, T.496, K.56.

that I am looking much better now than I did some time ago, and I find that I can read with much greater vigour than I could when I had no exercise but walking, in the inexpressibly dull country round Cambridge'.[47]

On 5 March 1843 (that is, in his second year) Thomson watched the college 'bumps' and felt a surge of Peterhouse loyalty when they were bumped by First Trinity.[48] He was well known as an expert solitary sculler, and was friendly with committed oarsmen in other colleges.[49] Thomson wrote, when pressed to join the first Peterhouse eight, 'I am very much tempted to join, but both on account of reading, & of what my father would think of me joining, I shall delay. I mean however to join the boat club, some time before I take my degree, perhaps this time next year.'[50] Ten days later he agreed to join the club and row in the second boat.[51] 'They wish me to pull in the races next term, but I shall not do so, as the exercise would be so much that I should be sleepy in the evenings.'[52] In the next few weeks he changed his mind, confiding to his diary on 2 April, 'I have been thinking on the boat more than anything else, all day', and on 10 April, 'After chapel I took tea with Cookson, and, after exhausting mathematics, we started boating.' After a long discussion Thomson 'nearly managed to persuade him' that he might row in the Easter Term 'without committing suicide mathematically, physically & morally'.

Preparing for the races took more time than he had usually spent in boats. Between 13 February and 16 March Thomson apparently sculled on only half-a-dozen occasions, and certainly spent more time on his other pleasures – music, talking, and pottering about. From the last week in March onwards he sculled or rowed in the eight nearly every day, but on 15 April came a shock. After rising late, as usual, he 'pulled dreadfully uncomfortably in a 4... Attributed my distress to new bread.' Three days later, things were worse. 'Resolution failed as usual', and he rose late. He pulled, but 'Airey's stroke from the 1st post to the Plough astounded me and I

[47] T.206, T.209, and T.213, April and 6 May 1842, William to James Thomson.
[48] CUL Add. MSS 7342, NB 29, Diary of William Thomson, February–October 1843.
[49] This group consisted of Field, Hemming, and Stephen of St John's, and Gutch of Sidney Sussex, plus Thomson. Thomson called them 'the Fleet'.
[50] NB 29, 14 March 1843.   [51] NB 29, 24 March 1843.
[52] T.233, 24 March 1843, William to James Thomson.

got horribly done after Grassy. What shall I feel when I pull in 1st boat? I must endeavour to get into good condn . . . I am trying to get out of pulling in the 1st.' For some weeks he usually retired and rose early, 'trying to train ferociously'.[53] The climax came in the middle of May.

The boat racing has commenced in earnest. On Wednesday we had not much racing but kept easily our place on acct. of the Johnians being bumped by Caius. Yesterday the odds were strongly in favour of Caius bumping us, but we astounded the university by keeping away. We had a glorious pull for it, and I shall remember for my whole life, the work of 7 minutes last night. My pleasure at keeping away was beyond any thing I have ever felt. We shall have another hard pull tomorrow, as Caius means to bump us and so I must have plenty of sleep. I always take 9 or 10 h before the race, and I have to go to Hopkins at 7 tomorrow. (Strikes 10 and so good night. I have been reading a very little German tonight.)[54]

This, the last diary entry for the May Term, is almost the last reference to boating in a journal that petered out in Michaelmas. Many years later Thomson, recalling his days rowing, remarked that he 'had found it too exciting', and in the racing period he 'could do no reading'. In November 1843 Thomson won the Colquhoun silver sculls, but that was his last serious venture on the Cam.[55] He was too ambitious intellectually, and too fond anyway of a range of other pastimes, to submit himself to the strenuous régime needed.

In the 1920s an observer in the Cambridge Psychological Laboratory analysed the pains, processes, and pleasures of rowing, assessing a Cambridge rowing eight and a college boat club in ways that illuminate what Thomson wrote about his river experiences.[56] Victory is marvellously elevating, but it is rare, and at best follows a lot of misery: 'the cold, the heat, the sun in his eyes, the wind, the rain, splashing, too much lunch, too little sleep the night before . . . blisters on his hands, an oar handle that seems too thin or too thick'. An aggressive self-confident temperament is needed to conquer

---

[53] NB 29, 20 April 1843.   [54] NB 29, Sunday 14 May 1843.

[55] S. P. Thompson, *William Thomson*, vol. 1, pp. 59–62. Colquhoun, a Scot, gave a prize for Cambridge oarsmen. After some years on the Thames, it was held on the Cam for the first time in 1843.

[56] P. E. Vernon, 'The Psychology of Rowing', *British Journal of Psychology*, 18 (1927–8), pp. 316–31, from which the quotation that follows comes.

discomfort, but the last thing wanted is a boat of *individuals*, seeking personal glory or seeking to impose their wills on others. For generations rowing enthusiasts like W. B. Woodgate had been saying similar things about the folly of tolerating egotists in a crew. Man–of–war discipline was recommended for 'mutineers', such as strokes who resented being told by the coach to row faster, or maybe slower, and 'declined to be dictated to. In each case the boat was instantly ordered ashore, and the grumbler was asked to step out.' He was replaced, and only a grovelling apology brought reinstatement, and perhaps not as stroke.[57] 'It is', wrote Vernon,

> especially profitable to consider the boat . . . as an organism . . . if one man slacks, the whole boat feels heavy and dead . . . if one man relaxes the pressure of his feet on the stretcher or brings his oar through the water too high or too low, the balance is lost and the whole boat rolls over to one side. On the other hand, when the boat has really reached the stage of going well, such slight deviations from the normal are immediately compensated for by minute, often unconscious adjustments on the part of the rest of the crew. There is therefore very close interconnection between the members, yet there is but little verbal intercommunication while on the river; indeed, there are few things more objectionable in rowing than the man who tries to coach other members of his own boat.[58]

Constant practice – to the outsider the most noticeable feature of Cambridge rowing – is therefore necessary to achieve total harmony of movement and spirit, and to persuade oarsmen to subdue their individuality for the sake of the boat as a whole. 'Stroke is supposed to determine the rate of striking, when spurts shall be made, and so on; actually he is quite unable to do so unless all the members of the crew are so closely intercoordinated with one another that each one quite naturally seems to want to do what all the rest do.' Victory through comradeship is intensely pleasurable, but it has to be worked for. William Thomson describes the sweat and the exaltation, yet it may be that desire for other pleasures and for mathematics was not the only reason for his spending only one term in the Peterhouse eight. He strikes us as too dedicated a loner, too much the ruminative introvert, to commit himself to a crew for

[57] Woodgate, *Boating*, p. 84.
[58] Vernon, 'The Psychology of Rowing', p. 319, and p. 320 for the next quotation.

long. Sculling satisfied him for longer – a quite different pursuit, in which success 'depends entirely and absolutely upon yourself' and an ability to survive a 'sense of utter isolation'.[59]

As P. E. Vernon makes clear, in the training of an eight the role of the coach is all-important, requiring the talent to stimulate the confidence and aggressiveness of the group, by encouragement that does not lead to complacency and criticism that does not seem like nagging. Thus some coaches acquired legendary reputations in Oxbridge boathouses. About 1860 the young don Leslie Stephen coached the Trinity Hall eight. 'None could rival his wind and fire and his long legs could keep up with the boat mile after mile along the tow-path as the crew paddled down the river towards Ely.[60] Clad in a filthy shirt and grey flannel trousers with a large purple patch in the seat, and damning the eyes of any cox on the river who did not give way, the Rev. Leslie Stephen was a sight to make Victorian eyes blink.'[61] Above all, 'he knew when to slang a man and when to praise; and his fertile mind was always thinking out new ways of improving rowing technique so that he never grew stale'.

At university races eight-oar boats have always been used, but craft of various sizes were raced in the early years on the Cam – four, six, eight, and ten oars being mentioned. These early boats were descended from those used and sometimes raced by Thames watermen, which were built for strength, safety, and carrying capacity rather than speed.[62] As the competitive spirit increased, year by year, boats became lighter and faster (and also less seaworthy), changes being effected by boatbuilders on the Cam and Isis and other rivers in Britain – testimony to the widespread popularity of boating; news of improvements in design was spread widely by *Bell's Life in London*, the sporting weekly. From the 1830s onwards boats of lighter wood and construction were introduced, the traditional gang-board down the vessel's middle was abolished, and the top strakes were removed from the hull. Outriggers made a

[59] Lehmann, Nickalls, and Davis, *Rowing*, p. 159.
[60] Nowadays coaches ride bicycles and have an easier time than the crews they exhort.
[61] Annan, *Leslie Stephen*, p. 29, and p. 31 for the next quotation.
[62] For what follows, see Woodgate, *Boating*. pp. 102–6, 142–51; Rowe, Pitman, Serocold, *et al.*, *Boating and Punting*, pp. 14–17; and Dodd, 'Rowing', esp. pp. 287–90. A technological history of Cam boating has yet to be written.

narrowing of beam possible (by reducing the length of oar inside the boat). They are said to have been used in Canada in 1828, and after sundry experiments were employed by both teams in the Boat Race of 1846. Harry Clasper, a Tyneside boatbuilder, had a part in this invention, and also in the greatest single innovation, the keel-less boat. He built one in 1847, but more significant ventures came from another Tyneside man, Mat Taylor, a ship's carpenter and accomplished sculler. He worked as a trainer and boatbuilder for the Royal Chester Club, and together with the club captain (from a Liverpool firm of shipbuilders) constructed the keel-less eight in which the club won two races at Henley in 1856.[63] Its performance was observed by the Oxford Boat Club president, who at his own expense got Taylor to build a similar craft in which Oxford 'rowed clean away from Cambridge from start to finish' in the 1857 race.[64] Keel-less boats were generally adopted, and in 1858 Cambridge won in one built by Taylor. The last great innovation of Victorian times was the sliding seat. The advantages of 'sliding' had been known for a long time, and there are reports of rowers putting lard on fixed seats on the Tyne and the Ouse at Bedford, though friction made it impossible to keep up the movement for long. First used in Chicago in 1857, the sliding seat is said to have been adopted by a competitor at the King's Lynn Regatta in 1870. In the Boat Race they were used for the first time in 1873.

Thus there evolved a variety of light craft for pleasure and racing, quite different in shape from the traditional Thames wherry for cargo or passengers.[65] In Cambridge they were usually named after their number of oars – eights, fours, and pairs – though there were also skiffs and gigs among the smaller boats, and 'funnys', two-oared vessels.[66] Extraordinary dimensions were attained; racing eights 58 feet long might have a beam of less than 2 feet and a depth at the stern of only 6 inches. In 1888 it was written that 'the cost of a racing eight, with all fittings, is about £55. Some builders will build at as low a price as £50, especially for a crack crew, or an important race, because the notoriety of the vessel, if successful, naturally acts as an

[63] One of Taylor's Chester boats is in the Science Museum, South Kensington.
[64] Quoted in Treherne and Goldie, *University Boat Race*, p. 81.
[65] For this paragraph, see Woodgate, *Boating*, pp. 142–52, and p. 148 for the quotation.
[66] One was bought by William Thomson in 1842: see p. 653 above.

advertisement.' Sculling boats might cost as little as £12. Prices were up to 10 per cent less than they had been in the middle of the century owing to competition; so William Thomson's second-hand funny was probably a bargain at £7 in 1842.

The motor for this technological advance was competition, especially the increasing influence of the Boat Race.[67] Held nearly every year from 1839 onwards, it became an annual event in 1856. The lower Thames best suited both universities, and for some years the course was from Westminster to Putney, a location near the centre of London naturally being most convenient for spectators. But steamers were a nuisance there, and in 1845 the race was moved up-river, to the course from Putney to Mortlake that it has had ever since. Even there steamers were still an annoyance. The swell from one put the Oxford crew off their stroke in 1858, and in 1865 the Cambridge boat was stove in by a tug after the race ended: at length the Thames Conservators disciplined steam traffic. The new lighter and keel-less boats were inherently unseaworthy, and in 1849 the Cambridge boat 'was so inadequate that under hard pressure it buried amidships, and collapsed at both ends'.[68] The usual timing of the race, Easter, added to river hazards while suiting the university rowing-year; in 1859 the Cambridge boat sank in a north-east gale, Putney Reach being 'a perfect sea'. The art of rowing became ever more complex, as the authors of several lengthy monographs did not weary of telling their readers. The crew had to watch boat, wind, and tide while trying to beat their rivals and of course to row in unison. The quality of the winning crew of 1852 was said to be clear at a distance.

> When the eye first caught a glimpse of Oxford heaving into sight from behind a point a mile away, it was perceptible that there were on each side four oars blent into one. And the way in which the wrists clicked home with a vicious wrench of the elbows grazing the ribs told that the last dip of the stroke had as full a grip of the water as the entering dip.[69]

On the other hand Cambridge, losing in 1864, showed 'feather under water, bucketing recovery, hang at the finish, bent arms, and

---

[67] For what follows, see in general Treherne and Goldie, *University Boat Race*, pp. 19–161.
[68] Treherne and Goldie, *University Boat Race*, p. 55.
[69] Treherne and Goldie, *University Boat Race*, p. 63, and p. 108 for the next quotation.

19 The Boat Race. A drawing of 1840 showing inter-collegiate races, viewed from the north bank of the Cam near where Victoria Bridge now stands, and looking across Midsummer Common to King's College Chapel.

such like violations of first principles'. Many essays analysed rowing styles, and the alleged contrast between the approaches of the two universities was dilated upon.[70] Lighter boats meant that the stroke favoured by Thames watermen was no longer appropriate, and in 1842 Oxford ceased to rely on them for advice. But the new long stroke took time to perfect. Thirty years later the sliding seat caused even larger difficulties; a standard manual devotes twenty-one pages to the new skills needed.[71]

University rowing reached its apogee after 1870. For enthusiasts the entire year was filled with activities, from the freshman's first hesitant strokes under a coach's guidance in a 'tub pair' at the beginning of the Michaelmas Term, through intensive training, to the river competitions in the Lent and Easter Terms, with the University Boat Race as the focus of effort for a tiny minority and of attention for everybody else.[72] Training was more onerous than it

[70] See for example 'Oxford and Cambridge Rowing' and 'Rowing Styles', in Richard A. Proctor, *Rough Ways Made Smooth. A Series of Familiar Essays on Scientific Subjects* (London, 1880), pp. 148–77.

[71] Walter Bradford Woodgate, *"Oars and Sculls", and How to Use Them* (London, 1875), pp. 87–107.

[72] Rowe, Pitman, Serocold, *et al.*, *Boating and Punting*, pp. 162–81.

had been for Thomson's generation, the demands of the new technology being part of the reason. It involved, at least in theory, in the winter 'Réveille at 6.30 to 7.0 am, tub and rub down with rough towels or flesh brush . . . to open the pores of the skin, then a brisk walk of a mile, or thereabouts, before breakfast': then the recommended breakfast consisted of grilled steak or cold meat, dry toast, egg, and watercress. A similar purpose – to create energy but not excessive weight – lay behind other meals prescribed by experts for men intending to spend long hours on the river.[73] Pundits worried lest time not spent on the river might hang heavily, though while he was in Cambridge or Oxford the oarsman at least had his lectures, 'his fixed tale of work to get through'. The period of seclusion at Henley or Putney, harassed by newspaper reporters interested in the crew's intensive training, and lacking even a billiard table, sounds tedious indeed. 'I may, therefore, offer the oarsman a piece of advice which is sound in spite of its copybook flavour, and that is, that he shall cultivate a habit of reading, and, if possible, of reading good literature', recommended one expert. He also suggested spending ten minutes a day practising writing and spelling.[74]

Rowing enthusiasts sensibly pointed out that students needed plenty of exercise. 'Their wants will hardly be supplied by taking "constitutionals" along straight roads bounded by turnip-fields, in a country so flat that a tall man has an extensive view.' But boating would not continue as mere recreation if it lacked the stimulus of college competition, which in turn depended on the Putney race. 'A blue blade is the highest ambition of all rowing men. It is the fellowship of the Cam, and the main incentive to row.'[75] These comments appeared in a lengthy volume addressing the alleged cost of rowing to undergraduates' health and well-being, a controversy sparked off by a correspondence in *The Times* in autumn 1867. The investigation was an interesting parallel, hitherto unremarked, to the contemporary 'overstrain' controversy over the advanced schooling of young women. After reviewing copious

---

[73] Woodgate, *"Oars and Sculls"*, pp. 124–49. There are many other books of advice.

[74] Lehmann, Nickalls, and Davies, *Rowing*, Isthmian Library, pp. 140–1.

[75] H. A. Morgan, tutor of Jesus College, Cambridge, quoted in J. E. Morgan, *University Oars, being a Critical Enquiry into the After Health of the Men who Rowed in the Oxford and Cambridge Boat-Race, 1829–1869* (London, 1873), p. 341; p. 337 for Young's letter, below.

evidence Dr J. E. Morgan, himself a veteran Oxford oar, found the Boat Race not guilty of causing the premature death of normal strong young men, though like many others he regarded the Cam as less healthy than the Isis because it consisted very largely of stagnant sewage.[76] The most telling contribution to the debate came from F. J. Young (Christ's 1866 to 1874), who rowed in the Cambridge boat at Putney in 1869:

> There is only one objection to the training, and I should not be giving you my whole opinion if I did not state it; it is not exactly physical, but still results from the bodily exercise. It is this – during the time of training, and for some time afterwards, all study is almost impossible. Although the body is in an apparently perfect state of health, and capable of any exertion, the mind is almost incapable of doing anything. I do not know whether this proceeds from exhaustion or excitement, perhaps both.

It was a frequent Cambridge aphorism that 'a rowing man is not a reading man'. Rowing lured to Cambridge many men who were good for nothing else: in the 1870s and 1880s Jesus College was full of them, and from among them came Steve Fairbairn's cheerfully philistine autobiography: 'I stayed up six years and attended one lecture. It didn't interest me.'[77] But the evidence of degree results is inconclusive; it does not suggest decline over the fifty years when training became more intensive, or in other words that it became harder for men determined on honours to achieve them. In Boat Race crews there were two honours men in 1836,[78] and three in 1860 and again in 1880. Perhaps the explanation is that intellectually ambitious oarsmen were willing to sacrifice other pleasures to rowing. Also, William Thomson's Peterhouse career shows that one did not have to work hard *forever* to do well in the tripos; years one and two might be taken easily, and placing the Boat Race about Easter meant that until 1882 it occurred several months after triposes in January; and from 1882 onwards there were several months between the race and triposes in June that might be given over to revision.

[76] R. P. P. Rowe's judgement was that 'if you upset in the Cam, send your clothes to the wash'; the Cam was 'unsavoury and somewhat gelatinous': *Boating and Punting*, pp. 47, 57.
[77] *Fairbairn of Jesus* (London, John Lane, 1931), p. 35.
[78] The second Boat Race.

THE CULT OF THE RIVER

For William Thomson and his friends in the 1840s an intense pleasure that could nevertheless be given up, thirty years later rowing was for some an obsessive lifelong pursuit. A reason, in addition to technological advance and the impulse to competitiveness, was the influence on dons of the athleticist cult that overtook some public schools after 1850.[79] Though not all dons or colleges were strongly affected (or for that matter all schools and their masters) at its most intense the new fervour was the defining characteristic of man and institution, as we may see in the lives of two men at Jesus College: H. A. Morgan was tutor from 1863 to 1885 and master from 1885 to 1912, while E. H. Morgan was dean from 1865 to his death in 1895.[80] Both previously masters at Lancing College (they were not related) they devoted their lives to games of many sorts – the satisfactions are after all often similar – but above all to rowing, H. A. explaining that 'athletes were too much for self-glorification', but 'boating was the ideal, no pots or personal rewards, all for the honour of the College and the University'. H. A. Morgan rowed for Jesus College for ten years and afterwards coached for many more, a familiar figure on the Cam towpath, as he exhorted his crew from his white horse Gehazi. Increasing the college enrolment because of the appeal of its boating prowess, he (wrote Charles Whibley) 'then endowed it with . . . a soul of energy and patriotism . . . a just cause of pride in their College, and warmed their courage at the fire of his own enthusiasm'. Tony Mangan avers that while H. A. 'was a glorified headmaster with a taste for sport, E. H. Morgan was a glorified games-master with an obsession for it'. Described by one undergraduate as 'one of Nature's bullies' with a 'voice like a bull', E. H. seems to have been an insensitive man who filled his college with boating louts, and drove matriculations down in consequence. It is with E. H. and his kind that boat clubs came to be equated with drunken hooliganism.

Yet from Cambridge rowing also came a much more subtle and

---

[79] Mangan, *Athleticism*.

[80] For what follows see J. A. Mangan, 'Oars and the Man. Pleasure and Purpose in Victorian and Edwardian Cambridge', *British Journal of Sports History*, 1 (1984), pp. 245–71, from which the quotations are taken.

sophisticated mystique best demonstrated in the attitudes of Rudolph Chambers Lehmann, the most famous Cambridge oarsman of the period 1850–1900. His rowing poems capture the delight of gliding vigorously between the willow-clad banks of the Cam:

> To make the rhythm right
> And your feather clean and bright
> And to slash as if you loved it, though your muscles seem to crack.
> And, although your brain is spinning,
> To be sharp with your beginning,
> And to heave your solid body indefatigably back . . .
> To sink yourself and be
> Just a unit, and to see
> How the individual withers, and the crew is more and more;
> And to guard without omission
> Every glorious tradition
> That the ancient heroes founded when they first took up an oar.[81]

Lehmann came from a mercantile and artistic family with German and Scots antecedents. His father, a prosperous businessman, was also an accomplished violinist whose friends included Joachim, Brahms, Dickens, and Wilkie Collins.[82] For his son, the literary life was as natural as the water he rowed on, and his inheritance enabled him to embrace both without constraint. At Trinity he gained a second in the Classical Tripos (1878), was President of the Cambridge Union, and an early editor of *Granta*, who nurtured this seed-bed of literary talent for seven years. But like the hero of his volume of comic Cambridge letters he spent as much time with his feet on the stretcher as under his desk.[83] Lehmann was captain of the First Trinity Boat Club,[84] and rowed in the university trial eights.

---

[81] 'Style and the Oar', *Selected Verse* (London, Blackwood, 1929), pp. 76–7.
[82] R. C. Lehmann, *Memories of Half a Century* (London, Smith Elder, 1908), and John Lehmann, *Ancestors and Friends* (London, Eyre and Spottiswoode, 1962). John Lehmann, author and editor of *New Writing* was R.C.L.'s son; his other children included Beatrix, actress, and Rosamond, novelist.
[83] R. C. Lehmann, *Harry Fludyer at Cambridge and Conversational Hints for Young Shooters* (London, Chatto and Windus, 1904).
[84] The original Trinity Boat Club (later called 'The First') was founded in 1825. In view of Trinity's size and the popularity of rowing, it was understandable that it came to have rivals. A second club existed from 1831 to 1838, and another bearing the name Second Trinity Boat Club from 1840 to 1876. The Third Trinity Boat Club dates from 1833, when it was composed of ex-pupils of Eton and Westminster. See W. W. Rouse Ball, *History of the First Trinity Boat Club* (Cambridge, Bowes and Bowes, 1908).

Later, he eagerly coached the boat-race crews of both universities until middle age and wasting disease, and he made three visits to coach Harvard too. 'Water sports', writes his son, 'were the passion of his life',[85] and he built his house on the Thames at Bourne End so as to pursue them. The boat-house accommodated a variety of craft, from the eight he was currently coaching to a randan[86] for family picnics. In the house oars and other rowing memorabilia stood near much-read sets of Dickens, and the Thames fraternity in their Leander caps visited as often as contributors to *Punch* – Lehmann being one himself for many years. The *belles lettres* Lehmann composed sprang from memories of youthful strength and victory on the river. Boat Race day was 'the most important day of the year ... a great spring festival ... if Cambridge won, the crops would grow; if Oxford beat them, the future seemed dangerous and dark'.[87]

The banks of the rural Thames were then inhabited by similar 'devotees of the arts of the river', who scorned 'the meretricious advantages of motor and accumulator'. For them rowing was linked to notions of the genteel and cultivated life. 'Of all our great sports', wrote R. C. Lehmann, 'none is, I think, so completely free from the sordid taint of professionalism.'[88] During Henley Regatta, wrote a celebrant of the Thames's civilised way of life, there are 'no book-makers with their depraved features and yelling noise'; 'young athletes' are cheered on by 'college chums and boating friends' and 'ladies and gentlemen are the rule, not the exception'; while 'on the lovely reach at Henley ... there is no dust, nor smell of sodden turf, and comparative freedom from swindlers and roughs'.[89] But rowing was not confined to this narrow and exclusive circle. In the late Victorian leisure-boom nearly every river had its rowing clubs, regattas, and riverside hotels, and they were above all phenomena of the Thames, whose beautiful upper reaches were visited with increasing ease, in train and steamboat, by

---

[85] John Lehmann, *The Whispering Gallery* (London, Longman, 1955), p. 24, and pp. 3–57 generally. See also Eric Halladay's essay in *Dictionary of National Biography. Missing Persons*, edited by C. S. Nicholls (Oxford University Press, 1993), p. 396.

[86] A wide-beamed boat, common on the Cam in the 1820s and 1830s.

[87] J. Lehmann, *The Whispering Gallery*, pp. 33–4, and p. 34 for the next quotation.

[88] *The Complete Oarsman* (London, Methuen, 1908), p. 3. This work of nearly 400 pages is the largest guide to the pursuit.

[89] George Dunlop Leslie, *Our River* (London, 1881), p. 204.

millions living nearer its mouth. The half-century before the First World War was the apogee of this river-culture, reflected in E. V. Gregory's painting *Boulter's Lock on Sunday Afternoon* (1895), Jerome K. Jerome's *Three Men in a Boat* (1889), and Kenneth Grahame's *The Wind in the Willows* (1908). From a handful of rowing clubs in the 1830s, the number grew to 60 in 1879 (when the Amateur Rowing Association was founded) and to 457 in 1890, 301 of them in the London area.[90]

Thus the choice of the Putney–Mortlake course for the annual Boat Race proved within a few decades to have entirely unpredicted consequences. By the 1880s it rivalled the Derby as a popular national entertainment, while paradoxically continuing at the same time to be an inspiration and challenge for the purely local concerns of two universities. The change was gloomily noted by Charles Dickens Jr in his *Dictionary of the Thames*.[91] Thirty or so years before there had been comparatively few spectators, little betting, and no publicity; it 'kept alive that idea of sport for its own sake'. But 'it was all too good to last'. As rowing grew more popular, more people became interested. 'Then the newspapers took the subject up, and the graphic reporter ... and the extraordinary multiplication of sporting newspapers ... let loose any number of touts on to the towing-path ... the whole character of the race was changed.' Dickens, writing in 1885, noted the 'ludicrous' character of the interest that the race aroused for weeks before it occurred. Gossip is invented by reporters, and eagerly devoured. 'Cabmen, butcher boys, and omnibus drivers sport the colours of the Universities', which 'fill all the hosiers' shops', and there is much talk of prospects. On the day itself thousands go to the river 'who do not know one end of a boat from the other'. They do not care 'that all they are likely to see is a mere glimpse of the two crews as they dash by'. Many 'go to the Derby on exactly the same principles'. His comments getting more fastidious as they proceed, Dickens avers that the removal of the race 'from metropolitan waters would not be lamented by the real friends of the Universities, or lovers of genuine sport'. Rosamond Lehmann's memories of life in Buckinghamshire

[90] Mason, *Sport in Britain*, p. 291.
[91] Quoted in Christopher Dodd, *The Oxford & Cambridge Boat Race* (London, Stanley Paul, 1983), pp. 74–6.

add to these impressions of the Boat Race's prominence as national entertainment. One Edwardian spring her father was coaching the Cambridge crew from a launch, megaphone in hand, the boats' movement watched by the village children on the river bank. Suddenly

> gang warfare breaks out all over Bourne End; partisan frenzy leads to coarse tauntings, black eyes, bloody noses. Rude boys and girls parade upon the towing path, plucking off each other's pale or dark blue rosettes, stridently chanting:
>
> > Cambridge the winner!
> > Oxford the sinner!
> > Put 'em in a match box
> > And float 'em down the river![92]

BALL GAMES

FOOTBALL

In one of the few references to football in Cambridge before the 1840s Christopher Wordsworth wrote that 'About 1632 John Barwick at St John's, "would frequently recreate himself with bodily exercises and those violent enough, such as pitching the Bar, and playing at football, at which latter game, having the misfortune to break a player's collar-bone, he would never play again".'[93] These few words refer to a game played throughout England in the Middle Ages and afterwards. In fact it was not a game in the full modern sense. It did not possess a widely accepted set of rules, and its conventions varied greatly from area to area or even village to village. It was played on streets, or on fields that a modern footballer might find familiar in shape and size, or over wide expanses of countryside, between teams of a few men or gatherings of many hundreds, with balls that were small and hard or inflated pigs' bladders cased in leather; and depending on local custom the ball might be kicked or thrown or carried. Often manhandling was allowed – hence perhaps the injury mentioned in the St John's

---

[92] Rosamond Lehmann, *The Swan in the Evening. Fragments of an Inner Life* (London, Collins, 1967), pp. 42–3. I have altered some spellings in the verse.
[93] Christopher Wordsworth, *Social Life*, p. 179. Christopher Wordsworth, grandson of the Master of Trinity of the same name, was the poet's great-nephew.

account.[94] In the eighteenth century and later the game was under attack for the noise and disturbance, the damage to person and property, the affront to respectable opinion, caused by what an inhabitant of Derby called 'this relic of barbarism'.[95] Thus in *Sports and Pastimes of the People of England* (1801) Joseph Strutt wrote that 'the game was formerly much in vogue among the common people, though of late years it seems to have fallen into disrepute and is but little practised'.[96] Still, we are told that 'between 1835 and 1857 ... the game, saving consequent refinements in detail, was reconditioned and made into an effective instrument for modern use'.[97]

Cambridge, as it happened, played a large part in this refurbishment, which however started not in the university but in the public schools. Early in the century public schoolboys were left very largely to their own devices outside the classroom. They got up to much that headmasters might disapprove of, yet could not always control. Football was a suspect activity, and headmasters sometimes discouraged it – Keate at Eton and Butler at Shrewsbury being examples we know about, Butler denouncing it as 'only fit for butcher boys'. But from about 1840 teachers intervened far more closely in their pupils' leisure, to discipline unruly energies into acceptable patterns, very largely of course on the games field. Football of a suitably non-violent character was encouraged, and by the middle of the century at the latest it was played at all schools.[98] Schools tended to develop their own versions of the game, since until the coming of the railway network it was not possible to organise away fixtures, contest occurred within schools not between them, and uniformity was not necessary.[99] Still, Montague Shearman was able, while describing the game as it was in the middle of the century, to separate the 'kicking' game played almost everywhere from the 'hacking' or 'collaring' game at Rugby. In the kicking game the ball was kicked but not opponents, and handling

---

[94] Robert W. Malcolmson, *Popular Recreations in English Society 1700–1850* (Cambridge University Press, 1973), pp. 34–40.

[95] Malcolmson, *Popular Recreations*, pp. 138–45, 168.

[96] Quoted in Percy M. Young, *A History of British Football* (London, Stanley Paul, 1968), p. 61.

[97] Young, *British Football*, p. 62.

[98] Young, *British Football*, pp. 63–74; Mangan, *Athleticism*; John Chandos, *Boys Together. English Public Schools 1800–1864* (London, Hutchinson, 1984), pp. 332–40.

[99] At the end of the century some leading public schools still played their individual versions of the game: see Shearman, Oakley, Smith, *et al.*, *Football*, pp. 36–84.

the ball and manhandling the other team were limited or forbidden practices. Only at Rugby was running with the ball and shin-kicking (or hacking) permitted, and even after the rules of 1846 barbarities were permitted on the Warwickshire field that were distasteful to teams elsewhere.[100]

Undergraduates from football schools started the game at Cambridge. The first football club was founded about 1840, when seven men drew up rules to assimilate different school practices; one of the men was Edgar Montagu, ex-Shrewsbury.[101] The club did not last, but in 1846 two more Old Salopians, Henry de Winton (Trinity) and J. C. Thring (St John's) 'persuaded some Old Etonians to join them and formed a club. Matches were few and far between, but some were played on Parker's Piece.'[102] This club too soon folded, and in 1848 yet another was founded. But, recorded a Trinity undergraduate involved, H. C. Malden,

> the result was dire confusion, as every man played the rules he had been accustomed to at his public school. I remember how the Eton man howled at the Rugby for handling the ball. So it was agreed that two men should be chosen to represent each of the public schools, and two, who were not public school men, for the 'Varsity... We were fourteen in all, I believe. Harrow, Eton, Rugby, Winchester and Shrewsbury were represented. We met in my rooms after Hall, which in those days was at 4.0 pm; anticipating a long meeting, I cleared the tables and provided pens, ink, and paper. Several asked me on coming in if an exam. was on! Every man brought a copy of his school rules, or knew them by heart, and our progress in framing new rules was slow... The new rules were printed as the 'Cambridge Rules', copies were distributed and pasted up on Parker's Piece, and very satisfactorily they worked.

Perhaps these rules were adopted for some games.[103] But the variety of practice that Malden described in fact continued for some time. Cambridge football was a modest game in the 1850s, and not a

---

[100] Shearman, *Athletics and Football*, pp. 271–5; Young, *British Football*, p. 63. Sometimes the less violent form of football was called the 'dribbling' game.

[101] See his letter of 1899 quoted in J. Basil Oldham, *A History of Shrewsbury School 1552–1952* (Oxford, Blackwell, 1952), p. 232.

[102] N. L. Jackson, *Association Football* (London, 1899), pp. 26–7 for what follows.

[103] Oldham, *Shrewsbury School*, p. 233. The only known copy of these early University Football Club rules seems to be in the library of Shrewsbury School.

challenge to the sovereign pursuit, rowing. T. G. Bonney, an undergraduate at St John's from 1852 to 1856, recollected that football 'in winter and cricket in summer occupied the "dry-bobs"', and he 'often played football on Parker's Piece, without uniform or regular organisation', very few colleges, if any, having grounds of their own.[104] Bonney and his friends made little impact on his Cambridge contemporary, John Venn, who wrote that football was 'left to boys . . . I never saw the game played, and . . . no friend of mine ever practised it'.[105]

A few years later Venn would certainly have noticed football. By 1870 there were in addition to the university team, clubs at St John's, Jesus, and Corpus, all three colleges having football grounds while some games were still played on Parker's Piece. There were also Cambridge clubs for Old Harrovians and Old Etonians, and the Eton side was thought by some to be the strongest in Cambridge. At any rate some of these clubs were able to field two teams. Still, the fixture-list was necessarily brief; in Michaelmas 1869 (the first term for which details can be traced) the St John's first team played only six times.[106] The Rugby game was played in Cambridge, and several varieties of the kicking game: 'At both Universities non-Rugby schools played their own school games still, and generally joined in a sort of Association game played two or three times a week on Parker's Piece at Cambridge, in the Parks at Oxford.'[107] In Michaelmas 1869 the St John's team played Rugby against Jesus and Eton, with thirteen on each side, Rugby against the university, with teams of fifteen, and a return Rugby match against the university with teams of twelve. It also played an Association game (or something like it) against Corpus with teams of eleven. There was considerable fluidity in Cambridge in what the report calls 'a healthy and inexpensive amusement'.

In the 1850s and 1860s clubs were founded all over Britain, as enthusiasm rippled outwards from school and university clubs.

---

[104] 'A Septuagenarian's Recollections of St John's', by T. G. B[onney], *The Eagle*, 30 (1909), pp. 304–5.
[105] John Venn, *Early Collegiate Life*, p. 280. Venn was an undergraduate at Gonville and Caius from 1853 to 1857, and a fellow from then until his death in 1923.
[106] *The Eagle*, 6 (1869), pp. 254–6. For advice on this crucial article and other football technicalities I am indebted to Robert Cook of the University of Sheffield.
[107] A. C. M. Croome, ed, *Fifty Years of Sport: Oxford and Cambridge* (2 vols., London, Walter Southwood, 1913), vol. II, p. 66.

These amateurs in the Lincoln, Sheffield, or Dingley Dell clubs played by the rules of the school that inspired them, or as agreed by a local association. Chaos threatened. J. C. Thring, in the 1860s an assistant at Uppingham (where his brother was headmaster) was concerned at the possible effects of differences on 'a game so manly and played with so much spirit'; he published an attempt at consensus rules 'lest too frequent spills and too heated personal encounters might lead to results not compatible with the dignity and honour of maturing manhood'.[108]

A similar wish to bring unity to the game led to the formation of the Football Association in 1863 by representatives of some public schools and metropolitan clubs.[109] In framing the rules the gathering had before them a draft drawn up by a committee of the Cambridge University Football Club in October 1863. This draft reflected support for the kicking game, in that handling the ball was totally forbidden, though however much the drafting committee wished to depart from the Rugby tradition,[110] the game remained popular in Cambridge in the 1860s. At all events, this Cambridge draft formed the basis of the FA rules agreed on 1 December, and for this reason an historian of the game has written that 'As was Rome in relation to the institution of Christianity, so was Cambridge in respect of football.'[111] The association was trying to unite all footballers, and its rules reflected an attempt to include both the dribbling and handling traditions.[112] But they did prohibit hacking, which was denounced by the president as 'dangerous as well as painful' and 'very brutal'. Failing to get the ban rescinded, the Blackheath club, very strongly Rugby in sentiment, withdrew from the association;[113] the divergence into two discrete games really dates from that point. The Rugby Football Union was founded in 1871, and local diversity of rule was eroded as clubs affiliated to one national grouping or another. In Cambridge two distinct teams were formed in 1872 and 1873. The first Inter-University Rugby

---

[108] J. C. T[hring], *Rules of Football: The Winter Game* (London, 1862).
[109] For what follows see Jackson, *Association Football*, pp. 24–40.
[110] Strangely, the drafting committee of nine included two Rugbeians.
[111] Young, *British Football*, p. 86.
[112] The FA rules required throwing in from touch instead of kicking in as the Cambridge draft suggested; and they allowed fair catches while Cambridge forbade all handling.
[113] Paradoxically, when in 1871 the RFU was formed one of its first actions was to forbid hacking.

A Cricket-Match on Fenner's Ground.

STIRRING THE STUMPS.

Cricket on Parker's Piece.

20 Two views of Cambridge cricket, drawn in 1859. On Fenner's Ground is the pavilion built in 1856. The drawing of Parker's Piece shows the houses of Regent Street, and on the left the tower of St Paul's church in the Hills Road.

game was played in 1872, and the first Association Varsity game in 1874.

CRICKET

'There is no more entrancing sport than cricket, and nowhere does cricket present itself in a more entrancing form than at Cam-bridge.'[114] This typical expression of delight in the game is taken from a book largely written by Cambridge's most famous Victorian player, while the boards around its detailed bulk are decorated with the university coat of arms, as though it had invented the game. Yet in Victorian Cambridge cricket never had as many participants as rowing, and colleges did not give the historian the feeling that they were organised for the sake of taking part in it, as when viewed in a certain light they did with respect to oarsmanship. In part the explanation is that of course cricket is a summer pursuit, and rowing a year-long one. Matriculants from schools where nothing in particular was played were recruited into the novices' boats in October, and so the pattern of their undergraduate leisure became set. And while the Cam was as good a stretch of water (sewage apart) as you might find, cricketers had no special turf until the late 1840s, and played on Parker's Piece.

The origins of Cambridge cricket and football were very similar; they were brought to the university by matriculants from the Great Schools,[115] though cricket came earlier, or at least seems to have been the first to come to Cambridge in a regulated form developed from an inchoate stick-and-ball game. Cricket recognisably evolved by the sixteenth century, as a popular game in south-east England, and was taken up as an aristocratic pursuit soon after 1660 in a process hard to elucidate.[116] Cricket was played in the university by the early eighteenth century; regulations of 1714 forbade

---

[114] W. J. Ford, 'Cambridge University Cricket', in K. S. Ranjitsinhji, *The Jubilee Book of Cricket* (Edinburgh, 1897), p. 112. These sentences are based on H. S. Altham and E. W. Swanton, *A History of Cricket* (fifth edn, 2 vols., London, Allen & Unwin, 1962), vol. 1 (by Altham), pp. 19–59; and Christopher Brookes, *English Cricket. The Game and its Players through the Ages* (London, Weidenfeld & Nicolson, 1978), pp. 1–66.

[115] The public schools regarded as pre-eminent, and which were emulated by others; the list always included Eton, Harrow, Charterhouse, Rugby, Shrewsbury, Westminster, and Winchester, and sometimes St Paul's and Merchant Taylors' also.

[116] These sentences are based on Altham and Swanton, *History of Cricket*, vol. 1 (by Altham), pp. 19–59; and Brookes, *English Cricket*, pp. 1–66.

undergraduates to visit 'a coffee-house, tennis-court, cricket-ground, &c. between 9 and 12 a.m.' (the hours of college tuition).[117] By about 1750 Old Etonians had established the dominance of Cambridge cricket they were to keep for a long time, but the fondness for the game shown by Henry Venn, an undergraduate from 1742 to 1746 at St John's and Jesus and 'one of the best players in the University',[118] suggests its general popularity.

When the university cricket club was founded in 1820, 25 undergraduates joined, and there were 47 such members two years later, plus 2 dons.[119] There were games between club teams that were quite informal, sometimes only 7 or 8 on each side turning up to play. In the early years there was a shortage of first-class matches; the club played the Cambridge town club every year, and Bury St Edmund's, while sometimes King's (that is, Etonians) played the rest of the university. There were no county engagements, however. In 1827, there occurred the first of the Oxford v. Cambridge matches. Held again in 1829 and once more in 1836, the series became annual from 1838 onwards. The teams never met at Cambridge, one problem being the lack of a good private ground in the early years. All matches were held at Lord's, except the second, in Oxford; London was convenient for both universities, just as the Thames was for the Boat Race. But the cricket match drew fewer spectators than the race, and in the university itself cricket was not always taken seriously. Wishing to play, G. R. Dupuis (King's 1854 to 1857) was refused leave of absence from afternoon chapel by the dean, and only succeeded when he asked the provost. In the 1830s the XI had no ground staff of professionals and no distinctive uniform. H. S. Altham's judgement is that 'the average University Eleven down to the sixties would have had no chance whatever against any of the good county sides'.[120]

In the 1820s the cricket club leased a piece of land in Barnwell, but for a few years only; building-leases commanded more money than the club could afford, and even as grassland plots were very expensive. So for some years all university and college matches had

---

[117] Christopher Wordsworth, *Social Life*, p. 67; see also Cooper, *Annals*, IV, pp. 278–80.
[118] Later a famous Evangelical clergyman.
[119] For what follows, see W. J. Ford, *A History of the Cambridge University Cricket Club 1820–1901* (Edinburgh, Blackwood, 1902), pp. 1–13.
[120] Altham and Swanton, *History of Cricket*, vol. I, p. 114; Ford, *History of the C.U.C.C.*, pp. 8–9, 40–1.

to be played on Parker's Piece, described by the cricket club's historian as a 'huge village-green'. F. H. Norman, a keen under-graduate cricketer at the end of the 1850s, reported that

> The seat of the University cricket was in Parker's Piece: I cannot say I enjoyed that. The fieldsmen of the different matches were all jumbled up together ... and the hits of one game crossing those of another, which was both disconcerting and dangerous. But it was a splendid lively ground, and not too true – very good to learn on.[121]

We are told that 'there also haunted "The Piece" a class ... of rather seedy-looking professionals, provided with bat, ball, and stumps – no net – ready and anxious to bowl to any passer-by for a casual shilling; and often was he who journeyed up to Fenner's for athletics invited to stop and "'Ave a few balls", if a specially bright and warm day accidentally appeared during the rigours of a Cambridge March'.[122] It was believed that 'so large a sward, intersected by footpaths, public property with "rights of way" innumerable, and no facilities for gate-money, was hardly the fit home for a University Club capable of measuring its strength with the strongest sides'. The MCC (Marylebone Cricket Club) came to play the university on several occasions but refused to return 'owing to the noisy and ill-mannered chaff to which they had been subjected', perhaps from the townspeople to whom Parker's Piece was fully open.[123]

A more suitable ground came the club's way in 1848, when F. P. Fenner gave it exclusive use between May and September of a field he leased from Caius, to the east of what is now Gonville Place, and overlooked by the gaol, since demolished. Fenner's field, six acres in extent and on the edge of built-up Cambridge, was more private than Parker's Piece and also smoother; F. P. Fenner's boast was 'Put a stump where you will and when you will, measure 22 yards, and you can play a game on any ground' in his field.[124] At first players did not think it as perfect as that, and the captain of the Cambridge 1850 XI complained that he 'was knocked down senseless by a ball in the eye' that bounced off the grass. The ground had originally been two

---

[121] Quoted in Ford, *History of the C.U.C.C.*, p. 13.
[122] Ford, 'Cambridge University Cricket', p. 340.   [123] Ford, *History of the C.U.C.C.*, pp. 6, 10.
[124] Ford, *History of the C.U.C.C.*, p. 10, pp. 10–11 for the next two quotations, and pp. 9–31 for these paragraphs generally.

fields, and the ditch between them was still there. 'In the course of half a century', wrote W. J. Ford in 1902, 'alterations and improvements innumerable have been made, till the ground, as it now is, is not to be recognised by its earliest or indeed its later users.' The club's income was small, and there was often friction with F. P. Fenner over money. For some years there was no pavilion, and the wooden one built in 1856 was uncomfortable; 'nor was there any water in the lavatory except what was fetched by members in a can from a tap close by'.[125] Building the pavilion loaded the club with a debt of £300 which was not paid off for some years, while there was a constant need to find salaries for the professionals employed to coach the gentlemen of the CUCC (Cambridge University Cricket Club). In the 1860s the club had at least four professionals all of whom played for the Cambridgeshire county team. William Buttress was as a bowler 'probably as good as anyone in England' until drink weakened his delivery and shortened his life (he died at forty-one), while George Tarrant was a bowler of 'speed and destructiveness', and Thomas Hayward and Robert Carpenter were 'such a pair of batsmen as no other county could claim'. Though essential to improve the strength of university cricket, they 'were often absent – on leave – to fulfil first–class engagements elsewhere'. When the club demurred at their absence, 'they threatened to transfer their services to Oxford'.[126] Always short of money, the club faced acute crisis in 1870. The wooden pavilion was dilapidated, but a new one could not be contemplated until something better than annual tenancy could be arranged. In 1873 the opportunity came, when F. P. Fenner having left Cambridge, Caius granted a long lease in return for a modest rent. A brick pavilion was built. Its predicted cost was £1,500, but by 1877 the total had risen to £3,800, owing to 'difficulties in connection with drainage, erection of fences, and making of roads'.[127] A subscription headed by the Prince of Wales settled the debt.

In the long run the club's finances were improved by the popularity of cricket in Cambridge. Since about 1840 it had been growing with the matriculation of pupils from schools that were

---

[125] Ford, *History of the C.U.C.C.*, p. 17, quoting T. E. Bagge, a player of *c.* 1860.
[126] Ford, *History of the C.U.C.C.*, pp. 15–16; Altham and Swanton, *History of Cricket*, vol. 1 (by Altham), pp. 101–3.   [127] Ford, *History of C.U.C.C.*, p. 24.

pushing it in the athleticist boom, and a few colleges laid out cricket grounds. After 1870 the rise of cricket suddenly accelerated. More colleges prepared grounds and engaged professionals. The first edition (1889) of the 6" Ordnance Survey map of Cambridge shows eleven cricket grounds serving fourteen colleges, in addition of course to Fenner's. Enough enthusiasts paid the UCC subscription of one guinea to enable it to employ a dozen professionals by the 1890s, and to buy the freehold of Fenner's in 1894 in partnership with the athletic club. By the end of the century cricket was perhaps second only to rowing in popularity. Every college had its ground and the services of a professional. Matriculants came up from cricketing schools and joined their college club, and some never rose higher: 'there is an absolute dearth of any element corresponding to "house feeling" in schools',[128] and spectators were few, but still, 'grounds are charmingly good, bowling delightfully bad, hospitality unlimited, and cricket rather free-and-easy'. Players noticed in college games were swept off to Fenner's to play in the Freshers match, and if good enough were placed in a university XI, and perhaps eventually in *the* XI, to play Oxford, the MCC, or the first-class counties. For some, university cricket was a full-time occupation in the summer, rather than a pastime. Playing, and being coached by the Fenner's professionals, meant, it was said, that 'the "blue", or prospective "blue", is so much occupied with University cricket – he may perhaps even do some "reading" as well – that he has but little time to devote to club and college cricket ... he is the servant of the University for the time being, and the slave of the captain'.

Other opportunities for cricket were offered to proficient players by the many Cambridge clubs, the Crusaders, Hawks, Pilgrims, Magpies, Jackdaws, and others, who took on any suitable XI, wore distinctive colours, and sometimes had their own club-rooms. The most famous, the Quidnuncs, had no more than fifteen members, and played against 'the different public schools and various garrisons and regiments' because no local team was good enough; while the Perambulators and Etceteras were confined to alumni of the Great Schools and played college XIs. The Varsity team itself was virtually

---

[128] Ford, 'Cambridge University Cricket', p. 346 for this quotation and pp. 340–48 for these paragraphs generally.

a Great School preserve; for example, of the ten men in the 1881 XI whose schools can be traced seven had come from Great Schools, four of them from Eton.[129] In fact, a disproportionate number of Cambridge cricketers were Etonians. The engaging and too brief memoirs of one such, Lord Hawke, suggest that his three Cambridge years were devoted to cricket, football, athletics, his militia battalion, the Beefsteak Club, and avoiding the Proctors; he left without taking a degree.[130] He served in the Green Howards till 1894, but his life was dominated by his captaincy of Yorkshire cricket from 1883 to 1910. An ardent believer in the amateur philosophy embodied in the Cambridge University Cricket Club, he is chiefly famous for his plea, 'Pray God, that a professional should never captain England.'

A NOTE ON PUNTING

In his pages on punting in the 1903 edition of the Badminton Library volume P. W. Squire wrote that 'when boating for pleasure a punt possesses many advantages' over craft that were rowed.[131]

> The punter faces the direction in which the craft is travelling, and he or she can have a good view of the scenery; the position for punting is less cramped than that for rowing, and the stroke is more varied; the sitters can be more at ease than in a skiff, which must always be properly 'trimmed'. The punt is also better adapted for luncheon and tea, which is a great convenience on a journey, and obviates the necessity of reaching an hotel at any special time.

All this is true, and though P. W. Squire might well have admitted that it is much harder to learn punting than rowing, his words serve to explain why punting is so popular on the Cam today. But he does not mention Cambridge punting at all, the reason being that as far as we can tell it hardly existed on the Cam, at all events as a pleasure pursuit, before the beginning of the twentieth century. Its absence is puzzling, especially since the Cam offers an intrinsic advantage to

[129] In addition there were two Harrovians and one Rugbeian. The other three came from Repton, Marlborough, and Uppingham.
[130] Martin Bladen Hawke, *Recollections and Reminiscences* (London, Williams & Norgate, 1924), pp. 34–49.
[131] Rowe, Pitman, Serocold, *et al.*, *Roweing and Punting*, 2nd impression (London, Longmans, 1903), p. 235.

the punter – the causeway that was laid down in the middle of the river centuries ago in the absence of a towpath near the colleges, to allow horses to walk upstream pulling barges.

From earliest times flat-bottomed boats that were poled rather than rowed have been used in shallow waters for transport, fishing and hunting. Just as happened with rowing boats, working craft became adapted for pleasure. Leisure punting is well attested in the nineteenth century on the Thames, the Isis, and other rivers.[132] It was common at Oxford: but not Cambridge, though for workaday *commercial* purposes punts were often to be seen on the Cam and neighbouring streams. Punts could be poled up reaches where there were only four inches of water, and the Fens were ideal waters for them.[133] Such work-punts were of various designs, to some extent depending on boatyard traditions, but they were usually very solidly constructed. They were about 16 feet long and 4 feet wide, double-ended (and therefore very square in appearance) so that they did not need to be turned round in narrow channels. They were often called 'garden punts'. Undergraduates were shown amusing themselves in one of these heavy craft in the *Copperplate Magazine* in 1792; implausibly garbed in academical dress, they are on the classical punter's stretch of the Cam, above Clare Bridge and next to King's College lawn, the chapel being clear in the background.[134] But there are few references to such punters in Victorian Cambridge. In the most sympathetic of Cambridge autobiographies, Charles Darwin's granddaughter writes about her childhood in the 1890s in Newnham Grange (now part of Darwin College), whose garden fronted the Cam – a pleasant site since it was upstream from the filth of the river in central Cambridge: 'we were all able to swim early, and grew up knowing how to manage boats by instinct: row-boats and canoes; but not punts, for there were then none on the Cam.' She mentions, however, enjoying 'the best games of pirates in an old, square, flat-bottomed boat, which the gardener used when he was cutting the reeds in the river'.[135] This boat is also

[132] R. T. Rivington, *Punting, Its History and Techniques* (Oxford, R. T. Rivington, 1983), esp. pp. 1–43.
[133] This sentence is based on conversations with Jack Ravensdale, the doyen of Fenland historians until his death in 1994.   [134] Rivington, *Punting*, pp. 160–1, and illustration 57.
[135] Gwen Raverat, *Period Piece. A Cambridge Childhood* (London, Faber, 1952). p. 232. The garden punt is shown, in drawings by Gwen Raverat herself, on pp. 33 and 231.

described by Gwen Raverat's younger sister, as 'a garden punt generally kept moored near the landing stage', and needed 'to rescue balls hit into the river from the lawn above'. It was used, too, 'as a kind of water-borne cart or floating wheel-barrow... It was frequently water-logged and needed constant baling-out. The two flat ends might be used as seats, but except for having a flat bottom it bore little resemblance to the elegant slim punt of today.'[136]

It seems that the first true pleasure punt was not seen on the Cam until shortly before 1900. It was built for two Pembroke undergraduates, Dammers and Howard, to a design that owed something to Dammers's memories of punting holidays on the Thames. Two punts are thought to have been imported from the Thames about 1902.[137] Many others quickly followed or were built in Cambridge. Punts spread in a surge of popularity that reminds us of the rage for the safety bicycle in Cambridge twenty years previously; 'by 1907 they had largely replaced the rowing boats for river outings and picnics'.[138] The mystery of the pleasure punt's late arrival in Cambridge is a problem of historical absence: the dog that did not bark. Such questions are the hardest to answer, and there have been few attempts at explanation. The true cause was surely the filthy state of the river in the nineteenth century, its use as a sewer outfall meaning that it grew more disgusting as the town developed.[139] 'There is a tale of Queen Victoria being shown over Trinity by the Master, Dr Whewell, and saying, as she looked down over the bridge: "What are all those pieces of paper floating down the river?" To which, with great presence of mind, he replied: "Those, ma'am, are notices that bathing is forbidden".'[140] However beguiling the upper reaches of the Cam might have been, nobody would have wished to linger in a punt in the centre of town, or to drive the punt-pole into the oozy bed of the river. Proper sewage works were not constructed until 1895: the first pleasure punts reached the river a few years later.

---

[136] Margaret Elizabeth Keynes, *A House by the River. Newnham Grange to Darwin College* (Cambridge, Darwin College, 1976), p. 74.
[137] Rivington, *Punting*, p. 155.
[138] Enid Porter, *Cambridge Customs and Folklore* (London, Routledge & Kegan Paul, 1969), p. 234.
[139] *VCH Cambridgeshire*, III, pp. 104–5.
[140] Raverat, *Period Piece*, p. 34.

Chapter 19

LEISURE FOR TOWN AND GOWN: MUSIC, DEBATING, AND DRAMA

MUSIC

MUSIC 1760–1832

On Sunday 12 March 1843 William Thomson wrote in his diary that 'after hall, I went over to practising along with Airey, & played the Canadian Boatsong as a duetto'.[1] Thomson was playing a 'cornopean', as the cornet was at first called; the instrument, essentially a valved version of the posthorn, had been invented in France about fifteen years earlier, reaching Britain about 1834. The cornet was characteristic of the improvement in instruments that occurred between 1700 and 1850 and accompanied the extension of interest in music, as a leisure pursuit, to large numbers in the middle and working classes. This was a striking cultural phenomenon of the epoch, akin to the spread of literacy and a taste for books.[2] Cambridge – town and gown – participated in it, and as we shall see William Thomson was a notable figure within it.

Music had for long been established in the Cambridge syllabus, but was as an academic subject disparaged and despised by dons for whom it was a cherished leisure pursuit. (Something similar was later to happen with English literature.) Winstanley describes it as the 'Cinderella among the faculties', and points out that early in the nineteenth century it was said that 'this faculty does not form part of the University and has only a slight connexion with it'.[3] Neither doctors nor bachelors of music were members of the Senate. For

---

[1] CUL MSS Add. 7342: NB 29, diary of William Thomson.
[2] Much of this section draws upon E. D. Mackerness, *A Social History of Music* (London, Routledge, 1964), esp. pp. 87–198.
[3] For what follows, see *Unreformed Cambridge*, pp. 77–8. Biographical details in these pages are taken from *The New Grove Dictionary of Music and Musicians* (20 vols., London, Macmillan, 1980).

both degrees the qualification was the composition of a piece of solemn music, approved by the Professor of Music; it was usually performed in Great St Mary's on Commencement Sunday.[4] Candidates had to have their names on the books of a college but did not have to reside. Very few music degrees were taken, and at all events in the eighteenth century graduates were mostly 'church organists or choirmasters who hoped to advance themselves in their profession by the acquisition of an academic distinction'.[5] The three men who served as professors between 1755 and 1836 (John Randall, Charles Hague, and John Clarke-Whitfeld) were themselves practitioners rather than scholars; or at least it might be said that they did not possess the sort of learning needed for reputation at Cambridge. Since all three had merely musical degrees they could not even enter the Senate House (reserved strictly for MAs) to present candidates for the BMus or DMus. The title professor itself was used by the university in a Pickwickian sense, as for a professor of fencing. The professors received no stipend, and were paid by fees for musical degrees; these being few and fees low, the professor earned only £47 between 1836 and 1850. Fortunately he had other wide musical activities.[6] But all three men named are worth mentioning as composers – Clarke-Whitfeld especially, with two oratorios to his credit, much influenced by Handel.[7]

Music's fortunes were very similar at Oxford.[8] Strong interest among both town and gown, in college, choir, and chapel, contrasted with the marginal status of musical degrees and the professors – who, nevertheless, had greater achievements to their name than we might suppose. In both universities the prominent place of music in university ceremonial suggests that music was more esteemed than its academic practitioners, and praise of music uttered in the Sheldonian Theatre in July 1773 expressed affections felt in Cambridge too: 'To calm the boisterous passions. To relieve the anxieties of the world – To inspire cheerfulness – To appease the nervous when irritated . . . to kindle in our Souls the bright flame of

---

[4] Commencement occurred at the end of June and the beginning of July.
[5] Winstanley, *Unreformed Cambridge*, p. 78.
[6] PP 1852–3, HC xliv [1559]: *Graham Commission Evidence*, p. 136.
[7] *The Crucifixion* and *The Resurrection*.
[8] See S. L. F. Wollenberg, 'Music and Musicians', in Sutherland and Mitchell, *The Eighteenth Century*, pp. 865–87. The quotation occurs on p. 865.

Devotion; and to raise the Mind to a sensibility, and love of order. Those will not surely have misspent their time, in acquiring the knowledge of Musick, who apply it to these Purposes.'

Features of the Cambridge year were subscription concerts, held fortnightly in term from October till the following spring. Often they were held in the Town Hall. Professor Hague, perhaps typically among Cambridge musicians, mounted them in his private house, in Bridge Street; tickets for his series of twelve cost three guineas for men and two for women, while tickets for individual concerts cost 5s.[9] Many such series were held in the 'concert rooms' of public houses. The Black Bear, in Market Street, had a 'Music Club' to embrace its subscription concerts.[10] Richard Hurd, a young graduate of Emmanuel (he was later the Bishop of Worcester) attended a 'weekly concert of Musick at the Tuns' (the Three Tuns in Market Hill) in February 1741:

> The Room was made very comfortable by a couple of good fires & a considerable number of Candles. After a little chat among the Auditors & a few preparatory flourishes among the performers, we were most elegantly entertain'd with a very fine Sonata. Whether Corelli's, Vivaldi's, or Geminiani's is not very material to determine: 'tis enough yt the musick was good, & we pleas'd.[11]

Indistinguishable from these subscription concerts in scale and musical content were the 'benefits' upon which Cambridge's professional musicians relied for much of their income; in the 1780s we know of at least sixteen benefit concerts for the Mahons, a local musical clan.[12] Thus almost a century after Hurd's visit to the Three Tuns Mr Registrary Romilly recorded in his diary:[13]

> Dr Carnaby dined in Hall with me: – in the Evg. to Concert at the Hoop[14] for benefit of Mrs Matthews (widow of our late Org[anis]t):

[9] See for example, *Cambridge Chronicle*, 7 November 1801.
[10] CUL: Cam Collection, Musical Society at the Black Bear, Programmes 17 February 1789–8 May 1809 (Cam.a.789.1).
[11] *The Early Letters of Bishop Richard Hurd 1739–1762*, ed. Sarah Brewer, Church of England Record Society, 3 (Woodbridge, Boydell, 1995), p. 36.
[12] Frida Knight, *Cambridge Music* (Cambridge, Oleander Press, 1980), p. 53. See also, for example, *Cambridge Chronicle*, 20 February 1808: Nicholls's annual benefit concert, with visiting performer Signora Griglietti.
[13] Bury, *Romilly's Cambridge Diary 1832–42*, p. 26, Wednesday 16 January 1833.
[14] It stood between the Round Church and Jesus Lane, with its entrance on Bridge Street.

Dr Carnaby[15] at the Piano: pretty ballad of his about 'a peaceful cottage': – chorusses in the Messiah well sung – Found it pleasant enough; sat all night next Mrs Prest[16] – Harraden[17] admired to me the beauty of his boy (a chorus singer) – as plain as his Father: – young Matthews sung rather nicely in Avison's beautiful 'sound the loud timbrel' – thin Post opened his mouth in a Chorus but I heard no voice from it.

Professional musicians (numbering some scores, perhaps) played at these concerts and at student parties, taught music, ran the one or two music shops in the city, and sold musical instruments or hired them out to dons and students.[18] Among these professionals should be counted the organists and lay clerks of King's, Trinity, and St John's; one such (in the 1790s) was John Bennett, the grandfather of Sterndale Bennett, the composer and Cambridge professor. This college music world is lightly sketched in the memoirs of William Glover, a Trinity boy chorister in the 1820s and 1830s.[19] He records that though Samuel Matthews, the Trinity organist, was kindly in private he was a martinet with the choir, in the practices that preceded each morning's school:

> We attended service at chapel on Sundays and 'surplice days', that is, on Saints' Days and the evening previous. On Sunday, we went to chapel at eight a.m.; breakfasted; went to Trinity Church generally at eleven; then to St John's[20] at five, and finally to Trinity Chapel service at six. I am wrong. I said 'finally', but it is an actual and maniacal fact that our friends positively desired our presence, unofficially, at St Mary's late service.

Glover adds: 'There was also a town choral society in which we were the only trebles employed. At this society I first heard the great works of Handel, Beethoven, and Mozart performed with band

---

15 Probably William Carnaby (1772–1839), organist of Hanover Chapel, London. Two weeks later Carnaby failed to become Trinity's organist, being defeated by T. A. Walmisley, Professor of Music 1836–56: see *Romilly's Cambridge Diary 1832–42*, p. 28, 1 February 1833.
16 Probably the wife of Samuel Prest of Stapleford Lodge, six miles south of Cambridge.
17 Richard Harraden, artist and compiler of *Cantabrigia Depicta*.
18 See *Cambridge Chronicle*, for example 15 November 1783 (Morris Barford's music shop, Petty Cury), 4 March 1786 (Anthony Manini), and 21 March 1807 (Poole teaches harp and has one to hire).
19 William Glover, *The Memoirs of a Cambridge Chorister* (2 vols., London 1885), esp. vol. I, pp. 142–51. The quotations are from p. 143.
20 Until 1856 the three colleges shared their choirs, which greatly added to the workload.

accompaniments. Such a society is an invaluable institution in any town.' This choral society (the date of its foundation is unknown) was essential for large-scale productions.

Glover's words remind us that a greater amount of music at Cambridge, as elsewhere, was performed by *amateurs* – citizens, dons, and undergraduates. Thus the diarist Romilly, who was a musical enthusiast, visited the opera in London but got his pleasure in Cambridge from amateur music, even if we count as professional the anthems to which he listened attentively in church. Visits to masters' lodges were always enlivened by amateur singers. After a visit to Sidney master's lodge Romilly records, 'Mrs Phelps sung a duet with the giantess, who afterwards sang "O thou that tellest very well indeed" – Mathison and other musical men came in the Evening.'[21] Larger events might take place in the Town Hall (i.e. the Guildhall): 'Went to the Amateur Concert at the Town hall, a ticket having been kindly given me by the secy Mr McDonnell of Magd. – I thought the performance very good: a freshman of King's made his first appearance as a singer: he sang "the Pilgrim of Love" & was rapturously received.'[22]

Musical incidents at an evening in Trinity lodge when it was occupied by that familiar couple Dr and Mrs Whewell are described by John Bacchus Dykes, an undergraduate at St Catharine's, and a well-known Cambridge musician.

There is a piece of etiquette kept up at Trinity Lodge, which I believe is kept up nowhere but at court – viz: that no *male* sits down all the evening. So of course I had to stand on my legs all night. We had some music during the evening: – Walmisley and Blow played a magnificent P.F. [pianoforte] duett of Onslow's, which took up nearly half an hour, and which acted as a nice accompaniment to conversation! Then some lady who was staying at the lodge sang a song, and very nicely she sang it. This being finished, I saw, from the other end of the room, Mrs W. apply her glass to her eye, and take a sweep of the room, and stop in the direction where I was standing. I immediately began talking very vigorously to some young ladies near whom I was, – but it was all no go. I was petrified by Mrs W. coming up to me and saying, 'Mr Dykes, will you go to the P.F. and

[21] Bury and Pickles, *Romilly's Cambridge Diary 1842–1847*, p. 100, 29 May 1844.
[22] 14 March 1849.

sing something'. I, of course, had to say, 'Certainly, Madam', and then began to rack my brains for something to sing. Of course I dared not sing anything comic, so I luckily thought of that song of Kreutzer's – 'Ah from out those gloomy vallies' with which, by the bye, Walmisley was delighted.[23]

Cambridge was far more fortunate than other small market towns in possessing the Senate House for concerts, from 1730 onwards, and there was the Town Hall too. Musical possibilities were further extended when the Barnwell theatre was built by William Wilkins junior in 1814 and when the Town Hall was enlarged in the 1840s. In the Senate House, and in Great St Mary's, Handel's oratorios were often performed.[24] They were as popular in Cambridge as elsewhere in Britain for their combination of memorable harmony with religious sentiment. Likely to attract maximum audiences, *Samson, Judas Maccabaeus,* and of course *Messiah* were ideal for a great charitable purpose of town and gown, Addenbrooke's Hospital. Acquiring in the course of time status as *patriotic* music, *Messiah* was the obvious work to celebrate George III's return to sanity in 1789. A. H. Mann, visiting Cambridge, wrote: 'Passing St Mary's Church I heard music. Dr Randall was rehearsing Handel's anthem "My heart is indicting". I was charmed and could not leave until the music had ceased. This was preparatory to the celebration day on which the King was to go to St Paul's to return thanks for his mental recovery.'[25]

Music was an essential part of the proceedings at Commencement, at the end of June. Writing in 1854 about events that took place a half-century or more earlier, Henry Gunning recalled that Commencement, 'was at that time the gayest season in the University. A nobleman scarcely ever took his degree except on the Monday in that week; and I recollect that on one occasion, when Dr Pearce was Orator, eleven persons took their degrees in right of nobility.'[26] During Commencement the Pot Fair was held on Midsummer Common, and on the Saturday evening before the

[23] J. T. Fowler, *Life and Letters of John Bacchus Dykes* (London, 1897), pp. 29–30, quoting from a letter of May 1845. Dykes's prominent part in the Cambridge University Musical Society is treated below.

[24] For what follows, see Knight, *Cambridge Music*, pp. 50–2.

[25] Quoted by Knight, *Cambridge Music*, p. 54. The king's recovery was merely temporary.

[26] Gunning, *Reminiscences*, vol. 1, 26, and pp. 26–9 for what follows.

festivities there was a promenade across Stourbridge Common, and a ball for the gentry of city and county. The following day, Commencement Sunday, 'the college walks were crowded. Every Doctor in the University wore his scarlet robes during the whole day. All the noblemen appeared in their splendid robes, not only at St Mary's and in the college halls, but also in the public walks.' There were public dinners for hundreds (sometimes thousands) in college courts, firework displays, and as in 1811 the ascent of a hot-air balloon. Among the most popular entertainments were concerts of secular music in the Senate House, and of sacred music in Great St Mary's. When a new Chancellor was installed at Commencement, an ode was composed and set to music. For Grafton's installation in 1769 Thomas Gray composed an ode out of gratitude to Grafton for appointing him Professor of Modern History though he thought such odes were 'by nature doom'd to live but a single day'.[27] In search of a doctorate, the composer Charles Burney hoped to set Gray's ode to music, and was advised to suit the University's taste: 'Out roar Old Handel if you can.'[28] Owing to a contretemps Burney withdrew, and the ode was set by John Randall, the Professor of Music. It was the highest-profile task of his career.

When the Duke of Gloucester was installed at the Commencement of 1811, the ode, written by William Smyth, Professor of Modern History and set by Professor Hague, 'was performed in an exquisite manner by the most celebrated vocal and instrumental performers'.[29] For the five concerts players and singers were as usual at Commencement brought in from London and elsewhere, to reinforce local talent for this most important festival, and to give Hague a 'band' of twenty players. Among the singers, for example, was the most celebrated soprano of the age, Angelica Catalani. The concert programmes give a glimpse into the musical taste of dons and citizens.[30] As we might expect, Handel dominated the morning of sacred music, in the shape of excerpts from five oratorios, and

[27] Paget Toynbee and Leonard Whibley, eds., *Correspondence of Thomas Gray* (3 vols., Oxford University Press, 1935), vol. III, Gray to Beattie, 16 July 1769, p. 1070.
[28] Roger Lonsdale, *Charles Burney. A Literary Biography* (Oxford University Press, 1965), p. 77.
[29] Cooper, *Annals*, IV, p. 497.
[30] See Cambridgeshire County Library: Cambridgeshire Collection, *Cambridge Commencement. Grand Musical Festival, 1811* (Cambridge, 1811).

there were excerpts too from Haydn's *Creation*. The four evening 'miscellaneous concerts' in the Senate House were varied indeed. The first, a typical example, comprised symphonies by Haydn and Mozart, a bassoon concerto by an untried composer named Holmes, two glees and a ballad, two arias from unnamed Italian operas, and a recitation by J. P. Curran, *The Deserters' Meditations*. Another lavish musical festival was mounted during the Commencement of 1824, when Rossini, the most famous opera composer in Europe, accompanied Catalani in the Senate House. There were twenty-eight players in the orchestra; to pay for imported artists, and to provide funds for Addenbrooke's Hospital, tickets were more expensive than usual, at between 7s and £1. The takings totalled £2,560, of which the hospital got one-fifth.[31] There were equally grand musical occasions in 1835, when Camden was installed as Chancellor, and in 1847 when Queen Victoria visited the city and university and the Prince Consort was installed as Chancellor.[32]

T. A. WALMISLEY AND WILLIAM STERNDALE BENNETT AND CAMBRIDGE UNIVERSITY MUSICAL SOCIETY

In 1836 the university acquired a far more talented Professor of Music than any of his predecessors.[33] This was Thomas Attwood Walmisley; educated for a musical career from an early age, he was appointed organist of Croydon parish church at sixteen (in 1830) and his success there led to appointment as organist at Trinity and St John's in 1833. Soon acting as deputy to the ageing Clarke-Whitfeld, he succeeded him as professor in 1836, when he was only twenty-two – and also an undergraduate, having matriculated at Corpus Christi in 1834. Few other professors have been appointed in like circumstances.[34] Graduating in 1838, Walmisley was the first Professor of Music with a BA (albeit an ordinary degree) and, after

---

[31] P. J. Warren, Grand Musical Festival Cambridge 1824 (typescript in Cambridgeshire Collection, Cambridgeshire Library, rev. edn 1981).

[32] Knight, *Cambridge Music*, pp. 61–2, 71; 'E.B.C.', *Victoria and Albert at Cambridge. The Royal Visits of 1843 and 1847 as they were recorded by Joseph Romilly, Registrary of the University* (Cambridge University Library, 1977).

[33] What follows is based on the detailed biography by Nicholas Temperley in the *New Grove Dictionary of Music and Musicians*.

[34] Though a non-graduate, Thomas Okey was elected Professor of Italian in 1919.

he took his MA, the first to be able to enter the Senate House in his own right. He was also the first musical professor to give lectures, speaking to the university at large rather than to musical specialists.

Nicholas Temperley regards Walmisley highly as a composer. His Evening Service in D minor (probably 1855) is said to be 'one of the highpoints of English cathedral music'. Easily discouraged, Walmisley gave up composing ambitious orchestral pieces when Mendelssohn remarked: 'No. 1! Let us first see what no. 12 will be!' upon being shown his First Symphony. Yet he was a more accomplished composer than Cambridge had so far seen, while his appreciation of J. S. Bach's works (then largely unknown in Britain) led him to perform some in Cambridge. His skilful direction of the Trinity and St John's joint choir made it one of the best in Britain, and he was an organist of surpassing quality. While still a very young man he had a national reputation, yet remained in Cambridge. Sensitive and easily depressed, he sought escape in college port, and alcoholism was probably responsible for his death at the age of forty-two.

We may see the influence of Walmisley's musicianship in the slow increase in the number of music graduates after 1840,[35] and in undergraduate music-making. A group inspired by Walmisley in Trinity has attracted notice: and so should the playing of Thomson and his friends. Thomson's 1843 diary attests the pleasure he took in playing his cornopean, sometimes with friends, more often alone in his room when relaxing for half an hour before setting to work, or when taking time away from it. 'In the evening was rather idle, on account of having all my music lying open, on the chimneypiece. In future I shall keep it out of the way at reading time', was one promise not always kept. 'It is quite delightful to feel perfectly careless for a while. I have been playing the cornopean nearly constantly, to make up for missing it 3 days', he records after his last session with Hopkins before the Easter break.[36] Some time in the Lent Term 1843 a group of music-loving friends founded the Peterhouse Musical Society (PMS).[37] The prime mover was George

---

[35] Between 1800 and 1840 there were 12 B.Mus. graduates, and between 1840 and 1875, 24. Frida Knight, *Cambridge Music*, p. 68.
[36] CUL Add. MSS 7342: NB 29, Diary of William Thomson, 15 February and 6 April 1843.
[37] NB 29, 21 February 1843.

Edmund Smith who entered Peterhouse in 1841 but died of consumption in 1844.[38] Another exact contemporary of Thomson at Peterhouse, William Blow, was an accomplished violinist. Others were beginners. Thomson's friend J. L. Airey of Pembroke was invited to attend a PMS concert in the May Term 1843. He heard G. E. Smith producing 'such a soft and mellow tone' from his cornet that he made up his mind to play that instrument. Finding that Sippel, an instrument seller and music teacher of King's Parade, was linked to the society, he hired a cornet and took lessons from him – an anecdote showing the symbiotic relationship between music shops and amateur players. By Michaelmas 1843 Airey was ready to play second cornet in the society orchestra. An early concert, possibly in February 1843,[39] was followed by supper and 'certain hilarious proceedings on the college roof, which nearly wrecked the enterprise'.[40] Moving to the Red Lion Hotel in Petty Cury because Peterhouse did not have a room large enough, the society gave a concert in December 1843; what must surely have been its maximum strength of eleven (including Thomson on the French horn) played Haydn's First Symphony, the overtures to *Masaniello* and *Semiramide*, the *Elisabethen waltzes* of Strauss, and some quadrilles – an eclectic programme typical of Cambridge (and British) music-making in that epoch.

About this time the society changed its name to the Cambridge University Musical Society (CUMS), giving its first concert under this name in May 1844. G. E. Smith was the first president, William Blow the second, and William Thomson the third. John Bacchus Dykes of St Catharine's, described by Thomson as 'incomparable', was another early member, and a conductor of the society; taking holy orders, he became precentor at Durham and became one of the most famous Victorian hymnologists, composing *Horbury* (the tune of 'Nearer, my God, to thee'). Alfred Pollock, who was very briefly a Peterhouse undergraduate, played the oboe, and after he became a solicitor in London played in the Crystal Palace orchestra. Still, most members were necessarily modest performers. The society

---

[38] Much of what follows draws upon Silvanus P. Thompson, *William Thomson*, vol. I, pp. 69–76, an account which quotes the reminiscences of Thomson and others extensively. See also Gerald Norris, *Stanford, the Cambridge Jubilee and Tchaikovsky* (Newton Abbot, David & Charles, 1980), pp. 7–13.   [39] See NB 29, 23 February.

[40] Silvanus P. Thompson, *William Thomson*, vol. I, p. 69.

quickly tapped enormous musical enthusiasm in the university; in the Lent Term 1846 there were 426 members. Peterhouse was still the college with the largest number among the committee and the 'full' (that is, playing) members – 7 out of 12. Among the other full members was Walmisley.

The society used to have what Thomson called 'delightful quartette evenings',[41] in which Mozart, Handel, Beethoven, Weber, and Mendelssohn were played. That tradition continues. But from the first there were also larger gatherings, semi-annual concerts given in the Guildhall – enlarged in the 1840s. Mozart, Handel, and Haydn were still played, but as elsewhere in Britain in the mid-Victorian years the favourites were Spohr and Mendelssohn, whose oratorios were very often performed.

From 1856 onwards these concerts were conducted by William Sterndale Bennett, aged forty-seven, Walmisley's successor as professor.[42] Spending his childhood in Cambridge, where he was a King's chorister, he was admitted to the Royal Academy of Music before he was ten on the recommendation of the Vice-Provost of King's as a 'prodigy'. Early in manhood remarkable as a pianist, he is said by Nicholas Temperley to rank 'as the most distinguished English composer of the Romantic school'; he was much admired by Schumann and Mendelssohn, and the latter greatly influenced him. In 1853 he was offered a conductorship at the Leipzig Gewandhaus, a considerable honour for an Englishman, but turned it down. Bennett was thus the first Cambridge Professor of Music to enjoy an international reputation. In the university he continued Walmisley's practice of lecturing, and he replaced the outdated and sometimes risible exercises for the music degree with examinations, though the Music Tripos was not taken until 1948.

Like his predecessors, Bennett fostered the amateur tradition in the university. He discovered, wrote his son, that 'the band and chorus of the University Musical Society presented, at the time, rather a motley crew'.[43]

---

[41] In a letter to Professor C. V. Stanford of December 1888, quoted in Silvanus P. Thompson, vol. 1, pp. 70–1.
[42] What follows is based on J. R. Sterndale Bennett, *Life of William Sterndale Bennett* (Cambridge University Press, 1907), and Nicholas Temperley's detailed biography in the *New Grove Dictionary of Music and Musicians*.
[43] Bennett, *William Sterndale Bennett*, pp. 268–70.

College choirs were at hand to assist; good solo-singers were generally attainable; among the members were men of intellectual ability, to whom the study and practice seemed to present little difficulty; the north of England, from which Cambridge draws so many of her students, contributed its due share of musical fervour. General culture and enthusiasm were, however, far in advance of actual performance, which was, and remained for many years, rough and imperfect.

But Bennett 'proved himself a most capable leader of irregular forces'.

Upon amateurs who found themselves for the first time under the influence of his musical personality the impression was very forcible. The presence of a master was felt... Bennett's face, stern as it was, never betrayed the least sign of displeasure, or of his having taken any particular notice of failures and imperfections past remedy...

When the music was over he appeared in another aspect. He had the faculty, strengthened no doubt by long experience with pupils, of finding a few expressive words of temperate approval or encouragement... little treasures in the memory of those to whom they were addressed.

By the power of his personality, Bennett raised the CUMS to new heights of achievement. In 1857 he conducted Mozart's *Requiem*, and two years later, Beethoven's *Mass in C*. New works by Wagner and Schumann were introduced, among the frequent performances of Spohr and Mendelssohn.[44] When Bennett died in 1875 undergraduate music-making was perhaps far more polished and sophisticated than in the 1840s, yet Thomson's part in founding the University Musical Society should not be forgotten. It was his gift to the university to which he always acknowledged his debt.

THEATRE

STOURBRIDGE FAIR AND THE UNIVERSITY'S AUTHORITY

Dr Farmer [the Master of Emmanuel] never failed to be present... he with his friends, George Stevens, Isaac Reed, Malone, and one or two others, (whom Dr Barnes used to designate the *Shakespeare*

---

[44] Gerald Norris, *Stanford, The Cambridge Jubilee and Tchaikovsky*, p. 15.

Gang) were accustomed to occupy that part of the pit which is usually called 'The Critic's Row', and which was scrupulously reserved for them. They seemed to enjoy the play as much as the youngest persons present... Dr Farmer and his friends rarely left before the whole performance was concluded; the party joined loudly in the mirth which the fairies of those days never failed to produce, in the midst of which the hearty and very peculiar laugh of the Doctor could easily be distinguished.[45]

Thus Henry Gunning recorded his memories of the visits that were made to Cambridge each September by players from Norwich and elsewhere in the last decades of the eighteenth century. They were one of the chief attractions of Stourbridge Fair, which ever since the Middle Ages had been mounted on common land outside Cambridge between the Newmarket Road and the river. Garlic Row, which still exists, takes its name from produce sold at the fair, and was its central thoroughfare. In the late Middle Ages the fair was the greatest in Europe, and though it was in decline by the early eighteenth century Daniel Defoe described it as 'the greatest in the whole nation' and by report as mightier than the fairs at Leipzig, Frankfurt-am-Main, Nuremberg, or Augsburg.[46] At the time Gunning was referring to in his memoirs, the 1780s, the fair was still a major regional centre for a bewildering variety of goods from ironmongery to hops, but it was becoming more significant as entertainment – a 'fair' in the modern sense – and it is as a festive season offering a 'mixture of dwarfs and giants, conjurors and learned pigs', that Gunning presents it.[47] In *A Step to Stir-Bitch Fair*, printed in 1700, Ned Ward describes the fair as a place 'where vice, merchandize, and amusements draw the Cambridge youth, London traders, Lynn whores and abundance of ubiquitarian strollers, all contributing something to either the pleasure or profit of one another'.[48]

Despite its changing character, the fair was a pinnacle of the university year, as it had been for centuries. Opened by the

---

[45] Gunning, *Reminiscences*, vol. I, pp. 172–3.
[46] *A Tour Through England and Wales*, vol. I, p. 80. Defoe describes the fair in detail.
[47] Gunning, *Reminiscences*, vol. I, p. 171.
[48] Quoted in Sybil Rosenfeld, 'The Players in Cambridge, 1662–1800', p. 26, in *Studies in English Theatre History* (1952), pp. 24–37, a valuable article exploiting the university archives, and from which much that follows is drawn.

Vice-Chancellor with panoply and feasting in the middle of September, it was the effective start of the Michaelmas Term. The university enjoyed (or claimed) jurisdiction over the fair, and so did the city authorities: there were town-and-gown disputes as well as friction between showmen and authority. Most relevant for our purpose is the permission that entertainers of any description had to get from the university. The Vice-Chancellor set up a court of summary jurisdiction, where the Commissary acted as magistrate and offenders were charged by the Proctors. From the records of this court in the eighteenth century, writes Sybil Rosenfeld,

> we learn the names of many itinerants who exhibited animals, freaks, mechanical wonders and waxworks or who gave conjuring, rope-dancing and equestrian performances. In these pages we meet a heifer with two heads, a learned horse and pig, a mermaid, a man's skin stuffed with hay, the panopticon, the camera obscura, musical clocks, Mount Vesuvius and all sorts of popular marvels.[49]

So for the Proctors September 1751 was enlivened by checking the licence of a 'learned French dog from Paris' which 'reads, writes and casts accounts by the means of typographical cards' and 'has been shown at Charing Cross London'.[50] Very many showmen failed to obtain licences to exhibit such marvels, and were fined amounts ranging from 1s 6d to 11s in the Commissary's Court, in addition to expenses of 3s 6d. Such modest sums were no deterrent, and seem themselves to have been regarded as licences.

The Proctors were also concerned with 'plays' in the usual sense, and they were treated differently from mermaids and the like. As in Shakespeare's day, theatrical companies had legally to have either a royal patent or a licence from the Lord Chamberlain or Master of the Revels, and in Cambridge they had also of course to obtain the university's sanction. Thus in 1672 the university declared that Martin Powell showed 'a Patent under the Seale of Sir Hen: Herbert to act Comedies and by the said Patent had acted, in this faire contrary to the statutes of the University';[51] and in 1676 the

---

[49] Quoted in 'The Players in Cambridge', p. 25.
[50] H. C. Porter, 'The Players Well Bestowed? Stourbridge and Barnwell Theatres 1740–1814', p. 215, *Cambridge Review*, December 1984, pp. 214–18. This substantial article draws on local newspapers and playbills, and complements Rosenfeld's study.
[51] Quoted in Sybil Rosenfeld, 'The Players in Cambridge', p. 22.

Duke of Monmouth asked the Vice-Chancellor to permit the duke's own licensed company to play during the fair, and so recognised the university's authority. Players who did not seek it were fined even while, it seems, they were licensed by the Lord Chamberlain – though in the seventeenth century fines were on a par with the modest ones paid by rope-dancers. In 1701, however, the university's attitude became much more severe, for reasons hard to specify but certainly including jealousy of the city's jurisdiction. In July the well-known Norwich actor Thomas Doggett entered into a bond for £500 not to act during the September fair. Nevertheless the corporation gave his company permission to perform, and a temporary theatre was built. The Vice-Chancellor was Richard Bentley, a man whom Doggett was foolish to cross. Doggett was imprisoned, the theatre was demolished, and sixty-two MAs were given proctorial powers to patrol the fair.[52] This was a battle won by the university, but it was hard to win the war. In September 1705 the Senate approved a grace restating the university's rights and privileges because 'certain players have lately caused an house to be erected by Paper Mills,[53] pretending it was out of the Jurisdiction of the University, and have given out that they will act there'.[54] That such fulminations were ineffective was suggested by the author of 'The Long Vacation, a Satyr address'd to all disconsolate Traders' (1708):

> The Actors too, must take the pleasant air
> To Oxford some, to Sturbridge some repair,
> And quite debauch the hopeful Students there.[55]

In 1730 a grace complained that another play booth had been built near Paper Mills, and threatened a fine of £1 for any 'Member of this University, of what standing or Degree soever' who attended a performance. In August 1736 the fine was doubled, when yet another play booth was prepared for the forthcoming fair by Joseph Kettle; presumably the university was finding it increasingly difficult to prevent its own members from enjoying themselves at

---

[52] C. H. Cooper, *Annals*, 4, pp. 45–6.
[53] Paper Mills was the area immediately to the east of the Leper Chapel on the Newmarket Road, near where Ditton Fields now begins.
[54] Quoted in Rosenfeld, 'The Players in Cambridge', p. 27.
[55] Cooper, *Annals*, IV, p. 46.

the theatre. Joseph Kettle was not deterred either. In March 1737 the Senate petitioned the House of Commons to complain that

> a House hath lately been built, within the precincts of the University, for the Acting of Plays and Interludes, and hath accordingly been made use of for that Purpose, notwithstanding the Vice Chancellor and Heads of Colleges, did discourage, and, to the utmost of their Power, endeavour to prevent, the building the said House; and that many Inconveniences and Mischiefs will arise, and the Manners of the Youth committed to their Care be in great Danger of being corrupted, if Playhouses should be established among them.[56]

The counter-petition of Joseph Kettle stated that he had 'at his own great Expence, built a commodious Playhouse, on his own Land . . . for the entertainment of the Company who should come to Sturbridge Fair'; and his claim to continue it was supported by 'Gentlemen and Inhabitants of the Town and County'.

Plainly a permanent theatre was at stake, not a mere flimsy playbooth, and there was a demand in Cambridge for it. The truth was that with rising middle-class incomes the theatre boomed in the eighteenth century. In other East Anglian towns plays were performed in inns, and in 1736 Ipswich led the way in constructing a purpose-built theatre; during the next forty years Norwich, Lynn, and Yarmouth followed suit. The university was setting its face against popular demand. On this occasion, however, the university won, aided by Walpole's government which feared the political effects of the great independence theatre had enjoyed for a decade. The Licensing Act of 1737 ended the licence and patent system for provincial companies,[57] and declared that actors were to be treated as rogues and vagabonds. Though in practice companies continued to exist on sufferance, they were always liable to be imprisoned if an informer lodged a protest with a magistrate, and occasionally highly respectable actors found themselves locked up. In addition, by the act the texts of plays had to be approved by the Lord Chamberlain, censorship that lasted until the 1960s. Another act of 1737[58] forbade

---

[56] Cooper, *Annals*, IV, p. 227, and pp. 227–32 for the details and quotations that follow.
[57] P.G. Acts 10 Geo. II, c.28. Companies were still able to act under licence in London.
[58] P.G. Acts 10 Geo. II, c.19: *An Act for the More Effectual Preventing the Unlawful Playing of Interludes within the Precincts of the Two Universities . . . in England.*

the performance of all plays and operas within five miles of the two university towns, the Vice-Chancellor's Court having the power to punish actors with one month's hard labour. But, crucially, the university was also by implication given the power to license performances, and eventually drama was to be staged again at Stourbridge in the 1760s. For a quarter-century after 1737, however, the university's ban appears to have been broken only by a few pantomimes, such as *Harlequin's Frolic, or Jack Spaniard Caught in a Trap*, put on in 1748.[59]

THEATRICAL COMPANIES AND CAMBRIDGE

Provincial England was criss-crossed by the tours of theatrical companies.[60] Even towns with established theatres, such as Norwich, could not sustain a season of more than three or four months; the Norwich company, for example, would commonly take its repertory and properties to Lynn, Yarmouth, Ipswich, Colchester, Bury, and Stourbridge in the course of a year, visiting some centres twice so that the tour-map is a bewildering web.[61] Norwich, a comparatively prosperous troupe, were fortunate enough to be able to transport their effects in waggons. Along East Anglia's roads they would meet bands of literally 'strolling' actors, who sometimes carried their rudimentary scenery on their backs. For such men and women, lacking any permanent stage, life was precarious indeed, at the mercy of creditors, weather, and fickle audiences. Dickens's account of Mr Vincent Crummles's company in *Nicholas Nickleby* (1838–9) suggests how a small group of friends and relations, happily doubling up to allocate a large cast of roles between them, might sustain themselves through vicissitudes by a self-conscious sense of professionalism. The picaresque character of the stroller's life is also sketched in the memoirs of a Cambridge man, John Brown. Born in 1796, the son of a Barnwell butcher, he worked for some time in his youth as a journeyman shoemaker, and was at the age of sixteen a soldier in

[59] Rosenfeld, 'The Players in Cambridge', p. 29.
[60] For this paragraph see Sybil Rosenfeld, *Strolling Players and Drama in the Provinces 1660–1765* (Cambridge University Press, 1939), pp. 11–34.
[61] Elizabeth Grice, *Rogues and Vagabonds or the Actors' Road to Respectability* (Lavenham, Suffolk, Dalton, 1977), p. 29, prints a map of the Norwich tour network.

Kent. Deserting, he met a travelling company, and said to the manager that he 'should be glad to do anything'.

> On this he asked if I could read; and my answer was – 'Yes, tolerably well'. It was now daylight; so taking a book from his breast pocket, he asked me to read a speech of 'Henry', in *Speed the Plough*. When I had finished, he said – 'That will do excellently well; so you study that part by to-morrow night. We are going to do the regular drama in a barn where we always get good houses; and it strikes me that you will take amazingly.'[62]

Learning his part in two hours, John Brown acted well enough, and learned many others too until the company broke up at the end of September. Restless, quick-witted, and self-confident, possessing literary tastes and some education, he was perhaps typical of the lower reaches of a profession with David Garrick at its top.

An account of Stourbridge Fair published in 1773 says that despite the 1737 act, 'a Company or two of Players are allowed to perform during the Fair'.[63] This significant relaxation of the university's attitude seems to have taken place in the 1760s, since a more or less continuous flow of performances started about 1762. In 1765, for example, a company from Ely put on *Andromache* followed by a pantomime, *Pygmalion, or Harlequin Enchanter*, *Richard III* (perhaps in a modified version), *The Devil to Pay*, and *The Provok'd Husband*. This medley was typical of the provincial theatre of the day, in which Shakespeare, pantomime, and comedy were popular and, like the music of the day, repertories included plays that have been continuously staged since – yet also others that are now forgotten.[64] Programmes were changed each evening, and charges were 2s in the pit and 1s in the gallery. Companies from Sussex, Huntingdon, Norwich, and elsewhere visited the fair in following decades, usually paying fees of a few shillings to the Commissary's Court, and often cautiously evading the 1737 Licensing Act's

---

[62] John Brown, *Sixty Years' Gleanings from Life's Harvest. A Genuine Autobiography* (Cambridge, 1858) pp. 51–2.

[63] *An Historical Account of Stourbridge, Bury and the Most Famous Fairs in Europe and America* (1773), quoted in Sybil Rosenfeld, 'The Players in Cambridge', p. 31. These paragraphs are based on this article, pp. 29–36, from which the quotations are taken.

[64] Allardyce Nicoll, *A History of English Drama 1660–1900* (rev. edn, 6 vols, Cambridge University Press, 1952–9), vol. II, pp. 59–60.

prohibition of playing for gain by staging 'interludes' that were technically free between musical items that were charged for.

Frequent visitors were Mrs Waklyn's troupe. Mrs Waklyn, veteran of a well-known theatrical family, staged pantomimes, farces, burlettas, and ballad operas at Stourbridge, and also rope-dancing, tumbling, and slack-wire performances. This eclectic offering had rivals in 1774 in the shape of James Whitley's company. Whitley was the proprietor of theatres in Nottingham, Derby, Shrewsbury, and Stamford. He reappeared in 1775, announcing that he had engaged accomplished actors from York for the exalted university audience he expected, and advertising his temporary booth as 'the most commodious and extensive of the two erected this season for Histrionic Representations'. This was a point of contention between Whitley and his rival, William Bailey, manager of the Norwich company. Bailey assembled for Stourbridge actors from London, York, and Edinburgh, as well as Norwich, and erected a booth that was, he claimed, drier and warmer than Whitley's. Violent storms were a hazard. In 1772 Bailey's booth had been 'entirely blown down, and many other booths there were much injured'.[65] Pickpockets were another danger. In the 1776 season one woman in Whitley's crowded audience lost 10 guineas. Whitley brought stars to the fair in 1777, when the Covent Garden actors Wilson and Lee Lewes came for large salaries to play Cholerick and Clodio in *The Fop's Fortune*, Grub and Chapeau in *Cross Purposes*, Hardcastle and Young Marlow in *She Stoops to Conquer*, and Falstaff and the Prince of Wales in *Henry IV* – good examples of the range that actors were expected to cover in the short season. These were benefit performances for local charity schools and Lee Lewes himself, events often paralleled in the musical seasons in the centre of Cambridge.

Whitley visited the fair for the last time in 1779. For more than thirty years from 1782 onwards the Stourbridge season was dominated by the Norwich players, one of the most important provincial companies; they prospered under the direction of the Wilkins family of proprietors while successive actor-managers took the players on the road; William Wilkins senior (1751–1815), a

---

[65] Cooper, *Annals*, IV, p. 366.

Norwich-born architect, was proprietor and patentee of the Norwich Theatre Royal and founded a chain of East Anglian theatres that were inherited by his son William Wilkins junior, an eminent architect; the two Wilkins, father and son, were behind the building of permanent theatres at Barnwell. The staging in 1783 of a pantomime, *The Elopement; or, Harlequin's Trip to Stirbitch Fair*, was an attempt to please local taste, perhaps successful, since in this season the players were patronised by Lady Halton, Sir John Hynde Cotton, and the mayor and corporation. The tantalisingly few references we have to university reactions to Stourbridge suggest a warm welcome for its addition to Cambridge's amenity. By the side of Gunning's enthusiasm may be placed the words of Richard Denison Cumberland, an undergraduate at Magdalene College. Spending some months in Cambridge in the summer of 1773, he wrote to his brother on 22 September that 'Cambridge which for these 3 months past has been the dullest Place on earth' was enlivened by Stourbridge Fair. 'The Fair open'd on Saturday & last Night I was at the Play Booth we had the Clandestine Marriage[66] & the Citizen.[67] The first tolerably acted, but the Farce equal to anything of the kind I ever saw in Town, the Characters of young Philpot & Maria inimitably well performed & upon the whole gave great satisfaction.'[68]

THE BARNWELL THEATRES AND DRAMATIC EVENINGS

Plays and other entertainments at Stourbridge Fair were mounted in substantial structures for which the usual description, 'booth', seems an inadequate word.[69] The booths of the mid-eighteenth century, though standing for the three-week fair season only, had boxes and a gallery, which implies some substantial wooden parts, like indeed some of the fair stalls. These theatres were erected on the north side of the Newmarket Road to the west of Garlic Row. In the 1770s theatre booths were built on the opposite side of Newmarket Road

[66] A comedy (1766) by George Colman the elder, and Garrick.
[67] A farce (1761) by Arthur Murphy.
[68] Clementina Black,ed., *The Cumberland Letters* (London, Secker, 1912), p. 48. Cumberland, who matriculated at Magdalene in 1771, graduated LL B. in 1780. He became a clergyman. Richard Cumberland the dramatist was his third cousin.
[69] These paragraphs are based on Porter, 'The Players Well Bestowed?', pp. 216–18.

near the Cheese Fair;[70] this site was advertised as being warmer and drier than the others. But the destruction of Bailey's booth in a storm in September 1772 showed the need for a permanent theatre. In the 1780s one was constructed, of wood, most probably where the theatre booths had stood. The theatre was built in a horseshoe, with two rows of boxes. The architect was local, Charles Humfrey senior, frequently an assistant to James Essex.[71] Presumably the venture could only go ahead because any objections the university had were overcome, and no doubt consumer demand had much to do with its conversion; Gunning tells us that 'the house was generally well filled, and on some evenings crowded in every part, especially when the Lord Lieutenant, or the Members of the town and University, bespoke the play'.[72]

There was an unfounded fire-scare in the new theatre in September 1802, natural perhaps in a wooden building lit by oil-lamps; four people were trampled to death in the panic.[73] Considered unsafe, the theatre was demolished in 1807 and replaced the following year by a new structure, in Sun Street (now the first part of Newmarket Road) next to the Sun Tavern.[74] Both Wilkins, father and son, worked on the design. Like its predecessor the horseshoe-shaped auditorium had two rows of boxes. In the event the theatre was used for only a few seasons, 1813 being its last; in an area close to the city where land was much in demand for property development, it was sold in November 1815, and very soon the bricks and mortar of the rising suburb of Barnwell covered the spot.

In the same year William Wilkins II (1778–1839)[75] inherited his father's leases on theatres in Norwich, Cambridge, Bury, Colchester, Yarmouth, Ipswich, and Lynn. They yielded an income from rentals paid by acting companies of more than £1,100 in 1815; they had doubled since 1800. The younger Wilkins, East Anglia's versatile architectural genius, and fellow of Caius 1803–11,[76] added the running of this property empire to his design practice. He designed the New Theatre in Barnwell in 1814, just before his

[70] A row of 'autocentres' now covers the site.   [71] See chapter 1, pp. 13, 18.
[72] *Reminiscences*, vol. 1, p. 172.   [73] Cooper, *Annals*, IV, p. 474.
[74] On a modern map the theatre would be situated at the junction of East Road and the Newmarket Road, on the south side of the Elizabeth Way roundabout.
[75] For this paragraph, see Liscombe, *William Wilkins*, esp. pp. 81, 121–2, 216–18.
[76] For his activities in Cambridge see chapter 1, pp. 18–26, 29, 33–5.

father's death. It was – indeed is – nearer the city than its two predecessors, being in the half-mile of Newmarket Road between East Road and Jesus Lane. The theatre was opened in September 1814, for the fair season. The *Cambridge Chronicle*,[77] praising its 'great taste and elegance', pointed to the 'four Giallo Antiquo marble pilasters' supporting the proscenium, and the figures of 'Apollo and Minerva visiting the Muses' on the frieze. 'Upon the whole we believe . . . this theatre to be the best provincial theatre in the kingdom, and (the differences of magnitude considered) it vies with any of the theatres in the metropolis. In point of hearing, it is superior perhaps to any, the least whisper on the stage being heard in every part of the house.' It was in this theatre that drama was staged in Regency and early Victorian Cambridge. (It became the Theatre Royal in 1849.[78]) Next to the theatre Wilkins built a house for his own occupation.[79] Wilkins sank a great deal of money into his theatres, building another at Bury in 1819[80] and remodelling three others. But a source of income when he took them over, the theatres became by the 1830s an expensive hobby that had to be subsidised by Wilkins's architectural practice. The effects of his financial mismanagement were aggravated by economic slump, and financial worries were said to have hastened Wilkins's death in 1839.

VICTORIAN BARNWELL AND THE CHALLENGE TO THE UNIVERSITY'S AUTHORITY

Barnwell theatre served several publics: the county, shopkeeper, and university clients (dons and undergraduates) in the circle, and the more numerous occupants of the cheaper seats in the pit. What was offered to these mixed audiences? For the opening night of a typical Stourbridge season, Wednesday 15 September 1830, the manager of the theatre announced that 'Mr Power (of the Theatre Royal, Covent Garden)' had been engaged to take the part of Dennis

[77] Quoted by Porter, 'The Players Well Bestowed?', p. 218.
[78] It became a mission hall in 1878, and continued in that role until the 1920s, when it became the Festival Theatre. After use by the army during the Second World War, it was bought in 1948 by the Arts Theatre, which later used it as a studio workshop and wardrobe store. Though its exterior is recognisably original the interior has been much altered.
[79] He later built a more imposing residence, 'Lensfield', where the Chemistry Laboratory now stands.
[80] Now owned by the National Trust, it is the only Georgian theatre in Britain with its original internal structure.

Brulgruddery in George Colman the Younger's comedy *John Bull, or an Englishman's Fireside* (1803), and the role of Teddy in the 'entirely new farce' *Teddy the Tiler*. Tickets, 4s for boxes, 2s 6d for the pit, and 1s for the gallery, might be bought at J. Taylor's shop opposite Sidney Sussex College. The performance would begin at 6.30. 'No Admittance behind the Scenes on any account whatever.'[81] The following evening *Teddy the Tiler* was repeated, and a 'petite-comedy', *More Blunders than One; or the French Valet*, and a 'comic interlude', the *Irish Tutor*, introduced. During the four weeks of this season some fifty different entertainments were offered, a wide repertory indeed for a company of a dozen or so. Thirty plays were performed only once, and the rest only twice or (very occasionally) three times. Two or three plays were presented each evening, and usually there was a comic song as well, sung by one of the actors, versatile indeed. *As You Like It, The Merchant of Venice*, and *Richard III* were staged, no doubt in abridged form, and Cambridge was also given Massinger's comedy, *A New Way to Pay Old Debts* and Otway's tragedy *Venice Preserved*. The other offerings are now unknown save by archaeologists of the theatre. There were a few melodramas whose description sounds very operatic – *The Brigand, Charles XII*, and *The Robber's Wife* – and as many musical 'burlettas', comic or serious – *The Corporal's Wedding, or the Husband's Mistake*, and *Thirty Years of a Gambler's Life*. Thirty were comedies or farces – *The Master's Rival; or, a Day's Fun in France*, and *Perfection, or the Lady of Munster*. This varied medley corresponded in its emphasis to the national dramatic taste as described by its historian; in other words, Cambridge preferred what is rather oddly called the 'illegitimate drama' to the 'legitimate'.[82] Perhaps to our eyes the strangest presentation was not dramatic at all: a 'moving panorama' of Algiers, the shores of Asia, the island of Rhodes, the European shore of the Bosphorus, and Constantinople. This gratification of audiences very largely starved of visual representation was offered four times. The final performances, on 15 October, were for the benefit of George Smith, the actor-manager of the Norwich company that had as usual appeared at Barnwell during the fair.

George Smith's company returned in the 1830s, and in 1840 their

---

[81] This account is based on the playbills in Cambridgeshire County Library, Cambridgeshire Collection, C.76.8.   [82] Nicoll, *English Drama*, vol. IV, esp. pp. 78–99.

programme was similar to 1830's in its variety and emphases, though hardly any of the actual plays staged then were repeated, which is presumably a tribute to the fecundity of the early Victorian drama. A 'panorama' was once again popular, 1840's choice being nearer home than Constantinople: 'The Liverpool & Manchester Rail-Road, Its Tunnel, Excavations, Bridges... Liverpool Station... Entrance of the Tunnel at Edge Hill... Tunnel by Gas-Light... A Moving Train of the different Classes of Carriages, with their Engines... A View of Manchester.' (The railway came to Cambridge in 1845.) One great difference from 1830 was that 'in consequence of the engagement for six nights only of three "Stars"', the first week was given over to excerpts from eight operas.[83] The week made an uneven impression on a writer in the local newspaper. On the first night attendance was thin, and the performance 'languid'. The orchestra (evidently a scratch local team, not mentioned in the playbills) was wobbly on the first three evenings. *Guy Mannering* was a 'poor adaptation' and the *Devil's Bridge* a 'trumpery affair', though *The Beggar's Opera* and Bellini's *La Sonnambula* were admired choices that were said to have called forth the best performances. Even then, however, the correspondent handed out criticism as well as praise. One of the three stars, Frederick Shrivall, had a 'rich and mellow' falsetto, but his acting was 'passionless'. His colleague Alban Croft's bass voice was sometimes inappropriate; 'neither is his person stage-built, nor his motion gainly'. His wife was strikingly attractive, and 'certain youthful members of the university' showered bouquets of flowers onto the stage at her final curtain. Her Amina was 'chaste, original and vivid', but in somnambulism scenes she 'exhibited perhaps too much *timidity* in the motion with too much flexion of the body to be true to nature'.

In the second and third weeks some evenings were 'bespeaks', or under the patronage of the Lord Lieutenant, the Garrick Club (a local amateur dramatic society), the Cambridge Freemasons, and the Mechanics Conservative Association – a way to whip up meagre attendances. The *Cambridge Chronicle* suspected a similar motive in the staging of the lurid melodrama *Jack Sheppard*, thought to be an

---

[83] For what follows, *Cambridge Chronicle*, 1, 19 and 26 September 1840.

unfitting choice for 'the very excitable locality of Barnwell'. Still, it seemed foolish to thin the 'boxes to a few pounds, in order to put £10 in the gallery and £8 in the pit'. One gets, in these brief sentences, a hint that Barnwell shared in the decline in the fortunes of the professional theatre that marked the age, and which its historian finds difficult to explain.[84]

Stourbridge Fair was in decline as a centre of commerce in the eighteenth century, and the Barnwell Enclosure Act, though it protected established fairground rights, led to building on the newly enclosed land and the construction of brickworks; the loss of space for stallholders was aggravated by the building of the railway in 1845. More important were new methods of retail distribution. A revealing passage in Josiah Chater's manuscript diary shows that in 1850 he bought stock for his Cambridge haberdasher's shop to sell to fairgoers, but from Yorkshire dealers rather than from Stourbridge itself.[85] It was reported in 1859 that the fair was 'wretched for business', apart from horses, hops, and wood. But Stourbridge participated in the Victorian leisure boom, especially on 'horse-fair night', when a thousand visitors were attracted by the cake-stalls, peep shows, cheapjacks and boxing booths, and the dancing booth erected on the bowling green opposite the Globe Inn, Paper Mills.[86] They also came for the theatre: horse-fair night was often crowded, and boisterous.

By the middle of the century the university had ceased to mark the opening of the fair with spectacular ceremony, and the long-standing dispute with the city over jurisdiction at Stourbridge was settled by Sir John Patteson in 1855, as part of a wide-ranging arbitration. He decided, among many points in the town's favour, that the university should cease to have powers over fairs and markets in the borough.[87] This reduction was confirmed by s. 15 of the Act of Parliament of 1856 that resolved matters which had long been in dispute between borough and university.[88] The Commissary Court

---

[84] Nicoll, *English Drama*, vol. IV, pp. 58–78.
[85] Honor Ridout, *Sturbridge Fair in the Eighteenth Century*, 1992 (Dissertation in Cambridgeshire Collection), pp. 25–6. Stourbridge Fair was ceremonially abolished in 1933 after many years as a minor horse-fair, with entertainments.
[86] *Cambridge Chronicle*, 1 October 1859.
[87] Cooper, *Annals*, V, pp. 192–201. The relevant section is 8, p. 194.
[88] L. & P. 19 & 20 Vict. c. 17: *An Act to Confirm an Award for the Settlement of Matters in Difference between the University and Borough of Cambridge*.

sat for the last time in 1855. But the university retained authority over theatrical performances. A long campaign to free the drama from the restrictions of the 1737 act resulted in an Act of Parliament in 1843 that lifted most of them,[89] while giving to the two Vice-Chancellors the power to deny licences to theatres within fourteen miles of Oxford and Cambridge.[90] This power was retained, with respect to Cambridge, by section 8 of Patteson's adjudication. The 1856 act (s.16) required the consent in writing from the mayor and Vice-Chancellor for any 'public exhibition or performance' held outside the Long Vacation. This meant that while the Barnwell theatrical season might begin earlier than Stourbridge Fair, it could not finish later than early October save with the university's consent. But since the theatre had to be licensed anyway it relied on the university's goodwill throughout the year.

The fortunes of the Norwich circuit declined in the 1840s, as William Wilkins's son W. Bushby Wilkins tried to restore profitability with a succession of actor managers; but the problems defeated even T. D. Davenport, who had much stage experience in Britain and America and is thought to have been the model for Vincent Crummles.[91] In 1850 the theatre was leased by Edward Hooper, who had taken up the stage after a career as a naval officer. Hooper brought a new vigour to the Theatre Royal, Barnwell, and after his death in 1865 a succession of lessees and managers kept up the momentum.[92] With the university's sanction the season was sometimes started in August, and Hooper filled seats by slashing prices as soon as he took over, putting 'more money into the treasury . . . than has been received for many a year'.[93]

Among Hooper's problems was the social mixture of the Barnwell audiences. When the pit overflow moved upstairs there were complaints: 'amidst ladies and gentlemen of good social and Masonic connexion, were ushered pot-house revellers, reeking with the pungent odour of the "Shakespeare", rude and dirty

---

[89] Nicoll, *English Drama*, vol. IV, pp. 4–5. The Lord Chamberlain's censorship was retained in 1843.
[90] P.G. 6 & 7 Vict. c. 68: *An Act for Regulating Theatres*. Section 10 related to the two universities.
[91] Elizabeth Grice, *Rogues and Vagabonds*, pp. 159–71; H. T. Hall, *Cambridge Dramatic Album* (Cambridge, 1868), p. 83.
[92] These paragraphs are based on the files of the *Cambridge Chronicle*, 1850–70, and the playbills in the Cambridgeshire Collection, c.76.8. See also H. T. Hall, *The Cambridge Dramatic Album* (Cambridge, 1868), pp. 96–112.   [93] *Cambridge Chronicle*, 25 September 1852.

coprolite diggers, as well as notorious street-walkers and brazen-faced harridans', wrote a correspondent in 1863.[94] The dramatic taste of these groups in fact overlapped quite a lot, and Hooper and others showed their skill in catering to it, with inevitably some ups and downs. 'Sensation is the order of the day, and it has been clearly demonstrated that Cambridge is not a whit behind the age in encouraging exciting and sensational dramas', wrote the theatre critic in 1869.[95] The repertory was very similar to what had been staged in the 1830s and 1840s, as we may see by looking at a typical evening – 6 September 1852.

The evening began with an exotic melodrama, described as 'a heavy affair', but popular enough to be staged three times in the season.[96] This was *Ingomar the Barbarian*, 'translated from the German'; Ingomar was 'leader of a band of Alemanni', and also appearing were the Timarch of Massilia and citizens called Neocles and Amyntas. Characteristically, there was afterwards an abrupt change of mood, when Kate Kirby gave her usual dance, with a 'Comic Pas de Trois'. (Her other specialities were clog dances and Irish jigs.) Another interlude was offered by Herr Deulin and his sons, 'whose bodies have been twisted into positions which would apparently have insured the disjointure of any snake', including 'apparent impossibilities on the tightrope'.[97] (On later evenings the Deulins danced 'their extraordinary stilt polka', and displayed their 'Marble Grouping or the Grand Exhibition Statuary'.[98]) The evening of 6 September concluded with the 'laughable farce', *My Master's Rival*; Mr Fitzroy, who one hour before had played a merchant called Polydor, now took the part of Sir Colly Cowmeadow.

Hooper effected an 'improvement in the quality of the *corps dramatique*', by recruiting actors from London.[99] In 1852, for example, five came from Madame Vestris's Lyceum Theatre and five more from other London houses to form a company of about a dozen. Very popular was the Shakespearian actor G. V. Brooke. The Theatre Royal was 'crowded to suffocation' when he played

[94] *Cambridge Chronicle*, 19 September 1863.   [95] *Cambridge Chronicle*, 4 September 1869.
[96] *Cambridge Chronicle*, 9 October 1852.   [97] *Cambridge Chronicle*, 4 September 1852.
[98] The playbill refers to the 1851 Crystal Palace exhibition.
[99] *Cambridge Chronicle*, 25 September 1852.

Othello in 1853, and 'crowded to excess, and *mirabile dictu*, money was turned away from the door' on Brooke's return in Hamlet in 1854.[100] Amy Sedgwick's reception in 1860 made the *Chronicle* judge that despite the liking for 'melodrama with alliterative titles, abounding in bloodshed, blue fire, and startling tableaux ... some affection still lingers in Cambridge for good acting and genuine comedy'. 'Mr Hooper's enterprise and exertion in his desire to please the public' was rewarded too at popular 'bespeaks' like that patronised by the borough's MPs when ladies wearing the pink and white of Cambridge Conservatism crowded the theatre, and many latecomers had to stand in the aisles.[101]

Takings fell sharply on wet evenings because patrons objected to walking so far from the town centre. There was never enough money to commission new scenery. 'We can recollect it nearly twenty years, and we think it has lasted long enough', it was written in 1852; seven years later the lessee was asked to substitute 'new canvas for the present battered and worn out apology for scenery'. The building itself needed repair in the 1860s too.[102] But of course the theatrical season was too short; for much of the year the auditorium was empty. Also, the management wanted to attract gown as well as town; but when the theatre was open students were mostly absent from Cambridge. The last night of the season occurred right at the start of Michaelmas Term and it was described as 'undergraduates' evening'; though they were often rowdy they gave the manager a tantalising glimpse of the extra profit that might come his way. But the Vice-Chancellor would not countenance the professional theatre becoming a prominent feature of the Cambridge autumn, and stimulating student high jinks in Barnwell; the brothels there worried the Proctors already. In October 1864 many citizens of standing 'requisitioned' the Vice-Chancellor to extend the season by one week: the modest request was refused. 'The exceptional state of affairs pertaining to the Drama in this locality scarcely befits the nineteenth century', complained the manager John Coleman as he took the season's final curtain.[103] Still, while the

---

[100] *Cambridge Chronicle*, 8 October 1853 and 14 October 1854.
[101] *Cambridge Chronicle*, 18 September 1852, 8 September 1860, 21 September 1861.
[102] *Cambridge Chronicle*, 9 October 1852, 8 October 1859, 11 July 1868.
[103] *Cambridge Chronicle*, 1 and 15 October 1864.

university held back the *professional* theatre, undergraduates promoted *amateur* drama, at least at the end of our period.

STUDENT THEATRE: THE ADC

The first amateur dramatic society in Cambridge was for town, not gown: the Shakespeare Club, founded in 1830 by W. H. Smith, a printer of Rose Crescent. It seems to have flourished for about four seasons. Then in 1833 one of the quarrels that mark the annals of Victorian small-town life occurred; Smith founded a new society, the Garrick Club, and appears to have taken the strength of the original one to it.[104] Perhaps the quarrel had something to do with undergraduate members, since the Garrick stressed its refusal to have them. The membership roll published in 1836 contains 140 names, of whom 11 were dons or resident MAs. A sample reveals a sprinkling of professional men, and a preponderance of shopkeepers and tradesmen.[105] Until 1842, the club staged productions in the Barnwell theatre on a few evenings each year. The plays it chose were very similar to the theatre's professional repertory. A commentator praised the 'clever performances' in the drama *The Wreck Ashore* and the farce *My Neighbour's Wife*, staged on 11 and 12 August 1834; they gave 'much pleasure' to the 'numerous and respectable audiences', and the 'efforts of the performers to gratify their friends were decidedly successful'.[106] A similar desire to please may be detected in the formation of no fewer than four more non-university theatrical societies in Cambridge in the next twenty years. The most important was the Amateur Theatrical Society, founded in 1854 by Harry T. Hall, a man of independent means and much energy, and an enthusiast for art and literature.[107] The

[104] This passage is based on *Album of the Cambridge Garrick Club* (Cambridge, 1836), esp. pp. 23–4, and Florence Ada Keynes, *By-Ways of Cambridge History*, 2nd edn (Cambridge, Heffer, 1956), pp. 128–30.

[105] The list may be found in *Album of the Garrick Club*, pp. 217–20. The sample is of the 9 life members, and the 27 annual subscribers whose names begin with A and B. Of the 23 whose occupations can be traced in the poll-books and elsewhere 4 were dons. Charles Claydon, the butler of Trinity College, was another member. There were also a gentleman, a banker, two attorneys, and a schoolmaster. Besides five printers, sellers or binders of books there were two innkeepers, a silversmith, a draper, a tailor, a brazier, a builder, and a seller of chinaware.

[106] *Cambridge Chronicle*, 15 August 1834.

[107] He gave a collection of Shakespearian literature to the city library. On Hall, see the detailed obituary in the *Cambridge Chronicle*, 20 July 1894.

709

theatrical society was founded to raise money for Crimean War soldiers and their families. It continued long after under firm direction; dramas and farces like those in the Barnwell repertory were staged on several evenings a year, and a few professional actors were engaged to stiffen local amateur talent. The society also offered more Shakespeare than Barnwell, and in 1864, 'the Tercentenary of . . . the poet and dramatist of the world', *The Merchant of Venice* and *As You Like It* were given in April 'in aid of the London Shakespeare Memorial, and under the sanction and authority of the National Shakespeare Committee'.[108] Audiences were large. 'A popular farce was thrown in after each play. Except for some interruptions from a few noisy members of the university, the performances passed off with great spirit and to the satisfaction of the audiences.'[109] Thus in drama, as in music, the city possessed an active and diverse culture which the university contributed to, but did not dominate.

No doubt many undergraduates staged in their rooms, without programmes or playbills, dramatic productions of which we can know nothing. The first of which we appear to have certain information was *Much Ado About Nothing*, produced in the Hoop Inn in March 1830 with a cast of Apostles and others. Stafford Augustus O'Brien was Benedick, and J. M. Kemble was Dogberry.[110] 'Conceive Milnes doing the elegant and high minded Beatrice like a languishing trull', wrote Kemble to another Apostle W. B. Donne.[111] Some of the same men soon afterwards appeared in *The Rivals* in rooms in Trinity and King's, and perhaps these enthusiasts were followed by others. We know that about 1850 Alfred Thompson[112] tried to form an amateur dramatic society, but the first such association to last was the Amateur Dramatic Club, the

---

[108] Harry T. Hall, *The Cambridge Dramatic Album* (Cambridge, 1868), p. 23, and pp. 5–27 for this passage generally.

[109] H. T. Hall in *Shakespearean Fly Leaves*, quoted in F. A. Keynes, *By-Ways*, 2nd edition, p. 129.

[110] O'Brien and Kemble were Trinity undergraduates. On the Apostles, see note 148

[111] Quoted in Peter Allen, *The Cambridge Apostles. The Early Years* (Cambridge University Press, 1978), p. 101. See also for these sentences F. C. Burnand, *The 'A.D.C.' being Personal Reminiscences of the University Amateur Dramatic Club, Cambridge*, 2nd edn (London, 1880), pp. vii–xi. Donne, a scholar of Gonville and Caius, did not graduate owing to scruples over the religious tests. For some years Examiner and then Licenser of Stage Plays, he also wrote on the drama.

[112] Thompson was an undergraduate of Trinity from 1850 to 1855. Among a variety of occupations, he designed more than 5,000 costumes for the English stage and wrote many comedies and light operas.

The Little Theatre at "the Hoop."
"But soft! what light thro' yonder window breaks
"It is the East and Juliet is the sun."
(Romeo and Juliet. Act 2. Sc. 2.)

21 The Little Theatre at 'the Hoop', drawn in 1859.

'ADC', whose moving spirit was Francis Cowley Burnand. Burnand, the son of a London stockbroker, claimed descent from the playwright Hannah Cowley, delighted in the stage from an early age, and composed a farce that was performed in his house at Eton.[113] It is not surprising that, in Burnand's first term at Trinity, Michaelmas 1854, the notion occurred to him that 'much more amusing than cards, drinking, and supper, would be private theatricals, with, of course, supper to follow'.[114] A few weeks later a group of undergraduates performed a farce written by Burnand, in his rooms opposite Trinity Gate, over a grocer's.[115] The players then considering a public performance, perhaps in the Bull Inn or the Barnwell theatre, Burnand went to request the necessary permission from the Vice-Chancellor, Dr Guest, of Caius. Guest is described by Burnand as 'a short, wizened, dried-up, elderly gentleman, with little legs and a big head, like a serious Punch doll, wearing his academical cap, and with his gown hitched up under his elbows';[116] he assumed that a Greek or Latin play was intended, and was

---

[113] Francis C. Burnand, *Records and Reminiscences. Personal and General* (2 vols., London, Methuen, 1904), vol. I, esp. pp. 95–117.
[114] Burnand, *The 'A.D.C.'*, p. 2. What follows is taken from this source, pp. 1–40.
[115] The premises were swept away soon after, as Salvin began to build Whewell's Court (1859–60).
[116] Burnand, *The 'A.D.C.'*, p. 8. The words on Guest are very misleading.

711

puzzled by the one Burnand did mention, *Box and Cox*. He referred the matter to the heads of houses, who refused permission.

But Burnand learned that the Athenaeum Club, a society for aristocratic undergraduates,[117] was planning to stage a play in the Red Lion Hotel in Petty Cury. Irritated that aristocrats could go ahead with what had been denied his circle, Burnand pushed for the creation of a dramatic club, which might justify their activities by the Athenaeum's precedent. The club was formed in 1855, and a stage built in two unused rooms at the Hoop Inn, Jesus Lane. The first productions, one evening in the Easter Term 1855, were two farces and the 'burlesque tragic opera', *Bombastes Furioso*. Eleven of the seventeen founder-members came from Trinity, and at least half the membership in later years was from Trinity too, as was an even larger proportion of the committee. Trinity was the biggest college; even so, there was a lot of justice in the complaint (in *Granta* 1889) that the ADC was a 'social clique', and no more than an 'appanage' of Trinity.[118]

The original premises were tiny.[119] The larger room, measuring 34 feet by 22 feet, contained the stage and the auditorium. An audience of fewer than seventy crammed in on benches. The stage was only 4ft above the floor, and so any character going through the trap had to go onto all fours to disappear. There was a gap of only two inches between the back scenery and the wall, and players could not behind the scenes get from one side of the stage to the other. The smaller room, the 'green room', was also used for dressing and properties.[120] With success it became possible to construct a much larger stage and auditorium, each about 40ft long, from the Hoop's billiard rooms.[121] The old premises became the green room. The present much larger theatre was constructed in 1935 on the same site after serious fire damage, and there were more improvements in the 1970s.

[117] Burnand describes it (*The 'A.D.C.'*, p. 24) as consisting of 'dukes, earls, and other titled members of the aristocracy who had kindly consented to come up to the University and patronise the ancient Institution'.

[118] I owe these facts to an unpublished paper by H. C. Porter, 'The Early Years of the A.D.C.' (1994).

[119] For what follows, see Burnand, *The 'A.D.C.'*, pp. 27–267.

[120] A drawing of 'the Little Theatre at the Hoop' was published in the *Cambridge Scrapbook* (1859); it is reproduced in Laurence and Helen Fowler, *Cambridge Commemorated. An Anthology of University Life* (Cambridge University Press, 1984), p. 22.

[121] At one time they had been the debating-chamber of the Union.

Thinking of themselves at first as being 'in the catacombs' under threat of 'Neronic persecution' at the hands of the Proctors, the club 'had a speaking tube run through from the Hoop bar to our green-room ... and outside the windows of the stage we had a ladder placed, by which the performers could have descended into a yard below; and so out into the street, dressed in our caps and gowns, which would hide the theatrical costumes underneath'.[122] They thought of having passwords and masonic signs for admission, both to be changed each evening; but they settled for tickets, to be sold by the handful of members (there were only seventeen at first). On the handbills the actors hid behind pseudonyms like K. Arrots and B. Agpipes – typical of the rib-nudging clubby atmosphere, very much that of the in-group, of the ADC in its early days. The Proctor's visit soon came, but when he saw that there were 'no signs of revelry or drinking', and had the club's activities described to him, 'he was much interested, considerably assured, owned that our object was laudable, and our efforts ... absolutely beneficial'.[123] Gradually dons themselves came to enjoy the performances, though a little shamefacedly at first, as if they were visiting a 'naughty French play' – the club being exceedingly careful however not to taint farces with anything likely to bring a blush to the cheek of a Proctor. After a few years the ADC became an accepted part of the university scene, and tutors were even willing to allow players to return to college or lodgings as late as 1.0 am on performance evenings. A visit by Edward, Prince of Wales, in March 1861[124] marked authority's acceptance of the club. The theatre was 'filled with the members of the University, and ladies and gentlemen from the county, and several who had come expressly from London'.[125] It was the first time that non-undergraduates were present, and that actors played under their own names. 'The pieces selected for representation were Mr Planché's drama *Not a Bad Judge*, Mr Maddison Morton's farce *A Thumping Legacy*, and a new burlesque extravaganza, called *The Fair Maid of Wapping, or The Tragical Tale of William Taylor.*'[126]

[122] Burnand, *The 'A.D.C.'*, p. 36.
[123] Burnand, *The 'A.D.C.'*, pp. 55–7 and p. 57 for the next quotation.
[124] He was studying at Trinity and living in Madingley Hall.
[125] *Drawing Room*, quoted in Burnand, *The 'A.D.C.'*, p. 213.
[126] *Era*, 9 March 1861, quoted in Burnand, *The 'A.D.C.'*, p. 214.

In the twentieth century the ADC boards have been a proving-ground for the West End, but at the beginning the members had no links whatever with the professional stage, and nobody even knew an actor. Burnand was accepted as an authority on the strength of a farce written at Eton and performed on a benefit night in Worthing. For some years the ADC did not know that they should pay royalties to dramatists. Very oddly it seems to us, there is no hint of contact with the Barnwell actors, though the university's distrust of the theatre was perhaps a sufficient reason. Even stranger, perhaps, given the amount of music and song in ADC stagings, was the lack of any co-operation with the Cambridge University Musical Society. Burnand's explanation that 'musicians are such uncommonly difficult people to deal with, – when, that is, theatrical people are dealing with them',[127] is too delphic to tell us much. Music at plays was provided by four local professionals led by 'White-headed Bob', a violinist.

The ADC contained 'sporting men, serious men – not *too* serious, but with ecclesiastical tastes – reading men, lounging men, political debaters at the Union'.[128] It was limited to forty (later sixty) members, who had to be Cambridge residents or graduates though members of Oxford University were also able to join. In the early years non-residents sometimes took leading parts; this was called the 'star system', and was a way of strengthening a wobbly company. Members did all the carpentry, stage-mechanism, and painting themselves, and their enthusiasm overflowed onto the stage, when members 'ignorant of the principles of the art of scene-shifting' obstructed those whose business it was.[129] After performances there were 'pleasant, cheery evenings' in Malcolm Street, when 'rough-and-ready repartee ... knock-down blows from a cudgel ... were exchanged amid shouts of uproarious merriment'. Today we may associate the ADC with with productions of Brecht, Chekhov, and Shakespeare. By contrast, Burnand averred that in its early days its purpose was exclusively student fun. 'We aimed low, and hit the mark exactly. Our selection of pieces does not show any great ambition. We only wanted to amuse, and – be amused.'[130] But in

---

[127] *The 'A.D.C.'*, p. 58.   [128] Burnand, *The 'A.D.C.'*, p. 99.
[129] Burnand, *The 'A.D.C.'*, p. 226, and p. 94 for the next quotation.
[130] Burnand, *The 'A.D.C.'*, pp. 64–5.

22 Chapman as Widow Pottle, and Finch as John Duck, in a production of James R. Planché, 'The Jacobite', in November 1864.

fact plays of quality were produced, alongside farces and comedies with punning titles and lots of noisy business, as in *Turkish Waters, A Tail of Coarse-Hair*, put on in November 1857. Three Sheridan plays were staged in the 1860s, and there were productions of dramas from the pen of J. W. Clark, a don friendly to the ADC, and of major plays by Tom Taylor.[131]

The ADC season lasted for three or four evenings each term. At any rate in the early days the prompter was as important as any player. All parts were taken by members, including the female roles.[132] Burnand and a couple of other enthusiasts dropped their studies for several weeks in the Easter Term 1856 to act with Captain Morton Price's 'small company of non-professionals playing for charities, local and otherwise, at various provincial theatres'.[133] After graduating Burnand took the ADC to act in Brighton in 1860 and 1864. He was the life and soul of the club, and wrote some of their scripts, including his favourite dramatic form, the burlesque. A parody of a well-known piece, the burlesque included song, comic business, and much local reference designed to appeal to undergraduates. In Burnand's *Alonzo the Brave*, for example, which was remotely based on Goethe's *Faust*,[134] Faust sends for a Proctor to investigate noise outside his study; 'the hit of the evening', on 3 December 1859, was the entry of 'Augustus Guest, dressed as a proctor, accompanied by his two bulldogs'. The Proctor cuts short his conversation with Faust to chase a student seen without his cap and gown in the street below. After singing a solo the Proctor exits dancing, with the bulldogs. Though in the 1990s students prefer their comedy to be more subtle, in 1859

> This was encored six times at least – the Proctor and attendants becoming wilder and wilder in their antics. It was without exception the funniest thing, of its kind, I ever saw on the 'A.D.C.'

---

[131] H. C. Porter makes this point in his unpublished paper, 'Francis Burnand and the early repertoire of the Cambridge A.D.C.' (1994), to which I am indebted.

[132] There is an album of photographs of ADC actors in the 1870s, by William Farren, in the Cambridgeshire Collection (C.76). Some players in female roles are more realistic than one might expect.

[133] Burnand, *Records and Reminiscences*, vol. I, p. 280. Burnand got an *exeat* for this absence of several weeks by telling his tutor it was for 'a matter of *serious* importance'. His ability to ignore lectures throws light on the easy life of a 'non-reading man'; Burnand was to take the ordinary BA.

[134] There is a Phil May caricature of Burnand as Mephistopheles in *Records and Reminiscences*, vol. I, p. 278.

stage, and, considering its appropriateness, I am not prepared to say that it was not the most genuine spontaneously funny thing I have ever seen on any stage. The point would perhaps be lost on a mixed audience, and when we played *Alonzo* away from the 'A.D.C.' Theatre, we invariably cut out the Proctor and Co.[135]

But 'a strong party existed among the Dons unfavourable to the "A.D.C."', and they disliked burlesques most. A gathering of twenty-five college tutors resolved in 1871 that the ADC's plays had 'become highly detrimental to the discipline and studies of the University, and that they are strongly disapproved of by the parents of many Undergraduates who take part in them'.[136] They wished to close the club down altogether. It was saved by John Willis Clark, a graduate of Trinity[137] and since 1861 an honorary member of the ADC. 'He paid a personal visit to the Tutors of Colleges, and pointed out that, while it might be possible to discountenance, it would be extremely difficult to suppress' the ADC, 'and that it would be far better to allow the Club to continue under proper sanction and supervision, than to leave it to develop as an illegal and secret society'.[138] Accepting this argument, the tutors drew up rules for the society which it perforce accepted in a 'Concordat' in 1871. Performances were confined to three evenings in Michaelmas, were to include no burlesques and close by 10.30, and be performed by university residents only (thus excluding graduates like Burnand). Texts had to be approved in advance by a tutors' committee.[139] Since about 1866 Clark had been sympathetically guiding the club to give up 'one-act low comedy farces' and to turn to 'three-act dramas and high comedies',[140] such as *Ruy Blas*, *The Rivals*, and *The School for Scandal*.

Clark also wrote several plays for the society, became its treasurer

---

[135] Burnand, *The 'A.D.C.'*, pp. 192–4, and p. 203 for the next quotation.
[136] Memorial of College Tutors, c. October 1871: CUL, Cam. b. 871.1, The ADC and the Tutors. Alteration in Rules, with letters on the subject, 1871–8. This folder, despite its place in the Cam Collection in the Rare Books Room, consists of manuscript material by J. W. Clark and others.
[137] Clark was elected fellow of Trinity in 1858 but refused to be ordained when the rule required; he gave up his fellowship but was allowed to continue to have rooms in college. He was appointed superintendent of the Museum of Zoology in 1866, and Registrary in 1891.
[138] G. B. Tatham, 'The "A.D.C."', in *Fasciculus Ioanni Willis Clark dicatus* (Cambridge University Press, 1909), p. 556; what follows is drawn from this essay.
[139] These rules are printed in Burnand, *The 'A.D.C.'*, p. 264.
[140] G. B. Tatham, 'The "A.D.C."', in *Fasciculus*, p. 557, and p. 564 for the next quotation.

in 1880, and negotiated the loan from Mortlocks' bank that made possible the ADC's purchase of its theatre's freehold in 1882. The summit of the serious drama was a production of *King Henry IV, Part 1* in Michaelmas 1886, the club's only venture into Shakespeare: 'it was the audience who failed and not the actors, and the play . . . was given to scanty houses'. It lost money, and was in any case hard to produce on a fifteen-foot stage. The club returned perforce away from drama to comedy for the rest of the century, and even to burlesque again on occasion; a Proctor appeared again in R.C. Lehmann's 'original mythological musical extravaganza' *Jupiter LL.D*, staged in June 1894.

DEBATING

THE CAMBRIDGE UNION SOCIETY

In 1843 John Moultrie, the rector of Rugby, published 'The Dream of Life', described by Thomas Seccombe in the *Dictionary of National Biography* as an 'autobiographical meditation in verse'. In this shadowy imitation of the *Prelude* Moultrie described the 'keen conflicts of contending wit' in the Cambridge Union Society, the university debating forum, whose early meetings he had attended when he was a commoner at Trinity College from 1819 to 1822:

> those nights and suppers of the gods –
> Feasts of the hungry soul, when, at the close
> Of some well argued, eloquent debate
> Held in the 'Union', which with lengthen'd roar
> Of cheers had shaken Petty Cury's roofs,
> Startling the jaded shopman from his sleep, –
> The leaders of the war on either side.
> (Their strife suspended) to my neighbouring rooms
> Adjourn'd, to sup on oysters.[141]

Discussion, a constant undergraduate activity which is reflected in this epoch in (for example) Christopher Wordsworth's Trinity diary, led naturally in Georgian Britain to formal debating: a model was provided by parliament, the palladium of a venerated constitu-

---

[141] John Moultrie, *Poems* (new edn, 2 vols., 1876), vol. 1, pp. 420–1. Moultrie, a reflective, taciturn, and somewhat indolent man, was 'a listener not a talker' at the debates, 'noticeably, and it may be said, notably, silent': see Derwent Coleridge's memoir prefacing vol. 1 of the *Poems*, p. xx.

tion devoted to liberty, on whose benches many undergraduates aspired one day to sit. We know of three debating societies in existence during the French wars, and maybe there were more; the three came together to form 'the Union' (hence its name) in 1814.[142] It first began its weekly meetings in February 1815, in what an early debater many years later recalled as a 'low, ill-ventilated, ill-lit apartment, at the back of the Red Lion Inn – cavernous, tavernous – something between a commercial room and a district branch meeting-house'.[143]

From the first the society debated literary and political questions such as the government's Irish policy, and they made the Vice-Chancellor, James Wood, very uneasy; Wood, the Master of St John's, went to a Union meeting in March 1817 with the Proctors.[144] They ordered the members to disperse and not to re-assemble. In the chair was William Whewell, Second Wrangler in 1816 and within sight of his Trinity fellowship. In his first public action he struck the pompous note he was to keep to throughout life: 'Strangers will please to withdraw, and the House will take the message into consideration.'[145] Later a Union deputation visited Wood, who refused to allow political speeches, and added that some Union members' studies 'had been checked and their prospects blighted, by the attention and attendance which they had been obliged to bestow on the society' (whose meetings in fact lasted for no more than two or three hours a week). Winstanley and later writers have been sharply critical of Wood's over-reaction to the Union's activities, forgetting that in 1817 the entire British Establishment quaked in fear of revolution. Four years later the then Vice-Chancellor, Christopher Wordsworth of Trinity, permitted the resumption of debates provided that there was no discussion of political questions current within the preceding twenty years; this rule was obviously difficult to enforce, and in any case it was dropped about 1830.

Wood certainly seems to have been afraid without cause. When

---

[142] What follows is based on Cooper, *Annals*, IV, pp. 516–17, and Winstanley, *Early Victorian Cambridge*, pp. 25–8.

[143] T. Wemyss Reid, *Life, Letters and Friendships of Richard Monckton Milnes, First Lord Houghton* (2 vols., London, 1890), vol. II, p. 160. Houghton uttered the words quoted at the opening of the Union's present premises in Round Church Street in 1866. The Red Lion Hotel stood in Petty Cury; its last fragments were demolished in 1970.

[144] They were (1816–17) William Okes of Caius and William French of Pembroke.

[145] Quoted in Winstanley, *Early Victorian Cambridge*, p. 26, as also for the next quotation.

in the 1970s the Union debates of the 1820s were closely examined, the conclusion was that the prevailing opinion was 'anti-Establishment', natural enough to young but conventional men when a Tory government was in power; their liberalism, it was said later by one of them, Charles Merivale, was largely that of 'the so-called Whigs, who except for two or three popular crotchets to which they had incautiously pledged themselves during their long exclusion from the responsibilities of office, were little other than rather free spoken Tories, who claimed the privilege of speaking evil of dignities to which they were at heart as devotedly attached as their rivals'.[146] Peter Allen judges that 'entirely typical' of such men, 'in his taste for disputation, his political partisanship and his ability to blend liberal rhetoric with conventional social values', was Benjamin Hall Kennedy – brilliant classicist undergraduate at St John's from 1823 to 1827, and in later life headmaster of his old school, Shrewsbury, before returning to Cambridge as Regius Professor of Greek forty years after his Union speeches.

On the right was a small number of Tories, chief perhaps being James Farish.[147] Perhaps the most interesting name on the left was John Sterling, chiefly known to us as the subject of Carlyle's biography.[148] At Cambridge, Carlyle tells us, Sterling became the 'acknowledged chief' in the Union, which offered 'much logic, and other spiritual fencing and ingenuous collision'. A radical, Sterling 'ruffled the general young imagination into stormy laughter' with his attack on 'the anti-superstitious side of things', the Church of England's 'black dragoon in every parish'.[149] The views of the middle-opinion majority between these extremes are reflected in the voting figures for some representative debates in these years.[150] 'Is an Elective Monarchy a beneficial form of Government?' was

---

[146] Merivale is quoted in Allen, *Cambridge Apostles*, p. 33, to which (pp. 27–34) these paragraphs are indebted.

[147] James Farish graduated BA at Trinity College in 1825 and MB in 1828; he became a surgeon.

[148] Born in 1806 in Scotland, Sterling matriculated in Trinity College in 1824. He was a distinguished debater, and one of the original 'Apostles', the intellectual coterie that began within the Union Society, but he did not take a degree. He was introduced to Coleridge by his tutor, Julius Hare, and devoted much energy to his thought. Variously a writer and journalist, and briefly a clergyman, Sterling's life was undermined by restless and unfocused ambition and cut short by tuberculosis in 1844. On Sterling's loss of faith, see chapter 10, pp. 369–70.

[149] Thomas Carlyle, *Life of John Sterling* (1851), Part 1, chapter 4.

[150] These facts are taken from Allen, *Cambridge Apostles*, pp. 33–42.

defeated by 121 to 54, as was by 94 to 7 'Are any dangerous results to be apprehended from the general diffusion of knowledge among the lower orders of Society?', and by 46 to 9 'Was Parliamentary Reform upon the principle that *Elections* should be *annual*, that the Vote should be by *Ballot*, and that the *right of voting* should be enjoyed by *every man who could read*, desirable in the year 1805?'. (The retrospectivity of this topic was an entire masquerade and a good example of the ineffectiveness of the 'twenty-year' rule.)

The flavour of a debate was described by 'EB' of Christ's College in the *Athenaeum* for 14 June 1829.[151]

Suppose this to be Tuesday, the —th day of—, and behold the 'Union' in all its glory. A long, low room, with three or four rows of benches down the sides, and the President's chair at one end, exhibits a muster of perhaps two hundred members. Tables with candles stand in the centre, and the orators are generally congregated near them. After some minutes spent in private business, the President announces, that 'the question for this evening's discussion is, – ought the claims of the Roman Catholics to have been granted previous to the year 1808? The opener is at liberty to begin.' *(Order, order!)* My friend Williams rises, with his eyes upon the ground, and his hands upon the ballotting-box. *(Hear, hear, hear!)* – 'Mr President, I should not have proposed this question to the society, had I thought that it was commonly discussed elsewhere on the proper grounds. This question is, in fact, a contest between the people and the aristocratic monopolies, which scarcely even pretend to represent the people,' etc. etc., and so on for half an hour. Then rose Mr Billingsgate, a soft-voiced young gentleman of large fortune, and a fellow-commoner; yet, though a fool, a favourite with the society. 'I protest, Sir, against the use of such expressions as those which have been expressed by the honourable gentleman. They are decidedly unconstitutional; I say, Sir, they are decidedly unconstitutional. I maintain, Sir, that the House of Commons does fully and fairly represent the people. By the people, I do not mean the rabble, but persons of birth, influence, fashion and fortune. The glorious constitution, Sir, is composed of three powers, all exactly equal to each other, and yet no two of them superior to the third. I consider that the speech of the honourable gentleman was decidedly unconstitutional, and in favour of the bloody papists, and ought to

151 Quoted in Allen, *Cambridge Apostles*, pp. 43–4.

have been interrupted from the chair.' *(Hear, hear, hear and loud laughter.)* Then am I seen to rise, or some moderate, well-informed, and eloquent member, and the assembly is stilled into silent expectation. The discussion is restored to its proper path, the opposing arguments are admirably balanced, and the whole question is settled in one rolling accumulated peroration.

An evening of this kind seldom terminates without a supper party.

In March 1829, at the height of the national controversy over Catholic Emancipation, there was a Union debate on the question – a stormier evening[152] than the one 'EB' was to describe a few months later. Diehard Protestants and Tories, calling themselves the Brunswick Club (in fancied support for George IV) turned up in strength. Richard Monckton Milnes wrote that he 'had intended to have spoken, but the tumult grew so great about 10 o'clock, that it was impossible to make a word heard – and the room was so full that there was a division into the yard – this was a most noisy proceeding – all kinds of cheers and groans mingled together'. At last the tellers 'appeared at the windows' announcing the defeat of the Emancipation motion by 10 votes. But while 'the yell of the victory of the Brunswickeers' was still heard a mistake was announced; 'the change of countenance was ludicrous . . . the canvassing on that side had been most vigorous'.

The most acute assessment of early Victorian Union debates we possess, by Leslie Stephen, describes their confusing mixture of deep conviction, light-heartedness, and play-acting.[153] On one occasion, in 1848, 'the chartist ardour burnt in the bosoms of a small minority'. One such, in fact Richard Sedgwick[154] 'prayed for an army of French republicans to re-enact Pride's Purge, and inoculate the British populace with the true social virus. The Conservative majority of course groaned at his monstrosities and cheered the next speaker', who described Louis Philippe as the wisest French king

---

[152] What follows is taken from Allen, *Cambridge Apostles*, pp. 48–9.
[153] Leslie Stephen, *Sketches from Cambridge by a Don*, pp. 58–69, from which the quotations that follow are taken.
[154] See Percy Cradock, H. Wilson Harris, Arnold McNair, *Recollections of the Cambridge Union 1815–1939* (Cambridge, Bowes and Bowes, 1953), pp. 37–8. Richard Sedgwick, nephew of the first Adam Sedgwick, the geologist, and father of the second, the zoologist, graduated at Trinity College in 1850 and became a clergyman – for a long period at Dent, the geologist's village.

ever and denounced his rebellious subjects. Sedgwick irritatedly brandished a decanter. 'The president put a motion for his instant expulsion, which was carried by acclamation, and immediately enforced by a unanimous charge from the overwhelming majority. The radicals defended for a moment a difficult angle in the staircase, but were soon swept tumultuously into the street amidst tremendous cheers.' Debates were relaxation, and necessarily at times frivolous. 'Exuberant animal spirits and youthful vanity' impel the undergraduate to the Union 'as soon as he is taken out of the traces which bind him to the drudgery of his studies'. Recalling the occasion when he 'denounced the Prime Minister of the day as "a contemptible sneak" (or words to that effect)', Stephen reminded his readers that the 'youthful eagle essaying his preparatory flights' in 'half-conscious imitation of his paternal models' should not be regarded too critically.

American commentators thought that debating was taken less seriously than in Harvard or Yale, where large numbers of undergraduates were fascinated with oratory – a reflection of a difference from British culture that Dickens mocked in *Martin Chuzzlewit*. Bristed reported that in the early 1840s interest was aroused in Cambridge by 'aspirants' to the name of orator, ambitious Small-College men, and a hard-working Trinity Scholar or two (Bristed himself was a member) that in the early 1840s 'got up stirring political debates – democracy against aristocracy, toleration against church exclusiveness, old common sense against Young England – and soon had crowded houses for nights in succession'.[155] But debates had sometimes to be adjourned for half an hour for lack of speakers, and vacant offices were hard to fill. 'In general', declared William Everett, debates were 'death itself', one reason being the British cult of self-deprecation that led men expert on a given topic to take the heart out of their potentially forceful utterance: 'I didn't mean to speak to-night, and I haven't much to say.'[156]

But though the media have always regarded the debates as the Union's most important feature, they were not in fact why most members paid the modest subscription – in the 1840s £1 entrance

[155] *Five Years*, vol. I, p. 164.   [156] *On the Cam*, pp. 107–8.

fee and 10s a term, membership however being free after eight terms. Thus for £5 members got the Union library containing more popular literature than any local circulating library, a great range of newspapers and magazines, and comfortable reading and writing rooms. Compared with these delights William Thomson, for example, thought the debates did not have 'much interest in them'.[157] 'Its five hundred members', wrote William Everett, making constant use of it from day to day, never, perhaps ... reading for amusement anything not supplied by it, and yet to a vast extent wholly careless of who controls it, or what it does as a society', were content to leave its committee and their two clerks to run it.[158] These reading members provided a large part of the £9,000 spent in 1865 on a new Union building, on its present site behind the Round Church. The design was awarded in a competition to Alfred Waterhouse, aged thirty-five, a rising architect who began a long involvement with bricks and mortar in Cambridge (and Oxford) with his Union building. Waterhouse studied the Oxford Union, designed in extravagant Gothic by Benjamin Woodward and William Wilkinson a few years before, but produced for Cambridge 'a simple but attractive building with decoration pared to a minimum'. The use of high-class sub-contractors and the addition of a complete set of furniture designed by the architect 'showed that this was no pinch-penny job'.[159]

[157] CUL Add. MS 7342, William Thomson to James Thomson, T.179, 26 October 1861.
[158] Everett, *On the Cam*, p. 106.
[159] Colin Cunningham and Prudence Waterhouse, *Alfred Waterhouse 1830–1905. Biography of a Practice* (Oxford, Clarendon, 1992), p. 66. The front elevation of the 1865 building (which was extensively altered in the 1880s) is illustrated in plate 62.

APPENDICES

Appendix I. The composition of the University of Cambridge

Ia. 1795

College	Founded	Masters and fellows	Fellow commoners	Scholars	Pensioners	Sizars	Noblemen	Total undergraduates
Peterhouse	1284	22	2	—	16	8	—	26
Clare College	1326	21	3	15	8	8	—	34
Pembroke College	1347	17	3	7	22	7	—	39
Gonville and Caius College	1348	27	3	31	—	2	—	36
Trinity Hall	1350	13	6	14	24	1	—	45
Corpus Christi	1352	11	—	13	8	3	—	24
King's College	1441	59	1	11	—	—	—	12
Queens' College	1446	20	7	18	—	4	—	29
St Catharine's College[a]	1473	18	1	15	2	2	—	20
Jesus College	1496	17	1	2	33	—	—	36
Christ's College	1506	16	8	—	23	11	—	42
St John's College	1511	62	20	35	27	16	2	100
Magdalene College	1542	14	—	—	19	16	—	35
Trinity College	1546	67	42	25	80	18	—	165
Emmanuel College	1584	14	16	16	19	18	—	69
Sidney Sussex College	1596	11	2	—	13	9	—	24
Total		409	115	202	294	123	2	736

[a] Catharine Hall until 1860

Source: *Cambridge University Calendar for the Year 1796* (Cambridge, 1796), pp. 2–93. NB. Although the calendar was published in 1796 it is stated in the preface that the lists of names were taken from the college boards in the period before October 1795 (p. iv).

Ib. 1850

College	Founded	Masters and fellows	Fellow commoners	Scholars	Pensioners	Sizars	Ten-year men	Noblemen	Total undergraduates
Peterhouse	1284	24	3	—	41	3	3	—	50
Clare College	1326	22	—	22	28	—	—	—	50
Pembroke College	1347	14	—	3	16	3	1	—	23
Gonville and Caius College	1348	30	2	16	90	—	2	—	110
Trinity Hall	1350	13	9	8	33	—	—	—	50
Corpus Christi	1352	10	2	19	40	3	4	—	68
King's College	1441	62	—	9	—	—	—	—	9
Queens' College	1446	19	2	9	46	17	28	—	102
St Catharine's College[a]	1473	12	8	—	57	2	12	—	79
Jesus College	1496	18	7	9	43	—	—	—	59
Christ's College	1506	16	2	13	62	2	3	—	82
St John's College	1511	58	4	41	200	55	48	—	348
Magdalene College	1542	15	4	14	38	3	2	—	61
Trinity College	1546	61	21	17	444	38	3	2	525
Emmanuel College	1584	15	2	7	74	4	8	—	95
Sidney Sussex College	1596	12	—	10	15	2	4	—	31
Downing College	1800	4	9	—	—	—	2	—	11
Total		405	75	197	1,227	132	120	2	1,753

[a] Catharine Hall until 1860

Source: Cambridge University Calendar for the Year 1850 (Cambridge, 1850), pp. 200–347.

SOURCES OF APPENDICES II–VIII

St John's College Archives

C3.4, Fellows' Register 1735–75
C3.5, Fellows' Register 1775–1824
C3.6, Fellows' Register 1824–60
C3.7, Fellows' Register 1860–1965

Emmanuel College Archives

FEL. 7.3, A list of the Masters and Fellows of Emmanuel College, since the foundation AD 1584.

Pembroke College Archives

BB.6–9, Order Books 1735–1839
BE.I, Order Book 1839–86

Much personal information summarised in the tables has been drawn from J. and J. A. Venn, *Alumni Cantabrigienses*.

Appendix II. *Quality of degree of masters elected, 1751–1870*

	1751–60	1761–70	1771–80	1781–90	1791–1800	1801–10
1	—	—	—	2	1	1
2	1	—	—	4	2	1
3	—	—	1	—	2	1
4	1	1	1	—	—	—
5	—	1	—	1	—	—
6	2	1	1	—	1	—
7	4	3	3	1	1	—
8	1	—	1	—	1	—
9	—	1	—	—	—	2
10	—	—	—	1	—	—
Total	9	7	7	9	8	5

	1811–20	1821–30	1831–40	1841–50	1851–60	1861–70
1	4	1	1	3	—	1
2	3	2	3	5	5	1
3	2	—	2	1	—	—
4	—	—	—	—	—	—
5	—	—	—	—	—	—
6	—	—	—	—	—	—
7	1	—	—	—	—	—
8	1	—	—	—	1	—
9	1	—	—	1	—	—
10	—	—	—	—	—	—
Total	12	3	6	10	6	2

Legend
1 Senior Wranglers, Senior Classics, and Prizemen
2 Wranglers and Classics Firsts
3 Senior optimes
4 *In comitiis prioribus*
5 Junior optimes
6 *In comitiis posterioribus*
7 Poll degree (include *ad baptistam* degrees)
8 MAs and doctorates (no BA noted)
9 LL B and MD
10 Oxford degrees

Appendix III. *Quality of degree of the fellows of three colleges, elected 1751–1870*

IIIa. Foundation fellows of St John's College

	1751–60	1761–70	1771–80	1781–90	1791–1800	1801–10
1	1	2	4	3	3	3
2	1	3	11	12	15	15
3	—	—	—	—	—	—
4	8	10	5	4	1	4
5	6	9	4	1	1	—
6	5	3	—	3	1	1
7	—	—	—	1	—	—
Total	21	27	24	24	21	23

	1811–20	1821–30	1831–40	1841–50	1851–60	1861–70
1	5	5	9	6	8	12
2	12	14	20	20	15	24
3	—	4	5	2	4	6
4	—	2	—	2	—	—
5	—	—	—	—	—	1
6	1	2	1	—	—	—
7	—	—	—	—	—	—
Total	18	27	35	30	27	43

Legend
1 Senior Wranglers, Senior Classics, and Prizemen
2 Wranglers or Classics Firsts
3 All 'Double Firsts' (i.e. Wranglers and Classics Firsts, etc.)
4 Senior optimes
5 Junior optimes
6 Poll degree
7 MA (no BA noted)

IIIb. Fellows of Emmanuel College, excluding Gillingham and Dixie fellows

	1751–60	1761–70	1771–80	1781–90	1791–1800	1801–10
1	—	—	1	—	—	—
2	2	3	1	2	4	2
4	1	2	3	4	2	3
5	3	1	1	1	1	—
6	1	—	1	2	2	1
Total	7	6	7	9	9	6

	1811–20	1821–30	1831–40	1841–50	1851–60	1861–70
1	—	—	—	—	1	3
2	5	3	4	2	—	3
4	6	4	3	—	—	—
5	1	2	—	—	—	—
6	—	—	—	—	—	—
Total	12	9	7	2	1	6

Legend
1 Senior Wrangler, Classics First or University Prize
2 Wranglers
4 Senior optimes
5 Junior optimes
6 Ordinary degree

IIIc. Fellows of Pembroke College (excluding Grindal and Lany fellows)

	1751–60	1761–70	1771–80	1781–90	1791–1800	1801–10
1	—	4	2	1	2	1
2	3	2	2	8	7	4
3	—	—	—	—	—	—
4	5	2	3	2	—	1
5	2	—	—	—	—	—
6	1	—	—	—	—	—
7	—	1	1	—	—	—
Total	11	9	8	11	9	6

	1811–20	1821–30	1831–40	1841–50	1851–60	1861–70
1	2	—	2	2	2	1
2	6	8	8	4	4	7
3	—	2	1	—	—	—
4	2	—	—	—	—	—
5	—	—	—	—	—	—
6	—	—	—	—	—	—
7	—	—	—	—	—	—
Total	10	10	11	6	6	8

Legend
1 Senior Wranglers, Senior Classics, and Prizemen
2 Wranglers or Classics Firsts
3 All 'double firsts' (e.g. Wranglers and Classics Firsts)
4 Senior optimes (including 3 *in comitiis prioribus* 1751–60)
5 Junior optimes (including 1 *in comitiis posterioribus* 1751–60)
6 Poll degree
7 MA (no BA noted)

Appendix IV. *Undergraduate colleges of fellows of St John's and Emmanuel Colleges elected 1751–1870*

IVa. St John's College: Foundation, 'restricted', and Platt fellowships

	1751–60	1761–70	1771–80	1781–90	1791–1800	1801–10
1	—	1	1	1	—	—
2	—	1	—	—	—	—
3	—	—	—	—	—	—
4	—	—	—	1	—	—
5	—	—	—	—	—	—
6	—	—	—	1	—	—
7	45	41	45	44	45	47
Total	45	43	46	47	45	47

	1811–20	1821–30	1831–40	1841–50	1851–60	1861–70
1	—	—	—	—	—	—
2	—	—	1	1	—	—
3	—	—	—	—	—	1
4	—	—	—	—	—	—
5	—	—	1	—	—	—
6	—	—	—	—	—	—
7	45	43	57	56	43	58
Total	45	43	59	57	43	59

Legend
1 Christ's
2 Trinity
3 Emmanuel
4 Queens'
5 Magdalene
6 Corpus
7 St John's

IVb. Emmanuel College: elected, Gillingham, and Dixie fellows

	1751–60	1761–70	1771–80	1781–90	1791–1800	1801–10
1	—	—	—	1	—	—
2	2	1	1	—	—	1
3	—	—	—	—	—	—
4	—	—	—	1	—	—
5	12	8	10	12	13	7
Total	14	9	11	14	13	8

	1811–20	1821–30	1831–40	1841–50	1851–60	1861–70
1	—	—	—	—	—	—
2	1	—	—	1	1	—
3	—	—	—	—	1	—
4	—	—	—	—	—	—
5	11	11	7	7	7	7
Total	12	11	7	8	9	7

Legend
1 Christ's
2 St John's
3 Queens'
4 Clare
5 Emmanuel

Appendix V. *Quality of degree in 'restricted' followships*

Va. Quality of degree of those elected to 'restricted' fellowships in St John's College (Beresford, Rokeby, Simpson, Keton, Fell, and Thimbleby fellowships), 1751–1870

	1751–60	1761–70	1771–80	1781–90	1791–1800	1801–10
1	—	2	—	—	—	—
2	2	1	1	1	2	1
3	—	—	—	—	—	—
4	1	1	—	—	3	2
5	1	—	2	—	—	—
6	6	1	2	2	1	5
7	—	—	—	—	—	—
Total	10	5	5	3	6	8

	1811–20	1821–30	1831–40	1841–50	1851–60	1861–70
1	—	1	—	2	—	—
2	4	4	3	3	3	6
3	—	—	—	—	2	1
4	2	—	1	—	1	—
5	—	—	—	—	—	—
6	1	—	1	1	—	—
7	—	—	—	—	—	—
Total	7	5	5	6	6	7

Legend
1 Senior Wranglers, Senior Classics, and Prizemen
2 Wranglers or Classics Firsts
3 All 'Double Firsts' (e.g. Wranglers and Classics Firsts, Wranglers and Natural Sciences Firsts, Wranglers and Moral Sciences Firsts, Wranglers and Theology Firsts, Wranglers and Civil Law Firsts)
4 Senior optimes
5 Junior optimes
6 Poll degree
7 MA (no BA noted)

736

Vb. Quality of degree of those elected to 'fully restricted' fellowships in St John's College (Constable, Halitreholme, Bailey, Lupton, Ashton, Hebblethwaite, Dee, and Gregson fellowships) 1751–1870

	1751–60	1761–70	1771–80	1781–90	1791–1800	1801–10
1	—	—	1	1	—	1
2	2	4	2	6	2	2
3	—	—	—	—	—	—
4	2	1	3	—	2	2
5	—	—	—	—	1	2
6	4	—	—	3	4	—
7	—	—	—	—	—	—
Total	8	5	6	10	9	7

	1811–20	1821–30	1831–40	1841–50	1851–60	1861–70
1	—	2	3	1	—	—
2	2	5	6	7	6	8
3	—	—	—	1	—	1
4	8	1	2	—	1	—
5	—	—	—	—	—	—
6	—	—	—	1	—	—
7	—	—	—	—	—	—
Total	10	8	11	10	7	9

Legend
1 Senior Wranglers, Senior Classics, and Prizemen
2 Wranglers or Classics Firsts
3 All 'Double Firsts' (e.g. Wranglers and Classics Firsts, Wranglers and Natural Sciences Firsts, Wranglers and Moral Sciences Firsts, Wranglers and Theology Firsts, Wranglers and Civil Law Firsts)
4 Senior optimes
5 Junior optimes
6 Poll degree
7 MA (no BA noted)

Appendix VI. *Status on matriculation of undergraduates later elected to fellowships, 1751–1870*

Note: the numbers in each column relate to the status on matriculation of fellows elected during the decade in question

VIa. St John's College: foundation, 'restricted', and Platt fellowships

	1751–60	1761–70	1771–80	1781–90	1791–1800	1801–10
1	19	25	29	29	26	32
2	26	18	17	18	18	15
3	—	—	—	—	1	—
Total	45	43	46	47	45	47

	1811–20	1821–30	1831–40	1841–50	1851–60	1861–70
1	30	27	37	27	22	40
2	15	16	22	30	21	19
3	—	—	—	—	—	—
Total	45	43	59	57	43	59

Legend
1 Pensioner
2 Sizar
3 Fellow commoner

VIb. Emmanuel College: 'elected', Gillingham, and Dixie fellowships

	1751–60	1761–70	1771–80	1781–90	1791–1800	1801–10
1	9	5	5	7	8	2
2	4	4	6	6	5	5
3	—	—	—	1	—	—
4	1	—	—	—	—	1
Total	14	9	11	14	13	8

	1811–20	1821–30	1831–40	1841–50	1851–60	1861–70
1	8	10	4	6	9	7
2	3	1	3	2	—	—
3	—	—	—	—	—	—
4	1	—	—	—	—	—
Total	12	11	7	8	9	7

Legend
1 Pensioner
2 Sizar
3 Fellow commoner
4 Unknown

Appendix VII. *Length of tenure of foundation fellows of St John's College,*
1751–1870

	1751–60	1761–70	1771–80	1781–90	1791–1800	1801–10
1	2	2	1	3	4	3
2	12	12	9	10	8	8
3	5	11	6	4	3	3
4	—	—	4	3	4	5
5	2	2	4	4	2	4
Total	21	27	24	24	21	23

	1811–20	1821–30	1831–40	1841–50	1851–60	1861–70
1	2	9	8	3	8	5
2	6	7	15	8	8	19
3	5	5	2	5	3	5
4	—	2	2	2	1	3
5	5	4	8	12	7	11
Total	18	27	35	30	27	43

Legend
1 Up to 5 years
2 Up to 11 years
3 Up to 25 years
4 Over 25 years
5 Unknown

Appendices

Appendix VIII. *Later occupations of fellows elected 1751–1870*

VIIIa. Fellows of St John's College

	1751–60	1761–70	1771–80	1781–90	1791–1800	1801–10
1	38	37	37	36	31	35
2	3	4	1	2	4	3
3	1	—	—	—	—	—
4	2	—	6	6	7	8
5	—	1	—	—	2	1
6	—	—	—	1	1	—
7	1	1	2	2	—	—
Total	45	43	46	47	45	47

	1811–20	1821–30	1831–40	1841–50	1851–60	1861–70
1	30	31	38	26	10	11
2	4	6	6	24	21	33
3	—	—	—	—	—	—
4	7	4	6	4	7	9
5	—	1	3	1	2	3
6	—	—	—	—	1	2
7	4	1	6	2	2	1
Total	45	43	59	57	43	59

Legend
1 Anglican clergymen and schoolmasters (includes missionaries)
2 Non-Anglican clergymen, academic careers in Cambridge and elsewhere, schoolmasters, astronomer
3 Landed gentlemen (includes sheriffs and JPs)
4 Lawyers, physicians
5 Diplomats, civil servants, army and navy officers, Members of Parliament
6 Actuaries, bankers, businessmen and merchants, civil engineers
7 Early death, unknown

VIIIb. Emmanuel College

	1751–60	1761–70	1771–80	1781–90	1791–1800	1801–10
1	13	7	7	10	11	7
2	1	—	2	1	1	—
3	—	—	—	—	—	—
4	—	2	—	—	—	—
5	—	—	—	—	—	—
6	—	—	—	1	—	—
7	—	—	2	2	1	1
Total	14	9	11	14	13	8

	1811–20	1821–30	1831–40	1841–50	1851–60	1861–70
1	8	9	5	4	8	2
2	2	1	1	2	1	2
3	—	—	—	—	—	—
4	1	1	—	—	—	2
5	—	—	1	—	—	—
6	—	—	—	1	—	—
7	1	—	—	1	—	1
Total	12	11	7	8	9	7

Legend

1 Anglican clergymen and schoolmasters (includes missionaries)
2 Non-Anglican clergymen, academic careers in Cambridge and elsewhere, schoolmasters, astronomer
3 Landed gentlemen (includes sheriffs and JPs)
4 Lawyers, physicians
5 Diplomats, civil servants, army and navy officers, Members of Parliament
6 Actuaries, bankers, businessmen and merchants, civil engineers
7 Early death, unknown

Appendices

VIIIc. Pembroke College

	1751–60	1761–70	1771–80	1781–90	1791–1800	1801–10
1	8	7	5	8	7	3
2	1	1	1	1	1	—
3	—	—	1	—	—	—
4	—	1	—	2	2	3
5	1	1	—	—	1	—
6	—	—	—	—	—	1
7	5	1	1	—	—	—
Total	15	11	8	11	11	7

	1811–20	1821–30	1831–40	1841–50	1851–60	1861–70
1	6	3	7	2	4	4
2	3	1	4	2	1	2
3	—	—	—	—	—	—
4	—	5	1	2	1	2
5	—	—	—	—	—	—
6	—	—	—	1	—	—
7	1	1	—	—	—	—
Total	10	10	12	7	6	8

Legend
1 Anglican clergymen and schoolmasters (includes missionaries)
2 Non-Anglican clergymen, academic careers in Cambridge and elsewhere, schoolmasters, astronomer
3 Landed gentlemen (includes sheriffs and JPs)
4 Lawyers, physicians
5 Diplomats, civil servants, army and navy officers, Members of Parliament
6 Actuaries, bankers, businessmen and merchants, civil engineers
7 Early death, unknown

Appendix IX. *The literary productivity of fellows*

IXa. The literary productivity of the foundation fellows of St John's, elected between 1751 and 1870

Cohort	Size of cohort	Number of publishing fellows	Number known to have published during their fellowship
1751–60	21	2	1
1761–70	27	2	2
1771–80	24	2	—
1781–90	24	1	—
1791–1800	21	8	3
1801–10	23	11	5
1811–20	18	7	5
1821–30	27	13	7
1831–40	35	23	9
1841–50	30	16	10
1851–60	27	16	7
1861–70	43	19	8
Total	320	120	57

IXb. The literary productivity of St John's fellows elected between 1831 and 1840

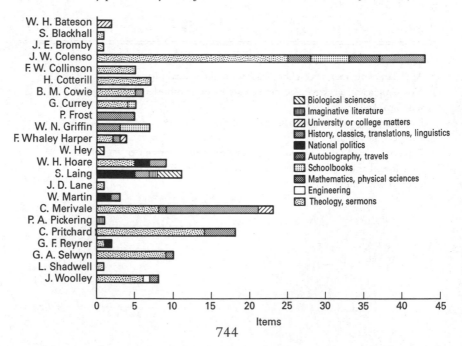

744

Appendix X. Scholarships and sizarships, 1850

College	Open scholarships	Restricted scholarships	Value of scholarships	Exhibitions	Value of exhibitions	Sizars
Peterhouse	38	30	£2.50–£30	—	—	4
Clare College	41	4	£5–£50	—	—	3
Pembroke College	14	16	£5–£80	c.8	—	3
Gonville and Caius College	13	32	£8–£60	—	—	—
Trinity Hall	16	—	£12.60–£52.50	—	—	—
Corpus Christi	23	30	£2.50–£40	—	—	6
King's College	—	10[a]	£27	—	—	—
Queens' College	15	—	£15–£50	—	—	24
St Catharine's College	30	13	£2–£35	—	—	1
Jesus College	19	30	£2–£60	—	—	—
Christ's College	52	2	£10–£17	c.40	£1–£35	4
St John's College	32	92	?	c.75	£8–£100	54
Magdalene College	16	21	£3–£77	12	—	4
Trinity College	68	4	£47	c.20	£6–£100	32
Emmanuel College	—	21	£10–£53	—	—	4
Sidney Sussex College	24	12	£5–£26	—	—	4
Totals	401	317	—	c.155	—	143

[a] By the statutes of King's College all scholars of Eton were entitled to fellowships at King's, and a scholarship at the college was held for three years before automatic election to a fellowship. The Graham Commission commented that 'this law of succession removes all stimulus to exertion'.

Source: PP 1852–3, HC xliv [1559]: Graham Commission Report, pp. 185–96.

Appendix XI. *Percentages voting at two parliamentary elections*

College	1826 election		
	Fellows for Palmerston (no. of fellows)	Non-fellows for Palmerston (no. of non-fellows)	Percentage difference between fellows and non-fellows
Caius	73 (11)	30 (53)	43
Christ's	67 (9)	33 (33)	34
Clare	16 (16)	19 (31)	− 3
Corpus	25 (8)	33 (21)	− 8
Downing	83 (6)	0 (2)	83
Emmanuel	0 (12)	30 (64)	− 30
Jesus	62 (13)	50 (40)	12
King's	39 (28)	32 (19)	7
Magdalene	43 (7)	71 (17)	− 28
Pembroke	31 (13)	31 (26)	—
Peterhouse	36 (14)	36 (25)	—
Queens'	40 (15)	25 (32)	− 15
Sidney	17 (6)	44 (25)	− 27
St Catharine's	44 (9)	31 (16)	13
St John's	83 (46)	60 (260)	23
Trinity	61 (36)	58 (349)	3
Trinity Hall	43 (7)	13 (15)	30
Overall percentage	50 (256)	49 (1,028)	1

Appendix XI (*cont.*)

| | 1831 election | | |
College	Fellows for non-reformers (no. of fellows)	Non-fellows for non-reformers (no. of non-fellows)	Percentage difference between fellows and non-fellows
Caius	36 (17)	65 (55)	− 29
Christ's	17 (6)	55 (44)	− 38
Clare	63 (16)	61 (38)	2
Corpus	30 (10)	76 (29)	− 46
Downing	17 (6)	25 (8)	− 8
Emmanuel	50 (12)	65 (54)	− 15
Jesus	40 (15)	60 (48)	− 20
King's	39 (23)	52 (23)	− 13
Magdalene	13 (8)	36 (25)	− 23
Pembroke	50 (12)	62 (21)	− 12
Peterhouse	62 (13)	50 (38)	12
Queens'	85 (13)	65 (46)	20
Sidney	92 (12)	59 (27)	33
St Catharine's	88 (8)	65 (26)	23
St John's	64 (36)	68 (287)	− 4
Trinity	39 (46)	44 (412)	− 5
Trinity Hall	80 (5)	60 (10)	60
Overall percentage	51 (258)	56 (1,191)	5

Note. I am grateful to Natasha Glaisyer for help in compiling this appendix

BIBLIOGRAPHY

MANUSCRIPTS

British Library, London

Additional MSS

35377: Letters of Philip Yorke

Cambridgeshire County Library, Lion Yard, Cambridge

Cambridgeshire Collection

C.76: Album of photographs of ADC actors
C.76.8: Playbills

Cambridgeshire County Record Office, County Hall, Cambridge

Parish enclosure award maps

St Andrew the Less (1807)
St Andrew the Less, Barnwell (1811)
St Giles (1804)

Cambridge University Library, Cambridge

MSS Additional

6819: Diary of Joseph Romilly, 1837–8
6836: Diary of Joseph Romilly, 1855–6
6840: Diary of Joseph Romilly, 1859–62
7342: Kelvin-Stokes Papers

Bibliography

Cam Collection

Cam.a.500, 5/124: printed petition
Cam.a.789.1: Musical Society at the Black Bear, Programmes
Cam.b.871.1: The ADC and the Tutors
Cam.c.848.47: volume of newscuttings

University Archives

Degr. 9: Joseph Romilly, Graduati Cantabrigienses (1846)
Degr. 10: Henry Luard, Graduati Cantabrigienses (1873)
VCV 41: Diary of William Frere

Emmanuel College Archives, Emmanuel College, Cambridge

2.2.16: Cicero, *De Oratore*, printed, interleaved with notes by William Bennet
2.3.19: Sophocles, *Electra*, printed, with MS notes by William Bennet
3.2.21: William Bennet's Register, vol. 1 (1773)
STE. 1.6: Steward's Accounts 1759–72
FEL. 7.3: List of the Masters and Fellows of Emmanuel College

Pembroke College Archives, Pembroke College, Cambridge

BB.6–9: Order Books 1735–1839
BE.I: Order Book 1839–86

Royal Archives, Windsor

Letters of the Prince Consort as Chancellor of the University [CUL microfilm
    MSS 3547, 3548]

St John's College Archives, St John's College, Cambridge

C3.4: Fellows' Register 1735–75
C3.5: Fellows' Register 1775–1824
C3.6: Fellows' Register 1824–60
C3.7: Fellows' Register 1860–1965
C5.4: Conclusion book 1846–72
D33.10.21: Lists of college suppers for servants, 1864–9
JB 3.1: First Junior Bursar's Account, 1807–29
M.I.3: Abstract letter book of James Wood, 1808–1836

749

Bibliography

TU.1.1.2: Letter book of James Wood 1792–1807
TUI.3.2: Payments to bedmakers and laundresses, 1839–53

Trinity College Archives, Trinity College, Cambridge

MS 0.11.8: Diary of Christopher Wordsworth (October 1793–April 1794)

NEWSPAPERS AND JOURNALS

Cambridge Chronicle
Cambridge Independent Press
Cambridge Intelligencer
Hansard
Illustrated London News
The Times

ACTS OF PARLIAMENT

L. & P. 57 & 58 Vict. c. lx: *Cambridge University and Corporation Act*
L. & P. 19 & 20 Vict. c. 17: *An Act to Confirm an Award for the Settlement of Matters in Difference between the University and Borough of Cambridge*
P.G. 10 Geo. II, c. 19: *An Act for the more Effectual Preventing the Unlawful Playing of Interludes within the Precincts of the Two Universities . . . in England*
P.G. 10 Geo. II c. 28: *An Act for the more Effectual Punishing of Common Players of Interludes*
P.G. 6 & 7 Vict. c. 68: *An Act for Regulating Theatres*
P.G. 19 & 20 Vict. c. 88: *An Act to make further Provision for the Good Government and Extension of the University of Cambridge*
P.G. 21 & 22 Vict. c. 44: *An Act to give to the Universities of Oxford, Cambridge, and Durham, . . ., Power to sell, enfranchise, and exchange Lands . . ., and also to grant Leases*

PARLIAMENTARY PAPERS

PP 1833, HC xxvii (189): *Number of Electors Inrolled in Each County, City, Borough or Place . . . Under 2 William IV, c. 45*
PP 1835, HC viii (547): *Report from Select Committee on Bribery at Elections*
PP 1837–8, HC xliv (329): *A Return . . . from Every County, City and Borough in England and Wales, of the Number of Electors Registered . . . 1836 and 1837*
PP 1840, HC ix (258): *Minutes of Evidence . . . Select Committee on the Cambridge Borough Election Petition*
PP 1843, HC vi (316): *Minutes of Proceedings . . . Select Committee on the Cambridge*

750

Bibliography

Borough Election Petition

PP 1846, HC x (686): *Report of the Select Committee on Legal Education in England and Ireland*

PP 1852–3, HC ix (185): *Minutes of Evidence . . . Select Committee on the Cambridge Borough Election Petition*

PP 1852–3, HC xliv [1559]: *Report of Commissioners Appointed to Inquire into the State, Discipline, Studies, and Revenues of the University and Colleges of Cambridge: Together with the Evidence, and an Appendix (Graham Commission Report and Evidence)*

PP 1861, HC xx [2852]: *Report of the Cambridge University Commissioners*

PP 1873, HC xxxvii (iii) [C.856–II]: *Report of the Commissioners appointed to Inquire into the Property and Income of the Universities of Oxford and Cambridge and of the Colleges and Halls therein [Cleveland Commission], vol. III, Returns from the University of Cambridge, and from the Colleges therein*

BOOKS, ARTICLES, AND ESSAYS

'Account of the Sixth Anniversary Meeting of the Cambridge Camden Society, 8 May 1845', *Ecclesiologist*, 4 (1845), pp. 1–28

Ackermann, James. *A History of the University of Cambridge, Its Colleges, Halls, and Public Buildings* (2 vols., London, 1815)

Akenson, Donald H. 'Pre-University Education, 1782–1870', in W. E. Vaughan, ed., *A New History of Ireland, vol. V, Ireland under the Union, 1801–70*, pp. 523–37

Album of the Cambridge Garrick Club (Cambridge, 1836)

Allen, Peter. *The Cambridge Apostles. The Early Years* (Cambridge University Press, 1978)

Allibone, Jill. *Anthony Salvin. Pioneer of Gothic Revival Architecture, 1799–1881* (Columbia, Mo., University of Missouri Press, 1987)

Altham, H. S., and Swanton, E. W. *A History of Cricket* (fifth edn, 2 vols., London, Allen & Unwin, 1962)

Altholz, Josef L. 'The Warfare of Conscience with Theology', in *The Mind and Art of Victorian England* (Minneapolis, Minn., University of Minnesota Press, 1976), pp. 58–77

Anatomy of a Controversy: The Debate over Essays and Reviews, 1860–64 (Aldershot, Scolar, 1994)

Ambrosoli, Mauro. *John Symonds. Agricoltura e Politica in Corsica e in Italia (1765–1770)* (Turin, Einaudi, 1974)

Anderson, C. Arnold and Schnaper, Miriam. *School and Society in England. Social Backgrounds of Oxford and Cambridge Students* , Annals of American Research (Washington, D.C., Public Affairs Press, 1952)

Bibliography

Anderson, R. D. *Education and Opportunity in Victorian Scotland. Schools and Universities* (Oxford, Clarendon, 1983)

Annan, Noel. *Leslie Stephen. The Godless Victorian* (2nd edn, London, University of Chicago Press, 1986)

Anson, Sir William R., ed. *Autobiography and Political Correspondence of Augustus Henry Third Duke of Grafton* (London, 1898)

Anstruther, Ian. *Oscar Browning. A Biography* (London, John Murray, 1983)

Apology for Christianity, in a Series of Letters Addressed to Edward Gibbon, Esquire, An (Cambridge, 1776)

[Appleyard, E. S.], *Letters from Cambridge* (1828)

Arnold, Reverend F. *Oxford and Cambridge, their Colleges, Memories and Associations* (1873)

Arx, J. P. Von. *Progress and Pessimism: Religion, Politics and History in Late Nineteenth Century Britain* (Cambridge, Mass., Harvard University Press, 1985)

Ashton, Rosemary. *The Life of Samuel Taylor Coleridge* (Oxford, Blackwell, 1996)

Atkinson, Thomas. 'Struggles of a Poor Student Through Cambridge', *London Magazine and Review*, ns, 1 (1825), pp. 491–510

Avis, Paul. *Anglicanism and the Christian Church. Theological Resources in Historical Perspective* (Edinburgh, T. & T. Clark, 1989)

Babbage, Charles. *Passages from the Life of a Philosopher* (London, 1864)

Baker, J. H. *An Introduction to English Legal History* (London, Butterworth, 1971)

Baker, Thomas. *History of the College of St. John the Evangelist, Cambridge*, ed. by J. E. B. Mayor (Cambridge, 1869)

Ball, W. W. Rouse. *Cambridge Notes Chiefly concerning Trinity College and the University* (2nd edn, Cambridge 1923)

   Cambridge Papers (London, Macmillan, 1918)

   History of the First Trinity Boat Club (Cambridge, Bowes and Bowes, 1908)

   A History of the Study of Mathematics at Cambridge (Cambridge, 1889)

Bamford, T. W. *Thomas Arnold* (London, Cresset, 1960)

Banham, Martin, ed. *Plays by Tom Taylor* (Cambridge University Press, 1985)

Barber, Lynn. *The Heyday of Natural History 1820–1870* (London, Jonathan Cape, 1980)

Barker, Edmund Henry. *Parriana: Or Notices of the Rev. Samuel Parr, LL.D . . .* (2 vols., London, 1828)

Barker, Ernest. *Traditions of Civility* (Cambridge University Press, 1948)

Barker, Juliet. *The Brontes* (London, Weidenfeld, 1994)

Bartholomew, Michael. 'The Moral Critique of Christian Orthodoxy', in Gerald Parsons, ed., *Religion in Victorian Britain: II, Controversies* (Manchester University Press, 1988), pp. 174–82

Bayley, C. J. 'University Reform', *Edinburgh Review*, 89 (April, 1849), pp. 499–517

Bebbington, D. W. *Evangelicalism in Modern Britain. A History from the 1730s to the 1980s* (London, Unwin Hyman, 1989)

Becher, Harvey W. 'Voluntary Science in Nineteenth Century Cambridge University to the 1850s', *British Journal for the History of Science*, 19 (1986), pp. 57–87

'William Whewell and Cambridge Mathematics', *Historical Studies in the Physical Sciences* , 11 (1980–1), pp. 1–48

'William Whewell's Odyssey: From Mathematics to Moral Philosophy', in Menachem Fisch and Simon Schaffer, *William Whewell. A Composite Portrait* (Oxford, Clarendon, 1991), pp. 1–29

'William Whewell and the Preservation of a "Liberal Education" in an Age of Challenge', *Rocky Mountain Social Science Journal*, 12 (1975), pp. 59–70

Beckett, J. V. 'Landownership and Estate Management', in G. E. Mingay (ed.), *The Agrarian History of England and Wales, vol. VI, 1750–1850* (Cambridge University Press, 1989), pp. 545–640

Bellot, Hugh Hale. *University College, London, 1826–1926* (University of London Press, 1929)

Bendall, Sarah, Brooke, Christopher, and Collinson, Patrick. *A History of Emmanuel College* (forthcoming)

Bennett, J. R. Sterndale. *Life of William Sterndale Bennett* (Cambridge University Press, 1907)

Besant, Walter. *Autobiography* (London, Hutchinson, 1902)

Best, G. F. A. *Temporal Pillars. Queen Anne's Bounty, the Ecclesiastical Commissioners, and the Church of England* (Cambridge University Press, 1964)

Bicknell, John W. 'Mr Ramsay was Young Once', in Jane Marcus, ed., *Virginia Woolf and Bloomsbury: A Centenary Celebration* (Basingstoke, Macmillan, 1987)

Birch, Thomas. *The Life of Dr John Tillotson* (London, 1752)

Black, Clementina, ed. *The Cumberland Letters* (London, Secker, 1912)

Blake, Henry John Crickitt. *The Cantab, or, A Few Adventures and Misadventures in After Life* (Chichester, 1845)

Boase, Frederic. *Men of the Time* (7 vols., Truro, Netherton and Worth, 1892–1921)

Bolton, Arthur T. *Architectural Education a Century Ago* (London, Sir John Soane Museum, [1930])

Bonney, T. G. *Memories of a Long Life* (Cambridge, Metcalfe, 1921)

[Bonney, T. G.] 'A Septuagenarian's Recollections of St John's', by T. G. B[onney], *The Eagle* , 30 (1909), pp. 304–5

Boswell, James. *Life of Johnson* (Oxford University Press Standard Authors edition, 1953)

Bibliography

Boulger, James D. *Coleridge as Religious Thinker* (New Haven, Conn., Yale University Press, 1961)

Bourne, Kenneth. *Palmerston: The Early Years 1784–1841* (London, Allen Lane, 1982)

Bowles, William Lisle. *Fourteen Sonnets* (1789)

Bradley, James E. 'Religion and Reform at the Polls: Nonconformity in Cambridge Politics, 1774–1784', *Journal of British Studies*, 23, 2 (1984), pp. 55–78

    Religion, Revolution and English Radicalism. Non-Conformity in Eighteenth-Century Politics and Society (Cambridge University Press, 1990)

Brauer, George C. *The Education of a Gentleman. Theories of Gentlemanly Education in England 1660–1775* (New York, Bookman Associates, 1959)

Brent, Richard. *Liberal Anglican Politics. Whiggery, Religion, and Reform 1830–1841* (Oxford, Clarendon, 1987)

Brewer, John. *Party Ideology and Popular Politics at the Accession of George III* (Cambridge University Press, 1976)

    'The Wilkites and the Law, 1763–74: A Study of Radical Notions of Governance', in John Brewer and John Styles, *An Ungovernable People* (London, Hutchinson, 1980), pp. 128–71

Brewer, Sarah, ed. *The Early Letters of Bishop Richard Hurd 1739–1762*, Church of England Record Society 3 (Woodbridge, Boydell, 1995)

Bristed, Charles Astor. *Five Years in an English University* (1st edn, 2 vols., New York, 1852)

    Pieces of a Broken-Down Critic. Picked Up by Himself (4 vols: in 1, Baden-Baden, 1858–9)

    The Upper Ten Thousand: Sketches of American Society (London, 1852)

Brooke, Christopher N. L. *A History of Gonville and Caius College* (Woodbridge, Boydell, 1985)

    A History of the University of Cambridge, vol. IV, 1870–1990 (Cambridge University Press, 1993)

Brooke, Christopher N. L., Highfield, R., and Swaan, W. *Oxford and Cambridge* (Cambridge, 1988)

Brooke, John Hedley. 'Indications of a Creator: Whewell as Apologist and Priest', in Menachem Fisch and Schaffer, Simon, eds., *William Whewell. A Composite Portrait* (Oxford, Clarendon, 1991), pp. 149–73

Brookes, Christopher. *English Cricket. The Game and its Players through the Ages* (London, Weidenfeld & Nicolson, 1978)

Brooks, Peter Newman, ed. *Christian Spirituality. Essays in Honour of Gordon Rupp* (London, SCM, 1973)

Brown, Abner William. *Recollections of the Conversation Parties of the Rev. Charles Simeon* (London, 1863)

Bibliography

Brown, John. *Sixty Years' Gleanings from Life's Harvest. A Genuine Autobiography* (Cambridge, 1858)

Browne, Janet. *Darwin, vol. I, Voyaging* (London, Jonathan Cape, 1995)

Browning, Reed. *The Duke of Newcastle* (New Haven, Conn., Yale University Press, 1975)

Brydges, Sir Samuel Egerton. *Autobiography, Times, Opinions and Contemporaries* (2 vols., London, 1834)

Bullock, F. W. B. *A History of Training for the Ministry of the Church of England . . . 1800 to 1874* (St Leonard's-on-Sea, Budd & Gillatt, 1969)

Burnand, Francis C. *The 'A.D.C.' being Personal Reminiscences of the University Amateur Dramatic Club, Cambridge* (2nd edn London, 1880)

Records and Reminiscences. Personal and General (2 vols., London, Methuen, 1904)

Butler, Joseph. *Works. To which is Prefixed . . . some Account of . . . the Character and Writings of the Author, by Samuel Hallifax* (2 vols., Oxford, 1820)

Bury, J. P. T., ed., *Romilly's Cambridge Diary 1832–42* (Cambridge University Press, 1967)

Bury, M. E. and Pickles, J. D., ed. *Romilly's Cambridge Diary 1842–1847* (Cambridgeshire Record Society, 1994)

Butler, K. T. B. 'A "Petty" Professor of Modern History: William Smyth (1765–1849)', *Cambridge Historical Journal*, 9 (1947–9), pp. 217–38

Cam, Helen. 'John Mortlock III, Master of the Town of Cambridge', *Proceedings of the Cambridge Antiquarian Society*, 40 (1944), pp. 1–12

'*Quo Warranto* proceedings at Cambridge, 1780–1790', *Cambridge Historical Journal*, 8 (1944–46), pp. 145–65

Cambridge Commencement. Grand Musical Festival, 1811 (Cambridge, 1811)

Cambridge Commencement. Grand Musical Festival, 1824 (Cambridge, 1824)

Cambridge Staircase, A (London, 1883)

Cambridge University Calendar for the Year, 1746, 1802, 1803, 1826, 1830, 1850, 1865

Cannadine, David. *G. M. Trevelyan. A Life in History* (London, Harper Collins, 1992)

Cannell, D. M. *George Green, Mathematician and Physicist, 1793–1841: The background to his Life and Work* (London, Athlone, 1993)

Cannon, John. *Aristocratic Century. The Peerage of Eighteenth-Century England* (Cambridge University Press, 1984)

Cantor, Geoffrey. 'Between Rationalism and Romanticism: Whewell's Historiography of the Inductive Sciences', in Menachem Fisch and Simon Schaffer, *William Whewell. A Composite Portrait* (Oxford, Clarendon, 1991), pp. 67–86

Carlyle, Alexander. *Autobiography* (3rd edn, Edinburgh, 1861)

Bibliography

Carlyle, Thomas. *Life of John Sterling* (1851)

Carpenter, Edward. *Thomas Sherlock 1678–1761* (London, SPCK, 1936)

Carus, William. *Memoirs of the Life of Charles Simeon* (London, 1847)

Chadwick, Owen. 'Charles Kingsley at Cambridge', in *The Spirit of the Oxford Movement: Tractarian Essays* (Cambridge University Press, 1990), pp. 104–34

    The Spirit of the Oxford Movement (Cambridge University Press, 1990)

Chadwick, Owen. *The Victorian Church*, Part 1 (London, A. and C. Black, 1966)

Chandler, Michael. *Life and Work of John Mason Neale* (Leominster, Gracewing, 1995)

Chandos, John. *Boys Together. English Public Schools 1800–1864* (London, Hutchinson, 1984)

Chitty, Susan. *The Beast and the Monk. A Life of Charles Kingsley* (London, Hodder & Stoughton, 1974)

Christian Kalendar for the Use of Members of the Established Church Arranged for the Year of Our Lord God MDCCCXLV, A, 'by a Lay member of the Cambridge Camden Society' [S. N. Stokes] (Cambridge, 1845)

Christie, Ian R. *Wilkes, Wyvill and Reform. The Parliamentary Reform Movement in British Politics 1760–1785* (London, Macmillan, 1962)

Clark, J. C. D. *English Society 1688–1832: Ideology, Social Structure and Political Practice during the Ancien Régime* (Cambridge University Press, 1985)

Clark, J. W., and Gray, A. *Old Plans of Cambridge* (2 parts, Cambridge, Bowes and Bowes, 1921)

Clark, John Willis and Hughes, Thomas McKenny. *The Life and Letters of the Reverend Adam Sedgwick* (2 vols., Cambridge University Press, 1890)

Clark, W. G. 'Cambridge Life according to C. A. Bristed', *Fraser's Magazine* , 49 (1854), pp. 89–100

Clark-Kennedy, A. E. *Stephen Hales, D.D., F.R.S., An Eighteenth-Century Biography* (Cambridge University Press, 1929)

Clarke, M. L. *Paley. Evidences for the Man* (London, SPCK, 1974)

Clay, Christopher. 'Landlords and Estate Management in England', in Joan Thirsk, ed., *The Agrarian History of England and Wales, vol. V, 1640–1750, Part 2, Agrarian Change* (Cambridge University Press, 1985)

Clive, John. *Thomas Babington Macaulay. The Shaping of the Historian* (London, Secker & Warburg, 1973)

Cole, G. A. 'Doctrine, Dissent and the Decline of Paley's Reputation, 1805–1825', *Enlightenment and Dissent*, 6 (1987), pp. 19–30

Coleman, John. *Players and Playwrights I Have Known* (2 vols., London, 1890)

Coleridge, S. T. *The Constitution of the Church and State* (1829)

Colley, Linda. *In Defiance of Oligarchy: The Tory Party 1714–60* (Cambridge

University Press, 1982)

Colvin, H. M. *A Biographical Dictionary of British Architects 1600–1840* (London, John Murray, 1978)

Complete Oarsman, The (London, Methuen, 1908)

Conington, John. 'The English Universities', *North British Review*, 14 (November 1850), pp. 169–201

Consideration of Some Recent Strictures on Paley's Evidences of Christianity, A (Cambridge, 1898)

Cooper, Arthur Nevile. *Quaint Talks about Long Walks* (London, 1904)

Cooper, C. H. *Annals of Cambridge*, vol. IV (Cambridge, 1853); vol. V (Cambridge, 1908)

Costello, W. T. *The Scholastic Curriculum at Early Seventeenth-Century Cambridge* (Cambridge, Mass., Harvard University Press, 1958)

Country Parson's Advice (1860)

Cox, George W. *The Life of John William Colenso, D.D., Bishop of Natal* (2 vols., London, 1888)

Cradock, Percy, Wilson Harris, H., McNair, Arnold, *et al.*, *Recollections of the Cambridge Union 1815–1939* (Cambridge, Bowes and Bowes, 1953)

Craig, F. W. S. *British Parliamentary Election Results 1832–1885* (London, Macmillan, 1977)

Crawley, C. W. *Trinity Hall. The History of a Cambridge College 1450–1975* (Cambridge, Trinity Hall, 1976)

Craze, Michael. *History of Felsted School* (Ipswich, Cowell, 1955)

'Critical Notice: William Smyth, *Lectures on Modern History*', *Christian Examiner and General Review*, 29 (1840–1), pp. 366–73

Croker, J. W. *Correspondence and Diaries* (3 vols., London, 1884)

Crook, Alec C. *From the Foundation to Gilbert Scott. A History of the Buildings of St. John's College, Cambridge* (Cambridge, St John's College, 1980)

Crook, J. Mordaunt. *The Greek Revival. Neo-Classical Attitudes in British Architecture 1760–1870* (London, John Murray, 1972)

Croome, A. C. M., ed. *Fifty Years of Sport: Oxford and Cambridge* (2 vols., London, Southwood, 1913)

Crowther, J. G. *British Scientists of the Nineteenth Century* (London, Kegan Paul, 1935)

Cumberland, Richard. *Memoirs* (2 vols., London, 1807)

Memoirs, edited by Henry Flanders (1856)

Cunich, Peter, Hoyle, David, Duffy, Eamon, and Hyam, Ronald. *A History of Magdalene College Cambridge 1428–1988* (Cambridge, Magdalene College, 1994)

Cunningham, Colin and Waterhouse, Prudence. *Alfred Waterhouse 1830–1905* .

Bibliography

Biography of a Practice (Oxford, Clarendon, 1992)

Curtis, Mark. *Oxford and Cambridge in Transition 1558–1642* (Oxford, Clarendon Press, 1959)

Darwin, Charles. *On the Origin of Species by Means of Natural Selection*, World's Classics Edition (Oxford University Press, 1929)

Darwin, Charles, and Huxley, T. H. *Autobiographies*, ed. Gavin de Beer (Oxford University Press, 1974)

Darwin, F. and Seward, A. C. *More Letters of Charles Darwin* (2 vols., London, 1903)

Davie, George Elder. *The Democratic Intellect. Scotland and Her Universities in the Nineteenth Century* (Edinburgh University Press, 1961)

Davies, Richard. *The General State of Education in the Universities with a Particular View to the Philosophical and Medical Education* (1759)

Defoe, Daniel. *A Tour Through England and Wales* (1724), Everyman's Library (2 vols., London, Dent, 1928)

Dening, Greg. *History's Anthropology: The Death of William Gooch*, Association for Social Anthropology in Oceania, Special Publications no. 2 (Lanham, Md., University Press of America, 1988)

De Morgan, A. *A Budget of Paradoxes* (London, 1872)

De Quincey, Thomas. *Recollections of the Lakes and the Lake Poets*, ed. David Wright (Harmondsworth, Penguin, 1986)

De Selincourt, Ernest and Shaver, Chester L., eds. *The Letters of William and Dorothy Wordsworth: Vol. I, The Early Years 1787–1805* (2nd edn, Oxford University Press, 1967)

Desmond, Adrian, and Moore, James. *Darwin* (London, Michael Joseph, 1991)

Diamond, Alan, ed. *The Victorian Achievement of Sir Henry Maine: A Centennial Reappraisal* (Cambridge University Press, 1991)

Dickinson, H. T. *Britain and the French Revolution, 1789–1815* (London, Macmillan, 1989)

　Liberty and Property. Political Ideology in Eighteenth-Century Britain (London, Weidenfeld, 1977)

Dictionary of American Biography (20 vols., Oxford University Press, 1928–36)

Dictionary of Australian Biography (12 vols., Melbourne University Press, 1966–90)

Dictionary of National Biography (63 vols., London, 1885–1900); *First Supplement* (3 vols., London, 1901); *Second Supplement* (3 vols., London, 1912)

Dictionary of National Biography. Missing Persons, ed. C. S. Nicholls (Oxford University Press, 1993)

Dictionary of Scientific Biography (18 vols., New York, N.Y.: Scribner, 1970–92)

Disney, John, ed. *The Works of John Jebb ... with Memoirs of the Life of the Author* (3 vols., London, 1787)

Distad, N. Merrill. *Guessing at Truth. The Life of Julius Charles Hare* (Shepherdstown, W. Va., Patmos, 1979), pp. 3–34

Dodd, Christopher. *The Oxford & Cambridge Boat Race* (London, Stanley Paul, 1983)

'Rowing', in Tony Mason, ed., *Sport in Britain. A Social History* (Cambridge University Press, 1989), pp. 276–307

Doolittle, I. G. 'College Administration', in L. S. Sutherland and L. G. Mitchell, eds., *The History of the University of Oxford, vol. V, The Eighteenth Century* (Oxford, Clarendon, 1986), pp. 227–68

Downes, Kerry. *Hawksmoor* (2nd edn, London, Zwemmer, 1979)

Dozier, Robert R. *For King, Constitution, and Country. The English Loyalists and the French Revolution* (Lexington, Ky., University Press of Kentucky, 1983)

Dunbabin, J. P. 'College Estates and Wealth 1660–1815', in L. S. Sutherland and L. G. Mitchell (eds.), *The History of the University of Oxford, vol. V, The Eighteenth Century* (Oxford, Clarendon, 1986), pp. 269–301

Dunbabin, J. P. 'Oxford and Cambridge College Finances, 1871–1913', *Economic History Review*, 2nd series, 28, 4 (November 1975), pp. 631–47

Dyce, Alexander, ed. *Recollections of the Table-talk of Samuel Rogers* (New Southgate, 1887)

Dyer, George. *Memoirs of the Life and Writings of Robert Robinson, Late Minister of the Dissenting Congregation, in St Andrew's Parish, Cambridge* (London, 1796)

Privileges of the University of Cambridge; together with Additional Observations (2 vols., London, 1824)

'E.B.C.' *Victoria and Albert at Cambridge. The Royal Visits of 1843 and 1847 as they were recorded by Joseph Romilly, Registrary of the University* (Cambridge University Library, 1977)

Ehrman, John. *The Younger Pitt. The Years of Acclaim* (London, Constable, 1969)

Eliot, George. *Scenes of Clerical Life* (1858)

Adam Bede (1859)

Elliott, Clark A. *Biographical Dictionary of American Science: The Seventeenth through the Nineteenth Centuries* (London, Greenwood, 1979)

Empson, William and Newman, Francis W. 'Academical Test Articles', *Edinburgh Review*, 88 (July, 1848), pp. 163–93

Engel, A. J. *From Clergyman to Don. The Rise of the Academic Profession in Nineteenth-Century Oxford* (Oxford, Clarendon, 1983)

Essays and Tales by John Sterling (2 vols., London, 1848)

Everett, William. *On the Cam. Lectures on the University of Cambridge in England* (London, 1866)

Fairbairn, Steve. *Fairbairn of Jesus* (London, John Lane, 1931)

Farmer, Richard. *Essay on the Learning of Shakespeare* (1767)

Farren, Robert. *Cambridge and its Neighbourhood* (Cambridge, Macmillan, 1881)

Fasciculus Ioanni Willis Clark dicatus (Cambridge University Press, 1909)

759

Bibliography

Fauvel, John, Flood, Raymond, Shortland, Michael, and Wilson, Robin, eds. *Let Newton Be!* (Oxford University Press, 1988)

Fawcett, Henry. 'On the Exclusion of Those who are not Members of the Established Church from Fellowships and Other Privileges of the English Universities', *Macmillan's Magazine*, 3 (1860–1), pp. 411–16

Feingold, Mordechai. *The Mathematicians' Apprenticeship. Science, Universities and Society in England, 1560–1640* (Cambridge University Press, 1984)

Feingold, Mordechai, ed. *Before Newton. The Life and Times of Isaac Barrow* (Cambridge University Press, 1990)

Fenwick, Gillian. *Leslie Stephen's Life in Letters. A Bibliographical Study* (Aldershot, Scolar, 1993)

Ferguson, J. P. *An Eighteenth Century Heretic. Dr. Samuel Clarke* (Kineton, War., Roundwood, 1976)

Fink, Z. S. *The Early Wordsworthian Milieu* (Oxford University Press, 1958)

Fisch, Menachem and Schaffer, Simon, eds. *William Whewell. A Composite Portrait* (Oxford, Clarendon, 1991)

Forbes, Duncan. *The Liberal Anglican Idea of History* (Cambridge University Press, 1952)

Force, James E. *William Whiston: Honest Newtonian* (Cambridge University Press, 1985)

Ford, W. J. 'Cambridge University Cricket', in K. S. Ranjitsinhji, *The Jubilee Book of Cricket* (Edinburgh, 1897), pp. 338–65

A History of the Cambridge University Cricket Club 1820–1901 (Edinburgh, Blackwood, 1902)

Forman, P, Heilbron, J. L., and Weart, S. 'Physics *circa* 1900: Personnel, Funding and Productivity of the Academic Establishments', *Historical Studies in the Physical Sciences*, 5 (1975), pp. 1–185

Forster, R. H., Harris, W., Stammers, A. D., and Day, G. L. *History of the Lady Margaret Boat Club, St John's College, Cambridge, 1825–1926* (Cambridge, Johnian Society, 1926)

Fowler, J. T. *Life and Letters of John Bacchus Dykes* (London, 1897)

Fowler, Laurence and Fowler, Helen. *Cambridge Commemorated. An Anthology of University Life* (Cambridge University Press, 1984)

French, Stanley. *Aspects of Downing History*, vol. II (Cambridge, Downing College Association, 1989)

The History of Downing College (Cambridge, Downing College Association, 1978)

Frend, William. *An Address to the Inhabitants of Cambridge and its Neighbourhood, Exhorting Them to Turn from the False Worship of Three Persons to the Worship of The One True God* (St Ives, Hunts., 1788)

Peace and Union Recommended to the Associated Bodies of Republicans and

Bibliography

Anti-Republicans (St Ives, Hunts., 1793)

Thoughts on Subscription to Religious Tests, and a Letter to the Rev H. W. Coulthurst (St Ives, Hunts., 1788)

Friedman, Terry. *James Gibbs* (New Haven, Conn., Yale University Press, 1984)

Frothingham, Paul Revere. *Edward Everett. Orator and Statesman* (Port Washington, N.Y., Kennikat Press, 1971, repr. of 1925 edn)

Froude, J. A. *Thomas Carlyle. A History of the First Forty Years of His Life, 1795–1835* (new edn, 2 vols., London, 1895)

Galton, Francis. *Memories of My Life* (London, Methuen, 1908)

Gascoigne, John. 'Anglican Latitudinarianism and Political Radicalism in the Late Eighteenth Century', *History*, 71 (1986), pp. 22–38

Cambridge in the Age of the Enlightenment. Science, Religion and Politics from the Restoration to the French Revolution (Cambridge University Press, 1989)

'Church and State Allied: The Failure of Parliamentary Reform of the Universities, 1688–1800', in L. Beier, D. Cannadine, and J. Rosenheim, eds., *The First Modern Society: Essays in English History in Honour of Lawrence Stone* (Cambridge University Press, 1989), pp. 401–29

'Mathematics and Meritocracy: The Emergence of the Cambridge Mathematical Tripos', *Social Studies of Science*, 14 (1984), pp. 547–84

'Politics, Patronage and Newtonianism: The Cambridge Example', *Historical Journal*, 27, 1 (1984), pp. 1–24

'The Universities and the Scientific Revolution: The Case of Newton and Restoration Cambridge', *History of Science*, 23 (1985) pp. 391–434

Gash, Norman. *Mr Secretary Peel* (London, Longmans, 1961)

Sir Robert Peel (London, Longmans, 1972)

Gazeley, John G. *The Life of Arthur Young 1741–1820* (Philadelphia, Pa., American Philosophical Society, 1973)

Geyer-Kordesch, Johanna, Weatherall, Mark, and Kaminga, Harmke. *The History of Medicine in Cambridge: Education, Science and the Healing Arts* (Cambridge, School of Clinical Medicine, 1990)

Gibbon, Edward. *Autobiography*, World's Classics Edition (Oxford University Press, 1907)

Gill, Stephen. *William Wordsworth. A Life* (Oxford University Press, 1989)

Gillispie, Charles Coulston, *Genesis and Geology* (Cambridge, Mass: Harvard University Press, 1951)

Girouard, Mark. *Life in the English Country House. A Social and Architectural History* (New Haven, Yale University Press, 1978)

Glover, William. *The Memoirs of a Cambridge Chorister* (2 vols., London 1885)

Goldman, Lawrence, ed. *The Blind Victorian. Henry Fawcett and British Liberalism* (Cambridge University Press, 1989)

Grattan-Guiness, I. 'Mathematics and Mathematical Physics from Cambridge,

1815–40: A Survey of the Achievements and of the French Influences', in P. M. Harman, ed., *Wranglers and Physicists: Studies on Cambridge Physics in the Nineteenth Century* (Manchester University Press, 1985), pp. 84–111

Gray, Arthur and Brittain, Frederick. *A History of Jesus College, Cambridge* (London, Heinemann, 1960)

Green, George. *An Essay on the Application of Mathematical Analysis to the Theories of Electricity and Magnetism* (Nottingham, 1828)

Green, V. H. H. 'The University and Social Life', in L. S. Sutherland and L. G. Mitchell, eds., *The History of the University of Oxford, vol. V, The Eighteenth Century*, (Oxford, Clarendon, 1986), pp. 309–58

  The Young Mr Wesley. A Study of John Wesley and Oxford (London, Arnold, 1961)

Greene, Mott T. *Geology in the Nineteenth Century. Changing Views of a Changing World* (Ithaca, N.Y., Cornell University Press, 1982)

Grice, Elizabeth. *Rogues and Vagabonds or the Actors' Road to Respectability* (Lavenham, Suffolk, Dalton, 1977)

Gross, E. J. *Chronicle of the College Estates*: Part 2 of John Venn, E. S. Roberts, and E. J. Gross, *Biographical History of Gonville and Caius College*, vol. IV (Cambridge University Press, 1912)

Grosskurth, Phyllis. *John Addington Symonds* (London, Longmans, 1964)

Guerrini, Anita. 'The Tory Newtonians: Gregory, Pitcairne, and Their Circle', *Journal of British Studies*, 25 (1986), pp. 288–311

Gunning, Henry. *Ceremonies Observed in the Senate House of the University of Cambridge* (Cambridge, 1828)

  Reminiscences of the University, Town and County of Cambridge from the Year 1780 (2 vols., London and Cambridge, 1854)

Hall, Harry T. *The Cambridge Dramatic Album* (Cambridge, 1868)

Hallifax, Samuel. *A Sermon Preached before the ... House of Commons ... on Monday, January 30, 1769; Appointed to be Observed as the Martyrdom of King Charles I* (Cambridge, 1769)

  Three Sermons Preached before the University of Cambridge, Occasioned by an Attempt to Abolish Subscription to the XXXIX Articles of Religion (Cambridge, 1772)

Hamilton, William. 'On the State of the English Universities, with More Especial Reference to Oxford' (June, 1831), pp. 386–7, reprinted in William Hamilton, *Discussions on Philosophy and Literature, Education and University Reform* (London, 1852), pp. 386–434

Hanham, H. J. *Elections and Party Management: Politics in the Time of Disraeli and Gladstone* (London, Longmans, 1959).

Hans, N. *New Trends in Education in the Eighteenth Century* (London, Routledge, 1951)

Bibliography

Hare, Augustus J. C. *Memorials of a Quiet Life* (2 vols., London, 1872)
 The Story of My Life (6 vols., London, 1896–1900)
Hare, Julius Charles. *Charges to the Clergy of the Archdeaconry of Lewes . . . from the year 1840 to 1854* (3 vols., Cambridge, 1856)
 Miscellaneous Pamphlets (Cambridge, 1855)
 The Mission of the Comforter (2 vols., London, 1846)
 Sermons Preacht on Particular Occasions (Cambridge, 1858)
 'Sketch of the Author's Life', in *Essays and Tales by John Sterling* (2 vols., London, 1848)
 The Victory of Faith and Other Sermons (Cambridge, 1840)
 Vindication of Luther Against His Recent English Assailants (Cambridge, Macmillan, 1855)
Hare, Julius Charles and Hare, Augustus W. *Guesses at Truth by Two Brothers* (2nd edn, first series, London, 1838; rev. edn, London, 1866)
Hargreaves-Mawdsley, W. N., ed. *Woodforde at Oxford 1759–1776* (Oxford Historical Society, NS, 21, 1969)
Harman, P. M., ed. *Wranglers and Physicists: Studies on Cambridge Physics in the Nineteenth Century* (Manchester University Press, 1985)
Hawke, Martin Bladen. *Recollections and Reminiscences* (London, Williams & Norgate, 1924)
Hazlitt, William. 'Mr Coleridge', in *The Spirit of the Age*, first published 1825 (Oxford University Press, World's Classics edn, 1904), pp. 35–47
Hearnshaw, F. J. C. *The Centenary History of King's College London 1828–1928* (London, Harrap, 1929)
Heitland, W. E. *After Many Years* (Cambridge University Press, 1926)
Heitzenrater, Richard P., ed. *Diary of an Oxford Methodist, Benjamin Ingham, 1733–1734* (Durham, N.C., Duke University Press, 1985)
Henriques, Ursula. *Religious Toleration in England 1787–1833* (London, Routledge, 1961)
Hervey, Thomas. *Life of the Rev. Samuel Settle* (Colmer, Hants., 1881)
Hilken, T. J. N. *Engineering at Cambridge University 1783–1965* (Cambridge University Press, 1967)
Historical Account of Stourbridge, Bury and the Most Famous Fairs in Europe and America, An (1773)
Hodgson, Francis. *Leaves of Laurel* (1812)
Hogg, Thomas Jefferson. 'The Universities of Oxford and Cambridge', *Westminster Review*, 15 (July, 1831), pp. 56–69
Hole, Robert. *Pulpits, Politics and Public Order in England 1760–1832* (Cambridge University Press, 1989)
Holmes, Geoffrey. *The Making of a Great Power. Late Stuart and Early Georgian Britain 1660–1722* (London, Longmans, 1993)

Bibliography

Holmes, Geoffrey and Szechi, Daniel. *The Age of Oligarchy. Pre-industrial Britain 1722–1783* (London, Longmans, 1993)

Holmes, Richard. *Coleridge: Early Visions* (London, Hodder & Stoughton, 1989)

Holroyd, M., ed. *Memorials of G. E. Corrie* (Cambridge, 1890)

Holt, Richard. *Sport and the British. A Modern History* (Oxford, Clarendon, 1989)

Holtby, Robert T. *Daniel Waterland 1683–1740. A Study in Eighteenth Century Orthodoxy* (Carlisle, Thurman, 1966)

Home, Henry, Lord Kames. *Elements of Criticism in Three Volumes* (1762)

Hopkins, Hugh Evan. *Charles Simeon of. Cambridge* (London, Hodder & Stoughton, 1977)

Hopkins, William. *Remarks on the Mathematical Teaching of the University of Cambridge* (Cambridge, c. 1854)

Hort, A. F. *Life and Letters of Fenton John Anthony Hort* (2 vols., London, 1896)

Houston, R. A. *Scottish Literacy and the Scottish Identity. Illiteracy and Society in Scotland and Northern England, 1600–1800* (Cambridge University Press, 1985)

Howard, H. F. *An Account of the Finances of The College of St. John the Evangelist in the University of Cambridge 1511–1926* (Cambridge University Press, 1926)

Huber, V. A. *The English Universities*, an abridged translation by F. W. Newman (3 vols., London, 1843)

Huch, Ronald K. *The Radical Lord Radnor: The Public Life of Viscount Folkestone, Third Earl of Radnor (1779–1869)* (Minneapolis, Minn., University of Minnesota Press, 1977)

Hughes, Graham W. *With Freedom Fired: The Story of Robert Robinson, Nonconformist* (London, Carey Kingsgate Press, 1955)

Hughes, T. S. *Discourses by William Samuel Powell D.D. and James Fawcett B.D., with Some Account of their Lives* (London, 1832)

Hyman, Anthony. *Charles Babbage. Pioneer of the Computer* (Oxford University Press, 1982)

Irving, Washington. *The Sketch Book of Geoffrey Crayon, Gent.* (1819–20)

Jackson, N. L. *Association Football* (London, 1899)

Jacob, Margaret C. *The Newtonians and the English Revolution 1689–1702* (Sussex, Harvester, 1976)

James, Montagu Rhodes. *The Western Manuscripts in the Library of Emmanuel College* (Cambridge University Press, 1904)

James, Robert Rhodes. *Albert, Prince Consort* (London, Hamish Hamilton, 1983)

J. C. T[hring]. *Rules of Football: The Winter Game* (London, 1862)

Jerram, James, ed. *The Memoirs and a Selection from the Letters of the Rev. Charles Jerram* (London, 1855)

'John Smith (of Smith Hall)' [John Delaware Lewis], *Sketches of Cantabs* (London, 1849)

Bibliography

Jones, W. H. S. *A History of St. Catharine's College once Catharine Hall Cambridge* (Cambridge University Press, 1936)

Jowett, Benjamin. *The Epistles of St. Paul to the Thessalonians, Galatians and Romans. With Critical Notes and Dissertations* (2 vols., London, 1855)

Joyce, Thomas. 'College Life at Cambridge', *Westminster Review*, 35 (April, 1841), pp. 456–81

J. R. J[ackson] 'The First Athletic Sports in Cambridge', *The Eagle*, 16 (1891), pp. 358–61

Kelly, Thomas. *A History of Public Libraries in Great Britain 1845–1965* (London, The Library Association, 1973)

Kelty, Mary Ann. *Reminiscences of Thought and Feeling* (London, 1852)
Visiting My Relations, and its Results; A Series of Small Episodes in the Life of a Recluse (London, 1851)

Kemble, J. M. 'British and Foreign Universities: Cambridge', *British and Foreign Review*, 5 (July, 1837), pp. 179–181

Ker, Ian. *John Henry Newman. A Biography* (Oxford, Clarendon, 1988)

Ketton-Cremer, R. W. *Horace Walpole* (3rd edn, London, Methuen, 1964)

Keynes, Florence Ada. *By-Ways of Cambridge History*, (2nd edn, Cambridge, Heffer, 1956)

Keynes, Margaret Elizabeth *A House by the River. Newnham Grange to Darwin College* (Cambridge, Darwin College, 1976)

King, Elizabeth. *Lord Kelvin's Early Home* (London, 1909)

Kingsley, Charles. *Alton Locke. Tailor and Poet* (1st edn., 2 vols., London, 1850)
The Roman and the Teuton (new edn, London, 1875)
Three Lectures . . . on the Ancien Régime as it Existed on the Continent before the French Revolution (London, 1867)
Two Years Ago (Cambridge, 1857)

Kingsley, Frances Eliza, ed. *Charles Kingsley. His Letters and Memories of His Life* (2 vols., London, 1877)
ed. *Charles Kingsley* (abridged one-volume edn, 1883)

Kirke-White, Henry. *Remains*, (rev. edn, Cambridge, 1839)

Knight, Frida. *Cambridge Music from the Middle Ages to Modern Times* (Cambridge, Oleander, 1980)
University Rebel. The Life of William Frend (1757–1841) (London, Gollancz, 1971)

Langdon-Brown, Walter. *Some Chapters in Cambridge Medical History* (Cambridge University Press, 1946)

Langford, Paul. 'Old Whigs, Old Tories and the American Revolution', in P. Marshall and G. Williams, eds., *The British Atlantic Empire before the American Revolution* (London, Frank Cass, 1980), pp. 106–30

Larmor, Joseph. 'Obituary of Lord Kelvin', *Proceedings of the Royal Society of London*, Series A, 81 (1908), pp. iii–lxxvi

Bibliography

Latham, H. 'University Expences', in *The Student's Guide* (1862), pp. 50–66

Lawlor, Edwina G. *David Friedrich Strauss and His Critics* (New York, Peter Lang, 1986)

Leader, Damian Riehl. *A History of the University of Cambridge: Volume I, The University to 1546* (Cambridge University Press, 1988)

Lees-Milne, James. *The Age of Adam* (London, Batsford, 1947)

Lehmann, John. *Ancestors and Friends* (London, Eyre & Spottiswoode, 1962)
   The Whispering Gallery (London, Longmans, 1955)

Lehmann, Rosamond. *The Swan in the Evening. Fragments of an Inner Life* (London, Collins, 1967)

Lehmann, Rudolph Chambers. *The Complete Oarsman* (London, Methuen, 1908)
   Harry Fludyer at Cambridge and Conversational Hints for Young Shooters (London, Chatto and Windus, 1904)
   Memories of Half a Century (London, Smith Elder, 1908)
   'Style and the Oar', *Selected Verse* (London, Blackwood, 1929), pp. 76–7

Lehmann, R. C., Nickalls, Guy, Davis, G. L., *et al. Rowing*, Isthmian Library, no. 4 (London, 1898)

Le Keux, J. *Memorials of Cambridge: A Series of Views of the Colleges, Halls and Public Buildings* (2 vols., London, 1841–2)

Le Mahieu, D. L. *The Mind of William Paley. A Philosopher and his Age* (Lincoln, Nebr., University of Nebraska Press, 1976)

Le Neve, J. *Fasti ecclesiae Anglicanae, 1541–1857*, compiled by Joyce M. Horn, David M. Smith, and Derrick S. Bailey (8 vols., London, Institute of Historical Research, 1969–96)

Leslie, George Dunlop. *Our River* (London, 1881)

Lewis, Georgina King. *John Stoughton D.D. A Short Record of a Long Life* (London, 1898)

Lewis, Wilmarth Sheldon, ed. *The Correspondence of Horace Walpole* (48 vols., New Haven, Conn., Yale University Press, 1937–83)

Lincoln, Anthony. *Some Political & Social Ideas of English Dissent 1763–1800* (Cambridge University Press, 1938)

Liscombe, R. W. *William Wilkins 1778–1839* (Cambridge University Press, 1980)

Little, Bryan. 'Cambridge and the Campus. An English Antecedent for the Lawn of the University of Virginia', *Virginia Magazine of History and Biography*, 79 (1971), pp. 190–201

Litvack, Leon. *John Mason Neale and the Quest for Sobornost* (Oxford, Clarendon, 1994)

Loane, Marcus. *Cambridge and the Evangelical Succession* (London, Lutterworth, 1952)

Lobel, M. D. and Johns, W. H., eds. *Atlas of Historic Towns*, vol. II (London, Scolar, 1975)

Bibliography

Lockhart, J. G. *Life of Sir Walter Scott* (10 vols., Edinburgh, 1882 edn)

Lonsdale, Roger. *Charles Burney. A Literary Biography* (Oxford University Press, 1965)

Lough, A. G. *John Mason Neale – Priest Extraordinary* (Newton Abbot, A. G. Lough, 1975)

Lukis, W. C., ed. *The Family Memoirs of the Reverend William Stukeley, M.D. and the Antiquarian and other Correspondence of William Stukeley, Roger & Samuel Gale, etc.* (Surtees Society Publications, vols. 73, 76, 80, 1882–7; vol. 73, (1882)

Lyell, Charles. 'State of the Universities', *Quarterly Review*, 36 (June 1827), pp. 221–37

Travels in North America (2 vols., London, 1845)

Macaulay, James. *The Gothic Revival 1745–1845* (Glasgow, Blackie, 1975)

Mackerness, E. D. *A Social History of Music* (London, Routledge, 1964)

McKitterick, David. *Cambridge University Library. A History: The Eighteenth and Nineteenth Centuries* (Cambridge University Press, 1986)

McLelland, Vincent Alan. *English Roman Catholics and Higher Education* (Oxford, Clarendon, 1973)

Macleod, Roy and Moseley, Russell. 'Breaking the Circle of the Sciences: The Natural Sciences Tripos and the "Examination Revolution"', in Roy Macleod, ed., *Days of Judgement. Science, Examinations and the Organization of Knowledge in Late Victorian England* (Driffield, N. Humberside, Nafferton Books, 1982), pp. 189–212

McWilliam, Colin. *Lothian* (Harmondsworth, Penguin, Buildings of Scotland series, 1978)

Maitland, Frederick William. *The Life and Letters of Leslie Stephen* (London, Duckworth, 1906)

Township and Borough (Cambridge University Press, 1898)

Malcolmson, Robert W. *Popular Recreations in English Society 1700–1850* (Cambridge University Press, 1973)

Manchester, A. H. *A Modern Legal History of England and Wales, 1750–1950* (London, Butterworth, 1980)

Mangan, J. A. *Athleticism in the Victorian and Edwardian Public School: The Emergence and Consolidation of an Educational Ideology* (Cambridge University Press, 1981)

'Oars and the Man. Pleasure and Purpose in Victorian and Edwardian Cambridge', *British Journal of Sports History*, 1 (1984), pp. 245–71

Martin, Robert Bernard. *The Dust of Combat. A Life of Charles Kingsley* (London, Faber, 1959)

Martin, Theodore. *The Life of His Royal Highness the Prince Consort*, 5th edn (5 vols., London, 1875–80)

Bibliography

Mason, Tony, ed. *Sport in Britain. A Social History* (Cambridge University Press, 1989)

Masson, David, ed. *Collected Writings of Thomas de Quincey* (Edinburgh, 1889–90)

Mathew, W. M. 'The Origins and Occupations of Glasgow Students, 1740–1839', *Past and Present*, 33 (April, 1966), pp. 74–94

Maurice, F. D. 'Introduction', in Julius Charles Hare, *Charges to the Clergy of the Archdeaconry of Lewes . . . from the Year 1840 to 1854* (3 vols., Cambridge, 1856), vol. 1

Mayor, J. E. B., ed. *Cambridge under Queen Anne* (Cambridge, 1911)

Mayor, J. E. B., ed. *History of the College of St. John . . . by Thomas Baker* (2 vols., Cambridge, 1869)

Meadley, George Wilson. *Memoirs of William Paley* (1st ed. Sunderland, 1809; 2nd edn Edinburgh, 1810)

Memoirs of the Life and Writings of Mr William Whiston (1st edn, London, 1749)

Memoirs of the Life of Dr Trusler (Bath, 1806)

Merivale, Judith Anne, ed. *Autobiography of Dean Merivale with selections from his Correspondence* (London, 1899)

Middleton, Conyers. *A Letter to Dr. Waterland, containing some Remarks on his 'Vindication of Scripture'* (London, 1731)

Middleton, Richard. 'The Duke of Newcastle and the Conduct of Patronage during the Seven Years War, 1757–1762', *British Journal for Eighteenth-Century Studies*, 12 (1989), pp. 174–86

Mildert, William van. *A Review of the Author's Life and Writings*, in *The Works of the Rev. Daniel Waterland* (10 vols., Oxford, 1823)

Miller, Edward. *Portrait of a College. A History of the College of Saint John the Evangelist Cambridge* (Cambridge University Press, 1961)

Mills, W. H. 'Schools of Chemistry in Great Britain and Ireland, 6: The University of Cambridge', *Journal of the Royal Institute of Chemistry*, 77 (1953), pp. 423–31, 467–73

Milner, Mary. *The Life of Isaac Milner, D.D., Comprising a Portion of his Correspondence . . . hitherto Unpublished* (London, 1842)

Mingay, G. E., ed. *The Agrarian History of England and Wales, vol. VI. 1750–1850* (Cambridge University Press, 1989)

Mitchell, Jeremy C. and Cornford, James. 'The Political Demography of Cambridge, 1832–1868', *Albion*, 9 (1977), pp. 242–72

Monk, John Henry. *The Life of Richard Bentley, D.D.* (2 vols., London, 1833)

Moody, T. W. and Beckett, J. C. *Queen's, Belfast 1845–1949. The History of a University* (2 vols., London, Faber, 1959)

Moore, David Cresap. *The Politics of Deference* (Hassocks, Sussex, Harvester, 1976)

Moorman, Mary. *William Wordsworth. The Early Years 1770–1803* (corrected 1st edn Oxford University Press, 1965)

Bibliography

William Wordsworth. A Biography. The Later Years 1803–1850 (Oxford University Press, 1965)

Morgan, J. E. *University Oars, Being a Critical Enquiry into the After Health of the Men who Rowed in the Oxford and Cambridge Boat-Race, 1829–1869* (London, 1873)

Morris, Christopher. *King's College. A Short History* (Cambridge, King's College, 1989)

Moule, Henry Carr Glyn. *Charles Simeon* (London, 1892)

Moultrie, John. *Poems* (new edn, 2 vols, 1876)

Murphy, James. *The Religious Problem in English Education. The Crucial Experiment* (Liverpool University Press, 1959)

Murphy, Michael J. *Cambridge Newspapers and Opinion 1780–1850* (Cambridge, Oleander Press, 1977)

Namier, L. B. and Brooke, J., eds. *The History of Parliament: The House of Commons, 1754–1790*, 2nd edn (3 vols., London, Secker & Warburg, 1985)

Newman, Francis W. 'University Reform', *Prospective Review*, 5 (February, 1849), pp. 1–15

Newman, J. H. *Historical Sketches* (3 vols., London, 1872)

New Grove Dictionary of Music and Musicians (20 vols., London, Macmillan, 1980)

Nichols, John. *Literary Anecdotes of the Eighteenth Century* (9 vols., London, 1812–16)

Nicoll, Allardyce. *A History of English Drama 1660–1900* (rev. edn, 6 vols., Cambridge University Press, 1952–9)

Nockles, Peter. 'Church Parties in the Pre-Tractarian Church of England 1750–1833: The "Orthodox" – Some Problems of Definition and Identity', in John Walsh, Colin Haydon, and Stephen Taylor, eds, *The Church of England. c. 1689–1833. From Toleration to Tractarianism* (Cambridge University Press, 1993), pp. 334–59

Noll, Mark A., Bebbington, David W., and Rawlyk, George A., eds. *Evangelicalism. Comparative Studies of Popular Protestantism in North America, the British Isles, and Beyond, 1700–1990* (Oxford University Press, 1994)

Norris, Gerald. *Stanford, The Cambridge Jubilee and Tchaikovsky* (Newton Abbot, David & Charles, 1980)

Norris, John. *Practical Discourses Upon the Beatitudes of Our Lord* (1728)

'Obituary of George Peacock', *Proceedings of the Royal Society of London*, 9 (1859), pp. 536–43

O'Gorman, Frank. *The Emergence of the British Two-Party System 1760–1832* (London, Edward Arnold, 1982), pp. 1–22

Voters, Patrons and Parties. The Unreformed Electoral System of Hanoverian England 1734–1832 (Oxford, Clarendon, 1989)

'Old Jonathan' [J. A. Doudney]. *Try and Try Again* (London, 1863)

Bibliography

Oldham, J. Basil. *A History of Shrewsbury School 1552–1952* (Oxford, Blackwell, 1952)

Otter, William. *The Life and Remains of the Rev. Edward Daniel Clarke, Professor of Mineralogy in the University of Cambridge* (2nd edn, 2 vols., London, 1825)

'Our Chronicle', *The Eagle*, 6 (1869), pp. 254–6

Owen, Dorothy M. and Leedham-Green, Elisabeth. 'Who deue wilbe a register . . .', *Catalogue of an Exhibition of University Archives* (Cambridge University Library, 1984)

Paley, Edmund. *Life of William Paley*, in *The Works of Edmund Paley* (4 vols., London, 1838), vol. I, pp. xv–ccxvii

Works (4 vols., London, 1838)

Parsons, Gerald, ed. 'Biblical Criticism in Victorian Britain: From Controversy to Acceptance', in *Religion in Victorian Britain, II, Controversies*, pp. 239–44

Religion in Victorian Britain (4 vols., Manchester University Press, 1988)

Partington, W., ed. *The Private Letter-Book of Sir Walter Scott* (London, 1930)

Paz, D. G. *The Politics of Working-Class Education in Britain 1830–50* (Manchester, 1980)

Peacock, George. *Observations on the Plans for a New Library . . . by a Member of the First Syndicate* (Cambridge, 1831)

Observations on the Statutes of the University of Cambridge (London, 1841)

Pearson, Karl. *The Life, Letters, and Labours of Francis Galton* (4 vols., Cambridge, 1914–30)

Peile, John. *Christ's College*, College Histories Series (London, 1900)

Pevsner, Nikolaus. *Cambridgeshire*, Buildings of England series (Harmondsworth, Penguin, 2nd edn, 1970)

Some Architectural Writers of the Nineteenth Century (Oxford, Clarendon, 1972)

Phillips, John A. *Electoral Behavior in Unreformed England. Plumpers, Splitters and Straights* (Princeton University Press, 1982)

Philpott, Henry. *Remarks on the Question of Adopting the Regulations Recommended by the Syndicate Appointed February 9, 1848* (Cambridge, 18 October 1848)

Piggott, Stuart. *William Stukeley, an Eighteenth-Century Antiquary* (Oxford University Press, 1950)

Pinney, Thomas, ed. *The Letters of Thomas Babington Macaulay* (7 vols., Cambridge University Press, 1974–)

Plumptre, E. H. 'Memoir of J. C. Hare', in J. C. and A. W. Hare, *Guesses at Truth by Two Brothers* (rev. edn, London, 1866)

Plumptre, Robert. *Hints Respecting some of the University Officers, Its Jurisdiction, Its Revenues, & etc.* (Cambridge, 1782)

Porter, Enid. *Cambridgeshire Customs and Folklore* (London, Routledge & Kegan Paul, 1969)

Porter, H. C. 'The Players Well Bestowed? Stourbridge and Barnwell Theatres

Bibliography

1740–1814', *Cambridge Review* (December, 1984), pp. 214–18

Porter, Kenneth Wiggins. *John Jacob Astor. Business Man* (2 vols., Cambridge, Mass., Harvard University Press, 1931)

Porter, Roy. 'The Natural Sciences Tripos and the "Cambridge School of Geology", 1850–1914', *History of Universities*, 2 (1982), pp. 193–216

Powell, William S. *An Observation on the Design of Establishing Annual Examinations at Cambridge* (Cambridge, 1774)

Poynter, F. N. L., ed. *The Evolution of Medical Education in Britain* (London, Pitman, 1966)

Proctor, Richard A. *Rough Ways Made Smooth. A Series of Familiar Essays on Scientific Subjects* (London, 1880)

Pryme, George. *Autobiographic Recollections* (Cambridge, 1870)

Purnell, E. K. *Magdalene College*, College Histories Series (London, Robinson, 1904)

Ranjitsinhji, K. S. *The Jubilee Book of Cricket* (Edinburgh, 1897)

Raverat, Gwen, *Period Piece. A Cambridge Childhood* (London, Faber, 1952)

Ray, Nicholas. *Cambridge Architecture. A Concise Guide* (Cambridge University Press, 1994)

Reardon, Bernard M. G. *Religious Thought in the Victorian Age. A Survey from Coleridge to Gore* (new edn, London, Longmans, 1980)

Reboul, Marc. *Charles Kingsley. La Formation d'une personnnalité et son affirmation littéraire (1819–1850)*, Publications de l'université de Poitiers, Lettres et sciences humaines XIII (Paris, Presses Universitaires de France, 1973)

Reid, T. Wemyss. *Life, Letters and Friendships of Richard Monckton Milnes, First Lord Houghton* (2 vols., London, 1890)

Remains of John Tweddell . . . Being a Selection of his Correspondence . . . Prolusiones Juveniles . . . Some Account of the Author's Collections . . . Preceded by a Biographical Memoir of the Deceased . . . by the Rev. Robert Tweddell A.M. (2nd edn augmented, London, 1816)

Remarks on the Enormous Expence of the Education of Young Men in the University of Cambridge (London, 1788)

Remarks on the Mathematical Teaching of the University of Cambridge (Cambridge, c. 1854)

Reply to Some Reasons against the Expediency of Instituting a Public Examination of Students Previous to their Residence in the University, 6 December 1847. [UL Zz. 39. 11/14]

Report of the Commissioners Appointed . . . to Inquire into the Existence of Corrupt Practices in the Borough of Cambridge together with the Minutes of Evidence (London, 1853)

'Review of La Place, *Traité de Méchanique Celeste*', *Edinburgh Review*, 11 (1807–8), pp. 249–81

771

Bibliography

'Review of Richard Edgeworth's *Essays on Professional Education*', *Edinburgh Review*, 15 (1809–10), pp. 40–53

'Review of the Clarendon edition of Strabo's geography', *Edinburgh Review*, 14 (1809), pp. 429–41

Reynolds, Osborne. Memoir of 'James Prescott Joule', *Memoirs and Proceedings of the Manchester Literary and Philosophical Society*, fourth series, 6 (1892), pp. 1–196

Rivington, R. T. *Punting. Its History and Techniques* (Oxford, R. T. Rivington, 1983)

Roach, J. P. C., ed. *Victoria County History of Cambridgeshire, vol. III: The City and University of Cambridge* (Oxford University Press, 1959)

Robb-Smith, A. H. T. 'Medical Education at Oxford and Cambridge Prior to 1850', in F. N. L. Poynter, ed., *The Evolution of Medical Education in Britain* (London, Pitman, 1966)

Roberts, David. *The Town of Cambridge as it Ought to be Reformed* (Cambridge University Press, 1955)

Roberts, Gerrylynn K. 'The Liberally-Educated Chemist: Chemistry in the Cambridge Natural Sciences Tripos, 1851–1914', *Historical Studies in the Physical Sciences*, 11 (1980–81), pp. 157–83

Robinson, Duncan and Wildman, Stephen. *Morris and Company in Cambridge* (Cambridge University Press, 1980)

Robson, Robert. 'William Whewell, F.R.S. (1794–1866). I: Academic Life', in *Notes and Records of the Royal Society of London*, 19 (1964), pp. 168–76

Roby, H. J. *Reminiscences of My Life and Work, for My Own Family Only* (Cambridge, privately printed, *c.* 1912)

Rogerson, John. *Old Testament Criticism in the Nineteenth Century. England and Germany* (London, 1984)

Rook, Arthur. 'Cambridge Medical Students at Leyden', *Medical History*, 17 (1973), pp. 256–65

'Charles Collignon (1725–1785): Cambridge Physician, Anatomist and Moralist', *Medical History*, 23 (1979), pp. 339–45

'Medical Education at Cambridge, 1600–1800', in Arthur Rook, ed., *Cambridge and its Contribution to Medicine*, Publications New Series 20 (London, Wellcome Institute for the History of Medicine, 1971), pp. 49–63

'Medicine at Cambridge, 1660–1760', *Medical History*, 13 (1969), pp. 107–22

'Robert Glynn (1719–1800), Physician at Cambridge', *Medical History*, 13 (1969), pp. 251–9

'The Thackerays and Medicine', *Medical History*, 15 (1971), pp. 12–22

Rook, Arthur, ed. *Cambridge and its Contribution to Medicine*, Publications New Series 20 (London, Wellcome Institute for the History of Medicine, 1971)

Rook, Arthur, Carlton, Margaret, and Cannon, Graham W. *The History of*

772

Bibliography

Addenbrooke's Hospital, Cambridge (Cambridge University Press, 1991)

Rose, H. J. *Discourses on the State of Protestantism in Germany* (London, 1825)

The Tendency of Prevalent Opinions about Knowledge Considered (Cambridge, 1826)

Rosenfeld, Sybil. 'The Players in Cambridge, 1662–1800', in *Studies in English Theatre History* (1952), pp. 24–37

Strolling Players and Drama in the Provinces 1660–1765 (Cambridge University Press, 1939)

Rowe, Reginald P. P., Pitman, C. M., Serocold, C. P., *et al. Boating and Punting* (Badminton Library, 1898)

Rowing and Punting (2nd impression, London, Longmans, 1903)

Royal Commission on Historical Monuments (England), An Inventory of the Historical Monuments in the City of Cambridge (2 parts, London, HMSO, 1959)

Royle, Edward, and Walvin, James. *English Radicals and Reformers 1760–1848* (Brighton, Harvester, 1982)

Rule, John. *The Experience of Labour in Eighteenth-Century Industry* (London, Croom Helm, 1981)

Rupp, Ernest Gordon. *Religion in England 1688–1791* (Oxford University Press, 1986)

Ruse, Michael. 'William Whewell: Omniscientist', in Menachem Fisch and Simon Schaffer, *William Whewell. A Composite Portrait* (Oxford, Clarendon, 1991), pp. 87–116

Russell, Bertrand. *The Autobiography of Bertrand Russell* (3 vols., London, Allen & Unwin, 1967–9)

Russell, John, Earl. *Recollections and Suggestions 1813–1873* (London, 1875)

Russell-Gebbert, Jean. *Henslow of Hitcham. Botanist, Educationalist and Clergyman* (Lavenham, Suffolk, Terence Dalton, 1977)

Salt, Peter. 'Wyatville's Remodelling and Refurbishment of Sidney Sussex College, 1820–1837', *Proceedings of the Cambridge Antiquarian Society*, 81 (1993), pp. 115–55

Sargent, J. *The Life of the Rev. T. T. Thomason* (London, 1833)

Saunders, Laurance James. *Scottish Democracy 1815–1840* (Edinburgh, Oliver and Boyd, 1950)

Schaffer, Simon. 'The History and Geography of the Intellectual World: Whewell's Politics of Language', in Menachem Fisch and Simon Schaffer, *William Whewell. A Composite Portrait* (Oxford, Clarendon, 1991), pp. 201–31

Schneider, Ben Ross. *Wordsworth's Cambridge Education* (Cambridge University Press, 1956)

Searby, Peter. *The Training of Teachers in Cambridge University: The First Sixty Years 1879–1939* (Cambridge, Department of Education, 1982)

773

Bibliography

Secord, James A. *Controversy in Victorian Geology. The Cambrian–Silurian Dispute* (Princeton, N. J., Princeton University Press, 1986)

Sedgwick, Adam. *A Discourse on the Studies of the University* (1st edn Cambridge University Press, 1833; 5th edn, Cambridge, 1850)

Sedgwick, Richard Romney, ed. *The History of Parliament: The House of Commons 1715–1754* (2 vols., London, HMSO, 1970)

Seed, John. 'Gentlemen Dissenters: The Social and Political Meanings of Rational Dissent in the 1770s and 1780s', *Historical Journal*, 28 (1985), pp. 299–325

Seeley, J. R., ed. *The Student's Guide to the University of Cambridge* (Cambridge, 1862)

Sells, Arthur Lytton Lytton. *Thomas Gray: His Life and Works* (London, Allen & Unwin, 1980)

Sewell, William. 'The Universities', *Quarterly Review*, 59 (October, 1837), pp. 439–83

Sewter, A. C. *The Stained Glass of William Morris and his Circle* (2 vols., New Haven, Conn., Yale University Press, 1974–5)

Sharlin, Harold Isadore. *Lord Kelvin, The Dynamic Victorian* (University Park, Penn., Pennsylvania State University Press, 1979)

Shearman, Montague, Oakley, W. J., Smith, G. O. *et al. Football*, Badminton Library (new edn London, Longmans, 1899)

Shearman, Montague. *Athletics and Football*, Badminton Library (London, 1887)

Sheppard, Carol Anelli. 'A Brief History of *The Practical Entomologist* and its Contributions to Economic Entomology', *Entomological News*, 100 (1989), pp. 212–223

Shipley, A. E. *"J." A Memoir of John Willis Clark* (London, Smith Elder, 1913)

Shuckburgh, E. S. *Emmanuel College*, College Histories Series (London, 1904)

Shuckburgh, E. S. *Laurence Chaderton [and] Richard Farmer, D.D. (Master of Emmanuel 1775–1797)* (Cambridge, 1884)

Sicca, Cinzia Maria. *Committed to Classicism. The Building of Downing College, Cambridge* (Cambridge, Downing College, 1987)

Simpson, A. W. B., ed. *Biographical Dictionary of the Common Law* (London, Butterworth, 1984)

Sir Leslie Stephen's Mausoleum Book, with an introduction by Alan Bell (Oxford, Clarendon, 1977)

Slee, Peter R. H. *Learning and a Liberal Education. The Study of Modern History in the Universities of Oxford, Cambridge and Manchester, 1800–1914* (Manchester University Press, 1986)

Smith, Crosbie. 'Geologists and Mathematicians: The Rise of Physical Geology', in P. M. Harman, ed., *Wranglers and Physicists*, pp. 49–83

Smith, Crosbie, and Wise, M. Norton. *Energy and Empire. A Biographical Study of*

774

Bibliography

Lord Kelvin (Cambridge University Press, 1989)

Smith, Edward H. and Sheppard, Carol Anelli. 'A Heritage of Distinguished Journals,' *American Entomologist* (Spring, 1990), pp. 7–17

Smith, J. J. *A Letter to the Vice-Chancellor* (Cambridge, 24 November 1846) [Cam. c. 846. 17]

Smith, J. J. *A Letter to the Vice-Chancellor on the Late Rejection by the Caput of a Grace Respecting an Examination Previous to Residence* (Cambridge, 14 December 1847)

Smout, T. C. *A Century of the Scottish People. 1830–1950* (London, Collins, 1969)
A History of the Scottish People. 1560–1830 (London, Collins, 1986)

Smyth, Charles. *Simeon and Church Order. A Study of the Origins of the Evangelical Revival in Cambridge in the Eighteenth Century* (Cambridge University Press, 1940)

Smyth, Dame Ethel. *Impressions that Remained. Memoirs* (2 vols., London, 1919)

Smyth, William. *English Lyrics* (5th edn, London, 1850)
Lady Morley's Lecture (Leeds, 1840)
Lectures on History. Second and Concluding Series on the French Revolution (3 vols., London, 1840)
Lectures on Modern History, from the Irruption of the Northern Nations to the Close of the American Revolution (2 vols., London, 1840)
Some Reasons against the Expediency of Instituting a Public Examination of Students Previous to their Residence in the University, 3 December 1847, repr. in Whewell, *Of a Liberal Education*, 2nd edn, 1850, Part 2, appendix, pp. 139–41

Souden, David. *Wimpole Hall* (National Trust, 1991)

Southey, William. 'Hayley's Life and Writings', *Quarterly Review*, 31 (1825)

Speakman, Colin. *Adam Sedgwick. Geologist and Dalesman, 1785–1873* (Heathfield, Sussex, Broad Oak Press, 1982)

Squibb, G. D. *Doctors' Commons. A History of the College of Advocates and Doctors of Law* (Oxford, Clarendon, 1977)

Squire, P. W. 'Punting', in Reginald P. P. Rowe, C. M. Pitman, C. P. Serocold, *et al.*, *Rowing and Punting* (1903 impression)

Stair Douglas, J. *The Life and Selections from the Correspondence of William Whewell D.D.* (London, Kegan Paul, 1881)

Stanley, A. P. 'Archdeacon Hare's Last Charge', *Quarterly Review*, 97 (June 1855), pp. 8–9

Steers, J. A., ed. *The Cambridge Region* (London, British Association for the Advancement of Science, 1965)

Stein, Peter. 'Maine on Legal Education', in Alan Diamond, ed., *The Victorian Achievement of Sir Henry Maine. A Centennial Reappraisal* (Cambridge University Press, 1991), pp. 195–208

775

Bibliography

Stephen, Caroline Emelia, ed. *The Right Honourable Sir James Stephen. Letters with Biographical Notes* (private publication, 1906)

Stephen, James. *Essays in Ecclesiastical Biography* (2 vols., London, 1853; 5th edn, London, 1867)

    Lectures on the History of France (2nd edn, 2 vols., London, 1852)

Stephen, Leslie. *An Agnostic's Apology and Other Essays* (London, 1893)

    Essays on Freethinking and Plainspeaking (London, 1873)

    History of English Thought in the Eighteenth Century (3rd edn, 2 vols., London, 1902)

    'In Praise of Walking', in *Studies of a Biographer* (4 vols., London, Duckworth, 1898–1902)

    The Life of Henry Fawcett (London, 1885)

    The Life of Sir James Fitzjames Stephen (London, 1895)

    'Mr Matthew Arnold and the Church of England', *Fraser's Magazine*, NS 2 (October, 1870), pp. 414–31

    'Mr Voysey and Mr Purchas', *Fraser's Magazine*, NS 3 (April, 1871), pp. 457–68

    'Ritualism', *Macmillan's Magazine*, 17 (1867–8), pp. 479–94

    Sketches from Cambridge by a Don (London, 1865)

    Some Early Impressions (London, Hogarth, 1924)

Stephens, F. G. 'Thomas Woolner, R.A.', *The Art Journal* (1894), pp. 84–5

Stone, Lawrence. 'The Size and Composition of the Oxford Student Body 1580–1910', in L. Stone, ed., *The University in Society* (2 vols., Princeton, N. J., Princeton University Press, 1975), vol. 1, pp. 3–110

Stoughton, J. *Religion in England* (2 vols., London, 1884)

Stroud, Dorothy. *Sir John Soane, Architect* (London, Faber, 1984)

Stubbings, Frank. *Forty-Nine Lives, An Anthology of Portraits of Emmanuel Men* (Cambridge, Emmanuel College, 1983)

Sturrock, June. 'Wordsworth's Italian Teacher', *Bulletin of the John Rylands University Library of Manchester*, 67 (1984–5), pp. 797–812

Suess, Eduard. *The Face of the Earth* (1904–9)

Sully, James. 'Reminiscences of the Sunday Tramps', *Cornhill Magazine*, NS 24 (1908), pp. 76–88

Summerson, Sir John. *Architecture in Britain 1530 to 1830* (4th edn, Harmondsworth, Penguin, 1963)

Sutherland, L. S., and Mitchell, L. G., eds. *The History of the University of Oxford, Vol. V, The Eighteenth Century* (Oxford, Clarendon, 1986)

Sykes, Norman. *Church and State in England in the Eighteenth Century* (Cambridge University Press, 1934)

    Edmund Gibson. Bishop of London 1669–1748 (Oxford University Press, 1926)

    From Sheldon to Secker. Aspects of English Church History, 1660–1768 (Cambridge

University Press, 1959)

Symonds, John. *Remarks upon an Essay, Intituled the History of the Colonisation of the Free States of Antiquity, Applied to the Present Contest between Great Britain and her American Colonies* (London, 1778)

Tanner, J. R., ed. *The Historical Register of the University of Cambridge . . . to the year 1910* (Cambridge University Press, 1917)

Tatham, G.B. 'The "A.D.C."', in *Fasciculus Ioanni Willis Clark dicatus* (Cambridge University Press, 1909), pp. 552–67

Thirlwall, Connop. 'Introduction by the Translator', in Terrence N. Tice, ed., Friedrich, Schleiermacher, *Luke: A Critical Study* (Lampeter, Dyfed, Edwin Mellen, 1993)

  A Letter to the Rev. Thomas Turton . . . on the Admission of Dissenters to Academical Degrees (2nd edn, Cambridge, 1834)

Thirlwall, John Connop. *Connop Thirlwall. Historian and Theologian* (London, SPCK, 1936)

Thirsk, Joan, ed. *The Agrarian History of England and Wales, vol. V: 1640–1750, part 2, Agrarian Change* (Cambridge University Press, 1985)

Thompson, D'Arcy Wentworth. *Wayside Thoughts* (Edinburgh, 1868)

Thompson, Joseph. *The Owens College: Its Foundation and Growth* (Manchester, Cornish, 1886)

Thompson, Silvanus P. *The Life of William Thomson, Baron Kelvin of Largs* (2 vols., London, 1910)

Thompson, T. W. *Wordsworth's Hawkshead*, edited by Robert Woof (Oxford University Press, 1970)

Thomson, J. J. *Applications of Dynamics to Physics and Chemistry* (London, 1888)

Thomson, J. J. *Recollections and Reflections* (London, 1936)

Thomson, William, Lord Kelvin, 'Lord Kelvin and his First Teacher', *Nature*, 68 (29 October 1903), pp. 623–4

Thorne, R. G., ed. *History of Parliament. The House of Commons 1790–1820* (5 vols., London, Secker & Warburg, 1986)

Thorp, Margaret Farrand. *Charles Kingsley 1819–1875* (Princeton, N. J., Princeton University Press, 1937)

Thoughts on the Recommendations of the Ecclesiastical Commission . . . A Letter to W. E. Gladstone (1837)

T[hring], J. C. *Rules of Football: The Winter Game* (London, 1862)

Tice, Terrence N. Editor's Introduction to Friedrich Schleiermacher, *Luke: A Critical Study*, translated by Connop Thirlwall (Lampeter, Dyfed: Edwin Mellen, 1993)

Tillyard, A. I. *A History of University Reform 1800 A.D. to the Present Day* (Cambridge, Heffer, 1913)

Bibliography

Todhunter, Isaac. *William Whewell, D.D. Master of Trinity College Cambridge: An Account of his Writings with Selections from his Literary and Scientific Correspondence* (2 vols., London, 1876)

Tolles, Winton. *Tom Taylor and the Victorian Drama* (Morningside Heights, N.Y., Columbia University Press, 1940)

Torry, A. F. *Founders and Benefactors of St. John's College, Cambridge, with Notes, chiefly Biographical* (Cambridge, 1888)

Towers, Bernard. 'Anatomy and Physiology in Cambridge before 1850', in Arthur Rook, ed., *Cambridge and its Contribution to Medicine* (London, Wellcome Institute for the History of Medicine, Publications New Series 20, 1971), pp. 65–77

Toynbee, Paget, and Whibley, Leonard, eds. *Correspondence of Thomas Gray* (3 vols., Oxford University Press, 1935)

Treherne, George G. and Goldie, J. H. D. *Record of the University Boat Race 1829–1880* (London, 1883)

Treherne, George G. and Goldie, J. H. D. *Record of the University Boat Race 1829–1883* (London, 1884)

Trevelyan, G. M. *An Autobiography and other Essays* (London, Longmans, 1949)
Trinity College. An Historical Sketch (Cambridge University Press, 1943)
'Walking' in *Clio, A Muse and Other Essays* (2nd edition, London, Longmans, 1930), pp. 1–18

Trinity Man, A [John Martin Frederick Wright]. *Alma Mater; or, Seven Years at the University of Cambridge* (2 vols., London, 1827)

Twigg, John. *A History of Queens' College, Cambridge, 1448–1986* (Woodbridge, Boydell, 1987)

Underwood, Malcolm G. 'A Tutor's Lot', *Eagle*, 69 (1984), pp. 3–8
'Restructuring a Household. Service and its Nineteenth Century Critics in St. John's', *Eagle*, 72 (1990), pp. 9–19

University Pollbooks: 1831, 1835, 1865, 1870

Vaughan, Edward Thomas. *Some Account of the Rev. Thomas Robinson* (London, 1815)

Vaughan, W. E., ed. *A New History of Ireland, vol. V, Ireland under the Union 1801–70* (Oxford, Clarendon, 1989)

Veitch, John. *Memoir of Sir William Hamilton* (Edinburgh, 1869)

Venn, J. *Caius College*, College Histories Series (London, Robinson, 1901)
Early Collegiate Life (Cambridge, Heffer, 1913)

Venn, J. and Venn, J. A. *Alumni Cantabrigienses, 1752–1900* (6 vols., Cambridge, 1922–54)

Venn, J. A. *Oxford and Cambridge Matriculations 1544–1906* (Cambridge, Heffer, 1908)

Verey, David. 'George Frederick Bodley: Climax of the Gothic Revival', in Jane

Fawcett, ed., *Seven Victorian Architects* (London, Thames and Hudson, 1976)

Vernon, P. E. 'The Psychology of Rowing', *British Journal of Psychology*, 18 (1927–8), pp. 316–31

Vindication of Christ's Divinity: Being a Defence of Some Queries, relating to Dr. Clarke's Scheme of the Holy Trinity, in Answer to A Clergyman in the Country, A (1719)

Vindication of Niebuhr's 'History of Rome' from the Charges of the Quarterly Reviewer, A (Cambridge, 1829)

Wagner, Henry. 'Some Romilly Notes', *Proceedings of the Huguenot Society of London*, 8 (1905–8), pp. 340–7

Wakefield, Gilbert. *Memoirs* (2 vols., rev. edn, London, 1804)

Walker, Thomas Alfred. *Peterhouse* (Cambridge, Heffer, 1935)

Walpole, Horace. *Memoirs of the Last Ten Years of the Reign of George the Second* (3 vols., London, 1846)

Walpole, Hugh. *The Prelude to Adventure* (London, 1912)

Walpole, Spencer. *The Life of Lord John Russell* (2 vols., London, 1889)

Walsh, Benjamin Dann. *A Historical Account of the University of Cambridge, and its Colleges; in a Letter to the Earl of Radnor* (London, 1837)

Walsh, John. 'The Cambridge Methodists', in Peter Brooks, ed., *Christian Spirituality. Essays in Honour of Gordon Rupp* (London, SCM, 1973), pp. 249–83

'The Magdalene Evangelicals', *Church Quarterly Review*, 69 (1958), pp. 499–511

'"Methodism" and the Origins of English-Speaking Evangelicalism', in Mark A. Noll, David W. Bebbington, and George A. Rawlyk, eds., *Evangelicalism. Comparative Studies of Popular Protestantism in North America, the British Isles, and Beyond, 1700–1990* (Oxford University Press, 1994), pp. 19–37

'The Origins of the Evangelical Revival', in G. V. Bennett and J. D. Walsh, eds., *Essays in Modern English Church History in Memory of Norman Sykes* (London, A. & C. Black, 1966), pp. 132–62

Walsh, John, Haydon, Colin, and Taylor, Stephen, eds. *The Church of England c. 1689–c. 1833* (Cambridge University Press, 1993)

Walters, S. M. *The Shaping of Cambridge Botany* (Cambridge University Press, 1981)

Ward, W. R. *The Protestant Evangelical Awakening* (Cambridge University Press, 1992)

Wardale, J. R. *Clare College*, College Histories Series (London, 1899)

Warrington, John ed. *The Paston Letters*, Everyman's Library (2 vols., London, Dent, 1956)

Waterland, Daniel. *Advice to a Young Student. With a Method of Study for the First Four Years* (London, 1730)

Bibliography

Waterman, A. M. C. 'A Cambridge "Via Media" in Late Georgian Anglicanism', *Journal of Ecclesiastical History*, 42 (1991), pp. 419–36

Watkin, David J. 'Introduction' to reprint of Willis and Clark, *Architectural History of the University of Cambridge* (Cambridge University Press, 3 vols., 1988), vol. I, pp. vii–xx

The Life and Work of C. R. Cockerell (London, Zwemmer, 1974)

'Newly Discovered Drawings by C. R. Cockerell for Cambridge University Library', *Architectural History*, 26 (1983), pp. 87–91

Thomas Hope 1769–1821 and the Neo-Classical Ideal (London, John Murray, 1968)

The Triumph of the Classical. Cambridge Architecture 1804–1834 (Cambridge University Press, 1977)

Watson, Richard. *Anecdotes of the Life of Richard Watson, Bishop of Llandaff* (London, 1817)

Watson, Richard. *A Collection of Theological Tracts* (6 vols., Cambridge, 1785)

Westfall, R. S. *Never at Rest. A Biography of Isaac Newton* (Cambridge University Press, 1980)

Whately, Richard, ed. *Paley's Moral Philosophy* (London, 1859)

Whewell, William. *History of the Inductive Sciences* (3rd edn, 3 vols., London, 1857)

Of a Liberal Education in General; and with Particular Reference to the Leading Studies of the University of Cambridge (London, 1845; 2nd edn, London, 1850)

On the Principles of English University Education (London, 1837)

The Philosophy of the Inductive Sciences (2 vols., London, 1840)

Remarks on Proposed Changes in the College Statutes (23 September 1857)

Remarks on Some Parts of Mr Thirlwall's Letter on the Admission of Dissenters to Academical Degrees (Cambridge, 1834)

Reply to Observations on the Plans for a New Library. By a Member of Both Syndicates (Cambridge, 1831)

Some Reasons against the Expediency of Instituting a Public Examination of Students Previous to Their Residence in the University, 3 December 1847, reprinted in William Whewell, *Of a Liberal Education*, (2nd edn, London, 1850)

Two Introductory Lectures in Moral Philosophy (Cambridge, 1841)

White, James F. *The Cambridge Movement. The Ecclesiologists and the Gothic Revival* (Cambridge University Press, 1962)

White, Richard Grant. 'Charles Astor Bristed', *The Galaxy. A Magazine of Entertaining Reading*, 17, 4 (April 1874), pp. 473–84

Whiting, C. E. *The University of Durham 1832–1932* (London, Sheldon Press, 1932)

Wilberforce, R. I. W. and Wilberforce, Samuel. *The Life of William Wilberforce* (5 vols., London, 1838)

Bibliography

Willey, Basil. *More Nineteenth Century Studies. A Group of Honest Doubters* (London, Chatto & Windus, 1956)

Williams, Perry. 'Passing on the Torch', in Menachem Fisch and Simon Schaffer, *William Whewell. A Composite Portrait* (Oxford, Clarendon, 1991), pp. 117–47

Williamson, R. 'Sir Busick Harwood: A "Reappraisal"', *Medical History*, 27 (1983), pp. 423–33

Willis, Robert and Clark, John Willis. *Architectural History of the University of Cambridge* (4 vols., Cambridge University Press, 1886; the first three volumes reprinted by Cambridge University Press, 1988)

[Willmott, R. A.?]. 'Arnold and Smyth on Modern History', *Fraser's Magazine*, 26 (July–December, 1842), pp. 631–45

Wilson, David B. 'The Educational Matrix: Physics Education at early-Victorian Cambridge, Edinburgh and Glasgow Universities', in P. M. Harman, ed., *Wranglers and Physicists*, pp. 12–48

'Experimentalists among the Mathematicians: Physics in the Cambridge Natural Sciences Tripos, 1851–1900', *Historical Studies in the Physical Sciences*, 12 (1981–82), pp. 325–71

Winstanley, D. A. *The University of Cambridge in the Eighteenth Century* (Cambridge University Press, 1922)

Unreformed Cambridge. A Study of Certain Aspects of the University in the Eighteenth Century (Cambridge University Press, 1935)

Early Victorian Cambridge (Cambridge University Press, 1940)

Later Victorian Cambridge (Cambridge University Press, 1947)

Wollenberg, S. L. F. 'Music and Musicians', in L. S. Sutherland and L. G. Mitchell, eds., *History of Oxford, vol. V, Eighteenth Century*, pp. 865–87

Wood, Thomas. *Study of the Laws of England in the Two Universities* (Oxford, 1708)

Woodgate, Walter Bradford. *Boating*, Badminton Library (London, 1888)

'Oars and Sculls', and How to Use Them (London, 1875)

Woodhouse, Robert. *Elements of Trigonometry* (Cambridge, 1809)

Principles of Analytical Calculation (Cambridge, 1803)

Woolf, Virginia. *Moments of Being*, ed. with an introduction by Jeanne Schulkind, revised and enlarged edn (London, Hogarth, 1985)

To the Lighthouse (London, Hogarth, 1927)

Wordsworth, Christopher (Bishop of Lincoln). *Memoirs of William Wordsworth* (2 vols., London, 1851)

On the Admission of Dissenters to Graduate in the University of Cambridge. A Letter to the Rt. Hon. Viscount Althorp M.P. (Cambridge, 1834)

Wordsworth, Christopher. (Prebendary of Salisbury) *Scholae Academicae. Some Account of Studies at the English Universities in the Eighteenth Century* (Cambridge, 1877)

Bibliography

Social Life in the English Universities in the Eighteenth Century (Cambridge, 1874)

Wordsworth, William. *The Prelude. 1799, 1805, 1850. Authoritative Texts*, ed. Jonathan Wordsworth, M. H. Abrams, and Stephen Gill (London, W. W. Norton, 1979)

Wratislaw, Albert Henry. *Adventures of Baron W. Wratislaw of Mitrowitz. What He Saw in the Turkish Metropolis, Constantinople; Experienced in His Captivity . . . Literally Translated from the Original Bohemian* (London, 1862)

Historical and Statistical Sketch of the Slavonic Protestants, in the North of the Austrian Empire (London, 1861)

Lyra-Czecho-Slovanska. Bohemian Poems, Ancient and Modern, Translated from the Original Slavonic, with an Introductory Essay by A. H. Wratislaw (London, 1849)

The Native Literature of Bohemia in the Fourteenth Century. Four lectures Delivered before the University of Oxford on the Ilchester Foundation (London, 1878)

Observations on the Cambridge System, Partly in Reply to, Partly Suggested by Dr Whewell's Recent Educational Publications (Cambridge, 1850)

Patriotism: An Ancient Lyrico-epic Poem, Translated from the Original Slavonic (London, 1851)

Wyndham, H. Saxe. *William Lambe, M.D. A Pioneer of Reformed Diet* (London, The Vegetarian Society, 1940)

Yeo, Richard R. *Defining Science. William Whewell, Natural Knowledge, and Public Debate in Early Victorian Britain* (Cambridge, 1993)

'William Whewell's Philosophy of Knowledge and its Reception', in Menachem Fisch and Simon Schaffer, *William Whewell. A Composite Portrait* (Oxford, Clarendon, 1991), pp. 175–99

Young, Percy M. *A History of British Football* (London, Stanley Paul, 1968)

UNPUBLISHED THESES AND PAPERS

Cook, Daniel. 'The Representative History of the County, Town and University of Cambridge, 1689–1832' (University of London PhD thesis, 1935)

Enros, Philip Charles. 'The Analytical Society: Mathematics at Cambridge University in the Early Nineteenth Century' (University of Toronto PhD thesis, 1979)

Porter, H. C. 'Francis Burnaud and the Early Repertoire of the Cambridge A.D.C.' (1994)

Ridout, Honour. 'Stourbridge Fair in the Eighteenth Century' (Dissertation in Cambridgeshire Collection, 1992)

Taylor, Stephen J. C. 'Church and State in England in the Mid-eighteenth Century: The Newcastle Years 1742–1762' (University of Cambridge PhD thesis, 1987)

INDEX

Institutions of the University of Cambridge are gathered under Cambridge. Disciplines, faculties, and colleges are indexed separately. Oxford, and Oxford and Cambridge universities considered jointly, are under those headings. All other universities are under universities. Newspapers and journals are gathered under that heading. Cambridge buildings and streets are indexed separately. Numbers in italics refer to pages with illustrations.

Index

Bennett, John, 684
Bennett, William Sterndale, Professor of Music, 684, 691–2
Benson, Christopher, 490
Bentham, Jeremy, philosopher, 305–6, 427
Bentley, Richard, Master of Trinity, 150, 281, 695
Beresford, George, 78
Beresford, William Carr, Field Marshal, 487
Beresford Hope, A. J., 342, 487
Berkeley, George, Bishop of Cloyne, philosopher
Berridge, John, 315–17
Besant, Walter, 274–5
Betham, Edward, 102
Betjeman, John, poet, *Summoned by Bells*, 562
Bilsborrow, Dewhurst, 579–80
Bird-bolt Lane, 9
Bishop Wearmouth (Durham), 298
Black Bear Tavern, 481, 555, 683
Blackburne, Francis, 405
Blackstone, William, 190
Blake, Henry John Crickitt, 66–8
Blakesley, Joseph Williams, 251, 432, 495
Blick, Charles, 94, 141
Blomfield, Charles James, Bishop of London, 267, 432
Blore, Edward, 29
Blow, William, 632, 690
Blunt, John James, Lady Margaret Professor of Divinity, 268
Bodley, George, 40–2
Bond, Henry, 222
Bonney, Thomas George, 232, 254, 670
Botanic Garden, 9, 59, 206–7, *207*
botany, 209–12
Bowman, Thomas, 562
Bowyer, William, 70
Boyle, Robert, 150
Braithwaite, Gawen, 582
Branthwaite, Berney, 101–2
Brewster, Sir David, 519
Bridge Street, 555, 683
Bridgewater Treatises, 313
Bristed, Charles Astor: background and attitudes, 585–91; *Five Years at an English University*, 588; experiences at Trinity, 186, 593–4, 599–600, 603–10, 635–6; on college architecture, 82; on constitution of university, 85; views on sex at Cambridge, 103; on compulsory chapel, 272; views on Cambridge education, 610–12
Bristed, John, 586

Brockdish (Norfolk), 162, 572
Brockett, Laurence, 234, 572
Bronte, Patrick, 333
Brooke, Zachary, 98, 398–400
Brougham, Henry, 168, 427
Brown, James, 395
Brown, John, tutor, 119–20
Brown, John, actor, 697–8
Browne, Harold, 265–6
Browne, William, 151
Browning, Oscar, 87–8, 103
Brunswick Club, 722
Bryce, James, 424–5
Buffon, George-Louis Leclerc, Comte de, 149
Bunbury, Edward, 519
Bunsen, Christian Karl Josias von, 368–9
Burdon, Charles, 481
Burdon, William, 78
Burnand, Francis Cowley, 711–16
Burne-Jones, Edward, 41–2
Burney, Charles, 687
Burrough, James, 13, 15–16, 17–18
Burton, Decimus, 26
Bury St Edmunds, 235
Butler, Joseph, Bishop of Durham, 152, 406, 300, 304
Butler, Samuel, headmaster, 668
Butterfield, William, architect, 488
Buttress, William, 676
Byfield, George, 22
Byron, George Gordon, 6th Lord, poet, 185, 237–8, *English Bards and Scotch Reviewers*, 239

Caius, John, 195
Calgarth, Cumbria, 289
Cam, river, 678–80
Cambridge Architectural Society, 39–40
Cambridge borough: corporation, 50–2; Improvement Commissioners, 59; Magna Congregatio, 51, 93; maps, 7, 9; open fields, 9; parliamentary constituency, 389–90, 413, 416–17, 419–20, 479–85; railway, 9–10; settlement and townscape, 7–8, 43–4
Cambridge Camden Society, 36–40, 338–47
Cambridge Conservative Mechanics' Association, 481
Cambridge, University of
Commencement, 686–8
costume, *70*
degrees and examinations: awarding of degrees, 163, *180*, 256; degrees in

784

Index

Index

Index

Index

Index

Romilly, Sir John, 522
Romilly, Sir Samuel, 237
Rooke, George, 397
Roscoe, William, 237
Rose Crescent, 709
Rose, Hugh James, 366, 428
Rossini, Gioacchino, composer, 688
Rough, William, 580, 583
Royal Albert Almshouses, Hills Road, 40
Rugby School, 583
Rugby (Warwickshire), 718
Ruskin, John, author, 37, 40, 41
Russell, Bertrand, 175
Russell, Lord John, 95, 501–2, 507–8, 511, 517, 519–23, 530–1
Rutherford, Mark, author, 404
Rutherforth, Thomas, Regius Professor of Divinity, 397–9
Rutland, 4th Duke of, *see* Charles Manners

Sackville College, East Grinstead, Sussex, 347
Salthythlane, 7
Salvin, Anthony, architect, 38
Sandwich, 4th Earl of, John Montagu, 398
Sandys, Edwin, Archbishop of York, 564
Sandys, Francis, 22
Sargent, John, 333–4
Satterthwaite, James, 580–3
Saunderson, Nicholas, 151
Scarlett, James (Lord Abinger), 69
Scarsdale, Baron, Nathaniel Curzon, 135
Schleiermacher, Friedrich, 353, 36
Scholefield, James, Regius Professor of Greek, 336, 491–2
Scott, George Gilbert, architect, 28, 42–3, 342
Scott, James, 275–6
Scott, Sir Walter, author, 424
Seale, John Barlow, 123
Secker, Thomas, Bishop of Bristol, 401
Sedbergh Grammar School, 459
Sedgwick, Adam, Woodwardian Professor of Geology, 25, 96; character, career and geological achievement, 213–17, 459–60, 503–4; and Cambridge Camden Society, 39, 341–4; photograph, *214*; divinity Act, 262–3; on students at divine worship, 276; attitude to Paley, 312–13; on university curriculum, 460–2; as Chancellor's Cambridge secretary, 462; works for Palmerston's election, 474–8; opposes subscription, 495, 497–8; on university reform, 521–3; on college reform, 541–2
Sedgwick, Richard, 722–3
Selwyn, Charles Jasper, 487–8
Selwyn, William, Lady Margaret Professor of Divinity, 42

Senate House, 12, 14–17, *17*, 45, 686–8
Settle, Samuel, 323–4
Shadwell, Laurence, 114
Shaftesbury, 3rd Earl of, Anthony Ashley Cooper, philosopher, 304
Shakespeare Club, 709
Shaw-Lefevre, John George, 489–92
Shearman, Montague, 645, 647
Shedden, Thomas, 631
Sheridan, Richard Brinsley, playwright, 237
Sherlock, Thomas, Master of St Catharine's, 280–1
Shilleto, Richard, 131–2, 606
Shrewsbury School, 720
Shrivall, Frederick, 704
Sidgwick, Henry, 382–3
Sidney Sussex College, 7, 95, 98, 232, 261, 542
Silver Street, 134
Simeon, Charles, 275, 312, 322; character and career, 326–36
Sippel, Cambridge music teacher, 690
Smith, George Edmund, 690
Smith, George, 703–4
Smith, John Bainbridge, 632
Smith, John James, 512, 515–17
Smith, Robert, 151
Smith, Sydney, author, 591
Smith, W. H., Cambridge printer, 709
Smyth, Henry, 422
Smyth, William, Regius Professor of Modern History, 219, 236–43
Society for Constitutional Information, 410, 415
Sockbridge, Cumbria, 565
'Speculative' Club, 556
Spengler, Oswald, writer, 367
Spital End, 7
Spring Rice, Thomas, MP for Cambridge, 480, 482–3, 497
Squire, P. W., 678
St Andrew the Less, Church of, Barnwell, 115, 138
St Catharine's College, 13, 89, 98, 109, 134, 542
St John's College: advowsons and livings, 108–9; athletics, 64–6; building, 13, 35–6, 42–3, 141; chapel, 261; constitution and statutes, 141–2; fellows and fellowships, 95, 98–100, 105–9, 111–17, 136–7, 537, 542–3, 731, 734, 736–8, 741, 744–5; masters, 91, 397–400; Methodists, 317–20; NST lecturers, 232; political views, 476–8, 492; Rokeby judgement, 99–100, 106; rowing, 651;

794

Index